NEW BABYLON
NEW NINEVEH

To four who feared not.

NEW BABYLON NEW NINEVEH

Everyday Life on the Witwatersrand 1886 – 1914

CHARLES VAN ONSELEN

JONATHAN BALL PUBLISHERS
JOHANNESBURG & CAPE TOWN

Originally published in 1982 by
Longman Group Ltd,
England

Originally published in two volumes under the titles:
Studies in the Social and Economic History of the Witwatersrand 1886 – 1914
Vol 1 *New Babylon*
Vol 2 *New Nineveh*
Everyday Life on the Witwatersrand 1886 – 1914

This edition published in 2001 by
JONATHAN BALL PUBLISHERS (PTY) LTD
P O Box 33977
Jeppestown
2043

ISBN 1 86842 111 2

Design by Michael Barnett, Johannesburg
Typesetting by ALINEA STUDIO, Cape Town
Set in 10.5 on 12.6 pt Palatino
Cover reproduction and picture section by Triple M Design & Advertising, Johannesburg
Index by Naomi Musiker, Johannesburg
Printed and bound by NBD, Drukkery Street, Goodwood, Western Cape

Front cover photograph reproduced from *The Face of the Country* by Karel Schoeman,
published by Human & Rousseau, 1996.

PHOTOGRAPHIC ACKNOWLEDGEMENTS (PICTURE SECTION)
The Hatherley Distillery, horse-drawn tram and electric tram by courtesy of the State
Archives, Pretoria.
All the rest by courtesy of the Department of Historical Papers, William Cullen Library,
University of the Witwatersrand.

Contents

PART TWO NEW NINEVEH

Abbreviations

BWEA	British Women's Emigration Association
CAJ	Cabmen's Association of Johannesburg
CDU	Cab Drivers' Union
EDNLA	Employers' Domestic Native Labour Association
ILP	Independent Labour Party
MLA	Member of the Legislative Assembly
NZASM	Netherlands South Africa Railway Company
RUIC	Rand Unemployed Investigation Committee
S & DN	*Standard and Diggers' News*
SLC	Special Liquor Committee
TMA	Transvaal Miners' Association
WLVA	Witwatersrand Licensed Victuallers' Association
WNLA	Witwatersrand Native Labour Association
YMCA	Young Men's Christian Association
ZAR	Zuid Afrikaansche Republiek
Zarp	Zuid Afrikaansche Republiekeinsche Polisie

Foreword to the second edition

Johannesburg, a concrete encrustation on a set of rocky ridges, has never been loved by nationalists. Without fertile soil, striking natural vegetation, a lake, a mountain, a valley, a river or even an attractive perennial stream, it lacks the landscape of affection or mystery easily appropriated by myth-makers and nation-builders. A poorly-behaved urban delinquent, it only came into being through its supposedly inspiring ability to vomit up its mineral innards and its unfortunate habit of belching into the clear highveld sky. These anti-social habits attracted bad company in abundance and did little to endear the city and its nondescript surrounds to more genteel folks.

Nature's parsimony, in everything except the gold that it chose to bury more deeply here than anywhere else on earth, meant that the Rand could barely offer its earliest inhabitants a subsistence existence, let alone sustain the luxury of trade in bountiful products. Without a meaningful history of continuous settlement, there was no ready store of deep folklore, tales of derring-do, or great drama for appropriation by ideologues intent on finding an authentic experience of the soul with which 'the people' could identify.

Indeed, it is precisely because nationalist pickings remain so thin that so many triumphalist accounts are sprouted and peddled about the integrated slum that was first Sophiatown, then became racist 'Triomf', and is now once again 'non-racial' Sophiatown. In truth, much of the real story of the first 50 years of Johannesburg revolves around the contest between the narrowly-based economic self-interest of the mine owners and the relatively cosmopolitan labour force that served the industry. It was the immediate clash of class interests around the principal industry that did more to excite the passions of the citizenry than any supposedly primordial yearning for cultural expression or strivings for a more encompassing identity. Other groupings, ranging from small manufacturers, hawkers, retailers, traders and service workers through to the structurally unemployed and their cousins – the criminal classes – almost always found their interests rendered subservient to those of the dominant enterprise.

The city has never cradled a national political party of note of either the enfranchising or the disenfranchising variety. Its shallowly-rooted, first-generation bourgeoisie and the crass nouveau riche of subsequent generations have always felt more comfortable in the bank, the stock exchange and the sports stadium than they have in attending a church, sitting in a concert hall, walking through an art gallery, reading in a library or even serving in the ranks of their city council.

Nationalists, sensing that this was apathetic, difficult, perhaps even intractable human material with which to work and to try to fashion some grander consensus, have always ruled the rich and poor of Johannesburg from afar with a mixture of apprehension, contempt, disdain and neglect. The city, thank heaven, has usually returned the favour by being only lukewarm about the nationalists of the day, paying only lip-service to the ideology of the moment that came from 30 miles away. Johannesburg's industrialists had the brass, Pretoria the politicians with their snouts in the trough. The one paid and the other pronounced – it was never a marriage made in heaven.

When Johannesburg first emerged, the country's racially defined electorate, much taken with an ethnically-exclusive nationalism that was seemingly averse to Eurocentric ideas, was composed for the most part of semi-literate, poorly-educated rural folk who had little or no knowledge of the requirements of a modern industrial economy. Most of Johannesburg's citizens did not qualify for the vote. The members of parliament sent to the national assembly were – in terms of formal education – for the most part indistinguishable from the voters who had sent them there. The ruling party's strategy for the development of a manufacturing sector centred on a scheme based on agricultural production that guaranteed direct or indirect nationalist control.

This policy of nationalist economic empowerment was loosely based on the old Tsarist practice of confining the granting of concessions for industrial development to members of the landed Russian nobility. The concept itself had been sold to the pipe-smoking state president by two entrepreneurial east-European Jewish immigrant friends whom he lauded as 'patriots'. The granting of the initial monopolies, as well as the subsequent broadening of the patterns of ownership relating to them, was accompanied by a great deal of venality which frequently enveloped members of parliament and both Johannesburg and Pretoria reeked of corruption.

The country's civil service, confined almost exclusively to ethnic-nationals, was often as crass, illiterate, unskilled and inexperienced as the political administration it served. Indeed, so pronounced was the problem that at the most senior levels nationals were, for a time, replaced by specially recruited advisors and consultants from abroad who were paid market-related salaries. Most of these skilled administrators, 'Kruger's Hollanders', unambiguously European at a time when the locals were keen to run everything on their own, came to occupy these posts on a full-time basis – a development bitterly resented by the most strident of the ethnic nationalists.

In its desire to retain political control of all the most important structures in the country including the Johannesburg municipality, Pretoria's ethnic nationalists jigged the constitution of the mining city in a manner which, in effect, allowed the government of the day to appoint the mayor. Lacking a coherent, integrated city council with roots deeply embedded in local communities, Johannesburg's municipal services remained primitive in the extreme, further undermining any sense of civic pride. Large parts of the filthy city and the municipal market were a public disgrace. The drivers of the local horse-drawn cabs – rude, poorly-trained and given to fleecing the public – were notorious for their 'furious driving'. Public transport was hopeless. Unable or unwilling to develop or maintain the roads leading in and out of the country's foremost commercial centre, the government introduced a system of privatised toll gates that was loathed by industrialists, farmers, retailers and travellers alike.

Within Johannesburg itself – partly overrun by illegal immigrants, well-organised gangsters and motley undesirables drawn from Europe and Africa in equal measure – law-enforcement fell to new lows almost each year before the turn of the twentieth century. On the streets most of the police – consciously drawn almost exclusively from the ranks of the sons of the soil, from the ethnically dominant nationalists – were without proper equipment, remuneration or uniforms, badly educated, semi-literate and often commanded only their mother tongue or some very broken second language. In the courts prosecutors did creative and imaginative things – dockets, exhibits and evidence disappeared with alarming regularity and most ordinary policemen had financial interests in either brothels or illegal drinking dens; often both. In the dirty, overcrowded prisons overseen by officers at least as cynical and corrupt as those in the police, hundreds of inmates were herded into inadequate facilities that spawned violent anti-social gangs, whose members preyed remorselessly on the young and vulnerable.

History, as we now all know, does not repeat itself. Every now and then, however, it bears rereading with a sharp eye looking for underlying continuities – be they ideological, political, economic or social. If these few vignettes of the 1890s help sharpen our understanding of the modern Witwatersrand's predicament they will have served their purpose.

Charles van Onselen
Pretoria
March 2001

Preface to first edition

Ignorance has many virtues, amongst them the fact that it tends to produce a feeling of self-confidence which allows one to contemplate large
projects with a sense of complete equanimity. In the early seventies I
decided to undertake at least two studies based on the historical transformation of societies in south-central Africa engendered by the mineral
discoveries of the late nineteenth century. The first of these would concentrate on the social experience of black workers at the point of production – more especially on the gold mines of Southern Rhodesia. The
second would look at the experience of non-mining classes in a region
which was nevertheless dominated by extractive industry – the
Witwatersrand – and attempt to explore some of the wider world that
the mine owners made.

In 1976 the first of these studies appeared as *Chibaro: African Mine
Labour in Southern Rhodesia, 1900-1933*. The second, however, soon began
to exceed the bounds of a single volume and now stands complete as
Studies in the Social and Economic History of the Witwatersrand, 1886-1914.
Unfortunately, *New Babylon* and *New Nineveh* have been some time in the
making, and this can be partly accounted for by the fact that the task of
writing and researching the work was undertaken over a period of six
years in five different settings – Oxford, Geneva, London, New Haven
and Johannesburg.

Throughout this period and at all of these places I have enjoyed the
support of many colleagues and several institutions. Writing social history is both an expensive and an esoteric business and it needs a very
special sort of body to fund a man who is, amongst other things, set on
determining how many customers frequented a certain Johannesburg
brothel during the course of a certain summer's evening in 1897.
Amongst others who were willing to tolerate and even encourage such
mindless enquiries, however, were the Institute of Commonwealth
Studies at the University of London where I spent a happy year as a
Junior Research Fellow in 1975. Even more felicitous and intellectually
profitable were the three years which I spent as a Ford Foundation
Research Fellow at a sister institution – the Centre of International and
Area Studies at the University of London – between 1976 and 1979. In
addition, I have profited from being attached as a Visiting Fellow to the
South African Research Programme at Yale University during the fall
term of 1978, and – since 1980 – from my research affiliation to the
African Studies Institute at the University of the Witwatersrand.

Not all institutions, however, are willing to take so tolerant a view of social history or those who write it. Some, for reasons that are not always easy to understand, appear to be, if not obstructive, then at very least unduly defensive. Of such institutions which operate archival policies that are far more restrictive than those practised by most modern western governments, at least two deserve special mention – the Chamber of Mines of South Africa and Barlow Rand Ltd. Both these institutions take the view that the historical documents now in their possession constitute 'private' collections and that they are therefore at liberty to determine whom they will allow to have access to these archives. In a narrow legalistic sense there is undoubtedly considerable merit to this argument, but viewed from other perspectives it seems to be rather more open to question. Throughout the period under consideration in this study – 1890 to 1914 – the Chamber of Mines and, to a lesser extent, Barlow Rand's predecessors, played an unashamedly public role in the making and shaping of South Africa society. Public actions in some measure engender public responsibilities and the mere passage of time does not transform them into private behaviour. It is all the more unfortunate therefore that serious professional researchers should, on a somewhat arbitrary or selective basis, be denied access to documents which could help to shed valuable light on a past which belongs to all South Africans.

But the world – even the world the mine owners made – has more to offer than frightened custodians of the past; it also has many helpful guides to the present who are more than willing to assist a historian who has, all too frequently, lost his way. In the course of negotiating several unfamiliar archival paths, for example, I have frequently received the generous help of specialists who either made copies of their own research material available to me, or else pointed me in the direction of more fruitful sources. I am most grateful for their assistance and I hope that they will not take it amiss if I do not list their names here. Fellow professionals will find their help acknowledged at the point where it often counts most – the notes.

This historian, however, is also perfectly capable of losing his way between the look-alike airports of Africa, Europe and the United States. Here again, it has been my good fortune to have many good friends who have not only lent me valuable support during the course of my research but who, through their warmth and hospitality, have given me time to recover my sense of social direction at several crucial moments. Their homes have been my homes and I am greatly indebted to Guerino and Cora Bozzoli, Peter Delius, Stanley Freenberg and Rosa DeLauro, Keith and Dixie Griffin, Bill Johnson and Anne Summers, Diana Phimister, Richard Rathbone and – especially – Barbara Trapido.

Four other people – Tim Couzens, Shula Marks, Ian Phimister and Stanley Trapido – have helped, encouraged and supported me in so many different and valuable ways that I find it difficult to thank them adequately. I consider myself to be singularly privileged to have had these model professionals not only as advisers and informed critics but as friends. If there is any merit in this work then it is largely as a result of their unstinted efforts.

All authors are aware, however, that books are never simply the product of one person's enterprise, and I am also acutely aware of the help that I have received from three other friends – Barbara Cowap, Wendy Cullinan and Georgina Relly. It is their efficiency that has enabled me to spend many more hours writing than would normally be possible, and their remarkable skill and accuracy which have provided the publishers with a superb manuscript. I would like to offer them my sincere thanks.

Writing does not come easily to me – something to which most of the people mentioned above can testify. I find it to be a slow, difficult and demanding task and the final product seldom pleases me for more than a day or two. My greatest debt of all, therefore, is to those who are closest to me and my work. Nobody could ask for more than I have asked from Belinda, Gareth and Jessica. They, more than anybody else, have shared in the making of this work and it rightly belongs to them. It comes with my deepest gratitude.

C van Onselen
Johannesburg
July 1981

Introduction

Viewed from virtually any angle, the Witwatersrand, during the three breathless decades which separate the discovery of gold in 1886 from the outbreak of the First World War in 1914, constitutes something of an historian's dream. In a little less than 30 years, a republic founded on a modest agricultural economy was transformed into a colony boasting the world's largest and most technologically sophisticated gold-mining industry – a traumatic transition which was overseen by four different governments, punctuated by an attempted *coup* and, at one stage completely halted by a bloody conflict lasting two and a half years. Into this cauldron of capitalist development poured men, women and children drawn from all over the world, giving the Rand a cultural diversity and social texture that bubbled with excitement and vitality. And, as this new and remarkably complex industrial society was moulded, the entire process was recorded – often in a wealth of detail – in the annals of industry, government commissions of enquiry, the reports of municipal and state officials, the accounts of insiders and outsiders, and in any one of half a dozen newspapers.

Yet, for all its obvious appeal and vulnerability to imaginative attack, the social history of the Witwatersrand and that of its principal city, Johannesburg, has remained relatively intact. In the midst of an industrial revolution, timid historians – lamenting the absence of an indigenous aristocracy – have tip-toed through the tree-lined avenues of the northern suburbs, peering into the homes and lifestyles of the 'Randlords', attempting to put a romantic gloss on the ceaseless pursuit of wealth at a time when, elsewhere in the city, the dusty streets were bursting at the seams with a seething mass of struggling humanity. It is almost as if by concentrating exclusively on the exploits of a small number of ruling-class actors the people could be ignored, and the city would somehow be endowed with a mythical collective past which was more becoming to its present role as one of the major finance capitals of the world. Perhaps Herman Charles Bosman in his *A Cask of Jerepigo* had such historians in mind when he complained that:

> They are trying to make Johannesburg respectable. They are trying to make snobs out of us, making us forget who our ancestors were. They are trying to make us lose our sense of pride in the fact that our forebears were a lot of roughnecks who knew nothing about culture and who came here to look for gold.

xvii

Bosman, however, was far from pessimistic about the outcome of this process and he continued by pointing out that:

> We who are of Johannesburg, we know this spirit that is inside of us, and we do not resent the efforts that are being made to put a collar and tie on this city. Because we know that every so often, when things seem to be going very smoothly on the surface, something will stir in the raw depths of Johannesburg, like the awakening of an old and half-forgotten memory, and the brick-bats hurtling down Market Street will be thrown with the same lack of accuracy as when the pioneers of the mining camp did the throwing.

Amongst other things, it is the social historian's duty to help stir the raw depths of the city in the hope that Market Street might one day be restored to some of its former glory.

New Babylon, New Nineveh constitutes an extended and thematically linked exercise in historical materialism which seeks to set the experience of selected groups of ordinary people in Johannesburg within the wider context of the industrial revolution that engulfed the Witwatersrand at the turn of the century. By situating these groups within the emerging structures of the society and refracting their experiences through the process of class struggle, it seeks to demonstrate how, during these formative decades, the ruling classes gradually came to assert their control over the subordinate classes on the Rand and exercise a powerful influence over where they lived, how they spent their non-working hours, how domestic labour was allocated within their homes, and how they were to endure periods of unemployment. Hopefully, it represents not so much the grinding and grating of so many abstracted categories against the processes of history as the analytically informed chronicle of the warm, vibrant and intensely human struggle of people seeking to find a place of dignity and security within a capitalist world that encroached on them all too quickly.

A large part of the course and nature of this struggle was ultimately determined by the changing economic imperatives of the mining industry and by the mine owners' drive to accumulate capital during the series of spectacular booms and slumps which mark the period under examination. But, despite the industry's ever-growing strength, the mine owners did not always enjoy a free hand in their conflict with the subordinate classes; during the era of the Kruger Republic the state – through which this struggle was partly mediated – was, in the final analysis, dominated by an aspiring agricultural bourgeoisie. Much of *New Babylon, New Nineveh* is therefore concerned with charting the changing nature of the state between 1886 and 1914 – from one that gave preference to the accumulation of capital in the countryside before 1899, to one that came to favour the pursuit of profit by urban industrial enterprise after 1902 – and demonstrating how this, in turn, affected the lives of liquor sellers, prostitutes, cab drivers, washermen, domestic servants, transport riders, brickmakers and members of the working classes. In particular, this study attempts to pay some attention to the years immediately after the war, the so-called 'reconstruction period', during which the new governing class, largely freed from any direct electoral responsibility, replanned the Rand's principal city, and the state – during a crucial interlude – came to adopt an unashamedly instrumental role in shaping the future of an increasingly industrial society.

The resistance of the under classes to that shaping process – both at their places of employment and well beyond it – was at various times culturally informed, subtle, extensive and militant. Formal resistance, as expressed through petitions, deputations, demonstrations, marches and strikes, drew on strands as diverse as the English trade union tradition and Jewish experience of the Bund in Eastern Europe; while less formal resistance – but nonetheless well organised – as manifested in intimidatory displays, assaults or gang activities, could be influenced by aspects of Pedi youth culture, the Zulu regimental system, or the ethnic bonds uniting gangsters drawn from Manhattan's lower east side. But what was perhaps most impressive about this working class in the making was the manner in which its members borrowed, shared and adapted practices drawn from older settings and put them to work in the new environment. Cape 'Malay' cab drivers added their names in Arabic script to the petition of their Afrikaner counterparts addressed to President Kruger in the name of the 'working classes'; black washermen organised along Zulu military lines wearing turbans adopted from Asian *Dhobi* custom went on 'strike' when their livelihoods were threatened; while gangs of *Amalaita* 'houseboys' molesting white women in suburban streets took to wearing the red insignia of organised labour. In New Babylon the need to speak a common language – and to a limited extent even that came with the advent of *fanakalo* – was somewhat diminished as the social cement of class attempted to bond together the first generation of a new proletariat.

Finally, this study, in attempting to come to terms with the richness and complexity of the unfolding conflict on the Witwatersrand, and in trying to do justice to the simultaneous demands of both structure and process, has been inspired by the efforts of a remarkably talented group of scholars who have never ventured down the intellectual by-ways of Transvaal history. The influence which the works of Eugene Genovese, Herbert Gutman, Eric Hobsbawm, George Rudé, Gareth Stedman Jones and Edward Thompson have had on this author should nevertheless be very obvious to the more seasoned travellers in the fields of social history.

Ancient Nineveh and Babylon have been revived.
Johannesburg is their twentieth century prototype.
It is a city of unbridled squander and unfathomable squalor. Living
is more costly than one's wildest dreams. All the necessaries of life are
impudently dear. Miners of England and Australia, however poor may
be your lot, however dark your present prospects, let no man tempt
you to South Africa with tales of the wages that are paid upon the
Rand! The wages are high indeed, but the price the workers pay for
them is paid in suffering and blood.

A PRATT, *The Real South Africa* (1913)

PART ONE
NEW BABYLON

1

THE WORLD
THE MINE OWNERS MADE

Social themes
in the economic transformation of
the Witwatersrand, 1886-1914

The struggle for wealth is at no time an edifying spectacle.
Johannesburg has been a leaven in the land which has proved
by no means an unmixed blessing to South Africa. The financial
adventurer who has wandered to the Transvaal is not the type
of man who would demonstrate the highest side of European
civilisation to the Boers.
VIOLET MARKHAM, *NOTES FROM A TRAVELLING DIARY*, 1899

In 1870 the first stirrings of a new giant in the area north of the Vaal River became apparent when alluvial gold was discovered in the Murchison range of the Zoutpansberg district. Three years later there were further rustlings when more alluvial gold was discovered at Pilgrim's Rest in the Lydenburg district, and a little more than a decade later still, in 1884, there was an even more significant movement when the first reef deposit was uncovered at Barberton in the eastern part of the country. A mere 24 months later, however, the giant sat up uneasily for the first time when the most substantial reef deposits yet were discovered on the Witwatersrand.

At first, few international observers took the slow-moving Transvaal mining industry particularly seriously – and why should they have? In 1886, the year that the Rand was discovered, the new industry produced only 0,16 per cent of the world's gold output and was still clearly dwarfed by its more formidable Australian and American rivals. By 1898, however, the new giant was already firmly on its feet, without serious challengers, and producing no less than 27 per cent of the world's gold. By 1913 the Witwatersrand mining colossus bestrode the economic world, producing no less than 40 per cent of the world's gold output.

Highly visible from even the most far-flung of financial outposts, this imposing new profile of profit captured the attention and imagination of a whole generation of European capitalists. In 1890 the par value of capital invested in the Rand mining industry stood at 22 million pounds sterling, by 1899 it had reached 75 million pounds, and by 1914 it had climbed to a staggering 125 million pounds.[1]

This dramatic shift, as the Transvaal abruptly transferred its economic weight from its agricultural to its industrial leg over a brief period of 30 years, transformed the Witwatersrand and, in time, the whole of southern Africa. For a length of some 40 miles along the line of reef, from Springs in the east to Krugersdorp in the west, the accommodating ridges and depressions of the Witwatersrand became pock-marked with all the signs of an industrial revolution – mining headgear, ore dumps, battery stamps, reduction works, slimes dams and the frayed ends of railway lines. Besides, and in between these starker thickets of technology, the same revolution also spawned a series of urban sponges – the mining compounds and towns – that were called upon to absorb the ever-increasing numbers of black and white miners who made their way to the new goldfields at the turn of the century. And, in the midst of all of these developments, almost exactly half-way along the line of the reef outcrop, lay the social, political and economic nerve centre of the new order – Johannesburg.

Fathered by gold and mothered by money, Johannesburg's impatient and demanding parents scarcely allowed their charge time to pause in infancy or linger in adolescence before pushing it out onto the streets of the economic world. The tented diggers' camp of the eighties soon gave way to the corrugated iron structures of the mining town of the mid-nineties, and then to the more substantial brick buildings of an industrial city with suburban homes during the first decade of the twentieth century. By 1896 the 3 000 diggers of the original mining camp were lost in a town of 100 000 residents and, by 1914, these 100 000 were in turn becoming harder to find in a city with over a quarter of a million inhabitants. The inexorable pressure exerted by people, houses, shops, offices and factories pushed back the municipal boundaries from five square miles in 1898, to nine square miles in 1901, and then – more ambitiously still – to an enormous 82 square miles in 1903.

Given the company that the parents kept, it is scarcely surprising that the child lost its innocence at an early age. With white workers ranged against black, skilled miners against the mine owners and the Randlords against the state, Johannesburg was racked by class conflict during much of this period. By the outbreak of the First World War the city had been chosen as the centre of an unsuccessful attempted uprising against the government of the day, been occupied by the army of an invading imperial power, and subjected to at least three bouts of such serious industrial unrest that troops had to be called in to help maintain order. It was these turbulent events, the city's cosmopolitan immigrant population and the all-consuming worship of wealth which, in 1910, prompted the visiting Australian journalist, Ambrose Pratt, to comment: 'Ancient Nineveh and Babylon have been revived. Johannesburg is their twentieth-century prototype. It is a city of unbridled squander and unfathomable squalor.'[2]

The new Babylon and new Nineveh which Pratt saw all too clearly in 1910, however, had already been 25 years in the making and, as in any other city, its complex economic, political and social structures had all been erected at their own distinctive pace. Indeed, what characterised much of Johannesburg's early growth was its markedly uneven development; something which in turn reflected how closely the city was pulsed by the changing profitability of the mining industry during its formative decades. Predictably, Johannesburg's periods of greatest economic growth tended to coincide with the most noticeable investment spurts in the mining industry – 1888-89, 1895 (the great 'Kaffir Boom'), 1899, 1902-03 and 1908-09. Politically, the most dramatic change in the fortunes of the Rand were undoubtedly occasioned by the South African War (1899-1902); whilst the periods of greatest social re-structuring appear to have taken place during the three major depressions that were interspersed between the booms in the mining industry – 1890-91, 1896-97, and 1906-08.[3]

But to separate out artificially the social, political and economic components to the city's historical development in this way ultimately conceals more than it reveals; since it is precisely the linkages between these strands that are of most interest to those who wish to understand how the mining industry – directly and indirectly – came to govern important aspects of life beyond the mine shafts. This chapter then, by way of an introduction, seeks to illustrate a few of the ways in which the world the mine owners made affected the lives of some of the ordinary people on the Witwatersrand between 1886 and 1914.

THE FOUNDATIONS OF ECONOMY AND SOCIETY ON THE WITWATERSRAND, 1886-1891

The initial discoveries of gold on the Rand were made along the length of the reef outcrop as it stretched from east to west in the series of rocky ridges which gave the region its name. Both the fact that the reef protruded at the surface along this line, and that the gold itself was held within the matrix of a more friable and weathered conglomerate in its upper reaches facilitated the first – and easiest – phase of the production process. Hundreds of small-scale, under-capitalised 'diggers' simply excavated rows of trenches from which the gold-bearing reef was relatively easily removed by pick and shovel. From there the ore was transported to the steam-driven stamps where it was crushed, after which it was amalgamated with quicksilver before being retorted to yield its gold. However, it was particularly during the two latter stages of the production process – milling and recovery – that the diggers and others were made to realise just what a mixed blessing the new goldfields constituted. For while the Rand gold deposits had the inestimable virtue of being extremely regular and reliable, they also had the vice of being of an exceptionally low grade. This meant, as one observer has noted, that: 'From its inception, mining development on the Rand was both labour and capital intensive. A large labour supply, elaborate machinery, and chemical works were required to profitably recover gold from the low grade ore.'[4]

In the very first flush of development, however, the importance of this harsh economic reality did not fully dawn on hundreds of diggers who were in any case perhaps more interested in the speculative gains that could be made from the buying and selling of small claims, than in the more rigorous demands of productive mining. But speculation of its own accord has a limited economic momentum, and within 18 months of the fields being opened the infant industry made the first of its many demands for more substantial capital investment. The response to this cry for capital came in the boom of 1888-89 as several joint stock companies were floated – many of the more important ones drawing on the expertise and financial resources of capitalists who had earlier made their fortunes on the Kimberley diamond fields. This development, as small individual enterprises tended to give way to larger companies, heralded the decline of the digging community and in 1889 the Diggers' Committee gave way to the newly formed Chamber of Mines.

It was also during the latter stages of this first boom, and for a while thereafter, that a few of the more far-sighted mining financiers started systematically buying up land that was situated at some distance from – but parallel to – the original line of the reef outcrop. Quick to appreciate the significance of the fact that the reef dipped away steeply to the south, these astute investors realised that if shafts were sunk to the south of the existing diggings, then the gold-bearing reef would eventually be intersected at deeper levels. Thus throughout much of 1889 and 1890 larger companies such as H Eckstein & Co – later part of the powerful Wernher, Beit & Co – moved to acquire that property which would in due course make deep-level mining a reality on the Rand.[5]

But no sooner had this important element in the long-term future of the industry been assured than the goldfields were struck by what

4

seemed like a technological disaster. From mid-1889 producers discovered that gold-bearing reef drawn from below a depth of about 120 feet resisted amalgamation during the later stages of the recovery process. Whereas reef extracted from closer to the surface had had its gold freed by weathering and oxidisation, that drawn from lower down had its particles of the precious mineral firmly locked into the conglomerate by pyrite crystals:

> With no immediate solution at hand, yields of the producing mines declined sharply. This setback collapsed stock values and forced hundreds of companies to wind up. The crash ruined hundreds of small miners and promoters who sold off what assets they could. The buyers were larger operators with financial resources sufficient to ride out the fall, purchase additional mining ground cheaply, and invest in a solution to the refractory ores.[6]

This technologically triggered financial crisis might therefore have left the larger companies temporarily starved of investment capital, but it also left them poised for expansion when the first signs of economic recovery came. Those signs did not appear for at least two years, and throughout 1890 and 1891 the Witwatersrand and its principal mining town languished in a serious depression.

All of these events, the initial boom, the increasing hold of the mining companies, the purchase of the land to the south of the outcrop, and the subsequent slump, helped first to sketch, and later to fill out in bolder strokes, the outline of life in Johannesburg between 1886 and 1891; and, as might be expected, the earliest picture to emerge came almost as caricature. The discovery of gold and the boom that followed drew hundreds of diggers, miners, traders, adventurers, agents and speculators to a mining camp which, within months, gave way to a mining town loosely centred on the Market Square. Throughout 1888-89 the market and its surrounding dusty streets filled with produce merchants, traders, shops, offices, banks, bars, saloons and canteens, formed the focal point for incoming transport riders as well as members of the digging community who were dependent on food and mining supplies brought into the geographically isolated South African Republic by ox wagon. The clamour set up by all of this human activity competed uneasily – and largely unsuccessfully – with the continuous din of the nearby mining machinery to produce a veritable cacophony of sound. It was only in 1890 and 1891, when many of the more vulnerable newcomers to the Rand had settled down into their less familiar roles as unemployed workers, billiard markers, barmen, skittle-alley attendants, vagrants, petty thieves and burglars during the depression, that both the tempo and volume of this noise abated somewhat.

Beyond the dust and noise of the mining town, however, there were already to be detected the outlines of a few striking features which, during the following decade and a half, did much to influence Johannesburg's social development. Of these, two are of particular importance to the more detailed studies which follow this introductory essay. First, it is worth noting how overwhelmingly male-dominated the town was throughout the period leading up to the South African War. Initially uncertain about the economic future of the goldfields, and later about their political fate as *uitlanders* under the Kruger regime, Johannesburg's immigrant miners were for many years extremely reluctant to commit their wives and children to a settled life on the Witwatersrand. This, together with the expense and difficulty of getting to the Transvaal before the rail link with the Cape was established in January 1893, meant that early Johannesburg was largely devoid of working-class family life. Thus, while a few of the wealthy mine owners and a section of the commercial middle class soon set up home on the Rand, the large majority of workers had to be content with considerably less – the skilled white miners from Cornwall, Cumberland and Lancashire taking up residence in the town's numerous 'boarding-houses', and unskilled black workers from the Cape, the Transvaal and Mozambique being pushed into the repressive conformity of the mine compounds.[7]

Secondly, it is equally important to note the geographical distribution of these racially divided working-class institutions. The large majority of the Rand's boarding-houses were located either on the mining property itself, or in one of the town's two major working-class suburbs – Jeppe in the east and Fordsburg in the west. The mine compounds, which housed the black workers, were – without exception – situated on mining property. This meant that most working-class accommodation, like the line of reef which it followed, tended to extend along the east-west axis of the Witwatersrand. More significantly, however, it also meant that most workers – skilled and unskilled – lived close to the point of production, and that in early Johannesburg no great distance separated the place of residence from the place of work.

These clusters of workers, concentrated in the boarding-houses and mine compounds of the Witwatersrand, produced, reproduced and accentuated several elements of late nineteenth-century working-class culture – and, in the case of the white miners, elements of British male working-class culture in particular.[8] Drinking, gambling and whoring, which would probably have played an important part in the emerging working-class culture of the Rand in any case, became largely divorced from the broader mediating influences of family life, and thus assumed a central role in the lives of thousands of skilled and unskilled miners. This dependence of black and white workers on alcohol and prostitutes to lend some meaning to an otherwise alienated social existence was swiftly appreciated by the Transvaal ruling classes who, through a combination of strength and weakness, chance and design, came to operate a policy of social control which had its roots deeply embedded in the sociological realities of boarding-house and compound culture.[9] Put starkly, the Kruger government and the mine owners – sometimes acting jointly and sometimes of their own accord – encouraged black workers to consume alcohol, and tolerated the recourse of white workers to prostitutes in order to safeguard the long-term accumulation of capital in the industrialising state.

As early as 1881, President Kruger took the first somewhat optimistic step towards industrialising the Transvaal when he granted a concession for the manufacture of alcohol from locally grown products to the Pretoria-based entrepreneur, A H Nellmapius. This venture, which two years later commenced production as *De Eerste Fabrieken in de Zuid Afrikaansche Republiek Ltd*, initially experienced considerable difficulty in finding a market for the liquor manufactured from the agricultural surplus of Boer farmers. Once the Witwatersrand goldfields were discovered, however, the company's prospects were transformed overnight. In May 1889 it was noted of the distillery that, 'from a very modest beginning on a tentative scale, its success has become unprecedently rapid, and it is now developing itself into a great industry'.[10] Three years later, in 1892, *De Eerste Fabrieken* became a public company, and amongst the most prominent investors in the new venture were several of the Rand mine owners.

On the goldfields this growth of a 'great industry' in the countryside reflected itself in an explosion in the number of retail liquor outlets along the reef. The number of licensed canteens on the Witwatersrand rose from 147 in 1888 to 552 in 1892 – a threefold increase over a four-year period. To the delight of shareholders in what was by now the Hatherley Distillery, these canteens sold an ever-increasing quantity of cheap liquor to the Rand's thirsty miners during the following years. For some of the mine owners, however, this growth of the retail liquor trade proved to be a double delight. Mine owners with a financial interest in Hatherley could not only look forward to a handsome dividend from the distillery, but to the prospect of a more stabilised – if not more sober – black labour force since the many migrant workers who spent their wages on liquor saved less of their earnings than their more abstemious colleagues, and thus tended to labour underground for periods that were significantly longer than would otherwise have been the case. Thus, by 1892 the Randlords and the Kruger government were locked into a class alliance which, in rather different ways, was to the financial benefit of both the mine owners and Boer agricultural producers.

But if this class alliance on the question of the use and consumption of alcohol in the industrialising republic was consciously and aggressively fostered by the Randlords and the Kruger government, largely because of the direct profits which it could yield, then the same was not true of the more complex issue of prostitution. In the latter case, the official attitude of muted acceptance was gradually developed over a number of years, went largely unstated, and serviced the accumulation of capital in a more indirect way.

It was during the boom years of 1888 and 1889 that scores of prostitutes drawn from the southern African coastal regions first made their way inland to the new goldfields of the Witwatersrand. A few years later, and more particularly during 1892-93, these early arrivers were joined by a significant influx of 'Coloured' prostitutes – women who had been driven north of the Vaal by the progressive implementation of the Contagious Diseases Act in several of the leading Cape Colony towns. Almost all of these pioneers of vice found themselves positions as 'barmaids' in the canteens, or else openly plied their trade from the 'rooms' to be found at the back of the more notorious drinking dens. In either case, however, their presence on the premises was welcomed by the liquor retailers who, through their powerful trade organisation, the Witwatersrand Licensed Victuallers' Association (WLVA), acknowledged the ability of these women to draw customers to their businesses. Thus, although the Johannesburg Sanitary Board had the power to initiate prosecutions, and although some government officials objected strongly to the social effects of this trade in vice, there was little – if any – official action taken against prostitutes during the late 1880s or the early 1890s. A government anxious to protect a liquor industry that benefited its most powerful constituents, and a mining industry that sought to attract and stabilise a working class on the Witwatersrand, between them had good reasons for condoning this conspicuous inactivity.

Both prostitution and drinking, therefore, partly grew out of the male culture that was rooted in the boarding-houses and the mine compounds. But the fact that most of the Rand's labouring population was collectively housed in institutions closely tied to the line of reef had effects that reached beyond these two elements of working-class culture. It also helped to shape the limited economic opportunities which existed outside the confines of the mining industry, and as such assumed some importance for those blacks and whites who were seeking ways of resisting entry into the working class as unskilled labourers. It is within the context of this wider struggle against proletarianisation that employment in the fields of domestic service, the construction industry and transport during the period 1886-91 has to be seen.

Right from the moment of its establishment, Johannesburg evinced a notable demand for domestic servants of all colours and of both sexes.[11] Much of the early demand for black male servants in particular, however, came from the relatively small number of middle and ruling-class families who considered a team of 'houseboys' to be part of their colonial birthright. This, together with the absence of white working-class house-holds in any significant number, meant that while the demand for 'house-boys' within a certain narrow stratum of Rand society was always high, the overall size of the service sector for African males remained relatively small during these early years. While the majority of the Witwatersrand's skilled and semi-skilled white workers remained confined to the board-ing-houses, the possibility of blacks seeking to avoid labour on the mines by obtaining positions as 'houseboys' remained limited.

There was one domestic service, however, which the hundreds of boarding-houses did not provide for the immigrant miners, and it was this unavoidable omission which created an alternative economic oppor-tunity for certain blacks. Because the town lacked a major natural system of drainage which would allow for the ready removal of effluent, the Johannesburg Sanitary Board for several years prohibited the washing of clothing in residential areas since it feared that slops tipped into the dusty streets would soon come to constitute a serious health hazard for the European community. This, and the absence of any steam laundries, meant that for some time the labouring men of the Witwatersrand were called upon to do their own laundry in one of the streams on the out-skirts of the town – a tedious, time-consuming task which ate into the precious hours which the miners had set aside for their recreation.

From 1890 onwards, however, small groups of Zulu-speaking washer-men – often drawn from the same rural areas in Natal which supplied the Rand with many of its 'houseboys' – established themselves on the banks of the Braamfontein *spruit* in the vicinity of Sans Souci. These 100 or 200 turbaned men, who modelled themselves on the lines of the Hindu *Dhobi* or washermen's caste which they had seen at work on the East coast, soon dominated Johannesburg's hand-laundry business. Bound into an ethni-cally based organisation which in some respects resembled a medieval European craft guild, this association of *AmaWasha* quickly won formal recognition from the Sanitary Board, and its members did much to ease the domestic burden of the immigrant miners who were without recourse to the labour of their wives and daughters.

It was also largely for this reason – the absence of the European miners' wives and children – that the demand for white working-class housing on the Rand during this period remained limited. But if the limited call for small family cottages had a marginally depressing effect on the construc-tion industry, then it was more than compensated for by the demand for other types of structures as the mining camp started to give way to the mining town. The boom of 1888-89, in particular, saw the erection of a large number of shops, offices and workshops in addition to the many new structures of all types commissioned by the mining industry. All of this building activity occasioned a pronounced demand for bricks and it was this early need of the mining town which, as in the case of the laundry business, afforded yet another group of South Africans being pushed out of the countryside the chance of urban survival.

In late 1887 dozens of poor Afrikaner families – ex-*bywoners* who had either been driven off the land by natural disasters such as drought, or else who had become the early victims of the growing commercialisation of agriculture in the Transvaal hinterland – petitioned the State President for the right to manufacture bricks from the clay to be found on certain government land bordering the Braamfontein spruit to the south-west of the original mining camp. Kruger, aware of the difficulty which his unskilled countrymen experienced in obtaining employment of any kind in the mining industry, agreed to this request as a temporary measure which would in some way help to ease the plight of some of his most vulnerable burghers. The former *bywoners*, however, promptly built their homes on this property, and within months the site gave rise to a local industry of some importance as the landscape became dotted with clay diggings, puddle machines, kilns, stacks of drying bricks and scores of horses and carts. By the early 1890s, the Brickfields had started to assume an even more permanent aspect and became well known as a place of economic refuge for the Afrikaner poor.

It was during the course of this same search for a place of economic refuge that another group of burghers driven off the land found that they too could put some of their rurally acquired skills to good urban use. Shortly after the diggings were proclaimed, a few Afrikaners used what limited capital they had to acquire small hooded 'Cape carts' and horses, which they then proceeded to ply for hire in the town as cabs. Initially there was very little demand for such a cab service, not least because, as we have seen, the majority of the inhabitants lived close to their place of employment. But, as the mining town started to stretch out a little along its east-west axis, so first a modest and later a steady demand for cheap transport between the two outer suburbs and the inner business district developed. When the Johannesburg Cab Owners' Association was formed in January 1891, it attracted over 80 members – mostly Afrikaners, but also including amongst its numbers some 'Cape Coloureds' and a few European immigrants.

By then, however, the long-term prospects of running a successful transport business in the promising mining town had already been thoroughly assessed by the ubiquitous A H Nellmapius.[12] Early in 1889, at the height of the first boom on the Rand, the Pretoria entrepreneur approached the Kruger government with a request for a concession which would entitle him to operate an animal-powered tramway service in Johannesburg for a period of 30 years. Here, as with the liquor concession, the State President and his closest advisers were much taken with the idea of an urban industrial development which could provide an important market for Boer farmers – in this case, forage, mules and horses. The government thus granted the concession, but Nellmapius, always hard-pressed for cash, almost immediately sold it to a Rand mining company owned by Sigmund Neumann, Carl Hanau and H J King.

A few months later, in September 1889, Neumann and his partners – all well-known men in local financial circles – floated the Johannesburg City & Suburban Tramway Co Ltd. This venture, which its promoters believed would one day be allowed to operate a more profitable electric tramway system, attracted a considerable amount of speculative interest, and prominent investors included Porges & Co – yet another forerunner of the powerful Wernher, Beit & Co – and, in Europe, N M Rothschild & Sons. With its working capital readily secured, the company proceeded at once with the necessary survey and construction work, and in February 1891 the City & Suburban line which ran for a length of four and three-quarter miles along Commissioner Street, between Jeppe in the east and Fordsburg in the west, was opened to the public.

A year marked by depression, however, 1891 was possibly not the most auspicious moment at which to commence operations, and at the end of the 11 months the shareholders in City & Suburban could look at a gross profit which amounted to very little more than £2 000. It was largely this dismal return on their capital and the inability to pay a dividend which, late in 1891, prompted the directors to approach Kruger with a request that the company be allowed to electrify its line. For reasons which Nellmapius would have understood a lot better than the subsequent concession holders, the government turned down this request – perhaps the first, but certainly not the last occasion on which Kruger thwarted the desire of Rand mining capitalists and international bankers for immediate profits in order to protect the longer-term interests of his agricultural producers.

But if the ZAR government had shown its willingness to protect the interests of some of its more powerful supporters during a depression year, then it proved to be a lot less concerned about the economic fate of another – and more vulnerable – section of its constituency during the same year. The discovery of gold on the Witwatersrand had come as a major economic blessing to the country's transport riders; throughout the late eighties and the early nineties hundreds of burghers with limited capital and the requisite skills made a good, and at times even a lucrative living, by conveying mining supplies and foodstuffs between the coastal cities and the Transvaal. Indeed, so well did this business develop in the years before the railways reached the Rand that it caught the eye of the government as a potential source of revenue. Thus, in 1891, the State President persuaded a slightly reluctant *Volksraad* to impose a toll of 30 shillings on each wagon carrying loads of up to 6 000 lbs along the Republic's main roads. This measure, which would have been unpopular in the countryside at any time, must have aroused particular resentment during the depression and it was strongly resisted by the transport riders.

All of these occupations – transport rider, cab driver, brickmaker, washerman, 'houseboy', prostitute and liquor seller – point to an important sector of the rapidly emerging Rand economy which, although ultimately linked to the mining industry and its wider needs, could offer persons a living outside of the mainstream of the working class. Most of these positions, which depended on the deployment of a combination of unskilled or semi-skilled labour and a modest amount of capital, were filled by people drawn from within southern Africa, and most of the incumbents appear to have weathered the first really serious economic storm on the Witwatersrand. Admittedly, in 1890 the local press did complain about the activities of a gang of well-organised 'Zulu' burglars and it is possible that this was the first tell-tale sign of black unemployment which, a few years later, was to assume larger and even more organised proportions in the shape of *Umkosi Wezintaba* – 'The Regiment of the Hills'. But, in general, Africans and Afrikaners alike survived the depression of 1890-91 fairly well, and emerged relatively unscathed. The same, of course, was not true of those who were perhaps in the most vulnerable position of all – those who had only their labour to sell to a primary industry that was languishing in a trough of economic uncertainty: the skilled and semi-skilled immigrant miners drawn from the United Kingdom, Australia and elsewhere. It was these men who, throughout 1890, 1891 and a large part of 1892, were forced to turn to the most menial of casual labour or, where this proved to be unavailable, were made to suffer the pains of open unemployment. Above all other groups of workers on the Rand, it was the hundreds of unemployed miners who stood to gain most from a rapid recovery of the mining industry.

DEEP-LEVEL ECONOMIC DEMANDS FOR A NEW SOCIAL ORDER, 1892-1899

The financial crisis in the Rand mining industry brought about by the problems associated with the treatment of pyritic ore in 1889 meant that 'at a crucial time of moving into deep-level operations, the main source of funds for mining development began to dry up'.[13] From early 1890, therefore, the leading mining companies were called upon to deal with two major problems in order to secure their long-term viability – the one technical and the other financial. But, since the solutions to both of these problems were ultimately intertwined with the immediate need to restore investor confidence in the Rand, the mine owners could not afford to work on one to the neglect of the other and thus between 1890 and 1893 there was a significant re-marshalling of resources and a great burst of creative capitalist energy which ultimately helped to place the industry on a much firmer footing.

Late in 1890 sections of the mining industry started to experiment with an amalgamation and recovery technique which had first been developed and patented in Glasgow – the MacArthur-Forrest process. This technique, which relied on first dissolving the gold in a weak cyanide solution and then precipitating it with the aid of zinc metal shavings, immediately produced spectacular results. Whereas other methods of recovery retrieved between 60 and 80 per cent of the gold from crushed ore, the MacArthur-Forrest process yielded almost 90 per cent. This discovery – or at least its rediscovery and application on a larger scale in a new setting – not only ensured continued production, but provided the mines with bigger yields.[14]

Both the MacArthur-Forrest process and mining at deeper levels, however, called for new plant and equipment and thus exacerbated the mining companies' need for capital at a most unpropitious moment in the industry's history. Amongst the very first to appreciate the magnitude of this problem, and to take important steps towards its resolution, were the owners of the company that had earlier led the move to acquire deep-level properties – Wernher, Beit & Co. Between 1890 and 1892 Wernher, Beit & Co rationalised their holding in such a manner as to allow them to make use of the immediate profits generated by their outcrop mines to provide operating subsidies for their deep-level mines which, they suspected, would in time yield even larger and more continuous profits.

The rationale underlying this highly successful tactic was further refined and extended when Wernher, Beit & Co publicly launched Rand Mines Ltd in 1893. The venture offered nervous investors the opportunity to buy their way into a portfolio of shares carefully spread between deep-level and outcrop mines, the chance to benefit from the advantages that would flow from the pooling of administrative resources, and the right to share in the profits that would flow from the efforts of a team of exceptionally talented mine managers. In these respects Rand Mines was 'the prototype of the group system which in the twentieth century was to become the financial mainstay of the South African mining industry'.[15] Not surprisingly, this development was soon emulated by a half-dozen or so of the other leading companies on the Rand and this in turn gave rise to a number of new mining houses – amongst them, Cecil Rhodes' and Charles Rudd's Consolidated Gold Fields of South Africa Ltd. In retrospect it can be seen that: 'The nine main gold mining groups in the 1890s all owed their origin, therefore, as much to the financial crisis associated with the collapse of the first great investment boom as to the financial exigencies of deep level mining.'[16]

Through the early nineties these two major developments – the success of the MacArthur-Forrest process on the one hand, and the emergence of the group system on the other – interacted in a mutually reinforcing way to breathe new life into the mining industry. The steadily returning confidence of 1893 gave way to a sharp upturn in share prices in late 1894, and by mid-1895 the Rand was enjoying an unparalleled boom. Several of the leading companies, including Wernher, Beit & Co and Consolidated Gold Fields, made use of this exceptionally favourable financial climate to unload some of their less promising shares in outcrop mines onto the market, and to rationalise further their holdings. By late 1895 the major mining companies on the Rand were more committed to a future that was built around deep levels than ever before.

But despite the spectacular recovery of the stock market, many of the mine owners – and more particularly those who had staked their fortunes on the future profitability of the deep levels – had cause for growing concern by 1895. As the development of the deep levels accelerated through the mid-nineties, so it became increasingly apparent that deep-level mining entailed costs which differed significantly from those of outcrop mining. There were several reasons for this. First, deep-level mining necessitated the employment of a much larger pool of unskilled black labour – and at a cost which could only be reduced if the hard-pressed ZAR administration was willing to assist the industry in the task of effectively disciplining and controlling its work force. Secondly, because of their geological nature, deep levels used far greater quantities of dynamite for rock-breaking operations than did outcrop mines. This problem was aggravated by the fact that the dynamite was supplied at a price through a company which enjoyed a monopoly – a feature which in turn could ultimately be attributed to Kruger's concessions policy. Thirdly, the cost of both coal and mining supplies was to an extent artificially inflated by another set of controversial government measures and this too tended to press harder on the deep-level mines than on the outcrops. Finally, the state's taxation policy – if not in principle, then at least in practice – tended to weigh more heavily on the deep-level than on the outcrop mines. Most of these economic grievances could in the final analysis be traced to political roots: 'The deep level capitalists and technical advisers argued that, with efficient government in the

Transvaal, the cost of native labour and explosives and coal and imported supplies could be so sliced that the costs of production on the Rand
could quickly fall by maybe 15 or 20 per cent.'[17]

Throughout the period 1893-95, as the leading companies continued to
shift the balance of their investments from outcrop to deep-level mines,
so the industry and its spokesmen – pushed by a growing sense of
urgency – unsuccessfully sought to resolve these difficulties and other
questions such as those surrounding the issue of the *bewaarplaatsen* by
appealing to the Pretoria administration.[18] When the great 'Kaffir Boom'
collapsed in September 1895, and the pioneer deep-level mine, the
Geldenhuis Deep, failed to yield a profit two months later, several of the
deep-level mine owners came to the conclusion that it was 'through the
unkind economic environment which Kruger's policies had created' that
'the high profits which their bold investments would normally have won
were being converted to losses'.[19] It was thus during the closing months
of 1895 that the plans of Otto Beit, Lionel Phillips, George Farrar, John
Hays Hammond and other mine owners meshed with the wider imperial ambitions of Cecil Rhodes, and the conspirators proceeded to invite Dr
Jameson to lead a military force to overthrow the Kruger government.

The Jameson Raid, which started out as a plot within the confines of
smoke-filled rooms in the houses of high finance, ended as a low-level
farce in the open veld near Krugersdorp. On the last day of December
1895 Jameson and his men surrendered to Boer forces and were marched
to Pretoria where they and members of the instigating 'Reform Committee' were made to stand trial for the armed invasion of the Republic.
The Raid, which had been meant to herald the advent of a new season of
economic confidence in the mining industry and its future, had precisely the opposite effect – it rocked rather than rescued the Rand. The recession which had started in late 1895 soon deepened into a full-scale
depression which lasted through 1896, 1897 and a large part of 1898.

What the Jameson Raid did manage to do, however, was to administer a severe political jolt to the Kruger government. The effect of this
alone would probably have been enough to make the government reconsider its attitude towards the mining industry and its needs, but the
emergence of a more compliant attitude on the part of the state was further facilitated by the ensuing depression. Between 1896 and 1898, the
Kruger government made serious, consistent and determined efforts to
improve the quality of its administration, and to accommodate the mine
owners' steadily escalating demands for a new order which could more
effectively nurture the growth of industrial capitalism. In some respects
then the Jameson Raid marked an important turning point in the history
of the Rand since, after that date, the Kruger state through its actions
– hesitant, grudging and deeply suspicious as they were – slowly start-

ed to admit the mining industry to a more important role in the political economy of the Transvaal.

Perhaps one of the first signs of this new – albeit gradually emerging – attitude on the part of the Pretoria administration came in 1896 when the government, after discussions with the mining industry that dated back to March 1894, promulgated the Pass Regulations to facilitate the control of black workers on the Witwatersrand. Leading spokesmen for the industry were forced to concede that this was a 'good law', although they did express serious reservations about the manner in which it was being enforced.[20] More significant by far, however, was the important concession which the Kruger government made when it agreed to the appointment of an Industrial Commission of Enquiry to examine the grievances of the mining industry in 1897. This very professional team of investigators, which included representatives of the mining industry, produced a wide-ranging and penetrating report which was severely critical of the government's economic policies. Although Kruger and his colleagues could not be expected to act immediately upon all of these recommendations – some of which contained serious implications for the Republic and its allies – the government did, despite the rapidly deteriorating political situation, manage to modify certain aspects of the Gold Law, and to arrange for a 10 per cent reduction in the rates charged by the Netherlands South African Railway Company.

Moreover, it was not only the mining industry's narrower and more immediate economic demands which the state inched towards accommodating in the years leading up to the South African War. After the Jameson Raid the Kruger government also took serious, and in some cases impressive steps, to meet the mine owners' ever-expanding demands for a social and political order that was more compatible with the wider needs of urban capitalism. From June 1898 the new State Attorney, J C Smuts, made vigorous efforts to reform and improve the quality of the police force on the Witwatersrand. As a result of these efforts the systematic theft of gold amalgam was partially checked, and – more importantly – the illicit sale of alcohol to black mineworkers was severely disrupted, so improving the efficiency of the industrial labour force. In August 1899 no less a person than Friedrich Eckstein, speaking on behalf of the mine owners at the monthly meeting of the Chamber of Mines, paid public tribute to the State Attorney and his Chief Detective for the success which they had enjoyed in suppressing the illicit liquor trade.[21]

Likewise, when militant unemployed white workers threatened to mount serious disturbances in Johannesburg during 1897, the government moved with 'commendable promptitude in regard to the question of relief to the indigent'.[22] Throughout late 1897 and most of 1898, the

Pretoria administration – with the active and grateful assistance of the mine owners – helped to control urban unrest amongst the working classes in the principal city on the Witwatersrand. Finally, in yet another political concession, Kruger increased Johannesburg's powers of local government when he granted it municipal status in late 1897. Although still somewhat circumscribed by the requirement that half the members of the town council had to be burghers, this move – when set within the context of the political climate created by mine owners and their powerful allies – can be seen as yet another gesture of reconciliation on the part of the Kruger government. When all of these actions are taken into account, it seems a little harsh to dismiss the government's policies towards the mining industry in the pre-war period as being simply those of 'neglect and obstruction'.[23]

By late 1898 a measure of confidence in the future of the Rand had been restored in public if not in private circles, and in 1899 there was a short spurt of investment in the mining industry. By then, however, the die had been cast and the Kruger government found itself ranged not only against the nervous and demanding mine owners, but against an increasingly interventionist British government which felt that its long-term imperial interests in southern Africa were seriously jeopardised by an independent *Zuid Afrikaansche Republiek*. In October 1899, after a political crisis which had lasted some months, Kruger's burghers found themselves pitted against the might of the British army in a conflict which, in the final analysis, hinged around gold and the future of the Republic's enormously profitable mining industry.[24]

In retrospect then, the period between 1892 and 1899 was one of crucial importance and severely fluctuating fortunes for the Witwatersrand and its inhabitants. The mining industry eased itself out of the slump of the early nineties to enjoy an unprecedented boom in 1895, only to have the deep-level mine owners overreach themselves in the Jameson Raid, and see the share market slide into a depression before speculative interest in the industry was once again briefly restored for a few months before the outbreak of the South African War.

This dramatic rise and fall in the economic tide over a period of seven years, however, constituted more than simply a cyclical movement from slump to boom and back to slump again. The depression of 1896-98, in particular, marked a structural shift of qualitative importance in the Rand's economy as a whole, and as such left a deep imprint on the lives of the ordinary people which we have been examining.

When *De Eerste Fabrieken* became the Hatherley Distillery in 1892 it put a partnership which had been developing between Boer agricultural producers and the mine owners ever since the opening of the goldfields onto a slightly more formal footing. Over the next three years, in particular, the Pretoria distillery produced an ever-increasing quantity of cheap alcohol which the Rand's many canteen keepers readily sold to the mining industry's expanding black labour force. As the real costs of deep-level mining became increasingly apparent during the middle of the decade, however, so the mine owners started to have second thoughts about the wisdom of using alcohol as one of the primary means of attracting and stabilising their supply of cheap labour. By 1895 it was estimated that between 15 and 25 per cent of the black labour force was always unfit for work because of drunkenness and, as the Chamber of Mines pointed out in its report of that year, this meant that 'the scarcity of labour was intensified, as companies able to get them had to keep far more boys in their compounds than were required on any one day to make up for the number periodically disabled by drink'.[25]

This growing contradiction, where on the one hand the mine owners sought to use and profit directly and indirectly from the sale of alcohol to their black workers, and on the other wished to reduce the cost and inefficiency of the labour force, became increasingly unmanageable as the deep-level mines approached the critical production stage. The leading mine owners accordingly shifted their stance from being in favour of the controlled use of alcohol in the years leading up to the 'Kaffir Boom' to the point where, shortly after the onset of the depression in 1896, they advocated the 'total prohibition' of the sale of alcohol to black mineworkers and others. When the Chamber of Mines informed the Pretoria administration of this change of policy and of its desire to have new legislation to meet it, it found members of the *Volksraad* to be divided over the issue. Whereas President Kruger and his closest supporters were strongly opposed to any move which would ultimately restrict the size of the market for Boer produce, others – including many of the 'progressives' who had serious reservations about the social and economic implications of the government's concessions policy – favoured the idea of 'total prohibition'. It was thus with some relief that the Chamber of Mines discovered that when Act No 17 of 1896 was eventually passed by the *Volksraad* it contained a 'total prohibition' clause which would be put into effect on 1 January 1897.

The mine owners and their 'progressive' allies, however, soon found that 'total prohibition' had to contend with a formidable array of opponents which included, amongst others, the State President and his Executive Committee, the well-connected owners of Hatherley Distillery and the many members of the Witwatersrand Licensed Victuallers' Association. Throughout 1897 and the first half of 1898 these parties made vigorous but unsuccessful attempts to get the Volksraad to sanction a return to the *status quo ante*. But if 'total prohibition' continued to hold firm in theory throughout this 18-month period, in practice the law was breached on a massive scale. Large and well-organised illicit liquor syndicates soon sprung up and through most of the 'prohibition' period East European immigrants – with the aid of a venal ZAR police force – continued to supply black miners with enormous quantities of cheap imported potato spirits. 'Total prohibition' was 'total' in name only.

From mid-1898, however, this situation started to change and the illicit liquor dealers and their allies in uniform found themselves on the defensive. There were two related reasons for this. First, the *Volksraad* reaffirmed its adherence to the principle of 'total prohibition' and this time the State President appears to have accepted the majority sentiment without qualification. Secondly, in an attempt to co-opt some of his 'progressive' opposition and accommodate the desire for reform, Kruger appointed Smuts to the position of State Attorney. The new State Attorney and a young colleague, F R M Cleaver, devoted their first months in office to the task of ridding Johannesburg's notorious police force of corruption. Thus, when an H Eckstein & Co-financed newspaper, the *Transvaal Leader*, appeared on the streets for the first time in 1899 with a well-orchestrated demand for immediate action against the illicit liquor syndicates, the state was in a much better position to respond than it had been earlier. And, as we have seen, by the time the war broke out even the mine owners were forced to acknowledge the Kruger government's achievement in this arena.

Unskilled black workers on the Witwatersrand during the 1890s therefore found themselves in the position where, before the deep-level mines went into production they were allowed – if not actually encouraged – to consume large quantities of alcohol, while after 1896 they were expected to exercise maximum restraint as the mine owners and the state sought to mould them into a more disciplined industrial labour force. The other major section of the working class, the skilled white immigrant miners, found that one of their major social outlets – recourse to prostitutes – experienced a broadly similar change in fortune over the latter half of the decade. But, for several reasons – not least of all the fact that prostitution and its associated effects cost the mining industry less than did alcohol – the Kruger government was left to tackle this task of reform on its own.

Between 1892 and 1894 Johannesburg's prostitutes were, for the most part, made up of women who hailed from the Cape Colony and who tended to ply their trade individually from the bars and canteens of the mining town. This comfortable local arrangement, however, was rudely interrupted by the explosive growth of the town during the 'Kaffir Boom' and by the rail links which the Rand developed with the east coast during the mid-nineties. In particular, the arrival of the railway line from Lourenço Marques in January 1895 did much to change this situation since it placed the Rand – via the cheap passages of the German East

African Shipping Line – within convenient reach of several continental ports. Scores of French, German and Belgian prostitutes, who had previously competed for customers in the relatively stagnant northern markets of the older European cities, now turned their attention to the new and rapidly expanding towns generated by the South African industrial revolution. In addition, dozens of Russo-American women and their gangster pimps, for a rather different set of reasons, also chose to abandon New York City during the same period and make their way to the Rand. By 1896, then, the picture had changed dramatically, and Johannesburg's prostitutes were largely 'continental women' who, with the aid of their pimps, openly solicited customers for the many brothels established in houses in the centre of town.

This burgeoning public trade in vice was to the immediate benefit of at least two parties in the town – the landlords, including 'men of repute, banking corporations and eminent firms' who derived inflated rents from letting properties to brothel-keepers, and retail liquor merchants who continued to benefit from the custom which prostitutes drew to the bars and canteens which they frequented.[26] In addition, the presence of prostitutes in such large numbers helped to make life on the Rand a little more bearable for single miners and, to the extent that it assisted in attracting and stabilising the industry's semi-skilled and skilled workers, it met with the tacit approval of the mine owners. Neither the mine owners nor any of their newspapers – neither of which were otherwise characterised by their reluctance to raise private or public questions about the moral well-being of sections of the working class – brought the issue of prostitution and its effects to the attention of the government, or embarked on any campaign to deal with organised vice in the mining town.

But not everybody in Johannesburg proved to be equally phlegmatic about these new developments. Several of Kruger's local officials, the non-propertied middle class, and more particularly the Rand's clergymen, were dismayed by the rapid spread of venereal disease, embarrassed by displays of public indecency, shocked by allegations of 'white slavery', and perfectly horrified to learn that some continental prostitutes were willing to accept black as well as white customers. From mid-1896, representatives of these groups put the Sanitary Board and the Pretoria administration under increasing pressure to draft legislation which would effectively destroy the 'social evil' on the Witwatersrand.

At first, however, neither the members of the Sanitary Board nor the State President and his Executive Committee were particularly anxious to take drastic steps against organised vice on the Rand – the former because they feared the political consequences of alienating powerful groups such as the landlords and the liquor merchants, and the latter because they were counselled about the naiveté of simply attempting to legislate prostitution out of existence by some of Kruger's senior Dutch advisers who had first-hand experience of such matters in Holland. But, as the 'social evil' became more entrenched in Johannesburg and pressure on the government increased, the issue could no longer be avoided, and in 1897 as well as 1898 the *Volksraad* enacted new legislation to deal with the problem.

Both of these laws, however, remained a dead letter. An ambivalent attitude about the value of such legislation in the office of the Johannesburg Public Prosecutor, the systematic bribing of the Morality Police and – above all – the power and pervasive influence of the gang of former New York City pimps, ensured that organised prostitution on the Rand continued to thrive for some time after this legislation was passed. It was only after Smuts and Cleaver mounted a carefully planned counter-offensive against the leading gangsters involved in the vice trade that there was a significant improvement in the situation. By August 1899 the Kruger government had taken impressive strides towards its goal of reforming the police force and smashing the hold of organised crime on the Witwatersrand.

The continuing vitality of the trade in sex and alcohol through the largest part of the nineties, however, revealed to what extent the pre-war Rand remained characterised by the features which we cited earlier – the predominance of a male population and its accommodation in distinctive institutions situated relatively close to the points of production. While the 'Kaffir Boom' did undoubtedly help to swell the size of Johannesburg's middle class it failed to persuade most of the white migrant workers about the wisdom of bringing out their wives and children to settle on the Rand. Thus, while the boom did force the expanding white population to spill over into the suburbs immediately surrounding Jeppe and Fordsburg, the vast majority of white miners continued to be housed in boarding-houses while their black counterparts remained confined to the compounds. As before, these social realities did much to influence the size and shape of opportunities in the service sector of the local economy – and more especially so for domestic servants and the members of the washermen's guild.

The rapid expansion of Johannesburg after 1892 produced a swift and pronounced escalation in the demand for white servants – either as 'cooks-general' in middle or ruling-class homes, or as cooks or house-maids in hotels and boarding-houses. This demand which peaked during the 'Kaffir Boom', however, did not immediately fall off in the depression which followed the Raid, and by late 1896 there was still a considerable shortfall in the number of specialist servants available on the Rand. In an attempt to alleviate the labour shortage and at the same time engineer a fall in the high wages that it was forced to pay its existing employees, the 90 members affiliated to the Witwatersrand Boarding-House Keepers' Protection Association organised a campaign to import specialist servants from London during early 1897. This move, which was vigorously opposed by members of the Witwatersrand's Hotel Employees' Union, does not appear to have met with any great success.[27]

Denied the flow of imported labour which they would have preferred, the boarding-house keepers and other householders turned instead to substituting cheap unskilled black labour for more expensive semi-skilled white labour as the mid-decade depression deepened. After 1897 there was therefore an increase in the demand for 'houseboys' and, for a variety of reasons, most of these positions came to be filled by Zulu speakers drawn from neighbouring Natal. By 1899 there were several hundred 'houseboys' at work on the Rand who could look forward to an average monthly wage of 80 shillings – a sum which already contrasted sharply with the 50 shillings which black miners on average earned each month. Although the mine owners remained silent about this on the eve of war, in time it proved to be a development which met with the strong disapproval of the mining industry.

But if the prospects for the wage-earning 'houseboys' generally improved during the years between 1892 and 1899, then those of the self-employed Zulu washermen tended to fluctuate somewhat more dramatically. While the period started on a cheerful enough note for the *AmaWasha* as the guild's membership rose from about 500 in 1892 to over 1 200 in 1895, it ended on a distinctly gloomier one as their numbers again fell back to about 500 by 1899. This rise and decline in the fortunes of the guild, however, did more than merely reflect the dominant influence of the 'Kaffir Boom' and the ensuing depression – it also marked an important structural change in the service sector of the local economy that could be traced back to certain developments that took place in 1895.

In 1895, at the height of the 'Kaffir Boom', the Witwatersrand's spring rains failed to materialise and during the drought that followed the Johannesburg Sanitary Board officials became alarmed at the dangerously low levels in the streams and 'pits' at the Zulu washing sites. In the interests of public health therefore, it was decided that the washermen should be removed to a new and more distant site on the farm 'Witbank' where they would be able to enjoy the use of a permanent and more abundant supply of clear water. This move, however, imposed a more taxing cost structure on the washermen's business and it was thus strongly opposed by most of the members of the guild. Eventually, after several unsuccessful appeals to the Sanitary Board and a week-long protest 'strike', the *AmaWasha* were forced to make the move to the new site in December 1896.

Neither the rapid growth in the number of washermen before this, nor the subsequent plan to have them permanently removed from the immediate vicinity of the town, escaped the attention of Johannesburg's leading financiers – including some of whom, like Otto Beit, had strong interests in the mining industry. In October 1895 the first of several companies to promote steam laundries was floated, and by April 1898 the town could boast a half-dozen such enterprises. Thus, by the time that the hapless Zulu washermen were eventually allowed to return to town in August 1897 – as a result of a series of lengthy legal battles fought largely on grounds of self-interest by the old site owners – they not only had to contend with the effects of the depression, but also with the growing competition of the capitalist industries which had sprung up during their absence at Witbank.

In certain important respects the story of the Zulu washermen during this period was also the story of another group of self-employed that we have been examining – Johannesburg's Afrikaner brickmakers. Between 1892 and 1895 both the brickmakers and the town's building contractors enjoyed the benefits of the upturn in the Rand's economy as the number of plans which the Sanitary Board approved for construction rose from 1 200 in 1894 to over 2 500 in 1895. By 1896 there were over 1 500 brickmakers and several thousand manual labourers of different races at work on the most important of the brickmaking sites on the banks of the Braamfontein *spruit*. Then, just at the moment that building activity in the town started to slacken off markedly after the Raid, the brickmakers were served with a final notice by the government to quit this central site in order to make way for a marshalling yard needed by the expanding Netherlands South Africa Railway Co. In July 1896, after a series of unsuccessful appeals to Kruger, the majority of the brickmakers reluctantly left Braamfontein and made their way to the alternative site which the government had provided them with on the farm 'Waterval', some six miles out of town.

As in the case of the washermen, this move imposed a new and more demanding cost structure on the brickmakers at a time when they were least able to defend themselves. The number of building plans approved by the Sanitary Board fell from 1 500 in 1896 to just over 1 000 in 1897, and then to a disastrously low 440 in 1898. In addition, the brickmakers – like the washermen – found that some of the mine owners were more than willing to move into the economic space which they had been forced to vacate. In 1896 H Eckstein & Co bought a controlling interest in the newly floated Johannesburg Brick and Potteries Co, and this highly mechanised modern industrial enterprise soon dominated the local market for bricks. Unlike the washermen, however, the small brickmakers were not allowed to re-occupy their old business sites at a later date, and this made their subsequent struggle against the developing hold of industrial capitalism even more difficult. Under the circumstances it was hardly surprising that there were hundreds of brickmakers amongst Johannesburg's unemployed between 1896 and 1898.

The fortune of many of the town's Afrikaner cab drivers during this period can be traced along the same economic graph which indicated gathering success during the early nineties followed by a sharp reversal in mid-decade. Between 1892 and 1895 most of Johannesburg's cabbies prospered as the arrival of the railways and the growth of the white population during the boom occasioned a greater demand for transport within the town. The cab owners, however, were not the only ones to detect this improvement and, in 1895, the owners of the City & Suburban Tramway Co approached the Pretoria administration with yet another request that it be allowed to extend and electrify its lines on the Rand. The Kruger government again rejected this request – not so much because it wished to defend its urban cab-driving constituents against the advances of mining or industrial capitalism, but because it wished to protect the tramway company as an important market for the products of its more powerful rural constituents. Thwarted in its desire to electrify the system, the City & Suburban Co decided instead to extend its horse-drawn lines by 25 per cent in 1896. As in the other cases we have been considering, this development came at a particularly bad time for the self-employed cab owners, who not only had to contend with the extended competition of a powerful company, but with the enormous rise in the prices of horses and forage after the rinderpest epidemic. Over a period of 12 months, four out of every ten cab drivers in the town were thrown out of work as the number of licensed cabbies in Johannesburg slumped from 1 200 in 1896 to 700 in 1897.

When the Afrikaner cab drivers and brickmakers made their way to the dole queues, however, they soon discovered that many of the places were already occupied by members of yet another group of formerly self-employed kinsmen – the transport riders. After the discovery of gold, the Kruger government made energetic efforts to provide the Witwatersrand with a set of rail links to the coast and by the mid-nineties several of these schemes had come to fruition. The arrival of the railway from the Cape in January 1893 was followed exactly two years later by the arrival of the line from Delagoa Bay in January 1895, and ten months later by the arrival of the line from Natal in October 1895. But, while the development of this capitalist infrastructure undoubtedly helped to fuel the spectacular growth of the 'Kaffir Boom', it spelt disaster for the geographically dispersed and badly organised transport riders who could only provide isolated instances of spontaneous resistance to the advent of steam transport north of the Vaal. It was the railway revolution of

1895, followed shortly thereafter by the rinderpest epidemic, that did most to render thousands of Afrikaner transport riders permanently unemployed and, of these, several hundred found their way to Johannesburg's working-class suburbs of Fordsburg and Vrededorp.

Both the extent and the nature of this rapid build-up in the numbers of unemployed on the Rand took the Republic's ruling classes by complete surprise. While obviously aware of the depression and some of its social consequences, the government and the mine owners were initially of the opinion that most of the unemployment in Johannesburg was of a cyclical nature that derived from a temporary loss of financial confidence in the mining industry, and that most of those affected were thus single skilled immigrant miners who would be readily re-absorbed into the workforce once faith in the future of the Rand had been re-established. It was only after a series of menacing incidents and an unruly mass protest march in the centre of the town during the last quarter of 1897, that the Kruger administration and the mining companies became aware of the fact that much of the unemployment was structural in nature – that it derived from the first great spasm of capitalist development on the Witwatersrand and that many of the whites most badly affected were unskilled married Afrikaners who could not readily be absorbed into the working class.

Once this dimension of the problem was appreciated, however, the mine owners moved in quickly to control the situation. Within four days of the protest march during which a leading local journalist had narrowly escaped with his life, H Eckstein & Co announced its intention of taking on 200 unskilled Afrikaners as surface workers on its mines. This gesture was soon followed by other mine owners, and within four weeks over 500 Afrikaners had been found such positions in the industry. In addition, most of the large mining companies made generous cash donations to the Rand Relief Fund in an attempt to stem the rising tide of social tension within the town.

The Kruger government too, as we have seen, moved 'with commendable promptitude in regard to the question of relief to the indigent'. Within a week of the march it announced its intention of building an 'industrial school' to train the children of poor burghers, the setting up of a project to employ the workless women of Vrededorp in a public laundry, and a scheme to employ unskilled Afrikaner males on the construction of the Main Reef Road. While the first two of these schemes never came to fruition, the Pretoria administration did spend no less than £30 000 on the public works programme between early 1898 and late 1899. It was thus the employment generated by the Main Reef Road construction works that did most to ease class antagonism within the town, and the mine owners – sensing this – eased up on their contributions to Rand relief agencies after September 1898.

The economic crisis and structural unemployment of 1896-98, however, extended beyond the confines of Johannesburg's white working-class suburbs. Drought and rinderpest in the countryside pushed more blacks from neighbouring Natal onto the Rand labour market at precisely the moment that the mine owners were reducing wages and giving employment preference to the longer-working Shangaan labourers drawn from Mozambique. This, together with a marked decline in the demand for 'shop boys', 'messenger boys', *togt* workers and the collapse of employment opportunities in the washermen's guild and brickfields, meant that there was not only a general build-up in the level of black unemployment of the Rand during this period, but that much of it was 'Zulu' unemployment.

But, unlike the poor whites, unemployed blacks always found it difficult to linger in the urban areas, and this was particularly true after the pass laws had been promulgated in 1896. It was largely because of this that many of the 'Zulu' unemployed and some hardened criminals moved into the protective surroundings of the Klipriversberg to the immediate south of Johannesburg where, under the leadership of a remarkable man known as Jan Note, they were organised into a quasi-military body known as the 'Regiment of the Hills' or 'Ninevites'. This organisation, which contained within itself certain mutually contradictory elements, was partially fired by a sense of social justice while at the same time being involved in a series of profoundly anti-social activities. Its members, who saw themselves as being in a state of rebellion against the government's laws, lived largely by robbing passing migrant workers of their wages or from the proceeds of well-organised burglaries in the towns. By the outbreak of the war, when most of its members made their way back to Natal, the Regiment of the Hills had become a well-established feature of the Witwatersrand's criminal underworld.

Looking back then, it can be seen that the Witwatersrand and its inhabitants experienced a great lurch towards modern industrial society between 1892 and 1899, and that in general this was a movement which was facilitated rather than frustrated by the Kruger government. As H J and R E Simons have pointed out in a much-quoted passage:

> Few agrarian societies were so richly endowed or well equipped as the Transvaal for an industrial revolution. The republic attracted educated and professional men from Holland or the Cape, and was beginning to produce its own specialists. Left to itself it would have developed an efficient administration, a network of railways and roads, and adequate supplies of water and power. Far from being intractable, the burghers expanded production to provide food-

stuffs for the Rand, built railways linking it to the ports, enacted an excellent mining code, kept order over unruly, rebellious fortune-hunters, repelled an armed imperialist invasion, and held the world's greatest military power at bay for more than two years.[28]

Neither the mine owners nor their powerful allies, however, were content either to accumulate capital at a pace that was dictated by a rural bourgeoisie, or to share more generously the proceeds of an industrial revolution with Boer agricultural producers. The war of 1899-1902 was not so much a dispute over the desirability of capitalism as a goal for the Transvaal, as a conflict between two competing bourgeoisies about the terms and paths along which it could best be sought.

RECONSTRUCTION, MINING HEGEMONY AND THE SOCIAL ORIGINS OF THE MODERN WITWATERSRAND, 1902-1914

While the South African War severely disrupted the mining industry and caused indirect losses estimated at £25 million as capital lay in enforced idleness for many months, the Rand mine owners and investors had every reason to be optimistic once restrictions on mining operations were lifted in December 1901. Several administrative measures enacted by the British government, 'the most important of which were the reduction of railway rates and the adoption of a new duty on dynamite in the 1903 Customs Union Convention', initially helped to reduce the industry's average working costs.[29] This, together with a development loan of £35 million to the new Colony, did much to restore confidence in the future of the Rand and 1902-3 saw a significant spurt of investment in the mining industry.

But, as had happened at least once before in the history of the industry, Witwatersrand geology brought the European investment balloon back to earth just at the moment that it threatened to float away from economic reality. Soon after the war it became even more apparent than it had been in the late 1890s that the grade of ore recovered from the Rand mines fell off rapidly as the reef was pursued at ever greater depths.[30] At first, the effects of this were partially offset by selectively mining the higher-grade sections of the reef, but this short-term strategy did not offer any long-term solution to the problem. To make matters worse, this difficulty presented itself at a time when the industry was already being forced to contend with an acute shortage of cheap black labour.[31] This in turn tended to force up African wages and thus contributed substantially to an increase in the average working costs of the mines – a feature which became particularly noticeable after 1903.

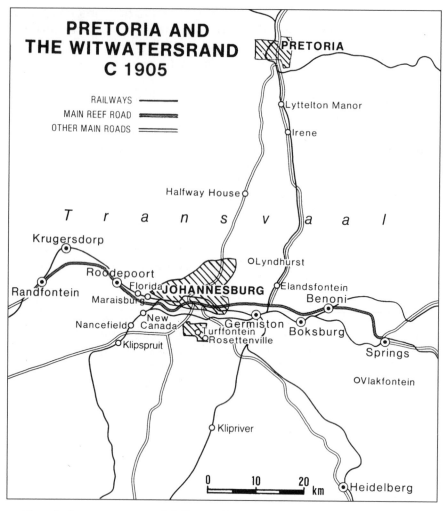

PRETORIA AND
THE WITWATERSRAND
C 1905

RAILWAYS
MAIN REEF ROAD
OTHER MAIN ROADS

Caught between a rapid falling off in the grade of ore being mined on the one hand and rising labour costs on the other, the post-war industry was soon confronted with a serious crisis of profitability. Normally, the way out of such a difficulty would have been for the producers to put up the price of their product and thus protect their profit margins. But, since gold was sold at a fixed price over fairly lengthy periods of time, the mine owners were denied this orthodox economic response. Instead, the mine owners countered in the only remaining way possible – they attempted to maximise output while minimising working costs.[32]

The programme to expand output took two related forms. First, the post-war industry mined gold 'at levels which increasingly approximated to the average grade of the deposits as a whole, rather than to the higher average grade of part of the deposits'.[33] This brought hitherto unexploited ground into production and widened the productive basis of the industry as a whole. Secondly, the mine owners introduced a series of technological innovations which greatly facilitated the programme of expanded production. Amongst these were the installation of tube mills, the extension of stamping capacity and the introduction of mechanised rock drills. Although some of these developments – notably the introduction of the rock drill – eroded the skills of the more highly paid white miners and thus contributed to the marked industrial conflict of this period, the programme as a whole was spectacularly successful and between 1901 and 1912 output rose at an average of 14,2 per cent per annum.

The attempt to minimise costs, however, proved to be far more difficult to manage. Apart from the few immediate post-war administrative successes noted above, and the economies of scale that flowed from a programme of expanded production, the mine owners at first had little to show for their efforts on this front. Despite the operation of the Witwatersrand Native Labour Association (WNLA), which the mine owners had specifically created to eliminate competition for unskilled labour within the industry and to hold down wages, the cost of African labour continued to rise alarmingly in the months after the signing of the Peace of Vereeniging. Early in 1903, therefore, the mine owners – with the active support of the post-war British administration – set out to explore new and radical ways of aiding the ailing industry and within 12 months the first of thousands of Chinese indentured labourers arrived on the Witwatersrand.

But not even the arrival of Chinese labourers in growing numbers after 1904 could immediately arrest the economic decline in the industry, and for several years the grade of ore mined continued to fall off more rapidly than did average working costs, thus exacerbating the industry's profitability crisis. Although the seriousness of this situation was to some extent masked by the tendency of the mine owners 'to distribute dividends in excess of figures justified by existing profit margins', most investors remained deeply sceptical and 'between 1902 and 1907 the market value of the shares of the 42 producing and dividend-paying companies on the Rand fell by over 50 per cent'.[34]

From about 1906, however, Chinese labour did help the industry to gradually recover its financial footing. The army of indentured labourers dramatically reduced the costly turnover of unskilled labour and enabled the industry to expand production at a crucial moment in its history. In addition, and at least as important, was the manner in which Chinese labour allowed the mine owners to undercut African labour, and after 1907 black wages in the industry declined in both real and monetary terms. All of this assisted the Rand in general, and the mines in particular, to recover from the serious economic depression of 1906-8, and in 1909 'almost as much foreign capital flowed into the mining industry as had come in in the previous three and a half years'.[35] After this turning point had been reached the policy of output maximisation and cost minimisation continued to gain momentum with increasingly beneficial results for the mine owners and their fellow investors. After a further round of industrial conflict in 1913-4, however, the mining industry found itself on the eve of yet another economic downturn.

While these booms and slumps in the fortunes of the mining industry did much to determine the pulse of economic life and the shape of society on the Witwatersrand between 1902 and 1914, not all of the fluctuations were of equal importance or significance. As in the pre-war era, it was the depression – this time of 1906-8 – that left the deepest imprint on the lives of those that we have been examining, and which most clearly marked the second great spasm of capitalist development on the Rand. But, unlike the Kruger era, this latter period was also characterised by radical political developments that were specifically designed to facilitate the emergence of a social infrastructure that was fully compatible with the needs of industrial capitalism.[36] And, of the three different governments that were responsible for the Transvaal between 1902 and 1914, it was the one that was free from any direct accountability to an electorate – the Milner administration – that intervened most directly to lay the foundations of modern industrial society on the Witwatersrand.[37]

When Johannesburg was fully re-opened to civilians in 1902 it immediately became the focus of attention for the Rand's working-class refugees whose financial resources had been exhausted by their prolonged and enforced stay at the coast.[38] Thousands of refugees, joined by hundreds of wartime immigrants, flooded back into the Rand's principal industrial city in a desperate scramble to find employment. The more fortunate of the skilled and semi-skilled male workers, aided by the early promise shown by the mining industry, succeeded in this search for jobs and quickly re-established themselves in their old quarters. But it was precisely this – the cautious re-entry of the majority of white workers into the Transvaal and their tendency to take up residence in boarding-houses, rather than in homes with their families – that initially caught the eye of politically sensitive observers, including one who was later to become British Prime Minister. In October 1902 James Ramsay Macdonald ventured the opinion that:

> President Kruger was perfectly right in refusing to recognise Johannesburg as a civic community which had settled into an organic part of the State. You have simply to walk through the wage-earning districts of the town to see the numerous working-

class dining rooms; you have simply to try and find a workman at home in Johannesburg, to discover that his home is only a bed-room, which he generally shares with a fellow workman, and that family life – upon which the state is built – may be said hardly to exist amongst great sections of the population. Men rent beds, not houses, in the Golden City.[39]

Had this eminent working class sympathiser visited the compounds spread along the Reef he would have discovered an even more alienat-ing and depressing absence of 'family life' amongst the black miners.[40]

Not all the white workers returning to the Rand, however, made their way to the boarding-houses or the mining companies' 'single quarters'. A significant minority of craftsmen and qualified artisans did indeed set up home in the more established working-class suburbs such as Jeppe, Troyeville, Belgravia and Fordsburg, thus contributing to a serious post-war housing crisis in a city that was already notoriously expensive to live in. At the other end of the scale, unskilled labourers and the unem-ployed – many of them Afrikaners – crowded into the lower end of Vrededorp or the 'Brickfields' where they contributed to a more threat-ening social problem. As the Commissioner of Police, E M Showers, reported in early 1902:

> These places are not laid out in any kind of order, and it is quite impossible to make any kind of arrangement for keeping any watch on the low class of people living in the place, or for an effec-tive guard over the property of people living in the Town.[41]

Post-war Johannesburg thus began to re-assert two of the features which had characterised it in earlier periods – a preponderance of adult males over females, and a tendency for the working classes to be clustered close to the points of production. In the latter period, however, the 'labouring classes and the dangerous classes' were pushed into closer proximity than ever before, and nowhere was this more evident than in the poorest south-western quarter of the city where parts of Fordsburg, Vrededorp, the Brickfields and the Indian location merged into one another.

The Milner administration proved to be remarkably sensitive to these social problems and the extent to which their possible political conse-quences could jeopardise the long-term development of industrial capi-talism on the Witwatersrand. In September 1902 the Governor of the Transvaal announced the appointment of a commission 'to enquire into and Report on the Johannesburg Insanitary Area Improvement Scheme'.[42] This scheme, piloted along the lines of the Westminster

Housing of the Working Classes Act of 1890, led to the effective demolition of the Brickfields and surrounding 'slum' areas, and their replacement by the commercial centre of Newtown. This was followed in 1903, with less success, by a commission to enquire into 'the scarcity of housing accommodation in Johannesburg, as especially affecting the members of the artisan working classes and those earning small salaries'.[43] In mid-1903 the Transvaal Immigration Department, in close co-operation with the London-based South African Colonisation Society, stepped up its efforts to introduce British female domestic servants to the Witwatersrand – a move calculated, amongst other things, not only to remedy the imbalance in sex ratios in the new colony, but to help displace black male domestic servants into the mining industry.[44] And, in October 1903, the administration approved new by-laws which enabled local authorities to deal more effectively with several 'private' locations for blacks in urban areas along the Reef.[45]

All of these measures were, in differing degrees, designed to help stabilise the Rand's skilled white proletariat, secure British hegemony, and facilitate social control by separating the labouring classes from the dangerous classes. But if it was the Witwatersrand in general that was the object of the administration's interest, then it was Johannesburg in particular that was singled out for special attention. It was here, more than anywhere else, that Milner and his colleagues were concerned to prevent the eruption of open class conflict, and, to this end, the administration constantly urged the mine owners to develop a wider appreciation of the needs of industrial capitalism. This pressure was particularly evident in two areas – the question of white working-class housing, and the related issue of town planning.

Between 1896 and 1899 the cost of building white working-class homes on the Witwatersrand rose substantially as a result of the high price of machine-made bricks and cement – factors which were, to a very large extent, under the direct control of the mine owners who dominated the latter industries.[46] This gave rise to a situation where the supply of houses fell well behind demand, thus aggravating the subsequent post-war housing shortage on the Rand. By 1903 the shortfall of houses was sufficiently pronounced for the members of the Johannesburg Housing Commission to debate seriously the feasibility of working-class housing being provided by the state or local government. After careful consideration, however, the commission came to the conclusion that the situation would best be alleviated through the initiative of 'private enterprise'.

As the part of 'private enterprise' best placed to help overcome the shortage, and as the employers who stood to lose most from the crisis in working-class accommodation, the mine owners paid some attention to the commission's findings. Over a 36-month period between 1903 and

1905 the H Eckstein & Co-controlled Johannesburg Brick and Potteries Co Ltd reduced the price of machine-made bricks on the Rand by 50 per cent, and still made a handsome profit. Responding to the fall in construction costs brought about by this and other factors, several mining companies reluctantly expanded their programme to provide housing for their European employees. Between 1902 and 1905, for example, Rand Mines, Consolidated Gold Fields and East Rand Proprietary Mines collectively spent about £400 000 on providing accommodation for married employees.[47]

But the eight hundred or so houses provided by these leading companies did not bring about a marked improvement in the overall position on the Rand, and a nervous reconstruction administration continued to push the industry to make further investments in its housing programme. In January 1906 Lord Selborne – Milner's successor in the Transvaal – again broached the subject with Lionel Phillips of Wernher, Beit & Co. The mine owners, however, constrained by the continuing and deepening profitability crisis in the industry, were unwilling to countenance any further expenditure in this direction. As Phillips put it in his reply to Selborne a few days later:

> When, therefore, you ask me to lead the way in providing more married quarters so that we may see a larger British population settled in the country and, at the same time, that the ultimate interests of the mining industry be furthered, I am obliged to answer, that while I am in full sympathy with your views, the moment is not propitious to consider any large and avoidable capital outlay.[48]

It was thus only after there had been an undoubted upturn in the performance of the industry, in 1909, that the mine owners and others were willing to resume their investment in working-class housing.

In 1910 the outgoing Transvaal government, still anxious to help find ways of getting hesitant white workers to commit themselves to a future on the Rand, appointed a commission of enquiry to examine the conditions under which certain titles to property were held in some of Johannesburg's residential areas. When this commission reported, two years later, it recommended that those tenants who were willing to pay in a modest predetermined amount should be allowed to acquire property previously held on leasehold terms under freehold conditions.[49] Significantly, this process of conversion was facilitated by the powerful Township Owners' Association, a body with exceptionally strong links to mining capital. By the same year – 1912 – some of the leading mine owners, such as R W Schumacher of Rand Mines, were also sufficiently confident about the future of the industry to allow white miners to buy certain houses from the company regardless of whether or not they intended remaining employees of Rand Mines.[50] The arrival of the latter situation, where the mine owners were willing to relax one of the means of control which they exercised over their more highly paid workers, was a measure of the degree to which the Witwatersrand's white proletariat was becoming stabilised, as well as de-skilled, by the outbreak of the First World War.

As we have already seen, however, it was not only the quantity and quality of housing provided for white workers that was of interest to the post-war Transvaal authorities, but its distribution through the city. Here again, it was Milner's reconstruction administration, and more particularly the man whom he appointed as Town Clerk in Johannesburg, Lionel Curtis, that was most actively involved in planning a secure future for industrial capitalism. Curtis, with his Mansion House Committee on the Dwellings of the Poor experience behind him, was always acutely aware of the class antagonisms that existed between London's east and west ends, and in 1901 he suggested that:

> What we have to fear and avoid is the creation of a similar state of things in Johannesburg – where the area north of the reef would be covered by the residences of the well-to-do, and by streets of shops supplying their wants – while the area south of the reef would be inhabited solely by the poorer employees of the mines and by an inferior class of local shopkeepers. There are, therefore, strong reasons based upon the broadest political ground for securing now and for ever that the various townships shall radiate from their economic centres, that each class shall bear the political and social burdens which should fall to their lot as members of an economic whole, and that one class should not be allowed to separate its life from another class with which it is bound up by an inseparable economic tie.[51]

Thus, in addition to being one of the prime movers to rid the inner city of its 'slum' areas, Curtis was anxious to ensure a more even spread of the working classes through the city. In order to bring this about the Town Clerk and his colleagues proposed that there be a substantial increase in the size of the city's boundaries and that, in order to offset the greater distance that would separate the worker from the point of production, Johannesburg be served by a modern system of cheap public transport.

Curtis's preliminary work on the scheme to have Johannesburg's municipal boundaries extended pre-dated any form of civilian administration on the Rand. In April 1901 he and the military officer in charge of the city, Major W O'Meara of the Royal Engineers, after reaching agreement on the broad outlines of the Acting Town Clerk's plans, arranged for the municipal boundaries to be extended to cover nine square miles. Five months later, in September 1901, Curtis won the endorsement of Milner's nominated town council for a far more ambitious scheme. When the outline of this latter scheme was sent to the Chamber of Mines for 'comment', however, it at first met with resistance from some of the mine owners who feared that any substantial extension of the boundaries would inevitably include mining property, and thus render the industry liable to pay rates. It was only after Percy FitzPatrick – at Milner's request – had explained the political advantages of the scheme to the less far-sighted of his colleagues, that the mine owners agreed to support the plan. In 1903 Johannesburg's municipal boundaries were extended to embrace an area of 82 square miles – a figure which differed radically from the modest five square miles which the town had covered when Kruger first granted it municipal status in 1897.

In the meantime, however, the Town Clerk's plan for an efficient public transport system to serve a greater Johannesburg had run into difficulties. The Transvaal Concessions Commission of 1901, unwilling to alienate powerful European financiers and local mining capitalists with large holdings in the City & Suburban Tramway Co, had acknowledged the legality of the concession originally granted by the Kruger government. The company's directors proceeded to put this finding to good use, and demanded substantial compensation from the town council before they would be willing to relinquish their right to operate a horse-drawn tramway system in the inner city. In June 1904, after several months of negotiation, an agreement was reached for the town council to acquire the assets and rights of the City & Suburban Co at a cost of £150 000; but even so it was only in February 1906 that the electric tram finally made its appearance in the streets of central Johannesburg. Shortly thereafter, the system was extended to serve the new working-class suburbs to the north-east of the city such as Kensington and Malvern.

Looking back then, it can be seen how, although it was under the immediate post-war administration that most was done to plan for the emergence of Johannesburg as a mature industrial city, it was only some years later that most of this planning started to take effect. Equally noteworthy was the manner in which the state was called upon to take the lead in designing an appropriate socio-economic infrastructure for the city between 1902 and 1906, and constantly having to spur the mine owners to greater efforts in the fields of housing, transport and town planning at a time when the mining industry was labouring under the strains of a profitability crisis.

Once the turning point of the depression had been reached, however, Johannesburg experienced an accelerated social transformation which was relatively smoothly channelled along the lines which had been laid down by the architects of reconstruction. A marked increase in the amount of working-class accommodation available in urban areas that were increasingly accessible, saw a fall in rents at a time when other factors were already producing a gradual reduction in the cost of living in the city.[52] In general, the period between 1908 and the outbreak of the war saw a marked decline in the number of single male workers based in the boarding-houses of the inner city, and a sharp increase in the number of working-class families located in the suburbs. In 1897 only 12 per cent of the Witwatersrand's European mine employees were married and had their families resident with them in the Transvaal; by 1902 this figure had crept up to 20 per cent, and in 1912 it reached 42 per cent.[53] It is thus largely against this backdrop – the emergence of the white working-class family in the suburbs of a more socially ordered colonial city – that we have to view the changing fortunes of the groups that we have been examining between 1902 and 1914.

At the outbreak of the South African War most of the Rand's 'foreign' pimps and prostitutes fled to the coastal cities where their wartime presence and subsequent behaviour attracted much adverse comment, and ultimately helped to usher in a new round of morality legislation in the various southern African colonies. As soon as Johannesburg was re-opened to civilians, however, many of these 'undesirables' promptly made their way back to the Witwatersrand, and in July 1903 the reconstruction administration – in an attempt to be seen to be coping with an old problem – passed Ordinance 46, the 'Immorality Act'.

But, if in theory the Transvaal was now well placed to restrict the growth of the *demi-monde* in its principal industrial city, then in practice the authorities did little to curtail the activities of those European women who sold sexual services to white working-class men. Aware of the social composition of the city and sensitive to the alienated existence led by most white miners, Milner and his most senior advisers were of the opinion that 'local conditions' formed an all-important consideration in determining how the policy to combat public vice was implemented. This sympathetic concern for the lot of the boarding-house residents, however, was not extended to the compound dwellers and such police action as there was, therefore, was largely directed against those white prostitutes who were willing to take black customers – a racist double-standard which helped to increase the cultural distance separating the two major ethnic components of the working class. The years between 1902 and 1905 thus saw the re-emergence of organised vice in central Johannesburg, albeit on a somewhat diminished scale, and with a clientele that was more effectively racially segregated than it had been before the war.

For an extremely intricate set of reasons, however, this situation started to change in important respects during the depression. A campaign against certain leading vice merchants by the police in 1906 was followed by a far more successful drive during 1907-8 when scores of prostitutes – for reasons that are unfortunately not clear – assisted the authorities by turning against their pimps. The state made use of this revolt by the prostitutes to obtain the evidence necessary to deport hundreds of for-eign-born 'undesirables' from the Transvaal, an offensive which was continued right up to the formation of Union in 1910 by a former Kruger official who was all too familiar with the problems of prostitution on the Rand, J C Smuts.

On the one hand then, the period 1906 to 1914 saw a decline in the more highly organised vice of the inner city – an administratively-led achievement that was supplemented by the fall in the demand for the services of prostitutes occasioned by the surge in the number of work-ing-class families being established in Johannesburg at the time. On the other, however, the same period saw an increase in the more loosely organised prostitution located in the older and poorer working-class quarters around the city centre. During the depression a significant num-ber of working women in Fordsburg and Vrededorp turned to casual sexual liaisons in order to supplement their meagre wages, and in many cases this later gave way to a full-time career of prostitution. By the out-break of the First World War, white Johannesburg's commercial sexual needs were being largely catered for by the daughters of the Rand's own proletariat – thus ending a dependency on 'continental' women that dated back all the way to the 'Kaffir Boom' of the mid-nineties.

The other major element of social control on the Witwatersrand that harked back to the mid-nineties – the use of alcohol to help stabilise black labour – also experienced a decline in the new era. When the British army occupied Pretoria, on 5 June 1900, a proclamation issued under martial law prevented any further manufacture or sale of spiritu-ous liquor in the town. This move effectively sealed off Hatherley Distillery as the major source of cheap liquor destined for the Rand's black mineworkers, and a few months later the military authorities fol-lowed up on this action with the large-scale arrest and deportation of for-eign-born illicit liquor dealers in Johannesburg.

These swift and decisive military measures won the immediate approval of the mine owners who, sensing that their allies were winning the war, at once took steps to ensure that the mining industry would not lose the peace. At precisely the moment that the Transvaal started to experience the transition from a military to a civilian administration, a new body which enjoyed the support of most of the mine owners – 'The South African Alliance for the Reform of the Liquor Traffic' – emerged to put pressure on the reconstruction government to exercise tight control over the retail liquor trade on the Witwatersrand. Milner, however, already had strong ideas of his own on the subject and needed little persuading about the virtues of 'total prohibition' for blacks. After the concessions commission had issued its report and recommended the cancellation of the Hatherley concession with generous compensation for its owners, the reconstruction government passed Ordinance 32 of 1902 which prohibited the distillation of spirits for commercial gain in the new colony.

In 1902 Milner and the mine owners therefore picked up where the Kruger government had left off and abandoned the use of alcohol as a device with which to help stabilise the mining industry's migratory labour force, although mine managers did – for some time – continue to make use of a weekly issue of 'Kaffir Beer' as one of the means of keeping control over their unskilled workers.[54] This renewed willingness to dispense with the carrot, however, was more than compensated for by an increase in the use of the stick. The reconstruction administration 'extended the pass department, created a system of courts to deal with masters and servants legislation' and 'introduced a scheme to register the fingerprints of all mining employees to help identify workers who had deserted', while the mine owners improved the capacity of their compounds to exercise physical control over the inmates.[55] In part then, the post-war ruling classes could afford to do without some of the more indirect forms of control over the Rand's black miners precisely because they exercised so much greater direct control over workers in the mining industry.

But, despite the enhanced law-enforcement capacity of the post-war state, the sale of alcohol to black miners by persons based outside the compounds did not cease to be a minor source of irritation to the mine owners between 1902 and 1914, and more especially so during periods of economic recession when 'poor whites' in areas of high unemployment turned to the illicit liquor trade to ensure their survival. Significantly, parts of Fordsburg and Vrededorp figured prominently amongst such supply areas after 1906. Within a decade, vibrant working-class communities which had once supplied the Rand with many of its transport riders, brickmakers and cab drivers, were reduced to providing the city with a disproportionate number of its illicit liquor dealers and prostitutes.

Black miners, however, were not the only group of African men on the Witwatersrand to attract official attention after the war. The shortage of cheap unskilled labour in the mining industry forced the reconstruction administration to look well beyond the usual sources of supply, and it was during the course of this search that the growing number of Zulu 'houseboys' on the Rand came to its notice. The presence of this sizeable pool of unproductive labour amidst a serious shortage of productive labour in the colony's premier industry proved to be too much of a temptation to resist, and between 1902 and 1906 Milner and the mine owners made two major attempts to dislodge the 'houseboys' from the kitchens and force them into the compounds.

First – and as we have already noted in another context – immediately after the war the reconstruction administration set about encouraging the immigration of white female domestics from the United Kingdom in the belief that Rand employers would give preference to white housemaids over black 'houseboys', and thus dispense with the services of their Zulu servants. This well-organised venture, the South African Expansion Committee and its successor, the South African Colonisation Society, enjoyed the personal support and financial assistance of several prominent mine owners and the ubiquitous Percy FitzPatrick acted as chairman of its 'advisory council'. Secondly, in 1904, E P Rathbone, editor of the journal *South African Mines, Commerce and Industry*, proposed to Johannesburg householders that they establish an Employers' Domestic Native Labour Association (EDNLA), along the lines of WNLA, in order to engineer a fall in the steadily rising wages of Zulu 'houseboys'. This move, which in the short run would achieve the overt objective of reducing 'houseboy' wages, would also have the long-term effect of rendering the domestic service sector of the local economy less attractive to African men and the scheme therefore received the support of 'many industrial and representative parties'.[56]

In the final analysis, however, both of these schemes failed in so far as they were designed to increase the flow of cheap labour into the mining industry. White domestic servants never came to the Rand in sufficient numbers for them to make a significant impact on the service sector of the economy, while those who did soon absorbed the values of a colonial society and refused to undertake menial, dirty or hard labour – thus leaving intact a role for the black 'houseboy'. Rathbone, for his part, discovered that while it was one thing to get a small number of mine owners to co-operate to form a monopsonistic association like WNLA within a single industry, it was quite another to get hundreds of individual employers to put their domestic labour arrangements at risk through an outside agency such as EDNLA. When 'houseboy' wages did eventually fall, between 1906 and 1908, it was as a product of the depression and an influx of black female and child labour, rather than as a result of any external attempt at manipulating the labour market.

The failure of these early attempts to alter fundamentally the structure of the service sector meant that for much of the interwar period Zulu 'houseboys' were, to an increasing extent, brought into immediate and highly personal contact with immigrant English working-class women who were either fellow servants in the homes of the affluent, or the

39

wives of white miners in the suburbs. This great cultural collision between black adult males who were responsible heads of household in their own right, and young white females newly exposed to colonial society, produced a highly explosive psychological mixture which gave rise to periodic outbursts of great sexual hysteria on the Witwatersrand between 1902 and 1914. It was these recurrent 'black peril' scares and, to a lesser extent, the partially organised resistance of the 'houseboys' to colonisation as expressed through *Amalaita* gangs, that contributed to the gradual but far from complete substitution of black male by black female domestic labour in the years leading up to the First World War.

The history of the other group of Zulu speakers that we have been following – the members of the washermen's guild – was even more troubled than that of the 'houseboys' in the post-war period. Between 1901 and 1905 the Milner administration sought to bring these small black businessmen under more effective control by attempting to get the *AmaWasha* to occupy a single segregated site under municipal supervision. Eventually these efforts succeeded in 1906 when the washermen – after a period of prolonged harassment – were expelled from the city's perimeter and made to occupy a site adjacent to the municipal sewerage farm at Klipspruit some 13 miles from the centre of Johannesburg.

This enforced move to an economic wasteland by administrative fiat did much to hasten the demise of the guild. It imposed a new and demanding cost structure on the Zulu washermen at the worst possible moment – the start of the depression – and thus left them vulnerable to the competition of a growing number of capitalist steam laundries as well as that of Chinese and Asian laundrymen who had been allowed to stay on in the city. To add to their difficulties the *AmaWasha* were also the victims of the Rand's rapidly changing social structure after 1909, as wives and black servants undertook a growing volume of domestic laundry within the confines of working or middle-class homes. All of these factors contributed to a steady decline in the average number of municipal washing licences granted to the members of the guild during this period. In 1905, the last year during which the Zulu washermen were permitted to operate on the outskirts of the city, this figure stood at 262, by 1914 it was down to 93 – a reduction of more than 60 per cent over a brief nine-year period.

Johannesburg's Afrikaner brickmakers, who had been forced to vacate the city centre in 1896, fared equally dismally after the turn of the century. For a brief period during 1902-3 the 'Waterfall Brickmakers' Association' prospered as its 30 to 40 members and their employees took advantage of the post-war housing boom. In the more taxing years that followed, however, the brickmakers suffered greatly as a result of being located six miles out of town – something which the Kruger government had promised to offset by providing a rail link to the city centre. High transport costs and the powerful competition provided by Eckstein's Brick & Potteries Co did much to destroy the viability of these smaller enterprises at Waterval, and by the onset of the depression in 1906 there were hundreds of Afrikaner brickmakers amongst Johannesburg's unemployed.

These brickmakers, however, did not want for familiar company in the depression dole queues. After the war many Afrikaners had successfully re-established themselves in the local cab trade while the town council and the City & Suburban Co struggled to reach agreement about the fate of the horse-drawn tramway system which Johannesburg had inherited from the Kruger government. But once this compromise had been reached, the cab drivers' days were numbered, and between 1906 – when the first electric tram appeared on the city streets – and 1909, some 600 cab drivers were thrown out of work.

This gradual build-up in the number of unemployed white workers in Johannesburg after the war, and then the more rapid increase during the depression, did not find the Transvaal's ruling classes entirely unprepared. Early in 1903 Milner and Curtis, with the support and financial assistance of the leading mine owners, had helped to launch the Rand Aid Association. This body, once again consciously modelled along the lines of a metropolitan institution – this time the Charity Organisation Society of London – was largely designed to co-ordinate the provision of temporary relief to those skilled and semi-skilled workers in the city who found themselves facing short periods of unemployment, and this role it filled with relative ease during the post-war recession.

From mid-1906, however, there was an enormous and sudden increase in the numbers of both skilled and unskilled workers without jobs in the city. Immigrant workers in the building and allied trades suffering the ravages of cyclical unemployment were now joined by hundreds of unskilled Afrikaner workers rendered jobless by more lasting structural changes in the local economy. This situation brought Johannesburg's unemployed English workers with their well-developed tradition of trade unionism and organisation into much closer contact – and competition – with their Afrikaner counterparts, and extended the resources of the Rand Aid Association to pose the ruling classes with a more formidable challenge.

In 1906, Selborne – under considerable pressure from concerned local government officials along the Reef – appointed the Transvaal Indigency Commission to examine the causes of widespread unemployment in the colony, and to suggest ways of overcoming it. This commission, subsequently taken over by the *Het Volk* government, did little to provide increasingly impatient men with work, however, and when English mineworkers went on strike in May 1907 the mine owners saw the possibility of combining political expediency with economic necessity by using unskilled Afrikaners as strike breakers. But, out of a complex mixture of fear and class solidarity, Johannesburg's Afrikaner unemployed hesitated before acting as scab labour and the majority of positions were thus filled by workers drawn from further afield. It was thus left to yet another body, the Rand Unemployment Investigation Committee, to supersede temporarily the politically suspect Rand Aid Association, and create a significant number of positions for militant unskilled workers on the mines and in the municipal service between March 1908 and the end of the depression.

The trauma of unemployment and the scars of the depression, however, left their unmistakable imprint on the class consciousness of the city's Afrikaners, and this reflected itself in their continuing search for an appropriate political home. Throughout the period 1908-14 poor Afrikaners in Vrededorp searched, largely in vain, for a place in a labour movement which could accommodate their distinctive needs as unskilled white workers. But, neither the nationalists of *Het Volk* who attempted to win their loyalty through a labour wing of the party, *Arbeid Adelt*, nor the trade unionists of the craft-dominated Labour Party could capture and hold the allegiance of these vulnerable workers, thus exacerbating the turbulence of working-class politics in the city. As late as May 1914, the Johannesburg Town Council, during the course of its evidence to the Relief and Grants-in-Aid Commission, noted that these workers 'had overturned every political party, and would overturn any political party which might be in power unless a remedy was provided to remove their appalling poverty and degration'.[57] A mere two months later, in July 1914, the first of several working-class leaders in Vrededorp joined the ranks of the newly established National Party.

For the unenfranchised black workers of the city, however, there was nowhere to turn for even temporary relief from the problems of poverty and unemployment. The use of Chinese indentured labour on the mines, structural changes in the local economy during the depression, and the dislocation caused by the Bambatha Rebellion in rural Natal, all appear to have contributed to growing 'Zulu' unemployment on the Rand after 1906. Confronted by the more effective repressive capacity of the reconstruction state and its successors, these unemployed men soon found themselves either locked up in prison, or else seeking shelter in the disused mine shafts, prospect holes or abandoned houses on the city's periphery – all well-established haunts of Jan Note's lumpenproletarian army.

But, whereas before the turn of the century some of the Ninevites' activities had been inspired by a sense of social justice and the desire to cling to aspects of a peasant lifestyle in a rapidly industrialising society, after the war Note's organisation appears to have become increasingly anti-social as the mining revolution produced its first significant numbers of fully proletarianised black workers. After 1910 the Ninevites hid themselves more effectively from the endless pass raids of the police by taking refuge in the mine compounds, from where they launched criminal sorties not only against white property in neighbouring towns, but against black migrant workers. It was as a result of these essentially apolitical activities that Note's army found itself locked in a confrontation with the forces of the state during much of 1912 and 1913. Denied orthodox outlets in a repressive and racially discriminatory state, the Witwatersrand's black unemployed turned to crime rather than politics for a solution to their problem.

CONCLUSION

When gold was discovered on the Witwatersrand in 1886 it hurtled Kruger's slumbering *Zuid Afrikaansche Republiek* into the modern era of industrial capitalism. Within months, rural notables who had previously presided over a slowly developing agricultural economy were called upon to exercise control over one of the fastest growing and most technologically sophisticated mining industries in the world. And, within little more than a decade, the near bankrupt ZAR was transformed into the wealthiest and most powerful state in southern Africa.

The vision of a journey from rags to riches via the path of industrialisation was not one which had entirely eluded the ZAR's overlords – indeed, Kruger's plans for the industrial development of the Transvaal pre-dated the discovery of gold on the Rand when he helped to christen the *Eerste Fabrieken* as *Volkshoop* in 1881. But what Kruger and his colleagues had always envisaged was the emergence of a state in which industry was the logical outgrowth of, and ultimately dependent on, the output of a dominant agricultural sector. Kruger's concessions policy was thus initially designed to foster the growth of a very particular set of enterprises – namely, those that converted the agricultural output of his Boer constituents into products which could be sold within the slowly developing markets of the Republic and its adjacent territories.

What the discovery of gold did, however, was to sweep aside the major assumptions on which the concessions policy had been predicated. Almost overnight the ZAR's rulers found themselves governing a state in which extractive industry rather than agricultural production constituted the mainstay of the economy. The concessions policy, originally designed to facilitate the accumulation of capital in the countryside by nationals, now had to be hastily extended to meet the changing demands of European capitalists in the urban centres of the Witwatersrand as the mining industry moved from outcrop diggings to deep-level production within the space of a decade.

Kruger and his colleagues' strategy for industrialisation was thus overtaken by events. Once committed to the concessions policy, however, the ZAR government found it virtually impossible to stage a retreat. If, after the discovery of gold, Kruger had simply abandoned the concessions policy as originally conceived and opened the Republic to the unrestricted competition of foreign products, he would have had to sacrifice important markets – such as those of the distillery and the tramway company – at precisely the moment that these enterprises were starting to channel a significant flow of funds back into the countryside. Moreover, after 1890 the government was faced with strong domestic opposition to the concessions policy from its 'progressive' rivals, while after 1896 criticisms of those concessions which adversely affected the cost structure of the mining industry were difficult to entertain in view of the political climate generated by the Jameson Raid.

It is within this wider context and on this broader testing ground that the ZAR government's strategy for industrialisation has to be reassessed. Kruger's concessions policy cannot simply be refracted through the rapidly changing demands of the mining industry and be said to have failed. If the policy was indeed a failure in so far as it did not relieve the growing pressure on the cost structure of the mining industry after the opening of the deep levels, then this 'failure' has surely to be offset against the 'success' which it enjoyed in attempting to serve agriculture. It is only once the evolving concessions policy has been situated within the political economy of the ZAR as a whole, and its strengths and limitations more rigorously examined through detailed case studies, that we will be able to arrive at a more balanced judgement of Kruger's strategy for industrialisation.

If, however, Kruger's vision of a republic founded on an agricultural base with an industrial outgrowth was eclipsed by the mining revolution, then it was Milner who – with the help of the mine owners – realigned the social, political and economic infrastructure of the Transvaal in such a way that it became an industrial state served by agriculture. But, whereas the economic and political aspects of the reconstruction programme have been subjected to close scrutiny – and more especially as they directly affected the mining industry – the social planning which the post-war administration put into the creation of a modern industrial state has been somewhat neglected.

As noted above, much of the Milner administration's efforts in the latter field were directed towards increasing social control over the Rand's population; by separating the labouring classes from the dangerous classes in 'slums' such as the Brickfields and the 'washing locations', and by attempting to distribute and stabilise white working-class families in the suburbs of an enlarged city. These strategies for separating the residential areas of various subordinate groups – on an intra-class as well as an inter-class basis – were in some cases buttressed by further divisions introduced at the place of work. It was, for example, Johannesburg's post-war administration which initiated the distinction between 'first' and 'second class' cabs in the city, a division which exacerbated the differences of colour and class in a trade which, in times of crisis, had tended to manifest a degree of interracial co-operation. Likewise, one of the effects of relegating the *AmaWasha* to Klipspruit in 1906 was to separate the Zulu washermen from those Asian *Dhobis* with whom they had been labouring in great harmony for several years. These, and other examples which may be drawn from changes in policy relating to the issuing of municipal hawking and trading licenses, suggest that it may be profitable to mount a more systematic examination of the manner in which the occupational and residential patterns of the subordinate classes on the Witwatersrand were brought into greater alignment during the first decade of the twentieth century.

Here again, however, the 'success' achieved by the Milner administration in the field of social planning during a period when it was largely freed of any direct electoral accountability, will have to be offset against the subsequent 'failure' of town councils more closely bound by local class interests to extend the Curtis initiative. When W C Scully visited Johannesburg in 1911 he was still struck by 'the sudden transition from splendour to squalor on the western side of the city', and by numerous 'slum-warrens' housing 'Europeans of various nationalities – Indians, Chinese, Arabs, Japanese, Kaffirs and miscellaneous Coloured people of every hue'.[58] These interracial 'slum-yards', which yielded their own distinctive sub-cultures, merit closer study, not only because of their intrinsic interest, but because they will heighten our understanding of the various ways in which they helped to inform – and in turn were informed by – the emerging culture of the city's black labouring population.

In much the same way, the changes in white working-class culture that accompanied the move from the boarding-houses of the inner city to the working-class homes of the suburbs need to be explored. In general, this shift heralded a decline in the male-centred leisure-time activities of drinking, whoring and gambling in various forms, and the rise of more 'balanced' family entertainment centred around the theatre, the cinema and communally organised sport and recreation. It also, however, helped to increase the growing social distance between white and black miners. Workers, who at one time had been drawn closer together by their need for alcohol and prostitutes as an escape from the privations of boarding-house and compound life, now found themselves inhabiting different social worlds, as white miners, in growing numbers, 'settled down' to family life. Lionel Phillips was certainly aware of all these dimensions – and of the new opportunity which they afforded the mine owners when, during the course of a letter to Lord Selborne in 1906, he noted that:

> The Recreation Hall and the opportunity for social intercourse and rational entertainments which it affords can also, I think, be made a valuable instrument in raising the tone of the working man. I intend personally to go to as many entertainments at the mines as possible, as I am a great believer in the effect of personal intercourse and if those men who are at the head of mining affairs attend functions of this order, the example will no doubt be followed by those employees and their wives who have not hitherto come into much contact with the miners, artisans and men of that class. With novel labour conditions, such as we have in this country, success will depend in no small measure upon the White man being superior in fact, as well as in name, and setting an example to the unskilled Kaffirs or Chinamen. An increase in the class of respectable married men, with their families, would undoubtedly tend in this direction, so I am entirely with you in this connection.[59]

From this and other evidence we have, it is clear that both ruling-class initiative and subordinate-class expression will have to be carefully charted and distinguished when the history of working-class culture on the Rand comes to be written.

It is only once this latter task is completed, and we can add our knowledge of the emerging working-class culture to our greater understanding of the de-skilling of white workers over the same period, that we will be in a position to appreciate more fully the nature and significance of the European miners' struggle during the first two decades of the twentieth century.[60] After the advent of deep levels, white workers not only gave their labour to the mining industry, they committed their whole lives – and those of their wives and children – to a future based on the Witwatersrand. Given this escalating commitment it is less than surprising that they responded with growing anger and violence when their livelihoods were put at stake in 1907, 1913 and 1922; nor is it surprising that they did not win the support of the majority of their fellow workers who had been left stranded in the shadows of the compound. Had they done so, they would have succeeded in launching an even more effective challenge to the world the mine owners made.[61]

2

RANDLORDS AND ROTGUT, 1886-1903

The role of alcohol in the development of
European imperialism and southern African
capitalism, with special reference to
black mineworkers in the Transvaal Republic

The presence or absence of an agricultural surplus has always played a
central role in the historical transition of pre-capitalist modes of production into capitalist modes. At the very least, the inhabitants of the new
towns and the emerging proletariat have to be fed by the food produced
on the land. The capacity of various systems to produce such an agricultural surplus during the transformation to capitalism, however, has varied significantly, as has the ability of the emerging social formation to
absorb it. In general though, it seems plausible to suggest that the development of European capitalism is as much punctuated by the absence of
an agricultural surplus as by its presence. It is largely, although not solely, for this reason that rising prices, starvation and food riots occupy such
an important chapter in European economic history.[1]

But having noted this broad pattern, social and economic historians
should also be prepared to pay close attention to those cases in which
substantial agricultural surpluses *were* generated. In Europe, as elsewhere, any one of a number of reasons could account for such surpluses
and often the contributing factors were regionally specific – for example,
land distribution, technological innovation or the cost of labour. It is not
simply the genesis or size of the surpluses that should be noted however, but their rather specific *quality*. Here it is important to realise that in
some respects agricultural commodities had almost unique properties
during the historical development of capitalism in the eighteenth and
nineteenth centuries. Unlike many such commodities today, fresh produce could not be stored for relatively lengthy periods, processed into
tinned foods, or transported across vast distances to the more certain
markets offered by affluent societies. Thus, during the European transi-

tion to capitalism, the producer was faced with a potentially substantial loss if he could not dispose of his agricultural surplus – a problem which still troubles the contemporary, producer, albeit to a lesser extent. Historically, it was precisely for this reason that producers sought ways of storing the value of their commodities, or minimising the losses they were likely to sustain in the event of over-production. Through distillation, agricultural surplus was converted into spirits and not only was part of its value maintained, but in some cases the price actually increased as the commodity matured. Capital accumulated through spirit distillation thus provided one of the clearest visible links between a declining agriculturally-based feudal regime, and a modern industrial capitalist order.[2]

In several parts of Europe such capital was initially accumulated through the creation and exploitation of local markets. During the eighteenth century in Rumania, for example, the Porte had prohibited the export of corn from any of the provinces. Faced with grain surpluses, The Rumanian landlords took to distilling spirits which they then used in paying their labourers. The remainder of the spirits they obliged villagers to buy at the public houses which they opened on their estates.[3] In Russia liquor leases were widely sold between 1712 and 1863. These leases proved to be 'a significant means of primary accumulation of capital', and 'were the origin of the later fortunes of the large industrial bourgeois families of the Yakolevs, Zlobins, Saposhnikovs, and Kokorevs'.[4] The Russian nobility were also not above the liquor trade and the prices Dolgoruki, Gagarin, Kurakin and Potemkin all earned a sizeable part of their income from the sale of spirits.

The development of such local markets, however, did not mean that producers came into direct contact with the consumers. Usually the spirits found their way to the new markets via the European publicans – the petty bourgeoisie. For this reason it was the publicans, rather than the producers, who came to figure prominently in the popular perception of the liquor trade – an understandable but unfortunate fact, given that many publicans were Jewish. In Russia and the Ukraine, for example, most of the canteens in the rural areas during the mid-nineteenth century were owned by Jewish businessmen. The *korchma* or tavern was a prominent part of peasant life and many Ukrainian folk songs of the time bemoaned the peasant's indebtedness to the local Jew. In the urban areas too, Jewish traders figured prominently in the sale of alcohol to factory workers.[5] This, amongst several other factors, made Jewish tavern keepers obvious targets of local hatred and resentment, and they suffered accordingly during the disturbances and programs of the nineteenth century. Among the many Jewish refugees who made their way to the Transvaal Republic and elsewhere at this time, there must have been more than a few *korchma* keepers.

But with or without the aid of an intermediary petty bourgeoisie, there were limits to type and quantity of spirits which producers could unload on local markets. Nowhere were these limitations more apparent than in the case of Germany. During the last three decades of the nineteenth century there was a substantial increase in the average yield of potatoes per acre in Prussia and Germany. This phenomenon was especially noticeable in the rye-and-potato economy which dominated the lighter soil areas of Prussia. The increased yield, however, was something of a mixed blessing, since it came at a time when the consumption of the potato as a vegetable was declining in the domestic households of Prussia and Germany. The Junkers, confronted with an increased potato crop amidst declining demand, turned to the time-honoured solution of distillation – a practice which, in the Prussian case, dated back at least to the seventeenth century. But this time the scale of the operation was qualitatively different, since a special steam apparatus for mashing silo potatoes had been developed in 1873, and large 'distillation domains' came into existence.[6]

The Junkers found, however, that their problems did not end with the large-scale conversion of potatoes into spirits. From 1880 onwards, the domestic markets of Prussia and Germany showed an increasing preference for the superior-quality alcohols that were being distilled from grain. By the 1890s producers were finding themselves with large stocks of potato spirits which sold extremely slowly in domestic European markets. It was largely for this reason that the producers turned to the less discriminating and captive colonial markets which the imperial powers had shared out amongst themselves after the Berlin Conference of 1884. This solution was greatly facilitated in the German case by the considerable political power and influence which the largest distillers enjoyed. The spirit producers and others saw to it that rail freight charges to the port of Hamburg were reduced, and that an annual subsidy to the value of £45 000 was paid to the German East African Steamship Company.[7] With such incentives to exporters, it was possible for Africa to become an outlet for enormous quantities of potato spirits in the late nineteenth century.[8]

Not all of Africa, however, was equally vulnerable to imperial penetration. The degree to which, and the speed with which, European economic forces could conquer and capture new markets was dependent on the extent and nature of underdevelopment in the various parts of the continent. In Mozambique, for example, there was a relatively well-established bourgeoisie which had long provided mercantile middlemen for Portuguese producers. For several decades these merchants had sold cheap Portuguese commodities – including alcohol – to Africans who constituted the local market. As middlemen rather than producers, they were willing to sell anything – not excluding German potato spirits – for a share of the profits.

What was true of Mozambique, however, was not true of the independent Boer Republics in southern Africa. These regimes had their own rural bourgeoisie in the form of white farmers who were themselves directly and actively involved in agricultural production. During the last quarter of the nineteenth century a considerable number of districts within the Republics were grain exporting, and in the villages and towns there was a sizeable market for spirits. Here too, the combination of agricultural surplus and local markets made distillation a real business possibility. Even a modest town like Harrismith in the eastern Orange Free State could house 'Demarillac's Distillery' which, in 1895, was worth over £4 000.[9] In the Transvaal, as early as 1870, 32 liquor licences were issued in Potchefstroom, 17 in Pretoria, 15 in Wakkerstroom, and 5 in Heidelberg.[10] Markets such as these, located in independent states, served by a local petty bourgeoisie and supplied by national producers, were usually protected from competition by high import duties.[11] That they were relatively inaccessible geographically, and of modest size by international standards, may also have rendered them less vulnerable to initial imperial economic penetration. Indeed, had this configuration of factors remained constant, the Transvaal Republic might have experienced a more gradual 'decline of feudalism and rise of towns', like that of Europe, in which capital accumulated from distillation contributed to the subsequent development of industrial capitalism. 'Factors', however, seldom remain constant, and they certainly did not do so in the Transvaal during the late nineteenth century.

In 1886 gold was discovered on the Witwatersrand. This discovery jolted the Transvaal into an era of rapid industrial development. An influx of fortune-seeking Europeans and an ever-expanding army of black mineworkers crammed themselves into mushrooming towns such as Krugersdorp, Johannesburg and Boksburg. Virtually overnight the Witwatersrand became one of the biggest, wealthiest and fastest-growing markets in sub-Saharan Africa. This expanding conurbation, with its numerically preponderant black population spread along the Reef, promised new rewards to national and international entrepreneurs. The stage was set for a battle of conflicting class interests in which the participants were drawn from throughout Europe, Mozambique and the Transvaal. At the very heart of that conflict lay alcohol and the African mineworker. As a Johannesburg newspaper editorial put it in 1892:

> Today, despite his faults, the Kaffir is a distinct source of support to many hundreds here; he is acquiring the habit of clothing himself

and he is becoming used to luxuries, thereby creating and increasing a trade that is a means of existence to a considerable section of the mercantile community. The covetous director, the interested temperance advocate, and the wily monopolist begin to see this, and they desire him for their own. They tell you they desire only to suppress drunkenness among natives, to secure a reliable labour supply for the mines, to regulate native passions, and to protect the public and the shareholder. Would that their motives were so noble! Unhappily there lurks behind their pretty speeches and still prettier sentiments the Policy of Grab.[12]

Clearly, there was no lack of contemporary awareness of the importance of the class conflict surrounding the issue of alcohol and black workers.

Who exactly, and what precisely, was involved in this conflict? Did these issues simply pass by a rural Afrikaner farming community that was thoroughly steeped in the conservatism of a Calvinist tradition? What were the objectives of the newly-emerging industrial bourgeoisie and what was the nature of its relationship with the temperance advocates? What was the role of the Afrikaner state? Were black workers simply passive consumers, or did they respond more actively? The remainder of this essay will seek to establish who these interested parties were and why they advocated particular policies at certain historical junctures – in short, it will seek to expose the political economy that underlay the 'Policy of Grab'.

THE BLACK WORKER AS CONSUMER
The rise of the liquor industry, 1881-1896

During 1873-4 several hundred diggers and prospectors made their way to the promising goldfields discovered at the small eastern Transvaal town of Pilgrim's Rest. Amongst the new arrivals there was a young Hungarian Jew by the name of Alois Hugho Nellmapius. Making good use of his expertise as a mining engineer, Nellmapius soon established himself as one of the most successful and prosperous diggers in the area. Nellmapius, however, had an economic eye capable of scanning broader business horizons than mining – which was perhaps as well, given the rather short life of the eastern Transvaal goldfields. While at Pilgrim's Rest, Nellmapius also started, and successfully ran, a mule caravan service which traversed the tsetse fly-infested country between the town and Delagoa Bay. The central purpose of this service was to provide mail links between country and port, but it would be surprising if Nellmapius's returning caravans did not also bring with them some of the cheap contraband Portuguese liquor which played such an important part in the life of the mining camp.[13]

Nellmapius used this early success to consolidate his career and diversify his interests. He became a successful farmer, and eventually came to run a large estate near Pretoria which earned the reputation of being a 'model' agricultural enterprise. His success and abilities soon attracted the attention of notables in the Transvaal and, in particular, he became the friend and confidant of S J P (Paul) Kruger. Nellmapius was the person primarily responsible for selling the idea of concession-granting to the President of the Republic.[14] Concessions, 'that is the handing out by the state to private individuals or private groups of the exclusive right to manufacture certain articles subject to certain guarantees, and in return for a substantial payment', became the cornerstone of early Transvaal industrial policy.[15]

On 3 October 1881 the *Volksraad* (Parliament) of the *Zuid Afrikaansche Republiek* (ZAR) – the Transvaal – passed Article 44. This granted A H Nellmapius a concession 'for the sole right to manufacture from grain, potatoes, and other products growable in the Transvaal, excepting tree-fruits and grapes, and the right to sell in bulk and bottle free of licence' such spirits.[16] The President's friend was granted this original concession for a period of 15 years on condition that the distillery was operational by 1 July 1882. Weeks before this latter date was reached, however, on 7 June 1882, Nellmapius (in return for a 20 per cent share) ceded the concession to a partnership comprised of himself, the cousins Isaac and Barnet Lewis, and Barnet's brother-in-law, Samuel Marks.[17] It was this partnership which gave birth to *De Eerste Fabrieken in de Zuid Afrikaansche Republiek Ltd* ('The First Factory Ltd') and in June 1883 a proud President Kruger personally opened the new distillery and christened it *Volkshoop* – 'The People's Hope'.

A director of the distillery at a later date, Hugh Crawford, was therefore largely correct when he noted that: 'The distillery was established, and its operations commenced before the goldfields of either Barberton or the Transvaal (Witwatersrand) were discovered, and at a time when the country was poor, its population small, and business very limited.' These early business realities, however, did not prevent the *Volksraad* from continuing to perceive the factory as *Volkshoop*. As the economic climate in the Transvaal changed in the mid-1880s, so the *hoop* of the *volk* grew. When asked to modify and confirm the terms of the concession on 23 June 1885, members of the *Volksraad* took the opportunity to make additional demands for development. In return for extending the monopoly for a period of 30 years to 30 June 1912, they insisted on the state receiving an annual payment of £1 000 and a guarantee that a glass factory and co-operage works would be erected at the distillery.[18] In return, the company was to continue to enjoy exemption from any other form of taxation.

These additional development requirements specified by the *Volksraad* extended the company's resources, and none more so than the glass factory which was ultimately constructed only in 1894.[19] However, the dramatically changed economic conditions in the Transvaal after the mid-1880s assisted the company. In particular, the rapid growth and development of the Witwatersrand goldfields transformed the prospects of business success for *Volkshoop* from probability to certainty. In May 1889 it was noted of the distillery that, 'from a very modest beginning on a tentative scale, its success has become unprecedentedly rapid, and it is now developing itself into a great industry'.[20]

The tangible proof of the emergence of a 'great industry' was to be found on the 4 000-acre site of the distillery on the banks of the Pienaars River, some ten miles east of Pretoria. On what was formerly Sammy Marks's Hatherley Farm, there arose a reservoir with a capacity of 170 000 gallons of water, a 30-horsepower plant for electricity generation, a four-storey central distillation plant, a boarding-house for accommodating white workers, houses for married European employees and a suitably prestigious separate house for the distillery manager. The buildings most likely to attract the attention of the Transvaal *burghers* (citizens), however, were the three large grain stores, each with a capacity of 5 000 bags. These stores, and indeed the entire factory site, could be viewed from managing director Marks's 'splendid residence' some one and a half miles away at Zwartkoppies.[21]

By 1889-90 the factory employed at least 50 white and over 100 African workers. In December 1889 the German distillation plant was working at full capacity, and producing 1 000 gallons of proof spirit per day from grain supplied exclusively by Transvaal burghers.[22] Even this output, however, was insufficient to maintain stocks, and the management embarked on a programme of expansion. New boilers, kilns, malting floors, stills and storage space were all being added to the factory when, in mid-December 1889, a fire broke out and disrupted production.

The setback caused by the fire proved to be less serious than it might have been, and the company merely lost two months' production. What concerned Marks and his colleagues more, however, was the fact that the distillery had been left uninsured and that the fire was considered to be the work of an arsonist. The owners of the factory were sufficiently convinced of this theory to offer 'a £2 000 reward for the apprehension and conviction of the person or persons implicated in the fiendish act'. In the months after the fire the reward remained unclaimed, the distillery was insured, and the owners took the opportunity of making a change in the factory management. Sammy Marks raided Demarillac's Distillery in

Harrismith – hailed at the time as 'one of the largest distilleries in the world' – for new managerial talent, and Thomas Strachan came to Pretoria to replace the previous manager, Stokes. Under Strachan's management a series of improvements were made and the business experienced steady expansion. The resources of the company were again stretched, however, when a second fire broke out in the four-storey distillery on 29 May 1891. But since the plant had just been insured for £6 000, and the maturing stock carefully isolated from the distillery proper, the effect of the fire was less serious than might otherwise have been the case.[23]

Nevertheless, in view of the excellent prospects of the company and the need for expansion, these setbacks left *De Eerste Fabrieken in de Zuid Afrikaansche Republiek* relatively starved of badly-needed capital. Marks's solution to this problem was to allow the company to go public. In November 1892, in exchange for £122 000 and shares, the holders of the concession made it over to *Eerste Fabrieken* Hatherley Distillery Ltd.[24] With the advantage of a listing on the London Stock Exchange, Hatherley Distillery was able to attract international as well as national capital, and the company was on the threshold of a period of spectacular expansion.

Seldom, if ever, could ambitious plans for industrial expansion have been launched into a safer or more sympathetic business environment. What more could capitalists ask for than a government-granted monopoly in a rapidly expanding market? As the sole producer in the Transvaal of cheap spirits for African consumption, Hatherley Distillery Found itself catering for a market of 14 000 black miners in 1890, 88 000 in 1897, and an enormous 100 000 by 1899. Privileged access to a market that expanded nearly ten times in as many years was an important part of the Hatherley success story.

It was not only the size of Hatherley's market that was important, however, but its quality. In particular, the fact that the majority of the 100 000-strong workforce was drawn from Mozambique was of the utmost importance. For at least several decades prior to the industrialisation of the Witwatersrand, the peasants and workers of Mozambique had been sold large quantities of wine and spirits – inferior-quality alcohol that flowed from the vats of metropolitan Portugal. There is substantial evidence to show that the more proletarianised Africans of southern rural Mozambique, and the black workers of the urban areas along the coast, were considerably addicted to alcohol by the early 1890s.[25] In 1894, the British Council in the territory, W A Churchill, noted how large quantities of spirits were sold in 'up-country stores', and that black workers 'spent the greater part of their wages in alcohol, known as "Kaffir Rum"'.[26] In the following year Churchill noted in his annual report that the landing agents in the ports often experienced the greatest difficulty in finding sober black workers. Indeed, this problem became so well known that ships from South Africa brought their own dockers with them to offload cargo in the Mozambique ports.[27]

The link between alcohol consumption in Mozambique and the recruitment of African miners for the Witwatersrand was also clear to observers in the 1890s. The syndrome of rural underdevelopment and peasant indebtedness ensured that the canteens of the countryside became good recruiting centres for Transvaal labour agents.[28] On the mines themselves the poverty and relatively advanced proletarianised status of an *isidakewa* ('drunkard' – also the African name for Charlie Chaplin), was readily apparent. 'In a store where the boy's belongings were hanging', noted one observer, 'a drunkard's sack was generally noticeable by its age, and leanness of aspect.'[29] Also, African miners returning to Mozambique were at least as likely to be carrying back gas-piping for use in domestic distilleries, as they were to be taking a gun.[30]

This link between alcohol and workers from Mozambique was of considerable importance to both Hatherley and the mining industry. The Pretoria distillery was catering not only for a rapidly expanding market, but also for one in which the potential consumers already had a well-developed predilection for the product. The mining industry, for its part, was quite content for its workers to spend their wages on Hatherley products if they so desired. For, the more money the mineworkers spent on liquor, the less they saved; and the less they saved, the longer they worked before returning to the peasant economies of their rural homelands. In other words, mine owners realised that wages spent on liquor helped lengthen the periods of migratory labour, and tended to produce a more stabilised labour force – in short, it facilitated the process of proletarianisation.

Few of these marketing realities escaped the attention of investors when the Hatherley Company went public in late 1892, and £350 000-worth £1 shares became available.[31] As possibly the only other large-scale investment opportunity in the Transvaal, the distillery attracted local mining capital seeking to spread and diversify its holdings. A significant proportion of the shares were subscribed to by South African mining capitalists, and throughout the 1890s the depth and extent of their holdings was reflected in the directorships of the company. Besides Sammy Marks, the board of Hatherley Distillery during the 1890s included, at various stages, the following mining capitalists: J N De Jongh (Executive Member of the Transvaal Chamber of Mines 1897-1909, President of the Chamber 1906-7), S Evans (mine manager associated with the Eckstein Company after 1898 and made a full partner in 1902); L Ehrlich (before 1894 director of the Ferreira, Modderfontein, Knight, Wolhuter, Main Reef and other Transvaal companies of the S Neumann Group); and A Epler (Executive Member of the Witwatersrand Chamber of Mines 1899-1909, and later Managing Director of Transvaal Goldfields Ltd).[32]

Where national capital went successfully, international capital was not slow to follow. Thus, Hatherley also came to have a significant number of English, French, Austrian and German shareholders.[33] The interests of these various European investors were safeguarded by individual members of the Hatherley board who acted as the agents of international capital. Director J H Curle (mining correspondent of the *Economist*), held an informal brief for English shareholders, while the Bavarian, Ludwig Ehrlich, looked after the portfolio of German investors. During the 1890s the Austrian, Adolf Epler, undertook this task not only at Hatherley but in other concerns as well, and was candidly described in a publication of the time as 'a representative of Foreign Capital in South Africa'. The French investors in *Eerste Fabrieken* looked to yet another director for their protection – Henri Duval, who was also the manager of the *Banque Française de l'Afrique du Sud* in Johannesburg.[34]

With the benefit of some of the most astute managerial talent available in the Transvaal, and the financial muscle provided by national and international capital, Hatherley Distillery set course for a period of spectacular development. Especially during the early 1890s, Hatherley Distillery was the undisputed master of the Witwatersrand liquor market.

Table 1 Eerste Fabrieken Hatherley Distillery Ltd, profitability 1893-99

Year	Gallons sold	Net profit or loss	Dividend declared
1893	272 616	+ £47 404	16%
1894	316 046	+ £48 399	16%
1895	386 281	+ £98 274	20%
1896	298 130	+ £69 569	12%
1897	63 191	– £46 988	–
1898	153 594	+ £10 490	–
1899	86 998	+ £2 737	–

[Compiled from data contained in *Special Liquor Committee of the Chamber of Mines, Report, 1898*, p 111, and *Command 624*, June 1901, p 73.]

Any industry which could yield dividends ranging from 12 per cent to 20 per cent was, however, likely to attract the envious attention of competitors, and the large new market in the Transvaal had not escaped the notice of other spirit producers. In theory, Hatherley's monopolistic position was absolutely secure. Besides being the sole producer of grain spirits in the ZAR, the company, through its privileged exemption from excise duty, was in a position to undercut any imported spirits. For example, 'Cape Smoke', the notorious cheap brandy produced in the western Cape, could not compete on the legal Rand markets because of high import duties.[35] Through diligent reading of the fine print in inter-state treaties, however, one group of spirit producers in southern Africa *did* find a weakness through which they could attack Hatherley Distillery's dominant position. The Treaty of Commerce entered into by the Transvaal and Portugal in 1875, ratified in Pretoria in 1882, and not due to expire until 1902, made provision for the produce of Portugal to enter the ZAR free of duty.[36] It was this chink in the legal armour of Kruger's Republic that producers in Mozambique exploited fully in the mid-1890s. After 1894, and especially after 1895, once the railway line from Delagoa Bay to the Witwatersrand had been opened, Hatherley's firm hold on the Transvaal market was seriously undermined by cheap-er spirits originating from two very different sources.

First, rum 'which was distilled at a fraction of the cost at which grain spirit is produced', undercut Hatherley products.[37] In Mozambique, pro-ducers such as the *Companhia do Assucar de Moçambique* turned their atten-tion to the profits to be derived from rum distillation. In 1894 the *Com-panhia's* distillery at Mopea produced 5 000 gallons of rum specifically for the Rand market.[38] The following year saw such an expansion of rum dis-tillation that the *Companhia* exhausted its supplies of sugar. With excess distillation capacity on hand, the *Companhia* approached the Portuguese government for permission to import additional quantities of sugar from Natal.[39] The fact that the president of the *Companhia*, Frederico Ressano Garcia, was also a minister in the Portuguese government no doubt helped ensure that this permission was granted. Since members of the Portuguese ruling elite were personally involved in the manufacture of spirits, and the ZAR's rail outlet to the sea was at stake, it is perhaps not surprising that the Transvaal government admitted this trade because of 'high political considerations'.[40] In the following years the *Companhia* consistently manu-factured spirits from sugar drawn not only from Mozambique, but from Natal and Mauritius as well. By 1896 the *Companhia* was still expanding rum production and sharpening its competitive edge through price reduc-tions – the latter being achieved by replacing European personnel at the Mopea distillery with African artisans.[41]

The pattern of expansion to be seen in the *Companhia do Assucar's* activities was repeated at other distilleries throughout Mozambique. In 1895 the distilleries of Portuguese East Africa exported 84 528 gallons of spirits to the ZAR; in 1896 this rose to 255 157 gallons; in 1897 to 357 260 gallons; and by 1898 it had reached 456 000 gallons.[42] This business bonanza, perhaps without precedent in the economic history of Mozam-bique, saw the ownership of several distilleries change hands.[43] New capital was attracted to distilleries that could produce alcohol at three shillings a gallon, and command a wholesale price of eight shillings a gallon on the Witwatersrand. Profit margins of this order also warranted investment in new plant and equipment, and the large French company at Lourenço Marques, the *Societé Française de Distillerie*, expanded its activities in 1895. The *Societé* built a large new distillery on the banks of the Inkomati River, 100 yards from the Transvaal frontier, at the border village of Ressano Garcia.[44] This venture too received the blessing of the Portuguese government.

Second, Hatherley's grain spirits were undercut by cheaper German potato spirit. Indeed, so cheap was the German potato spirit that it undercut even the sugar-based imports from Mozambique.[45] But because of the high import duties in the ZAR, German potato spirits could not penetrate the market directly – like 'Cape Smoke', they would simply have ceased to be cheap if imported in the orthodox manner. Both Prussian producers and Transvaal importers therefore had to find a way round this problem if they wished to share in the profits that could be made in the ZAR. Well aware that this customs barrier had already proved vulnerable on the eastern border with Mozambique, international capitalists set to work, weaving the sort of legal magic by which the potatoes of Prussia became converted into the 'produce of Portugal'. It was in this latter guise that thousands of gallons of German and Prussian potato spirits flooded into the Transvaal from 1894 onwards.

During the 1890s German liners took on their cargoes of potato spirits at the port of Hamburg. From there, they would fan out into two large southward arcs that embraced the west and east coasts of Africa respectively. The liners *Thekla Boben*, *Hausa*, *Bida* and *Ilorin* worked the Atlantic, and discharged their cargoes in ports from Lagos in the north to Luanda in the south.[46] The ships of the German East Africa line, however, worked with a slightly different routine. After taking on their cargoes, the liners *König*, *Herog*, *Kanzler*, *Admiral* and *Reichstag* would first make for the port of Lisbon. There, they would lie overnight with their cargo of Prussian potato spirit. Then, after a suitable number of hours had elapsed, they would receive a 'certificate of naturalisation' from a port official and, from then on, the cargo would be 'produce of Portugal'.[47] Thereafter the ships would head east through the Suez Canal, and then south into the Indian Ocean. In the 1890s the most important port of call on the southern run was Lourenço Marques. It was in this latter port that the liners discharged the bulk of their cargo of potato spirit – alcohol that was partly destined for local consumption within Mozambique, and partly for the Witwatersrand.[48] The extent of this traffic between 1894 and 1903 is clearly evident from Table 2.

Table 2 Imports of plain *aguardente* through Lourenço Marques, 1894-1903

Year	Quantity in litres
1894	195 038
1895	182 182
1896	517 709
1897	215 297
1898	195 129
1899	123 839
1900	32 681
1901	28 771
1902	15 977
1903	108

It should be noted that large quantities of the same 'fire-water' were also offloaded at the ports of Inhambane, Chinde and Quelimane.

[Table derived from A Freire D'Andrade, *Relatorios solne Moçambique*, Lourenço Marques 1907, p 40.]

The Transvaal liquor consumer of the 1890s was thus likely to be drinking spirits coming from one of three basic sources: Hatherley, any one of several Mozambique distilleries, or Germany. Seen another way, the consumer could also, in order of declining cost, be drinking either grain, sugar or potato spirits. He would also, however, be drinking a good deal more than plain alcohol and, in terms of the cost to his health, he was likely to be paying a good deal more than he bargained for. Even in their 'pure' form direct from the distilleries, these spirits contained a high proportion of amylic alcohol. This latter form of alcohol, also known as fusel oil, was a poisonous by-product of the fermentation process. Samples of Hamburg potato spirit, taken in West Africa in 1902, revealed a proportion of fusel oil by weight which varied from 1.26 per cent to 4.4 per cent. When a Transvaal chemist analysed spirit from the same source in 1895, he declared it 'unfit for internal use'.[49] Spirits that started their manufactured life unfit for human consumption in their 'pure' form hardly improved as they passed through the hands of various other intermediaries in the Transvaal.

Most of the spirits which entered Johannesburg first found their way to the wholesalers: firms such as Meskin and Davidoff, Vogelman and Friedman, Kantor Ltd, T Friedman Ltd, I Herzfeld Ltd, or Blum & Co Ltd.[50] A couple of these firms, Kantor and Blum, dealt only in bulk supplies of spirits which they sold directly to smaller bottling concerns. The majority, however, opted for the higher profits to be made through processing the raw spirits into the fiery commercial brands that apparently satisfied the tastes of black and white consumers on the Rand.

Firms involved in the processing business, such as Meskin and Davidoff, required three things in addition to raw spirits: a large supply of bottles, various chemicals and essences, and a stock of forged cork tops and brand labels. The first requisite was obtained through the endless collection of 'empties' from the canteens and back streets of Johannesburg; at a later date some were undoubtedly supplied from the glass works of Hatherley. The second was purchased from a local firm of wholesale chemists – P J Peterson & Co.[51] The third requisite – forged labels – came from the firm responsible for printing the *Standard and Diggers' News* – Messrs Matthew and Walker. These forgeries, frequently making use of well-known brand names, suggested that the spirits were manufactured in various European countries such as Scotland, France or Holland. Several different forgeries were printed on a single sheet, and the customer could then cut out the label which he considered appropriate to his product.[52]

Armed with these prerequisites the firms then set about manufacturing various brands of liquor according to recipes that were widely known within the trade. 'Kaffir Brandy', price 16/6d per dozen bottles in 1899, was prepared according to the following formula: 15 gals Delagoa proof spirit, 15 gals water, 1 gal cayenne pepper tincture, ½ lb mashed prunes, 1½ oz sulphuric acid and 1 oz nitric acid. This 'brandy' was coloured through the addition of a suitable quantity of burnt sugar. 'Kaffir Whisky', price 14/6d per dozen bottles in 1899, required the following ingredients: 100 gals of Delagoa Bay proof spirit, 1 gal tincture of prunes, 3 lbs glycerine, 1 pint green tea, ½ oz acetic acid, 20 drops of creosote and 12 drops of oil of cognac. 'Dutch Gin for Kaffirs', price 15/6d per dozen bottles in 1899, required the following: 100 gals Delagoa Bay proof spirit, 1 gal sugar syrup, 1 lb tincture of orange peel, 4 oz turpentine, 1 oz juniper oil and ½ oz of fennel. To this concoction was added bead without colouring (an additive partly composed of sulphuric acid), and then the entire quantity of 'gin' was filtered through charcoal.

For the benefit of European consumers in the working class some of the recipes were varied slightly, and the processing was made a little more sophisticated. Whisky, for example, was prepared in exactly the same way as 'Kaffir Whisky' except that it was filtered more frequently. Further, a layer of oak sawdust, when available, was added to the whisky in order to imbue it with a distinctive flavour. The *Transvaal Leader* warned its white Johannesburg readers in 1899: 'Do not be aghast at the prospect of drinking sulphate of copper and green tea, acetic acid and oil of Neroli as Martell's Five Star Liqueur Brandy; you have done it often enough.' Basically, white and black workers, however, were required to pay slightly more for their 'refined' taste. Whereas 'Kaffir Ginger Brandy' sold at 16/6d per dozen bottles, the same quantity of 'White Ginger Brandy' cost 22/6d.[53]

The fact that these different types of 'liquor' were sold in vast quantities through public outlets was well known at the time. As early as April 1890, the *Standard and Diggers' News* devoted an entire editorial to the subject. It pointed out how, in a neighbouring colony (probably Mozambique), Hennessy and Martell's XXX Brandy has been analysed, and found to consist of potato spirit, fusel oil, burnt sugar, spirits of nitre and oil of cognac. The editorial continued:

> We cannot prove that what is drunk here as retailed in like these samples, but he would be a bold man who would bet on the purity of the liquor ordinarily retailed in Johannesburg. A public officer is absolutely needed to deal with such matters.[54]

This plea for a public analyst fell upon deaf ears, as did a further appeal two months later. Although subsequent legislation did make legal provision for a public analyst there was no such official in 1895, and as late at 1898 the situation was still unremedied. The government of the ZAR knew only too well that if an analytical chemist started probing the composition of Rand liquor, then the finger of guilt would ultimately point not only to the wholesalers of Johannesburg, but to influential capitalists in Lisbon and Hamburg as well. That was a political price which the Transvaal government was unwilling to pay. The liquor was thus allowed to pass unchallenged from the wholesalers to the retail outlets spread across the Witwatersrand – the canteens.

There was no shortage of canteens in the industrialising republic. As early as 1888 there were 393 licensed canteens throughout the Transvaal and of these, no fewer than 147 were in the more concentrated Witwatersrand area. A mere four years later, in 1892, the number of licensed canteens on the Witwatersrand had jumped from 147 to 552. And it is estimated that at the zenith of the liquor trade in 1895, between 750 and 1 000 canteens could be found in the area between Krugersdorp in the west and Nigel in the east. Even by 1898, when the licensed retail liquor trade had declined substantially, there were 495 recognised outlets in the magisterial districts of Krugersdorp, Johannesburg and Boksburg, and in the same year the Licensing Board had to deal with 165 new applications.[55]

Numerically significant from an early date, this petty bourgeoisie was quick to recognise its class interests and to organise accordingly. As early as 1888 the canteen keepers of the various mining districts had got together to form the Witwatersrand Licensed Victuallers' Association (WLVA). By March 1890 WLVA had 100 members, and the executive was considering applications from a further 40 prospective members.[56] The Association protected members when their licenses were threatened, petitioned the state to liberalise the liquor laws in an attempt to expand the size of its legal market, and sought to limit competition by exercising control over the numbers of retailers entering the trade.[57] While the canteen keepers were without the international connections or power that the liquor producers enjoyed, they were a local and national force to be reckoned with.

While the organisational power of the retailers was undoubtedly impressive, it should not be forgotten that the liquor trade also operated within a wider context, which tended to produce its own constraints. A colonial ruling class which had established a state by conquest, and which held out hopes for an industrialising economy, was never likely to endorse a *laissez-faire* policy wholeheartedly. In theory, the right of the canteen keepers to sell unlimited quantities of spirits to the growing number of black workers was severely circumscribed. According to the regulations, the Liquor Licensing Boards strictly vetted all new applications for licences and issued only those which were considered to be in the public interest. The liquor law of 1889 made it clear that a canteen keeper could sell alcohol to an African only on the production of a permit signed by a white master, and that the police and courts could enforce these requirements. Other less onerous constraints derived from the wrath of employers, or the hostility of 'public opinion' which objected to an unfettered trade that produced large numbers of drunken, noisy and, at times, violent black workers. The barriers that these supposed constraints erected, however, were less than formidable in the harsher light of practice.

The attitudes of the Witwatersrand Liquor Licensing Boards to the scores of applications reaching them throughout the 1880s and early 1890s can euphemistically be described as 'open' and 'flexible'. During the first decade of mining development, virtually any applicant who could raise the necessary fee was granted a retail liquor licence. Strong petty-bourgeois representation on the early Licensing Boards ensured a considerable degree of overlap between what was perceived as 'business' and what passed for the 'public interest'. In July 1889 the Boards were taken to task by the local press for not balancing the number of retail outlets in Johannesburg against the 'public interest':

> In one corner of this town, within two minutes of the Exchange, there are no less than from 10 to 12 licensed drinking shops. If the whole town is looked over it will be found that purely drinking dens are out of all proportion to the requirements of the people, and outside the town the conveniences for Kaffirs in procuring drink are legion.[58]

Even after limited state representation on the Boards was provided for in late 1892, there was little change in this basically liberal attitude on the part of the local authorities.[59]

Occasionally, it is true, objections *were* made to the granting of canteen licences. The more honest of these petitions, such as that of the Braamfontein Ratepayers' Association to the Johannesburg Liquor Licensing Board in 1894, categorically spelt out the threat that canteens presented to local property values. Usually, however, this real objection was hidden beneath eloquent concern over 'social nuisance' or 'health'. Even in such cases, however, the aspirant canteen keeper stood a good chance of getting the objection overruled if he could elicit the support of a local notable.[60] The pre-1896 canteen keeper could thus look for protection to a basically sympathetic Licensing Board; at the very least, the number of retail liquor licences granted on the Rand kept abreast of the expanding population.

The canteen keepers of this era had little reason to greatly fear 'public opinion'. Certainly there was a constant stream of individual complaints to stem the volume of liquor sales, or to diminish drunkenness. Such organised public protest as there was occurred mainly during the initial period of rapid expansion in 1891-2, and was largely the work of two bodies.

Particularly in 1892, both the Labour Union and the Transvaal Temperance Alliance briefly acted as media of 'public opinion'. The geographical segregation of the races was not so marked at this time, and the Labour Union became concerned when its white members were attacked by drunken black miners. Thus, in November of that year the Union organised an 'anti-drink demonstration' which attracted about 700 whites and several local organisations – the one notable absentee was a representative from the powerful Chamber of Mines.[61] The Union, however, soon found that it had more important concerns and turned its attention to other issues. The Transvaal Temperance Alliance, for its part, appears to have had an equally transient effect on liquor policy. Several factors could account for this failure. It is possible that in the frenzied atmosphere of a money-making town, poorly endowed with middle-class moral custodians, few people were willing to devote time to such matters. By August 1892 the Alliance could muster only 70 members. However, it is equally plausible that the Alliance failed because it attracted a leadership that had concerns other than temperance matters. Perhaps it was simply a combination of common sense and coincidence that led to the formation of the Alliance in 1892 – the same year that the Hatherley Distillery Co went public. It would be stretching matters too far, however, to make coincidence also account for the fact that the Alliance was presided over by William Hoskin. As chairman of the local Chamber of Commence, Hoskin's concern over canteens and African sobriety was unlikely to be totally divorced from his other interests – in black spending patterns on the Witwatersrand.[62] For obvious reasons, merchants would be pleased if African wages spent in canteens could somehow be diverted into traders' tills.

This weakness of 'public opinion' and the strength of the Licensed Victuallers' Association as an almost dominant fraction of the local petty bourgeoisie, combined to give canteen keepers on the Witwatersrand considerable room for economic manoeuvre. But, important as these factors undoubtedly were, they were perhaps ultimately less significant than yet another factor – the deep-seated ambivalence of mining capitalists towards the liquor trade as this stage.

Mine owners were aware that alcohol helped them secure and control black workers, and they were therefore most reluctant to countenance any attempt to close canteens. In fact, the mining capitalists found that they had to act as a brake on 'public opinion' which was tending to demand total prohibition for all Africans. At a large public meeting held in 1891 to discuss the liquor traffic, the capitalists and their spokesmen unsuccessfully tried to persuade the audience that total prohibition for black workers was 'premature'. Similarly, in the same year, a mining commissioner could state in court, without fear of contradiction in capitalist circles, that 'nearly everyone is agreed that total prohibition would be disastrous to the native labour position'. When there was further loose talk about 'total prohibition' in 1892, the *Standard and Diggers' News* warned its readers in an editorial that it was the liquor trade 'alone that ensures the Fields a labour supply. Constrict it, and the Rand's real troubles will begin.'[63] As late as 1895 the *Annual Report of the Chamber of Mines* made it clear that, while the capitalists wanted stricter control of the liquor traffic, they did not favour total prohibition.[64]

This apparently tolerant attitude of most mining capitalists towards the canteens was not a casual by-product of *laissez-faire* boardroom philosophy. Far from it: the mine owners took their cue from the hard school of practical experience. In particular, they were guided by their mine managers, the men in the lower echelons of the industry who had the most immediate experience of the problems involved in obtaining and controlling African labour.[65] It was these mine managers who were most aware that alcohol could 'attract' labour to the miserable compounds and that it assisted in the proletarianisation of migrant labour – all without direct cash cost to the company. In fact, a significant number of mine managers actually operated an industrial variant of the notorious *dop* system – the *tot* system, which formed part of the wages of the agricultural labourers in the Cape. When the use of alcohol in the control of black mineworkers was debated in the local press in 1891, it was noted that:

> ... at Kimberley [diamond mines] familiarity with the glass has built moderation in the black man, while it is admitted that better work is got out of him when he sees the prospect of a cheering glass at the end of a day's labour. That is very generally admitted on these Fields also, where the permit system is largely taken advantage of by employers of coloured labour. At not a few works permits are regularly issued for supplies to the native hands, the reasonableness of the request for stimulating refreshment being amiably admitted on the grounds that the 'boy' so humoured and so refreshed is the better labourer.[66]

Chamber of Mines' policy and ideology up to 1895 were firmly rooted in practice.

The mine managers' attitude towards the canteens might have crystallised most clearly on the issue of labour control, but several of them also had a more direct and immediate interest in the success of the retail liquor trade. As early as 1889 it was reported that one could 'see the names of managers of gold companies attached to the applications for canteen licences near the claims, and in recommendation thereof'.[67] It is possible that in some cases the mine managers had little option but to make such recommendations, since they were merely responding to directorial pressure from higher up in the industrial hierarchy. At the Spes Bona, George Goch and Henry Nourse mines, for example, the canteen keepers on the mining property were all closely related to mining directors. With such powerful backing it would have been a foolish mine manager who withheld his 'recommendation' for a liquor licence. But in most cases the mine managers got involved in the canteen business of their own volition in order to supplement their incomes. While the number of canteens close to the compounds was relatively small and the competition limited, the managers could expect fairly good returns from their 'shares' in the liquor business. As the number of canteens grew, however, so competition increased, and the managers had to act more vigorously in order to ensure that 'their' canteen still got its share of the trade. By 1895 some of their methods, and those of their subordinates, the compound managers, aroused the resentment of the WLVA. A deputation from the WLVA to the Chamber of Mines complained that 'on some mines natives are ordered to go to a particular canteen in which some employee of the company has a pecuniary interest...'[68] Thus the mine managers were *not*, at this stage, fundamentally opposed to the consumption of alcohol by their employees.

All these factors facilitated the emergence and entrenchment of the retail liquor trade during the first decade of the Witwatersrand's development. Finally, however, it was the state which made a vital contribution to these developments. In the eyes of Kruger and his government, Hatherley Distillery occupied a position of twofold importance. First, the distillery lay at the very centre of the State President's concessions policy and his strategy for industrialisation. Kruger was proud of his *Eerste Fabrieken*, and also a particularly close friend of its major shareholder, Sammy Marks. The President's attachment to Marks and the distillery was at least strong enough for him to spend one Christmas holiday at Hatherley. Second and more important, the *Eerste Fabrieken* provided a steady and expanding market for large quantities of the burghers' grain and fruit – a point which Kruger unfailingly brought to the notice of the distillery's critics.[69] As a producer who personally supplied large quantities of citrus for Hatherley's 'Orange Wine' from his farm *Boekenhoutfontein*, the State President had first-hand experience of this fact, which would also have appealed to other members of the Afrikaner rural bourgeoisie.[70] Whilst these fundamentals of business life remained constant, the state's attitude towards the canteen keepers was hardly likely to be one of uncompromising hostility.

In the early 1890s it was not simply a question of the state being unwilling to act against the liquor retailers; often it was *unable* to do so. Johannesburg had a population of about 25 000 people in June 1899. The entire population of the magisterial district, spread over a considerable area, was served by a police force of 35 men – of which only half was on duty at any one time. Not only was this 'Zarp' force (ZAR police) very small, but it was also very disorganised. There were no rules, regulations, codes or laws which allowed the Commandant of the police to discipline his ill-uniformed men. Salary gradations in the lower and middle ranks were non-existent, and a sergeant with five years' experience received as much as a newly appointed constable. To make matters worse, the salaries were very poor and most irregularly paid – on one occasion in 1895 the Zarps were forced to go on 'strike' in order to obtain their earnings. All this, together with the fact that ZAR nationals alone were eligible to serve in the force, meant that the police could attract only men of the most doubtful calibre. Poor illiterate Afrikaners, drawn from the most proletarianised stratum of rural society, were ill-suited to law-enforcement duties in a brash mining town dominated by foreign workers, traders and capitalists. The force was 'one of the greatest scandals in the State' and, in 1894, the Commandant of Police, D E Schutte, wrote an open letter in which he publicly admitted:

> I acknowledge the *rottenness* of the entire police force, but decline to accept the disgrace attached thereto, having striven to reorganise the same, but failed through lack of support.[71]

Clearly, the police force hardly represented the strong arm of the state.

Commandant Schutte's problems, however, did not end with the personnel of the Zarps, since his force was also somewhat hampered by the liquor law. A decision handed down by the High Court made it very difficult to obtain a conviction against any canteen owner who sold liquor to black workers without a permit. By 1891 the Court held that only licensees could be prosecuted for this offence and, since most canteen keepers had employees who undertook the actual serving of alcohol, convictions were few and far between.[72] In the lower courts, at least one magistrate took the opportunity, in passing sentence, of severely criticising the law which made it so difficult for the police to set up successful 'traps'.[73]

The canteen keepers were not slow to exploit any of these weaknesses, nor to open up others. They approached the badly paid policemen and succeeded in bribing a large number of Zarps.[74] The 'business insurance' provided by bribery was supplemented by other more practical precautions. Most canteen keepers employed a 'gang of spies to watch the approach of the police from every possible corner and frustrate their movements'.[75] These 'spies' and 'sentries' constituted the early rudiments of a petty-bourgeois business army which was to adopt a more organised form, and assume a more aggressive posture during the class war of 1897-9.

Because of the weakness of the state, the ambivalence of the mining capitalists, the studied indifference of the Afrikaner ruling class and the sympathy of the petty-bourgeois-dominated Licensing Boards, the retail liquor trade boomed before 1896. The boom, however, was not without its costs. It killed hundreds of workers – black and white – who consumed that working-class poison passing commercially as 'liquor'.[76] It was 'a common thing', noted one contemporary observer, 'to find "boys" lying dead on the veld from exposure and the effects of the vile liquids sold them by unscrupulous dealers'.[77] The Superintendent of the Johannesburg Cemetery was more than familiar with notices of interment that listed the cause of death as 'alcoholic poisoning'. He was reported to have surveyed one such corpse and remarked: 'Several of these every week – the cursed stuff burns their insides, and they never recover after a drinking bout.'[78] The same liquor also contributed to the many murders in the mining town, as well as to the large-scale 'faction fights' that broke out amongst black workers of different ethnic origin. It was also responsible for the enormous social problem of drunkenness or, in the idiom of the day, it created 'hordes of drunken Kaffirs'.

These human costs of the liquor industry left the alliance of class interests in the ZAR relatively unmoved. There was, however, another cost which moved them more – the cost to capital. Thus, while no commercial or industrial leaders were willing to complain or protest about the number of working-class *deaths* caused by alcohol, they were more than ready to abhor the cost to capital in terms of inefficiency and lowered productivity. In the short term, the deaths of the workers did not matter to the capitalists; the dead miner of today was bound to be replaced by the Lancastrian, Cornishman, Zulu or Shangaan of tomorrow. What *did* matter was that those who were alive should form the core of a sober, productive and efficient labour force. Given the level of alcohol consumption, however, not even that could be guaranteed, and thus the capitalists' wage bills were unnecessarily increased.

Now, this unnecessarily high wage bill had been a feature of the mining industry since at least the late 1880s. By the mid-1890s, however, the Witwatersrand mines were experiencing the important financial and structural changes which were associated with the transition from earlier forms of mineral exploitation to deep-level mining.[79] Significantly less speculative than earlier ventures, deep-level mining offered the industry a long-term future; but in turn it demanded a more realistic cost structure. It is thus significant that during this period of readjustment, in 1895, the Chamber of Mines complained that:

> … drunkenness was on the increase at the mines, and that, in consequence, the scarcity of labour was intensified, as companies able to get them had to keep far more boys in their compounds than were required on any one day to make up for the number periodically disabled by drink.[80]

The percentage of the black labour force 'disabled by drink' each day was officially estimated by the mine owners to be of the order of 15 per cent, but others put it as high as 25 per cent.[81] It obviously added significantly to the item which was already the single largest mining cost on the Rand – African wages.

By 1895-6 it was becoming very clear to mine owners that a massive contradiction had found its way into the capitalist development of the Transvaal: any further expansion in a large and very profitable liquor industry would be at the expense of the very motor of capitalism, the mining industry. This contraction was not without irony, since individual mining capitalists had themselves helped to create the Hatherley liquor machine which now jeopardised their long-term profits. Two contemporary writers, Scoble and Abercrombie, put this succinctly at the time, noting of the Pretoria distillery:

> This is the temple [Hatherley] where are distilled those nectars which goad the Kaffirs of the reef to deeds of derring-do, and it

would certainly have paid the present concessionaires, who have large mining interests, far better never to have started it could they have secured instead a concession for 'total prohibition'.[82]

But although the contradiction itself may have become fully visible in 1895, there is no doubt that mining capital, as opposed to individual mining capitalists, had for some time past taken into account its longer-term profitability requirements. It was this secondary strand of thinking amongst mine owners, the recognition of the longer-term need for a sober and efficient working class, which underpinned the 'ambivalence' of mining capital noted earlier. Thus, from an early date the Chamber of Mines, while not in favour of 'total prohibition', undertook a series of actions which attempted to control the black worker's liquor consumption. At the very time that Hatherley, individual mining capitalists, mine managers and the canteen keepers were allowing a contradiction to develop whereby the black man on the Rand was primarily a liquor *consumer*, capital, as embodied in the Chamber of Mines, was establishing those footholds from which it could ultimately destroy the developing contradiction, and ensure that the African was primarily a *worker*. It is to this latter set of actions that we now turn.

Before 1896, in order to secure the cheap and sober black workforce which alone could guarantee profits, the Chamber of Mines could choose to fight on any one of three fronts. First, it could go for a head-on confrontation with the producers of alcohol – particularly Hatherley, which was the major supplier. Second, it could put pressure on the state to administer the liquor laws more efficiently. Third, it could conduct a campaign against the petty bourgeoisie which, to an increasing extent, was expanding its control of the canteen business. Of these three, the first front was obviously the most difficult to fight on. Hatherley's central role in Kruger's industrialisation strategy, the distillery's importance for the grain market and the State President's friendship with Sammy Marks all combined to rule out that possibility. The Chamber therefore concentrated its efforts on the second and third fronts.

The Chamber of Mines sought to undermine the canteen keepers' position at the very source of petty-bourgeois power – the Liquor Licensing Boards. Using 'public opinion' which showed growing concern over the 'hordes of drunken Kaffirs', the Chamber attempted to apply the brake to the process of granting retail licences. By April 1890 the state was already on the defensive, and the government agreed that in future all licences granted by the Boards would have to be ratified in Pretoria. The large public meeting of 1891 held in order to discuss the liquor traffic generated further activity by the mining capitalists. The mine owners and their spokesmen got public support for a motion demanding that no new liquor licences be granted in mining areas, and that existing licences should not be renewed. They then arranged for this and other resolutions on the liquor question to be taken to Pretoria by a deputation under the leadership of mine owner, George Goch.[83]

Through exercising continual pressure for what it chose to term 'local representation', the Chamber also succeeded in getting its President appointed to the Johannesburg Liquor Licensing Board in 1895. Delighted with its success in Johannesburg, where it described the new system as 'working well', the Chamber tried to expand its power base to include Krugersdorp and Boksburg. The politicians of Pretoria, however, were wary of the expanding power of the mining capitalists, and the government resisted further Chamber of Mines pressure in this direction. By the mid-1890s the Liquor Licensing Boards were becoming increasingly politicised, and they were simply one of several arenas in which mining capital was pitted against the Afrikaner ruling class. This emerged with even greater clarity in the wake of the Jameson Raid in December 1895. In 1896 the government refused to allow the incoming President of the Chamber of Mines, J Hay, to replace Lionel Phillips on the Johannesburg Board. Instead, the government pointedly allocated his seat to H F Pistorius, President of the Chamber of Commerce, and by so favouring the petty bourgeoisie, underlined its continued suspicion of mining capital.[84] In general, battle honours on this front were shared since the government tended to play off the petty bourgeoisie, or fractions of it, against the advances of mining capital.

On the second front – the attempt to get more efficient state action against illicit liquor sales – the Chamber of Mines enjoyed slightly greater success. Here, away from the politics of committees and on the open ground of 'public opinion', the Chamber could harness more support. In particular, it attempted to exploit the groundswell of white annoyance at the amount of public drunkenness and violence amongst black workers. Individual members of the Chamber of Mines frequently raised these issues in the columns of the local press, and they were also active at public meetings. At the 1891 meeting they got support for motions which demanded that the government change the rules of evidence as they affected liquor cases, and that offenders should be given prison sentences in addition to fines.

This type of Johannesburg-residents-cum-Chamber-of Mines 'public opinion' was not the stuff of which spectacular victories were made. Not only was this a subordinate strand of thinking *within* the Chamber, but what was 'public opinion' to the Chamber of Mines was not necessarily 'public opinion' to the *Volksraad*. Nevertheless, the ideological offensive of individual activists within the Chamber of Mines should not be underrated. Locally the effect of this 'public opinion' could be seen, and nowhere more clearly than in the court of Magistrate van den Berg.[85]

Between September 1899 and June 1891 the average fine for selling liquor to a 'native' without a permit increased five times, from £10 (or one month in prison), to £50 (or three months).[86] Perhaps more important still was the long-term effect of the Chamber's campaign. This early offensive laid the foundations from which a strong attack could be launched on the canteen keepers in 1897-9. Before 1895, however, the Chamber of Mines could not claim a general success on this front, as was clearly indicated by the continuing liquor boom.

By 1891 the Chamber of Mines was also worrying at the state on another front, attempting to obtain an efficient and corruption-free police force which could deal with the large-scale theft of gold amalgam by white workers, and the enormous consumption of illicit liquor by black workers. On this issue, the tactic of the Chamber was to exploit the strains of disunity within the Afrikaner ruling class. In particular, the mine owners attempted to make use of the growing Afrikaner 'progressive' opposition to President Kruger.

The 'progressives' did not constitute a party as such, but formed rather a loosely-knit Afrikaner political alliance in broad opposition to the Kruger administration. Two of the central figures in this alliance were the widely respected Lukas Meyer, and Ewald Esselen, a former judge of the High Court. Under their guidance the opposition of this group became increasingly well-organised and effective between 1890 and 1892. In clear and outspoken terms they denounced corruption, maladministration, and government policies on the franchise, railways and concessions. In the 1893 election they achieved their greatest advance when their presidential candidate, General Piet Joubert, almost succeeded in defeating Kruger.[87]

Kruger responded in 1894 by devising a scheme by which he hoped to upstage his new Afrikaner political rivals. Seeking to take some of the wind out of the 'progressive' sails, he offered Ewald Esselen the post of State Attorney. Esselen accepted the offer, leaving behind him a lucrative £5 000-a-year law practice. The gamble which Kruger had taken in appointing this Scottish-trained lawyer, who was broadly opposed to his policies, was quickly spotted by the Chamber of Mines.

The Chamber noted with some approval Esselen's first act on taking office – the separation of the hitherto single post of State Attorney and Head of Police. The mine owners had long suspected that previous police commandants were personally involved in the illicit liquor traffic; Esselen's action gave them more room to manoeuvre.[88] Once the departments were separated the Chamber of Mines felt free to approach the State Attorney about the problem of the police. The mine owners suggested to Esselen that a special force of detectives be established to deal exclusively with the problem of gold thefts and illicit liquor sales. In order to overcome the old problem of low salaries and police corruption, it was proposed that the 'specials' be jointly paid by the state and the Chamber of Mines.[89] Esselen agreed to these proposals, and in order to implement the scheme he recruited Andrew Trimble from the Cape colonial service as Chief Detective. By August 1894 things seemed to be working quite well. 'Specials' such as Charles and Freddy Ueckermann, who were based in Pretoria and reported directly to the State Attorney, regularly raided illicit liquor dens in Johannesburg and received one-third of the fines imposed on canteen keepers.[90]

At this stage the Chamber of Mines had every reason to be optimistic. Its indirect incursion into Afrikaner politics seemed to be reaping dividends. Throughout September and October 1894 the 'specials' put the canteen keepers under great pressure.[91] At one stage, in a desperate attempt to come to terms with the new legal regime, the WLVA even went so far as to agree to close all 'Kaffir Bars' on Sundays. For his part, Andrew Trimble tried to extend this initiative and secure its effectiveness by policing the police. In January 1895 he arrested the senior detective in Johannesburg, Donovan, on a charge of accepting bribes from a canteen keeper named Greenstone.[92] He then persuaded State Attorney Esselen to arrange for Donovan's dismissal from the police force.

The Chamber of Mines, however, had chosen to make its indirect advance into a most sensitive area – one that involved intra-ruling class politics, and one which also ultimately affected the economic interests of the Afrikaner bourgeoisie. No sooner did Trimble's campaign get under way, than opposition groups started agitating for the Chief Detective's removal. The canteen keepers, particularly the Chairman of the WLVA, Foote, and a nephew of Sammy Marks's, S Heymann, consistently travelled to Pretoria, where they lobbied against the confirmation of Trimble's appointment. Their agitation came at a fortuitous moment. Kruger and his supporters were becoming disenchanted with their policy of *toenadering* (conciliation) towards the 'progressives'. When Trimble's appointment came up for ratification before the *Volksraad* and Esselen chose to make it an issue of confidence, Kruger saw his opportunity for getting rid of both men. The appointment was not confirmed, Esselen resigned, and Kruger appointed one of 'his' Hollanders, Dr H Coster, as State Attorney. Coster's first action was to reappoint Donovan, the very man Esselen had sacked, as chief detective in Johannesburg.[93] The Chamber's first attempt to exploit cleavages within the Afrikaner ruling class was less than a complete success.

By late 1895 the Chamber of Mines was faced with this bitter disappointment and it had achieved only limited success on other fronts. The retail liquor trade boomed, and 1895 saw an all-time high in Transvaal alcohol consumption – the contradiction within capitalist development was at its most acute. Confronted with what it could only consider as a series of unsavoury realities, the Chamber realised that the time was ripe for a more radical approach to the liquor problem. On 6 July 1896 the Chamber of Mines called a special meeting to consider the 'liquor question', and from it emerged a new stance. The mine owners jettisoned their old demands for stricter and more efficient *control* of a system which allowed black workers access to alcohol through employer-issued permits. The capitalists were now willing to abandon any benefits which they might have reaped from the operation of their own industrial variant of the *dop* or tot system. Instead, the meeting directed the *Volksraad*'s attention to 'the immediate necessity for legislation by which the sale of intoxicating liquors to natives in the mining districts and surrounding fields shall be totally prohibited'.[94] In calling for 'total prohibition' the Chamber of Mines had finally reached a position which a section of Johannesburg's 'public opinion' had reached at least five years earlier. Slowly, reluctantly, and only after numerous other courses had been tried, the Chamber of Mines had to abandon the exploitation of alcohol as a means of social and economic control over black workers.

Having achieved ideological fusion with 'public opinion' in pursuit of 'total prohibition', the Chamber of Mines was in a stronger position to challenge the Kruger government. It again sought out the discordant group within the Afrikaner ruling class – the 'progressives'. This time it used the local *Volksraad* member, Geldenhuis, to lobby for a 'total prohibition' clause in any new legislation on liquor. Geldenhuis in turn joined forces with another well-known Volksraad 'progressive', J P Steenkamp, and with Chief Justice J G Kotzé. These three, with the aid of other *Raad* members, ensured that when Act 17 of 1896 was passed it contained a 'total prohibition' clause. This time, for a variety of complex reasons, the divisions within Afrikaner politics had been capable of rapid exploitation and had yielded a handsome dividend. Hereafter, the Chamber of Mines clung tenaciously to the 'total prohibition' clause under all circumstances.

In general the Chamber of Mines could look back on the years before 1896 as something of a failure, since their black workers had been treated primarily as consumers for the benefit of the liquor industry and its allies. Equally, however, the Chamber could look forward to 1 January 1897, when the 'total prohibition' clause would become effective. As the last weeks of 1896 slipped by, the mine owners had every reason to believe that they were on the verge of a golden age in which they would have sober, efficient and cheap labour.

STALEMATE – THE BLACK WORKER AS WORKER AND CONSUMER
The Peruvian connection and the rise of the illicit liquor syndicates,
1897-1899

In order fully to appreciate and understand the problems of the liquor producers in this second period, it is necessary to recapitulate what had occurred in the months immediately before.

As viewed from Sammy Marks's position in the Hatherley board-room, 1896 and especially 1897 were bad years for business. Ever since the opening of the Lourenço Marques railway line in 1895, increasing quantities of Delagoa Bay rum and German potato spirits had found their way to the Witwatersrand. The Pretoria distillery's grain spirit simply could not hold its share of the market against the cheaper imported liquor. In 1896, for the first time in its history, Hatherley found itself with falling sales, and between 1895 and 1896 net profits fell from £98 274 to £69 569. The principal producers and wholesalers in Mozambique had become increasingly well organised. In order to protect their own profit margins, the firms in Portuguese East Africa had got together to form an 'Alcohol Trust' in 1896. Members of the 'Trust' agreed to 'sell only an equal number of gallons each, in proportion to the demand' and, more important, they had agreed on 'a uniform price'.[95] In effect, two giant competitors were challenging each other for the Transvaal market – a situation far removed from the cosy concession that Marks and his partners had bought nearly a decade earlier. Then, as if this picture of business-woe was not already dark enough, came the growing talk of 'total prohibition'. No sooner had the rumours of 'total prohibition' been circulated than the 1896 liquor act had been passed. When 'total prohibition' came into force on 1 January 1897 Hatherley Distillery was required to make the traumatic transition from being a squeezed competitor to being a producer with virtually no market at all. Overwhelmingly dependent on its liquor sales to black workers, Hatherley was totally unprepared for such a dramatic setback. The lowered profit margin of 1896 looked hand-some beside the net loss of £46 988 sustained in 1897.

In attempting to overcome this increasingly depressing situation, Marks and his fellow directors could have adopted any one of three basic strategies. First, they could have fought a defensive battle in order to retain what had been theirs in the past – monopoly production for a black retail market unhampered by cheaper imports. In practice this would have involved getting 'total prohibition' lifted, and at the same time stopping the Delagoa Bay trade in spirits. As a supplement to this strategy, the Pretoria distillery would have to continue to supply, to the best of its ability, the illicit liquor dealers who continued to operate despite the nominal 'total prohibition'. Second, by adopting innovative and creative marketing strategies they could try to redefine 'their' market. Here the most logical move would be to try switching to the European retail liquor trade in the hope that this would compensate for the 'lost' African market. Third, Hatherley itself could attempt to get into the rum and potato spirits business – an aggressive move that would protect the distillery from price-cutting should the African market be resuscitated to its full former strength. In practice this would mean going 'multi-national' and somehow reaching agreement with the powerful 'Alcohol Trust' in Mozambique. Given the magnitude of the problems facing Hatherley, the directors could not afford to dismiss any of these possibilities. Making full use of the business brains on his board, as well as their wide range of contacts, Marks started to work on all of these strategies.

Four months before 'total prohibition' was due to be enforced, the managing director opened his campaign to defend the Pretoria distillery. He wrote to the government on 6 August 1896, protesting about the new liquor law and pointing out that it severely damaged the concession which he and his partners had been granted. Six weeks after 'total prohibition' came into effect, on 19 February 1897, Marks again wrote to the government in similar vein. Neither of these initiatives brought any response from an unsympathetic administration, and Marks realised that he would have to approach them yet again. On 30 April 1897 he wrote his strongest letter, containing a final plea, and making new proposals. The managing director on this occasion first chose to remind the *Volksraad* of the capital invested in the distillery, and of the fact that the glass factory had been erected almost solely at its insistence. Marks followed up this rather stinging reminder with yet another telling point. He pointed out to the *Raad* that the poisonous duty-free spirits which came into the Transvaal made a mockery of its concession to him, and that it hardly qualified as the 'produce of Portugal'. Having established his case, Marks then proceeded to put forward his proposals. He suggested that the state undertake more rigorous quality-control measures against the liquor sold on the Rand – a blow aimed directly at cheap potato spirits – and requested permission to import, duty-free, blending materials and essences required for his business. Finally, he asked that the distillery be compensated for the losses which it had been forced to sustain as a result of government measures.[96] Virtually all of this appeal was ignored.

The absence of a positive government response might have disappointed Marks, but it could hardly have surprised him. After all, it was only a matter of months since the *Volksraad* had voted for the 'progressive' measures contained in the liquor act. Marks knew as well as any man in the Transvaal that Kruger was personally sympathetic to the canteen keepers and to Hatherley, but that he could not muster sufficient support to reverse the relevant clauses in the act. If Marks was to get the *Volksraad* to act then he had somehow to increase the State President's and his supporters' political leverage. In order to do this Marks probably worked through his nephew who was also the manager of Hatherley's Johannesburg branch, S L Heymann.

Samuel Heymann started his working life as an apothecary in a small village near Moscow before making his way to South Africa. In the 1870s, at the age of 19, he 'marched like a modern Dick Whittington from Cape Town to Kimberley, and thence to Pretoria, and presented himself to his uncle, Mr Sam Marks'.[97] Subsequently he worked his way up from a 'subordinate position' in the Hatherley organisation to the post of Johannesburg director. Heymann was a very influential figure in local business circles, and politically ambitious. As a credit-granting wholesaler he held considerable power over canteen keepers and was a member of the Chamber of Commerce as well as being Vice-President of the WLVA[98] He was politically active as a lobbyist during the Trimble affair, and on at least one occasion stood for office in local elections. For all these reasons he was well placed to be Sammy Marks's campaign manager, and when the distillery's books subsequently showed that, during 1897 sums from £20 to £40 were paid to unnamed persons to organise petitions calling for an end to 'total prohibition', there could be little doubt that most of the organisation was undertaken by Samuel Heymann.

In order to avoid raising the suspicions of the two most hostile *Volksraad* members, Steenkamp and Burger, these petitions were so worded as to make no mention of 'Hatherley Distillery'.[99] Although the exact fate of these petitions is unknown, it seems probable that they entered the political currency of the time, and that they played their small part in the liquor commissions of 1898 and 1899.

At the same time that he was writing to the government and organising a petition programme, Marks was also making important changes within the distillery itself. In particular, he ensured that there was a shift in production away from cheap spirits and towards the manufacture of quality liquor more suitable for European customers. This move neatly supplemented his request to the government for tighter quality control of spirits sold on the Witwatersrand, and he underlined his seriousness in this regard by arranging for the recruitment of top-class distillers in Europe. By early 1897 these new distillers – R van Eibergen Santhagens from the Netherlands, Le Farge from France, and H Coffey from Scotland – were at work at Hatherley.[100]

Neither of these two broad courses outlined above, however, were in themselves sufficient to place Hatherley on a sound economic foundation. Individually these strategies were inconclusive, and collectively they had the disadvantage of being time-consuming. By mid-1897 it was abundantly clear to Marks and his colleagues that their long-term security lay in making a quick and definitive entry into the Delagoa Bay trade, which was still the major supplier of the now illicit liquor market in the Transvaal.

Sammy Marks's first move was to contact the two Lourenço Marques wholesalers at the very centre of the 'Alcohol Trust' – Hunt and Auerbach, and Joost and Gubler. It is probable that the former of these firms acted as the wholesale outlet for the *Societé Française de Distillerie*. The latter firm certainly acted in that capacity for the Mopea Distillery which belonged to the *Companhia do Assucar*. Messrs Joost and Gubler were also involved in the potato spirits business since they acted as the local representatives of the German East Africa Line and, perhaps significantly, their business premises also housed the Imperial German Consulate. Through these firms and another intermediary, *Baron d'Inhaca*, Marks tried to establish exactly how much capital Hatherley would require to get control of the largest liquor producer in Mozambique. By early December 1897 the board of Hatherley Distillery knew that they needed at least £50 000 to acquire a controlling interest in the French company's distilleries at Lourenço Marques and Ressano Garcia, and to protect their vulnerable Mozambique flank.[101]

Knowing how much to raise was one thing. Knowing how to raise it was another. In looking for a solution to this problem Marks and his colleagues could be confident that the Paris *Bourse* (Stock Exchange) would be interested in the prospect of a large company, especially one with a good record like Hatherley, taking over the French company. If they did not know it themselves, then Henri Duval of the *Banque Française de l'Afrique du Sud* in Johannesburg would certainly have told them. The directors therefore decided to raise the capital through a new share issue. It seems likely that many of the 75 000 £1 shares made available to the public were placed in Paris. At the same time the Pretoria company decided to establish a permanent 'Paris Committee' of four members – a structure which had a precedent in the form of a similar 'London Committee'. By the end of 1897 Sammy Marks was the chairman of a company with listings in Paris and London, and with an issue share capital of close on half-a-million pounds.[102]

From this stronger base, negotiations for the acquisition of the French company could continue. On 12 January 1898 the chairman of the French company, Mr Villar, and the secretary of his Ressano Garcia Distillery, Mr Paul Regnet, were both present at a meeting of the Hatherley board. By this time, the *Societé de Distillerie*'s price had risen by £10 000 and the deal was finally concluded at £60 000. By 31 January 1898 Hatherley Distillery was in formal control of the Harmonia Distillery in Lourenço Marques and the newer distillery at Ressano Garcia.

Since 1895 Hatherley had been forced to drop its prices in an attempt to compete with the cheaper imported spirits – a factor which had no doubt made a substantial contribution to the shrinking profits in Pretoria.[103] Having bought control in the largest company in Mozambique, Marks now had access to the 'Alcohol Trust', and he could set to work on the price problem with the interests of the parent company in mind. By March 1898 the 'Alcohol Trust' had reached a new price and marketing arrangement that met with Hatherley approval. The new terms effectively limited the competition of all the Lourenço Marques distilleries bar one, and that of the Mopea Distillery to the far north. With virtually all the distilleries catering for the Witwatersrand market in line, the 'Alcohol Trust' was ready for a move into Johannesburg. By mid-1898 the 'Trust' had established a large depot in Kruis Street, where its wholesale activities were managed by J F De Villiers.[104]

All this success in Mozambique still did not satisfy the Hatherley board who had been stung out of any possible complacency by their loss of £46 000 in 1897. In particular, they remained worried by the threat posed by one of the smaller factories in Lourenço Marques, Dyball's Distillery. It was for this remaining competitor which was still outside the 'Trust' that Sammy Marks developed a special costless strategy. Marks instructed the firm of Hunt and Auerbach to take out an option to buy Dyball's on behalf of Hatherley Distillery. In practice, however, Marks and his colleagues did not have the slightest intention of buying the distillery. Instead, they merely made use of the option to suspend spirit production at Dyball's and to prolong the negotiations for as long as possible. This strategy was made clear to Hunt and Auerbach in a letter from the secretary at Hatherley, J P H Faure, on 2 April 1898. Although it cannot be conclusively proved, it seems possible that Marks's scheme eventually worked. Dyball's, on the strength of the option, certainly suspended production until June 1898, a sacrifice of at least three months' output. By 1899 there is no evidence of a 'Dyball's Distillery' in active production in Lourenço Marques.[105]

Capital, business acumen and ruthless determination all contributed to the relative ease with which the Pretoria financial generals had captured Mozambique. Their task, however, had also been made easier by the comparative indifference of the Portuguese capitalists – a surprising development given the latter group's interest in spirit production in the early 1890s.

The indifference of the Portuguese capitalists dated back to 1896. During the year not only had the 'total prohibition' clause been passed in the Transvaal, but the Cape farmers had experienced a particularly bad wine harvest. Prominent Portuguese capitalists and the Lisbon administration decided that this was an opportune moment to break into the wine market of southern and central Africa. A senior civil servant was sent to tour the region and to report on the business prospects. In the wake of this report a large wine depot was opened in Lourenço Marques, and a wholesale business under S F Belford was established in Pretoria. Belford not only sold wine reasonably successfully, but also tried to get a 'wine concession' from the Transvaal government.[106] To put it at its crudest: Pretoria's capital had succeeded in getting into Mozambique because Portuguese capital was partly intent on establishing itself in Pretoria. On the one hand, new industrial capital wished to monopolise spirit production for the African market, while on the other, older mercantile capital hoped to dominate the European wine market offered by settler societies. Whatever the cause of these developments, they suited Hatherley in the short run. In 12 months Sammy Marks steered his enterprise from a £46 000 loss to a £10 000 profit (1898).

The battle waged for the ownership of the means of production in Mozambique between 1897 and 1898 revealed several things. For one, it showed the capacity of South African-based capital to move into profitable sectors of economies in adjacent countries before the South African War. More fundamentally, it demonstrated that larger capital had to consume smaller capital when the former was faced with a declining rate of profit. Most important for present purposes, however, it showed that the capitalists knew that they still had access to a market for their product – why else fight for spirit production in a period of so-called 'total prohibition'? The fact that the market remained accessible after 1897 was not primarily due to the efforts of the capitalists themselves. For that vital condition the owners of the distilleries, the capitalists, had to thank another class – the petty bourgeoisie who owned the canteens.

When 'total prohibition' came into effect on 1 January 1897 at least half the canteens in the mining areas of the Transvaal closed down.[107] The new law and the stiffer penalties it contained simply frightened the more timid half of this sector of the petty bourgeoisie out of business. Many of the other canteen keepers, however, took heart. What other Rand businessmen could point to a market in which competition had been reduced by 50 per cent at a stroke? Moreover, canteen closures had the effect of reducing supply while demand remained at least constant. In practice this pushed up prices and profit margins. In 1898 a bottle of Delagoa Bay spirits cost 6d to produce, the Transvaal importer sold it for 2/6d per bottle, and the illicit liquor dealer sold it to African consumers at 5/- or 6/- per bottle.[108] Higher profit margins, in part a by-product of prohibition itself, ensured the persistence of the illicit liquor market on the Witwatersrand.

Some of these liquor sales took place in 'kaffir eating houses' and stores in the vicinity of the mining compounds. Often the quantities sold here were relatively small, and the trade was organised on a somewhat spasmodic basis. In several cases an essentially law-abiding storekeeper would bolster his sales through occasional trading in a commodity which yielded a handsome profit. In other cases, canteen keepers would cater essentially for the legal European trade and occasionally sell the odd bottle of spirits to Africans at the back door. These outlets, however, were largely insignificant and they constituted merely the tip of the illicit iceberg. More important by far were the large and well-organised syndicates which developed in an illicit trade that could yield profits of 100 to 150 per cent. These syndicates formed the very core of the illicit liquor business, and as early as March 1897 conducted a trade which the Chamber of Mines branded as 'rampant'. With the passage of time they became even more entrenched, and it was they who formed the nucleus of a petty-bourgeois army which defied the state and the mine owners between 1897 and 1899. But in order to appreciate fully who was involved in these syndicates, why they developed and how they operated, it is necessary to turn to earlier decades and another continent.

As suggested earlier, spirit production and the liquor trade had played an important role in the development of European capitalism. Within that trade Jewish communities had figured prominently – especially in the petty-bourgeois function of *korchma* keepers. Precisely because they were exposed in such visible class and ethnic positions, these communities were frequently persecuted, and pogroms forced thousands to emigrate to many countries during the nineteenth century. With the economic development which followed in the wake of the discovery of diamonds (1867) and gold (1886), southern Africa became an increasingly attractive refuge for such emigrants. Many of the Jewish refugees who came to Africa must have been generally aware of the role liquor could play in a developing economy, whilst yet others probably had personal experience of the trade. But, as is generally the case with immigration and developing economies, there was no simple equality of opportunity for these different waves of Jewish refugees. In general, the greatest opportunities arose for those who came earliest, in the 1860s and 1870s, at the very start of modern industrial capitalism, when the class structure was least developed. The later arrivals of the 1880s and 1890s who came into a socio-economic system with a more developed class structure, had to make do with more modest possibilities, and often ended up working for their ethnic kinsmen from Germany, Poland or Russia.

Given this broad and schematic outline, we can bring at least one new, albeit speculative, dimension to our understanding of events in the Transvaal. Now it is perhaps easier to see why the Hungarian Jew, Nellmapius, would have been so quick to appreciate the value of a liquor concession. Similarly, we can appreciate why three Russian Jews – Isaac Lewis, Barnet Lewis and Sammy Marks – were willing to go into partnership with Nellmapius when the opportunity arose. These men, amongst the first immigrants of the 1870s, came to a Transvaal which was, if not 'feudal', then at least pre-capitalist. As entrepreneurs present from the very outset of industrial development in the area, they rapidly established themselves as respected members of the emerging capitalist class. Nellmapius was one of the most prominent and powerful businessmen of his day, and at his death in 1893 President Kruger complimented him as 'a true patriot of the Transvaal'.[109] Like several of his Russian predecessors Sammy Marks accumulated considerable capital from the liquor business and came to head an 'industrial bourgeois family'.

This small and in part highly successful first wave of Jewish immigrants to the Transvaal was followed by a second wave of Europeans when gold was discovered in the mid-1880s. The men of this latter period saw their opportunities in the mushrooming towns of the Witwatersrand. Without the means, and without the personal access to the Afrikaner ruling class that would have enabled them to become capitalists, these men sought to accumulate their initial capital as a petty bourgeoisie. In particular, it was they who opened canteens and, as the *korchma* keepers of the pre-prohibition era, they sold spirits to black peasants who had come to the towns for a spell of wage labour. These immigrants, men like Herschfield, chairman of the Licensed Victuallers' Association (WLVA), might not have been 'respected' in the way that liquor capitalists like Sammy Marks were 'respected', but they were certainly a force to be reckoned with by the state and the mine owners.

The third wave of Jewish immigrants who entered the ZAR in the mid-1890s, however, were much less fortunate than their countrymen who had arrived earlier. For these poorest of East Europeans, not even the petty-bourgeois path to accumulation remained open. By 1895 the Chamber of Mines and WLVA had, for very different reasons, both agreed that no more canteen licences should be issued, and the 'total prohibition' law had followed in 1896. Poor and with every prospect of remaining penniless, these unfortunate immigrants were pushed into the life of the lumpenproletariat. As perhaps the most visible, dispossessed and unsuccessful group of whites on the Witwatersrand, they were the unhappy recipients of the most vicious class and race prejudice that society could muster:

> The stranger in Johannesburg cannot but ponder on the spectacle of a Kaffir respectably arrayed in good European clothing walking in the middle of the street, with a brass ticket strapped on his arm, while on the neighbouring footway may be seen, and even smelt,

some representative of European civilization, perhaps a 'Peruvian' from Poland or Russia, who has apparently not found it convenient to change his clothing or indulge in unnecessary ablutions since his entry into the country.[110]

For most of these 'very low class of Russian and Polish Jews, "Peruvians"', life in Johannesburg might have been totally miserable, but it certainly was not lonely. In 1899 it was estimated that there were over 7 000 'Russian Jews' on the Witwatersrand.[111]

After 1897 there developed amongst these different classes of Jewish immigrants various more or less explicit marriages of economic convenience depending ultimately on the liquor trade with black workers. The capitalist liquor producers, Marks and the Lewis brothers, remained in business largely because of the activities of the petty-bourgeois canteen keepers. The converse was, of course, equally true. In practice the producers and the retailers seldom met face to face, since both parties operated through another group, the merchant capitalists who acted as wholesalers. The most explicit marriage of convenience, however, took place between the petty bourgeoisie and the 'Peruvians' of the lumpenproletariat. Members of the former group had no desire to jeopardise their liquor licences through being caught personally selling alcohol to Africans, whilst the latter were so poor that any opportunity to earn money came as an offer which they could not refuse. The canteen keepers therefore:

> ... engaged newly arrived young Russian Jews, at what might appear to them princely remuneration, agreeing in the event of the latter being trapped and prosecuted, to pay the fines, or, if they were sent to prison, to pay them a lump sum of release as compensation.[112]

It was this latter arrangement, often reinforced by kinship ties, and here termed the 'Peruvian Connection', that formed the white base line of a pyramid of business exploitation.

The size of the illicit liquor syndicates and their exact mode of organisation varied considerably. A small minority of these businesses were entirely dependent on the driving force, skill and organisational ability of one man. H Max, for example, kept on the move continually, and never sold liquor from the same spot for more than a day or two. In some cases this type of 'mobile canteen' on a wagon had to be drawn by as many as ten oxen. Other canteen keepers, such as Tiversky of the 'Old Grahamstown Bar' or H Joffe of the 'Old Kentish Tavern', operated from a single business base and such men would employ three or four 'Peruvian' assistants at most.[113]

The majority of medium-to-large businesses were syndicates in the more real sense that they constituted a partnership in which two, three, or four 'big men' were involved. The partnership of Judelsohn, Nathan and Cohen, for example, owned the Californian Hotel, the 'Station Bar', and the 'Ferreira's Gate Bar'. Similarly, the partnership of Friedman, Pastolsky and Katzen owned the 'Old Park', 'Jumpers' and 'Wolhuter' Bars.[114] Syndicates of this size had several 'Peruvians' and dozens of black liquor 'touts' on their pay-roll.

The largest of this type of syndicate in the late 1890s was that of Finestone, Lediker, Sacke and Schlossberg. As was often the case, some of the members of the syndicate were related (Finestone and Sacke), and the social cement of kinship contributed to the cohesiveness of the partnership. By April 1899 this syndicate was reported as having no fewer than ten illicit liquor outlets on the Rand, with a collective monthly turnover of about £46 000. Out of this, the syndicate had to pay a monthly bill for police bribes of £2 000, and this left the partners with a monthly profit of the order of £8 000. This syndicate, and another reputed to have made £18 000 during three months' trading in 1898, would probably have employed at least a score of 'Peruvians' as front men.[115] Although its size was vital, the Finestone syndicate had additional features which made it important in the financial life of Johannesburg. Like many other criminal organisations in capitalist systems, the syndicate controlled a financial empire spanning both legal and illegal business activities. Finestone was 'a prominent member of the Stock Exchange', and together with his other partners held a share in five hotels, described as 'some of the most adequately and expensively equipped establishments on the whole line of the Reef'.[116]

The biggest syndicates of all, however, revealed some of the classic hallmarks of organised crime. In the finest tradition of the criminal underground, the most powerful syndicates were 'family businesses' which dominated particular territories. Anybody who wished to open an illicit liquor canteen in the Boksburg-Benoni district, for example, would have had to come to terms with one such powerful family syndicate. But, as was explained in 1899:

> The rules are somewhat onerous. Firstly, the consent of the syndicate has to be obtained, without which the new business would not flourish for a week. Then the new-comer has to purchase his liquor at a certain wholesale store in Johannesburg [probably Friedman's]. Finally, the syndicate takes a large share of the profits. So that to start a liquor syndicate is sowing seed on the hard and unfertile rock of the Syndicate Monopoly.[117]

Just as the notorious Nathansons ruled Boksburg, so the Joffes ruled

Krugersdorp and Randfontein, while the mighty Friedmans controlled central Johannesburg.

At the head of a family syndicate stood the 'Liquor King' and if, like Sam Nathanson, he had sons, then he would be assisted by the 'Princes'. Immediately below this 'royal family' and within the syndicate proper, there followed a hierarchy of 'Peruvians' who constituted the King's 'loyal men'. It was the business army of 'Peruvians' who organised most of the day-to-day operations in the drinking dens – men such as Sol Pastolsky who was described as 'General Commanding Officer' of the area around the New Heriot Mine. Similarly, the 'Peruvian' in control at the Nourse Deep Mine was known as 'Commandant Schutte', a humorous title which his namesake at the head of the Zarps might have found a little less amusing.[118]

Outside this immediate corps of loyal 'Peruvian' troops, the King could also place some reliance on the vast number of state officials whom he had bribed. The task of these venal officials was twofold. First, they had to ensure that no action was taken against the King's syndicate. Secondly, they had to harass the business operations of unwelcome competitors or enemies who managed to muscle their way into the King's territory. The degree of control which the King had over 'his' state officials was a matter of considerable prestige, since it accurately reflected the extent of his real power. Thus, in Johannesburg, King Friedman could claim, with considerable justification, that he was 'the real boss' of the Zarp 'Liquor Department'.[119]

But Friedman's control over the local state apparatus paled into insignificance when compared with that of 'King Nathanson' in Boksburg. Sam, or Smooel Nathanson as he preferred to call himself, was the original big gangster and racketeer on the Witwatersrand. Leaving behind a record of arson and fraudulent bankruptcies, Nathanson moved from the Cape Colony town of Prince Albert in the late 1880s in order to capitalise on the fresh possibilities in Johannesburg. On the Rand he found new respectability. At one stage he was President of the Johannesburg Old Hebrew Congregation, and as late as 1894 the names 'Mr and Mrs S Nathanson' figured proudly in the local press as the donors of a prestigious gift at a society wedding. The money for the gift probably came from Sam's expanding criminal operations, and it was these activities which ultimately led to Sam's fall from social grace. But predictably enough Smooel Nathanson's biggest opportunities arose when 'total prohibition' was introduced in the mid-1890s. It was then that he developed into a fully-fledged slum landlord and racketeer in the illicit liquor business.[120]

The hold which Nathanson developed on the East Rand first became apparent in 1893-4, when a motley crew of unsuccessful canteen keepers and a venal ex-Zarp detective appeared in court, accused of criminally libelling state officials. This group, comprising Messrs Globus, Shapiro, Cooper and van der Hoepen, wrote anonymous letters to Chief Magistrate van den Berg in Johannesburg and to the *Volksraad*, in which they pointed out some of the ways in which Nathanason corrupted and controlled Boksburg officials. When these charges were investigated they were found to be substantially correct. Embarrassed by findings, the Johannesburg Public Prosecutor finally withdrew his charges. But the damage had been done. The Mining Commissioner, the Public Prosecutor, and the local magistrate at Boksburg had all admitted to receiving a considerable amount of money and 'presents' from Smooel Nathanson.[121] The government's response to these disclosures was to take no action against the officials concerned or Sam Nathanson: it slowly formulated new penalties for those found guilty of bribing state officials.[122] In consequence of this leisurely approach Nathanson's control of the district became increasingly entrenched, and by 1899 the local press was confident enough to report that:

> You need no concealment in the Boksburg district; the place is a patch of the blackest villainy in the Republic. There is not one single official connected with the supervision, licensing, and control of liquor selling, from the highest magistrate to the lower constable, who does not deserve to be cashiered.[123]

Little wonder then that Smooel could walk around his district and call himself '*Landdrost* of the Detectives of Boksburg' or, quite simply and accurately, 'The Boss of Boksburg'.

Nathanson and the other 'liquor kings' of the late 1890s used their armies constantly, both to defend and to expand their empires. Like Sammy Marks, they worked on 'public opinion' by paying 'Peruvians' and other poor whites to put their signatures to petitions calling for an end to 'total prohibition'. Their political activities ensured constant movement between their districts and Pretoria, and by 1898 State Attorney J C Smuts described them as 'becoming a power at all elections'.[124] More important and equally sinister was the impressive way in which they could wield power when things went wrong for the syndicate. Any 'Peruvian' finally trapped by the police and brought to court was likely to benefit from strange developments which frequently took place. On at least one occasion a bottle of gin which was to be used in evidence, as if 'by some miracle ... turned to water when brought to Court'.[125] If the material exhibits in the case did not change, then the 'Peruvian' could always look forward to unscheduled disappearances among the African witnesses for the prosecution. By late 1899 the police had to protect their 'trap boys' from pre-trial syndicate approaches by imprisoning them until the case was heard. Of course not all witnesses could, or would, come to an agreement with the syndicates. In such cases the witnesses stood the risk of less profitable and more permanent 'disappearance'. On several occasions the syndicates were suspected of organised killings on the Witwatersrand.[126]

But there were also limits to syndicate power, and the actual organisation of the drinking dens revealed this most clearly. The King would always make certain that he took out wholesale liquor licences only for those stands from which the syndicate could have guaranteed access to adjacent properties. He would also take the precaution of warning the 'Peruvians' that only *legal* sales of alcohol should take place from the licensed property. Failure to ensure this would place the licence itself in jeopardy, and in the event of successful prosecution would ultimately kill the goose that laid the golden egg.

Once the above concession to the law had been made, however, the King could set about organising the rest of his defensive strategy on the 'adjacent stand' to the licensed property. First the 'adjacent stand' – be it house or vacant property – would be linked to the licensed property by means of an underground tunnel. Thereafter the entrances to these tunnels would be hidden with the aid of elaborate false partitions and trap-doors. The carpenters and electricians would then be called in to arrange for the final protection of the unlicensed property: on vacant stands high fences would be erected along the perimeter of the property, with strategic 'look-out' posts at each of the corners; from these posts 'Peruvian sentries' would keep constant watch for the approach of the Zarps.

The dens, with an irony that the mine owners would not have appreciated, were often called 'compounds'. Many such 'compounds' and houses were further protected through the installation of a system of electric bells on the unlicensed property. This technologically sophisticated system, pioneered by one 'Fred Poplar' Cohen and widely used during prohibition, gave swift warning of the approach of any unsympathetic Zarp. In several instances final precautions were taken at the actual point of sale itself. 'Peruvian' Silverman, for example, seated himself inside a specially constructed wooden compartment into which had been cut peep-holes and the smallest of serving hatches. This arrangement enabled him to see the customer, receive the cash and dispense a bottle of spirits while remaining hidden. With such elaborate precautions it is hardly surprising that many of the illicit liquor dens were called 'forts', and that they had to be 'rushed' by the police.[127] In a very literal sense it was the *army* of the petty bourgeoisie that held the state and the mine owners at bay between 1897 and 1899.

This rapid and solid entrenchment of the liquor syndicates after 1897 did not escape the attention of the state. The *Volksraad* realised to its embarrassment that 'total prohibition' was 'total' in name only. Even if the state *had* wanted to turn a blind eye to the massive illicit liquor trade it would not have been allowed to do so. Sammy Marks constantly reminded members of the *Raad* of their obligations under his concession, while the retailers exercised their own particular brands of coercion and persuasion. The mine owners for their part made their bitter complaints well known in evidence to the Industrial Commission of Enquiry in 1897.[128] By the end of that year such insistent pressures could no longer be ignored, and the administration felt compelled to act. Early in 1898 the State President appointed the Acting State Attorney, Schagen van Leeuwen, and the Inspector General of Customs to a special Liquor Commission. The appointment of this commission must have removed some of the immediate pressure on the hard-pressed administration.

The *Volksraad*, however, was not the State President, and the members of the *Raad* certainly did not feel or respond to exactly the same pressure as Kruger. The appointment of the Liquor Commission, therefore, offered different opportunities to these two branches of the government. As far as the *Raad* was concerned the task of the commission was clear – it had to find ways of defeating the illicit liquor syndicates, and to suggest ways of enforcing the Liquor Act of 1896. For Kruger, personally sympathetic to the liquor industry, the commission offered an opportunity to renew his battle with a *Volksraad* which basically favoured 'total prohibition'. If the Liquor Commission produced suitable findings, then the State President would have valuable ammunition in his fight against the 'progressives', and a chance to protect the fortunes of his *Eerste Fabrieken*. With a two-man commission, one of whom was a 'loyal' Hollander, Kruger had every reason to be confident about the findings of the enquiry.

By mid-March 1898 the confidential report of the commission had been completed. Basically its findings represented a compromise between the views of the *Volksraad* and those of the State President. As the report put it: 'The commission is of the opinion that a moderate use of drink by the natives, under the control of or on behalf of the Government and the mine managers must in every way effect an improvement.' In order to achieve this 'moderate use', the commission proposed the adoption of a modified Gothenburg system – a type of state monopoly which seemed to work successfully in Sweden. It suggested the liquor should be sold to 'natives' in the Transvaal, but that:

> This should not take place by means of money, but by cards, or tickets, which would have been purchased by the companies from the Government, and which after being stamped with the authority of

the mine managers, would again be sold to the coloured people; the latter could then, as it were, themselves exercise control over the use of drink by natives.[129]

This scheme was to be supplemented by increased quality controls, better law enforcement, and a chain of state canteens which would be the sole retail liquor outlets on the Witwatersrand. The commissioners must have hoped that this degree of 'control' would satisfy the mine owners, that the 'progressives' would be pacified by the proposed onslaught on 'abuses', and that Kruger and Marks would feel content about the prospects for Hatherley Distillery. On paper at least, the perfect compromise had been reached and the contradiction which had so plagued the development of capitalism in the Transvaal would be shortly resolved.

On 31 March 1898 the Rand mine owners were then startled to read in the *Johannesburg Times* 'that the establishment of a State monopoly in liquor was under consideration'.[130] After this press leak the state felt obliged to let the mine owners know the hitherto confidential findings of the Liquor Commission, and on 14 April Dr van Leeuwen detailed the government's proposals in a letter to the Chamber of Mines.

The mine owners were most dissatisfied with these proposals. In particular, the Chamber of Mines held two strong objections. First, it felt that there was insufficient 'local control' in the scheme – the mine owners would not have enough power to determine how many canteens there were to be, or where they were to be sited. Second and more important, it doubted the capacity of the state to administer the scheme successfully. The bribery and corruption of the police force were already clearly evident; what would happen when the officials of the ZAR were directly in charge of the canteens? In fact, the mine owners were so frightened by the prospect of uncontrolled *legal* sales of alcohol to black workers that they were willing to settle for the unsatisfactory status quo. On 20 April 1898 the Chamber wrote back to the State Attorney reiterating its support for 'total prohibition', and calling for the effective enforcement of Act 17 of 1896.

The mine owners followed this letter with a petition along the same lines addressed to the *Volksraad*. This was a move calculated to exploit the divisions within the Afrikaner ruling class on the liquor question. The Chamber's uncompromising opposition to the principal recommendations of the Liquor Commission, as well as the mine owners' direct appeal to a *Volksraad* so recently committed to 'total prohibition', drastically reduced the State President's room to manoeuvre. When the amended liquor law was debated in the *Volksraad* later in 1898 the 'total prohibition' clause was retained by 18 votes to 8.[131] The recommendations of the 1898 Liquor Commission were never implemented.

These events, however, made it clear to the mine owners – if they needed reminding – that the State President and his closest allies were deeply committed to *Eerste Fabrieken* and the liquor trade. The Chamber could therefore expect another move in the same direction in the not too distant future. The mine owners were also distressed by these developments because they did not offer the industry any immediate relief from the activities of the illicit liquor syndicates. Black miners would continue to be good alcohol consumers and bad workers. Faced with this dismal prospect the mining capitalists decided on a radical initiative to shape the future in their favour. Early in May 1898 the Chamber of Mines approached van Leeuwen and asked the government whether it had any objection to the mine owners coming to a direct settlement with *Eerste Fabrieken*. Such a settlement, it was suggested, would meet the interests of the mine owners, the government and the distillery. The State Attorney, no doubt with Kruger's full approval, indicated his support for a new move to circumvent the impasse on the 'liquor question'. The Chamber of Mines at once set about establishing a 'Special Liquor Committee' – the mine owners' belated equivalent of the ill-fated government Liquor Commission.

The Special Liquor Committee (SLC) had every reason to be optimistic about its direct approach to the Pretoria distillery. The SLC was fully aware that many of the most powerful capitalists in the liquor industry were also deeply involved in the mining industry. As the Committee later put it in their report to the full Executive Committee of the Chamber of Mines:

> Your committee recognises the value of the fact that the Directors of the Hatherley Company are gentlemen who are also largely interested in the Mining Industry, and believe that if some reasonable return could be assured to the Company in lieu of that trade which, however unjustifiably, its shareholders had come to reckon upon as their due, the Chamber could count upon their loyal support in the direction indicated.[132]

Clearly, in this limited respect the contradiction within the capitalist development of the Transvaal was a strength rather than a weakness.

In an effort to exploit these interlocking interests, the SLC first tried to establish what price the Hatherley Board would want for the outright sale of the liquor concession. The distillery directors made it clear that the sale of the factory would involve 'a very large sum indeed', since the company had every prospect of monopoly profits until at least 1912. Denied this most desirable solution of all, the SLC tried another approach. It offered to pay the distillery an annual sum of £10 000 not 'to manufacture the spirit now used in the native trade'. The proposal, whereby one set of capitalists envisaged paying another set of capitalists *not* to produce, revealed in stark outline the contradiction besetting economic development in the Transvaal. In fact it was a contradiction of such magnitude, and it would cost so much to resolve, that the mine owners saw no reason why capital should pay for it. Instead, they proposed that the black working class should pay for its resolution! In their report-back to the Executive Committee of the Chamber of Mines, the SLC suggested that the fee that Africans paid for passes should be raised from one shilling to two shillings. The state, after collection of this additional revenue from the workers, would then pass on the annual compensation of £10 000 to Hatherley.[133]

When it had completed its preliminary enquiries and deliberations, the SLC passed on the above recommendation, as well as others for the reform of the liquor trade, to the state. This time it was the turn of the government and Sammy Marks to be unenthusiastic. The major proposals of the SLC, like those of its predecessor (the government Liquor Commission), met a quick death. The state, the liquor producers and the mining capitalists simply could not reach an agreement satisfying all parties, and by June 1898 it was still a case of 'business as usual' in the liquor industry.

While 'business as usual' had an obvious appeal for the Liquor Kings, the *Volksraad* was less than pleased. Members of the *Raad* were dismayed at Zarp corruption, and embarrassed by the flagrant violations of the liquor law of the Witwatersrand. Although it was somewhat frustrated, the *Volksraad* continued searching for a solution to these problems. When the *Raad* debated the amended liquor law in 1898 it took the opportunity of calling in Commandant Schutte, and severely reprimanding him over the poor performance of the police. But perhaps the most important step towards solving these problems came when Kruger replaced State Attorney Dr van Leeuwen with J C Smuts. From mid-1898 onwards Smuts applied himself to the problem of stamping out corruption amongst the Zarps. His immediate efforts were concentrated at the most senior levels of the police force. When Chief Detective Robert Ferguson was caught buying gold amalgam and passing in on to Count Sarigny in November 1898, Smuts arranged for his immediate dismissal.[134] Shortly after this the officer in charge of the ZARP Illicit Liquor Department – Inspector Donovan of Trimble affair fame – was also replaced. These and otherchanges in personnel followed until by mid-1899 Smuts was satisfied that he had reliable, efficient and uncorrupt officers in control of the ZARP. Under the Smuts regime the post of Chief Detective was occupied by Officer De Villiers, and the illicit liquor section was headed by Detective Thomas Menton.[135]

These reforms, while welcome in themselves, did not go far to remove the fears and anxieties of the mine owners. The changes in Zarp personnel were largely confined to the most senior levels, and in the lower ranks, where the salaries were least adequate, police corruption remained a pervasive problem. Moreover the mining capitalists feared the possibility of yet another Kruger initiative to get 'total prohibition' lifted. Most serious of all, of course, was the fact that the Liquor Kings continued to undermine the productivity of black workers through the large-scale sale of spirits. These factors, as well as the rapidly escalating political tension in the Transvaal during 1899, left the mining capitalists decidedly nervous and insecure. Believing that the best form of defence was attack, they decided to launch a new ideological offensive. In April 1899 the first copies of an Eckstein & Co-financed newspaper, the *Transvaal Leader*, were sold on the streets of Johannesburg. It was this newspaper which became the primary cudgel of the mining capitalists in the open class conflict which formed a prelude to the South African War.

Almost from its very first issue the *Transvaal Leader* set out on a 'liquor crusade' against the business armies of the petty bourgeoisie. Virtually every issue during May, June and July of 1899 contained some sensationalist exposure or other of the illicit liquor trade. No effort was spared in disclosing the names of those involved in the syndicates, and no attempt was made to conceal the hatred and contempt felt for their 'Peruvian' employees. The activities of the firms at the heart of the wholesale trade were well publicised, as were the practices of those who bottled various concoctions under the seal of forged labels. Newspapers readers were treated to detailed descriptions of defensive arrangements inside 'Peruvian forts', and told the exact nature of the links with the adjacent stands. On several occasions even the activities of mine and compound managers who were implicated in the illicit trade were reported. The *Transvaal Leader* also took it upon itself publicly to lecture Emmanuel Mendelssohn, editor of the rival *Standard and Diggers' News*, on his 'responsibilities' to the 'public'.

On the face of it, the *Transvaal Leaders'* campaign had every appearance of a no-holds-barred, full-scale exposé for the benefit of the new court of 'public opinion'. Yet amidst all these revelations about the liquor trade and the inefficiency of the state there *was* one significant omission. Not once during all the months of the campaign did the *Leader* devote so much as a single line to the activities of the liquor producers – the capitalists. At least one shrewd reader, W S Cohn, spotted the deliberate omission in the mine owners' game and pointedly asked the editor:

> But how is it that you have never shaped your enquiries in the direction of the 'Big' syndicate here [Hatherley and the Alcohol Trust], as they are the people who are supplying all these illicit dealers with the liquor?[136]

Clearly the mine owners and their agents were at war with the petty bourgeoisie and not with the capitalists; there happened to be such an embarrassing overlap between liquor capitalists and mining capitalists. Eckstein & Co would have understood the problem, as would their editor of the *Leader*, Samuel Evans. Evans was a manager in the company *and* on the board of Hatherley Distillery.

But this class war of 1899 was not confined to an exchange of ideological ammunition in the editorial columns of the *Transvaal Leader*. Certainly the editor and his principals had reasons for whipping 'public opinion' into a frenzy on the 'liquor question', but they also wanted *action*. To this latter end the editor engaged the services of an ex-detective named Baxter.[137] Making full use of Baxter's expertise, the editorial staff of the *Leader* embarked on a programme of violence directed at the Liquor Kings and their 'Peruvians'. On Sunday mornings they would set out on carefully planned expeditions, and 'rush' the illicit liquor dens. They succeeded in smashing thousands of bottles of spirits; they tore down false partitions inside the 'forts' and ripped out trapdoors. This pioneering example of violence for the capitalists' cause was soon followed by the mine managers themselves, who also hired private detectives for the same purposes.[138] All this destruction and disruption placed the Liquor Kings on the defensive, assisted the mine owners in their quest for a productive black labour force, and made excellent copy for the Monday-morning edition of the *Leader*.

Most of the justification offered for this open confrontation derived from a single incident which, fortunately enough for the *Transvaal Leader*, came very early on in its 'liquor crusade'. On 29 April 1899, Mrs Applebe, wife of the Wesleyan minister in Fordsburg, and a companion by the name of Wilson, were viciously attacked by a gang of men while on their way to choir practice at the local church. The woman's condition remained critical during the following days, and rumour had it that the Liquor Kings had paid gangsters to attack her because she had supplied information on their activities.[139] On 2 May, when her condition had further deteriorated, the *Leader* ran a sensational editorial entitled 'Blood upon their hands!' in which it openly accused the Kantor syndicate of Fordsburg of being behind the assault. The sense of moral indignation which this aroused in the white public was complete when the minister's unfortunate wife died on the following day.

Despite the offer of a £500 reward by State Attorney Smuts for information leading to the prosecution of Mrs Applebe's assailants, no substantial evidence was ever offered to the police, and the criminals remained undetected.[140] The whole affair, however, helped stampede 'public opinion' in the direction suggested by the *Leader*. Within days of the death there occurred a rash of public meetings. Local church congregations passed resolutions supporting the *Transvaal Leader's* campaign, and on 10 May a great public meeting was held in Johannesburg at which the illicit trade was roundly condemned.[141] At the same meeting ministers of religion sat astride their highest moral horses, striking out blindly at the enemy; in the wake of the gathering at least one of them was sued for criminal libel by Emmanuel Mendelssohn. The most important meeting of all took place at Potchefstroom on 17 May. There the members of the Dutch Reformed Church met in formal session and decided to send a deputation to Pretoria to discuss the illicit liquor trade with the State President.[142]

Amid all this pure-white moral outrage, however, there were also significant signs of black activity. African leaders, more concerned with the health and welfare of their black kinsmen than with Mrs Applebe, took the opportunity to mobilise their followers. Among these leaders were some who became prominent in the African political struggle of later decades. Saul Msane (compound manager of the Jubilee Mine) and Sebastian Msimang were among those who addressed an 800-strong working-class gathering in the Wesleyan Native Church, Albert street, on 16 May 1899. Resolutions calling for 'total prohibition' and strict enforcement of the liquor law were passed, and according to the *Leader*: 'It was remarkable that, although the boys working on the mines were largely represented, there was not a single vote against the resolutions.' On the following evening Msane was again active, this time as chairman of a meeting of 'educated natives', held at the Independent Presbyterian Church in the Braamfontein location. Here a similar set of resolutions was proposed by the Revd Tsewu and accepted by the meeting.[143] The *Transvaal Leader* gleefully reported on these resolutions which so accurately mirrored the official Chamber of Mines' policy on the liquor trade.

With 'public opinion' at fever pitch in a community already deeply anxious about the possibilities of war with Great Britain, there was always the danger that the 'liquor crusade' would get completely out of hand, produce witch-hunting and lead to indiscriminate violence. Since the attention of the 'public' was so ruthlessly fixed on the problem of the 'Peruvians', the Jewish community became particularly anxious. Jews knew and understood the syndrome at work all too well. In his letter to the editor of the *Leader* on 5 May 1899, William Cohn warned the newspaperman of some of the possible consequences of his 'crusade':

> In your efforts to diminish this deplorable traffic there is a grave danger of creating a large amount of anti-semitic feeling, a feeling, which I may safely say, is already beginning to show signs of existence. The mischief caused by articles appearing in the Berlin *Kreuz Zeitung* and the St Petersburg *Novoe Vremia* and *Grazdanin* is well

within my memory. Surely there are sufficient existing troubles and disputes in this State without introducing another, which would bid fair to eclipse all others in the intensity of its race hatred.

Within ten days the Chief Rabbi, Dr Hertz, was in the midst of a controversy about Jewish involvement in the liquor trade, and desperately trying to pour oil on increasingly troubled waters.[144]

In several cases the warnings and cautions came too late. At the Rietfontein Mine the manager took it upon himself to administer a thrashing to a liquor seller, and was promptly discharged when the case was brought to court. Egged on by the shrill cries of the *Transvaal Leader*, other self-appointed vigilantes set about prosecuting the war of the mine owners and attacked 'Peruvian forts'. On Sunday 21 May, for example, the Wesleyan minister in Johannesburg, the Revd Scholefield, led his congregation in an attack on a neighbouring shebeen.[145] More serious and destructive were the series of not-so-mysterious fires which happened to break out in the illicit liquor dens and hotels during May and June 1899.[146] Caught by the wave of popular hatred, African workers also took the opportunity to settle their debts with their nearest and most visible exploiters – the petty bourgeoisie:

> ... at one of the mines 600 boys destroyed the illicit liquor store, together with all the elaborate equipment of electric alarms and signals with which the store and adjoining premises were fitted. The reason given by the natives for this action was that the store was too much of a temptation to them, so that all their money was spent on drink.[147]

Again, the mine owners and the *Leader* must have been pleased with this working-class action which tackled the 'forts' of the illicit liquor syndicates rather than the spirit factory of the mining-cum-liquor capitalists.

With 'public opinion' in high dudgeon Smuts also saw the opportunity to push more strongly against the illicit trade. Knowing that Kruger would be on the defensive, the State Attorney gave his support to the *Leader's* 'liquor crusade'. In Johannesburg two of Smuts's public prosecutors, Cornelis Broeksma and Mostyn Cleaver, both identified themselves with the newspaper campaign. During the weeks which followed the State Attorney spent much of his time and energy in combating the syndicates, and senior members of his new department set a personal example. When there were no prosecutions forthcoming from the Fordsburg district, the State Prosecutor, Dr F E T Krause, cycled around the area in an attempt to establish what was happening on the streets.[148]

Much of the State Attorney's effort, however, was frustrated by the high level of corruption among low-ranking Zarps. To circumvent this problem, Smuts adopted a suggestion which had been aired most recently by the Chamber of Mines at a large public meeting on 15 May 1899. Within Chief Detective de Villiers's department he set up a special task force under the direction of Tjaart Kruger. Men from the 'specials', such as Detective Goldberg, were selected for their particular knowledge of the liquor traffic. It became the sole objective of this nucleus of uncorruptibles to smash the big syndicates.

The initial response of the syndicates to the 'liquor crusade' had been one of the reasonably self-confident indifference. During the early days of the campaign the Lediker syndicate had even attempted a confidence trick: it took the representatives of the *Transvaal Leader* on a public relations tour of its legitimate business fronts.[149] After the Applebe murder, however, the syndicates were forced into a more aggressive stance, and they resorted to their trusted methods of threats, bribes and corruption. Just when these methods seemed to be holding their own, the syndicates were confronted with the new and substantial challenge presented by the 'specials'.

Early in June 1899 Tjaart Kruger received two threats in anonymous letters which warned him to take the greatest care if he were to be so unwise as to extend his activities to Boksburg. The leader of the 'specials' read these letters as coming from King Nathanson himself, and decided to take up the challenge. On Saturday 3 June Kruger sent two of his Pretoria-based detectives, Heysteck and Pelser, to Johannesburg in the utmost secrecy. At Park Station they were met by Detective Goldberg, a man with personal knowledge at the Nathanson family's business methods. From there the three detectives made their way to the South Rose Deep Mine where the manager supplied them with three compound 'boys' for trapping purposes. From the mine the detectives and 'boys' set out for Smooel Nathanson's biggest 'fort' – the one behind the Railway Hotel at Germiston known to African workers as 'Pudding'.

At the 'fort' the detectives supplied the compound 'boys' with marked coins, and then sent them in as 'traps' to buy liquor. As soon as the 'boys' re-emerged with the alcohol, the detectives 'rushed' the 'fort'. They made progress without hindrance until they reached a final door, and then they were confronted not by Smooel himself, but by Prince George Nathanson accompanied by no fewer than 20 'Peruvians'. At this point the Prince warned the detectives that, dead or alive, they would not be allowed into the heart of the 'fort'. A vigorous fight ensued. Unable to get at the marked coins, the detectives decided instead to arrest the Prince and two of the 'Peruvians' on a charge of obstructing the course of justice. The Prince was dragged off to the local charge office shouting, 'Look here you special bastards from Pretoria, I have more money than you think, I can cover you with money, and I shall go to Pretoria and you will all have to work for me at half-a-crown a day.'

The detectives had missed the King, but George Nathanson and two employees subsequently appeared at the Boksburg Police Court, where they were each sentenced to a fine of £20 or three months' hard labour. In late June it was rumoured that King Sam Nathanson was so annoyed by the 'treacherous' behaviour of Detective Goldberg in the case that he was willing to pay £2 000 to get this 'special into trouble'.[150]

The Kings were put on the defensive by this new rigid arm of the state, and they were wary of the heavier sentences which seemed to form part of the Smuts campaign.[151] On 4 July 1899 the entire syndicate network was shocked by the news of the latest state success in the battle against the illicit liquor trade. The sharpest operator of all on the Witwatersrand, the King of the Liquor Kings, Nathan Friedman, had been arrested by Chief Detective de Villiers, following a raid on the Wiltshire Bar. Despite several attempts to pervert the course of justice, Friedman ultimately appeared in court, and in August was sentenced to ten months' imprisonment without the option of a fine.[152] This unprecedentedly harsh sentence left the syndicates sorry, the detectives delighted, and the Chamber of Mines reasonably content. At the August monthly meeting of the Chamber, Eckstein, on behalf of the mine owners, paid public tribute to the ceaseless energy and recent success of the State Attorney and his Chief Detective.[153]

The purr of content from the Chamber of Mines, however, proved to be somewhat premature. The syndicates might have lost some important battles but they had certainly not lost the war. Their hidden allies, Kruger and the liquor producers, had been left relatively unscathed. The deep divisions within the Afrikaner ruling class on the liquor question always left the syndicates with the hope of rescue by government forces fighting behind the lines. From June 1899 onwards the syndicates placed increasing faith in those allies. Pretoria might have been the seat of the State Attorney and the hated 'specials', but it was also the home of the State President.

In the wake of the Applebe murder and the public meetings to which it gave rise, several deputations made their way to Pretoria. Of these the most important was one headed by the Dutch Reformed Church in mid-May. On Thursday 25 May 1899 the Revd Louw and 300 members of the church assembled in Pretoria to petition the State President about the liquor traffic. At the state buildings the deputation was met by the noted enemy of Hatherley Distillery, the Chairman of the Second *Volksraad*, H P Steenkamp. Steenkamp thanked the church for the work that it had done in fighting the liquor evil. He also informed the deputation that the *Raad* had decided to establish yet another commission to examine the whole problem, and that the State President would hear them personally. At this point the Commandant-General of the ZAR, General Piet Joubert, arrived to offer the State President's apologies – Kruger's health did not allow him to meet the churchmen on such a cold morning!

The churchmen, however, were not to be shrugged off so easily, and that evening they regrouped, together with several representatives of the mining industry. At 7.00 p.m. the enlarged deputation marched down Church Street towards the State President's home. Unable to avoid the burghers any longer, Kruger met their spokesmen and curtly informed them that he was entirely opposed to the present liquor laws, and that the best way round the whole problem was to create a state monopoly along the lines of the Gothenburg system. These answers did not satisfy the churchmen, who then asked to meet the President separately from the mining industry representatives.

Kruger met the churchmen again at the Executive Council chambers at 9.00 p.m. He told members of the deputation that he sympathised with their good intentions, but that he was still of the opinion that a state liquor monopoly was the best solution to the problem. Somewhat wearied by the whole day's anti-liquor agitation, he then proceeded to express his considerable annoyance to the Revd Louw. He complained bitterly that the deputation had hampered certain approaches that he planned to make to the *Raad*, and that the *Uitlanders* (foreigners) in the Transvaal would make great political capital out of the fact that they undertook their agitations on the Queen's birthday![154]

As soon as news of the *Raad*'s new Liquor Commission got out, the syndicates switched their attention from Johannesburg to Pretoria. Knowing that Kruger and the liquor capitalists favoured a state monopoly in which Hatherley was to be the sole producer, they lobbied anew for the removal of the 'total prohibition' clause. A mere two weeks after Nathan Friedman had been sentenced, the Liquor Kings succeeded in getting the information they longed for. On 26 August 1899 a disgusted *Transvaal Leader* told its readers:

> The syndicates are boasting of approaching changes in the Law as if they were as good as accomplished already, and they seem to know the mind of the *Raad* Liquor Commission before even that body has reported to the *Raad*. Prohibition, it is said, is to go by the board.[155]

A week later the commission reported to the *Raad*. It suggested that prohibition be lifted, that Africans be entitled to two drinks a day – one in the morning and one in the evening – but that nobody should be allowed to sell a black man a bottle of liquor.[156] These findings no doubt delighted the syndicates: if the proposals for what amounted to a new industrial *dop* system ever came into being, they would be able to expand their empires through the loopholes which they were bound to find in the new legislation.

At the same time, and for the same reasons, these findings must have been bitterly disappointing to the mine owners. As the clouds of war threatened to break, and the mining capitalists scurried for the protection of Cape Town, they could look back not on three years of 'total prohibition', but on three years of total frustration. What the *Volksraad* and the law had so faithfully promised them in 1896, the Liquor Kings, the 'Peruvians' and the Zarps had denied them over the succeeding years. Economic roots dating back at least to the 1880s had given rise to a political plant whose foliage had become hopelessly entangled. Every time that the stem of the alliance between the Chamber of Mines and the *Volksraad* was pulled in one direction, that of the State President and the liquor capitalists moved in another, and all the time the parasitic liquor syndicates continued to bloom. The mine owners knew that as long as Kruger and Hatherley Distillery survived, they would be confronted by a stalemate in which Witwatersrand Africans would be both liquor consumers *and* unproductive workers. They also knew that while there was war, there was hope.

THE BLACK WORKER AS WORKER
The spoils of a war fought for the mine owners, 1899-1903

Prohibition, the 'specials' and the 'liquor crusade' of the *Transvaal Leader* all helped to make 1899 one of the less successful years for Hatherley Distillery. Yet, despite the outbreak of war with Great Britain in October, which further undermined business, the Pretoria factory continued to manufacture spirits, and at the end of the year managed to show a profit of £2 737. *South Africa*, financial journal and capitalist mouthpiece in the city of London, assured its readers that, given the circumstances, 'this result cannot be regarded as other than satisfactory'.[157]

Under Sammy Marks's skilful financial tutelage the trading year for Hatherley in 1900 was no less satisfactory – again, given the circumstances. Catering for the climate of insecurity, Marks arranged for a sum of £25 000 to be taken out of the distillery's funds and secured as a special investment. Even after this had been done, the distillery showed a gross profit of over £16 000 for the 12 months; although the shareholders were not paid a dividend they had every reason to be content with an enterprise which could point to a net profit of over £9 000 in such trying times.[158]

A trading year, however, was not the same as 12 months of war, and viewed in other perspectives 1900 was not a good one for the Pretoria company. Early in the year there had been a considerable amount of fighting in the vicinity of the factory, and the company was fortunate that very little permanent damage was done to plant and equipment. However, once Pretoria fell to the British forces on 5 June 1900, damage of a more lasting type was done to the distillery. Under martial law the Military Governor issued a proclamation prohibiting the manufacture and sale of all spirituous liquors.[159] Under the same order, Sammy Marks was forced to close the glass factory at Hatherley, and this meant dismissing all employees. This latter action involved the company in additional expense, since all the skilled workers were on contract and demanded compensation for their enforced redundancy. The Hatherley directors sharply contested these decisions, but their combination of threat and plea left the Military Governor totally unmoved. This early proclamation gave the first indication of how the imperial authorities were to view the liquor industry in their newly acquired mining colony.

Initially the liquor capitalists were not greatly perturbed about the long-term consequences of this closure. Their ultimate confidence was reflected in the press release which the London Committee issued to English shareholders:

> The cessation of business, however, is only of a temporary nature, and when things have settled down there is every reason to anticipate that under the British Flag the Company will have a bright and prosperous future.[160]

Six, sixteen and twenty-six months later the distillery and the glass factory were still closed 'in obedience to proclamations issued by military authorities'.[161] In the end Hatherley Distillery never did re-open – a fate which the Transvaal gold mines certainly did not share. At some point between June 1900 and February 1903 British and other shareholders made the rather painful discovery that the imperial army had fought a war for the mine – and not the distillery-owners.

The closure of Hatherley did not dramatically disrupt the liquor trade on the Witwatersrand during the first nine or ten months of the war. Existing stocks and a much-reduced but continuing supply of liquor from the Pretoria distillery were sufficient to keep the syndicates in business. Black workers continued to buy, at new and even more exorbitant prices, the only 'cheap' liquor they could afford – Hatherley spirits or 'Nellmapius' as it was more commonly known. Both the syndicates and the black workers, however, got a foretaste of the imminent new dispensation when the ZAR government took over the running of five mines in April 1900. The wages of the 12 000 black workers were unilaterally reduced from 60 to 20 shillings per month, and the ZAR war administration further illustrated its no-nonsense capitalist approach by cancelling all liquor licences in the vicinity of the mines.[162]

More glimmerings in the new capitalist dawn were to be seen soon after the British forces occupied Johannesburg on 1 May 1900. Martial law was declared; within a month an important syndicate leader was arrested, and made an example of:

> ... a certain Joffe [Barry from Krugersdorp] known on the Rand as the Liquor King, was sentenced to a heavy fine and several years' imprisonment, with the result that the whole trade was paralysed.[163]

In fact the whole trade was not 'paralysed', but the Kings had received a near-fatal blow. Further problems arose for the syndicates as the army swept through Johannesburg, rounding up what the British administration called 'undesirable immigrants'. These lumpenproletarians from Russia, Austria, Germany, Italy, Spain and France were unceremoniously bundled onto trains, and despatched to Cape Town. There, at least one party 150-strong was put aboard the *Howarden Castle* and sent to Europe.[164] Amongst these 'undesirable immigrants' of July/August there were several 'Peruvians', and this further undermined the illicit liquor business. By September it was reported that the shebeens had 'been pretty well stamped out by the heavy penalties imposed'. The illicit liquor trade, however, was never totally eradicated – not even under the harsh regime of martial law. In February 1901, Colonel Davis, the Military Commissioner of Police, still had to devote a part of his day to it.[165] In general, however, there was no doubt that the Witwatersrand was becoming a better place for mining companies.

From their wartime base in Cape Town the mine owners watched the achievements of the imperial army with undisguised admiration. The closure of Hatherley, the trial of Joffe and the deportation of the 'undesirables' were gifts that only a war could bestow so swiftly and generously. In less than three months the Military Governor had succeeded in achieving what the Chamber of Mines and the *Volksraad* had failed to accomplish in three years.[166] The joy of the mine owners, however, was the joy of caution. They knew that the Transvaal would not always be under martial law, and that the British army would not always be there to do the work of the state. What they had to do, therefore, was to ensure that the gains of war did not become the losses of peace. To this end they spent their seaside days lobbying the imperial administration, and building up an ideological offensive against any future legislation which might allow alcohol to be sold to black men in the Transvaal. The ghost of the *Volksraad*'s 1899 Liquor Commission continued to haunt the Chamber of Mines in its wartime home.

In July 1900, a mere four weeks after Johannesburg had been occupied, a large deputation of mine owners and commercial men approached the then Government of the Cape, Sir Alfred Milner. The mining men described their pre-war liquor problem on the Witwatersrand in some detail to Milner, and expressed their wish that 'total prohibition' be maintained and effectively enforced. Milner gave the deputation a most sympathetic hearing and assured the businessmen that whoever took over the Transvaal's affairs after the war would probably be capable of clearing up the entire liquor question to their satisfaction within six months.[167]

A nod and a wink from a governor – even a British governor – did not completely satisfy mining capitalists. What would Sammy Marks and the producers of 'Cape Smoke' do once business was resuscitated and they got access to the markets of a united South Africa? For this and other reasons, the men of the Chamber of Mines threw their weight behind a new organisation which emerged exactly as the Transvaal was making the transition from a military to a civilian administration. 'The South African Alliance for the Reform of the Liquor Traffic' united men 'keenly interested in the moral and material welfare of South Africa, mine owners, mine managers, merchants, ministers of religion and private citizens'.[168] It would appear that within the alliance the men interested in the 'material welfare of South Africa' made considerable use of those interested in the 'moral welfare' of the country. It was the ministers of religion who undertook most of the agitation and public relations for the 'alliance' – men like the Revd Andrew Brown and the Revd J T Darragh, the founder of St John's College in Johannesburg. During June and July of 1901 they wrote articles at home and abroad outlining the aims and objectives of the movement.[169]

First, the alliance wished to seize the moment and secure the victories of the Military Governor. As the good Revd Darragh put it to his English audience:

> Reforms which it would be well-nigh impossible to introduce into an old and complex civilisation can now and here be attempted with the minimum of opposition and friction. We are making a fresh start, and it will be some compensation for the sufferings of the last two years if the start is made on sane, well-considered lines. We have perfect confidence in the ability, integrity and honesty of purpose of the Administration, but amid the multiplicity of claims which will be clamouring for attention, it is just possible that this golden opportunity for settling the liquor problem may be overlooked till it is too late.[170]

Second, and more fundamental, the alliance sought a state monopoly for the production and sale of liquor.

The idea of a state monopoly of this sort was not new to the mine own-ers – indeed it was very similar to the Kruger proposals of 1898-9. This time, however, the mining capitalists knew that the monopoly would be run by a state in which they had greater power, and that it would be backed by an administration which would more effectively guarantee the productivity of their black workers. In fact, the mine owners had such confidence in the competence of the incoming administration that many hankered after the old industrial *dop* system of pre-1897. With British backing, the use of alcohol as a means of socio-economic control again became a real possibility. Significantly, therefore, the alliance did *not* favour 'total prohibition', and again the capitalists left it to the churchmen to explain. The Revd Darragh told an English audience which was perhaps not fully familiar with the realities and history of the industry, what exactly it was that the mine owners contemplated:

> Many thoughtful persons feel that the mining native should be spe-cially considered. His work, especially underground, is disagree-able, monotonous and exhausting. The East Coast natives in par-ticular [Mozambicans] who furnish the largest number of under-ground workers, are used to stimulants from boyhood, and it seems unfair to deprive them altogether of what they regard as a solace ...[171]

Like other clergymen in the alliance, the Revd Darragh was capable of doing a more than passable imitation of a Minister of Mines.

As the Transvaal moved from military administration to imperial gov-ernment, the mine owners had placed their money on a win/win com-bination which guaranteed dividends. Either they could get 'total prohi-bition', which would ensure them a productive labour force, or they could retain the right to use alcohol as a lever of socio-economic control in a regime backed by an efficient administration. All that remained was the 'anxious' wait to see whether the approach through Milner or the deployment of the South African Alliance ultimately triumphed. In prac-tice the wait turned out to be less than nerve-racking.

In April 1901, within weeks of his arrival in Pretoria as High Commis-sioner, Alfred Milner was petitioned by the South African Alliance on the liquor question. The alliance again underlined the benefits that had come with martial law, and urged strong government control. For his part, Milner expressed sympathy with the new movement, and suggested that they also approach Joseph Chamberlain. Additional pressure brought to bear on the Secretary of State for the Colonies would neatly supplement the alliance's well-advanced public agitation in England. Having yet again expressed his understanding of the mining capitalists' problems, Milner set to work on his task of reconstruction.

In October 1901 Milner set up the Liquor Licensing Commission in Johannesburg to administer the resumption of the retail liquor trade.[172] As chairman of the commission he appointed a yeomanry officer, Major Macpherson, and to assist him, a committee of Johannesburg business-men. This military-cum-civilian licensing board was designed to pro-duce exactly the type of conservative change that Milner and the mine owners envisaged. Initially, it kept all bars, canteens, and bottle stores closed, and only allowed liquor to be sold in hotels and restaurants between 12 noon and 9 p.m.

Milner made this exceedingly modest revival of the liquor trade even safer when, on 10 December 1901, he used his powers of proclamation as High Commissioner to gazette new liquor laws for the Transvaal.[173] His proclamation embodied the principle of 'total prohibition' for Africans, and laid down stiffer penalties for the contravention of the law than had existed under the old ZAR government. Milner saw this law as a gift benefiting *all* the classes most closely involved in the reconstruction of capitalism on the Rand. With the fervour so characteristic of imperial ideology, he wrote to Chamberlain:

> … undoubtedly the greatest benefit which it is in the power of the Government to confer, alike upon mine owner and native, is the suppression of the illicit drink traffic.[174]

And to put the issue beyond any doubt at all, this proclamation was followed by Ordinance 32 of 1902 which prevented the distillation of any spirits for commercial gain within the Transvaal.

Between them these measures ensured an orderly transition to liquor retailing, and limited the opportunities for illicit dealers. When the bars reopened in Johannesburg in January 1902 they had to operate within restricted hours and provide a meal of some sort with any alcohol they served. Liquor licences came under the control of the Imperial Liquor Commissioner, and except for a brief period of public drunkenness when the bottle stores reopened in mid-1902, there were no major disruptions on the Witwatersrand. In December 1901 Milner noted with pleasure the mine owner's claim that only one per cent of their black workforce was now absent owing to liquor consumption on any one day, as against the ten to fifteen per cent average during the pre-war years.[175] This increase in productivity, coupled with the newly reduced wage rates for African workers, left the mine owners comparatively happy. The Transvaal was becoming a safer place for mining capitalism.

The happiness of the mining capitalists was also the sorrow of the liquor capitalists. The thoroughness of the British 'reforms' and the closure of Hatherley Distillery left Sammy Marks and his colleagues far from satisfied. Marks's financial acumen, the concession, and the large number of British shareholders in the distillery all meant that Milner could not simply brush the liquor capitalists aside. In mid-1901 *South Africa* warned Milner not to see the Pretoria business as simply another Kruger concession, like the railways or dynamite:

> The Hatherley Distillery has all along been an honest concern, with an honourable management, and as such is entitled to the highest consideration at the hands of the new Transvaal authorities.[176]

To make the new revolution of the mining capitalists secure, the British administration had to eliminate the Pretoria distillery at the same time that it was 'reforming' the Rand.

Within 12 months of the outbreak of war, in October 1900, the imperial government appointed the Transvaal Concessions Commission to examine the monopolies granted by the ZAR. Sammy Marks and his partners gave evidence before this commission in Pretoria, stressing that the concession had been legally granted, and that the company had kept to all the conditions attached to the grant. When the commission reported in June 1901 it found accordingly, and recommended that if the concession were cancelled the owners should be compensated.[177]

As soon as the commission reported, Sammy Marks authorised Isaac Lewis to undertake the detailed negotiations for compensation. As a figure less closely associated with Kruger than Marks, Lewis proved a wise choice. Between June 1901 and early 1903 he worked ceaselessly to extract the best possible settlement for the Hatherley shareholders. In particular, Lewis had to pursue two related objectives: first, he aimed to get a settlement as soon as possible, an objective which was basic to the shareholders' interest; second, he was intent on getting a settlement with the Milner regime rather than the Legislative Council which would succeed it – the British were likely to be more generous towards international shareholders than the local bourgeoisie who were bound to follow them.

By the end of 1902 Lewis had wrapped up his negotiations with the Milner administration, and in February 1902 details of the settlement were printed in the Hatherley Directors' Report for 1902. From the distillery's point of view the settlement appeared to be a relatively generous one. The shareholders were to be paid a cash settlement of over a quarter of a million pounds for the cancellation of the concession. In addition, stocks on hand could be sold, exempt from excise duty, and some of the liquor at Ressano Garcia and Lourenço Marques was also to be imported duty-free. In London, *South Africa* told British investors in the distillery that 'shareholders are to be congratulated on the result of the negotiations'.[178]

When these basic conditions were confirmed in the Legislative Council in July 1903 not everybody was pleased: 'Several members severely criticised the bargain, which passed only because the Government was already committed to the terms.' The resolution of the contradiction within the capitalist development of the Transvaal had to be paid for, and not all were happy with the asking price. In this case, however, the mining capitalists' and tax-payers' sorrow was the distillers' delight. Why exactly Marks and his partners were so satisfied emerged from the detailed analysis of the settlement which *South Africa* offered its readers:

> According to the balance-sheet made up to 31 December, 1902, the total assets stood at £600 000, against liabilities amounting to £475 000. At this time, the concession and goodwill stood in the accounts as representing £117 319 7s 5d which must now, in consequence of the amount the Government has agreed to pay, be increased by £180 555 12s 7d or as little as £1 12s 6d per share. In addition to this, the company will, considering the very favourable conditions granted them, undoubtedly make a large profit on the sale of the 320 000 gallons of liquor they have in stock, so that when the affairs of the company come to be finally liquidated, the return made to holders of shares should be an extremely good one. To the fact that they are today in this very satisfactory position shareholders are to a very great extent indebted to Mr Isaac Lewis ...

No wonder that the financial journal could take a broad perspective and conclude: 'At this result, holders of shares in this the first industrial company formed in the Transvaal have nothing of which to complain.'[179] The owners of Hatherley Distillery went out of business with a smile, if not a chuckle.

CONCLUSION

The paths that states tread on their way to economic development often have local distinguishing characteristics, but they are seldom unique. The direction which the Transvaal took from the mid-nineteenth century onwards was certainly not unique – at least not in the initial period. Indeed, its quasi-feudal mode of production gave rise to certain patterns which can readily be traced in European economic history. One of the clearest of these patterns relates to the production of agricultural surplus and its consumption. By the late 1870s, and certainly by the early 1880s, the Boer farmers who had conquered the area north of the Orange River were producing sizeable grain surpluses. Like some of their European predecessors, this rural bourgeoisie sought to accumulate capital through the process of distillation, and by selling alcohol spirits to the town and villages which formed the modest local market.

But the Transvaal was not destined to remain a modest local market. Once gold was discovered on the Witwatersrand in the mid-1880s, there was a rapid and sustained increase of population within a relatively concentrated area. African and European miners, many of them with a developed taste for alcohol, poured into the towns spread along the line of the Reef – towns such as Krugersdorp, Johannesburg and Boksburg. This massive new market transformed the economic prospects of Hatherley Distillery and those of the grain producers who supplied it. From a modest 'first factory' in the Transvaal there emerged a large modern industrial enterprise enjoying the support and protection of a significant section of the Afrikaner ruling class.

Afrikaner farmers and distillery owners, however, were not the only parties interested in alcohol consumption on the Witwatersrand. Alcohol was also a matter of central concern to the new industrial bourgeoisie who owned the mines, particularly insofar as it affected their cheap black labour force. To their delight, the mining capitalists discovered that the black Mozambicans who formed the majority of the African labour force had an especially well-developed liking for alcohol. It was this liking, or partial addiction to alcohol that mine owners exploited to procure a labouring population from basically peasant economies. In 1906 F Perry, one-time chairman of the Witwatersrand Native Labour Association (the mine owners' labour recruitment agency), noted that Mozambicans 'have always been fond of strong drink', and he continued:

> They brew themselves many kinds of native spirits, and the potent liquors of European manufacture threw open to them new vistas of enjoyment. A few of them had found their way to the diamond fields. To the Witwatersrand goldfields, which were nearer to them they came in great numbers, especially after the construction of the Delagoa Bay Railway. Their earnings were spent, not on cattle but on whisky and gin. Thus, a period of work, instead of supplying them with the means of settling down, only gave them a period of drink and idleness. Afterwards they had to return to work in order to earn the coin wherewith to gratify their cultivated taste. In this way they have come nearer than any of the other South African races to supplying the material of an industrial, as distinguished from an agricultural population.[180]

In short, alcohol was a distinct aid in proletarianising African peasants.

Not surprisingly, therefore, there was an economic marriage of convenience – a class alliance – which bound the Afrikaner rural bourgeoisie and the mining capitalists between 1886 and 1896.

From the earliest years of the industry, however, the mine owners were also aware that alcohol was not an unqualified blessing. Spirits might have assisted the capitalists in procuring a cheap labour force, but the resulting drunkenness seriously undermined the productivity of the workers. By 1896, that is at about the same time that the mine owners were making the transition to deep-level mining which would ensure the long-term future and profitability of the industry, this problem of drunkenness had reached enormous proportions. Not only were the workers consuming vast quantities of locally produced spirits; they were also drinking so many gallons of cheaper imported potato spirits from Germany that their productivity was seriously impaired. The cost and inefficiency that resulted from this extensive drinking, at a vital transitional stage in the gold-mining industry's history, forced the new industrial bourgeoisie to take remedial action. It was at this point that the mine owners started exploiting divisions within the Afrikaner ruling class, and successfully advocating a policy of 'total prohibition' for African workers. When this policy was adopted it brought to an end the formal class alliance which had existed between the Afrikaner rural bourgeoisie and the mining capitalists

Both the distillery owners and an important part of the Afrikaner ruling class stood to lose much through 'total prohibition', which denied them legal access to what had formerly been their most important market. Thus, between 1897 and 1899, the liquor producers and powerful elements of the Afrikaner bourgeoisie made several attempts to have the policy of 'total prohibition' reversed – in effect they made constant attempts to resurrect the old class alliance in explicit legal form. These attempts, however, had little chance of succeeding since the interests of the mining capitalists had undergone a fundamental change. Unofficially and illegally some of the essential features of the old order remained intact. In the towns the petty-bourgeois army of canteen owners, dominated by Russian Jewish immigrants and aided by the corrupt arm of the state in the form of the police, continued to supply African workers with vast quantities of spirits. *De jure* the old order might have ended on 1 January 1897 when 'total prohibition' came into effect; *de facto* it persisted well into 1899.

This stubborn persistence of elements of the old order remained a constant source of irritation, frustration and unnecessary cost to the mine owners between 1897 and 1899. But this new industrial bourgeoisie took heart when war broke out between Britain and the ZAR in October 1899. The mine owners knew that the imperialists would use an efficient

British administration to secure the interests of foreign capital, and to make gold mining the undisputed economic master of the Transvaal – indeed that was the very purpose of the war. And their hopes proved to be fully justified. Within 36 months the army and the British administration had closed Hatherley Distillery and compensated its owners, passed legislation to prevent any further distilling, deported 'undesirable immigrants', smashed the illicit liquor syndicates, and then rendered the entire black workforce on the Witwatersrand more productive and efficient on newly reduced wages. Gone were the remnants of the *ancien régime* – the last remaining links of the old class alliance. From the end of the war, an economically and politically subject Afrikaner bourgeoisie could construct no further form of class alliance. With the aid of imperial intervention mining capitalism had been installed as the dominant mode of production in southern Africa. In all systems of capitalism – but perhaps especially in colonial regimes – alcohol has more to do with profits than with priests and is concerned with money rather than morality.

3

PROSTITUTES AND PROLETARIANS, 1886-1914

Commercialised sex in the changing social formations engendered by rapid capitalist development in the Transvaal during the era of imperialism

'Prostitution', so the folk wisdom has it, 'is the oldest profession in the world.' Unfortunately this common-sense maxim does not constitute a particularly solid foundation on which to build a more scholarly examination of commercialised sex. By implication it suggests that in any society there would always be a certain number of women who would seek to earn their living by selling their bodies – a view akin to that which holds that while there is alcohol there will always be alcoholics. For social scientists the problem with using these home-spun wisdoms is that while they may contain a residual element of truth, they ultimately force any systematic enquiry to centre around the pathology of the individuals concerned. While such approaches may be helpful and even profitable within certain disciplines, they are of extremely limited use to the social historian since they persistently beg the all-important questions about the nature and structure of societies in which prostitution manifests itself to any significant degree.

It is precisely with this concern for social structures in mind that most students of Victorian society have conducted their enquiries into vice and arrived at the general conclusion that 'large-scale, conspicuous prostitution was a by-product of the first, explosive stage in the growth of the industrial city'. 'Prostitution', wrote Richard Evans, can be seen as a 'functional consequence of the rise of the urban society created by early industrial capitalism'.[1] Viewed from this latter vantage point, the social historian can scan the historical horizons of the early Transvaal with greater ease since it was here, more than anywhere else in the country, that South Africa's most explosive capitalist development took place between 1886 and 1914. Moreover, since the central thrust of this local development came *after* that of the major industrial nations elsewhere, it meant that the flesh markets of southern Africa were opening up for prostitutes at precisely the moment when those in Europe were starting to experience a decline.² It is only once these broad structural signposts are recognised that it becomes easier to chart and follow the historical paths of vice in Johannesburg.

If it was the glitter of gold and the pursuit of profit that first attracted hundreds of diggers to the Witwatersrand in the mid-1880s, then it was the sustained and changing demands of a fully-fledged mining industry over the next two and a half decades which continually transformed that society. As the original diggers' camp gave way to a miners' town, and then to a more settled working-class city, so – amongst many other distinctive developments – the sexual composition of Johannesburg underwent a fundamental change. The almost exclusively male digging community of the 1880s gave way, by the mid-1890s, to a town which – although still overwhelmingly dominated by migrant miners of all colours – had a more notable female component; and then, from the turn of the century onwards, to an established city with an increasingly well-balanced gender ratio.

But this sexual revolution was not achieved without its own set of social costs and concomitant traumas. When the Johannesburg Sanitary Board first conducted a census, in July 1896, the results revealed that 25 282 white males and 14 172 white females resided within a radius of three miles of the Market Square – a ratio of 1.78 men to every woman in the most developed part of the city. An even more marked imbalance was found to exist amongst the black inhabitants of the city. In this case, the 12 961 black males in inner Johannesburg outnumbered the 1 234 black females producing a ratio of 10.50 men to every woman. Even this ratio paled into insignificance, however, when the African miners housed in the compounds within a three-mile radius were also taken into consideration. On the latter basis, black males outnumbered black females by 40 855 to 1 678, producing a ratio of 24.34 men to every woman.³

Given this fundamentally warped social fabric, it is less than surprising that Johannesburg, especially during the mid-1890s, offered substantial opportunities for prostitution. During the 1896 census, 114 'continental women' openly returned their profession as that of 'prostitute'. This honest or brazen contingent, however, merely constituted the core of a body of full-time professional prostitutes that was reliably estimated to be in excess of 1 000 women – the vast majority of these comprising recent immigrants from Europe. While a figure of this order might not appear as being intolerably high for a young mining town when viewed from the comfort of a retrospective historical glance, it constituted a more visible and urgent problem to the Victorian contemporaries of the Witwatersrand. The presence of 'women of ill-fame' in these numbers meant that there was one whore for every 50 white inhabitants of the city or, expressed more dramatically, 10 per cent of all white women over the age of 15 in Johannesburg were prostitutes.[4]

Furthermore, this trade in sexual favours also developed other features which tended to evoke public concern. Perhaps inevitably, prostitutes and brothels attracted a fringe element of petty criminals, thieves and gamblers to the city centre where they constituted something of a social nuisance. Even more threatening to the middle and upper classes, however, were the 200-300 pimps, 'white slavers' and professional gangsters who controlled Johannesburg's prostitution business by the mid-1890s. It was largely as a result of the efforts of this latter group that commercialised sex and police corruption came to assume a highly organised form in the city. When J A Hobson later looked back on some of the factors which had indirectly contributed to the making of the South African War, he noted that a system of bribery and blackmail 'was practised by the Johannesburg police in dealing with illicit bars and disorderly houses, resembling that which Tammany police established in New York'.[5] Whether or not he intended it to be so, Hobson's choice of analogy was singularly apt since, behind much of the local corruption, there were indeed American gangsters who had had first-hand experience of Tammany Hall.

Public soliciting by prostitutes, pervasive police corruption and rampant racketeering did not settle easily on the shoulders of those in authority in the Transvaal. When President S J P Kruger granted the Johannesburg Sanitary Board powers of local government in 1887, the constitution, in two separate articles, made specific provision for the 'punishment of prostitutes' and the suppression of 'houses of ill-fame'. But, by the middle of the following decade, it had already become clear to members of the Pretoria government that these local by-laws were, in themselves, totally inadequate for dealing with the problem of large-scale prostitution as it now manifested itself in the principal city of the Republic. In three successive years, through three successive pieces of legislation – Law No 2 of 1897, Law No 22 of 1898 and Law No 11 of 1899 – the Kruger government attempted to arm itself with the necessary statutory weapons with which to fight organised vice in Johannesburg. Not even this battery of laws, however, succeeded in ridding the Rand of its 'social evil' problem.

Immediately after the war, the incoming British administration under Lord Milner found it necessary to promulgate the Immorality Ordinance of 1903 in a renewed attempt to combat prostitution, and this was followed by the Crimes Prevention Ordinance of 1905, a measure which was at least partially used to restrict the activities of pimps. Two years later, when General Botha's *Het Volk* government first took office, it too recognised the need to take further action against offenders of the public morals and passed the Immigrants' Restriction Act of 1907. Although admittedly framed with other intentions in mind, it was this law that was widely used by the Transvaal police to deport pimps, prostitutes and other 'undesirables' from the Witwatersrand.

This barrage of legislation over a ten-year period indicated just how serious a problem prostitution was considered to be in the early years on the goldfields. The continuous need for new measures, however, also showed how deeply the 'social evil' had embedded itself within the social structure, and how difficult it was to dislodge. Indeed, it was precisely because the problem proved to be so persistent that many men in high office at the turn of the century were of the opinion that it was both futile and inadvisable to seek the total eradication of prostitution from society. Believing that 'the virtue of the *monde* is assured by the *demi-monde*', they and the police argued instead for the 'regulation' and 'control' of the traffic in commercialised sex.[6] Thus is was that while all the morality legislation in the Transvaal sought in principle to eliminate prostitution from the state, in practice the authorities for the most part operated a policy of selective enforcement – a policy of social control.

This essay, then, will attempt to analyse the dynamic and diverse functions of commercialised sex over the initial two-and-a-half formative decades of the Witwatersrand's capitalist development. Through a detailed case study, which explores the origin and development of large-scale prostitution during the early years of an industrial revolution, it is hoped to illustrate the limits of a policy of repression on the one hand, and that of social control on the other. In short, this essay will seek to show how various intermediaries sought to manipulate and profit from the relationship that existed between prostitutes and proletarians in the period prior to the development of a fully stabilised working class on the Witwatersrand.

HERITAGE OF THE CAPE – DAUGHTERS OF THE OLD PROLETARIAT, 1886-1896

When the township of Johannesburg was first proclaimed on the Witwatersrand, in October 1886, it sparked first a national and then an international scramble for the goldfields. Amongst the very first parties to reach the new Promised Land of Profit were diggers drawn from the *Zuid Afrikaansche Republiek*'s neighbouring states on the subcontinent – Natal, the Orange Free State and the Cape Colony. It was also amongst these early arrivals that the town's first ladies of fortune were to be found, and they soon attracted the disapproving attention of President Kruger's local officials. Within months of the mining camp's establishment, Special Landdrost Carl von Brandis appealed to Pretoria for assistance in his struggle against these women who had already succeeded in spreading venereal disease through much of the town. A year later, in 1889, his appeal was echoed by a fellow magistrate when Landdrost de Beer requested the government to pass legislation which would enable them to deal with the 'hundreds' of prostitutes at the diggings. The Kruger government's view of the matter, however, was presumably that the powers conferred on the local Sanitary Board in 1887 were sufficient for dealing with the problem since no additional legislation was forthcoming from Pretoria.[7]

It is possible that in later years Kruger and his colleagues came to regret this early legislative inactivity for, while the *Volksraad* pondered over these appeals from Johannesburg, legislation was being promulgated elsewhere in southern Africa – legislation which ensured that prostitutes would not only continue to be 'pulled' towards the goldfields, but that they would also be 'pushed' northwards.

In 1885 the Cape parliament passed the Contagious Diseases Act a mere 12 months before its British equivalent was repealed in London under pressure from the women's movement led by Josephine Butler. This controversial piece of legislation, like the Westminster statute on which it was modelled, made provision for the proclamation of scheduled towns, the registration of prostitutes and their compulsory medical examination; and by the early 1890s both Cape Town and Port Elizabeth had been proclaimed as scheduled areas in terms of the Act. The enforcement of 'CD' regulations at these coastal towns was understandably unpopular amongst women, and in consequence many prostitutes migrated to various inland centres, including the mining town of Kimberley which was blessed with a considerable number of bachelors. This comparatively minor influx of prostitutes to the diamond fields, however, simply succeeded in raising the wrath of the local middle classes who thought that the town had long since seen the last of its 'rough and ready' days.[8] Thus, in late 1891, partly out of a genuine desire to curb the further spread of venereal disease and partly out of other more class-bound reasons, the city's medical practitioners agitated to have Kimberley declared a scheduled area in terms of the CD Act.[9] This renewed threat to the 'women of ill-fame', together with the extension of the railway to Johannesburg in late 1892, ensured that several prostitutes yet again chose to move northwards.

In Johannesburg these relatively late arrivers from the Cape joined the ranks of the true pioneers of prostitution, and by 1893 these two streams – the 'earlier' and the 'later' – were converging to produce a growing ethnic diversity amongst the prostitutes on the goldfields. While a small number of these women were black, the largest contingent by far was composed of 'Cape Coloured' and white women. Despite the presence in Fordsburg of a small number of Japanese ladies of questionable virtue,[10] this meant that most of the town's prostitutes of the early 1890s shared one important feature – the overwhelming majority of them were drawn from within southern Africa. The Rand's first hawkers of vice were thus in large measure the residual product of Cape commercial capitalist development in the nineteenth century. In short, they were the daughters of South Africa's old proletariat.

But regardless of whether they were young or old, black or white, these prostitutes tended to develop a new link with commercial capital when they moved to the Witwatersrand. Most of the prostitutes in Johannesburg in the early 1890s chose to attach themselves to any one of the hundreds of canteens or hotels which abounded in the mining town. Not only did such places offer 'rooms' in a town where accommodation was always at a premium, but they also constituted a centre to which hard-drinking miners gravitated and therefore tended to provide the 'women of ill-fame' with a steady stream of customers. While the hard-ened full-time professional whores entrenched themselves in the prem-ises to be found at the rear of the canteens, those part-time prostitutes on their way up or down the social scale often gained employment as bar-maids within the establishment itself.[11] This close linkage between an emerging retail liquor trade and prostitution was not, of course, without historical precedent, and on the Rand this relationship was encouraged by canteen keepers for exactly the same reasons as elsewhere – namely, that the presence of barmaids and prostitutes tended to attract male cus-tomers to the establishment and increase liquor consumption.[12]

The local canteen keepers were not slow to organise themselves into a protective professional association. Indeed, by 1888 they had already bound themselves into the Witwatersrand Licensed Victuallers' Association (WLVA), and this formidable body soon wielded consider-able economic and political power within the local community. Through their mouthpiece, the *Licensed Victuallers' Gazette*, members of the WLVA made it clear that canteen keepers were by no means opposed to prosti-tution, and that if the state were to take any action against the 'social evil', it should do so by means of a Contagious Diseases Act which would give rise to a system of controlled brothels.[13]

It was this strong overt and covert support for prostitution that came from the canteen keepers and other interested groups – such as landlords who benefited from high brothel rents – which discouraged the Sanitary Board from taking legal action against any of the 'women of ill-fame' in early Johannesburg. From the quarterly police returns in 1891, for example, it is evident that there was not a single conviction for prostitution in the town, and as late as 1893 Landdrost N J van den Berg was still unsuccessfully urging the Sanitary Board to use the powers it had at its disposal in order to initiate prosecutions.[14] But if Pretoria proved to be hard of hearing when it came to the problem of prostitution on the Rand in the early 1890s, then Johannesburg was positively deaf and nothing came of such appeals.

While such administrative deafness held a clear appeal for canteen keepers and others, it obviously also conferred a great boon on the people most directly threatened – the prostitutes themselves. For as long as prostitution was more or less openly tolerated in the town and unrestrained by legal action, so long prostitutes could command most of their earnings and be free of the insatiable demands of blackmailing policemen or parasitic pimps who posed as their 'protectors'. What is striking about prostitution in Johannesburg during this early period, therefore, is not only the linkage between the trades in sexual favours and alcohol, but the relative absence of large-scale *organised* prostitution. Most of the daughters of South Africa's old proletariat who turned to prostitution on the Rand before the mid-1890s were individual operators who found that they could conduct their trade largely on their own initiative, and certainly without the professional assistance of pimps and madams. This, however, was a situation which was to change rapidly and dramatically from 1895 onwards.

GIFTS FROM THE OLD AND NEW WORLDS – THE DAUGHTERS OF EUROPE 1895-1899

From about 1892, when the first deep-level mines were established along the line of reef, it became increasingly clear to many outside of southern Africa that the Witwatersrand goldfields were going to prove to be not only a substantial, but a lasting proposition. As the price of tin fell in Cornwall, and as some Australian goldfields faltered and failed, so many of the 'hard rock men' set their sights on new targets and made their way to the Rand mines which, by then, had been expanding for more than half a decade. While this flow of skilled workers to the mines gained momentum through much of 1893 and 1894, it was really in 1895 that the greatest influx of all occurred.[15]

Men, mines and money all combined to produce an explosive growth mixture, but it was the added spark provided by the arrival of the railway line from the east coast which really helped to make 1895 one of the truly memorable boom years on the Rand. The advent of the rail linkage between Delagoa Bay and the Transvaal, however, did much more than merely assist in the economic transformation of the principal town on the goldfields. By providing a more immediate link between the Rand and Lourenço Marques, the railway also succeeded in placing Johannesburg – via the cheap fares of the German East African Shipping Line – in more direct contact with the ports and prostitutes of Europe. Thus it was that Johannesburg, from the mid-1890s onwards, was opened not only to the Old World's cheap liquor but also to many of its cheap women who were slowly being denied a role in the maturing industrial states of Europe.[16]

Many, if not most of the women who chose to avail themselves of a passage on the East African Line were drawn from within Germany itself. Here, a policy which concentrated on the expansion of heavy industry tended to exclude female workers from the labour market, and consequently increased the number of structurally dislocated women who sought economic refuge in prostitution. To at least some of these women, more often than not drawn from working-class or artisan families, emigration to the Transvaal must have presented itself as an increasingly attractive proposition as their numbers grew towards the turn of the century. But, as always, there was no democracy of poverty and a policy of selective repression partly directed against 'foreign' prostitutes in Hamburg in 1894-5 ensured that many Austro-Hungarian women undertook the walk to the docks even more readily than their German sisters.[17]

The Great Depression of 1873-96, however, was no respecter of European boundaries, and elsewhere on the continent, too, problems of unemployment and under-employment made themselves felt as large-scale enterprises consolidated their operations at the expense of small craft industries. In some of the wine-producing areas of southern Europe the effect of the depression was further exacerbated when phylloxera attacked the grape vines during the early 1890s. Inevitably, this too contributed to the syndrome of rural female unemployment, growing poverty and a drift towards urban prostitution. The net result of these developments was to ensure that German prostitutes making the journey to southern Africa were not short of French and Belgian companions.

But not even Belgium, France and Germany exhausted the northern supply areas from which the Witwatersrand's 'women of ill-fame' were drawn since, in the 1890s, Johannesburg also boasted a contingent of 'Russian' prostitutes. Somewhat surprisingly, however, this latter group did not reach the goldfields via Hamburg and Delagoa Bay, as might be expected, but from New York via London, Southampton and the Cape ports. Although Johannesburg's 'Russian' whores had Old World origins, they were, in a more immediate sense, the product of developments in the New World.

After 1881, in particular, Jews in parts of the western Russian empire such as Poland, and in the neighbouring Hapsburg provinces of Galicia and Bukovina, experienced hardship and persecution which, by way of comparison, dwarfed the torments of industrial Europe. Poverty, to the point of endemic starvation, combined with a new round of Russian pogroms to take an awesome toll of lives in Jewish communities. Faced with this truly appalling situation, thousands of men and women from within these regions decided to emigrate to the United States of America. Here, as elsewhere, however, there were the quick-witted and the unscrupulous who were willing to feed on the ignorance and desperation of others, and many of these female emigrants found themselves tricked, recruited or forced into the trade in vice. But, irrespective of the exact route by which they entered the trade in commercialised sex, the result was often the same – the hard life of a prostitute in New York's immigrant quarter on the lower east side.[18]

While it is true that prostitution in New York pre-dated these European mass migrations, there can be no doubt that organised vice developed particularly rapidly during the late nineteenth century, and that few things did more to facilitate its emergence than pervasive municipal corruption. After 1868 the Tammany Society tightened its grip on the machinery of local government and ground out a succession of spectacularly corrupt mayors for New York City – 'Boss' Tweed, 'Honest John' Kelly and Richard Croker. These men, with the enthusiastic aid of an equally venal police force, parcelled out various of the city's wards in accordance with their ability to yield 'protection' money, and by so doing succeeded in turning public office into a series of private financial domains. Since there was nothing inherently incompatible between the rule of Tammany Hall and the existence of organised vice which was willing to pay its way, brothel and saloon keepers found that they could conduct their businesses openly and confidently – right up to 1891 that was.[19]

In 1891 a 'Massachusetts minister of Puritan ancestry', Dr Charles Parkhurst, was elected as President of the Society for the Prevention of Crime in New York. With the assistance of a private detective and a specially recruited set of 'agents', Parkhurst at once set about investigating and exposing police corruption within the city. These revelations about the connections between organised vice and a venal police force embarrassed even Tammany Hall and soon produced a logical sequel in a thoroughly corrupt system when, in 1892, Parkhurst was summoned to stand trial on a charge of malicious slander. So convincing was the evidence which Parkhurst and his associates led, however, that the Grand Jury was forced to acquit the President of the Society for the Prevention of Crime and tacitly concede to the existence of massive police corruption. With this victory behind him, Parkhurst found new influential allies who were willing to push for a full-scale enquiry into Tammany Hall and ultimately these agitations bore fruit when, in 1894, the state appointed the Lexow Commission to investigate police corruption in New York City. When the Commission finally issued its report, the findings more than justified Dr Parkhurst's allegations and resulted in the radical reorganisation of the city's police force. As far as Tammany Hall itself was concerned, however, the major blow really fell even earlier when its candidate in the November 1894 municipal elections, Richard Croker, was defeated by Judge van Wyck.[20]

But it was not only politicians and policemen who fell before the Parkhurst/Lexow onslaught. Pimps and prostitutes too felt the sting in the tail of the new Van Wyck administration, and the years between 1892 and 1895 were not the happiest ones for those involved in organised vice on the lower east side. Indeed, from late 1894 hundreds of 'undesirables' – including scores of Jewish pimps and prostitutes – chose to abandon New York and make their way to England. London, however, proved to be something of a disappointment. Not only did the British capital possess its own well-developed trade in vice which made for serious competition, but it also failed to live up to some of the other expectations of the volatile immigrants from the Bowery. Thus, when these well-travelled Russians and Poles heard of the exciting new opportunities developing in the southern hemisphere, they did not hesitate to move yet again. While some of their colleagues in the trade opted for South America, many of the former New York pimps and prostitutes decided to make their way to the goldfields in Kruger's republic.[21]

The advance guard of this American contingent was already actively involved in prostitution on the Witwatersrand by late 1895. Over the following two years, however, their numbers were substantially augmented by the arrival of dozens of the more professional 'white slavers' and their entourages from London. When this group first became highly visible to the public in 1898, even the worldly-wise court reporter of the local *Standard and Diggers' News* was left somewhat bemused:

> There are more things in Johannesburg than are dreamt of in the ordinary man's philosophy. For instance, there is here a large and thriving colony of Americanised Russian women engaged in the immoral traffic, who are controlled by an association of macquereaus of pronounced Russian pedigree embellished by a twangy flashy embroidery of style and speech acquired in the Bowery of New York City, where most of them, with frequent excursions to London, have graduated in the noble profession.[22]

Clearly, the composition of the mining town's underworld was capable of leaving at least one observer surprised.

If the 'ordinary man' was somewhat amazed by the cosmopolitan nature of the local underworld, however, then there was at least one man in town who was not – Sanitary Superintendent A H Bleksley. As a former Sanitary Inspector in Kimberley, Bleksley had been actively involved in the attempts to get that city declared a 'scheduled area' in terms of the Contagious Diseases Act in 1891. When he later came to Johannesburg on promotion, the new Sanitary Superintendent could not have failed to notice how the town was attracting not only some of the former Cape prostitutes with whom he was familiar, but also new arrivals drawn from Europe and elsewhere. This, together with his hope that the Kruger government would eventually implement a CD Act of its own, led Bleksley to conduct a rough census of the town's brothels in October 1895.

Bleksley's survey, although it hardly yielded accurate numbers, did reveal that, at the most conservative estimate, there were 97 brothels in the town, and that these were occupied by some 195 prostitutes.[23] While this did show a move away from the former situation, where individual prostitutes tended to operate from single rooms in canteens or hotels, it still meant that on average there were only two to three prostitutes in each brothel. Further information about the brothels was yielded when some of Bleksley's subordinates took the trouble to indicate the 'nationality' of the 'ladies of pleasure' in each establishment. This latter set of observations indicated just how cosmopolitan Johannesburg's *demi-monde* had become and is reproduced in Table 3.

A year later, in October 1896, Bleksley repeated the exercise and when he once again conducted an impressionistic numerical survey of immorality in Johannesburg, the Sanitary Superintendent found that the town had at least 133 brothels, which were said to be occupied by some 392 prostitutes.[24] On this occasion, however, Bleksley's inspectors did not attempt to provide a breakdown of the brothels by 'nationality'. Instead, the town's officials chose to include the 'location' in their census and provide details about the ethnic composition of Johannesburg's prostitutes. According to the Sanitary Superintendent's tabulations there were 91 white, 83 Coloured and 48 black women involved in full-time prostitution in October 1896. It is likely, however, that these figures – like those for the previous year – hopelessly under-estimated the real number of women involved in the town's trade in vice.

Table 3 Brothels in central Johannesburg, by nationality, October 1895

Number of brothels	'Nationality'
36	French
26	Unknown
20	German
5	Russian
2	Austrian
2	Belgian
2	American
2	Cape Coloured
1	English
1	Australian
97	Total

But whatever the true number of prostitutes in town was, what concerned some of Johannesburg's citizens more was the fact that their number was increasing and that their existence was becoming painfully manifest. Like their Victorian counterparts in Europe, the local middle classes were not so much outraged by the existence of vice, as by the *public* existence of vice. Thus, as the number of European prostitutes in the town became increasingly visible after 1895, so sections of the public and press became more vocal in their expressions of concern. During the trades carnival in November 1896, for example, 'a carriage load of gaudily dressed women' joined the 'industrial procession' and, much to the disgust of the *Standard and Diggers' News*, 'was cheered all along the line'. Such behaviour spoke 'poorly for the good taste of the populace', warned the newspaper, since 'the *demi-monde* was there for gaiety, and not for advertisement'. The 'ladies of pleasure', however, excelled themselves a few months later when several of their number accosted members of Kruger's *Volksraad* who were visiting the mining town, and the *Diggers' News* was forced to write of the 'Public Shame'.[25] The feelings of the *Raadsleden* were not recorded.

These more spectacular forays by the town's prostitutes were conducted from their bases in that part of central Johannesburg which the more daring of the popular performers at the Empire Theatre referred to as 'Frenchfontein'. It was in this area, between Bree Street in the north and Anderson Street in the south, and Kruis Street in the east and Sauer Street in the west, that the vast majority of the town's brothels were located in the mid-1890s. In Frenchfontein, 'at the sinking of the sun, and sometimes in the full glare of the noon-day', there were daily scenes which the middle classes found more abhorrent. From the doors, windows and verandahs of brightly painted houses with large distinctive numbers on their gate posts, women – in various stages of undress – called out endearments and invitations to passing men. Other equally unambiguous offers came from the ladies employed in the large number of 'cigar shops' in that quarter of town.[26]

But, depending on the circumstances in which they found themselves, the 'ladies of pleasure' were also capable of making more subtle approaches to potential customers. Printed cards bearing the name of the prostitute as well as that of her brothel – 'Monte Christo', 'Phoenix', 'Spire House', etc – were often handed out at places where there were large gatherings of men, such as the railway station or race meetings. During periods of sporadic police repression, such as in late 1898, more urgent ways had to be found of communicating a change of address to customers. Under a 'Notice of Removal' in the morning paper, 'Senorita Gabriella' informed her 'pupils' of her new address, and assured them that when classes recommenced on 1 November it would be at 'moderate terms'. So confident were the former New York pimps about the permanence of some of their brothels, however, that they allowed their advertising for the 'Green House' at number 20 Sauer Street to take on a slightly more lasting form. The Bowery gangsters had special 'false coins' struck and these tokens – which also circulated freely in the gambling dens which they controlled – 'bore a décolleté bust on the obverse and the name of the house on the reverse side'.[27]

As always, however, much of the gossip about the delights of the *demi-monde* was circulated not by coin or card, but by word of mouth amongst the male population at barber shops, canteens and race meetings. In addition, cab drivers and rickshaw-pullers were another ready source of information about the pleasures and pitfalls of Frenchfontein and, for a suitable sum, these public transporters were more than willing to act as guides.[28] The single greatest source of information about the painted ladies and their prices, however, came from the proprietors of the painted houses – the professional pimps.

Johannesburg's pre-war pimps, given the collective appellation of *macquereaux* by the local press, were in fact a far more cosmopolitan lot than this designation implied. While there certainly were Frenchmen within the ranks of this large parasitic army, there were also many pimps drawn from the other national groups represented on the Witwatersrand. Characterised by their bitter internal feuding, rivalry, treachery and violence, the 250-300 strong *macquereaux* were dominated by the 100 or so East European pimps, and within them, in turn, by the hard core of 50-70 'Bowery Boys' who preferred to refer to themselves as 'speculators'.[29] In the pecking order of pimpdom, the tough New Yorkers were followed firstly by the 50-60 French *souteneurs* who frequented the *'Ne Plus Ultra'* and 'Golden Lion' bars in the city.[30] Thereafter came the 20-40

German pimps who, more often than not, bore the name 'Louis', after the continental fashion.[31] The rear guard of the *macquereaux* was constituted from a miscellaneous collection of continental, English and Australian pimps, and possibly even one Afrikaner merchant of vice.[32]

Impressive as this list of pimps may have been, however, it still did not exhaust all the possibilities which the early Witwatersrand had to offer. After 1895 there were, at the very least, a dozen or more black touts and pimps who worked in close co-operation with some of Johannesburg's newly arrived French prostitutes. Most of these African men, of whom we know little more than their unrevealing Christian names such as John, Tom and Moses, acted as language brokers for these continental women and by so doing ensured that the cheaper non-racial brothels in town received their share of custom from black miners. Working on a straightforward commission basis, the touts received a sixpenny share out of the ten-shilling fee which the French prostitutes charged each of their black clients.[33] While most of these dealings between black middle-men and the continental whores remained largely impersonal and of a contractual nature, there is also evidence to suggest that on occasion they matured into the fuller and more complex love-hate relationships which characterise interactions between pimps and prostitutes.[34]

In addition to the black *macquereaux* and the scandalous sights of Frenchfontein, there were also other less visible – but more serious – signs which pointed to the explosion in commercialised vice in the mid-nineties. Whilst the presence of venereal disease amongst the town's population had been a cause for official concern as early as 1888, its spread appears to have been especially rapid after the first prostitutes fleeing the Contagious Diseases Act in the Cape established themselves on the Witwatersrand in 1893-4.[35] The fact that the subsequent influx of continental women in 1895-6 was accompanied by an increase in the number of European medical practitioners who offered 'special treatment with guaranteed success in all kinds of syphilitic diseases' did little to check the spread of VD. Since the presence of syphilis often went undetected until the development of the Wasserman test in 1907, limited value could be attached to the medical certificates which Dr Alfred Liebaert of Belgium or Dr Roberto Villetti of Rome issued to prostitutes in the larger brothels on a fortnightly basis.[36] As a result of all these developments, both syphilis and gonorrhoea became firmly established in sections of the black and white working class after 1895.[37]

It was not only the workers' health which suffered when the daughters of Europe came to town in large numbers. There were also other prices to pay. By late 1896 a significant portion of central Johannesburg was devoted exclusively to organised vice and, as one of the morning newspapers lamented at the time, 'our best residential streets and our most important thoroughfares are dedicated to it'.[38] But if the *Standard and Diggers' News* was saddened by this use of urban housing, then the same was hardly true of landlords and property owners. These latter parties soon made the joyous discovery that brothel keepers were willing to pay substantial cash rentals for such houses in order to avoid embarrassing questions or unnecessary legal complications. As a direct consequence of this development, rents in the central part of the town climbed beyond the reach of those who earned more modest incomes, and to their considerable annoyance, working-class and lower-middle-class families found themselves being pushed out to Johannesburg's more peripheral suburbs.[39]

The proprietors of Frenchfontein, however, the men who were in large measure responsible for this working-class exodus, were no mere slum landlords. Indeed, another local newspaper, *The Critic*, claimed in October 1896 that the properties on which 'houses of ill-fame' were located were often 'registered in the names of persons of repute, of banking corporations and eminent firms'.[40] When these allegations are more closely examined, by setting the addresses of known brothels against the property register of the time, *The Critic's* claims are largely vindicated. C D Rudd, mining magnate and intimate business associate of Cecil Rhodes, appears to have been the owner of at least three such properties; the *Banque Française de l'Afrique de Sud*, a Wernher-Beit associated enterprise, owned several such houses, as did the Rand Investment Co, the Real Estate Corporation of South Africa and African Cities Properties Trust Ltd.[41] Given this interest which commercial capital developed in organised vice, it is not difficult to see why landlords figured amongst those who supported a petition in favour of the status quo when, in 1897, the *Volksraad* first indicated its intention to promulgate legislation against those owners of property who allowed their premises to be used as brothels.[42]

Nobody – least of all those in official positions – could have failed to notice the dramatic transformation which took place in the heart of the town once the 'gay ladies' of Paris and their associates established themselves in the mining capital of Kruger's Republic. Thus, when Landdrost van den Berg was again approached with a set of complaints by some of the residents of Ferreirastown, in April 1895, he took the opportunity to personally draft a set of regulations for the control of prostitution in Johannesburg. The Criminal Landdrost then forwarded his proposed by-laws to State Attorney Esselen in Pretoria, only to have them returned with the suggestion that they be first approved by the local Sanitary Board.[43]

Members of the Johannesburg Sanitary Board turned, in the first instance, to their Chief Inspector, A H Bleksley, who immediately conducted the first of his two surveys of local immorality. It was partly

Bleksley's influence, as well as the members' own awareness of their canteen-keeping and property-owning constituency which helped to shape
the Board's policy on prostitution. While drafting its own regulations in
August 1895 then, the Sanitary Board took the view that it was the object
of local government to *control*, rather than eradicate sexual vice – a line
of reasoning not dissimilar to that which underlay most nineteenth-century CD Acts. When during the following month the Board took the precaution of sending a copy of its draft regulations to the Johannesburg
Protestant Ministers' Association for its comment, however, it ran
straight into another strand of late nineteenth-century thinking – that of
Christian feminism. The local clergy, schooled in the reasoning of
Josephine Butler and her feminist colleagues in Britain, objected vigorously to the enshrining of a legal 'double standard' which sought to deal
with prostitutes whilst ignoring their male customers. Moreover, the
ministers were particularly appalled by the customary provision which
allowed for the compulsory medical examination of women who were
suspected of suffering from venereal disease.[44] The Sanitary Board, however, chose to overlook these objections when it forwarded the draft regulations to the new State Attorney in December 1895.

The new State Attorney in Pretoria, Dr Herman Coster, was not immediately taken with the Johannesburg Sanitary Board's regulations for
controlling brothels. A recent immigrant from Holland, Coster doubted
strongly whether there was any value at all in attempting to legislate on
questions of morals. The State Attorney's first inclination, therefore, was
to do nothing about the suggested by-laws which he was confronted
with. Such was the influx of prostitutes into Johannesburg over the following months, however, that Coster soon found this to be an unviable
strategy.

In April 1896 the Landdrosts and the Commissioner of Police in Johannesburg were signatories to a letter pointing out the by now 'urgent'
need for legislation to cope with the problem of immorality in the mining town. At this point the State Attorney's attitude started to waver, and
the turning point came when both Dr Alfred Liebaert and the Transvaal
Medical Association submitted supporting memoranda which pointed
out the advantages of a system of state-controlled prostitution. Thus,
when President Kruger and his Executive Committee met on 18 July
1896, the members – largely at the prompting of Dr Coster – agreed that,
in principle, Johannesburg's *demi-monde* should be governed by a system
of 'controlled brothels'. The Executive Committee concluded its deliberations on the question by referring the draft regulations back to Johannesburg for a series of relatively minor amendments.[45]

But just as this game of legal shuttlecock between Pretoria and Johannesburg threatened to come to a close, a new set of complications arose

which further prolonged the mining town's administrative agony. Dr Herman Coster resigned from his position as State Attorney to be replaced by a new man – Dr Schagen van Leeuwen. As the third man to hold this office within a matter of months, the Acting State Attorney was as capable as any of his predecessors of having his own ideas of how Johannesburg's moral life should be governed. While it is unclear what exactly van Leeuwen's reservations about the Sanitary Board's regulations were, he too delayed ratification of the by-laws. This procrastination in Pretoria simply perpetuated the legal impasse on the Rand where local prosecutors tried in vain to convict offenders of the public's morals under a 300-year old Roman Dutch statute.[46]

Amidst this riding tide of confusion, the church now rose to add its voice. Witwatersrand clergymen of all denominations had, for some time, been deeply distressed by the prospect of the Kruger government recognising and controlling brothels rather than choosing to eradicate them. When, during the last quarter of 1896, the editor of the pro-government *De Volkstem*, Dr F V Engelenburg, chose to give the system of regulated vice support in the columns of his newspaper, it acted as a catalyst for a debate within clerical circles on the Rand. In particular, the Johannesburg Protestant Ministers' Association and the Young Men's Christian Association – the YMCA – felt that the church should take a more active role in the debate on these moral issues. It was largely for this reason that the churchmen agreed that an interdenominational deputation should seek a meeting with the State President and his Executive Committee as a matter of urgency.[47]

This deputation, under the leadership of the Revd P J Meiring of the Dutch Reformed Church and Mr Norman McCulloch of the YMCA, met with Kruger and his colleagues on 6 October 1896. Also present at this meeting – possibly at the invitation of the government – were A H Bleksley and two colleagues representing the interests of the Johannesburg Sanitary Board. During the discussion which followed, however, it was the arguments of the clergymen rather than those of the town officials which did most to convince the State President. In essence, Meiring and McCulloch persuaded Kruger of the desirability of following a policy of 'total prohibition' in relation to brothels. Furthermore, the clergymen impressed upon the State President the need for truly urgent action on the question of immorality which by now had remained unresolved for a period of 18 months.[48]

But if Kruger was by now totally convinced of the need to eradicate all brothels on the Rand, then the same was not true of all of his executive. In particular, it was again a Hollander – this time the State Secretary, Dr Leyds – who counselled caution and advocated a system of 'state regulation modelled on European lines'. After an 'animated discussion' within the Executive Committee, however, it was decided to refer the regulations back to Johannesburg yet again, this time with the instruction that they should be made more stringent – quickly.[49]

The Johannesburg Sanitary Board's canteen-keeping and property-owning constituency had not changed in the interim. Moreover, Bleksley and the rest of his deputation must have reported back to their colleagues on the continuing divisions amongst members of the Executive Committee on the issue of how best to cope with the town's problem of prostitution. For all of these reasons, the Sanitary Board again chose not to advocate a policy of total suppression when it once more submitted its revised draft regulations on brothels to Pretoria on 13 October 1896. This time, Kruger was galvanised into action. Casting aside the advice of the Hollanders which had so long restrained him, the State President now demanded that the Sanitary Board immediately furnish his government with a set of regulations which aimed at the total eradication of prostitution in Johannesburg.[50]

News of Kruger's radical and uncompromising response to the Sanitary Board's latest attempts simply to 'control' vice came as a welcome revelation to Johannesburg's hitherto beleaguered clergymen. In particular, it was the members of the Protestant Ministers' Association who immediately took steps to create a suitably supportive local climate in which to sustain the State President's initiative. Within days of Kruger's move, the Revd Meiring and Norman McCulloch of the YMCA wrote to the State President, both to congratulate him and to inform him that they had helped to launch the 'Transvaal White Cross Purity League' – in essence a local branch of the more famous chastity league founded in Britain in 1882 by the feminist Ellice Hopkins.[51] Although the clergymen succeeded in getting only about 200 young men to take the 'purity pledge', the League did make some headway in other directions. It was, for example, the White Cross Purity League which arranged for the publication, in English, of the Revd C Spoelstra's 'open letter' to the editor of the *Volkstem*, Dr F V Engelenburg, originally entitled *Teedere Zaken: Een Debat over het Prostitutievraagstuk in die Zuid Afrikaansche Republiek*. Under its new title, *Delicate Matters*, the little booklet soon sold 2 000 copies and must have reached a reasonably wide audience in the rough mining town.[52]

When the *Volksraad* did meet early in the following year, it did not bother to wait for the Johannesburg Sanitary Board's submission and lost no time at all in passing legislation which met with Kruger's requirements. As the *Standard and Diggers' News* put it: 'Every line of the law exhibits the stern and uncompromising attitude of His Honour the President who, Elijah-like, will hear of no half measures, and characteristically takes the shortest route to the end he has in view.'[53] In addition, the Commissioner of Police set up a special 'Morality Squad' under Detective J J Donovan in order to ensure that Law No 2 of 1897 would be enforced once it had been properly gazetted.

This flurry of activity and the new sense of purpose in the administration did not go unnoticed in some of the more timid circles of Frenchfontein. When many of the prostitutes chose to leave town on the night of 8 March 1897, however, they received anything but a cheerful send-off at Park Station. A mob composed of white workers, unemployed miners and petty criminals jostled and jeered the ladies of the night, looted their luggage for liquor, and were only prevented from doing more serious damage when the station master instructed the police to draw their batons and prepare to charge the crowd. By the following morning – when the new law came into force – over 300 prostitutes and their associates had fled Johannesburg for the Cape or Natal, 'resulting in an abundant supply of empty domiciles in and about town'. In Cape Town, to which the majority of these women had made their way, the Premier, Sir Gordon Sprigg, greeted their arrival with some distaste, and warned the Transvaal authorities that the lot of virtuous women in Johannesburg would not be made any easier now that the prostitutes who catered for the miners' baser needs had departed from the Rand.[54]

Sprigg need not have worried. For while it was true that hundreds of 'gay ladies' had deserted the Reef, many hundreds more who were made of sterner stuff had chosen to remain behind and ply their trade. Working on the assumption that even in Kruger's Republic past behaviour was often the best guide to future action, these remaining pimps and prostitutes were willing to take their chances under the new dispensation. As business people, these merchants of vice took the view that Law No 2 of 1897 simply increased unavoidable occupational hazards and raised necessary overhead expenditure on police bribes. The more hardened professionals of the *demi-monde* felt therefore that the answer to the *Volksraad*'s legislation lay not in escape or submission, but in even more rigorous planning and organisation. Thus, while the inhabitants of Frenchfrontein could hardly be accused of being disorganised in earlier years, their activities assumed new dimensions of precision in the period between 1897 and 1899.

In the underworld, organisation came most readily and most naturally to those who had previous experience of it – in this case, the former immigrant gangsters of New York City. The 'Bowery Boys', who ever since 1895 had always constituted something of a distinctive grouping within the town, soon organised themselves into a more structured gang which served to protect their gambling and vice interests in the southwestern quarter of Frenchfontein. By mid-1897 these 'slouch-hatted bullies', who dominated the cafés and canteens of western Commissioner Street, and who whisked out their six-shooters 'for no provocation at all', were said to have established a thorough-going 'reign of terror' in that part of the town. Given the readiness with which these American pimps produced their revolvers and the fact that the local police were unarmed, it comes as less than a surprise to learn that the Zarps seldom troubled the 'Bowery Boys', and that throughout 1897 and 1898 members of the Morality Squad tended studiously to avoid the larger brothels in their search for offenders of the *Ontucht Wet* – Law No 2 of 1897.[55]

The Americans, however, were also experienced enough to know that it was probably unwise to rely on fire-power alone as the exclusive means with which to protect their *bagnios*. For this reason the 'Bowery Boys' embarked on a programme of blackmail, bribery and corruption which, in the first instance, was directed at the most obvious and vulnerable target – the badly paid members of the Morality Squad.[56] This counter-offensive by the pimps proved to be so effective that, within months of the passage of the *Ontucht Wet*, the former New York gangsters had succeeded not only in getting most members of the Morality Squad on their payroll, but also part of the staff attached to the Public Prosecutor's office. This meant that throughout the best part of 1897-8 the 'Bowery Boys' found themselves in the privileged position of having their own brothels protected by the legal arm of the state, while – at the same time – they could call upon the self-same officers of the law to harass or close down the operations of rival vice merchants.[57]

Although the 'Bowery Boys' grew in strength throughout this period, there can be little doubt that their organisation made its greatest strides from mid-1898 onwards when it came under the most professional criminal management possible. In late August 1898, Joe Silver, a Polish-American pimp, and his prostitute/wife, Lizzie Josephs, arrived on the Witwatersrand from London. During the early 1890s, as a young Jewish immigrant on the lower east side, Silver had led a successful double life in New York City by acting as an 'agent' for the Revd Charles Parkhurst's Society for the Prevention of Crime while, at the same time, being deeply involved in the Bowery underworld. After the set-back to Tammany Hall in 1894, Silver had made his way to London where he had become an important figure in the 'white slave' traffic – assisting in the recruiting and seduction of young women in the East End and then 'exporting' them to various countries, including South Africa, as prostitutes. A cunning, ruthless and violent man, Silver was soon the undisputed leader of the former New York gangsters, and earned for himself the unofficial title of 'King of the Pimps' in Johannesburg.[58]

With his undisputed talent for organising, however, Silver was anxious to push the 'Bowery Boys' to new professional heights and for this reason he was instrumental in the formation, in late 1898, of the 'American Club'. While the official name purposely did not distinguish it from the many other immigrant clubs in the town, the 'American Club' in practice constituted something rather different – an association of Polish-American Jewish pimps which, in the local *demi-monde*, was more simply and accurately known as the 'Pimps' Club'. Amongst the names of the 50 founding members of the 'American Club' there were several, in addition to that of Joe Silver, which were to become notorious on the Witwatersrand over the next decade – Salus Budner, Joseph Epstein, Abraham Goldstein, David Krakower, Louis Shivinsky and Sam Stein.[59]

Predictably enough, the members of the club elected Joe Silver as the first 'president' of the pimps' association, and then went on to choose one of his closest henchmen, Salus Budner, as 'secretary' of the organisation.[60] In the latter case, the pimps allowed themselves the luxury of a display of Yiddish-cum-underworld humour by promptly allocating Budner the new alias of 'Joe Gold'. Perhaps the 'Bowery Boys' would have been less amused, however, if they had known that 'Silver and Gold' immediately proceeded to set up a 'secret committee' within the executive of the 'American Club', and that it was from within this latter group that the affairs of the pimps' association were really controlled.[61]

Most of Silver's personal as well as his brother pimps' business was conducted from the hired premises of the 'American Club' in Frenchfontein. It was here, at the club house, that the 'Bowery Boys' most frequently met to discuss the daily vicissitudes and requirements of Johannesburg's competitive vice trade – the hiring of suitable houses, problems with landlords, boundary disputes between rival pimps and the need to bribe different policemen. Since a good deal of this business directly and indirectly revolved around the venal Zarps, it was not an uncommon sight to see detectives entering or leaving the club premises in Frenchfontein. Indeed, so close was Special Morality Constable Hendrik Cuyler's association with the pimps, that he even consented to having his picture taken with some of them whilst standing outside the club.[62] It was also from within these premises, however, that the most secret plans of the 'American Club' emanated, and these schemes invariably centred around the question of where and how to procure new 'girls' for the brothels under the control of the Polish pimps.

During the mid-1890s the demand for prostitutes on the Rand escalated rapidly as the male population of the goldfields mushroomed with the development of deep-level mining. The pimps of Johannesburg, however, soon made the discovery that this increase in the demand for sexual services in the community did not simply parallel any demographic increases in the town. Clients of larger brothels looked forward to a regular change in the personnel of their favourite establishments and this alone occasioned the need for a regular turnover of prostitutes. In addition, the ranks of the prostitutes were also thinned out by the normal processes of attrition associated with the trade – age, disease or death. For these reasons the 'Bowery Boys' and other groups of pimps within the town found that they had to pay constant attention to the problem of providing their brothels with an adequate supply of new young 'girls'.

It is certain that some attempts were made to recruit local women into the trade in vice – a procedure which appealed to the *souteneurs* because it had the virtue of being relatively cheap. In such cases the pimps would usually send out the oldest and most trusted of their prostitutes – the madams of their houses – to the town parks and recreation areas where seemingly attractive propositions would be put to badly paid white domestic servants or other young white women.[63] Given the chronic shortage of mature women on the Rand at this time, however, this practice hardly produced a solution to the pimps' problem, and for this reason they were forced to look further afield in their search for new recruits. In the course of this latter search the pimps found that the older social formation of the Cape Colony tended to yield a slightly readier supply of poor, vulnerable or marginalised women. Small numbers of Coloured domestic servants who had already been seduced by white men could occasionally be recruited from Cape 'boarding-houses', while job adverts placed in the Colony's newspapers – via bogus 'employment agencies' – sometimes succeeded in luring naïve European women into the Transvaal 'houses of ill-fame'.[64]

Not even these forays to the south, however, could keep pace with the Rand's demand for sexual services during the mid-1890s, and for this reason the 'Bowery Boys' and other groups of local pimps were forced to turn to the older societies of Europe for the bulk of their supplies of prostitutes. At least some of these European recruiting operations worked along the same lines as those employed in the Cape. Advertisements placed in British or continental newspapers offered young women an assisted passage to South Africa in order to take up well-paid positions as 'barmaids' or 'domestic servants' in Johannesburg.[65] Needless to say, once these women had been 'escorted' to the Rand by the madams of brothels posing as 'agents', the vulnerable job aspirants were pressed into an entirely different line of service to that which they had perhaps imagined when they first set out on their journey.

In other cases the 'Bowery Boys' extended the area of their direct recruiting operations by pushing the boundaries back into the heartland of eastern Europe. In mid-1898, for example, 'Bessie Levin', acting on behalf of David Levinsohn of the 'American Club', was sent on a long trip which took her well to the north-east of her and her pimp's native

Poland. In the small Lithuanian village of Vilna Krevo the procuress met and offered a 15-year-old girl named Fanny Kreslo employment in London as a shop assistant at a salary of 100 Roubles a year. When the same proposition was subsequently put to the Kreslo parents they readily agreed to the 'employment' of their daughter on these terms and the two women then set off for England.

On their arrival in London Miss Kreslo was informed by Levin that her 'employer' had suddenly departed for South Africa, and that the two of them should follow him to the Rand. Isolated, vulnerable, penniless and speaking only Russian, the Lithuanian girl agreed to accompany the older and more experienced woman on the further journey south. Once in Johannesburg, Levinsohn and Levin placed the girl in a brothel at 35 Anderson Street and informed her that if she wished to make her way back to Russia it would be necessary for her to earn the money for her passage by prostituting herself. After allowing Miss Kreslo the luxury of having a Polish-speaker as her first sexual partner, the pimp and his madam then proceeded to provide the young Russian woman with a wider variety of Asian, black and white customers. It was only after several months – and after the backbone of the 'American Club' had been broken – that the young woman was released from her position as a 'white slave'. In mid-1899 the police, after learning of Fanny Kreslo's age, rescued her from the house in Anderson Street and arranged for the prosecution of Levinsohn and Levin.[66]

The same terrifying combination of cynical deceit and violence characterised many of the other 'white-slavery' operations of the 'Bowery Boys'. During 1897-8, while still in London and living under the alias of 'James Smith', a 'draper', Joe Silver and his Polish associates conducted their business from the 'American Hotel' in Stamford Road, Waterloo. Working from there, Silver, Joseph Anker, Beile Feirerstein, Jacob Shrednicki and others would undertake excursions into the East End, where the men would pose as eligible bachelors amongst immigrant Jewish girls employed in the rag trade. Such meetings would be followed by a preliminary amount of 'courting' during which the procuress, Beile Feirerstein, would present herself as adviser and confidante of the young East European women. Thereafter, the pimps would attempt to administer as much alcohol as possible to their 'fiancées' before seducing or raping them. After a further set of psychological and physical assaults, the victims would be forced on to the local streets to gain experience as whores prior to being 'exported' under escort to countries such as the Argentine or South Africa.[67]

Although the 'Bowery Boys' were, by far, the largest and best organised syndicate of 'white slavers' operating on the Rand between 1897 and 1899, they were by no means the only pimps trafficking in prostitutes on a substantial scale. Following closely in the footsteps of the Polish vice merchants were the scores of French pimps to be found in Johannesburg during this period. Within this latter group, however, it was once again a set of immigrant gangsters with first-hand experience of New York under Tammany Hall who provided the *souteneurs* with their most able leaders. Amongst the most noteworthy of these Franco-Americans were Paul Durenmatt, Leon Lemaire, Auguste Roger, François Saubert and – perhaps most notorious of all – a woman who had once called herself Mrs Bertha Hermann but who now chose to refer to herself as Mathilda Bertha.[68]

Mrs Bertha Hermann was first drawn to the attention of the western world when, in the mid-1890s, the famous muck-raking journalist, W T Stead, outlined the importance of this 'French Madam' in his book entitled *Satin's Invisible World Displayed* – an account of corruption in New York City based on the findings of the Lexow Commission. While in New York Mrs Hermann had run four brothels which, over a seven-year period between the late 1880s and the early 1890s, had required the handing over of 30 000 dollars in bribes to the Tammany police in order to remain in business. This alone made Mrs Hermann a valuable witness in the criminal proceedings which followed the eclipse of Tammany Hall. Indeed, so vital did Bertha Hermann's testimony become, that the New York police arranged for her to be kidnapped and railroaded around Canada and the western United States in an unsuccessful attempt to avoid the prosecution of certain senior officers. After this somewhat harrowing experience, the by now famous 'French Madam' developed an understandable urge to travel the world more widely under another name. In Johannesburg, Mathilda Bertha and François Saubert ran, amongst others, a large brothel at number 19 Sauer Street – a house adjoining a similar establishment managed by Joseph Silver.[69]

Given their earlier shared experience of the New York underworld and the over-arching imperatives of the vice trade, it was always likely that the Franco-Americans would run the 'white slavery' part of their business in a way which closely resembled that of the 'Bowery Boys'. Young servant girls from Brussels or Paris would be lured to the Rand with bogus offers of lucrative employment and, once removed from their more familiar environment, would be seduced or raped before being turned out into the streets in order to make a living. In other cases, however, the *souteneurs* and their female agents would recruit young girls from professional 'white slavers' – the Parisian counterparts of Joe Silver and his associates.[70] These specialists no doubt managed to generate their own 'supplies' by exercising the familiar combination of deceit and violence over those rendered vulnerable through poverty and ignorance.

The parallels between the business operations of the Franco-Americans and the 'Bowery Boys', however, transcended any similarities which might have existed in their basic recruiting operations. The well-organised and efficient manner in which they ran their larger brothels after the passage of the *Ontucht Wet* in 1897 also bears comparison, and perhaps one of the more revealing illustrations of this is offered by an institution which fell under French management – 'Sylvio Villa'.

Situated on the corner of De Villiers and Rissik Streets, 'Sylvio Villa' undoubtedly constituted early Johannesburg's most famous brothel. For well over a decade, from 1895 when it was first opened until 1906 when it was finally closed down by the British authorities, this *bagnio* held the pre-eminent position in the local *demi-monde*. During its heyday, between 1897 and 1899, 'Sylvio Villa' operated with a staff of no less than 15 persons – five men and ten women. At the head of the house stood the owner and managing pimp, the 'speculator' Auguste Roger. Below Roger, and assisting him, were a team of four full-time pimps who did the rounds drumming up business for the Villa, and a 'madam', Alice Muller, who in her various court appearances preferred to refer to herself as a 'modiste'. Between them, these touts in turn exercised varying degrees of control over the nine working women of the establishment – Evette Verwey, Suzanne Dubois, A Dumas, Blanche Dumont, Marie Buffaut, Jeanne Dubois, Marie André, Jeanne Durett and Georgette Carpentier. For the sake of convenience, these latter-named ladies chose to see themselves as 'housekeepers', 'milliners', 'musicians' and 'florists' in their legal affairs.[71]

The services of these nine women, who may more accurately be referred to as being French-speaking rather than 'French', proved to be in considerable demand during the 'naughty nineties'. As level-headed business women, however, the inhabitants of 'Sylvio Villa' were willing to offer their customers more than the erotic mystique of the foreigner – they were also able to produce certificates which testified to the fact that they had recently been medically examined and found to be free of contagious disease. The pleasure of their company could be purchased at the rate of £1 'short time', or £5 per night. While these competitive prices obviously assured the nine ladies of the night a measure of cash income, it would appear that the bulk of their earnings accrued to the 'management'. All the working women of the house were called upon to pay Alice Muller the sum of £4 per month for the provision of food and accommodation, a fee which excluded the additional costs they were called upon to bear for clothing, washing and ironing, and medical expenses. The levying of the £4 'board and lodging' fee alone would have yielded the 'madam' and her 'speculator' a gross income of £1 728 per annum.[72]

In addition to this, however, each of the prostitutes at 'Sylvio Villa' had a separate verbal contract with the 'management' which specified what percentage of her income had to be handed over to the 'madam'. While we unfortunately do not know exactly what this figure was in each individual case at the De Villiers street *bagnio*, we do know that Suzanne Dubois was called upon to hand over in excess of a quarter of all her earnings to Alice Muller. But, whatever this proportion was, it is sure to have produced Roger and his associates a handsome collective income during the course of the year since this popular brothel was hardly ever short of business. In this latter respect we are more fortunate since, from the observations of two detectives who were sent to observe the comings and goings at the French house during its prime, we know more or less precisely how many customers were entertained at 'Sylvio Villa' during the evenings over a two-week period in late 1897.[73] This information is reproduced in Table 4.

Table 4 Number of clients calling at the 'Sylvio Villa' brothel, 29 November 1897-12 December 1897

Day of the week	Date	Hours premises observed	Number of customers
Monday	29 Nov 1897	8.30 p.m. – 1.35 a.m.	21
Tuesday	30 Nov 1897	8.30 p.m. – 1.55 a.m.	41
Wednesday	1 Dec 1897	7.45 p.m. – 2.40 a.m.	52
Thursday	2 Dec 1897	7.45 p.m. – 1.53 a.m.	38
Friday	3 Dec 1897	7.35 p.m. – 2.05 a.m.	62
Saturday	4 Dec 1897	8.05 p.m. – 1.30 a.m.	96
Sunday	5 Dec 1897	7.20 p.m. – 1.10 a.m.	8
Monday	6 Dec 1897	7.25 p.m. – 10.35 p.m.	18
Tuesday	7 Dec 1897	7.25 p.m. – 1.10 a.m.	21
Wednesday	8 Dec 1897	7.30 p.m. – 9.50 p.m.	11
Thursday	9 Dec 1897	7.25 p.m. – 1.25 a.m.	20
Friday	10 Dec 1897	7.15 p.m. – 12.11 a.m.	26
Saturday	11 Dec 1897	7.40 p.m. – 1.10 a.m.	54
Sunday	12 Dec 1897	7.35 p.m. – 9.50 p.m.	7

From this it is clear that the nine women of 'Sylvio Villa' may have been 'ladies of pleasure' in name, but that in practice there must have been much hard work and little pleasure in their activities – and at no time more so than during the period which followed the month-end pay-day for mine labourers and other workers. From the same set of police observations we also know that most of these customers came to the brothel in parties of three, and that the average visit of a client to 'Sylvio Villa' took between 20 and 45 minutes to complete. Commercial sex could be obtained at a price which included a measure of fear and haste.

At least some of the fear – and certainly much of the haste – which accompanied this alienated sexual activity derived from the harassing tactics which many of the pimps of the larger brothels adopted. Since it was in the pimps' interests to ensure as large a turnover as possible, they constantly 'encouraged' customers to complete their business in a hurry. For essentially the same reason, many pimps urged the women under their control to accept black clients, since Africans, largely new to the need for this type of service and its strange cultural setting, seldom lingered on the premises. As one pimp put it: 'Kaffirs were better to encourage than white men' since 'they paid their money and did not want to stop drinking and smoking in the house'.[74]

In addition to having this time constraint placed upon them by the pimps, clients at *bagnios* were also apprehensive about the possibility of being relieved of their valuables while visiting the premises. Although such robberies did undoubtedly occur, it was fear of the resident pimp's violence, as well as the humiliation of a subsequent court appearance, that did most to ensure that the majority of such thefts remained unreported.[75] All of these factors contributed to the development of tensions between brothel patrons drawn largely from England and pimps who, in the main, hailed from the continent and Eastern Europe. It is therefore not very difficult to see why it was that on at least one occasion, in April 1898, a crowd of white miners and unemployed workers chose to attack a group of 'foreign' pimps whom they had managed to trap on the more public terrain of Park Station.[76]

Of course, neither these manifestations of highly organised vice, nor the scandalous scenes to which they occasionally gave rise, escaped the notice of those state officials who had been entrusted with the task of scrutinising the public's morals after the passage of the *Ontucht Wet* of 1897. Pretoria's problem was, however, that local government officials saw in the flagrant violations of the Morals Law only what they wanted to see. For some, such as the Commandant of Police, G M J van Dam, the continued flauntings of Frenchfontein pointed to the need for more rigid enforcement of the *Ontucht Wet*. For others, including some of the state's most senior officers, the persistence of prostitution underlined the futility of morals legislation and emphasised the need to follow more pragmatic policies. In practice these conflicting views were obviously extremely difficult, if not impossible, to reconcile, and nowhere was this problem more apparent than in the office of Johannesburg's Senior Public Prosecutor – Dr F E T Krause.

Frederick Krause, in later life a Member of Parliament for *Het Volk* and subsequently Judge President of the Orange Free State, was a member of one of South Africa's most distinguished and talented families. After an initial university training at Victoria College in Stellenbosch, F E T Krause proceeded to the University of Amsterdam where he obtained his doctorate in jurisprudence in 1893. On his return home, Krause made his way to the South African Republic where, as part of Dr Herman Coster's legal team, he assisted in the prosecution of the Jameson Raid 'reformers'. It was immediately after this assignment, in May 1897, and a matter of eight weeks after the controversial *Ontucht Wet* first came into operation, that he was appointed to the position of principal public prosecutor in Johannesburg.

Krause, who married late, at the age of nearly 40, spent a good part of his life as a bachelor and perhaps this, together with his experience on the Continent, helped shape his attitudes on the problems of prostitution in society. Certainly the influential Hollanders with whom he spent much time on the Rand, notably Herman Coster and Schagen van Leeuwen, were strongly opposed to President Kruger's attempts to legislate on questions affecting public morals. In any event, Krause took the decided view that prostitution was 'a necessary evil' in society and it was this outlook which came to govern his official actions on questions of immorality.[77]

The first indication of the Senior Public Prosecutor's attitude came within weeks of his assuming office when Commandant van Dam, after lengthy consultations with Krause, issued new instructions to Detective J J Donovan, the man in charge of the Morality Squad. As Krause later recalled:

> The instructions received by Donovan with my knowledge and consent were … that where houses suspected by the police to be brothels were found, they must only take the initiative against such a house when a bona fide charge was made against the house, or if it was discovered to be a disorderly house; in other words, where they found that excessive drinking was going on, or where there were frequent rows.[78]

In effect this policy meant that, contrary to the spirit and letter of the *Ontucht Wet*, official efforts throughout much of 1897 and 1898 were directed towards 'controlling' rather than eliminating sexual vice in Johannesburg.

As we have seen, the idea that prostitution was a 'necessary evil' and that it probably helped exercise a measure of social control over the mining population of the Witwatersrand, was not a new one.[79] What *was* new was the presence in Johannesburg of a senior state official who thought along these lines, and who was only willing to act within this prescription. F E T Krause, however, soon found out that he was not alone in offering resistance to the full-scale implementation of the Morals Law. In October 1897, the first important case to be heard under the new act came before Mr Justice Jorissen in the Circuit Court, when a French prostitute named Louise Roger was charged with having unlawful sexual intercourse with a black man. In his summing up, the Judge offered such a powerful criticism of the *Ontucht Wet* and its consequences for the many Africans who were confronted with a life of enforced celibacy on the Rand, that members of the jury – perhaps mistakenly – came to the conclusion that they could only find the accused 'not guilty'.[80] The decision, together with Krause's own predisposition about the functioning of the Morals Act, further confounded Kruger's and the church's efforts to eradicate vice from Johannesburg in the period leading up to the South African War.

This hesitancy on the part of the state and the judiciary had swift and largely beneficial consequences for the real rulers of Frenchfontein – the well-organised pimps. Predictably, it enhanced the need for, and the possibility of, bribing the poorly paid members of the Morality Squad who now enjoyed greater discretionary power in determining what exactly it was that made for a 'disorderly' house. This situation, in which a good measure of arbitrary power devolved upon those in most immediate contact with prostitutes and pimps, proved to be the ideal host culture for massive corruption. While the police continued to arrest the more vulnerable small-scale vice merchants in order to create a smoke-screen of activity and produce a steady flow of bread-and-butter convictions under the *Ontucht Wet*, the really large gangs which could afford to pay the necessary bribes – such as the 'Bowery Boys' – remained marvellously immune from prosecution. Not even these diversionary tactics, however, could succeed in concealing the magnitude of police venality, and over a 20-month period, between mid-1897 and late 1898, the Morality Squad experienced a change of leadership on no less than five occasions as officers and men alike fell under the suspicion of accepting bribes and acting corruptly. Not all of these officers chose to fall from power with grace and silence, and at least one of them – J J Donavan – made such serious allegations about F E T Krause's administration of the Morals Act that by mid-1898 even the Senior Public Prosecutor fell under the Pretoria government's suspicion.[81]

The State President and his closest colleagues, who from June 1898 onwards included a new young State Attorney by the name of Jan Christian Smuts, could not have failed to have noticed these distressing developments. Within weeks of the passage of the *Ontucht Wet* in early 1897, the *Standard and Diggers' News* ran an editorial pointing out that the Morals Act was, to all intents and purposes, a 'Dead Letter'. Thereafter, and for the next 18 months, the newspaper, under the guidance of its edi-

tor, Emmanuel Mendelssohn, consistently drew attention to the preva-
lence of prostitution, 'white slavery', police corruption and the hold
which the 'Bowery Boys' exercised over the local underworld.[82]

But, if the presidential eye perhaps did not scan the editorial columns
of the Rand's English press, then there can be no doubt that the presidential ear heard the articulate voices of Afrikaner and other clergymen
during the same period. In late September 1898, almost two years after
they had first gone to Pretoria as part of an interdenominational delegation to complain about Johannesburg's immorality, the Revd P J Meiring
and Norman McCulloch of the YMCA again called a public meeting to
discuss the continuing evils of Frenchfontein. Amongst the many public-
spirited citizens and committed Christians who attended this gathering
at the YMCA to contribute to what the press termed 'a lively discussion',
a reporter from the *Standard and Diggers' News* noted the presence of one
'Joseph Silver' who introduced himself to the meeting as a 'citizen of the
United States'. Displaying a degree of *chutzpah* which probably left even
his 'American Club' colleagues bemused, the 'King of the Pimps' proceeded to tell the unsuspecting audience that it would be futile to
attempt to rid the town of prostitutes, and that it would be more practical if 'this class of unfortunates' were confined to one part of Johannesburg. The majority of those present, however, apparently disagreed
with this view and at the end of the evening the good citizens elected yet
another interdenominational delegation to wait upon the State President, and urge upon him the need to clean up the town.[83] With uncharacteristic humility, Silver did not make himself eligible for election.

When the Revd Meiring and the members of his delegation met the
State President and his Executive Committee in the Transvaal capital on
13 October 1898, their renewed pleas met with an immediate and positive response. Kruger, with the enthusiastic support of his new State
Attorney, J C Smuts, was now more willing than ever to contemplate
decisive action against the vice syndicates of the Witwatersrand and at
once undertook to have a more stringent *Ontucht Wet* drafted. When this
new legislation – in the form of Act No 23 of 1898 – became law in mid-
December 1898, it not only contained clauses designed to cope with the
problem of 'white slavery'; it also made provision for the possible banishment of moral offenders from the South African Republic.[84]

The members of the delegation, however, were more painfully aware
than most that the proposed new legislation would in itself offer no real
solution to the problems posed by Frenchfontein – what *was* needed,
above all else, was strong, fearless and effective administration of the
laws. It was for precisely this latter reason that the clergymen were
pleased to have been afforded the opportunity of having a further set of
private discussions with the State Attorney after their initial hearing. The

delegates seized this chance to offer Smuts a detailed account of the pervasive police corruption in Johannesburg. Smuts, for his part, promised to undertake a detailed examination of the Morals Law on the Rand and, if need be, to radically reorganise the police and the office of the Public Prosecutor.[85] Armed with this pledge and a new sense of optimism, the clergymen withdrew from Pretoria.

Smuts, true to his word, immediately set about examining the manner in which the *Ontucht Wet* was being implemented in Johannesburg and, within 48 hours of his meeting the clergymen, J J Donovan was dismissed from the police force. Over the course of the next three weeks, however, the State Attorney's investigations into corruption took him through such an incredible maze of charges and counter-charges that he came to the conclusion that none of the police – or indeed the First Public Prosecutor for that matter – were above suspicion. As a result of his probing, Smuts was made to realise that if the amended Morals Act was to stand a chance of being successfully employed against the vice syndicates, then the state would require a new and independent team of law-enforcement officers on the Rand. With this latter requirement in mind, the State Attorney started to look around for a suitable candidate to lead a new legal team in Johannesburg. The person he chose for this daunting task was a determined and talented young South African by the name of Mostyn Cleaver.[86]

When F R M Cleaver was appointed to the position of Second Public Prosecutor in Johannesburg during the first week of December 1898, Smuts made it clear that the new man was to be relatively independent of the existing structures within the Public Prosecutor's office as regards to implementation of the *Ontucht Wet*, and that for these purposes he would report direct to the State Attorney in Pretoria. This arrangement was met with obvious resentment in the Public Prosecutor's office – and not least of all by F E T Krause and his closest assistant, Cornelis Broeksma. Krause, in an apparent attempt to be deliberately provocative, continually referred to Cleaver as 'my assistant' while somebody else in the office – probably Broeksma – reported him to Pretoria 'as having spoken unprofessionally of his Superiors in the Department'. When these efforts to humiliate and isolate Cleaver failed, a further attempt to neutralise his effectiveness on morals cases was made by burdening him with an excessive load of the department's more mundane work.[87]

The Second Public Prosecutor's problems with his fellow officials, however, were not confined to his closest colleagues – they soon spread beyond Krause's office. Members of the police force, who had even more reason to be threatened by Cleaver's presence than Krause, proved so hostile that the young Second Prosecutor felt that he was 'surrounded by enemies and spies'. Commandant van Dam in particular was deeply offended by Cleaver's suggestion that virtually all the members of his Morality Squad were corrupt and untrustworthy. Confronted with this active resistance on all sides, the Second Public Prosecutor was forced into developing his own supportive staff structure. With Smuts's support and encouragement, therefore, Cleaver employed a trusted former school friend, L B Skirving, to assist him with the prosecution work, while he hired a private detective, Arendt Burchardt of the Rand Detective Agency, to undertake the necessary police work.[88]

Quite fortuitously, the establishment of the Burchardt-Cleaver-Skirving legal team came at an important moment in the history of Johannesburg's *demi-monde*. In late October 1898 one of the leading 'Bowery Boys', David Krakower, and two of his fellow gangsters, Henry Rosenchild and Morris Rosenberg, decided that their membership of the 'American Club' was proving to be unduly restrictive of their business activities. The three pimps therefore decided to break with the 'Bowery Boys' and to operate as an independent team within Frenchfontein. This decision did little to endear the new group to their erstwhile colleagues in the 'American Club'. Krakower himself, however, was clearly willing to live even more dangerously. Shortly after the break with the 'Bowery Boys', he absorbed the President of the 'American Club's' wife/prostitute – Lizzie Josephs – into his vice network by offering her police 'protection' at the rate of £6 per month.[89]

These provocative actions presented an unmistakable challenge to the authority of Joe Silver and his colleagues – and the 'Bowery Boys' were not slow in formulating a reply. Within days of these developments the 'president' set plans in motion for the punishment of Krakower, whom he had known since their days together in New York City eight years earlier. First, Silver tracked down Lizzie Josephs and then he re-established his personal control over her by assaulting her severely. Thereafter he and his colleagues 'persuaded' Lizzie and other women to testify to Krakower's extortionary proclivities before constables of the Morality Squad who were already on the 'American Club' payroll. On the basis of these sworn affidavits the constables then proceeded to the public prosecutor's office where, avoiding Cleaver and the strictures of the *Ontucht Wet*, they succeeded in getting a warrant for the arrest of Krakower and his associates on a charge of 'theft by means of fraud'.[90]

Krakower, however, was far from being defeated, and when his case was heard in Johannesburg's Second Criminal Court, on 6 December 1898, it caused a minor sensation. Working through the medium of his exceedingly able lawyer, L E van Diggelen, Krakower succeeded in offering, for the first time, a detailed public account of the inner workings of the 'American Club'. In addition, van Diggelen – through the skilful cross-examination of the police and other witnesses – made certain that the court's eyes never lost sight of the hand of Joe Silver in the events that were recounted before it. Largely as a result of these efforts by van Diggelen, Krakower and his co-accused were found not guilty and discharged – to the embarrassment and anger of the 'Bowery Boys', members of the Morality Squad and the man who had led the state's case, Public Prosecutor Cornelis Broeksma.[91]

The boss of the 'Bowery Boys', of course, had more reason than most to be angered by this decision. Besides having had to suffer the humiliation of a defeat at the hands of his enemy, his own vulnerability to prosecution had been increased by the exposure of his role as President of the 'American Club'. With a characteristic combination of flair and cheek, Silver now attempted to retrieve the situation by writing a letter to the editor of the *Standard and Diggers' News* in which he outlined his proposed course of action:

> … my name having been freely mentioned as one belonging to the pimping fraternity, so that I can only express my desire to hold a mass meeting during the next few days, with the object of discussing the desirability of having these shameless ruffians driven out of our midst.
>
> Johannesburg has of late become the refuge of the above mentioned class, and the unrivalled home in South Africa of people who trade on prostitution, and unless we take some further steps to remove them, they will before long eat themselves into the community so deeply that the cure will be an impossibility.[92]

The proposed mass meeting never materialised, and if this letter fooled anybody, it certainly did not fool Mostyn Cleaver.

The Second Public Prosecutor had, in fact, observed the Krakower trial and its outcome with mounting optimism. Cleaver saw in the growing bitterness of the Krakower-Silver division an unparalleled opportunity for the state to strike a powerful blow against organised vice on the Witwatersrand. If Krakower and others could only somehow be persuaded to give direct testimony against Silver and some of his closest aides, then the 'American Club' would lose much of its organisational strength. But, while it was one thing to get those confronted with charges to give evidence against the 'Bowery Boys' when they were already in difficulty with the law, it was quite another to get them, voluntarily, to give evidence against the President of the 'American Club' when they were free men. In short, getting Krakower to defend himself against Silver was not the same as getting him to attack the 'King of the Pimps'. Cleaver therefore saw his first task as that of having to find a way in which to place Krakower, Rosenberg and Rosenchild under renewed pressure, and the best way of doing this was to have them re-arrested on new charges under the modified Morality Act.

On 29 December 1898 the three Polish-American pimps duly reappeared in Johannesburg's Second Criminal Court charged with procuration. While L E van Diggelen again appeared for the defence, Cleaver chose to lead the state's case personally on this occasion and, at the end of the first day's proceedings, Landdrost Dietzch adjourned the hearing to 6 January 1899. Even this restricted court appearance, however, was sufficient to convince van Diggelen and his clients that the prosecution's case had been prepared with unusual thoroughness and that it was almost inevitable that the accused would be found guilty. For his part, Cleaver now used the intervening period to place Krakower and his fellow accused under even greater pressure, and to encourage them to do a deal – namely, that in return for their willingness to give evidence against Silver and his associates in the future, the state would consider dropping the charges they were now confronted with. At some point during the first week of January 1899 David Krakower agreed to these terms.[93] This was the opening that Cleaver had been waiting for.

The Second Public Prosecutor, with the assistance of L E van Diggelen, now questioned Krakower about the workings of the 'American Club' in order to establish who, besides Silver, were the moving forces behind the 'white slave' traffic on the Witwatersrand. After obtaining this information, Cleaver drove home his advantage to discover that Lieutenant Murphy – the man whom Smuts had had replace J J Donovan as head of the Morality Squad – was in the pay of the 'Bowery Boys'. It was also in the course of this latter revelation that Cleaver discovered that, between them, Silver and Murphy had 'framed' two uncooperative Morality Squad constables named Maritz and Van Vuren, resulting in their suspension from duty.[94]

Cleaver then moved swiftly and with surgical precision. Deliberately by-passing the local office, he approached Smuts for the warrants necessary to arrest his suspects and for permission to select his own police force with which to execute the orders. Then, at nine o'clock in the evening on Monday 9 January 1899, he, and a special posse of armed and mounted police under the direction of Morality Constable S G Maritz, raided 45 Anderson Street and other addresses in the city's vice quarter. By midnight, the four leading 'white slave' traffickers on the Witwatersrand – Joe Silver, Sam Stein, Lizzie Josephs and Jenny Stein – were all in custody in the local police cells. So too were four other leading 'madams' employed by the Silver syndicate – Lillie Bloom, Florence Maud de Lacey, Annie Schwartz and Bessie Weinberg.[95]

The following day, after obtaining an additional set of warrants from the State Attorney by telegraph, Cleaver rounded off his operation by searching the premises of the 'American Club' and Sam Stein's safety deposit box for further evidence. Thereafter, with both suspects and evidence secure, he succeeded in sealing off the two gangsters' most obvious escape route by persuading Smuts to issue instructions which would ensure that the 'Bowery Boys' would be denied bail when they appeared in court. Thus, when Silver and Stein did appear in court briefly on the morning of 10 January 1899, they were duly refused bail and informed that their case had been remanded until 2 February. Not even this achievement, however, was enough to satisfy the relentless and careful planning of the Second Public Prosecutor. Fearing that the remaining 'Bowery Boys' would succeed in bribing the poorer burghers who would inevitably form part of a local jury, Cleaver then arranged that while the preliminary examination of Silver and Stein would take place in Johannesburg, the trial itself would be held in Pretoria.[96]

This unusually swift and thorough offensive by the state left the members of the 'American Club' stunned – but only briefly. Within 48 hours of their President's arrest, Secretary 'Joe Gold' and two other 'Bowery Boys', Wolf Witkofsky and Harris Stadtman, decided to pay a call on at least one person who was likely to be an important witness in any Silver trial – David Krakower's 'wife', Sadie Woolf. When the initial offer of a bribe failed to secure that reluctant lady's co-operation, the three 'Bowery Boys' attempted to concentrate the madam's mind by suggesting that she take an extended trip out of town if she wished to continue enjoying good health and a long life. While this suggestion went some way towards intimidating the former New York City prostitute, the proposition had precisely the opposite effect on her pimp/'husband' when it was subsequently relayed to him. Knowing that he now enjoyed the protection of the state, Krakower simply assaulted the Secretary of the 'American Club' on the first occasion which presented itself.[97]

The 'Bowery Boys'' attempt at a counter-offensive, however, was soon made to extend beyond the immediate confines of David Krakower. During the latter half of January 1899, 'Joe Gold' and selected henchmen systematically worked their way through Frenchfontein alternately encouraging and threatening witnesses to give only evidence favourable to Silver in the forthcoming hearings. But their task of finding suitably compliant and credible witnesses was made virtually impossible by the efforts of the indefatigable Cleaver. During the same period the Second Public Prosecutor was equally hard at work protecting witnesses, engaging in plea-bargaining, and methodically eliminating perjurers from within the ranks of the Morality Squad. Largely as a result of this, the 'Bowery Boys' were forced into paying an increasing amount of attention to Cleaver himself and, shortly before Silver's trial, the Second Public Prosecutor started receiving offers of substantial bribes. When this failed to elicit the required response, Cleaver's mail commenced to yield a predictable blend of blackmailing letters and notes containing death threats.[98]

Neither these crude strong-arm tactics indulged in by the 'Bowery Boys', nor the more subtle and skilful letter of appeal which Silver and Stein later directed to Landdrost Dietzch from their cell in the Johannesburg prison brought any relief to the beleaguered 'President' and his colleague. On 6 February – after almost a month's imprisonment – the preliminary examination got under way in the Third Criminal Court, and when the hearing ended eight days later, on 14 February, the two prisoners were committed for trial at the next session of the Pretoria assizes.[99] But even this news offered Silver and Stein little consolation since the precise date on which the assizes were to convene had yet to be determined by the State Attorney. Thus, while Smuts and Cleaver used the remainder of February, all of March and the first week of April to complete outstanding prosecutions against former members of the Morality Squad on charges of perjury and corruption, the two gangsters grew increasingly despondent waiting to hear the exact date set for their trial.[100]

Silver and Stein eventually appeared before Justice Esser in the Pretoria High Court on 18 April 1899, charged on several counts under the Morality Act of 1898. By that time, however, Mostyn Cleaver had succeeded in completely cutting off any access which the 'Bowery Boys' had to police witnesses who might formerly have enjoyed some credibility. But the Second Public Prosecutor had used the time put at his disposal by the State Attorney to do more than simply erode the possible case for the defence. He had also managed to build up an enormously convincing case for the prosecution. By making use of the old combination of pressure and plea-bargaining, Cleaver got many of Silver's intimates – including Wolf Witkofsky, Lillie Bloom and Bessie Weinberg – to give evidence on the state's behalf. Perhaps most impressive of all was the manner in which the Second Public Prosecutor and his team tracked down one of the Presidents of the 'American Club's' former partners at the London end of the 'white slavery' operations, Jacob Shrednicki, and 'persuaded' him to give evidence about the leader of the syndicate's activities in the vice business. Thus, despite the fact that the two 'Bowery Boys' were ably defended by ex-Chief Justice J G Kotzé, Silver was found guilty after a trial lasting five days. While Sam Stein was fortunate enough to be discharged, Silver was sentenced to two years' imprisonment with hard labour, and subsequent banishment from the South African Republic.[101]

The last legal hope of the leader of the 'Bowery Boys' now lay in an appeal to the State President and his Executive Committee, but when representations were made on his behalf in early June, Kruger and his colleagues took the opportunity to endorse emphatically Mr Justice Esser's decision. Not even this, however, ended Joe Silver's problems with the Transvaal law. Early in August, while serving his sentence in the Johannesburg goal, Silver caught hold of an African cleaner, 'Jim', and sodomised him. While this assault, together with his previous reputation as a procurer, earned Silver's name a permanent place in South Africa's black prison gangs, it did him little good when he subsequently appeared before Mr Dietzch in the Third Criminal Court charged with committing 'an unnatural offence'. The 'Bowery Boy' was convicted and sentenced to a further period of six months' imprisonment which was to take effect after the completion of his first sentence of two years' imprisonment.[102]

Within days of this distressing development, however, the 'King of the Pimps' saw the first glimmerings of new hope for his release. The Kruger government, knowing the outbreak of war with Britain to be imminent, took the precaution of moving some of its long-term and more dangerous prisoners from Johannesburg to smaller Transvaal towns whose Republican loyalties were beyond doubt. On 26 September 1899 Joe Silver, in the company of 25 other prisoners, was moved to Potchefstroom in the western Transvaal where he promptly made an unsuccessful attempt to escape from prison.[103] But, as later transpired, this escape bid proved to be unnecessary since shortly thereafter the Boer authorities – hard pressed for all available manpower – were forced into releasing all the prisoners under their control. Silver seized the war's gift of freedom and made his way to the safety of the south where, over the next five years, he proceeded to leave his own particularly indelible mark on the criminal underworlds of Kimberley, Cape Town, Bloemfontein and Windhoek.

Cleaver's well-orchestrated attack on organised vice and police corruption during late 1898 and early 1899 had nevertheless met with at least some success. Through his efforts the most important principals behind the 'white slave' traffic had been exposed and dealt with, and at the time of the Pretoria High Court trial, 'train-loads of Silver's victims were sent over the border to Cape Town'. In August this action was followed by the further amendment of the Morality Law and the expulsion of dozens of 'foreign' pimps from the Rand. Moreover, Cleaver made sure that in the months leading up to the South African War Johannesburg was served, for the first time, by a relatively honest and efficient police force.[104]

But, while the state had certainly launched a powerful attack on the forces of Frenchfontein, it had by no means defeated the army of vice. Despite the expulsion of scores of prostitutes and pimps, hundreds more remained in Johannesburg and only departed for the coastal cities when the general exodus of refugees took place later in the year. Even then, however, some left more willingly than others. On 2 November 1899 the *Standard and Diggers' News* – vigilant to the end – drew the authorities' attention 'to a gang of Bowery 'hautboys' of American nationality still in town'.[105] If some of the New York City gangsters left the Rand reluctantly, they certainly did not do so under a cloud of pessimism. After all, in the prostitution business soldiers and miners were equally welcome as customers.

POLICIES OF PRAGMATISM – BRITISH CONTROL OF EUROPEAN WOMEN, 1902-1906

During mid-1899, at precisely the moment when Mostyn Cleaver was rounding-off his operations against the major prostitution networks on the Witwatersrand, the Cape Colony was engaged in a debate of its own about the role of the Contagious Diseases Act of 1885 and the control of sexual vice. There, certain feminists, clergymen and Members of Parliament who had long been opposed to the 'double standard' enshrined in Cape legislation had forced a select committee to re-examine the functioning of the CD Act in early 1899. When this parliamentary committee issued its report it found that not only did the act not play any material role in diminishing the spread of venereal disease, but that it continued to provide – via the notorious 'compulsory examination' clause – the means by which women could be humiliated. Largely as a result of this report a measure for the repeal of the CD Act was introduced into the Cape Parliament in August 1899, and it was only as a result of the strong personal intervention of the Premier, W P Schreiner, that the bill was eventually withdrawn.[106]

Schreiner must have felt that his conservatism was vindicated when, over the following four months, the Colony, and Cape Town in particular, was inundated with pimps, prostitutes and gangsters who had either been expelled from the South African Republic or who, along with thousands of others from the Transvaal, had chosen to seek refuge at the coast when war was declared in October 1899. In addition to this influx of 'undesirables' which derived from up-country, however, the port itself continued to disgorge its own share of newly arrived criminal elements from Europe who, instead of proceeding to the Transvaal as in the pre-war period, now tended to stay on in Cape Town.[107]

Briefly invisible, these denizens of the *demi-monde*, who included amongst their number former members of the 'American Club', soon became more apparent as large brothels, betting houses and gaming houses started to proliferate in wartime Cape Town. While this development was readily accommodated by several unprincipled landlords in search of higher rents – such as H J Dempers, an Afrikaner Bond Member of Parliament who let his city property as a brothel – it received a more hostile reception from others in the local community. In October 1901, after a series of public meetings at which grave reservations were expressed about the adequacy of a local by-law which the City Council had passed earlier in the year in an attempt to cope with the 'social evil', a group of concerned clergymen approached the Attorney General, T L Graham, with a request that new state legislation be promulgated to combat the growth of organised prostitution in Cape Town.[108]

When Graham took the precautionary step of cross-checking the clergymen's claims with the local police he was somewhat taken aback by his findings. In addition to discovering that sexual vice was more widespread than he had anticipated, he was also distressed by the revelation that 'a considerable traffic was being carried on in Cape Town between aboriginal natives and white European women'.[109] On the strength of this rather 'disturbing' evidence the Attorney General readily persuaded the government to introduce the 'Betting Houses, Gaming Houses and Brothels Suppression Bill' to parliament in October 1902. This bill, which was more frequently known by its short title, 'The Morality Bill', was largely modelled along the lines of the former *Zuid Afrikaansche Republiek*'s *Ontucht Wet*. In addition to making sexual intercourse between black males and white prostitutes an offence, it also made provision for the punishment of pimps by periods of imprisonment of up to two years, or for the inflicting of up to 25 lashes on the offenders. These latter clauses, as John X Merriman put it while guiding the bill through parliament, were specifically designed in order to get 'at these wretches through their skin'.[110]

Understandably, these harsh provisions held little appeal for the 'wretches' concerned, and when the Morality Act came into force on 1 December 1902 it sent several Cape-based pimps and prostitutes scurrying to other corners of southern Africa in search of more congenial business climes. Joseph Silver and his associates, for example, left Kimberley for Bloemfontein where their professional activities precipitated such a social upheaval that – within four months of their arrival, in March 1903 – the Orange River Colony was forced into passing its own ordinance to provide for the 'Suppression of Brothels and Immorality'.[111] Other vice merchants, again including former members of the 'American Club', decided that the time had come for them to chance a return to the Transvaal which was preoccupied with more pressing problems. Yet others, however, decided to head for the territory which was now most vulnerable of all – Natal.

Such an influx of pimps and prostitutes from elsewhere in southern Africa into Natal was not a novel experience for the British colony.

Indeed, as far back as March 1897, when Kruger had first introduced the *Ontucht Wet* into the Transvaal, a significant number of the departing prostitutes had made their way east and established themselves in Pietermaritzburg and Durban. This initial wave of 'undesirables', however, was soon followed by an even larger and more disturbing wave of *lumpen*-refugees when the war broke out in late 1899. On this latter occasion, R C Alexander, the Durban Superintendent of Police who kept a close watch on such developments, put the number of newly arrived prostitutes from the Rand in his city at 231. In addition to this, Alexander noted how, on average, five or six prostitutes disembarked from each German ship calling at the port during the war. This meant that in the relatively brief period between 1899 and 1902 over 300 'continental' women joined the ranks of those prostitutes who had previously been established in Durban.[112]

As in wartime Cape Town, and Johannesburg before that, this influx of vice merchants transformed the rent structure for housing in parts of central Durban. In this case the majority of premises hired to serve as brothels appear to have been owned by comparatively wealthy Asian landlords, and by one 'Latif Osman Rich' in particular.[113] But, as in the Cape and Transvaal before, it was not simply the question of housing which distressed the local authorities but the manner in which these 'continental' business women were willing to accept all paying customers on a non-racial basis. Natal settlers, along with most other white South African males, believed that such sex across the colour line permanently debauched African men, and that these erotic experiences subsequently triggered-off 'black peril' assaults on other European women. It was largely for this reason that Natal joined the elaborate post-war round of legislative musical chairs when it introduced its own Immorality Act in mid-1903.[114] Predictably enough, this law once again set in motion a cycle of movement in the flesh markets as several pimps and prostitutes chose to move to the Transvaal and other centres where they were perhaps less well known to the local police.

When the members of this latest and relatively minor influx of coastal vice merchants reached the Witwatersrand in 1903 they found that although the substantial part of Johannesburg's *demi-monde* had long since reconstituted itself, the prospects for selling sexual services nevertheless remained as promising as ever. In 1904 the large numbers of black and white miners in town without their wives were joined by an industrial army of Chinese indentured labourers, and all these 'unattached' males provided the 'ladies of pleasure' with a steady stream of customers. In addition to this, the war itself had of course brought with it the added 'bonus' of thousands of British troops and, in the wake of their departure, the residual force of the men of the South African Constabulary.[115] Clearly, in a town where there was such an overwhelming pre-ponderance of males over females, the continuing economic viability of Frenchfontein was beyond question.

· As in the pre-war period, however, this powerful demand for the serv-ices of prostitutes could not simply be met from local 'supplies', and thus it again called forth a highly organised response from the pimps and gangsters of Frenchfontein. Within weeks of Johannesburg being reopened to civilians in early 1901, the old 'white slavery' lines of supply – which during the war had temporarily terminated at the coastal cities – had been extended back into the Transvaal. Under the leadership of an old friend of Joe Silver's – Louis Shivinsky – former members of the 'American Club', including Abraham Goldstein, Joe Josephs and Robert Schoub, established a new pimps' association, the so-called 'Immorality Trust'.[116] With its leadership largely drawn from the ranks of the former 'Bowery Boys', the members of the 'Trust' now looked to the well-organ-ised 'white slave' dealers on the eastern American seaboard for many of their prostitutes.[117] In this they were largely assisted by the members of the New York Independent Benevolent Association, a notorious group of Jewish gangsters who preyed on the women of the vulnerable East European immigrant communities on Manhattan's lower east side.[118]

But it was the older and more established supply routes which stretched directly from Europe to southern Africa which continued to yield the greatest number of the Rand's 'white slaves' in the immediate post-war period. While Hamburg and the German East African Shipping Line still played a significant part in this traffic, it was Paris – above all other cities – which dominated the 'export trade' in women, sending prostitutes drawn from a dozen different continental countries to the Transvaal and other flesh markets spread across the world.[119] Although it is difficult to determine the names of all the intermediaries connected with the southern traffic in women, it is clear that at least one of those involved was the notorious George le Cuirassier.

During the first decade of the twentieth century George le Cuirassier, his mother and their associates were amongst the foremost 'white-slave' dealers in Paris – indeed, in Europe. Reported as being 'the general fin-ancier and boss of pimps and procurers' by an American Immigration Officer investigating the trade in women in 1909, Le Cuirassier was also said to have 'interests in dozens of Houses of Prostitution all over the globe, including France, Manchuria, Argentine, Mexico and the United States'.[120] Certainly, when the South African market expanded particular-ly rapidly after the outbreak of the Anglo-Boer War, Le Cuirassier had switched his business to Cape Town for several months, and it was while he was there that he was closely involved with Joseph Silver and other former members of the 'American Club'. In addition to managing a

District Six brothel under the names of 'George Hyman'/'Dacheau', Le Cuirassier personally supervised the movement of prostitutes between various southern African countries.[121] If there was anybody who knew who it was who put the 'French' into 'Frenchfontein', then it was likely to have been George le Cuirassier.

With his well-developed Far Eastern interests, however, it is also possible that Le Cuirassier would have known which of his colleagues in the trade it was who had helped Johannesburg to acquire a modest contingent of Japanese prostitutes in the post-war period.[122] Here again, it would appear that some of the former members of the 'American Club' were involved since G K Turner, a well-informed observer of the international 'white-slave' traffic at the time, noted how 'After South Africa the New York dealers went by their hundreds to the East' and that 'they followed the Russian army through the Russo-Japanese war'.[123] Thus, at the very moment that the agents of the Chamber of Mines were at work in China recruiting indentured labour for the Rand mines, the agents of organised vice were also at work in the Far East, recruiting some of the Japanese prostitutes who would be used to provide sexual services for the new workers. It was these latter female recruits, the so-called *Karayuki-San*, who, during the course of 1904-5, made their way to Fordsburg and joined up with the small number of Japanese prostitutes who had been established in that quarter of the town since at least 1894.[124]

This dramatic resurgence of the organised trade in prostitution did not escape the attention of some of Johannesburg's more experienced and vigilant observers of the *demi-monde* – such as Joseph Hertz. As leader of the Witwatersrand Old Hebrew Congregation, Hertz had been deeply shocked by the 'American Club' revelations in early 1899 when the extent of Jewish involvement in the 'white-slave' traffic had first become apparent, and had subsequently taken vigorous intracommunal measures to oppose it.[125] It was thus with some alarm that Rabbi Hertz saw familiar elements of the 'social evil' manifesting themselves again within the community, and he therefore readily agreed to participate in a private meeting which fellow clergymen and concerned citizens called to discuss the problem on 14 January 1902.

At this meeting, which drew together about 25 of the Rand's leading clerical, commercial and legal personalities, it was decided that the new Administrator of the Transvaal, Lord Milner, should be approached with a formal request that the police be instructed to enforce Kruger's old *Ontucht Wet* – Law No 11 of 1899. Hertz, who was elected as secretary to this committee of notables, accordingly drafted a petition outlining this request, taking the opportunity to point out that many vice merchants were already back in town while 'hundreds' of pimps and 'thousands' of prostitutes were at the coastal cities awaiting their first chance to return to Johannesburg. This document – whose signatories included, amongst others, St John Carr, Hugh Crawford (of Lewis & Marks), the Revd J T Darragh, Canon F H Fisher, The Revd J T Lloyd, Advocate Manfred Nathan, the Revd O Owens, H F Pistorius (Chamber of Commerce), E P Solomon and Harry Solomon – was dispatched for Milner's consideration in the third week of January.[126]

The imperial overlord took his time. On the final day of February 1902 Milner got his Assistant Private Secretary to send the petitioners a 12-line reply acknowledging receipt of their communication, and informing them that it was 'within the competence of the Municipalities of Johannesburg and Pretoria to make by-laws for the suppression of houses of ill-fame'. In addition, however, the Secretary was instructed to point out to Hertz and his colleagues that 'no permits to return to the Transvaal' would be granted to 'persons of known bad character'.[127] But the Administrator, either through neglect or deliberate oversight, failed to instruct the Permit Department to liaise with the Criminal Investigation Department on this matter, with the result that there was a continuing influx of 'undesirables' into Johannesburg during the following months.[128]

If, however, Milner silently cherished the hope that his inaction would dispose of the matter for the foreseeable future then he was mistaken, for before the year was out the issue was raised again and this time from a more powerful quarter. By mid-1902, with the 'social evil' much in evidence locally, senior officials in the Natal administration were becoming deeply distressed by tales of how black men engaged in migrant labour on the Witwatersrand were getting sexual access to 'continental women'. On 5 September the Governor of Natal, Sir Henry McCullum, wrote to the Administrator of the Transvaal expressing his concern about the matter and asking Milner about the possibility of the British authorities undertaking co-ordinated action to expel all 'foreign-born' prostitutes from the territories under their control. In addition, McCullum suggested that the moment had probably arrived when all the southern African colonies could share uniform legislation for the control of vice. This time, Milner, ever anxious to observe protocol, deflected the query to the Lieutenant-Governor of the Transvaal, Sir Arthur Lawley.[129]

Lawley, of course, was fully aware of the fact that if there were to be any action along the lines suggested, it would have to be initiated by the Administrator and his reconstruction 'cabinet'. The Lieutenant-Governor therefore simply passed the problem back to the government by asking the Attorney General, Richard Solomon, to draft his reply to McCullum. Solomon's reply no doubt reflected Milner's thinking on the subject at least as much as his own since it produced a familiar refrain: 'I see no reason for having a uniform law in South Africa for dealing generally with prostitutes,' noted the Transvaal Attorney General. 'It is purely a municipal matter and must be dealt with by each State with due regard to local conditions.'[130] Lawley reproduced this line of reasoning in word-perfect fashion when he replied to McCullum on 24 October 1902.[131]

Within four months of this successful evasion, however, Milner's policy on prostitution was again under scrutiny – and this time the questions came from a quarter that was less easily dismissed. Early in February 1903 Lord Onslow, Under-Secretary of State for the Colonies, wrote to Milner, drawing his attention to the manner in which the 'white-slave' traffic from Europe to southern Africa had somehow re-established itself, and enquiring what the 'permit system' was doing to disrupt this 'disgraceful' trade in women. Onslow concluded his letter with the suggestion that Milner might, via suitable 'religious or charitable associations', initiate rescue work amongst 'fallen women' in the Transvaal.[132]

This whisper from Whitehall concentrated the imperial overlord's mind wonderfully. Within weeks of the receipt of Onslow's letter, Milner's administration was actively seeking new submissions from the very Rand petitioners whom it had earlier sent away with a flea in the ear. The members of this 'Morality Committee' had, in the interim, been working on a revised version of the Cape Betting Houses, Gaming Houses and Brothels Suppression Act which – in line with the Administrator's earliest curt suggestion – they hoped to get the Johannesburg municipality to adopt. By the second week of March this draft legislation was being studied in the Attorney General's office, and in July the Transvaal administration promulgated Ordinance 46 of 1903, the 'Immorality Act'.[133]

Although chiefly concerned to outlaw *all* sexual intercourse between African males and European women – not simply that between black men and white prostitutes – Ordinance 46 was also designed to allow for the disruption of the organised trade in vice.[134] It thus contained measures specifically aimed at those owners of property who habitually allowed their houses to be let for purposes of prostitution. Moreover, clause 21 of the new Act made provision for the infliction of lashes on all males found guilty of living on the proceeds of prostitution. In legal terms at least, the Milner administration had demonstrated its intention of dealing with the 'white-slave' traffic and some of the attendant evils.

But, as always, the news of imminent and harsher repressive measures for the control of vice was greeted with a twofold response by the inhabitants of the *demi-monde*. On the one hand there were those veteran vice merchants who saw in the new Act the need to improve their professional organisation, and this they promptly did. From mid-1903 onwards, those brothels catering for African workers developed elaborate systems of lookouts, electric alarm bells and secret entrances to afford them better protection from sudden police raids.[135] On the other hand, however, there were those meeker brothers and sisters who had no taste at all for the harsher penalties contained in Ordinance 46. While many in the latter category made the familiar short journey to Cape Town, a few of the 'Bowery Boys' came to the conclusion that the time had come to move even further afield, and made their way back to New York City via Buenos Aires.[136]

The remaining East European and other pimps, however, were quick to appreciate that such trans-Atlantic trips were premature. With the exception of the clause prohibiting sex across the colour line, the Milner administration made little effort to implement the more stringent provision of Ordinance 46. From early 1902 to late 1905, Milner and Richard Solomon's view, that policies on prostitution had to be determined 'with due regard to local conditions', held sway. The Commissioner of Police, E H Showers, correctly interpreted this guideline to mean that in a place like Johannesburg – where there existed a high proportion of single or unaccompanied white workers – prostitution should be controlled but not eradicated.[137]

In practice this meant that for some time before and after the passing of the Immorality Act, Frenchfontein was allowed to flower in a manner which had last been seen between 1895 and 1897. While public exposure and soliciting by prostitutes was prohibited, brothels with up to ten and more women were allowed to operate openly provided that their business was conducted in a suitably restrained and discreet fashion. Amongst the two to three dozen brothels located in Anderson, Rissik, De Villiers, Loveday, Bree and other streets, there were two, however, that were particularly noteworthy. 'Sylvio Villa', still operating under its old trade name but now owned by George Ducoin, alias 'Canada', retained much of its pre-war popularity, while a new establishment managed by Theodore Hovent, at 1 Jeppe Street, was renowned for the variety of services it offered – the patrons being able to choose from a selection of no fewer than 17 'girls'. Under these flourishing business conditions, members of the 'Immorality Trust', as well as other pimps, accumulated considerable sums of capital which, in the case of the 'Bowery Boys', they eventually repatriated to New York City.[138]

Milner, however, had not forgotten the suggestion from Whitehall by Onslow that he might consider encouraging religions or charitable institutions to undertake reclamation work amongst the 'fallen women' of the Witwatersrand. Thus, shortly after the promulgation of Ordinance

46, he approached some of the clergymen on the 'Morality Committee' with offers of limited state aid for such work, and by late 1904 there were two 'rescue homes' operating in the Transvaal – the one Protestant and the other Catholic. At Irene, near Pretoria, a grant from the Beit Trust helped establish the 'House of Mercy', while at Norwood, in Johannesburg, Thomas Cullinan's generosity, aided by Milner's personal involvement in fund-raising activities, helped support a similar institution run by a French order, 'The Sisters of the Good Shepherd'. With a characteristically tough Victorian combination of Christian love and strenuous laundry work, however, neither of these institutions held great attractions for the former 'women of pleasure', and these reclamation efforts appear to have met with only modest success.[139]

This Milner marvel – whereby the authorities could on the one hand allow large brothels to operate in undisturbed fashion, and on the other encourage the reclamation of 'fallen women' – persisted throughout the period of his administration and for several months thereafter. Then, in late 1905, the quiet comfort of this position was rudely shattered when the man in charge of the CID on the Witwatersrand, Major T E Mavrogordato, happened to outline the 'local conditions' policy to Milner's successor, Lord Selborne. The Governor, shocked by the discovery that wealthy vice merchants were allowed to operate relatively openly in Johannesburg, immediately wrote a pointed letter to the Attorney General, Richard Solomon, enquiring as to why it was that pimps were not being prosecuted under the provisions of Ordinance 46. The Attorney General, embarrassed by these questions, deftly passed them down the line to the Commissioner of Police, E H Showers. As co-authors – with Milner – of the 'local conditions' policy, both Solomon and Showers, of course, knew the answers to Selborne's questions perfectly well. But, either unable or unwilling to spell out these answers to a new Governor, the Attorney General and Commissioner of Police chose instead to assure Selborne that they would at once launch a drive against the pimps on the Rand. Then, in order to demonstrate their irritation at being pushed into this predicament by a relatively junior officer, Solomon and Showers promptly 'deputed Mr Mavrogordato to deal with the pimps'.[140]

Mavrogordato responded as well as he could to this petulant challenge from above. Within a week of receiving his directive from the Commissioner of Police on 23 January 1906, Mavrogordato's men arrested the veteran vice merchant Louis Shivinsky, now a member of the 'Immorality Trust', on charges framed under Ordinance 46. No sooner had this notorious 'Bowery Boy' been let out on bail of £1 000, however, than he fled the country. This arrest and its expensive sequel, 'which caused considerable commotion in the camp of the pimps' was followed by further vigorous CID activity during February, March and April. By May 1906 Mavrogordato could report to Showers that, besides Shivinsky and George Ducoin of 'Sylvio Villa' fame, 15 other important pimps had fled the Transvaal, that nine of Frenchfontein's largest and best regulated brothels had been closed down, and – a bit hopefully – that 'the organisation of pimps hitherto complained of in Johannesburg has ceased to exist'.[141]

The Commissioner of Police, a little ungenerously, found these results from the CID to be 'disappointing'. Showers felt that although the established brothels had been closed down, few of the pimps involved had been successfully prosecuted, and that the results that had been achieved could as readily have been obtained by the uniformed branch of the police.[142] The Attorney General, suitably briefed by Showers, shared this opinion, with the result that over the following months the members of the Criminal Investigation Department remained under constant pressure to produce a stream of convictions under the Immorality Act.

Eventually, after nearly a year and a half of intradepartmental rivalry and tension – and only after Solomon and Showers had moved out of office – the Head of the CID made the admission which the former Milner men would so dearly have liked to have extracted from him. In May 1907 Mavrogordato wrote to the Acting Commissioner of Police, Colonel A O'Brien, pointing out that:

> The position with regard to Public Immorality has greatly improved within the last two years; formerly large brothels containing 10 or more women each were allowed to exist. These institutions are not in existence now and most of the prostitutes are single women who are living by themselves or in a house. Soliciting in the streets has been reduced to a minimum and I do not think that the streets could be cleaner in Johannesburg in any other part of the world [*sic*].[143]

When O'Brien passed on this message to the new Attorney General, Jacob de Villiers, it was accepted, bringing some relief to the hitherto beleaguered chief of the CID. In retrospect, however, Mavrogordato would probably have agreed that this judgement was perhaps a little naïve, and certainly a bit premature. Prostitution had been a feature of the mining town ever since it was founded, and for over a decade much of Johannesburg's vice trade had shown all the hallmarks of careful organisation. These features, which ultimately derived from the deeper social structures engendered by capitalist development on the Witwatersrand and in Eastern Europe on the one hand, and from the cunning career management of professional gangsters spread across the world on the other, were unlikely to be simply blown away by a police campaign over an 18-month period.

THE TRANSVAAL'S OWN – DAUGHTERS OF THE NEW PROLETARIAT, 1907-1914

In May 1907, only a few months after the Transvaal attained self-governing status, members of Mavrogordato's staff compiled a return giving the names and addresses of all known pimps and brothels in Johannesburg. Possibly as a result of genuine ignorance, but more likely as a result of the bribery of some of the members of the CID concerned, this list of 60 'houses of ill-fame' proved to be conspicuously thin on information relating to the inner city's vice district. In particular, this return managed to miss the names and business addresses of several veterans of vice still active in Frenchfontein, such as Harry Epstein, Abraham Goldstein, Joe Josephs and others; as well as those of dozens of younger Russo-American pimps who had made their way to the Rand in the immediate post-war period to become members of the 'Immorality Trust' – men such as Meyer Arenow, Isaac 'Itchky' Favours, Leon Rosenblatt and 'Chicago Jack' Linderstein.[144]

This unusual silence from and about the activities of the town's oldest and best-organised vice district persisted for several months. Then, from December 1907 to May 1908, as the Rand's post-war recession deepened into a full-scale depression, the foundations of the *demi-monde* were rocked by tremors which emanated from the most unexpected quarter. Either because they found the financial demands of some of the members of the 'Immorality Trust' too demanding during such hard times, or for some equally cogent but hidden reason, certain prostitutes 'made up their minds to throw off the yokes of their pimps'.[145] One of the first and most important pimps to be subjected to this startling attack from below was Harry Epstein, a founder member of the 'American Club'.

As a result of information passed to the police by certain prostitutes formerly under his control, Harry Epstein was arrested by members of the CID on 14 February 1908. A seasoned professional, Epstein's immediate response was to look for the best defence lawyer in town who had first-hand experience of morality cases. To the delight of the former 'Bowery Boy', he found that sufficient money could retain the services of a lawyer who not only had an outstanding knowledge of the Transvaal legal system, but one who felt – as a matter of principle – that the law should have a little as possible to do with questions of public morality. First as Public Prosecutor in Johannesburg under the Kruger regime,

and later as lawyer and Member of Parliament for the *Het Volk* government, F E T Krause proved himself to be a friend of Frenchfontein.[146]

Right from the outset Krause distinguished himself in his defence of
his pimp client. By constantly seeking remands – and being granted at
least eight such requests – he managed to drag out the preparatory
examination from mid-February to early April 1908. Then, when Epstein's trial finally commenced in the Witwatersrand 'C' Court on
21 May, Krause managed to employ successfully the same delaying tactic on a further six occasions. While these adjournments gave members
of the 'Immorality Trust' ample opportunity to work on prosecution witnesses outside the courtroom, Krause supplemented their efforts inside
the court by suggesting that all evidence which emanated from prostitutes was by its nature suspect and therefore inconclusive. An able bar-
rister under any circumstances, Krause found that his eloquent plead-
ings echoed particularly loudly in the ears of a presiding magistrate
who, ten years earlier, had been one of his juniors in the Johannesburg
Public Prosecutor's office – W G Schuurman. The result of all this was
that Epstein was eventually found not guilty on 17 June 1908, discharged, and refunded the £750 which he had been made to deposit with
the court as bail.[147]

Epstein celebrated his victory at law in a manner which his colleagues
in the pimping fraternity could only thoroughly approve of. On the
evening of his release from custody, he and the chief witness for the
defence at his trial, Mrs Max Kaplan, hired a cab and then drove to the
various houses of the prostitutes who had dared to give evidence against
him. Here, after jeering and taunting the crown witnesses, they proceeded to smash several windows before moving on to a celebratory dinner
held for 'Trust' members and their 'madams' at 42 Polly Street. The following morning Epstein called at Krause's office where he stole all the
papers pertaining to his case before shaving off his moustache and fleeing the country.[148]

But if Mavrogordato's men failed in the case of Epstein, then they
more than compensated with the successes which they managed to
achieve during the six-month long pimp/prostitute war which engulfed
Frenchfontein between December 1907 and May 1908. Largely because
of evidence made available to the CID by rebellious prostitutes, 17 of the
most important pimps in the local *demi-monde* were arrested during this
period. The ensuing court cases necessitated the calling of 150 witnesses,
of whom over 100 were prostitutes. 'The result', noted the newly-pro-
moted Deputy Commissioner of Police, 'was that 10 well-known professional pimps were convicted and sentenced to terms of imprisonment
varying from 6 to 12 months with lashes.'[149]

Even this onslaught did not succeed in finally destroying the

'Immorality Trust' and the remaining vestiges of the 'white-slave' traffic. In October 1908 Mavrogordato could still draw the Attorney General's attention to the presence of dozens of Russo-American and other pimps on the Rand:

> The pimps referred to make no secret of their calling. Some of them live together, and there are such places in Johannesburg as pimps' boarding-houses and pimps' clubs. Some of them take houses in the country where they are supposed to live privately and where prostitutes who are imported or those who are sick take refuge till they are fit to be put on the market.[150]

It was precisely because of such remaining supportive structures that Mavrogordato now appealed to the Colonial Secretary to agree to the deportation of all foreign-born pimps and prostitutes convicted under the Immorality Act.

The Colonial Secretary had little difficulty in understanding Mavrogordato's problem or in acceding to his request. As the former State Attorney in Kruger's government who had been responsible for sending Mostyn Cleaver to Johannesburg to do battle with the 'American Club' ten years earlier, J C Smuts probably had a better idea than most of his colleagues in the cabinet what the CID was up against. Thus, between early 1909 and mid-1910, in a period of frenetic activity before Union, Smuts and Mavrogordato made widespread use of the Transvaal's Crimes Prevention Ordinance of 1905 and the Immigrants' Restriction Acts of 1907 and 1908 to deport hundreds of foreign-born pimps and prostitutes to Mozambique and the neighbouring colonies. From there many of these 'undesirable aliens' made the long journey home to the ports and backstreets of Europe.[151]

This campaign, and the scores of 'voluntary' departures which occurred during the same period, did much to break the dominant hold which immigrant vice merchants had exercised over Johannesburg's *demi-monde* ever since the mid-1890s. By July 1910, when the CID again conducted one of its periodic surveys of Frenchfontein, it could only find 17 pimps and 48 prostitutes who qualified for the category 'foreign-born'. Of the pimps, seven were listed as being 'Jewish', four French, four German and two Portuguese, while the prostitutes included twenty 'Russian and Polish Jewesses', nine German, eight French and three other women. Although no doubt suffering from some of the same deficiencies as earlier police reports in this regard, it seems possible that the survey did reflect some of the broader trends at work in the *demi-monde* since it also noted how, for the first time, South African-born women constituted the majority of white prostitutes in the town.[152]

Johannesburg's western working-class suburbs of Fordsburg and Vrededorp had always known poverty. Indeed, Vrededorp had been especially set aside by the Kruger government in 1893 for those poverty-stricken burghers who had been pushed out of the Transvaal countryside during the accelerated capitalist development of the late nineteenth century. Before the South African War many of these Afrikaners had made a living from transport riding, brickmaking or cab driving. The arrival of the railways in the mid-1890s, the destruction caused by the war itself, the mechanisation of brickmaking and the introduction of the electric tramway in 1906, however, had all contributed to growing Afrikaner male unemployment in the post-war period. Then, as if these problems were somehow not enough for the poor to bear, the recession of 1904-5 deepened into the depression of 1906-8.

Many Afrikaner families attempted to compensate for this loss of male earnings by sending out their daughters to seek such work as was available in a town dominated by the mining industry. Avoiding the lonely and humiliating experience of having to enter domestic service in the affluent homes of their English overlords in the northern suburbs, these young women turned instead to the work to be found in the small factories, dress-making concerns, bottling plants and hand-laundries closer to their homes. These menial jobs, however, hardly offered a grand solution to the grinding poverty and bitter distress confronting these communities. Besides being badly paid – yielding cash wages of between 8 and 20 shillings per week – such employment also had the disadvantage of pushing young women into the company of older and more experienced male labourers. This contact in the workplace in turn gave rise to a certain degree of promiscuous behaviour and casual prostitution which, in the hardest years of the depression, more readily gave way to a full-time career in vice.[153]

This entry of the daughters of the new proletariat into the vice market was reflected in the Criminal Investigation Department's immorality return for 1907 which, for the first time, noted the addresses of a large number of brothels in Fordsburg and Vrededorp. What some members of the police found even more distressing however, was the presence of a number of teenage prostitutes in the latter suburb who readily sold their services to the local Chinese storekeepers.[154] While the sexual exploits of Maggie van Niekerk, 'Trickey' Beukes and the two Potgieter sisters were certainly known to members of the local community, the English press made certain that the more sensational cases – such as that of the prostitute Susan Broderick who became Mrs Ho King of Vrededorp – were more widely proclaimed as illustrations of the 'yellow peril' in Johannesburg.[155]

But the depression did not confine itself to the white suburbs in the cities. It had an equally devastating effect on black homesteads in the country. Here the prevailing economic climate, drought, a rebellion in Natal and a new round of cattle disease combined to force a significant number of African women to abandon the rural areas in their search for a livelihood between 1906 and 1908. Many of those women who made their way to the Witwatersrand, however, soon discovered that the one segment of the labour market which they could possibly penetrate – domestic service – was already dominated by African men who had been forced out into migratory labour by poll tax a decade earlier. It was thus largely as a result of the lack of job opportunities that a number of these women either took to beer selling or drifted into casual prostitution.

Predictably, much of this new vice was to be found in Johannesburg's black working-class areas – the town and mine locations – and by 1910 the police estimated that there were between 200 and 300 black women who could be categorised as full-time prostitutes. While these women gained most of their customers from the compounds which housed the black miners on the outskirts of the town, a small number managed to establish themselves in the old inner vice district where they drew customers of all colours. In this latter case, as with Mrs Ho King in Vrededorp, the solvent of poverty and the colour blindness of the *demi-monde* occasionally gave rise to its own distinctive chemistry – as when 'Black Annie Miller' forged her relationship with the Jewish pimp Reuben Waltmann.[156]

In retrospect, then, it becomes clear that Johannesburg's underworld of sexual vice was transformed by two sets of supplementary forces between 1907 and 1910. First, the police seized the opportunity offered them by rebellious prostitutes in 1907-8 to embark on an extensive campaign of deportations which, over the following years, rid the town of the majority of its so-called 'foreign-born' pimps and prostitutes. This move not only broke the decade-old dominance of *organised* vice, it also contributed to the marked decline in importance of the inner city's 'traditional' red light district – 'Frenchfontein'. Secondly, a set of economic and social forces stemming from the increased tempo in the proletarianisation of local black and white women produced a growing contingent of South African-born prostitutes in the city after 1906. In effect this meant that as visible organised vice gave way in the city centre, it tended to be replaced by the less obtrusive activities of individual prostitutes working in the poorer working-class suburbs or ghettos of Johannesburg.

The interaction of these two sets of forces, however, did not bring about a state of equilibrium in the supply of prostitutes on the Witwatersrand since the deportation of 'undesirable aliens' and the 'voluntary' exodus which accompanied it, appear to have exceeded the

number of native-born women entering the profession during this period. In addition, another more deeply rooted factor made an equally
important contribution to the marked decline in white prostitution in
Johannesburg in the years leading up to the First World War – a slacken-
ing in the demand for commercialised sexual services occasioned by the
changing social structure of a maturing industrial capitalist system.
Whereas in 1897 only 12 per cent of the employees on the Rand gold
mines were married and had their families resident with them in the
Transvaal, by 1902 the figure had risen to 20 per cent, and by 1912 it was
up to 42 per cent.[157]

These quantitative and qualitative changes in the *demi-monde* produced reasonably predictable responses from the other parties usually
most concerned about prostitution in the city – the police, the churches
and the local middle classes. The police, content with having destroyed
most of the organised vice in Johannesburg, were unwilling to countenance a further 'wholesale crusade' against prostitution and thus
allowed individual prostitutes to ply their trade provided that they did
not openly solicit business or knowingly spread venereal disease. The
churches, for their part, tended not to grieve about what they did not see.
With such remaining sexual vice as there was in the city neatly tucked
away in the locations or the working-class suburbs, the clergymen and
concerned citizens who had earlier been so vocal in their condemnation
of Frenchfontein fell strangely silent. In the remaining years before the
First World War one of the few things which the Witwatersrand Church
Council could find to complain about in the field of public morality was
'the exhibition in shop windows of pictures of semi-nude women' – the
faintest possible echo of the naughty nineties in Nugget Street.[158]

By 1914, therefore, Johannesburg had reached the point where, after
nearly a quarter of a century, the relationship between prostitutes and
proletarians no longer yielded a significant profit margin for organised
elements of the lumpenproletariat or their petty-bourgeois partners – the
landlords and the liquor merchants. But if the gangsters and small businessmen lost money as a result of the decline, then the state and the ruling classes lost something less tangible – one of the means by which they
had been able to attract, stabilise and control labour during the Rand's
earliest phase of industrial development.

The role which prostitution plays in a developing capitalist system is
thus a complex one, and one which spans the class spectrum of society
at different historical moments. In the Transvaal this role was made even
more complex by the fact that most of this development occurred during
the era of imperialism – that is, at a time when the world capitalist system's boundaries were being extended particularly rapidly. This meant
that in one small quarter of the Witwatersrand's principal mining town

there were, at the turn of the century, the social deposits of economic waves which had washed not only the shores of Africa, but of North America, South America, Europe and Asia as well. 'There are more things in Johannesburg', warned the man from the *Standard and Diggers' News*, 'than are dreamt of in the ordinary man's philosophy.'

CONCLUSION

If prostitution is largely a function of 'fallen women', then it is interesting to note in what sequence and in what numbers women 'happened to fall' in the Transvaal between 1886 and 1914. For nearly eight years, from 1886 to 1894, prostitution in Johannesburg was dominated by hundreds of 'coloured' women drawn from the larger commercial centres of the Cape Colony. The presence of these women – which was encouraged by the local canteen keepers – could be attributed to their advanced proletarian status, repressive legislation to control prostitution in the Cape Colony and their geographical proximity to a new area of capitalist expansion in the subcontinent.

The more permanent developments which accompanied the establishment of the deep-level mines and the arrival on the Witwatersrand of the railway from Lourenço Marques on the east coast, however, radically transformed this situation. The presence of a large proletarian army of mineworkers combined with the low cost of steamship travel from European ports to attract thousands of continental prostitutes to the Rand from 1895 onwards. These women were soon joined by hundreds of Russo-American pimps and prostitutes from New York City who had been equally quick to spot the business potential of the new Transvaal goldfields. Between 1895 and 1899 these highly professionalised vice merchants, in alliance with local landlords and property companies, transformed much of inner Johannesburg into the red light district of Frenchfontein.

The public explosion of sexual vice in the mining town soon earned the strong moral condemnation of parts of the salaried middle class in Johannesburg – in particular, sections of the press and the church. The agitation of these latter groups to have prostitution suppressed, however, did not meet with great success initially for at least two reasons. First, Johannesburg's capital-accumulating small businessmen, the canteen keepers and the landlords, exercised a powerful influence over local government with the result that the Sanitary Board sought ways to 'regulate' rather than eliminate sexual vice in the town. Secondly, senior members of Kruger's administration, drawing on the experience of government in Holland, were unconvinced that a policy of outright suppression would succeed in ridding the town of prostitution. It was thus only after the State President personally chose to sweep aside elements of opposition and hesitancy, and appoint a determined State Attorney, that serious attempts were made to eliminate public immorality on the Rand. From December 1898 until October 1899 J C Smuts and F R M Cleaver made vigorous, and at least partially successful efforts to smash organised prostitution in Johannesburg.

These efforts by the state to erode Frenchfontein were soon supplemented by a more powerful 'voluntary' exodus when war broke out in late 1899, and thousands of pimps and prostitutes from Johannesburg joined the throng of refugees who made their way to the coastal cities. There, the former Transvaal vice merchants were soon joined by new arrivals from Europe who were equally keen to exploit the wartime business opportunities offered by the presence of thousands of British troops. It was thus largely as a result of this influx of up-country pimps and prostitutes that the Cape, Natal, and to a lesser extent the Orange River Colony, all found it necessary to promulgate new and more repressive immorality legislation between 1902 and 1903.

This battery of racist legislation – the forerunner of the modern South African Immorality Act – caused a considerable amount of movement between the various flesh markets of the subcontinent as vice merchants sought the most congenial socio-legal environment in which to conduct their business. It was during the course of this search that many pimps and prostitutes found their way back to the Transvaal where, to their delight, they discovered that the post-war authorities were marvellously understanding of Frenchfontein. Milner, anxious to re-attract white workers to the reconstruction state as swiftly as possible and then stabilise and control the mining proletariat, deliberately ignored the vocal objections of the local middle class and turned a blind eye to the problem of prostitution. It was only after the direct and pointed intervention of Whitehall that the reconstruction government introduced its own post-war legislation to suppress prostitution, and even then the provisions of Ordinance 46 of 1903 were only selectively enforced.

Milner's successors, however, were more concerned about prostitution, and in particular about the problem of organised vice in Johannesburg. First under Selborne, and then under *Het Volk*, the state made vigorous and determined efforts to break the hold which Russo-Americans and European immigrants exercised over the *demi-monde*. From late 1907 onwards the more prominent pimps of Frenchfontein were forced to beat a constant retreat before a police attack which, during its initial stages at least, enjoyed the support of rebellious prostitutes. The successes of the state between 1907 and 1908 were further consolidated between 1909 and 1910 when the police – actively supported by the Colonial Secretary,

J C Smuts – managed to deport hundreds of convicted pimps and prostitutes from the Transvaal under the Immigrants' Restriction Acts of 1907 and 1908.

If these post-reconstruction campaigns effectively destroyed the dominance of organised vice in Frenchfontein, they hardly eliminated prostitution from the streets of Johannesburg. For at the very moment that the notorious continental women were being forced to leave the country in large numbers, the Transvaal was starting to yield its own corps of white and black prostitutes drawn from the ranks of the emerging indigenous proletariat. As the inner city was freed of organised vice, so the peripheral working-class suburbs and ghettos started to produce their own problems of small-scale prostitution. The latter manifestations of vice, however, did not draw the same amount of attention that prostitutes had done in earlier periods in the city's history.

The changing social structure of the Witwatersrand meant that the relationship between the inhabitants of the *demi-monde* and the mineworkers had declined to the point where it neither yielded significant profits for the petty bourgeoisie, nor presented the ruling class with an instrument of social control over the working class. Under capitalism, the marriage of prostitutes and proletarians is not without its own interested brokers.

4

JOHANNESBURG'S JEHUS, 1890-1914

Cabs, cabbies and tramways during the transition from private to public transport in the principal industrial city of the Witwatersrand

The town council will thus accept the duty of providing for
the welfare of workers with moderate incomes, to whom a cheap,
efficient and well-regulated tramway-system is
practically a necessity, tending as it does to remove
the disadvantages of residence at a distance from their work ...
MAJOR O'MEIRA, Military Mayor of Johannesburg, April 1901

The mining capitalist revolution that occurred on the Witwatersrand between 1886 and 1914 created and transformed Johannesburg. From a diggers' camp of about 3 000 adventures in 1887, there developed first a mining town with a population of over 100 000 people in 1896, and then, by 1914, an industrialising city with over a quarter of a million inhabitants. From the tented mining camp at the diggings in the 1880s, there grew the single-quarters and boarding-houses built of corrugated iron that clustered around the deep-level mines and city centre in the 1890s, and then the more substantial brick-built homes of the working-class and other suburbs by 1914. This dramatic surge and spread of population also reflected itself in other ways, for example in the changing municipal boundaries of Johannesburg. In 1898 the Town Council held jurisdiction over an area of five square miles; when the nominated Town Council under the occupying British forces first took control in 1901 this was extended to nine square miles; and by the time that civilian local government was firmly re-established in 1903 this had yet again increased to an enormous 82 square miles.

But these developments, crammed as they were into a 25-year period, embraced changes of nature as well as of number. The move of Johannesburg from tent-town, through its intermediate stages to a city with sub-urban homes, thus also saw the shift from an economic system that was dependent on European immigrant miners for its skilled labour to one characterised by a more socially stabilised proletariat in which the work-ing class reproduced itself on the Rand through the agency of the nuclear family. The move to the suburbs, which accompanied this latter devel-opment, became particularly pronounced after 1901 and was conscious-ly facilitated by the state, which saw in the geographical dispersal of the white working class a means of enhancing its social and political control in a rapidly maturing capitalist system.[1] While this working-class exodus from the high-rental areas of the city centre might have solved some dif-ficulties, it also created at least one other significant problem – it tended, by an ever- increasing margin, to separate the worker from his place of work. This in turn meant that a greater amount of time and effort had to be spent in the daily movement of the worker between his home and the point of production, and movement, like everything else, cost money. In Johannesburg, where this latter problem assumed increasingly urgent proportions between 1896 and 1906, the bourgeoisie and the working class alike drew at least some consolation from the fact that this obstacle was not without recent precedent in capitalist development.

In Europe, capital had at a much earlier date produced its own trans-formation of society which, by way of comparison, clearly dwarfed the economic unfolding of the Witwatersrand. Right from its inception, how-ever, the industrial revolution had confined the bulk of its urban prole-tariat to within the immediate bounds of the 'walking city'. This meant that while the working class for the largest part lived in the sordid, con-gested conditions that Engels and others described so well, it was not forced to spend a significant proportion of its income on daily transport to and from the manufacturing enterprises in which it laboured. Much of this changed from the mid-nineteenth century onwards when the work-ing class, for a complex set reason, started to become more widely dis-persed within European cities.

Starting in the 1870s many European cities attacked the problem of a more widely dispersed urban population through the implementation of a horse-drawn tram service within the inner city. It was the cheaper and more efficient technology that came with electricity, however, that revo-lutionised public transport during the following two decades. By the mid-1890s large industrial cities throughout the world, from Kiev to Kansas, were introducing the electric tram or 'trolley' to their inhabitants – both as a response to the dispersal of the working class, and as a means by which to facilitate that process further. So smooth was the transition from horse-car to trolley, and so efficient was the electric tram in its new function, that the cost of transport in metropolitan Europe and the

United States fell consistently in the two decades before the First World War.[2] Above all else, it was to this strikingly successful contemporary European experience that the Witwatersrand capitalist class looked in its search for a solution to the developing urban transport problem in Johannesburg between 1890 and 1914. The solution, when it did come to the Rand, was neither swift nor painless.

The electric tram first ran in the streets of Johannesburg in 1906, a good ten years after the possibility of its use was first seriously mooted. Even then, the fact that it eventually ran at all was only due to the momentous upheavals that had occurred in the intervening decade. It took a war to replace a rural bourgeoisie with urban-based capitalists as the ruling class of the Transvaal, a searching commission of enquiry by the British government, a cash settlement of £150 000 with the earlier horse-drawn tram company, the sacrifice of a sizeable cab-owning class and the structural unemployment of hundreds of cab drivers, for the electric tram to establish itself in Johannesburg. This essay will seek to illustrate the process of class struggle as it developed in the field of urban transport during an era of revolutionary capitalism.

URBAN TRANSPORT UNDER THE DOMINANCE OF A RURAL BOURGEOISIE, 1889-1899
Capitalist transport – the Johannesburg City & Suburban Tramway Company

It was A H Nellmapius, one of the Transvaal's wealthiest and most pro-gressive farmers who, in late 1888, first approached the State President with a view to securing the exclusive right to operate a tramway system in Johannesburg. As a close confidant of Kruger, and as one of the archi-tects of the Boer Republic's concessions policy, Nellmapius had already secured several such grants from the *Volksraad* in the past. At the centre of at least one of these previous concessions – the spectacularly success-ful *Eerste Fabrieken* or Hatherley Distillery – lay the idea that industrial enterprises in the new Republic should form a market for the produce of the Dutch farmers and, as such, should aid in the development of spe-cific linkages between the urban and rural sectors of the economy. Nellmapius's idea for a Johannesburg transport system, which revolved around the exclusive use of animal power harnessed to a tramway, again proceeded from this premise. Kruger had little difficulty in persuading the members of his *Volksraad* that a concession which would result in the burghers being able to sell large quantities of horses, mules and forage was worthy of their support. Thus, in early 1889, A H Nellmapius secured a 39-year concession to operate a horse-drawn tramway in Johannes-burg, one of the conditions being that no alternative power source be

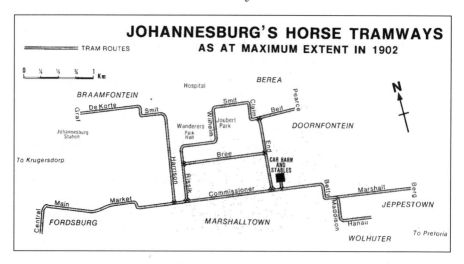

utilised in the system without the prior consent of the government.[3]

But if the tramway concession initially only half-aroused the interest of the *Volksraad* and its farming constituency, then it certainly succeeded in fully capturing the imagination and enthusiasm of the local capitalists. In April 1889, almost as soon as he had acquired the concession, Nellmapius sold a three-quarter share in it to a Rand mining company owned by Sigmund Neumann and his then partners, Carl Hanau and H J King. At the same time the concessionaire sold a further five per cent of his venture to Messrs Mosenthal Sons & Co of Port Elizabeth, 'one of the oldest and most prominent South African mercantile firms'. So swiftly did these events occur that Nellmapius requested that the *Volksraad* simply issue the original concession directly in the name of Sigmund Neumann.[4]

Neumann and his partners were well-respected entrepreneurs, and when they floated the Johannesburg City & Suburban Tramway Co Ltd with a capital of £125 000 on 19 September 1889, the £1 shares traded at a premium. The new issue immediately drew the support of other local capitalists and a man like Carl Meyer, for example, swiftly acquired 2 500 shares for himself. Mosenthal Sons showed their confidence in the venture by buying a further 7 500 shares to supplement the five per cent interest which they already held in the original concession. Elsewhere in the Cape, Natal and the Transvaal members of the public 'best acquainted with the conditions and prospects of the country' also purchased shares in the company 'long before it commenced active opeations'.[5] These swirls and eddies in the local financial currents, however, were soon swamped by the huge tide of European capital that flowed into the Johannesburg City & Suburban Co.

Immediately after the company was floated some of the most prominent groups in international mining and finance capital bought their way into the new Transvaal transport business. Porges & Co (later Wernher, Beit & Co) acquired 15 000 shares, while A Reimers & Co purchased a massive block of 30 000 shares within four weeks of the project's public launching. Here then, a section of mining capital – as it was to do again shortly afterwards in the case of Hatherley Distillery – showed its willingness to invest in secondary enterprise on the Rand at least half a decade before the more secure developments that came with deep-level mining took place.[6]

In France, together with Belgium acknowledged to be the most developed continental centre for horse-drawn and electric tramway enterprise, the *Banque Internationale de Paris* promoted the Johannesburg company and, amongst many other prominent investors, Messrs N M Rothschild & Sons bought 15 000 shares. In Brussels, where investors were apparently slower off the mark, the bulk of the investment only came in 1895 when a group around M Josse Allard, a prominent banker in the city and the Director of the Belgian Mint, acquired a large parcel of shares. By then, however, a 20-shilling share in the Johannesburg City & Suburban Co was trading at an all-time high level of 50 shillings.[7]

With its working capital requirements easily satisfied, the tramway company commenced its construction activities in July 1890, and by 2 February 1891, when the system opened, it could offer a service on a track that extended along Commissioner Street for 4.75 miles, between Jeppe in the east and Fordsburg in the west. By mid-1896 the system had reached the apex of its development with a line of track some 10.75 miles long, laid out in a series of loops designed to cover the inner city. In the same year, City & Suburban operated a fleet of about 35 trams, and employed a staff of over 200 workers – including 140 Cape Coloured tram drivers dressed in the distinctive blue and gold uniform of the company. Thereafter, the company's scale of operation remained more or less constant and six years later, by 1902, only one more mile of track had been laid bringing the total track distance covered to 11.75 miles.[8]

This pattern of growth in the company's activities was also to be seen in other areas of its operation. The basic fare of 3d per mile proved popular in Johannesburg, and right from the outset the service was well patronised. By 1896 the City & Suburban's fleet of trams was covering 1 000 miles per day through the town, and transporting a good two and a half million passengers during the course of a year. This volume of business showed itself in the company's turnover, and up to the mid-1890s in growing profits and dividends – see Table 5.[9]

Whilst this financial statement revealed a modest growth in the income of the company over an eight-year trading period, it also pointed to a high cost structure that tended to keep pace with any expansion in gross receipts.

Table 5 Johannesburg City & Suburban Tramway Co Ltd,
Financial Statement, 1891-98

Year	Gross Income	Costs	Gross profit	Dividend
1891	£14 511	£12 262	£2 488	–
1892	21 617	16 780	4 836	–
1893	27 162	20 507	6 655	4%
1894	29 484	22 780	6 703	4%
1895	41 374	27 490	13 883	6%
1896	–	–	–	10%
1897	–	–	–	7½%
1898	–	–	–	nil

The large majority of these costs derived directly from the fact that the tramway system was animal-powered. The working life of a tram-horse, relegated as it was to a strenuous round of endless stopping and starting, was about four years. From the mid-1890s the City & Suburban Co required a stable of over 200 horses to operate its trams, and new animals were constantly having to be purchased in order to keep the system up to strength. While this would have been an expensive business in the normal course of events, the situation was exacerbated through most of the 1890s by endemic horse-sickness which forced prices to remain at a high level.[10] To make matters worse, the local price of forage also remained high during the same period – not only because demand constantly outstripped supply, but because a series of severe droughts aggravated the situation. The company attempted to cope with this latter problem through a policy of bulk purchasing, its Doornfontein silo being built to hold a four-month supply of forage. But not even this solved the problem fully – the cost of forage consistently accounted for two-thirds of the company's expenses, and in 1896 the annual bill for that item alone ran to £18 000.[11]

These high costs did not cause the Transvaal farmers any concern. On the contrary, a market for burgher produce on this scale must have gone some way towards vindicating the *Volksraad*'s decision to grant Nellmapius the concession in the first place. From the City & Suburban's point of view, however, the problem was that the concession no longer belonged simply to Nellmapius. Once the concession had passed into the hands of the international capitalists, much of the unstated *raison d'être* for its existence also disappeared. Whereas a national capitalist like Nellmapius might live with a high cost structure which saw himself and his fellow burghers benefit from the prices for horses and forage, the same was not true for an international capitalist like Rothschild. While

Nellmapius could look forward to reaping profits at both the rural and urban ends of an integrated economic enterprise, the Rothschilds were confined to the dividends that could be directly extracted from the tramway company. It was largely for this latter reason that the international shareholders who dominated the company were deeply disturbed by a high cost structure that ate directly into profit margins.

The City & Suburban Co's profit margins between 1891 and 1898 was certainly worthy of concern. In three of those years it paid no dividend at all, while in the remaining period it declared a dividend which averaged out at only a little above five per cent. While such profits might arguably have been suited to a public utility, they were less than satisfactory for a private company in search of profit – especially one that had increased its capital from £125 000 to £210 000 in 1894. That City & Suburban was then still able to raise more capital on the strength of such a mediocre business performance revealed the extent to which there was a large speculative component in dealings in the company's shares before 1896. Especially during the early 1890s, shareholders in Europe had repeatedly seen modestly successful horse-drawn tramways profitably converted into electric systems based on the 'trolley'. The wonder of electricity not only cut costs by between 30 and 40 per cent, but also helped expand gross receipts for tramway companies by enabling them to provide a faster, more efficient and more frequent service for the travelling public.[12] It was largely this – the belief that the *Volksraad* would soon sanction the conversion from animal power to electricity – that continued to ensure European support for City & Suburban shares during the early 1890s.

In Johannesburg, the directors of the company were forced to nurture this belief, at first simply to maintain the short-term speculative buoyancy of the share market but later, and more urgently, out of a genuine desire to reduce costs and increase profits, and by so doing secure the long-term value of its appreciating shares. It was this set of overlapping reasons that twice within five years prompted the City & Suburban directors to approach Kruger's government for permission to electrify their tramway system. In 1891 their request was quickly dismissed, but in 1895 the State President, while again turning down their application, took time to explain that he was most reluctant to sacrifice a valued Boer produce market to electricity and higher company profit margins.[13] Neither of these refusals did the company much harm on the stock market, the shareholders choosing to interpret these dismissals from Pretoria as evidence of ambition being delayed rather than denied. Under these circumstances the level of City & Suburban shares remained high – right up to 1896.

Early in 1896 a group of four speculators – J P B Lombard, P J Botha,

F G de Beer, and a Californian named William G Keller – first saw their own vision of an electric tramway and the profits which it could produce. Since central Johannesburg was already served by a horse-drawn tram, however, the Lombard quartet was forced into composing an imaginative variation on a theme of urban transport. The group thus devised a scheme for an electric tramway which, while basically serving the ten-mile area *surrounding* Johannesburg, would also be linked to the city centre through two lines of access. The logic behind this seemingly strange idea only became slightly more apparent when it was understood that the system was to carry goods as well as passengers. But once it was further explained that the tramway was also to be linked to a system of low rates and free storage in the city centre for farmers conveying their produce to market, the whole idea seemed to assume a rounder and more rational form.

A scheme such as that proposed by Lombard and his colleagues would have held obvious attractions for the burghers of the South African Republic. As one contemporary observer noted:

> The gain to them would have been great, for it would have enabled their ox waggons to discharge their load ten miles outside the town and return homewards, instead of having to complete the journey and keep the oxen outspanned without food and water twenty-four hours on the market square.[14]

Armed with the nucleus of an idea that would have a clear appeal to the farmers, the speculators now turned their attention to Pretoria.

When the Lombard proposal was first put to the State President and his Executive Committee early in July 1896, Kruger was at once enthusiastic. 'The feature in the project that appealed to him most strongly', wrote someone who was closely involved in the negotiations, was 'the provision for the opening up of the Johannesburg market to the farmers.'[15] The State President was thus perfectly willing to envisage an elaborate two-tier transport system in the mining town – an inner core served by horse-drawn trams for the exclusive use of passengers, and a surrounding electric system which, while it would also carry passengers, would be largely devoted to carrying Boer produce to the market.[16] Both sections of such a system would have the merit of being of direct benefit to burgher agricultural production, and for this reason Kruger and his closest colleagues believed that they would have little difficulty in persuading the *Volksraad* to endorse the granting of such a concession. While giving the scheme his blessing, however, the State President also took the precaution of asking Lombard and his colleagues to deposit a sum of £5 000 in the National Bank as an indication of their good faith. It was in the course of their search for this money that the speculators, not surprisingly, found their way to the Johannesburg offices of the *Banque Française de l'Afrique de Sud.*

The French Bank, which had been founded in the early 1890s at the instigation of the local French Consul, Georges Aubert, had a reputation for being well connected and willing to look beyond mining for profit. Besides modest interests in local secondary enterprise, the *Banque Française* had also had the past good fortune of having made a highly profitable investment in one of Kruger's concessions – indeed, its local manager, Henri Duval, served on the board of Hatherley Distillery.[17] Furthermore, one of the most powerful principals in the French Bank, Baron de Gunzburg of Paris, had more than a passing interest in tramways during the mid 1890s.[18] For these and other reasons the *Banque Française*, on the strength of the promised concession, granted Lombard and his partners the necessary £5 000 which was duly deposited in the National Bank.[19]

With these preliminaries behind them, Lombard and his colleagues now proceeded to float a company through which they raised the capital which would ultimately turn the scheme into a reality. Nearly all the shares in this new enterprise were bought by a 30-member-strong syndicate in the United States of America. It was probably William Keller who succeeded in getting much of this financial support from his native state of California, but other shareholders also subscribed from as far apart as New York, Massachusetts, Kansas, Nevada and Montana.[20] At least £17 000 of this capital was soon spent in having routes surveyed for the electric tram in Johannesburg, and in orders for plant and equipment from the United States.

The first rumours of all this activity centred around the possibility of a new electric tram system for Johannesburg shook the directors of the City & Suburban Co rigid. They immediately realised that if the Lombard concession were granted and ratified, then the value of their own concession would be dramatically reduced, and that they would instantly forfeit the speculative support of the European shareholders which they had so long enjoyed. The chairman of the company, Julius Berlein, at once bought these considerations to the attention of Kruger's Executive Committee. On 18 July 1896 he wrote a lengthy letter to the State Secretary, F W Reitz, pleading that if any party had a moral right to the use of electricity then it was the City & Suburban Co, and further pointing out that if the Lombard concession were granted, then it would have the most serious repercussions for his European shareholders.[21] Berlein's approach to Pretoria proved ineffectual, and within weeks he was made to pay for his lack of success with his job. In August 1896 the City & Suburban Co, in a desperate attempt to shore up its position, appointed C S Goldmann as its new chairman.

Charles Goldmann personally went to Pretoria in order to impress on the State Secretary the large amount of foreign capital at stake in the company which now owned the first government tramway concession. Reitz, as befitted a cautious and correct bureaucrat, responded by calling for a list detailing all the names and holdings of European investors in the company. This information Goldmann handed to the State Secretary as soon as he was able to.[22] By then, however, it was already too late. Rumour of the Lombard concession had become public knowledge, and in two weeks' trading, between 12 and 23 September 1896, £125 000 was written off the stock exchange value of City & Suburban shares.[23]

This was a blow from which the Johannesburg tramway company never fully recovered, although Goldmann and his colleagues continued to make strenuous efforts to salvage the situation. A deluge of letters and telegrams from the French and Belgium governments now poured onto the State Secretary's desk, all urging that the Lombard concession be refused, and that the City & Suburban Co he given the right to electrify its lines.[24] In October Goldmann again asked the government for permission to convert his company's system from horse-drawn tram to trolley – this time attempting to coax compliance out of Kruger and his colleagues by offering the state a share in the company's subsequent profits.[25] But neither the stick of foreign pressure nor the carrot of financial incentive would make the State President and his Executive Committee budge. On 4 November 1896 a contract for the Johannesburg electric tram systems was entered into by the ZAR government with the Lombard group representing the American syndicate.

But if Goldman's appeals did not catch the attention of those higher up in the government, then they were certainly heard by those lower down in the echelon with their ears closer to the ground. The *Volksraad* had for some time been disturbed by the State President's concessions policy, and in 1895 had gone so far as to appoint a commission to enquire into the matter.[26] Members of the *Raad* now became concerned lest the besieged position of the City & Suburban Co culminate in the loss of a substantial market for burgher agricultural producers. Moreover, they felt constrained by the fact that the Lombard concession would operate in damaging opposition to the horse-drawn tramway company which they had fully examined and exonerated in the previous year. Thus, when the *Volksraad* met in December 1896, it narrowly passed a resolution denying Kruger's right to issue the electric tram concession independently. This political impasse heralded the advent of a new and protracted round of lobbying by all the parties concerned.[27] When the Lombard concession finally came up for ratification in July 1897 the members of the *Volksraad* – led by Messrs Labuschagne and Van Niekerk – again defeated the Executive Committee's proposal for an electric tramway system by 12 votes to 11.[28]

This defeat in the South African Republic's debating chambers left the

American syndicate thoroughly stranded amidst its substantial preliminary capital outlay. Over a year later – in October 1898 – William Keller
and his Californian cohorts were still unsuccessfully attempting to
recover their £5 000 deposit in the National Bank through the offices of
the United States Consul in Pretoria.[29] The City & Suburban Co, although
still in business, was in bad shape. Not only had it already lost a chairman, but in 1897 continental investors, unhappy with the way that earlier events in the Transvaal had tended to pass them by, had insisted on
the company opening offices in Brussels and Paris to keep the shareholders better informed.[30] Some of the first new information which those
shareholders received was not good. In the wake of the rinderpest epidemic and a pronounced increase in the price of forage, the company
issued no dividend at all in 1898. By the following year Belgian investors
were so concerned about the value of the shares that they had acquired
four years earlier, at 50 shillings each, that they sent a European tramways expert out to Johannesburg to investigate fully the operations of
the City & Suburban Co.[31] This commission exonerated the company and
pointed out that within the limitations imposed by the horse-drawn
tram, it was functioning as well as could be expected. It was by this and
other means in the late 1890s that shareholders in Brussels and Boston
alike made an elementary but painful financial discovery. In the Boer
Republic urban transport was under the control of a rural bourgeoisie.

PETTY-BOURGEOIS TRANSPORT – CAB OWNERS AND
CAB DRIVERS UNDER PRETORIA'S PROTECTION

From the late 1880s onwards at least part of Johannesburg's growing
transport needs were met through the initiative of small-scale private
enterprise. Most prominent of all in this sector of the urban economy
were the owner-drivers of horse-drawn cabs. These men, who plied their
small hooded 'Cape carts' through the dusty streets in search of fares,
formed an easily identifiable group with common class interests. In 1891,
over 80 of them co-operated to establish a Cab Owners' Association
when they petitioned the local Sanitary Board for better roads and the
setting aside of cab ranks.[32] The Association continued to serve its members in this form until 1896 when the organisation was reconstituted. By
then, private transport and its linked activities had grown to form an
important part of the local economy.

When the Sanitary Board conducted a census in 1896 it revealed that
there were 80 cab owners and 700 cab drivers resident within a three-
mile radius of the Market Square. In practice this figure was likely to be
substantially higher since most cab owners tended to keep their stables

further out of town, and a closer appreciation of the actual numbers directly involved in the business can be gauged from the fact that, in the same year, the Sanitary Board dealt with over 1 200 applications for cab-driving licences.[33] On its own, however, even the latter figure gives a misleading idea of the size and importance of the cab trade in Johannesburg. In order to get a more complete picture of the petty-bourgeois transport sector it would be necessary to include at least some of the 8 stable keepers, 16 farriers, 16 horse traders, 18 carriage trimmers, 26 coach builders, 43 harness makers, 70 produce merchants, 165 grooms, 325 stable boys and 504 blacksmiths who, in 1896, served cabbies in the city centre.[34]

Throughout the 1890s, but more especially so before 1896, the ranks of the Johannesburg cabbies contained within them men drawn from several different national, cultural and racial backgrounds. From scattered fragments it is known that a small number of these, perhaps between six and twelve, were black. Simon Untembu, for example, left Weenen in Natal in 1889 in order to take up cab driving in the city, and in the course of so doing deserted his wife and children. Untembu might have been alone in his attempt to get away from his family commitments, but he was certainly not alone in his desire to lead an independent economic existence. By 1894 there were sufficient black cabbies plying between the location and the town for them to ask the Sanitary Board to set aside a special rank for them. Although the large majority of their customers were fellow blacks, these cabbies – except when they were legally prevented from doing so during the smallpox outbreak of 1893 – also took fares from whites as and when they could find them. It was this practice of also touting for white customers that led a section of the local press, in the depression year of 1897, to demand that they be refused licences – a rather misguided way of trying to force them out of business, since the Sanitary Board had in any case always declined to lend them legal recognition in this manner. Despite a continuing measure of white hostility and some ambiguity surrounding their legal status, these black cabbies remained in business right up to the advent of British rule in the Transvaal.[35]

More prominent, more legally protected, and certainly more acceptable to the racist white community, were the numerous Coloured cabbies of Johannesburg with their allegedly 'inborn knowledge of horses, and their civility to superiors'.[36] These Coloured Muslims, so-called 'Malays', had made their way from Kimberley and Cape Town in increasing numbers after the discovery of gold, and by the mid-1890s there must have been between 200 and 300 of them at work as cabbies in the city. Although some of these immigrants may have been drawn to the unsympathetic South African Republic by the opening up of new opportunities in the horse-drawn tram service or cab driving, it seems at least as possible that others were forced out of the Cape by increasing talk and implementation of a policy of tramway electrification in the 1890s.[37] But whatever their initial motivation, cabbies from the Abdulla, Dollie, Domingo, Kamalaer and Salie families were amongst those who continued to play an important, albeit declining role, in Johannesburg's urban transport over the succeeding 25 years.[38]

In addition to these black and Coloured drivers, the city was also largely served by a cosmopolitan collection of white cabbies in the years before the South African War. Although generally more socially secure than their fellow-drivers in the European-dominated community, these white cabbies were nevertheless also susceptible to a measure of the prevailing prejudices – in their case dependent on their ethnic origins and their ability to communicate fluently with their passengers. Most acceptable were those English speakers drawn from Britain or the Cape Colony who, in the early 1890s, appear to have dominated the ranks of the white cabbies. Less acceptable were the growing number of Afrikaners who took to cab driving in the mid-1890s, and least acceptable were the first small number of Polish or Russian Jews – 'Peruvians' – who started to become cabbies between 1897 and 1899.[39]

Some of these white drivers, as in the case of their Coloured predecessors, were possibly drawn into petty-bourgeois enterprise by new economic possibilities during the early years of Johannesburg. From the mid-1890s, however, cab driving – for reasons that will transpire later – offered fewer rewards, and from then on it was likely to be hardship in a former occupation rather than financial opportunity as a cabby that forced new entrants into the profession. The arrival of the Natal railway on the Witwatersrand in 1895, as well as the locust, drought and rinderpest plagues of 1896-7, combined to attack the livelihood of transport drivers and poor farmers, and assisted in pushing them off the land and into the towns. For some of these destitute Afrikaners, equipped as they were with rural skills in the use of horse and cart, cab driving must have presented itself as one of the few ways of leading an independent economic existence in an otherwise hostile urban environment.[40] Similarly, it was a combination of skills previously acquired in the villages of Eastern Europe, and the necessity of finding a new way of earning a living after the Rand illicit liquor trade started to decline that forced the poorest Jewish immigrants to turn to cab driving after 1897.[41]

Despite their very diverse origins and the distinctive paths that they had followed in their entry into the transport business, the Johannesburg cabbies displayed a significant degree of class solidarity during most of the pre-war period. While it is true that the black and Coloured cabbies never played a part in the formal proceedings of the Cab Owners' Association, they were nevertheless fully incorporated into all the organised approaches that were made to the authorities. When the cabbies combined to approach the Sanitary Board in 1891, British, Dutch and Coloured drivers did not hesitate to sign a joint petition – at least one of the latter group signing in Arabic. Even after the Jameson Raid, when it would be reasonable to expect a certain amount of hostility between Boer and Briton, there was every sign of substantial co-operation, and in December 1896 African, Afrikaner, English and Coloured cabbies again combined to direct a common appeal to the State President and his colleagues as 'protectors of the working classes'. On the eve of the South African War, in February 1899, class interest was still strong enough for most of the prominent British, Dutch and Jewish cab owners to unite in an appeal to the town council.[42]

While some of this class solidarity undoubtedly derived simply from the pragmatic sharing of common economic interests in periods of stress, the bonds between the cab drivers were also strengthened by community ties throughout the 1890s. Most of those involved in the cab-driving business chose to keep their stables and equipment in Fordsburg from which they had easy access to the city centre and the forage supplies of Market Square. This meant that cabbies not only spent a considerable amount of time on the rank together, but they also tended to live in the same working-class suburb and to frequent the same recreational haunts. Thus, when their professional association was reconstituted in its new form in 1896 it was formally known as the 'Fordsburg Vigilance and Cab Owners' Association', and its meetings were frequently held in the Avenue Beer Hall of J Zeeman, a local publican who also operated a fleet of cabs.[43]

Although Fordsburg clearly formed the heart of cabby-country, the constituency also merged and extended into the adjacent areas of the 'Malay Camp', Brickfields and Vrededorp, where many of the poorer Coloured and Afrikaner cab divers lived.[44] The Fordsburg Vigilance and Cab Owners' Association recognised this, and through appointing prominent local Afrikaners such as S Venter, F W Axsel and J W Stegmann as office-bearers, allowed Dutch-speaking cabbies to identify with their professional association.[45] The fact that as burghers these latter members enjoyed the franchise, and that as a class cabbies were large and conspicuous consumers of Boer produce, combined to give the Cab Association considerable political muscle which the cab drivers used to defend themselves within the changing economic climate of the 1890s.

The early 1890s, marked as they were by the rapid growth of population in the mining town and the increased call for intra-city transport after the arrival of the railway in 1892 and 1895, were largely good years for Johannesburg's cabbies.[46] This relatively prosperous era, however, came to a rather prompt halt in 1896. While the general recession that followed on the Raid partly accounted for this, it was a series of more specifically aimed blows that did most to hurt the cab trade. Talk of introducing the electric trolley to the Rand simply alarmed the cabbies, but the actual extension of the horse-drawn tram line by 25 per cent in 1896, and the growing popularity of the bicycle amongst the working class in the same year, did immediate and lasting damage to their business.[47] Then, as if these new structural demands were somehow not enough, the cabbies were also asked to withstand the higher prices for horses and forage that came after the rinderpest. The cumulative effect of these blows was almost to halve the ranks of the cabbies. Whereas there were 1 200 licensed cab drivers in the town at the beginning of 1896, by the end of the following year there were only 700 cabbies left in the profession. This, as one local newspaper put it, was 'staggering shrinkage'.[48]

The Cab Owners' Association remained passive throughout much of this assault since the large and powerful economic forces that lay behind it were clearly beyond the sway of small-scale transport operators. The Association was, however, more inclined to accept and resist any additional challenges that might come its way during such troubled times. The most notable of such challenges in the mid-1890s came from a body that was well within the fighting weight of the organised cab drivers – the Johannesburg Sanitary Board.

In the period of prosperity that immediately preceded the Jameson Raid, the local authorities were put under considerable pressure by citizens who felt that cabbies were extracting extortionate fares from the travelling public. It was largely in response to these complaints that the Sanitary Board drafted a new set of regulations to govern the cab trade in late 1895. The draft regulations, which were referred to Pretoria for government approval in the normal manner, reduced the full fare for any second passenger on a journey by 50 per cent, but attempted partially to redress the balance by allowing cabbies to make a seasonal surcharge of 50 per cent on night fares between April and October.[49] The full significance of these proposed fare changes did not immediately strike the cab drivers in the balmy and prosperous summer days of 1895. When they made their appearance in the *Government Gazette* in the cooler and changed economic conditions of autumn 1896, however, they immediately concentrated the cab drivers' minds. Early in May – some two months before the regulations were due to be enforced – several of the more farsighted cab owners met in central Johannesburg and decided to send a deputation to the local authorities in an attempt to get the proposed tariffs amended.[50] This manoeuvre bought the cabbies time, but it did not bring them success. The Sanitary Board, more anxious than ever to deliver some relief to its constituency during the recession, was in no mood to listen to cabby complaints and dismissed the deputation's pleas.

By the time that the regulations appeared for a second time in the

Gazette in early September 1896, the recession had deepened and there was more widespread concern amongst the cabbies. This time a meeting of between 200 and 300 cab owners, held at the Mynpacht Hotel in Fordsburg, decided to bypass the local authorities and appeal directly to the State President and his Executive Committee.[51] The Sanitary Board immediately countered this move with its own representations, and found an unexpected ally in the pro-government *Standard and Diggers' News* which now also made an editorial call for the removal of the 50 per cent night surcharge.[52] Kruger and his colleagues, already beset with the more urgent problems surrounding the Lombard concession and the City & Suburban Tramway Co, nevertheless listened attentively to the cab drivers' submissions and promised to consider the Johannesburg tariffs.

From this point on the cab drivers never let the initiative slip from their grasp. They followed up the first deputation to Pretoria with a second, and kept up the pressure in the interim by sending Kruger and his colleagues a telegram. When neither of these supplementary measures produced a speedy decision, they set about organising a further petition that was signed by drivers of all colours and religious persuasions. This latter document they chose to present to the State President and the Executive Committee in December 1896 – that is, at exactly the time that the *Volksraad* was delivering its rebuke to Kruger over the Lombard concession, and expressing its fears about the possibility of a declining forage market on the Witwatersrand. By January of the following year the triumph of the cab drivers was assured, and in March 1897 the Sanitary Board was forced to revert to the schedule of tariffs that had operated in the city before the Jameson Raid.[53] To add insult to local-authority injury, Kruger not only restored the full fare for second passengers, but also allowed the cabbies to continue to make the 50 per cent surcharge on night fares.[54] Thus, in the mid-1890s Johannesburg's citizens discovered, as did others elsewhere, that in the Boer Republic urban transport was ultimately under the control of a rural bourgeoisie.

The cab drivers, through the tacit development of a class alliance with agricultural producers in the countryside, had unquestionably managed to score a notable victory over the local Sanitary Board and its constituents.[55] While this success largely derived from the exercise of orthodox political skills, it also owed much to the degree of unity which the cab-owning petty bourgeoisie had been able to display during a period of economic crisis. It was the presence of this overriding element of class solidarity amongst the cabbies that made their struggle of 1896-7 unique. For, at the very moment when the cabbies succeeded in uniting in common cause, the logic of capital set to work within their trade – ever increasing the division between owner and driver, and relentlessly fragmenting the petty bourgeoisie along more fundamental class cleavages.

Especially after 1896, the basic differences that divide employer from employee could be detected in the cab trade.

Cab owners – as distinct from owner-drivers – had formed part of Johannesburg's transport business since its very earliest days. In 1890 there were already five operators who owned sufficient cabs to make it worth their while to pay for individual entries in the local trade directory. Although it is difficult to estimate how many cabs such early owners kept on the streets, it is known that one of them, J de Vries, operated nine such vehicles in 1891. By the middle of the decade there were still only a half-dozen cab proprietors in the city and the largest of these, the American, Samuel Thornton, ran a sufficiently complex cab and livery stable business to necessitate employing a full-time manager.[56] However, despite the presence of these features, the cab trade still remained overwhelmingly dominated by owner-drivers throughout this period, and for this the Cape cart was largely responsible.

The small, two-wheeled Cape cart, drawn by a single horse, was in many respects ideally suited to the requirements of the hundreds of independently operating cabbies in early Johannesburg. Its outstanding virtue, of course, was its cheapness, and it was this factor, as much as any other, that lay behind the initial expansion of the private transport sector. For a capital outlay of £35-50 any prospective cabby could acquire a Cape cart as well as the necessary equipment and team of two horses that were required alternatively to service any hard-working cab. The simple design and modest size of the cart facilitated the rapid and easy harnessing of the horse, and by so doing reduced stable delays for the versatile man who wished to be a cabby. In addition, the vehicle had the added attraction of being relatively easy to clean and maintain. From the passenger's point of view, however, the Cape cart had less to commend its use as a cab. The cart was not particularly comfortable, it was fairly open and therefore exposed to the elements, and both ascent and descent from it were made difficult by its high body.[57] But while Johannesburg remained a largely male-dominated mining town not even these disadvantages could detract from the Cape cart's overriding utility as a cab.

The problem for the cart cabbies was, however, that the rough mining community of early Johannesburg started to give way to a more diversified and stabilised society in the mid-1890s, and that as this happened so their clientele changed. The arrival of the railways brought more women to the town, just as the workers started to desert the cabs for the bicycle or the City & Suburban tram. At about the same time, sizeable pockets of mercantile, trading and other groups started to congeal as a middle class in the society, and so came to supplement the small but ever-present stratum of truly wealthy families in the city. For the majority of people in these new categories, etiquette and class snobbery dictated that a 'proper' cab rather than a mere cart be called for when town transport was required.[58] It was this greater demand for comfort, style and elegance that ultimately proved to be the undoing of the old Cape cart.

By the mid-1890s coach builders and carriage trimmers in the city were already producing – in considerable numbers – the two vehicles that increasingly met the new demands of the cab trade. Of these, the most sought-after and expensive model was the Landau, which sported a fully enclosed carriage with glass windows, blinds and curtains. More widely used, however, was the cheaper Victoria with its well-sprung low body that could, if necessary, be completely covered by a retractable hood.[59] While both of these four-wheelers had the advantage of being able to carry more passengers, they had the disadvantage of having to be drawn by two animals – something which necessitated the acquisition and maintenance of *two* pairs of cab horses. This in turn meant that by 1898 the cost of a complete new turn-out was of the order of £200 – that is, about four times the previous price that had to be paid for entry into the cab trade.[60] Moreover, the cost of maintenance of a Victoria or Landau was higher than for a Cape cart, and it was said that such cabs required two to three hours of labour each morning before they were ready to be put on the rank.[61]

Capital costs and recurrent expenditure on this scale were probably beyond the financial reach of most independent cabbies in 'normal' times, let alone in the distinctly adverse economic conditions that generally prevailed after the Jameson Raid. Thus, although under some public pressure to convert to the fashionable new four-wheelers, many of the small operators desperately clung to their old economic life-line of the Cape cart, and by 1899 the unsympathetic *Standard and Diggers' News* was complaining loudly and calling for the 'removal of the weird procession of monstrosities that disgrace many parts of the town'.[62] Others, while they still had access to limited savings, sold their carts and proceeded to hire fully-equipped Victorias from Thornton's or Stegmann's at £14 per week – a precarious way of earning a living that was said to yield a 'profit' of between £2 and £3 per week. For a small but growing number of cabbies, however, the loss of the Cape cart heralded an unceremonious entry into the ranks of the working class. In return for 'board and lodging' and cash wages of between 40 and 60 shillings per week, these men sold their services as cab drivers to those proprietors who had survived the economic crisis of the mid-1890s.[63] As the South African War approached the Johannesburg cab trade was steadily splitting into its component parts of capital and labour – a process that was to reach its fullest, and perhaps most appropriate manifestation, in the years after 1900.

URBAN TRANSPORT UNDER THE HEGEMONY OF MINING
CAPITALISM, 1900-1914
Johannesburg's tramways – from private company to public utility

When British armed forces occupied Johannesburg in 1900 the city and its government were not – for the first time since the discovery of gold – ultimately subject to the approval of a rural bourgeoisie located in the Transvaal capital. Under the new dispensation the British government, in alliance with the Rand mining capitalists, came to exercise authority over the city and its inhabitants, and nowhere was the impact of the emerging industrial state more clearly visible than in the fields of urban planning and public transport. Any full appreciation of the changing role, function and ownership of Johannesburg's tramways, therefore, has to be firmly located in an understanding of the capitalist vision of the Witwatersrand that developed during the period of reconstruction.

Within a month of the occupation of the town, on 31 May 1900, a member of the Royal Engineers – Major W O'Meara – was appointed Acting Mayor of Johannesburg. A military man, in what was for some months essentially a military town, O'Meara was at first not unduly concerned about the fate of the city's former transport system. As a former intelligence officer, however, the Mayor would not have failed to notice that there was at least one 'war correspondent' around who *did* have a lively interest in the future role of trams in the town. As early as July 1900 C S Goldmann, in his interim guise as journalist, was hard at work representing the interests of the City & Suburban Co and attempting to pave 'the way for reviving electric tramway rights'.[64] But the chairman of the horse-drawn tram company was not the only one quick off the mark since, elsewhere, others too were already at work. In Cape Town, Lord Milner and Percy FitzPatrick – with no direct interest in tramways per se – were busy discussing the need for a full-scale investigation into all the concessions which had been granted by the Kruger government.[65] The resulting commission which, amongst others, investigated the Johannesburg Tramway Co sat down to its initial deliberations in the closing months of 1900.

The swift preliminary planning and manoeuvring by the incoming administration and its allies was further accelerated when the first British residents were allowed to return to the Transvaal in the early months of the following year. Milner, anxious that the path to civilian rule on the Witwatersrand should be made as smooth as possible, now looked around for an assistant who could help O'Meara in his role as Mayor of Johannesburg. It was in the course of this search that the Oxford old-boy network put forward the name of a promising candidate named Lionel Curtis, and it was this young man who did much to determine what the future role of tramways in the city would be.[66]

In several respects Curtis was an obvious choice for the position of Acting Town Clerk in the largest city of the newly conquered territory. Curtis had seen service as a despatch rider in the early months of the South African War and was thus already familiar with some aspects of what was a complex society. He also possessed a series of more pertinent qualifications, however, which could be directly harnessed to the job in hand. In the late 1890s he had gained insight into the problems of working-class housing and social engineering in Britain by serving on one of Octavia Hill's famous committees in London. This experience had left Curtis with a clear understanding of the importance of the geography of class and its related aspect of social control.[67] Moreover, as former Private Secretary to Lord Welby, Chairman of the London County Council, he had also had the opportunity to study carefully the official planning of local administration in a great city – and that in a country which in the late nineteenth century prided itself on the fact that it led the world in municipal government.

Thus in March and April 1901, Curtis and O'Meara – acting as complementary social and civil engineers – set about drafting detailed proposals about the future nature and government of Johannesburg.[68] The central consideration that underpinned these early discussions was most explicit. There was a clearly expressed need to avoid the emergence of a sharply demarcated central working-class area with its frequently associated problems of markedly different rating values, high rentals, and the development of an aggressive class-consciousness. Curtis had seen the difficulties which the absence of such a policy had produced in the East and West Ends of London, and was most anxious to avoid the potential for conflict which it carried within it. As the Acting Town Clerk later put it in an official version:

> What we have to fear and avoid is the creation of a similar state of things in Johannesburg – where the area north of the reef would be covered by the residences of the well-to-do, and by streets of shops supplying their wants – while the area south of the reef would be inhabited solely by the poorer employees of the mines and by an inferior class of local shopkeepers. There are, therefore, strong reasons based upon the broadest political ground for securing now and for ever that the various townships shall radiate from their economic centres, that each class shall bear the political and social burdens which should fall to their lot as members of an economic whole, and that one class should not be allowed to separate its life from another class with which it is bound up by an inseparable economic tie.[69]

In order to achieve this objective, Curtis and O'Meara proposed that Johannesburg's boundaries be substantially extended, that the population be more widely scattered within the new area, and that the design be made practical through the integrating linkages which a comprehensive tramway system would provide for.[70]

The principles involved in this grand design were approved by Milner and within weeks of its formulation the two original planners had the opportunity to implement a small part of their blueprint when they drafted a proclamation extending the city's boundaries from five to nine square miles. For the Acting Town Clerk, more accustomed to the measured political pace of a constitutional democracy, the speed and power of this form of government proved exhilarating. 'Just at present,' Curtis wrote in his diary on 25 April 1901, 'one gets things done with a stroke of the pen that in England would entail an act of Parliament and an exhaustive parliamentary enquiry.'[71] The full scheme, however, called for a municipal area embracing 82 square miles, and this could not – without raising serious political and economic problems – simply be achieved 'with a stroke of the pen'. This latter extension called for a more subtle and flexible approach.

As soon as the first nominated Town Council was appointed in May, Curtis and Mayor O'Meara immediately set about educating its members and soliciting their support for the proposals which the two had earlier drafted. The Acting Town Clerk, in particular, impressed upon his council members the need to include the mining property that lay to the south of the reef in any plans for a greater consolidated Johannesburg. Curtis's success in these efforts was only briefly interrupted by the *Report of the Concessions Commission* in June 1901. The commissioners, aware of the large amounts of European capital tied up in the City & Suburban Co, were unwilling to deny the validity of the original concession and recommended that the horse-drawn tramway enterprise be recognised and come to terms with.[72] The town councillors took this potential hurdle in their stride, and in September officially endorsed the 'Memorandum on the Present and Future Boundaries of Johannesburg' and had Curtis send a copy to the Chamber of Mines for its 'comment'.[73]

The Chamber of Mines was at first deeply suspicious about the memorandum and the purpose of its authors. Harold Strange and most of his fellow capitalists were opposed to any southward extension of the city's boundaries which would include mining property and thereby make the companies liable to pay rates and incur other financial obligations. The Chamber thus reacted negatively and with some hostility when it responded to the Town Council in October. Curtis and O'Meara, eager for any fray in which they enjoyed such powerful covert support, immediately issued a sharp rejoinder on behalf of the Council. Then, just when the stage seemed set for a long and acrimonious intra-ruling class battle, Milner intervened. Somewhat irritated by the mine owners' penny-pinching attitude, Milner now called on Percy FitzPatrick to persuade his colleagues in the industry of the long-term advantages contained in the proposal. This he proceeded to do and late in 1901 the Chamber of Mines withdrew its objections to the scheme.[74]

With this major obstacle out of the way, the Town Council now felt that it could confidently set to work on developing the necessary infrastructure for the Mayor and the Acting Town Clerk's scheme. In January 1902 it called for plans and tenders to be submitted for a new system of tramways in the city, and awarded the contracts to Messrs Mordey & Dawburn of England.[75] This time, however, the speed and swagger of the reconstruction momentum caused the Council to stumble since it failed to take sufficient cognisance of one unresolved issue – the fate of the City & Suburban Co.

C S Goldmann and his colleagues in the established tramways enterprise had been much heartened by the *Report of the Concessions Commission* in the previous year, and they now used its favourable recommendations as a base from which to fight a tenacious struggle against the new masters of the Transvaal. They constantly pressured the British administration for a decision on the fate of their company, and in June 1902 Milner, unable to avoid the issue any longer, conceded the legality of the original concession and acknowledged the right of City & Suburban to continue running horse-drawn trams in Johannesburg. The nominated Town Council, alarmed by this development, now rushed to its mentor and requested that it be granted the exclusive right to electric or mechanically worked tramways in the city. This Milner promptly did by issuing Proclamation No 39 which became law in the same month – June 1902.[76] The net effect of these decisions was simply to legalise a stalemate situation that had been developing for some time.

Both parties – the City & Suburban Co and the Town Council – now proceeded to use their respective rights as bargaining counters in an attempt to acquire the holdings of the rival since there was obviously no long-term future in two competing tramway systems within the city. When suitable terms could not be swiftly agreed upon, however, the opponents made unashamed use of the only other weapon available to them – time. The company, aware that its own operations hampered the city's planning and construction activities, hoped that any delay would increase public pressure on the Town Council and so facilitate a settlement.[77] The Council, for its part, was equally aware that the value of the horse-drawn tramway declined with each week that brought the electric trams closer, and thus looked to a sudden collapse by the company's principals. But, as so often happens in such evenly matched bouts, each contestant underestimated the other's capacity for resistance. In the end, it was only on 30 June 1904 that the Council acquired the undertaking and assets of the City & Suburban Co at a cost of £150 000.[78]

In practice, however, the price that the public were made to pay for the horse-drawn trams far exceeded the cash transaction which the Town Council negotiated. While the lengthy dealings between the Council and the company dragged on, the City & Suburban directors were understandably loath to spend any additional amounts on the maintenance or extension of the old tramway system. This meant that while the city was experiencing a rapid expansion and spread of population, its only available 'public' transport system was actually declining, and between 1903 and 1905 there was a steady decrease in the number of passengers which the horse-drawn trams carried each year. As a direct consequence of this inadequate service, many urban commuters were forced to turn to alternative forms of transport during this period. It was thus with a sense of some relief that the travelling public finally witnessed the running of the first municipal electric tram on 14 February 1906. But, although the number of passengers using the trams jumped from 3.5 million per year in 1904-5 to 14.5 million in 1906-7, the tramways offered an intermittent and restricted service for much of the period between 1906 and early 1908. Thereafter, there was a steady increase in the number of citizens making use of the electric trams and by 1914 the system was carrying over 30 million passengers annually.[79]

As soon as the Council had the nucleus of the new system established, however, it proceeded to pursue its declared policy of 'scattering' the white working population with some vigour. Aided by capital and land grants from the Malvern, Kensington and Braamfontein Estate Companies (at least one of which was wholly owned by mining capital), the Council extended the tramways to several new suburbs. Any additional capital costs which it incurred through such line extensions the Council recouped by imposing a special levy on ratepayers living in the newly connected working-class residential areas. These measures, when supplemented with a conscious policy of keeping fares relatively high until such time as the initial capital loan had been repaid, placed Johannesburg's electric tramways on a firm financial footing. In the first 14 years of its operation the new public transport system yielded a profit of over half a million pounds, and this sum was accordingly credited to the city's general funds.[80]

In summary then, it may be suggested that Johannesburg's transition from a privately owned horse-drawn tramway to an electrically operated public utility was far from smooth. It took a war, three years of hard negotiating, and a substantial cash payment to the City & Suburban Co for the reconstruction overlords to shake themselves free from a public transport system that had previously been designed to serve the needs of a rural bourgeoisie and its European capitalist partners. Once the British administrator and its industrial allies had become hegemonic, however, they made use of the urban transport system as part of a strategy of social control which was ultimately intended to reduce conflict between capital and labour. But it was during the transition between these systems that the tramways left most to be desired, and thus it was that between 1902 and 1908 there were still opportunities for a petty bourgeoisie looking to urban transport for its living.

JOHANNESBURG'S CAB TRADE IN THE POST-WAR PERIOD – RE-EMERGENCE, FRAGMENTATION AND DECLINE

As soon as significant numbers of refugees started to return to the Witwatersrand under the permit system, Johannesburg's dormant cab trade started-to revive. Indeed, so swiftly and securely did the private transport sector re-establish itself, that it is possible that by the end of 1902 there were more cabbies at work in the city than there had been in 1896. At least part of this early vitality in the post-war cab business derived from the fact that the horse-drawn tramway did not operate at all until Milner's decision in principle on the City & Suburban Co in June 1902. Thereafter, the cabbies simply reaped their share of the profits that became available during a period when the reconstruction government implemented its policy of 'scattering' the white working class whilst the public only had access to a declining horse-drawn tram service. Between 1902 and 1906, when the electric trams were introduced, there were always close on 800 licensed cab drivers in service in Johannesburg – see Table 6.[81]

But if the immediate post-war years brought the cabbies a period of great promise, then it also taxed them with its measure of problems. As might be expected in the wake of a war, forage and horses were in markedly short supply for some time, and throughout 1902-3 prices remained at record levels. In addition, the cost of repairs and mainte-nance both increased significantly after the war. The cost of having a horse shod, for example, rose from 6/- in 1899 to 8/- in 1903, and it was also in the latter year that it was estimated that the overhead costs for maintaining a four-wheeler cab and its horses ran to 40/- per day. As always, these costs pressed hardest on those who lacked capital, and under these conditions there was further consolidation in the trade as several large proprietors bought out many of the smaller and more vul-nerable cabbies. By early 1903 the luxurious Victorias cruised the streets of Johannesburg, virtually in total command of the cab trade, and hope-lessly outnumbering the three small Cape carts that somehow still sur-vived on the ranks.[82]

Not all the independent cabbies fell meekly before the economic onslaught, however; many simply passed on these higher costs to their customers and by so doing attempted to keep their profit margins intact. In the six months before the horse-drawn tramway resumed service, but also for a considerable time thereafter, there were consistent public complaints about cabbies refusing to accept engagements which they did not consider to be lucrative enough, or of drivers demanding excess fares. These practices frequently brought the cabbies into conflict with their clients, and during nine days in early 1902 no fewer than ten such complaints were lodged with the police. It was also in this same period that the most notorious case of such conflict was deliberately drawn to the public's attention by a local evening newspaper. On 13 January 1902 a leading Johannesburg socialite and member of the nominated Town Council, Colonel J Dale Lace, first assaulted an Afrikaner cabby named Theron for what he construed to be wilful disobedience, and then drove off with the man's cab. When Lace subsequently appeared in court and was found guilty of assault, *The Star* – through a series of provocative articles and editorials – attempted to justify the Colonel's characteristic bullying behaviour by pointing to public grievances against the cab trade.[83]

Table 6 Number of licensed cab drivers and cabs in Johannesburg, 1904-14

Six-month period ending	Number of cabbies licensed	Number of cabs licensed	Number of cabbies per licensed cab
31.12.04	945	575	1.64
30.6.05	–	587	–
31.12.05	799	618	1.29
30.6.06	853	530	1.61
31.12.06	606	406	1.64
30.6.07	623	417	1.49
31.12.07	558	368	1.51
30.6.08	523	373	1.40
31.12.08	490	367	1.34
30.6.09	476	363	1.31
31.12.09	389	337	1.15
30.6.10	437	328	1.33
31.12.10	424	344	1.23
30.6.11	485	368	1.32
31.12.11	483	378	1.28
30.6.12	477	367	1.30
31.12.12	401	336	1.19
30.6.13	400	384	1.04
31.12.13	349	277	1.26
30.6.14	343	298	1.15
31.12.14	302	297	1.02

It was partly because of such cases of conflict, but more particularly for the fundamental reason that the cab trade assumed an enhanced importance and power in the years before the introduction of the electric tram, that the reconstruction engineers regularly and vigorously intervened in the private transport sector. In the early months of 1902 Milner personally corresponded with members of the Refugee Committees at the coastal cities in an attempt to facilitate the prompt return of 'genuine cab proprietors'. But this benign and accommodating imperial involvement was not typical, and most of the state's intervention during this early period was directed towards 'tidying up' and controlling the cab trade. On two occasions within 12 months the Town Council debated elaborate draft regulations to govern the cabbies and their business, while the state obligingly turned these recommendations into law through the proclamation of Government Notice No 685 of 1902. Indeed, so extensive were these new by-laws, that the *Transvaal Leader* was moved to complain that 'the poor cabby has been legislated out of his business'.[84] What the *Leader* considered as ironic comment, however, was less than funny. For the most vulnerable cabbies in a racist state there was no humour in such a statement, only a chilling reality.

In the second week of January 1902 the reconstruction authorities arbitrarily withdrew the licences of all black cabbies operating in the city. When their documents were reissued a little later the cab drivers were informed that in future they would no longer be allowed to transport European passengers. 'At the stroke of a pen', Curtis and his colleagues created the 'second class cab' – a classification which, in the case of black cabbies, rested on the colour of the driver rather than on the quality of the vehicle or the service provided. Thus, after surviving more than a decade of legal twilight in Kruger's Republic, Johannesburg's black cabbies emerged into the unequivocal glare of formalised segregation under the Milner administration. Thereafter, the city's black cab drivers were restricted by law to accepting fares from only the poorest section of the urban population – their fellow Africans.[85]

It was this same device – the new classification – that Milner and his men employed to divide the ranks of the Malay cabbies. The 75 to 100 Coloured cabbies who owned vehicles that were considered to meet the required standard had their cabs rated 'first class', and were thus allowed to convey European passengers at the minimum rate of 2/6d per mile. The remaining cabbies, whose vehicles failed to meet the test set by the municipality's inspector, had their cabs classified as 'second class', and were thus restricted to transporting non-white passengers at the rat of 6d per mile. While the classification in this case did not derive simply from colour, since it was the cab rather than the driver that was supposedly under scrutiny, it nevertheless had the effect of penalising the poorest and most vulnerable Malays – those who had struggled hardest to make the transition from the old Cape cart to the new four-wheeled Victoria.[86] Moreover, since 'second-class' cabs were again restricted to conveying lower-income groups, it was difficult for these less fortunate Coloured drivers to accumulate sufficient capital with which to extricate themselves from their economic predicament.

In addition to these measures directed against the black and Malay cabbies, the new government also moved – in more subtle fashion – against the European drivers in its effort to rationalise and reorganise the city's cab service. Making use of the 'permit system' operating at the coastal towns, it sought to screen out unqualified or 'undesirable' white cabbies and prevent them from reaching the Rand. Its conspicuous failure in this regard, however, derived not so much from a lack of administrative zeal or skill, as from a series of complex problems that were clearly beyond its immediate influence. The manpower demands of the British army, the pace of demobilisation and the slow release of prisoners of war all combined to place experienced cabbies with a knowledge of Johannesburg in short supply. This, together with the pattern of European immigration to South Africa at the turn of the century, meant that most of those white cabbies who did find their way to the city after 1902 differed sharply in religious, cultural and class background from their predecessors in the trade.[87]

Poor East European Jews were no newcomers to South Africa. From the mid-1880s onwards oppressive Russian legislation, pogroms, demands by the Tsar's army and economic stagnation in the Pale of Settlement all had contributed to a steady flow of emigrants from Lithuania. The majority of these emigrants who made their way to the Witwatersrand were drawn from the small commercial centres situated in the agricultural areas that surrounded the larger towns of Kovno and Wilna. It was in their native Lithuania that most of these Jews acquired experience of petty trading, but a significant number of them had also been involved in the transport business – including cab driving.[88] This European background also came to reflect itself in the way in which these Lithuanians inserted themselves into the economic fabric of Johannesburg in the pre-war period – most turned to hawking and trading for a living, but a small number also took to cab driving.

After the recession of 1897 and the decline of the liquor trade, however, the poorest and most vulnerable of these Jewish immigrants were forced out of commerce and onto the Rand labour market. Shortly thereafter they were turned into wartime refugees, and it was while they were at the Cape between 1899 and 1902 that they were joined by new arrivals from Lithuania.[89] It was also during this period that most of these unskilled East European immigrants came to appreciate that their best chance of obtaining a permit for work in the Transvaal lay in presenting themselves as cab drivers. With the support and assistance of a small number of Jewish cab proprietors many of these immigrants succeeded in obtaining the necessary clearance certificates and made their way to the Witwatersrand. In Johannesburg it was this influx of new cabbies that was considered to be 'undesirable' by many of the local whites, and that was greeted with ill-concealed prejudice and contempt by the English press.

What these cabbies perhaps lacked in cash, they more than compensated for through close co-operation with their colleagues and by demonstrating a genuine concern for the wellbeing of their countrymen. Drawing from a rich Jewish cultural tradition in which the notion of *tsedaka* – social justice – played an important part, they were soon active in the many *chevras* or charitable associations on the Rand.[90] The Lithuanians rapidly discovered, however, that an enlightened social conscience alone did not provide sufficient professional protection in reconstruction Johannesburg. Anti-semitism, the Dale Lace assault, a barrage of local government legislation and a growing tendency for a few large proprietors to dominate the cab trade all persuaded the cab drivers to draw on another strand of their East European experience – that of the *Yiddisher Arbeiter Bund*, the union. Thus, when a Cab Drivers' Union (CDU) was formed in April 1902, the Jewish cabbies were amongst its most active and enthusiastic members.[91]

This move towards co-ordinated action by the drivers, together with a measure of shared apprehension about the Milner administration's moves to strictly regulate the cab trade, prodded the cab owners into action as well. In October 1902 the older and more established Cab Owners' Association was resuscitated and J Zeeman was elected as its first post-war chairman.[92] By the end of that year then, the Johannesburg cab trade had two professional associations which – amongst other things – represented divisions between older and newer immigrants, conservative and more radical elements, and capital and labour. In theory these divisions held considerable potential for conflict, but in practice they seldom produced major rifts.

One reason that lay behind the usually amicable relationship between the two associations was the fact that class differences within the trade were still not fully crystallised. A good number of owner-drivers chose to belong not to the CDU, but to the Cab Owners' Association. While such small self-employed operators had interests that differed in certain respects from those of the drivers, they were also not at one with the large cab proprietors, and this ambiguous situation tended to produce cross-cutting loyalties. At least as important a factor in reducing tension between the rival associations within the trade, however, was the fact that bonds of kinship, culture and religion tended to draw the two bodies together. Indeed, so strong were these ties by late 1904 when the CDU acquired the old Austrian Imperial Hotel premises for a social club, that in its application for a liquor licence the CDU committee made a point of stating that the building would be used by the 'Jewish Cab-owners and Drivers of Johannesburg'.[93]

It was largely this underlying unity between the CDU and the proprietors that enabled the trade to challenge Milner's nominated Town Council when it introduced Government Notice No 685 of 1902. This contentious legislation, amongst other things, made provision for the introduction of half-fares for the second and subsequent passengers on a cab journey – an old idea which the cabbies had resisted when the Sanitary Board first tried to implement it in 1896-7. On this occasion the small independent operators opposed the provision for exactly the same reason they had done six years earlier – namely, that it reduced their income. The large cab proprietors, however, had an additional reason for objecting to the clause, since its introduction came at precisely the same time that they were put under great pressure from the CDU to increase the £2 per week cash wage which they paid their drivers. This meant that the big cab owners were caught between the economic scissors of rising costs and falling revenue, and this was an argument which they successfully pressed home on the Union negotiators. Thus, when a joint meeting of the two professional associations was called to discuss the Milner proclamation on 15 January 1903, it drew more than 1 500 interested people to the Fordsburg Market Square.[94]

Partly as a consequence of this large gathering, a deputation was sent to the Town Council in order to put the cab trade's grievances. This delegation, led by CDU President W N Kingsley, put its case so forcefully and effectively that the Council agreed to withdraw virtually all those provisions in the legislation which the cabbies found objectionable. In March, Government Notice No 241 of 1903 came to replace the earlier proclamation and for the second time within a decade the organised cab trade had defeated the local authorities on the issue of tariffs. Needless to say this reversal of policy by Milner's nominees was greeted with derision and displeasure by many of the cab-users in Johannesburg.[95]

But despite the co-operation which brought about a victory on the half-fare issue, and despite the fraternity that lay behind the idea of the social club in Fox Street, there were also ongoing conflicts and tensions within the cab trade. Predictably perhaps, the most noteworthy of these differences lay between the two parties with the most divergent interests – the cab owners and their drivers. The drivers were deeply resentful of the small cash wage which they received in exchange for a working day which often averaged between 12 and 18 hours in length. As unskilled immigrants, however, they were also reluctant to confront their employers openly about this grievance. Instead, exploiting the absence of meters on their horse-drawn vehicles, the drivers made their own 'adjustments' to their wages by manipulating the amount of the takings which they handed over to the cab owner at the end of the day.[96]

The cab owners, aware of this growing practice, increased their vigilance and demanded that returning drivers hand over *all* the cash in their possession at the end of a shift. This in turn meant that drivers were often forced into handing over their 'tips' to their employers as well as their takings. The whole cash extraction ritual therefore produced great tension and resulted in heated arguments which frequently culminated in the dismissal of the cab driver. The drivers, ever resourceful, responded to this by forging themselves new licences and documents which they promptly presented to other cab proprietors in their search for alternative employment.[97] It was this smouldering post-war conflict which finally caught alight in full-scale class confrontation in 1905.

As early as January 1905 there were signs of substantial discontent in sections of the cab trade. In particular, cab drivers complained about being arrested for 'loitering' while attempting to secure a full complement of passengers for the journey to the race course at Auckland Park. At a series of mass meetings, attended by both owners and drivers, resolutions were passed requesting that the Town Council provide more cab stands, and that it provide more protection for cabbies by defining 'loitering' more precisely in the local statues. Over the next five months, however, nothing happened and the police continued to harass the drivers on race day – a most unpopular action since it disrupted the cabbies' work during a particularly busy shift on a day when they could normally look forward to a sizeable haul in 'tips'. In June 1905, the frustrated drivers again raised these grievances at a meeting, but the cab owners cautioned them about the need for patience and the importance of maintaining a united front in any further approaches that might be made to the authorities. Four weeks later – and with their grievances still unattended to – the drivers learned that the Town Council intended to introduce a new form of licence for cabbies modelled on that which was in use in London. This document, and a copy which had to be lodged with the municipal Inspector of Vehicles, had to indicate both when a driver had completed his period of employment and the reason for the termination of the contract. For many drivers, but especially for the Lithuanian cabbies, this action constituted the proverbial last straw.[98]

On 12 July the cabbies and a significant number of independent owner-drivers of cabs held an emergency meeting at Fordsburg at which the Lithuanians at once pressed for an official CDU strike until such time as all their grievances had been met. Although the Union leaders refused to give their official sanction to strike action, they and the small independent cab owners did agree to consolidate their alliance by electing a 36-man 'General Executive Committee' of cabmen. It was this committee, under the chairmanship of the 'Quiet little Napoleon of the Jehus', L Joffe, that decided that a strike should commence on the very day that the new licences were to be first issued – Saturday, 15 July 1905. Delighted with this decision, at least 300 drivers at once handed in their old licences to the Committee as an indication of their support for the strike.[99]

The strike started on a promising note for the drivers when, on the Saturday morning, a somewhat bemused Johannesburg awoke to find only six cabs plying for hire in the city. While members of the public searched for rickshaw-pullers to meet their transport needs, bands of strikers combed the city streets 'persuading' scabs about the folly of their ways and distributing handbills which outlined the cabbies' grievances and actions. At 11 o'clock hundreds of cab drivers, decked out in the distinctive colours of organised labour, met in the Fordsburg 'Dip' to take part in a procession to Von Brandis Square where they planned to hold a meeting. The strikers then marched behind the Red Flag and sang the *Marseillaise* as they made their way towards the city centre. But, at Von Brandis Square, the cab drivers met with an initial setback when they were dispersed by a contingent of mounted police even before they could commence their rally.

On the same afternoon, however, the strikers regrouped and held their meeting on the more familiar and secure ground of Avenue Road, Fordsburg. Here, the cabbies were given the cheering news that the drivers of horse-drawn buses – partly out of solidarity and partly out of fear of reprisals – had refused to convey large numbers of race-goers to Auckland Park. At the same time the strikers also listened to a warning from their leaders about the need to avoid violence – hardly inappropriate advice, since W N Kingsley of the CDU and one Mr Goldberg of the Cab Owners' Association had already been arrested for exchanging blows in a public place. That others too feared a breach of the peace by the strikers became clear later that evening when the police promptly arrested a prominent town councillor – J W Quinn – for loudly hailing a cab in Commissioner Street.[100]

Early on the following morning – Sunday – bands of strikers again roamed the city centre looking for any of the 30 drivers who had been bold enough to venture out and offer their vehicles for hire. Numerous arrests were made, for example, when Solly Levy, Harris Sollar and Harry Spencer stopped a 'non-union man's cab' in Rissik Street and used knives to slash the cushions and leather hood of the Victoria. It was in the afternoon, however, that the strikers once more gathered for a rally – this time near their base at the Moonlight Hotel in Commissioner Street. Here, a crowd of between 500 and 1 000 cab drivers and their sympathisers succeeded in blocking all traffic for several hours. But, as on the previous day, the strikers were again to be denied the right of a public meeting. No sooner did the Lithuanian founder of the short-lived Social Democratic Workers' Party – Yeshaya Israelstam – start his address to the crowd, than he was stopped by the police who asked him to produce his official authorisation to hold such a meeting.[101] By the time that Israelstam had solved this problem the crowd had dispersed, and that night the CDU instead held a meeting in the Trades Hall which was attended by about 400 drivers. At this meeting the cabbies discussed their campaign strategy and elected a deputation to wait upon representatives of the Town Council on the following day.[102]

On Monday morning, 17 July, when most of the white workers in Johannesburg again set out for their places of employment after the weekend, the cabbies were still out on strike. With transport still continuing to be seriously disrupted at the start of a working week, the attitude of both the press and public started to change significantly. Whereas the cab drivers' action had been received with some humour and amusement over the previous two days, there was now a more strident, aggressive and prejudiced tone to newspaper reports. The *Rand Daily Mail*, for example, published a list of 'Suggestions to the Municipality' which included recommendations that cabbies be made to wash and shave regularly and that they be required 'to know some English beyond "Nitchevo"'. There was also evidently some satisfaction at the fact that about two dozen strikers – most of whom were 'not of British nationality' – had been made to appear in the magistrate's court on the grounds of 'malicious damage to property' and other charges.[103]

Sensing this new mood of hostility towards the drivers, about 20 of the largest and most powerful proprietors in the Cab Owners' Association now took it upon themselves to put pressure on the city authorities to resist the strikers' demands. With a former cab proprietor and lawyer, B Alexander, acting as their spokesman, the owners sent a deputation to the Works Committee of the Town Council which strongly urged the retention of the London-style licence for cabbies. No sooner had the cab owners' delegation been dismissed, however, than the Works Committee received and granted a request to hear the cab drivers' case. L Joffe and W N Kingsley outlined what the cabbies' grievances were in general and then proceeded to argue particularly strongly that the new licences were 'on the lines of the native pass' and that they allowed 'employers who might be spiteful, the power to injure a man's character when the man did not deserve it'.[104] As far as the CDU, and the Lithuanian drivers in particular were concerned, the new licence forms had to be abandoned completely.

Caught in the crossfire of open class conflict, the Words Committee proceeded to attempt the impossible – it tried to satisfy both parties to the dispute. In order to get urban transport back to normal it immediately made full concessions to the drivers on the question of 'loitering' and on the issue of the need for more cab stands. In addition, it sought to appease the militant Lithuanians by agreeing to a change in the wording of the new licence and by assuring them that proprietors would not be allowed to enter prejudicial comments about drivers or 'secret marks' on the document. But in order to save some face and accommodate the cab owners, the Committee refused to entertain the CDU demand that the new licence be scrapped entirely.[105]

Since the Works Committee had gone so far towards meeting the cab drivers' demands, Joffe and Kingsley agreed to put the proposed concessions to the cabbies. At this point a rumour to the effect that the strike was over swept through the city, and this misinformation was given further credence by the publication of an incorrect press report. When the strikers met that night, however, they quickly dispelled such wishful thinking by voting overwhelmingly to continue their action until such time as the Council was willing to abandon the new licence entirely.[106]

On the following morning, Tuesday 18 July, between 60 and 70 owner-driven cabs appeared on the ranks, many as a result of the rumour that the strike was supposedly over. The large cab proprietors – I Moyes, N Kramer and B Davidson – immediately capitalised on this development by persuading the police to increase the number of men on duty at the cab stands. This act, which threatened to increase conflict, aroused great bitterness within the cab trade as a whole. The strikers, however, responded to it by sending out bands of roving pickets and by mid-morning they had succeeded in reducing the number of cabs plying for hire to about 20.[107]

With this successful counter-thrust behind them, and the strike entering its fourth day, Joffe and his General Executive Committee now decided to apply further pressure to the local authorities by sending a delegation of six representatives to the Inspector of Vehicles, Mr Jefferson. The Inspector, after listening to the cabbies' arguments, agreed to suspend the introduction of the new licences and proposed that the CDU again put their grievance to the full town council which was due to meet on the following afternoon. From Jefferson's words and actions it became clear to the drivers that the local authorities were about to accede to their major demand – and that the new licence be abandoned. But, as had happened once before, the story got afoot that the strike had been called off. This time the response in the trade was instant and by late afternoon close on 200 cabs were out on the streets plying for hire. For the second time that day it was left to the pickets to get the cabs and their drivers off the streets – a clear indication that sections of the trade were becoming impatient with the strike.[108]

That night, when a joint meeting of the 'small owners' and the cab drivers was held at the Moonlight Hotel, however, the Lithuanians again demonstrated that they were foremost among the ranks of the militants. In a lengthy speech delivered in Yiddish, B Slavin berated the large proprietors for their treachery in approaching the Town Council and the police in the name of the Cab Owners' Association. He was followed by yet another speaker who proposed that the owner-drivers 'leave the big cab-owners and do without them' – a development which did in fact materialise to some extent as several independent cabbies switched their affiliations to the CDU. At the end of the meeting resolutions condemning the large cab proprietors and supporting the strikers were carried 'with enthusiasm'.[109]

On Wednesday morning, 19 July – the fifth and final day of the strike – the cab drivers awoke to find themselves the subject of a vicious attack in the *Rand Daily Mail.* In an editorial the newspaper suggested that the Town Council adopt a firm stance against the strikers and that 'no licences be granted to men who are palpably little better in their appearance than the most filthy Kaffir'.[110] The effect that this verbal venom would have on members of the public and the town council undoubtedly worried the strike leaders. In addition, Joffe and Kingsley were becoming deeply concerned about the lack of strike funds and the difficulty they were experiencing in keeping non-union cabs off the streets. All of these problems contributed to making Wednesday a long and tense day for the General Executive Committee and their hardcore of Lithuanian supporters.

When the town council met in the afternoon its members at once retreated into a series of prolonged procedural manoeuvres. This intentional or unintentional filibustering took several hours, and it was late in the day before the Rand trade unionist, Peter Whiteside, managed to put the CDU's case to his fellow councillors. As evening fell, the cab drivers were still without a decision from the Council and, at this point, Joffe and his colleagues again conferred at their strike headquarters. Members of the General Executive Committee were of the opinion that the drivers were too poverty-stricken to continue the struggle, and that the effect of the strike was already starting to seriously undermine the condition of those horses that belonged to the sympathetic owner-drivers. Under the circumstances Joffe and Kingsley felt duty-bound to recommend a return of work, and to this end summoned a meeting of the strikers. In the courtyard of the Moonlight Hotel the cab drivers and the 'small owners' had already decided to return to work on the following morning when the news arrived that the town council had agreed to suspend the introduction of the new licences for a period of three months. This 'concession' was immediately interpreted as a victory by the strikers, and the celebrations in Commissioner Street lasted into the small hours of the morning.[111]

On the following day the Cab Owners' Association issued a sour 'official statement' to the press through its Secretary, J Harcourt-Stuart. The large proprietors felt that the drivers, in endeavouring to 'act without the sanction and co-operation of their masters, had made a mess of things and had alienated the sympathy of the public'.[112] But despite the Owners' opinion to the contrary, the men who came 'for the most part from downtrodden Russia' had succeeded in defending their economically precarious position with some skill and determination. The London-style licences were never reintroduced, which in effect meant that cabbies could continue to supplement their low wages by manipulating the amount of cash takings which they handed over to the proprietors. Moreover, since the Lithuanians had convincingly demonstrated their collective strength, large proprietors tended to exercise more caution in dismissing cabbies, and one consequence of the strike was the establishment of an 'Arbitration Board' which sought to settle all disputes arising between owners and drivers.[113]

Important and impressive as the strike of 1905 may have been, it also come in the twilight of the cab trade's powerful position within the local transport system. In the midst of a capitalist revolution, and without the protection which the old pre-war rural bourgeoisie afforded them, the bargaining power of those involved in horse-drawn transport was rapidly ebbing away. After 1905 the cab trade never again succeeded in halting or defeating the municipal government on any issue of substance. Indeed, thereafter – and especially between 1906 and 1909 – the cab trade declined steadily as the modern industrial city which Curtis and Milner had planned started to take shape.

In February 1906 the first electric tram ran through the streets of central Johannesburg. In the months that followed, it was swiftly extended to the most populous suburbs, and by December of that year – much to the cabbies' distress – it had already reached the Auckland Park race course. Despite its early lack of reliability and efficiency, the new system nevertheless succeeded in immediately carving off an enormous slice of the cab trade's business in what was already an economically depressed year. In six months, between June and December 1906, no fewer than 247 cab drivers were thrown out of work as close on 150 horse-drawn vehicles were permanently withdrawn from the ranks.[114]

Over the next two years the cab trade continued to contract, and a further 166 drivers lost their jobs as tramline extensions were made to yet more suburbs. But, despite the slow market erosion caused by the expansion of the electric system, the horse-drawn vehicles continued to serve a need by providing a flexible service which, free of a dependence on rails, could reach inaccessible parts of the city or take cross-town routes. The cab drivers must have known, however, that even this sector of their market was under threat from yet another post-war competitor – the motorised taxi.[115]

In December 1908 the cabbies' worst fears were realised when the town council announced that it had received its first application for permission to run a taxi service in the city. In a vain attempt to head off this competition, over 500 cabmen put their signatures to a petition protesting against this new development but, in February 1909, the first taxi duly made its appearance in Johannesburg. The fact that an ex-cab proprietor – B Golub of Terrace Road, Fordsburg – was a major shareholder in the Transvaal Taxi-cab Co Ltd did nothing to make this venture more acceptable to the Jehus, and neither did the competitive table of tariffs which the municipality announced shortly thereafter. In the latter half of 1909 it was the taxi, at least as much as the tram, that pushed a further 168 drivers into the ranks of the unemployed.[116]

This series of savage blows to the cab trade left ugly scars in several places. As the horse-drawn vehicles grew progressively less competitive, so the declining number of proprietors worked their drivers harder and longer for lower wages. Never an easy way of earning a living, by 1907 'cab driving was looked upon as the last resort of the destitute'. Poor, and confronted with the prospect of joblessness, at least some of the cabbies sought a way out of their predicament by supplementing their meagre incomes through developing links with prostitutes or illicit liquor sellers.[117] But, as the Transvaal Indigency Commission of 1906-8 revealed all too clearly, it was in Fordsburg and adjacent Vrededorp that the collapse of the cab trade took its heaviest toll. Much of the old bustle, vitality and social cohesion of these communities was lost and replaced by the open unemployment and tell-tale apathy that accompanies urban decay in capitalist societies. In 1913 the remaining active cabbies in Fordsburg – a suburb where the CDU eight years earlier had marched behind the Red Flag, and where before that the Vigilance and Cab Owners' Association had once been a single indivisible body – were sufficiently vulnerable for their fellow citizens to challenge their right to keep 'stables and kaffirs'.[118]

Within the cab trade itself the professional associations too went into a predictable decline after the introduction of the electric tram. By 1908 the separate owners' and drivers' organisations had been amalgamated into a single Cabmen's Association of Johannesburg (CAJ). To some extent this latter body continued to interest itself in the activities of organised labour on the Witwatersrand – as when, for example, it supported the strike of Krugersdorp cabbies against the introduction of a new municipal table of tariffs in 1908.[119] But, largely shorn of its Lithuanian component, the CAJ offered but a faint echo of the more vibrant and socially conscious voice of labour that had earlier been heard within the trade.

Already defeated by a combination of capitalist development and modern technology, the Cabmen's Association had no easily identifiable focus for its anger or despair. Instead, the CAJ made use of the dominant 'white labour policy' to turn on those 60 or more Coloured drivers who continued to operate 'first-class' cabs in the city. Between 1911 and 1913 the Cabmen's Association continually demanded that the local authorities take action against these remaining 'Malay' cabbies. Early in 1914 this racist agitation finally bore fruit when the town council duly legislated against Coloured cabbies accepting 'first-class' fares.[120] By then there were all of 300 drivers of horse-drawn cabs left in Johannesburg.

CONCLUSION

It is commonplace to suggest that the Witwatersrand experienced a capitalist revolution between 1886 and 1914. A number of scholars, through detailed and rigorous studies, have thrown light on that transformation, and through their efforts we now have valuable insights into the changing 'forces and relations of production', and the role of the state. Using the light shed by these enquiries, social historians are well placed to search for additional questions and answers that can further enhance our understanding of those formative years in the evolution of modern industrial South Africa. A detailed examination of the development of urban transport in Johannesburg can perhaps go some way towards illustrating the process of class struggle in one arena during that capitalist revolution.

It is possible that when Kruger and the *Volksraad* first gave A H Nallmapius a concession to run a horse-drawn tram service in Johannesburg they did not fully appreciate the size of the market which it would create for burgher agricultural produce. What is clear is that once the State President and his advisers did realise the value of the transport concession to their class constituents – the rural bourgeoisie and a section of the urban petty bourgeoisie – they defended it with the utmost determination. Kruger, contrary to the criticisms implicit in the writings of mining capitalists such as J P FitzPatrick and others, was no living anachronism opposed to modern technology per se. The State President was, however, fully aware of the fact that technology was not 'neutral', and that in a developing capitalist society it could be made to serve different class interests. Thus, Kruger was only willing to countenance the introduction of an electric tramway in the principal industrial city of his Republic if it could supplement or enhance the interests of his country-based ruling class. The longevity of the horse-drawn tram in Johannesburg offers evidence of burgher economic penetration into the new system rather than of the supposedly stubborn opposition of Boers to 'progress'.

The British imperialists, having smashed the old landed ruling class in the Transvaal, were equally aware that technology was not in any way 'neutral' in the class struggle. For Milner and his colleagues, however, Johannesburg was first and foremost an industrial capitalist city, and only thereafter an outlet for agricultural produce. It was thus in accordance with this new priority that Lionel Curtis and others planned the geography of class distribution within the modern city. Within this scheme the town planners made provision to 'scatter' the white working class over a wider area so that social control might be enhanced, and that the risks of class conflict might be reduced. Again, it was within the parameters of this design that the city required an electric tramway system which could provide for the cheap and efficient transport of workers to and from their places of residence. But, as Curtis and his colleagues discovered, the *ancien régime* did not end with the Peace of Vereeniging. In the boardrooms of Brussels, and in the backstreets of Fordsburg and Vrededorp, some of Kruger's oldest allies fought on until well after 1902. The class struggle moves at its own pace. In Johannesburg the electric trolley only came to town in 1906.

Joseph Silver, Johannesburg's most notorious pimp of the late 1890s. He was convicted of 'white slavery' in 1899 – importing women for use in local brothels. Born in Poland, but 'a citizen of the world', Silver later earned further notoriety in America, Europe, South America and southern Africa, for crimes ranging from assault through to bank robbery, burglary, theft, illicit diamond buying and police corruption.

Top: Members of the 'American Club' – immigrant gangsters drawn from New York's Lower East Side, who dominated the underworld vice syndicates in Johannesburg – at the height of the bicycle craze sweeping the world in the late 1890s.

Double page spread: The Hatherley Distillery, east of Pretoria, taken shortly after its official opening in 1885. Known as *De Eerste Fabrieken*, the 'first factory' in the Zuid Afrikaansche Republiek, it was a concesssion granted by President S J P Kruger and was designed to convert Afrikaner farmers' surplus grain and fruit into alcoholic spirits which could be consumed by, amongst others, African mineworkers on the Witwatersrand.

(Reproduced from Black Frontiers by S Kemp. London, 1932.)

Double page spread: **A morning market scene in early Johannesburg – Boer farmers taking advantage of new urban markets for their agricultural produce.**
(Reproduced from Pictorial Description of the Transvaal by H F Gros, 1888.)

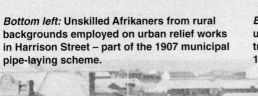

Bottom left: Unskilled Afrikaners from rural backgrounds employed on urban relief works in Harrison Street – part of the 1907 municipal pipe-laying scheme.

Bottom right: 'Rejected and dejected' – unsuccessful 'poor white' applicants for municipal trench-digging jobs in Johannesburg, during the 1906-08 economic recession.

A protest parade of Zulu 'washboys' – who modelled themselves along the lines of the Hindu Dhobi caste – taken in central Johannesburg in 1895.
(Originally published in The Sketch, Johannesburg, 2 October 1895.)

An African 'house boy'— the general factotum and domestic worker of the day. Positions as domestic servants were much prized after the Anglo-Boer War of 1899-1902, when the mine owners reduced the wages of black miners and eventually had to resort to the importation of even cheaper Chinese labour.

Johannesburg's relatively long-lived horse-drawn tramway – yet another of Kruger's concessions, designed to provide his rural constituents with an urban market for forage.

Electric trams, introduced to Johannesburg in February 1906 as part of Milner's modernisation of the urban infrastructure, to accommodate suburban expansion.

PART TWO
NEW NINEVEH

1

THE WITCHES
OF SUBURBIA

Domestic service on the
Witwatersrand, 1890-1914

*Perhaps it is not always easy for the white mistress to decide on
the best treatment for her native servant ... The rules are not
easily laid down, but they form an ethical code, an unwritten law,
which it is quite clear enough for her who runs a house to read.*
Imperial Colonist, November 1911

Viewed historically, the South African labour market has always been
dominated by the three major sectors of employment – mining, agriculture and domestic service. The twentieth-century emergence and rise of
secondary industry as an employer of labour has supplemented rather
than restructured this pattern. In the 1980s, as well as the 1880s, domestic service remains one of the most important sectors of a rapidly developing capitalist economy. Yet, despite this, it is largely in vain that one
scans the literature for any reflection of this reality. With the notable
exception of Jacklyn Cock's thorough examination of *Maids and Madams*,
there is little beyond a few local surveys by anthropologists to break the
monotony of the bleak academic landscape.[1]

This neglect may be more pronounced in southern African studies, but
it is certainly not confined to it. As late as 1909 domestic servants constituted the largest occupational grouping in England – being larger than
agriculture, mining or even engineering – yet it is only relatively recently that these neglected workers have received the more widespread
attention from scholars that they clearly deserve. Although we now have
David Katzman's suggestive work, we still do not have an exhaustive
study of domestic service in the United States of America.[2] In this latter
context, however, we do have the great advantage of a powerful novel

– Richard Wright's *Native Son*, which had such a significant effect on the subsequent writings of Frantz Fanon. Whilst there are also literary works that explore similar themes in Africa, notably by Doris Lessing, there is as yet no scholarly account of domestic service in the changing colonial context.

There seem to be two sets of related reasons behind this academic apathy, and both ultimately derive from the nature of domestic service itself. First, domestic servants serve, they do not produce. Not being commodity producers, their labour is difficult to evaluate in capitalist terms – which is why economists relegate their role to a discussion about the problems of national accounting. In addition, most servants live and labour in isolation. Well away from the production lines of factories or the more easily recognisable haunts and culture of the working class, they are fragmented as a group – features which do not readily earn them the curiosity of sociologists. Secondly, and largely because of these reasons, it is difficult to generate data about them. What is required, ideally, are the personal records and observations of those within the house itself – the employers and the servants. Thus a historian of 'The Domestic Servant Class in Eighteenth Century England' finds it easy to write about using 'the usual quarries of the social historian: diaries, memoirs, letters, magazines, newspapers, the accounts of travellers, and literary works'[3] No such simple solution exists for the social historian of the colonies, where problems of class, colour and literacy combine to place diaries, memoirs and letters of employers and servants at a premium.

Undoubtedly these are formidable problems, and in the South African case there are elements of them that are insurmountable. To do justice to all the subtleties and complexities that a history of domestic servants on the Witwatersrand demands is virtually impossible. But the questions and issues that remain are so important and insistent that they deserve even the most tentative of answers. How and why did domestic service manage to remain such a large and viable sector of the economy at a time when the demands of a powerful mining industry for labour seemed insatiable? What role did the state play in relation to this problem? How did white middle and working-class wives, often finding themselves for the first time in the position of being employers of domestic labour, control black male workers in the vulnerable intimacy of their homes? How did the first generation of African men, newly off the land as independent pastoralists, peasants and family-heads in their own right cope with roles which they considered to be largely female, in situations which sought to colonise them as 'boys'? What was the response of white female servants from a metropolitan background who found themselves plunged into a colonial nexus where they had to work side-by-side with black male servants? How, in Bertram Doyle's words, was 'the etiquette of race relations' forged in such a new and potentially explosive situation?[4]

This study will explore four broad areas in an attempt to answer some of these questions. First, it will examine the position of domestic service within the Witwatersrand labour market. Second, it will offer an outline of the roles, duties and conditions of service for servants. Third, it will attempt to specify some of the ways in which the state and employers sought to control domestic servants. Finally, it will attempt to analyse some of the responses of those who found themselves in domestic service.

DOMESTIC SERVICE IN THE WITWATERSRAND LABOUR MARKET
The period before the South African War, 1887-1899

In 1887 the Witwatersrand produced gold valued at £81 000. By 1899 that production had increased to a value of about £15 000 000 per annum. At the core of the Rand, Johannesburg, a mining camp with a population of about 3 000 of all races in 1887, was transformed to a mining metropolis of 100 000 inhabitants by 1899. Although it is difficult to document, it can be assumed that within that urban core a service sector developed with a demand for labour that at least matched this spectacular growth. What *is* known is that when a census was taken within a three-mile radius of Market Square in 1896, it revealed that central Johannesburg was served by: 3 253 domestic servants (largely black), 3 054 servants (white and Coloured), 402 cooks (white), 345 laundresses (Coloured), 341 waiters (white), 235 housekeepers (white), 219 nurses, 165 grooms, 146 'house-boys', 84 coachmen (black and white), 8 stable-keepers, 5 charwomen, 5 stewards, 4 mother's helps, 3 valets and 1 page.[5]

This rather stark statistical skeleton provided by the 1896 census is a reasonable departure point for a more detailed study of the domestic service sector prior to 1899. For within it lie several clues as to the particular lifestyle and class composition of white Johannesburg in the pre-war period. This is in turn necessary in order to develop a more sophisticated understanding of the particular patterns of demand for domestic servants.

At the apex of the town's social pyramid stood members of the haute bourgeoisie and their wives. The families of these merchant and mining capitalists were served by small numbers of specialist white servants such as stewards, valets and cooks, and larger numbers of white, black or Coloured laundresses, waiters and general servants. It would not be uncommon for such privileged households to have between four and six servants.

Below this small upper class came the more swollen ranks of the petty-bourgeois families and amongst these would number the 1 074 'wives' (as opposed to the 5 350 'housewives') noted in the census. The men of this class were predominantly drawn from the trading, shop-keeping and commercial world of the mining town. Depending on their income and social standing, which could vary enormously, these middle-class families would employ one or more white specialist servants. Most frequently this would be a cook or a housemaid, or in the case of a respectable unmarried man of middle age, a housekeeper. Almost invariably such a white servant would be assisted by one or more black general servants. The greatest of all petty-bourgeois employers of white servants, however, were the hotel and boarding-house keepers. It was essentially this group of entrepreneurs who catered for the needs of the bulk of the male working population who were without the services of their wives and daughters – the immigrant miners. As employers, it was they who gave work to the majority of white cooks, waiters, housekeepers, laundresses and housemaids. Here again the battery of white specialist servants was assisted by an army of black general servants.

The base of the pyramid was formed by the working-class households. Such households could assume one of two major forms. First, there were those cases where a group of four or six immigrant miners combined to collectively hire and occupy a house. In the better-off of such houses a housekeeper would occasionally be employed and assisted by a black general servant. More frequently, however, the miners' domestic chores would simply be undertaken by an African 'houseboy'. Secondly, there would be the less common case where a full working-class family occupied a home. Here the wives and daughters of the artisans, shop assistants, municipal workers or miners would undertake much of the domestic work with the assistance of a black general servant. In such homes it was also not uncommon for the family to take in a 'lodger' in order to supplement its income in an expensive city.

From this broad profile it is clear that, outside working-class homes, there was a fairly widespread general demand for white female labour through much of the 1890s. More particularly, there was a call for labour in the boarding-houses – the 1896 Johannesburg census listed 62 boarding-house keepers whilst in the same year the Witwatersrand Boarding-House Keepers' Protection Association claimed a membership of 90.[6] At the same time white women were in demand to serve as cooks, housemaids and nurses in the homes of the upper and middle classes. In both these cases, however, the demand was particularly pronounced in the early 1890s; that it, before the railways reached Johannesburg, and in the boom period that preceded the Jameson Raid of 1895. In the recession years, following the Raid and leading up to the outbreak of the South African War, there was a noticeable slackening-off in the demand for white female labour although the general level remained high. As late as

1899, it was noted that: 'Good white servants are not plentiful here, and the law of supply and demand has to be taken into consideration, and pretty seriously too.'[7]

Wage rates were tied to this slightly changing pattern in demand, remaining firm through the early 1890s, peaking slightly toward 1895-6 and then easing between 1897 and 1899. White nurses and housemaids commanded cash wages ranging between £4 and £5 per month, plus meals and a room in the house that were worth an additional £2 to £5 a month.[8] Most European women appear to have been acceptable as nurses but English, Irish and Scottish girls were 'always preferred as housemaids because they are smarter in appearance and work than their continental cousins'.[9] German women were widely sought as cooks, and at one stage around 1896 commanded cash wages of up to £10 per month in addition to meals and a room in the house. By 1898-9, however, their wages had been reduced to between £5 and £7 per month and some were reported to be 'glad to work at almost whatever is offered, since a situation means a home as well'.[10] On the rare occasions when a black or Coloured women was available for service in one of the above roles she would usually be offered the job, minus the offer of a room, and at a lower wage rate.[11]

Viewed from one of the South African coastal towns, or even England, these wage rates must have appeared most attractive to female domestics. In England, in 1895, for example, a woman of between 20 and 25 years of age working for a middle or upper-class family could still only look to an annual cash wage of between £15 and £18.[12] Johannesburg, however, was a town with a notoriously high cost of living, and moreover, one with such a marked imbalance in the sex ratios that no working-class woman ventured there lightly. Under these circumstances it is worth enquiring from where this labour market was supplied.

One source of supply was the employment bureau of the day that specialised in domestic servants – the registry office. In return for fees obtained from either party these offices would place employers and work-seekers in contact with each other. Such registry offices had long been a feature of places like Durban, Cape Town and Port Elizabeth, and either placed local workers or arranged for the 'importation' of suitable European domestic servants. In Johannesburg, the firm of Simpson Moncrieff was established as a registry office in January 1891, and by 1899 had been joined by a second agency, the South African Employment Bureau. Acting independently, or indirectly benefiting from the earlier efforts of the coastal agencies, these registry offices played a limited part in meeting Johannesburg's needs for specialist servants. But the overall scale of the problem was clearly beyond the capacities of the registries.[13] When servants' wages rose particularly rapidly in 1896 Richard Porter,

Secretary of the Witwatersrand Boarding-House Keepers' Protection Association, was sent directly to London in an attempt to recruit labour – an attempt which naturally met with strenuous local opposition from service workers.[14] In addition, because of the fees involved, the registry offices were usually the final resort of the frustrated employer or work-seeker. Thus both parties continued to place a great deal of trust in 'market forces'.

To the extent that employers looked to within the country for a growing supply of white female labour, their trust in 'market forces' was largely misplaced. It is true that in the worst recessions, such as that of 1890-2, some working-class families, with considerable misgivings, placed their daughters in domestic service.[15] It was also true that there were cases of young Afrikaner women going into service in the city. Martharina Christina van Wyk, for example, a 19-year-old girl from the Orange Free State, bound herself to a two-year contract with Mr Bekker of Hillbrow because her parents 'were too poor to support her'.[16] In both cases, however, the members involved must have been small. Full immigrant working-class families were the exception rather than the rule, and in town and country alike poor Afrikaner women were notoriously averse to going into service. It was partly for this reason that it was sourly noted in a Johannesburg newspaper in 1899 that 'Dutch girls as a rule know more about Paardekraal and inspanning a team of oxen than about domesticity'.[17]

In other ways, however, 'market forces' did not completely disappoint employers – although it hardly satisfied them either. Many foreign women who had made their way to Johannesburg independently to make a living or seek a fortune were willing to work as domestic servants for brief periods. For the large part composed of tough individualists drawn from the lumpenproletariat, these women were hardly suitable material for moulding into a docile servant class. They drifted in and out of domestic service between jobs as tea-room waitresses, barmaids or prostitutes.[18] With some justification then they were 'regarded with a certain amount of suspicion' or as being of essentially 'doubtful character'.[19]

With such volatile groups and uncertain sources of supply it can be appreciated why the demand for white female domestic labour in Johannesburg remained at a relatively high level throughout the 1890s. This, coupled with the fact that white women were considered to be unsuited to the rougher elements of housework in a sub-tropical climate also helps explain why it was that there was a steadily increasing demand for the labour of the largest group of servants of all on the Witwatersrand – African men.

The demand for black men as domestic servants in Johannesburg arrived at the same time as the first wagons of the 'Rand pioneers' trundled into the mining camp. Indeed, some of the small group of women involved had been far-sighted enough to foresee a 'servant problem' in their new environment and to take precautionary measures. Mrs Willie Rockey who arrived in 1886, for example, brought at least one domestic servant with her from the Cape Colony. For several years, however, women such as Mrs Rockey had to personally undertake a large proportion of the household chores.[20] When Archibald Colquhoun (later of Mashonaland) passed through Johannesburg in 1890 he noted:

> Service was almost unprocurable. Raw Kaffirs, who till a few months before had never seen the inside of a house, were pressed into service for which they had no natural bent, and the best one could hope for was an inferior type of Cape boy.[21]

This situation improved somewhat in the early 1890s, but demand again started to peak after 1893, reaching a high point in 1896. Even in the recession following the Jameson Raid, however, the general level of demand for black male domestic servants remained high – a trend that was no doubt aggravated by the employers' strategy of cutting back on white female domestics between 1897 and 1899.

The concomitant of this demand level was steadily rising wages. It would appear that between 1887 and 1892 the wage of an untrained 'houseboy' ranged between £3 and £4 with a monthly average being about £3 10s 0d. As their rudimentary skills developed, and as demand for their services increased after 1893, however, so 'houseboys' demanded higher wages. From 1892 to 1896 the range of wages widened to between £3 and £6 with a monthly average of about £4, a situation that remained relatively unchanged until the outbreak of the South African War in 1899.[22]

But, as in the case of white female domestic servants, 'houseboys' did not only receive cash wages – there were also other emoluments that had to be taken into consideration when attempting to assess their income. 'Here in Johannesburg,' noted the irritated leader-writer of the *Standard and Diggers' News* in 1898, 'the swarthy savage condescends to be taught the minimum of service for £4 per month with food, quarters, and gifts of clothing …'[23] These steadily rising real wages incorporating the payments in kind were, in many cases, exaggerated out of all proportion in the minds of the employers. Nevertheless, there was an increase in wages which annoyed white householders, the more so since the increases continued into a period when their own cash incomes were falling and when 'market forces' should have been reducing servants' wages. In an editorial in 1897, *The Star* surveyed 'Houseboy's Wages', and noted sadly that neither the advent of the railways nor a series of rural disasters in the shape of droughts, locusts and cattle diseases had been able to bring about an immediate and marked reduction in the wages of black servants. The rate of pay for domestic servants, *The Star* concluded, remained at a 'ridiculously high figure'.[24] It was in this context, and in the wake of the Chamber of Mines' successful reduction of African mineworkers' wages in 1896, that employers and public bodies openly debated the virtues of combination in an attempt to reduce 'houseboy' wages.[25] For the first, but not for the last time during a period of recession, Witwatersrand employers of domestic labour toyed with the idea of a Housekeepers' Protection Association. Householders as a group, however, were at least as fragmented as 'houseboys', and the wages held firm.

Cash wages, of course, are never the sole determinants of labour supply, and this is especially true of the colonial situation. But, to the extent that it is possible to separate out this variable, it would appear that the rising wages for domestic servants in Johannesburg were capable of eliciting a steadily increasing flow of labour from the countryside. If this was true for the years before 1895, then it was even more true for the period immediately thereafter when structural changes in town and country manifested themselves in the Witwatersrand labour market.

Prior to 1895 both black miners and 'houseboys' on the Rand had enjoyed rising cash wages but, in 1896, the Chamber of Mines implemented a wage cut for African mineworkers. Almost immediately *The Star* noted that: 'Since the reduction of mine boys' wages there has been a much larger supply of kitchen boys.'[26] After this reduction and over the succeeding years as the collective impact of the rural disasters noted above made itself felt, the domestic service sector must have become increasingly attractive to growing numbers of black workers who made their way to the Transvaal. By 1899 a Johannesburg domestic servant could look to a monthly cash wage of 80 shillings, while the black miner, for a similar period of labour earned, on average, 49 shillings and ninepence.[27] When relative conditions of service, health hazards and payments in kind are added to this cash differential, it can readily be appreciated why the domestic service sector must have proved increasingly attractive to many African workers in the late 1890s.

Between 1896 and 1899 this intersectoral competition for black labour on the Rand did not seriously threaten the Chamber of Mines, and there were three basic reasons for this. First, the size of the domestic service sector remained relatively small whilst the majority of the white residents were without their families and a settled home life. By 1899 there were probably, at most, 7 500 black domestic servants at work in Johannesburg. Secondly, in the wake of the natural disasters in the countryside during the mid-1890s there was a significant overall increase in the flow

212

of labour to the Rand – enough even to meet the Chamber of Mines' requirements at reduced wages. Between 1895 and 1899 the black labour force on the mines increased from 50 000 to over 96 000 workers. The third reason behind this rather untypical Randlord indifference to competition for labour emerges when the changing composition of the ranks of the 'houseboys' in the 1890s is examined. Who exactly Colquhoun's 'raw kaffirs' of 1890 were is unclear. What is clearer is that between 1890 and 1895 the 'houseboys' seem to have been more or less equally drawn from Zulus, Zulu speakers from Natal (hereafter collectively but incorrectly termed 'Zulus' for the sake of convenience), Basutos and Shangaans.[28] The twinned impact of wage reductions and rinderpest in 1896-7, however, constituted something of a wastershed. Thereafter, for a complex set of reasons, there appears to have been a set of readjustments and realignments in the labour market which manifested themselves in an increasing degree of ethnic job specialisation on the Witwatersrand.

While the general level of mine wages was reduced in 1896, wages could still cover a monthly range of between 30 and 70 shillings. Within this range, the best wages were paid to the semi-skilled 'drill-boys' who worked on the longest contracts. Before, but more especially after these reductions, Shangaans from the more proletarianised parts of southern Mozambique tended to monopolise these positions. A need and willingness to work for longer periods than most other black migrants, coupled with a previously acquired set of skills meant that these Shangaans came to be systematically favoured by mine managers towards the turn of the century.

Rinderpest for its part struck most powerfully at the comparatively wealthier cattle-keeping people of southern Africa. It was these latter people, especially those drawn from regions geographically adjacent to the Witwatersrand such as Zululand and Natal who were amongst the most anxious to earn cash and restock their herds after 1897 – as indeed they were after the turn of the century when a further set of cattle diseases such as lung-sickness and East Coast Fever attacked their herds.[29] It was these people without previously developed mining skills who were drawn to the position of 'houseboy'. Even food and quarters of bad quality, when combined with relatively high cash wages, offered migrants the prospect of being able to save. Moreover, and at least as important, was the fact that the position of the 'houseboy' was governed by a monthly engagement under the Masters and Servants' legislation as opposed to the longer fixed-term contracts of the mining industry. This meant – to the considerable annoyance of employers over the ensuing decade – that the 'houseboy' could move fairly freely, and that labour turnover consequently remained at a relatively high level.[30] It also meant that this pool of migrant labourers was not particularly attractive to mine managers at that time, and thus likely to receive proportionately lower wages as mineworkers. For a combination of these reasons, the 'Zulus' made the position of 'houseboy' on the Witwatersrand their very own to an increasing extent after 1897. By the outbreak of the war the words 'houseboy' and 'Zulu' had become almost synonymous on the Rand labour market.

It was under this very special set of circumstances that a gracious mining industry was willing to tolerate the growing intersectoral competition for labour and allow white Johannesburg its quota of 'houseboys' – a situation in marked contrast to the post-South African War period.

RECONSTRUCTION AND THE PERIOD THEREAFTER, 1902-1914

With the outbreak of war in 1899 the thousands of domestic servants in Johannesburg, along with their employers and other inhabitants of the city, joined the throng wishing to leave the Transvaal. The exit was not universally simple or painless. Several hundred 'Zulu' 'kitchen boys' were left stranded without money when their employers summarily decamped without paying them their wages. A minority of these were forced to stay on in the city, but the majority managed to join the march back to Natal and Zululand under the guidance of J S Marwick.[31] During the remaining years of the war many of these men worked for the imperial army at rates that were significantly higher than any previously ruling in southern Africa. The housekeepers, cooks and housemaids for the most part boarded the trains for the Cape – not always an uneventful trip since drunken refugees tended to force their attentions on female Coloured servants making the journey south.[32] Many of the employers spent the duration of the war in Cape Town, or if more opulent, in England.

Employers and servants alike returned to a Witwatersrand that was economically, politically, and socially transformed between 1902 and 1914. At the centre of these transforming processes lay a rapidly developing mining industry, and the successive administrations of the British, Transvaal and Union governments. In Johannesburg, however, these changes manifested themselves in ways other than simply the economic or political. As it had regularly done before 1899, the city once again more than doubled in size. From a population of about 109 000 of all races in 1902, the city grew to a point where by 1914 it had over 250 000 inhabitants of all races. But this time the change in Johannesburg – and indeed in other Reef towns – was more than demographic: it involved a fundamental change in the social composition of the city.[33]

In 1897, only 12 per cent of the white employees of the Witwatersrand gold mines were married and had their families resident with them in the Transvaal; by 1902 this figure had risen to 20 per cent, and by 1912 it was up to 42 per cent.[34] In the post-war period members of the working class for the first time, like the white middle and upper classes before them, could enjoy the privilege of family life in significant numbers. Put another way, this meant that between 1902 and 1914 there was a decline in the number of miners sharing accommodation or living in boarding-houses, and a marked increase in the number of working-class homes. This structural change affected the domestic service sector in at least two important ways.

First, the decline in collective working-class accommodation in one form or another brought about a reduction in the need for white special-ist servants – a feature that was especially noticeable after 1906 when the boarding-house business had contracted somewhat, and wives had done much to replace cooks and housekeepers. This trend was compounded when the service needs of middle and upper-class families, whose fami-ly structure had remained fairly constant, grew relatively slowly – demand being only in proportion to their limited size in the society as a whole. Second, the growth in the number of white working-class homes led to a marked increase in the overall demand for black domes-tic servants. It is these large-scale trends that form the backdrop against which we should seek a more detailed understanding of demand, sup-ply and wages of servants between 1902 and 1914.

Measures taken during the South African War did much to shape the domestic service sector of the Witwatersrand labour market in the immediate post-war period and the years leading up to the depression of 1906-8. Some members of the middle and upper classes returning to their northern suburbs homes from Cape Town or England took the pre-caution of taking along contract-bound white servants with them.[35] Others, however, placed their trust in the market and were bitterly dis-appointed. In April 1902, the demand for white female domestic labour in Johannesburg was described as being 'immense', and while the situa-tion improved somewhat in the following years, demand easily kept abreast of supply until at least the end of 1905.[36] Wages for European ser-vants reflected this demand by retaining their late-1890s level, and then rising slightly. By the end of 1905, a housemaid earned cash wages of between £4 and £5 per month, while a cook or 'cook-general' earned between £6 and £8 per month.[37]

The demand for black domestic servants after the war was no less pro-nounced. In this case the problem of a faltering supply was made worse by the continuing demands of the army and the military authorities' insistence on issuing a permit before a servant could be recruited from a neighbouring colony. Initially this procedure did much to impede the inflow of 'Zulus' who by now constituted the most natural reservoir of 'houseboys'. But the problem also went beyond this since even those Africans who managed to get into the city apparently held aloof from domestic service in the first months after the war.[38] This was hardly surprising since the £2 10s 0d to £3 10s 0d cash wages that employers were offering was below the pre-war level, and substantially below the erstwhile domestic servants' wartime earnings. But such was the demand for their services that wages were gradually forced back to the level of the late 1890s. By the onset of the depression in 1906, Johannesburg's 25 000 to 30 000 'houseboys' were once again earning cash wages of between £4 and £5 per month – a rate 30 per cent to 50 per cent higher than anywhere else in South Africa.[39]

White householders, however, were not the only ones to experience a serious shortage of labour after the war and nor were they the most important employers in the Transvaal. The Chamber of Mines, too, found itself faced with a 'shortage' of labour after the mines were reopened in 1901, and for reasons that were not entirely unfamiliar. In an effort to reduce costs the mine owners cut the wages of black workers and then discovered to their chagrin that a continuous supply of African labour was not forthcoming. But, unlike the weak and less organised householders, the Randlords were able to make their economic initiative hold. In 1904, with the aid and support of the government, they were able to secure vital supplies of indentured labour from China. This partial solution to their immediate problem, however, did not prevent the mine owners from continually casting covetous glances at other sectors of the Rand labour market that were better served by African labour. Neither did it prevent them from scouring the countryside for all available workers. Nor did it stop them from continuing to complain loudly about the 'shortage' of black labour.

All of these vociferous demands for cheap black labour were ultimately directed at the new British administration which was already beset with the problem of how best to politically stabilise and anglicise the Transvaal. The Milner administration undertook piecemeal solutions as best it could. In May 1902 a scheme was devised by which, for several months, black female domestic servants were provided to the citizens of Johannesburg from the military refugee camps.[40] Milner, with all the fervour of imperialism, however, was not really interested in piecemeal problem solving. What was required was a more imaginative and radical solution, and in this he was assisted by an Englishman, Sir John Ardagh.

In June 1902 Ardagh wrote to the Colonial Office pointing out how in southern Africa the number of males had always outnumbered the white females, and that this imbalance in the sex ratio was likely to be exacerbated by the number of soldiers settling in the Transvaal after the war. What was required to offset this, and at the same time help ease the domestic British 'problem' of a 'surplus' of women, was a system of female emigration to the colonies.[41] Milner seized on this idea for within it he saw the seeds of a solution to some of the most pressing problems with which he was confronted. For if female domestic servants and other wage-earning women from Britain could be encouraged to emigrate to South Africa, then they would assist in achieving several objectives. First, they could help ease the demand for domestic labour on the Rand. Second, if white domestic servants went in sufficient numbers they could replace the black male 'houseboys' who would then be available as workers for the gold mines. Third, if these women married and settled down they would contribute to the development of a stable and loyal British working class in the Transvaal.

What made these ideas even more appealing was the fact that the infrastructure for such a scheme had already been laid by the British Women's Emigration Association (BWEA). Flushed with the success of the imperial war, and partly financed by Rhodes and Rothschild, the BWEA had, in April 1902, set up a South African Expansion Committee (SAEC) in London which, in turn, was assisted by a branch in Johannesburg. The London Committee, under the patronage of Milner and Chamberlain, numbered amongst others as its members Lady Knightley of Fawsley, Mrs C S Goldmann and Mrs Lionel Phillips. The Johannesburg branch operated under the aegis of an 'advisory council' which included amongst its members Sir Percy FitzPatrick (President), F H P Creswell (Sec), R W Schumacher, J Wybergh, W Windham, Mrs Drummond Chaplin, Mrs Sidney Jennings and Mrs Harold Strange. Its day-to-day operations, however, were run by an executive committee composed of Mesdames Jennings, FitzPatrick, Marx, Matthews and Emrys Evans.[42] Neither of these committees could be accused of being unmindful of the interests of mining capital.

What Milner first did to put his scheme into operation was to create a 'Women's Immigration Department' in the Transvaal, and then to incorporate these various committees into his administration by granting them official recognition and financial assistance. In mid-1903, the London-based SAEC became independent of its parent body (the BWEA) under a new name – the South African Colonisation Society. As an advisory committee to what was by now the 'Transvaal Immigration Department', the Colonisation Society, amongst other things, vetted the applications received from potential immigrants, and then selected and forwarded suitable domestic servants to the new colony. The Johannesburg branch of the Colonisation Society, also in its capacity as an officially recognised advisory committee, received and vetted applications from would-be employers, and then in turn arranged for the reception of the immigrant domestic servants.[43]

Middle and upper-class Johannesburg at first embraced Milner's scheme with alacrity. The prospect of patriotism and parlour-maids at palatable prices smacked of a middle-class millennium. Along with lady helps, laundry-maids and even a few dairy-maids, Irish housemaids were requisitioned since they were considered to be 'generally stronger and less liable to illness than Scotch or English girls'.[44] Amongst members of the middle class in particular, however, the greatest demand of all was for that rare servant who would cook and undertake general household duties as well, the so-called 'cook-general'. At rates ranging between £48 and £72 per year (cash wages), plus the cost of a steamship passage for the servant (£12-£15), hundreds of applications were received from would-be employers. This demand is shown in Table 1 below.[45]

Table 1 Demand and supply of European female domestic servants during the reconstruction era

Period	No of applications from employers	No of servants supplied
1/7/02 to 30/6/03	1 200	502
1/7/03 to 30/6/04	866	367
1/7/04 to 30/6/05	565	173
Total	2 631	1 042

It is estimated that in the decade between 1902 and 1912 the SACS introduced a total of about 1 500 white female domestic servants to the Witwatersrand. What is also clearly evident from these figures, however, is the fact that there was a marked decline in the Society's activities after 1905. During the depression of 1906-8 the demand for white servants fell even more rapidly than it did before that, and when Premier Botha's *Het Volk* assumed office in 1907, it cut the subsidy to the Colonisation Society since, for obvious reasons, the new nationalist government saw no reason to assist English immigration to the Transvaal. Despite further generous financial assistance from various Rand mining companies after Union, the Colonisation Society was virtually moribund by 1912.[46]

There were, however, also more deep-seated social and economic reasons behind the failure of the Milner scheme – and reasons that lay both in Britain and on the Witwatersrand. During the crucial first three years of the scheme the Colonisation Society failed to supply both the quantity and quality of servant demanded in Johannesburg. The Colonisation Society attempted to recruit servants in Britain in precisely the decade during which women, in large numbers, were deserting the long hours, low wages and lonely labour of domestic service for work in industry.[47] Moreover, to a greater or lesser degree British servants tended to be specialists, and they thus viewed the more 'general' type of work being offered them in the Transvaal with suspicion, even though it held out the prospect of employment at considerably higher wages. The problem was well put in the *Annual Report* of the Colonisation Society in 1903:

> The great difficulty in the selection of girls of the servant class is chiefly the fact that the servant most in demand in the Transvaal is not known in England. What is required is a cook-general, but the English general servant is not, as a rule, a sufficiently good cook to fulfil the duties required, and those who are good enough cooks will not turn their hands to all the other work expected of them.[48]

It was largely in vain that the Society continually pointed out that 'All servants in the colonies are expected to be able to lend a hand to do anything that is wanted.'[49]

On the Witwatersrand a not entirely dissimilar set of factors also went some way to undermining the short and long-term viability of the scheme. The basic constraints imposed by labour in domestic service did not differ fundamentally in Johannesburg and London. Thus, the supply of immigrant servants was constantly diminished as women left paid household labour to seek a more independent and satisfying life elsewhere. While the Rand could not boast a well-developed sector of secondary industry, there was a keen demand for the cheap labour of women and waitresses in tea-rooms, assistants in shops or as clerical workers in offices or, to a lesser extent, in small factories.[50] Before 1906 several cooks were quick to spot that they could put their specialised skills to more profitable commercial use, and they promptly left private service to open their own boarding-houses.[51] But, in a society where men outnumbered women, marriage proved to be the greatest social and economic escape hatch of all from domestic service. Whilst such marriages might have contributed to Milner's policy of anglicisation, they certainly did not appeal to the servant-seeking middle class who came to refer to the Colonisation Society in derisive terms as a 'matrimonial agency'.[52]

The single greatest problem of all, however, made itself felt almost as soon as the immigrant servants set foot in the colony. It took white domestics no time at all to realise that in South Africa hard physical labour at low wages was first and foremost the province of the black man. 'The consequence,' *The Star* noted in retrospect, 'was that householders who engaged white domestic servants invariably had a male native to do what women term the rough work of a house.' This was all 'very well for people who could afford a staff of servants' but not for those of more modest means. In practice it meant that the white woman in service was 'not a domestic' but 'more of an administration official'.[53] The middle class simply could not afford the additional expense of a servant who was only willing to 'administer'.

This colonial reality destroyed the scheme insofar as it was designed to help reduce the overall demand for servants. Far from easing the situation, it in many cases actually exacerbated the problem since immigrant white domestics who went into the boarding-house business, or who set up their own homes, became employers of black labour in their own right. A young Scottish servant might still write home in mid-1903 that 'Lord Milner is trying to get the black boys back to the mines and out of service', but the imperial overlord himself and the mine owners must have known already that the scheme was failing.[54] As active and enthusiastic partners in the immigration scheme they watched in dismay as black men continued to swell the domestic service sector while the mines experienced a 'labour crisis'. By 1904 – the very year in which the imperial overlord and the Randlords were forced to turn to China for labour – there were 20 000 'kitchen boys' in Johannesburg alone, while the Witwatersrand mine compounds between them could only muster 68 000 black workers. This fact, when allied to the mounting inadequacy of the immigration scheme, must have proved exceedingly irksome to Milner and the mine owners, but they were not yet willing to acknowledge defeat.

The idea that an organised effort should be made to reduce the wages of Africans in domestic service was not a new one. Indeed, it had been around in one form or another on the Rand for the better part of a decade. Whenever such ideas had been mooted in the past, however, they had been advocated by relatively unorganised middle-class elements who sought to profit directly from a reduction in their servants' wages. Furthermore these middle-class sponsored schemes had been articulated at times when black labour supplies in the mining industry were increasing, and they had thus received no real support from the state, the Randlords or their allies. This lukewarm reception by other parties was not surprising since such middle-class schemes did not have as a primary objective an increase in the supply of mine labour, although a drastic reduction in wages may, indirectly, have produced such a result. All of this, however, was very different from the efforts made to enforce a wage reduction during the reconstruction era.

In the second half of 1904 incomes in several sectors of the Witwatersrand economy fell markedly as the post-war recession deepened. The resultant shortage of cash made itself felt in white working-class homes where there had been wage reductions, whilst the reduced turnover in commerce caused considerable concern amongst middle-class traders.

At such times white employers across a wide class spectrum must have been more than ordinarily resentful of paying wages – let alone wages that were still rising – to African domestic servants.[55] In addition, the 'shortage' of black mine labour was as acute as ever. This, then, was a singularly propitious moment for employers to co-operate in an effort to reduce 'kitchen boy' wages. When the Milner administration at the behest of its Native Affairs Department cut the wages of black government employees late in the year the mining capitalists seized their opportunity. On 23 November 1904, E P Rathbone, long-time ideologue for the Chamber of Mines and editor of the journal *South African Mines, Commerce and Industry* wrote to *The Star* with the encouragement of 'many industrial and representative parties' suggesting that it was 'absolutely monstrous that, through want of a little firm combination, the ridiculous wages paid to Coloured domestic servants should not be reduced'.[56]

Over the next 14 days Rathbone, with the generous assistance and strong editorial support of *The Star*, proceeded to expand on what his notion of 'a little firm combination' was. He, Major H M Downes, F Drake, G Kent and others proposed to float a registered limited liability company to be called the Employers' Domestic Native Labour Association (EDNLA). Like the mine owners' recruiting organisation, the Witwatersrand Native Labour Association on which it was modelled, EDNLA would eventually constitute a monopoly, all employers agreeing to employ 'houseboys' only at the newly reduced wage rate which was to be decided upon. EDNLA was to have a capital of £600 made up of £1 shares of which only ten shillings would be paid on subscription. The promoters calculated that a minimum of 1 000 householders would have to join EDNLA in order to make the scheme viable. In addition to fixing the wages of African domestic servants, EDNLA would also undertake to keep a register of information on efficiency, honesty and sobriety of servants thus enabling it to 'black-list' any undesirable 'houseboys'.[57]

But Christmas, 'kitchen boys' and companies apparently did not mix. Despite vigorous prodding by *The Star* and Rathbone the majority of white householders seemed to remain apathetic. Whether it was simply the festive season generally, or the fact that money was even tighter than usual at Christmas in 1904 is unclear, but few people seemed willing to subscribe to EDNLA shares. Rathbone soon discovered, as he put it, that 'what is everybody's business is usually nobody's business'. In late December he made one last attempt to salvage the scheme by appealing to the women's organisations in the suburbs to become involved, but again to no avail. The last stand of all in this great battle against the 'kitchen boys' and their wages was left to Rathbone's colleague – the redoubtable Major Downes. In late January 1905 the Major unsuccessfully attempted to revive the scheme as a 'Mutual Benefit Society' which required a mere half-a-crown as a subscription fee.[58]

White Johannesburg need not have despaired, however, for what the Major could not give them in a recession, the 'market' in a depression would. Just as 1896-7 had marked a watershed in the domestic service sector of the local economy in the 1890s, so the depression of 1906-8 constituted a landmark in the first decade of the twentieth century. In both cases structural changes in the labour market were inaugurated by a series of complex economic and political changes that took place in the town as well as the countryside, and in both cases they heralded the advent of a new period in which increasing supplies of labour produced a steady decline in the wages of domestic workers.

The scalpel of economic depression made its first cuts in the most predictable place – where labour was highest paid and least 'productive'. White female domestics, and especially the cooks-general, found that their services were amongst the first to be dispensed with by the middle classes. Although more skilled and competent than many black servants, they did less of the essential 'rough work' around the house, and were thus more vulnerable to dismissal. If these largely English-speaking women were the first fired, then they were also amongst the last to be re-hired in what became a relatively cluttered labour market, and this process in turn had a depressing effect on wages. From cash wages of between £6 and £8 per month in 1905, wages for cooks-general fell to between £3 10s 0d and £5 in 1907. A further sign of the times was the fact that the South African Colonisation Society – which had previously insisted on a minimum cash wage of £4 month for an immigrant servant – reduced the figure to £3 per month in 1907.[59]

If, however, the depression forced certain middle-class elements to forego the luxury of a semi-skilled 'cook-general', it did not make them abandon the idea of having a white servant. Showing a willingness to cut according to the new cloth, inhabitants of the predominantly English-speaking northern suburbs now cast around for white labour that was cheaper still. In this search their eyes came to rest, not for the first time, on the pools of urban poverty and largely Afrikaner distress in Fordsburg, Vrededorp and Newlands. Consciously adhering to the constructs of the dominant British ideology of the time, at least one middle-class woman of standing advocated that the wives and daughters of the less fortunate should be sent to the workhouse to qualify as white servants, and that charity should be avoided since it only tended to further degrade the poor.[60] *The Star*, always aspiring to subtlety, was content to chant a variation on a theme from Milner. Its leader writer suggested that Emily Hobhouse could best use her considerable influence amongst Afrikaners if she would persuade them to allow their daughters to enter domestic service and, by doing so, 'compel the Kaffir "boy" to seek employment for which he is naturally endowed'.[61] To their bewilderment and considerable annoyance, however, the middle and ruling classes uncovered that basic social fact that each of its generations has to rediscover for itself – namely, that during the severest of depressions and distress the poor prefer the communality of collective suffering to individual life-saving labour amongst alien classes. Afrikaner women, always reluctant to enter domestic service, were now more unwilling than ever to abandon their children, families and homes to work for their conquerors.[62]

But if the depression could not deliver urban Afrikaner women into service, then it did at least partly compensate the middle classes by producing an alternative supply of female labour from rural areas. Between 1906 and 1908 droughts, cattle diseases, the depression and an African rebellion in Natal and Zululand all combined to produce a new wave of proletarianisation that surged through the countryside and deposited thousands of African females in the cities. This influx of black women into Johannesburg was perceived by its white citizens partly in horror, and partly in hope. On the one hand many of these women – none of whom were subject to the pass laws – found their way to the notorious 'mine locations' in the city where they lived by prostitution, hawking, or beer brewing. On the other, however, there was the redeeming feature that a 'good number' – albeit without passes – entered into domestic service. The first signs of this new development in the labour market came as early as March 1906, when Martin's Agency indicated that it was ready to receive applications for a second 'batch' of 'Zulu Servant Girls' who were willing to serve under a 12-month contract.[63]

The white middle class considered this arrival of a significant number of African women in the city to be hopeful for other reasons as well. The depression had brought with it one of the recurrent waves of 'black peril' scares to Johannesburg. This state of near collective hysteria invariably manifested itself in a flood of accusations by white women – some with reason but for the most part without justification – that black men had, or had attempted to, sexually assault them. Leading middle-class elements now reasoned, as they did again in the subsequent scare of 1912-13, that if they could train this new pool of African female labour for service, then they could replace the 'houseboy' and so dispel the potential danger that lurked behind every kitchen cupboard. This outlook was further rationalised by the addition of familiar ideological notions which suggested that women were in any case 'naturally' more suited to this type of labour than men.[64]

The initiative in these matters was taken by the Church of England Mission. By February 1908, its Native Girls' Industrial School Committee had acquired a small cottage in Doornfontein where black women were instructed 'in all branches of housework, cooking and laundry work'. This Sherwell Street school started with only two pupils but within ten months there were so many applications for admission that the Committee had to make more ambitious arrangements. With the aid of Church funds, donations and money collected from Africans in the countryside and local mine compounds, a new property was acquired in Rosettenville in 1909, where the expanded St Agnes Native Girls' Industrial School could accommodate 40 pupils. Showing every sign of becoming a successful and worthwhile venture, the new institution now gained indirect state and mining house approval when it received the enthusiastic support of, amongst others, Lady Selborne, Mrs R W Schumacher and Mrs Albu.[65]

The St Agnes School started off promisingly enough with 37 pupils ranging in age from six to nineteen years being under the guidance of Deaconess Julia. It would appear that the majority of these girls were drawn from the mine locations since Deaconess Julia assured her public audiences that it was 'largely from this source that the girl domestic of the future would be drawn'. But despite the fact that the state provided bursaries for some of its pupils, the school did not prosper as was hoped. The three-year course must have sapped the financial resources of black parents, and most pupils left to seek work well before the course was completed. By late 1911 the school had produced a mere 20 graduates and its intake had declined to 25 pupils.[66]

From this it is clear that the depression and its immediate aftermath hardly produced an adequate supply of trained black housemaids. Neither did it bring about a radical change in the composition of the labour market in this respect – and that despite the fact that a 'good number' of untrained African women entered into domestic service. For although poverty might have brought thousands of black women into the city, only a minority of them ended up working in white households. The social and economic reasons for this lay with both prospective employees and employers.

African fathers, mothers and husbands had the most rooted objection to their female kin entering into domestic service during the first decade of the twentieth century. They believed, with good reason, that many women entering service would be seduced by white men and ultimately become immoral.[67] The black women themselves appear to have favoured making an independent legal or illegal living in the locations rather than sacrifice their working lives to the white masters and mistresses of the suburbs.[68]

The white mistresses for their part had good reasons for not wanting to employ black women as domestic servants. They believed African women to be 'ignorant' and more 'difficult to manage' than the black men to whom they were accustomed. One of their real fears, however, remained largely unstated or, at best, was stated in highly ideological form. White women were deeply disturbed by the possibility that black housemaids would develop sexual liaisons with their husbands. Unable or unwilling to confront their husbands directly, they stated instead that black females were grossly 'immoral'. Their fears were also shared by others. In 1908 the leader writer of *The Star* suggested that one cogent reason against the appointment of 'Kaffir Housemaids' was the fact that it increased the risk of a 'bastard population'.[69] Important as these reservations undoubtedly were, they were augmented by an equally persuasive economic argument – the fact that African women were simply no cheaper to employ than black men. Despite the depression, black women sought virtually the same wages from employers as other groups of servants on the Rand. Thus, while they introduced a new and growing element into the labour market they did not initially restructure it.[70] Some of the more significant re-structuring that did take place during the depression came from other quarters. More especially it came from the state and the employment of juvenile labour in domestic service.

Young African boys – 'piccanins' – had been employed as domestic servants in small Transvaal towns such as Middelburg since at least the turn of the century. Between 1902 and 1908, however, these Pedi tribesmen suffered a particularly severe set of rural disasters. In the years that their cattle were not struck by East Coast Fever, their crops were devastated by droughts and locusts.[71] These agricultural reverses significantly increased the supply of labour from this part of the country, and many more black boys made their way to the towns and cities in order to make a living. On the Rand, state-licensed labour agents were quick to spot this new flow of labour and capitalise on it. Particularly from the advent of the depression in 1906 firms such as B G Shepperson, P D de Villiers and Ross's systematically recruited 'piccanins' of between 10 and 15 years of age in the Pietersburg district of the northern Transvaal. These firms then supplied householders who, in exchange for a capitation fee of £2 and a train fare, acquired the services of a 'piccanin' who was bound by contract to them by cash wages of between 10 and 20 shillings per month 'according to size'.[72]

During the earliest months of the depression the government was content to allow this 'natural' functioning of the labour market to operate at its own pace. But when the Liberal government in Britain prevented the further recruitment of Chinese indentured labour for the Rand mining industry in November 1906, there was a new and urgent reason to facilitate this influx of juvenile labour from the northern Transvaal. Just as in the immediate post-war period it was believed that white female immigrant labour would release the 'Zulus' for work underground, it was now hoped that the influx of cheaper still 'piccanin' labour would help displace the 'houseboys' into the mine compounds. To achieve this objective, the government appointed H M Taberer as Director of the Government Native Labour Bureau in 1907.[73]

In mid-January 1908 Taberer announced to the Witwatersrand public that the labour bureau was willing to undertake part of the role of a registry office by supplying 'piccanins' for domestic service. Like the labour agents, the state obtained the bulk of these African boys from the Pietersburg district, and then forwarded them to a compound in Germiston where employers made their 'selection' – probably also 'according to size'. Unlike the independent agents, however, the bureau attempted to run its business with a slightly more responsible attitude. As far as was possible it attempted to recruit only those youths who were over 14 years of age – so that they could come under the control of the pass laws. This mixed blessing at least afforded some of the older lads a measure of legal protection that was denied to the 10 to 14-year-olds.[74]

The state scheme operated successfully enough for three weeks, and during this period it supplied householders with at least 150 'piccanins'. By mid-February, however, the scheme started to run into difficulties. The labour agents, and Shepperson in particular, complained that the state was destroying their delicate enterprises. In addition to this, the government started having reservations of its own. It found that the state had to charge a higher capitation fee than the agents to keep Taberer's scheme viable, and that it therefore tended to experience greater difficulty in placing its 'piccanins' than the independent agents. For both of these reasons Government Native Labour Bureau recruitment was stopped on 13 February 1908. Thereafter the administration was again content to resort to the cheaper workings of the 'market place'. The government instructed its native commissioners to 'encourage' youths to enlist for domestic service, while it once more allowed the independent state-licensed agents the undisputed right to supply the Witwatersrand market.[75] Although Taberer's formal scheme had failed, the latter arrangement continued to operate with government approval long after the depression.[76]

The influx of Pedi 'piccanins', the availability of a growing number of African women, the continuing arrival of black men from the countryside, the presence of a pool of unemployed European cooks-general, and the curtailment of demand for servants during a depression all left their mark on the service sector of the Rand labour market. From late 1907 through to 1909 there were indications of growing distress amongst the ranks of the 'houseboys' as suburban residents complained about an increase in petty theft by domestic servants. White householders constantly grumbled about the fact that their servant usually had some 'brother or sister' living in the back yard at 'their expense'. These and other tell-tale signs also showed that the market was becoming over-supplied. Gangs of African boys and older men roamed the streets in search of work. Labour agents who found that they could not dispose of their 'pic-canins' quickly enough were forced into the unusual practice of having to advertise. Perhaps most significant of all, however, was the fact in the winter of 1909, for the first time, there was no marked seasonal fluctuation in the labour supply to the domestic service sector.[77]

Employers took the opportunity presented by a swollen labour supply to make a series of complex substitutions which varied with their fears, prejudices and class position. Invariably, however, the consequence of such a labour substitution was cheaper service for the householder. White women were replaced by black men or Coloured women, while both of these could in turn be replaced by black women. All adult servants in their turn were liable to replacement by the cheapest labour of all – that of the 'piccanins'. Under these circumstances the wages of the single largest group of servants, the 'houseboys', could only move in one direction – down. What Milner, Rathbone and the Botha government between them could not achieve over eight years, the depression and a progressively underdeveloped countryside delivered in 24 months. Cash wages for 'houseboys' fell from a monthly average of 90 shillings in 1905 to 60 shillings in 1907, and then 50 shillings in 1908 – an overall reduction in their cash income of 46 per cent.[78]

As always, the realities of the depression lingered and helped to shape the post-depression era, 1909-14. Some of this continuing influence can be detected in the demand for white female domestic servants. After 1909, many of the middle classes again aspired to the services of a white servant but after their labour substitution experiences of the depression they were unwilling to revert to the pre-1906 wage rates. Their reduced offers were hardly capable of eliciting the much-prized cooks-general and, more often than not, such employers found that their wages tended to attract 'generals' rather than 'cooks'. By the time the recession of 1913-14 set in, these white female domestic servants were earning cash wages of between £2 10s 0d and £5 per month. At these wages it was hardly surprising to find that such women were in short supply.[79]

But if many in the middle class got the 'generals', then the remaining upper echelons of this and the ruling class got the 'cooks'. In the homes of the rich there was a strong and continuing demand for the genuine cook-general or the more specialist skills of a cook. In this case demand kept abreast of supply, and wages firmed in the post-depression period. From their all-time low of between £3 10s 0d and £5 during the depression of 1906-8, cash wages for cooks or cooks-general rallied to between £5 15s 0d and £7 per month in 1913.[80]

WAGE RATES OF DOMESTIC SERVANTS ON THE WITWATERSRAND 1890-1914

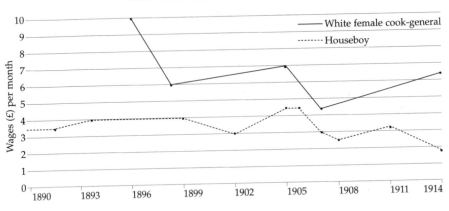

Just as many of the more privileged members of society wanted their white servants back after 1908, so too the lower-middle and working-class whites sought to recover their 'Zulu' servants in the post-depression period. From the summer of 1909 onwards the demand for 'houseboys' continued to firm through 1910 to 1912. This call for the black man's labour was most pronounced during 1911 and early 1912, and the resulting competition reflected itself in two public debates that arose during this period.

First, the 'kitchen boys" oldest enemies – the state and the mining industry – reared their heads. From 1907 to 1910 the mining industry had managed to increase its black labour complement by approximately 20 000 workers each year. Between 1910 and 1911, however, it had only acquired an additional 6 000 workers – a mere 30 per cent of the annual increase that it had sustained ever since the recruiting of Chinese labour had been stopped. Under these circumstances the Randlords and their allies invariably became nervous, and when they became nervous they had a habit of peering through the kitchen windows of Witwatersrand homes.

In October 1911 H C Hull, Treasurer of the new Union government, raised the issue in public when he questioned the large-scale unproductive use of black labour in domestic employment at a political gathering. Hull estimated that in the Witwatersrand-Pretoria area alone there were close on 150 000 'houseboys', and suggested that their employers should compensate the state for keeping this labour tied up at a time when industry needed all available African workers. He therefore proposed that householders should pay a labour tax of £3 per month for the privilege of keeping an adult male in domestic service. Although Hull's comments were made at a meeting in a rural area – and thus stated for the benefit of farm as much as mine owners – his proposals gave Rand householders a nasty shock and produced some heated responses. In the end, however, nothing came of these proposals.[81]

The second debate, which centred around domestic labour and technology, did not frighten Johannesburg citizens nearly as much as did the Union Treasurer. From mid-1911 onwards, retailers, the Johannesburg City Council and the press drew increasing attention to the possibilities offered by modern electric household appliances. The *Rand Daily Mail* spelt out part of its vision of the future in an editorial in May 1912:

> In New York the difficulty of securing domestic help has led to a wonderful extension of all labour-saving appliances, so that the house-wife can without any great hardship, do the work of the house, or flat, herself. Electric heaters and cookers, special methods for removing refuse, the provision of hot and cold water in every bedroom, and other inventions, lighten the usual household task so considerably that the absence of a servant is hardly felt. We feel convinced that much may be done along these lines to render the help of the male Kaffir unnecessary.[82]

But despite the great hope placed in the cooker-oven in particular, the Witwatersrand could not be recast in the mould of American capital so easily. In a society where domestic labour was cheap, household appliances were considered expensive, and thus South Africa continued to assume its own distinctive capitalist profile.[83]

Household appliances and the proposed Hull Tax thus left the 'houseboys' unscathed while the economy continued to gain strength between 1909 and 1912. From 1912 to 1914, however, the 'houseboys' once again found themselves under attack. In 1912 the Rand experienced its worst ever 'black peril' scare, and this was followed by a recession that continued until the outbreak of war. Yet another disastrous drought, this time in 1911, drove thousands more African women and children to the cities in search of a living.[84] On this occasion, however, black women came in such numbers that most of them appear to have been willing to accept lower rates for domestic employment than their male counterparts. Thus, for a combination of the old reasons of part-prejudice and part-economy, the 'houseboys' were again liable to substitution by cheaper labour and this showed itself in the changing cash wage rates. From the 50 shillings per month that they were earning at the end of the depression in 1908, 'houseboys'' wages rose to between 60 and 70 shillings by 1911-2. In the recession that followed, however, earnings fell back to between 40 and 60 shillings per month. When the Chamber of Mines undertook a survey of white working-class households in 1913, it found that black domestic servants were paid an average monthly cash wage of 37 shillings and sixpence.[85]

In this survey of the domestic service sector of the Rand labour market between 1890 and 1914, several noteworthy features emerge. First, it is striking to what extent the sector reflected the changing class composition and structure of a city in a maturing capitalist system. This can be seen particularly clearly in the changing demand for white and black servants. The demand for white servants was at its highest when the bulk of the population, the working class, was unable or unwilling to reproduce itself at the point of production – i.e. while 'single' migratory males lived in boarding-houses. Once the working-class family constituted itself in its classic nuclear form with wives and daughters after the South African War, there was an overall decline in the demand for white servants, although this trend was offset by the continuing aspiration of the middle classes to a European domestic servant. In a colonial society, however, even the white working class demanded servants and it is this factor that was largely responsible for the overall growth of the sector and the predominance of black servants.

In South Africa then, the white proletariat built the price of a black servant into the cost of reproducing itself, and this brings us to the second noteworthy feature – the marked conflict between the capitalists and the white proletarian's black servant during the mining industry's period of initial development. Mining capitalists had two good fundamental reasons for being resentful of black domestic servants between 1890 and 1914:

(a) As long as the white working class insisted on the employment of a black domestic servant as a condition of its reproducing itself, so long would the necessary means of subsistence of the most skilled part of the working class be 'artificially' high. It was for precisely this reason that the Chamber of Mines and its allies invariably drew attention to the wages of black domestic servants whenever the high 'cost of living' on the Witwatersrand was discussed.[86] Crudely put, the mine owners reasoned that if they could reduce the wages paid to black servants, they would ultimately be able to reduce the wage bill for the white working class, increase profits and thus benefit capital.

(b) The extremely competitive wages paid to black domestic servants, especially in the early years, increased the price of African labour and threatened labour supplies to the primary industry in the state. Mine owners resented this competition for unskilled adult male labour from a sector that was ultimately funded by themselves! This contradiction in capitalist development hampered profits, and the mine owners and the state consequently lost no opportunity to render the sector more unattractive, or to replace black men with the cheaper labour of women or children.

The third feature that emerges clearly from this survey is the long-term decline in the wages of black domestic servants. Since 'houseboy' wages were ultimately linked to the earnings of the white working class, they tended to reflect the changing wages of white miners. This was particularly clear during periods of recession or depression when the wages of white workers and domestic servants fell sympathetically. Growing proletarianisation in the countryside, coupled with increasing vulnerability to labour substitution by members of the opposite sex or other age groups meant, however, that 'houseboy' wages never recovered as much in periods of prosperity as they had lost in periods of recession. The fact that growing numbers of 'houseboys' were willing to work for declining cash wages points to both the conditions of service in household labour during this period and black South Africans' greater dislike of mine labour at wages that were also declining.

ROLES, DUTIES AND CONDITIONS OF SERVICE FOR DOMESTIC SERVANTS

A formidable number of variables in almost infinite permutations and combinations makes it rather difficult to generalise about this aspect of domestic service on the Witwatersrand between 1890 and 1914. The class of employer, the size and location of his or her house, the number of servants the family was willing to employ, the presence or absence of children and the individual fears, foibles and prejudices of the employer could all affect the duties of a servant. In addition, the class, colour, tribe, sex, age, experience and education of a domestic servant could all help determine the conditions of service he or she was employed under. These differences are important and they should not be minimised. They should not, however, be allowed to obscure such general patterns as do emerge in this area. In the following section an attempt will be made to explore the duties and conditions of service of some of the more important categories of domestic servants to be found on the Rand during this period.

House/parlour maid

Leading members of Johannesburg's commercial, financial and industrial bourgeoisie could afford to maintain a sizeable staff of specialist servants between 1890 and 1914 and no doubt thereafter as well. J W Quinn, baker, benefactor and town councillor, employed a cook, nurse and coachman in addition to several black servants in 1896. The financier, S J Cohen, kept a similar establishment in 1903 – only he employed a housemaid instead of a nurse. Max Epstein, a noted member of the Stock

Exchange, kept a similar staff to his financier colleague but went one further by employing a 'companion' for his allegedly neurotic wife. Amongst the largest complements of all, however, was that at 'Northwards' in Parktown, the home of Col J Dale Lace, mining magnate, town councillor and social patron *par excellence* of ruling-class society. In 1905, the staff at 'Northwards' comprised six white servants (cook, butler, coachman and three housemaids), and twice as many black servants to take charge of the 'rough' domestic work, stables and gardens.[87] In the homes of the Randlords, like the Ecksteins, a racially mixed staff of as many as 20 servants was not unusual.

In such establishments the role of 'housemaid' or 'slavey' was one of the lowest positions in the domestic hierarchy which a white female could occupy. Not only were the incumbents required to live in a modest room on the premises, but they also received amongst the lowest cash wages on the property. In the large and well-off Dale Lace residence, for example, the housemaids, in addition to their uniforms and 'beer money' of 14 shillings, received cash wages of between £4 and £5 per month. These wages were similar – and in some cases less – than those received by black servants in the same establishment and elsewhere in the city. This, coupled with the nature of the duties attached to the post, meant that there was never a ready supply of white housemaids on the Witwatersrand. For this reason employers invariably sought such labour from either the registry offices or the South African Colonisation Society. The immigrant housemaids, however, were as quick as any other Europeans to appreciate that in South Africa hard labour at low wages was considered to be 'kaffir work' and thus turnover in this category of employment remained at a consistently high level.[88]

The housemaid's routine duties involved a daily round of cleaning, sweeping, polishing, tidying and dusting. Johannesburg, which was notorious for its dust and dirt during the early years, ensured that these tasks were both demanding and time-consuming. In several of her chores, however, the housemaid was assisted by a black man – the making of beds, for example, appears to have been a commonly shared task. Other very demanding work, such as the cleaning of stoves or grates, was done largely by the black man with the assistance of the housemaid. It was usually at this point that the mistress of the house started to experience difficulties with her staff since what frequently started out as a joint housemaid-'houseboy' chore soon degenerated into a task involving only housemaid 'supervision'. This had the undesirable consequence of leaving the housemaid 'idle' and of generating considerable animosity between white female and black male servants. In addition to the chores outlined above it was also the housemaid's duty to assist in serving the family at meal times. Although it is difficult to be precise, it would appear that all of these duties made for a lengthy working day. Anna Herrmann, who was employed by the very demanding Cohen family, claimed that a normal working day started at 6 a.m. and ended at 10.30 p.m. Her case, however, does not appear to be typical since she was given added duties which housemaids were not normally expected to perform, and in the end she and a hard-worked cook both deserted the Cohen household to seek more congenial work elsewhere.[89]

Leisure-time activities posed difficulties for young female domestics in Johannesburg and this was particularly true between 1895 and 1908. A well-developed 'white slave' traffic in women and organised prostitution on a substantial scale were only two of the dangers that confronted the unwary. Equally menacing in its own way, however, were the low wages paid to housemaids in a city where there was a considerable preponderence of males over females. All of these factors combined to make the threat of lax moral behaviour and part-time prostitution on the part of the housemaids a matter of real concern to certain elements within the ruling classes. Thus, at different times the employers, the church and the state all undertook to organise activities which would steer female domestic servants clear of these dangers.

In 1898 Miss Plunkett's Club was set up in the city to help keep respectable young women out of trouble. After the war, the Women's Immigration Department and the South African Colonisation Society placed great emphasis on moral qualities in their selection of domestic servants for the Rand – a fact which pointed to the existence of similar problems in England. These organisations also made substantial efforts to ensure the welfare of these women once they had reached Johannesburg. Despite their precautions, however, 15 out of 500 such servants turned out to be 'morally unsatisfactory' between 1902 and 1904. The Church of England chose to make its effort through an organisation that had traditionally dominated domestic servants at 'home' – the Girls' Friendly Society; the major objective of the Society being 'to raise the standard of true, pure womanhood throughout the Empire'.[90]

The majority of the housemaids, however, seem to have followed the orthodox leisure-time activities of their class. On their Thursday afternoons off they would often visit their friends who were in service elsewhere in the city. As for the rest, they appear to have had their heads turned by the usual things that appeal to any younger generation. Paternalistic employers were concerned that they 'wasted' their time and money on pretty dresses, 'giddy' visits to the fortune-teller or on reading 'trashy novels'.[91]

The cook-general

In Johannesburg it was only the very rich who could afford the services of a fully qualified cook who, by 1905, could earn as much as £12 per month. The majority of the lower-bourgeois and upper-middle-class families therefore had to be content with the services of a cook-general and a relatively modest staff of black servants. In such homes the cook-general was frequently the only white servant employed, but the family would also enjoy the services of between three and five African male servants. The cook-general was thus likely to find herself at least partly in charge of, and responsible for, the work of the 'houseboy', 'garden boy', 'kitchen boy' and black 'coachman'.

The role and status of the cook-general as the only white servant on a staff of mixed races within the household was riddled with ambiguities and tension. Broadly conceived, there were two basic patterns of relationships that could develop, and each was enmeshed in its own problems. First, the employing family could perceive the cook-general primarily as a fellow *white* and only secondarily as a servant. If this happened the cook-general could often become a 'valued personal friend of both master and mistress'. It was vital that if the relationship was to be managed in this way, however, then the initiative for it should come from the mistress rather than the maid. For, if the cook-general of her own accord pushed too far and too strongly in this direction, then she was in danger of disregarding her servant status altogether and transgressing the class boundaries between herself and her employers. When this happened employers invariably became resentful and accused the maid of 'putting on airs' or of getting 'beyond her station'.[92]

Secondly, the employing family could choose to perceive the cook-general primarily as a *servant* rather than as a fellow white. This managerial style in effect left the white female domestic 'relegated to the society of black men'. If the first pattern of relationships had the danger of producing employer-based resentment, then the latter gave rise to employee hostility. Annoyed at having been pushed back into their class category with other black servants, the cooks-general tended to strike back by accusing the employers of not knowing how to treat them as *white* servants. These accusations they made all the more effective by pointing out that the *nouveau riche* middle classes of Johannesburg lacked the domestic managerial experience of the English ruling class to which they were accustomed. With biting accuracy they pointed to the recent and rapid class mobility of their employers by referring to them as a 'mushroom' or 'veld aristocracy'. As one shocked cook-general put it:

> Judge of my surprise on arrival at my new home when I recognised my lord and master as an ex-publican from Birmingham and my lady as the daughter of a well-known butcher to whose establishment I had often been on errands in the same neighbourhood.[93]

Clearly, class and class-consciousness partly forged in the old metropole could not always be effortlessly incorporated into the new colonial social structure.

These ambiguities in determining the exact status of the white servant also revealed themselves in other areas. Cooks-general who were fortunate enough to develop close relationships with economically privileged and liberal employers no doubt ate well enough, getting their share of what appeared on the family table. Other European servants, however, found that they were given a diet of special meat and second-rate vegetables with the result that they claimed to be 'nearly starving' for want of decent nourishment.[94]

In the question of accommodation the same range of possibilities opened up and ultimately a combination of employer's income, status considerations and employee's wishes determined whether or not the cook-general lived on the premises. In Johannesburg, middle-class homes were not designed to accommodate white servants and thus many cooks-general who did live in often had to make do with the smallest and least comfortable room in the house. Lower-middle-class employers found that they simply did not have the space to offer their white servants a room at all. In such cases the cook-general would hire a room in a 'respectable' working class suburb or in one of the racially integrated slum areas of older Johannesburg where she would then live with workers and servants of all colours.[95]

In theory, the cook-general had an awesome range of duties to fulfil. All the cooking and cleaning in the home were her responsibility and in addition she could be called upon to assist with the mending of clothes or doing of other 'needlework'. In some homes she would also be expected to do the washing and ironing, but this was a small minority of cases since most domestic servants – black as well as white – refused to undertake this hard specialised work in addition to their other duties. For washing and ironing then, the mistress had to look beyond the cook-general to the local steam laundries, Cape Coloured laundresses, or the Zulu craft guild that undertook much of the washing in the city.[96]

In practice, however, all the old ambiguities came into play to bedevil the problem of allocating duties to the cook-general. White women considered it to be 'undignified' to do 'such work as scrubbing floors, cleaning windows, washing up' and a score of other household tasks. This resistance or refusal to do hard unpleasant work produced considerable tension between mistress and maid, and the problem was only partially resolved by the employment of additional black servants to undertake such chores. Once the black men were employed, however, the cook-general would frequently fall prey to the temptation of delegating not only the 'rough work' to the 'houseboy' but an increasing proportion of her other duties as well. This in turn would spark off a new round of tensions between mistress and maid, and between the cook-general and an increasingly hard-worked and resentful 'houseboy'.[97]

But regardless of whether they actually performed their duties or merely supervised them, the cooks-general appear to have worked lengthy hours. This was at least partly due to the fact that they were responsible for meals and thus had to be on duty most evenings. The majority of these women started work between 5 and 7 a.m. and finished at some time between 9 p.m. and midnight. These were long hours and if they lived on the premises and there were tensions in the household, they could also be lonely hours. In a talk on 'Servants and their treatment' in 1912, Mrs W F Lance pointed out that she felt:

> … in sympathy with the young woman who went into a household where perhaps only one white maid was kept, where she had no one to speak to all day long, and her evenings were also spent alone.[98]

It was hardly surprising then, continued Mrs Lance, that women deserted domestic service for the comparative warmth and independence offered by working-class life in a factory.

Cooks-general appear to have spent their occasional evenings and afternoons off in much the same way as the housemaids although, being somewhat older than the latter, they were less frequently accused of 'wasting' their time or money. A popular haunt for the immigrant cook-general was the South African Colonisation Society Hostel in central Johannesburg where they would gather on a Thursday afternoon to collect their mail or meet their countrywomen.[99]

Children's nurse

In a mature capitalist system one of the major functions of the family, and more especially of its female members, is to socialise children. Precisely because the Witwatersrand did *not* constitute a mature capitalist system between 1890 and 1914 this family function could not be easily or simply fulfilled. There were three basic reasons for this. First, as we have seen, the sexual composition of the white proletariat was only gradually transformed to the point where it could reproduce itself. Second, this meant that there was a comparative shortage of white mothers, daughters, aunts and grandmothers to assist in the process of child-rearing and socialisation. Third, not even surrogate socialisation by a female domestic servant was a real possibility since, for a complex set of reasons, the historical process of proletarianisation had initially yielded a male-dominated service sector. Thus, when the predominant amount of child-rearing and socialisation was not directly undertaken by the mother, it was usually done by a black male servant. This delegation of responsibility for the child's socialisation, in a society deeply ridden with fear and race prejudice, produced a measure of guilt in the white family – and this was more especially the case where the child happened to be female. From the early 1890s until the outbreak of the South African War the overwhelming majority of 'nurses' in Johannesburg were 'Zulu' males and, so it was reported, most of them performed their duties in an 'excellent' manner. During this period the overall economic dominance of this sector by the 'Zulus', like that of their counterparts the 'kitchen boys', was not in question. Perhaps equally significant is the fact that while there was no serious alternative to this male labour there was no major ideological onslaught on their dominance of this role either.[100]

Immediately after the war, however, there was a sharp increase in the number of white wives and mothers in the Witwatersrand population. Now, for the first time, there was a significant and keen demand amongst the better-off families for the services of a professional child's nurse. The lower-bourgeois and upper-middle classes, however, found it hard to fill these positions with Europeans since the wages they offered were so low and since they expected nursemaids to undertake many 'housemaid' duties in addition to those of child-minding.[101] Thus while a small number of families managed to acquire the full-time services of a nanny, the majority had to continue to rely on their 'Zulu' nurses until at least 1908 and in some cases until very much later.

Between 1906 and 1908 the Witwatersrand experienced its first wave of really serious post-war 'black peril' scares. On this occasion there were also a small number of sexual assaults on very young white girls which contributed to the spreading hysteria. 'Black peril', the availability of the first limited number of black females in the service sector and a new attempt by the state and the Randlords to get the black man into the mining compounds combined to give weight to an ideological attack on the role of the 'Zulu' nurse. From late 1906 it was reported that there was a growing feeling that 'the Kaffir is not the person to be placed in charge of young children'. When *The Star* ran an editorial on 'The Servant Problem' to promote the use of 'piccanin' domestic labour in January 1908, it skilfully combined a growing public prejudice which it had helped foster as well as mining house interest, by suggesting that the 'kaffir' should be compelled to 'change the perambulator for the pick'.[102]

In the wake of these events a growing number of black women found employment as 'nurses' between 1908 and 1909. After the second wave of 'black peril' scares in 1912-3 there was a renewed demand for white nursemaids but such substitution as there was on this occasion usually involved black rather than white women. Right up to 1914, however, there were very many black males in employment as 'nurses' in Johannesburg homes.[103]

This gradual and incomplete process of substituting black females for male 'Zulu' 'nurses' between 1908 and 1914 was accompanied by its own particular brand of strident racist ideology. This was perhaps to be seen in its clearest and most bizarre form in the letters which a noted public correspondent, Philip Hammond, wrote to the press in 1909. Hammond assured his Johannesburg readers that if the appointment of a black nurse to a white child did not 'end in death' then it would certainly 'end in disfigurement'. 'The child', wrote Hammond, 'will absorb some of the attributes of the Coloured nurse. It will develop a cloudy and oily skin, often a blotchy face, and in many ways puzzle both mother and doctor ... '.[104] The effect of this 'extreme' form of racist ideology on its audience was interesting. On the one hand it was clear that very few people subscribed to Hammond's crude notion of the physical contamination of white children by black nurses. On the other, however, nobody dismissed his ideas as being totally unfounded or insane since the 'overstated' or 'extremist' views of the public correspondent simply revealed, in purer crystallised form, many of the shapeless ideas that floated freely and fully in the minds of most white South Africans. After all, it was only a year later that Sir Matthew Nathan in a public address to the South African Colonisation Society noted in the course of some remarks on the black nurse that: 'Just as the natives had a peculiar exterior so they had a peculiar character, and it was obvious that the British colonist did not want his child imbued with the ideas of a lower civilisation.'[105]

It was this latter and relatively subtle idea – that there were ultimately social prices to be paid for allowing one's children to be reared by people from another culture – that really concerned Witwatersrand mothers. Filled with guilt and prejudice, however, these white women removed their reservations from a *cultural* nexus and instead made them colour their *racist* perceptions. As a 'housewife' noted in 1907:

Many mothers have remarked the change for the worse in their sons' characters, never for a moment suspecting the freedom and close intimacy that there is between the lads and the native servants. Unconsciously the lads imbibe the loose ideas of morals from the natives, and these, unhappily, colour all their actions, to the distress of their parents and friends.[106]

It was for these reasons, amongst others, that the mothers wanted the black male servants removed as 'nurses' – wishing to replace them with the selfsame black females whom they considered to be too 'immoral' to associate with their husbands.

The 'houseboy'

While the rich had their cooks and specialist staff, and the middle classes enjoyed the services of their cooks-general and other black staff, the bulk of the white population – the lower-middle and working classes – made do with the services of the ubiquitous 'houseboy'. Above all others, it was this solitary general domestic servant who undertook the bulk of the domestic labour on the Witwatersrand between 1890 and 1914. Throughout these years the 'houseboy' was under close public scrutiny and even the most critical of observers, during the most stressful of circumstances, were fulsome in their praises of his attributes.

In the 1890s the first generation of Johannesburg 'houseboys' were considered to be noteworthy for their 'ignorance, but also for their amiable nature, general trustworthiness and especially for their capacity for hard work'.[107] As peasants newly off the land they were understandably untrained and 'ignorant' of European customs but sympathetic observers were quick to place these deficiencies in their correct perspective:

> A kaffir properly trained makes a capital servant, quick to learn, obedient, faithful, and apparently conscientious, if such a word may be used in this context. You would not take a man or woman from the country districts of England, Scotland or Ireland, and turn them into waiters, cooks and house-servants in a week or two.[108]

In retrospect, it would appear that it took about six or seven years for the Witwatersrand to acquire a pool of basically trained 'houseboys'.

After the South African War, once the 'houseboys' had acquired the most necessary domestic skills, the charge of 'ignorance' was seldom if ever raised and Mrs Lionel Phillips probably spoke for many when she praised these servants as 'an invaluable asset'. The Minister of Native Affairs was even more forthcoming. In 1912, at the height of the 'black peril' hysteria, he told white South Africans that 'rightly handled' the 'houseboys' were 'perhaps the best domestic servants in the world'. In the following year his words were echoed by a government commission of enquiry which found that 'as a rule, the native houseboy is an excellent servant, and frequently performs long and faithful service'.[109]

It is difficult to generalise about the duties of a 'houseboy' since, as we have seen before, duties tended to vary according to the class of the employer, the size and age of the family, the number of staff kept and the individual experience and attributes of the servant himself. In most homes, however, the 'houseboys' were responsible for the making of fires, cleaning stoves, sweeping, washing dishes, preparing morning and afternoon tea, keeping the yard clean, and doing such routine garden work as weeding and watering.[110] If the overwhelming majority of these duties were unskilled and centred on the kitchen, then the servant could be accorded the slightly lower status of 'kitchen boy'. In a significant number of homes, however, the 'houseboys' would assist in the preparation of meals or undertake the actual cooking of everyday meals for the family. In these latter cases the 'houseboy' was in fact no less than a regular black cook-general and, like the cook-general, would undertake to do the full range of household duties with the possible exception of washing and ironing.

In several Johannesburg middle-class families the 'houseboy' was also called upon to perform other tasks, such as acting as 'coachman' when the occasion demanded. Since it was an offence under the municipal by-laws to leave a horse and trap unattended in the streets, many mistresses made a practice of taking the 'houseboy' along with them on shopping trips so that he might play the role of coachman when necessary. In Johannesburg, a white woman out shopping with her 'houseboy', or sitting beside a black 'coachman', was a frequent enough sight to raise squeals of protest from articulate racists or unemployed white coachmen.[111]

But the 'houseboy's' duties did not end there. In many middle and some working-class homes he was also called upon to perform some of the more intimate functions of a body servant. Not only did they help their masters to dress and undress but, in the privacy of the house, they undertook tasks for the mistress which many Europeans felt should only be performed by a white female servant. Trusted 'houseboys' served early-morning coffee in the bedroom, sometimes assisted the mistress with the more difficult items of clothing while dressing, drew her bath and, on at least one occasion which Sol T Plaatje recorded in his famous essay *The Mote and the Beam*, sponged her back.[112]

The execution of these various duties brought the 'houseboys' into close contact with European women for a large part of their working day. 'White women', Mrs Lance pointed out in her talk in 1912, 'in many cases worked side by side with the boys from morning to night.' The nature and extent of this complementary labour, however, could vary according to the class of employer and the personalities of the parties involved. In working-class homes, where he was the only servant employed, the 'houseboy' would often work directly alongside the mistress of the house, but in lower-middle-class homes he might find himself working with either the mistress, or the cook-general, or both.

In many cases these working relationships were tolerably paternalistic or even amicable. Very many more, however, were characterised by friction and hostility or conscious disputes that arose from the unfair allocation of household chores. Depending on which of these patterns developed, and whether or not there were other black servants present, the life of a 'houseboy' – like that of a cook-general – could be more or less lonely and isolated.[113] In addition, and again like their cooks-general counterparts, the 'houseboys' worked long hours with the average day starting between 5 and 7 a.m. and finishing at some time between 6 and 9 p.m.[114]

The 'houseboys' remuneratioin for these long hours and varied duties was a cash wage and – as the employers never failed to point out – 'board and lodging'. In most cases the staple diet consisted of a daily ration of 'mealie meal' for porridge, occasional issues of cheap cuts of meat and whatever happened to be left over from the family table. Although it is difficult to be certain, it would appear that when cash wages declined after the South African War, 'houseboys' often demanded – and got – a slightly more varied diet with more frequent issues of meat.[115] Once again, however, this general pattern has to be offset against that ever-present minority of employers who appear to have fed their black servants particularly well.

The 'lodgings' which employers offered their black servants were, in the first instance, more for the convenience of the white family than for the comfort of the 'houseboy'. In fact, in many modest working-class homes before the First World War the 'houseboy' did not have a room at all but simply slept on the kitchen floor at night. In other homes the 'houseboy's room' was in reality part of the stables. On the majority of properties, however, there was usually a small single room without ablution facilities set aside in the back yard, and it was here that the majority of the black male servants on the Witwatersrand lived. The quality of this accommodation varied according to the usual factors, but with the average being somewhat closer to a hovel than a habitable room.[116]

The primary purpose of the servants' rooms, however, was to exercise control over the black domestics – and the 'houseboys' knew this only too well and resented it deeply. Thus in 1902, when the 'houseboys' returned to the Rand with some ready cash and new expectations after the war, a significant number of them refused to reoccupy the old hovels in the back yard. Knowing just how great the demand for their services was, the 'houseboys' pushed the employers into allowing them to live off the premises. What they then did was to club together and collectively rent a house within a Johannesburg suburb like Ophirton or Doornfontein, and live there free from the scrutiny of their employers. Yet others hired a room in a slum yard in old Jeppe or Doornfontein, or lodged themselves in the location.[117] Elements of this new pattern of independence in Johannesburg persisted right up to 1914, but never again on the scale of that immediate post-war period. Growing proletarianisation, but above all the declining cash wages for 'houseboys', progressively undermined these black servants' independence and ultimately drove them back to the employers' property.

In another area, however, the 'houseboys'' battle for independence never ceased and that was in their quest for adequate leisure time. To the considerable annoyance of many white families, the 'houseboys' insisted on having Sundays off and any employer invasion of this time was both deeply resented and strongly resisted. In addition, many 'houseboys' demanded a couple of hours off each afternoon in order to enjoy a meal and recover from a working day that had already seen about eight hours of labour.[118]

The importance of this leisure time to black male domestic servants who often worked in stringent isolation, in a culturally alien environment and under conditions of considerable tension cannot be overstressed. 'Houseboys' relaxed either by entertaining friends in their 'rooms', or by going to the slum yards or mine locations where they spent their time drinking, card-playing or whoring. Once these more basic needs had been met, however, they also took the opportunity to express and reassert themselves in the props of the invading culture that so relentlessly attempted to relegate them to the one-dimensional status of 'boy'. Outraged and threatened whites complained about the sights in Jeppe on a Sunday afternoon when domestic servants, 'attired in the most up-to-date costumes, and carrying canes and sticks', could be seen 'swaggering along using English language of the most appalling description'.[119]

The 'houseboys' however, were not merely taken with the form of 'western civilisation'; they also looked for substance. In particular, they longed to be educated in the hours when they were not at work. When the 'Transvaal Native Association' was formed after the war it received aid and support from two men who were thoroughly familiar with 'houseboys' and their aspirations – James Bold and John Parker, the partners in Parker's Registry Office. It was these men, and especially Parker as 'Honorary President' who, in 1905-6, encouraged the Native Association in its efforts to establish a meeting hall, library and night school for Johannesburg's black workers. Although this venture does not appear to have come to much, the 'houseboys' continued their struggle to become educated. In 1908 somebody else who was well acquainted with domestic servants, Miss M C Bruce of the St Agnes Native Girls' Industrial School, noted that: 'During the past half dozen years the Kaffir has been educating himself in his little tin shanty in our back yards to a degree that might astonish the average Johannesburger did he think about it.' Yet another observer, Ambrose Pratt, confirmed this during his visit to South Africa in 1910. Pratt was struck by what he termed the black man's 'intense desire' for education, and noted that: 'The vast majority of natives in domestic employment have books in their possession with which they are continually attempting to instruct themselves.'[120] Clearly, Johannesburg might have been 'the university of crime', as John X Merriman once called it, but for many 'houseboys' it was also a valued educational institution of another sort.

THE CONTROL OF DOMESTIC SERVANTS
The state

As we have seen above, the demand for white female domestic servants was at its most pronounced during Milner's reconstruction era. It was also during most of this period, between 1902-5, that the wages for European servants were rising. Under these circumstances it is perhaps predictable that employees would seek maximum mobility and that employers would do their utmost to prevent it. Invariably, such struggles are mediated through the law, and in most capitalist societies it is the masters rather than the servants who make the law. South Africa, however, was not merely a developing capitalist society, but also a colonial one, and for this reason it is of more than usual interest to see what role the state played in the attempt to control both black and white servants.

Between 1902 and 1905 several leading bourgeois families recruited their specialist domestic servants directly from England, and so too did the South African Colonisation Society. In return for forwarding the passage money for the journey to South Africa, the masters expected these servants to sign a contract of up to a year during which period the loan was wholly or partially repayable to the employer. The arrangement already contained the seeds of contradiction within it, as the Colonisation Society pointed out:

> ... for the women who are most suitable for emigration by independence of character, and love of enterprise and adventure, are precisely those who are most reluctant to bind themselves to an unknown employer in a strange country.[121]

Once these servants got to Johannesburg and found that they were required to do work that was considered to be socially unacceptable for a white woman, that the cash wages did not go as far as they thought they would, or that there were higher wages to be got elsewhere, they ignored their contracts and deserted.

On 12 March 1902 Elizabeth Knowles summarily left service at 'Northwards' after a disagreement with Mrs Dale Lace. Colonel J Dale Lace had little hesitation in having her prosecuted for what he believed to be a breach of contract. The magistrate, however, ruled that a contract signed outside the country was not binding in the Transvaal unless approved by a magistrate and registered within two months of the servant's arrival. Instead, he found Miss Knowles guilty under the Masters' and Servants' Act and gave her the nominal sentence of a £1 fine or two day's hard labour.[122] The decision, at exactly the time that the South African Colonisation Society scheme for large-scale immigrant labour had been launched, alarmed the employers considerably. *The Star* was quick to spot the danger and in an editorial appealed for a 'reform' of the law which would make such contracts binding.[123]

The law did not change, and the employers apparently did not learn from the Knowles decision. On 16 January 1903 the following notice appeared in the local press:

> Two German servant girls viz. ANNA HERRMANN and EMMA HOORMAN have deserted my service, being indentured to me for two years. All persons are hereby warned against harbouring them. If whereabouts are known please communicate with Criminal Investigation Department, Johannesburg.
> Siegfried J Cohen

Anna Herrmann was subsequently found working for Mrs Hermann Eckstein and prosecuted on 29 January 1903. Again the magistrate refused to uphold the contract and felt obliged to give Mr Cohen a lecture on the evils of lengthy contracts for white servants. This time the nominal sentence under the Masters' and Servants' Act was ten shillings and two days' imprisonment.[124]

But even this second decision was not enough for the richest, most stubborn and uncompromising employers of all. In September 1905 the Dale Laces once again brought out several servants from England under contract. Within three months all but one of these servants had left 'Northwards' for more tolerable conditions or higher wages elsewhere. When the last servant, a housemaid named Alice Shurville, gave notice of her intention to leave in January 1906, the Colonel refused to accept it and withheld wages that were due to her. Undaunted, Miss Shurville took her eminent employer to court, while he in turn attempted to defend the action on the basis of the contract. The magistrate awarded the housemaid her wages, a small amount for damages and the cost of the proceedings.[125]

By the time that this second Dale Lace case was decided upon the Colonisation Society's scheme for immigrant servants was virtually dead. Significantly enough, *The Star* did not make an appeal for the 'reform' of the law on this occasion. Instead it contented itself with the smug warning to employers that they had themselves to blame if they did not register their contracts with white servants in the Transvaal.[126] It was also clear by this time, from the remarks made by magistrates and the nominal sentences they imposed on European deserters, that the state was reluctant to deliver white servants into the hands of their employers. But if the state disappointed the employers in regard to a small number of white servants, then it more than compensated by harshly controlling the majority of servants who really made the system function – the black 'houseboys'.

From 1896 to 1914 the major mechanism which the state employed to control black labour on the Witwatersrand and elsewhere was, of course, the pass laws. The primary purpose of this repressive legislation was to channel black workers to the most important capitalist industry – the mines – and to ensure that they stayed on as cheap labour for the duration of their contracts. It was precisely for these reasons that the introduction and modification of pass law legislation invariably took place in periods of marked economic stress in the capitalist system. Thus, the first pass laws were introduced to the Rand in the wake of the Jameson Raid and the recession which is heralded. The black labour crisis in the post-war period, however, prompted the major revision, extension and sophistication of the pass laws by the Milner administration. Thereafter, the system was updated and modified whenever conditions demanded it – as for example during the depression in the wake of the departure of the Chinese labourers from the Rand in 1908.

Although these laws were primarily directed at industrial workers, they also applied to domestic servants. But since they were intended for the benefit of the former rather than the latter, they earned some hostility from the employers of domestic labour and the universal hatred of black workers. James Bold, of Parker's Registry Office, probably spoke for many in the service sector in 1906 when he said that:

> ... there can be no doubt that the native pass laws were framed to prevent the townspeople from obtaining domestic servants, or to render their employment so irksome to employers as to be prohibitory. Personally, I have no doubt that they are framed solely in the interests of the capitalists.[127]

A survey of the labour market reveals that the thrust of Bold's observation was close to the mark.

An important secondary purpose of the pass laws was to control the movement of black workers within the cities. In addition to a monthly pass to show that he was in regular employment, any African male who wished to proceed beyond the bounds of the municipality or to travel outside prescribed hours had to produce a 'special pass' signed by his employer. The laws thus severely restricted the free movement of blacks and, in the case of 'houseboys', must have markedly increased their feelings of isolation by tending to confine them to the suburbs. To make matters worse, these passes were constantly demanded by black policemen – men whom a commission of enquiry in 1913 found to be largely 'ignorant' and 'illiterate'.[128]

But the pass laws did not only isolate Africans; they also helped – albeit partly unintentionally – to humiliate them. In 1914, for example, a journalist with a keen eye noted how a stylishly dressed black man made his way through Joubert Park in a rather conspicuous manner until such time as he was accosted by a policeman.

> 'Where's your pass?' said the constable. All the rise and 'swank' taken out of him, the native humbly felt in his pockets for his pass, and after the constable was satisfied about it, he was allowed to proceed. But his step had lost its spring and lightness, and his eye its brightness too. He was a crushed and fallen man.[129]

The pass laws etched themselves deeply into the psyches of urban African men. Who then can wonder why they sometimes unleashed such deep, passionate and destructive urges in the men who were called 'boys'?

The remaining important control function which the passes served more directly was to provide a record of the 'character' of the black worker. When, for one or another reason the worker's contract came to an end, the employer would indicate his 'character' in the appropriate place on the pass. This white assessment of black performance was important to all African workers, but it was of special importance to the 'houseboy' who was in search not of cheap unskilled labour, but of semi-skilled employment at better wages in the intimacy of a European household. No doubt many employers gave their ex-servants adequate, fair or even excellent references. A great many others, however, deliberately spoilt their 'houseboy's' pass through the addition of spiteful or malicious comments. These gratuitous remarks had the effect of pegging or reducing the worker's subsequent wages, or of jeopardising his chances of getting other employment altogether.[130] Again this was potent fuel for the hatred that burnt in many a 'houseboy's' heart.

The employers

One of the most pervasive and successful ways in which householders attempted to control their domestic servants was through the manipulation of wage payments. In the years prior to the rinderpest, relatively independent 'Zulu houseboys' appear to have favoured a system of weekly cash wage payments. In an unstable mining camp with many unscrupulous employers who did not hesitate to defraud their employees of their wages, the advantages of this system to what were essentially short-term domestic servants was obvious. By 1896-7, when the process of proletarianisation in the countryside was more advanced, however, many Rand householders shifted to what they called the 'Natal system' – viz, paying their servants on a monthly basis. This meant, as an employer told his colleagues at a meeting of the Johannesburg Mercantile Association, that: 'The boys kept far more sober, they had a better hold on them, and they stayed longer.' After the South African War the monthly payment system appears to have become almost universal. But not even this was enough for some employers who further extended and 'refined' the system. As a matter of policy they kept 'houseboy' wages in arrears by anything from two to four weeks as a form of 'insurance' against instant departure by their domestic servants.[131]

In an equally deliberate attempt to defraud their employees of their wages, a significant number of employers also sought to provoke a mid-month confrontation with their servants. It is 'a common practice' for people to engage servants in Johannesburg, alleged a cook-general in 1905, 'and then to find the means to dispense with them before the month is up, for no other reason than to swindle the poor unfortunate women out of their pay'. A thousand and one 'houseboys' could have echoed these words in chorus, and there was no other single employer practice that produced a greater sense of injustice or provoked a more violent response from black male domestic servants than this one.[132]

Whilst the primary purpose of this employer stratagem might have been to refine robbery, it also had the indirect beneficial consequence of enhancing control over servants between pay-days. Servants, who were certainly aware of this employer-tactic, would have had to be abnormally passive and unusually restrained under provocation if they wished to get the chance of obtaining the wages due to them. Even total passivity, however, did not always guarantee the 'houseboy' his wages. The commission of enquiry in the wake of the great 'black peril' scare of 1912 found that in a significant number of cases employers had simply trumped up charges of sexual assault against their 'houseboys' in order to defraud them of their wages.[133]

More direct, but at least as crude, were some of the methods that employers used to control servants within their homes. We know from Jan Note – the founder of the most notorious black criminal gang on the Witwatersrand during this period – that when he went to be a 'kitchen boy' in Johannesburg in 1887 his employers threatened him with a revolver while giving him his instructions. Since his employers eventually transpired to be highway robbers this behaviour was perhaps not surprising. What is surprising, however, is how ready ordinary householders, including women, were to threaten 'houseboys' with guns.[134] In addition, not a few mistresses and their white female domestic servants appear to have been willing to strike or *sjambok* 'houseboys' who did not perform their duties adequately or quickly enough for their employers' liking.[135] Needless to say, such assaults did nothing to reduce the tension in what was already a highly charged atmosphere.

Employer control, however, also extended beyond the immediate work situation into the servant's 'private life'. This extension, as we have already noted in passing, was made possible largely through the manner in which domestic servants were accommodated. Male but more especially female domestic servants found that their sexual relationships were under the close, critical and constant scrutiny of their employers. This was particularly so in the case of white women who had a bedroom within the house itself – although it also applied to black and Coloured women who happened to occupy a room in the back yard of the premises. For obvious reasons this was yet another cause of friction and Mrs Lance, in her talk on the treatment of servants, made a point of suggesting that if householders gave their cooks-general a private sitting-room in addition to a bedroom in which to entertain their male friends, then employer-employee relationships would improve.[136] In addition to this moral surveillance, employers of all classes did not hesitate to invade and inspect their servants' rooms and goods if they suspected them of theft or any other misdemeanour.[137] Servants were always visible to their employers – during work and leisure hours alike.

Besides these cruder cudgels, employers also possessed a selection of more subtle instruments with which to control their black servants, and perhaps one of the most striking of these was to be found in the field of communication. With masters and mistresses unable to speak Zulu, and servants as yet unable to speak English, urban households gave rise to a jargon which one observer aptly termed an 'emergency language'. This 'language', which was later known as *fanakalo* – 'do it like this' – became the industrial *lingua franca* of southern Africa, was at the time almost universally known by the socially more significant name of 'Kitchen Kaffir'.

It was this Zulu-based jargon, interspersed with English and Afri-

kaans words, that served as the basic medium of communication between white mistresses and black servants in Johannesburg households.
While this 'Esperanto of South Africa' might have made simple commands possible it denied more subtle or complex communication and as
such it was the basis of much misunderstanding and conflict. Invariably,
however, the onus and responsibility for this lack of understanding was
made to rest with the servant rather than the master of mistress, and the
'houseboy' was frequently chastised for 'not knowing his own language'. In addition, many Europeans felt threatened by Africans who
spoke or attempted to speak English as this implied creeping equality
and thus insisted on blacks speaking 'Kitchen Kaffir'. Unable to communicate in their first language and saddled instead with a brittle and
bastard tongue, black servants had their dependent and colonised status
perpetually reinforced through appearing to be stupid, inarticulate and
incoherent. The 'language' might have been conceived in a kitchen, but
it was also *kaffir* – with all that that implied for white South Africans.[138]

If the element of control in the use of 'Kitchen Kaffir' was largely an
unconscious by-product in the use of language, then the same surely
cannot be said of the names which many white employers gave their
black servants. Like their Victorian predecessors who did not hesitate to
change 'their servants'' names arbitrarily if they happened to clash with
those of the 'family', European employers were quick to rename their
'Zulu' employees. In part, this was no doubt simply due to the difficulties which whites experienced with the pronunciation of Zulu names,
and some of the new names like 'New One' or 'Long One' were relatively innocent. But, whereas Victorian masters simply gave their servants
other randomly chosen Christian names to distance themselves from the
employees, many Witwatersrand household gave their servants the
names of commodities or objects. Names such as 'Saucepan', 'Shilling',
'Brandy', 'Sixpence' or 'Matches' not only distanced servants from
employers, they also humiliated them and ultimately denied their
humanity altogether.[139] Being a 'boy' must have hurt a man's pride; being
a boy-commodity must have crushed much of his remaining human dignity in what was already a servile position.

One of the remaining ways in which employers controlled their servants – white as well as black – but especially the 'houseboys', was
through gifts of cast-off clothing in an era when the use of servants'
uniforms was anything but widespread. This practice, however, was
beset with difficulties and produced a deep-seated ambivalence within
the minds of European employers. On the one hand, employers made
capital out of their gifts of second-hand clothing to servants by using it
as an ideological device with which to justify low cash wages.[140] It also
had the largely unconscious but nevertheless desirable consequence of

increasing the dependency of the servant.[141] Both of these procedures ultimately facilitated employer control, although in different ways.

On the other hand, however, black servants who dressed like their masters – indeed in what was, until very recently, the master's own clothing – were modelling themselves on Europeans and this had implications of aspirant if not actual equality. Between 1890 and 1914, when the Witwatersrand social structure was changing particularly rapidly and when personal class distinctions between workers and the petty bourgeoisie were not as visible or marked as they were in later years, nothing threatened Europeans more than this practice of blacks wearing 'white' clothes.[142] It was therefore predictable that one of the later proposals for dealing with the 'houseboy' 'black peril' threat was that:

> No native should be allowed to wear ordinary European dress during working hours, and employers should combine to this end. European dress gives him an inflated sense of importance and equality.[143]

When, very much later, 'houseboy' uniforms were introduced to the Witwatersrand, they undoubtedly served more than a simple utilitarian purpose.

The colonial masters' and mistresses' ideology

In the colonies, at least as much as in the metropolis, masters and mistresses spent an endless amount of time talking about their servants – and not infrequently such discussions took place in the presence of an apparently deaf-mute 'houseboy'. On the Witwatersrand, employers also addressed volumes of letters to the press on some or other recent dimension of the 'servant problem'. Here again the notions of the employers were subjected to the scrutiny of the cooks-general and the 'houseboys' and, on occasion, produced vigorous clashes in the correspondence columns of the local press. While it is difficult, if not impossible to assess to what extent these notions of the employing classes were internalised by the servants, it is important to have an idea of what some of these ideological constructs were. But since much of this ground has already been covered in passing, the discussion here will be necessarily brief.

'If the Kaffir is brother to anything', wrote one Charles O'Hara in 1912, 'it is to the anthropoid ape'. This view of Africans being more akin to animals than humans was not restricted to the lunatic fringe of racists in Witwatersrand society. In 1897 the pretentiously opinionated and self-styled 'progressive' newspaper *The Star* had run an editorial in which it claimed that: 'In South Africa in general the Kaffir is a mere naked savage, with not much more intelligence than a baboon, and not much more ambition.' On this, as on other occasions, it was left to the pro-Kruger and allegedly backward *Standard and Diggers' News* to defend the black 'houseboy' with some sane and well-reasoned perspectives. Partly because of these animal-cum-savage origins, African men were supposed to be highly sexed and uninhibited, and therefore constituted 'one of the most lustful savage races on earth'. [144]

It was considered, however, that if the 'noble savage' could be obtained immediately after his 'wild' youthful stage then he could be turned into 'a natural servant' since 'the instinct of the race makes for absolute obedience to their employers'. The problem with this was that it was all too difficult to obtain a 'kaffir' whose mind was *tabula rasa*. Usually he had already been interfered with before he entered service – most notably by the missionaries who gave him dangerous ideas of equality. Obviously then, the 'mission kaffir' made the worst possible type of servant.[145]

The best way of dealing with a black servant was as with a 'child' – firmly and fairly. In Johannesburg very cruel or brutal methods were perceived as being backveld or 'Boer' and unsuited to a modern city. With the passage of time, however, several citizens looked back with nostalgia to what they saw as the 'good old days' of servant control and discovered that they were, after all, 'Boer'-inspired. Mrs J L Robinson's letter to General Louis Botha on the 'houseboy' problems in 1907 is not untypical:

> I have been in Jo'burg for the last 15 years, and under the rule of the late President Kruger, we had nothing of this kind of thing to contend with. Then these Kaffirs were kept in their proper place, not allowed to strut about, dressed up to imitate the white man, nor to ride about in cabs, rickshaws and bicycles. They were not allowed to be insolent, and ask what wages they liked. It was the same in the Free State and other places.[146]

As so often in South Africa, English speakers helped forge and fashion an oppressive present and then, in retrospect, attributed it to an Afrikaner past.

Given the fairly consistent shortage of white female servants on the Rand before the First World War, it is understandable that mistresses were sorely perplexed by what they perceived as 'reasonless objections to "domestic service"'. These were all the more puzzling since it was said of housework that:

... there is hardly any work so much admired: it has the power which no other work within women's ken has, to hold homes together, to make lives happy, and almost to reconstruct the nation or spoil it. A woman who is a good housekeeper gets praise from thousands, and blame from none.[147]

Who was suited to such work? Well, 'a woman of no extraordinary amount of intellect' but 'with a well ordered mind and capable woman-ly hands'! As with all servants, such women should be well disciplined since it was well known that the 'weakness of a ruler makes bad sub-jects'. But a mistress who took an interest in her employees and who ensured fair and considerate treatment would never want for good ser-vants.

On the Witwatersrand, however, the mistresses had an additional ide-ological task to perform – they had to tell the white housemaids, espe-cially those newly arrived from 'home', how they should behave towards the 'houseboy':

They should be civil and kind, not dictatorial or imperious; but they should never allow any familiarity. They should not touch their hands, or sit in a room where there are boys, or do anything whereby an insolent native may take liberties. A girl is often inclined to think of a native boy as a 'thing', a 'machine', an 'ani-mal', not as a man, and if she never rouses any feeling he will usually do his work mechanically and never think of molesting her.[148]

Clearly, the 'etiquette of race relations' between servants had to be taught at least as much as it was 'naturally' acquired in a racist society. White householders taught well, but as we shall see, not all their pupils were willing to understand the lesson and 'feelings' were certainly aroused.

THE RESPONSE OF DOMESTIC SERVANTS AND THE RESISTANCE OF BLACKS TO COLONISATION
Universal patterns

In many cases white and black servants responded to the basic state instruments that respectively bound them to their employers – the con-tract and pass laws – by ignoring them and deserting from service. This drastic action, however, was seldom taken lightly, and the fact that ser-vants were willing to make considerable financial sacrifices rather than stay with their employers, testifies to the depth of their feelings. Anna Herrmann attempted to borrow 1 000 German marks in order to free herself from her contract with Siegfried Cohen before she finally deserted, and both she and the cook told the coachman that 'they would rather drown themselves than stop at the place'. Black male servants could be no less determined. In the mid-1890s an observer of Johannesburg life noted that masters would occasionally get a minor financial windfall since 'houseboys' tended 'to disappear one evening, not even taking the trouble to ask for their money' – money that was theirs and that sometimes included their savings as well as the wages that were due to them.[149]

But if these responses were driven by desperation, then there is abundant evidence to show that black servants also responded to the state's instruments of control in a variety of other ways. Those who were more passive, or perhaps it was simply that they had more faith in the law and money, paid shady lawyers or legal agents to help them negotiate thorny legal paths. Virtually from the moment the pass laws were introduced, however, others, through poverty, ingenuity or a sense of injustice, challenged the system in a more vigorous way. Black friends forged passes for one another – the literate helped the illiterate. Those who were not fortunate enough to have an obliging friend were forced into more contractual relationships in order to get their passes or 'characters' altered. In 1906, for a fee of half-a-crown, the Honorary President of the 'Transvaal Native Association' or his business partner at Parker's Domestic Registry Office would alter an unsuitable 'character' on a 'houseboy's' pass. No doubt for a slightly larger fee, lumpenproletarian elements in the city were willing to undertake the same task, or compose an entirely false testimonial for a 'houseboy'. [150]

A good number of servants could certainly have done with false testimonials. Housemaids and 'houseboys' alike appear to have indulged in their fair share of petty thieving, regularly taking food, clothing or alcohol from their employers.[151] While little can or should be read into these actions, these thefts do suggest a shortage of ready cash and, at very least, the value which servants attached to these positions in domestic employment. In a different category entirely were those cases in which 'houseboys' deliberately burgled the homes of ex-employers who had withheld their wages or 'spoilt' their passes.[152] Here was a single, clear and unequivocal statement about the chances of justice being obtained through the orthodox channels of the law and of the need for swift and full compensation.

Other and more oblique statements were made by the 'houseboys' in the day-to-day work situation – as expressed through their attitude towards their employers and work. It was a constant theme in employer ideology that black servants were becoming more 'cheeky' or 'insolent' and, since such arguments were invariably used instrumentally in an attempt to secure greater control over the 'houseboys', such statements should be viewed with a very critical eye. But, having noted this, the employer's objections should not be dismissed out of hand since there are two additionally noteworthy features about such complaints.

First, it is striking just how constant such complaints were; and it should be remembered that ideology feeds on a diet of fact as well as fiction. It is probable that a first generation of black domestic workers who were losing their base of rural independence and labouring for cash wages that experienced an overall decline *were* increasingly resentful of the situation in which they found themselves. Second, it is equally noteworthy how the volume of such employer complaints increased at periods of structural stress within the system – in particular, in 1896-7, 1902, 1906-8 and 1912-4.[153]

Thus it was in Heidelberg in 1902 that it was alleged that teachings of 'social equality' by an 'Ethiopian Methodist' minister were at the base of 'some disobedience on the part of native servants'.[154] Again, in the depressing year of 1906, at exactly the time that black domestic workers' wages were falling most rapidly and their home districts were being disrupted by the Bambatha rebellion, 'houseboys' were noted as being more truculent and difficult to manage. The *Transvaal Leader* recorded this unrest amongst 'a section of the Kaffir servants of the community' and further noted that only 'Zulu' and not Pedi or Shangaan 'houseboys' were affected.[155]

Essentially the same syndrome is to be detected where black attitudes crystallised and hardened into an outright refusal to work or, at least, to undertake certain tasks. By the very structuring of the roles, conditions of service and the allocating of work in Witwatersrand homes, such incidents were always liable to occur. What is again noteworthy, however, is the apparent frequency with which such incidents occurred during periods of more general crisis.[156] There thus appear to be more prosecutions of black domestic servants for refusal to work during the miners' strikes of 1913, and perhaps it is significant that the local press chose precisely the same moment to draw attention to the unease amongst white employers about the 'absolute disrespect' and 'insolence of native houseboys'.[157] *Prima facie* there is a good reason to believe that the changing material conditions of rural and urban life helped shape and pulse the consciousness of 'houseboys' at least as much as any other group of migrant workers in the city. From other more organised responses, it would also appear that it was the urban rather than rural milieu that became increasingly dominant in that process between 1890 and 1914. One pattern of rural and urban 'houseboy' response which did not undergo much change during this period was the rather more direct and unambiguous procedure of administering poison to a much hated employer. Usually such attempted murders – for they seldom succeeded – carried all the hallmarks of individual and hastily conceived schemes that were triggered by 'last-straw' provocative actions on the part of the intended victim. Household disinfectant or fly poison were added to the tea or coffee of white women who had insulted, assaulted or dismissed 'houseboys'.[158]

On at least one occasion, however, employers believed that there were more organised plans afoot by their 'houseboys' to murder them. In late 1898, in lower Doornfontein, a mistress became 'violently ill' after drinking tea made by her 'houseboy'. Subsequent observations and enquiries produced the rumour that a 'witch doctor' had instructed all his fellow tribesmen to poison their mistresses in this manner with herbs which he provided. This story caused 'considerable alarm' in the racially mixed community and a reporter sent to investigate the matter noted at the time that 'the ladies of the neighbourhood are now strongly inclined to make tea for themselves'.[159] Regardless of the truth of these allegations, it is clear that relations between black domestic workers and white mistresses were bad enough to sustain such a rumour and that employers were conscious of the fact that 'houseboys', if sufficiently provoked, could resist in ways that might well prove fatal.

'Houseboy' resistance, however, was not confined to the cities – as was to be expected with flows of migrant labour, it also spilled over into the countryside. Workers on the Witwatersrand, including domestic servants, constantly added new symbols, ideas and attitudes to their store of conceptual baggage which they then carried back to the rural areas and redistributed amongst their kinsmen.[160] Whilst it is not intended to explore these fascinating linkages in any depth here, the recounting of a single incident can help to re-alert us to the importance of the city's contribution to the struggle in the countryside.

During the depression in 1908 a Morolong 'kitchen boy', calling himself John Whitesun, left his employment in Johannesburg and made his way back to his home district of Mafeking. There, armed with a bullock's horn, a 'Queen's banner' with a coat of arms and with what were alleged to be 'Ethiopian' teachings, he joined forces with a Makwena herdsman named Cross Degomaile. From there, he and Degomaile – the latter now modestly renamed 'Jesus Christ' – proceeded to make their way first to Kanye and then ultimately to Taungs.

Preaching enthusiastically in the countryside, the pair of prophets soon attracted the attention of the white and black authorities in the region. They also found, however, that their prestige increased enormously when they were first arrested by the administration and then subsequently released as supposedly harmless lunatics. From then on an increasingly radical millenarian message attracted a growing number of supporters who were distinguished by the red cloth badges which they wore.

Events eventually came to a head when the prophets addressed a meeting of between 1 000 and 1 500 followers at Taungs on 24 July 1909. 'Jesus Christ' and his assistant told their black followers – in English, Dutch and Sechuana – that they 'remembered the rinderpest' and that Victoria had imposed a tax on them 'and that God was cross about it, and that was why the Queen died'. For the benefit of those who had worked in the old South African Republic, Whitesun also thought it worth mentioning that 'Paul Kruger used to give them 25 [lashes] and he was now getting 25 elsewhere [hell].' Then, most spectacularly of all, that the people 'were tired of the white man's rule', that there 'was going to be a bloody war', and that by sunset there would not be a single European left alive in Taungs. These prophecies did the nerves of the local whites of the district no good at all. Whitesun and 'Jesus' were promptly arrested and subsequently sentenced to four and a half and five years' imprisonment with hard labour respectively. In his summing up at the trial, the judge expressed the hope that 'when they come out of gaol they would discontinue preaching the Gospel'.[161]

In itself there is nothing startling about this rural protest movement – indeed it has many features in common with other such movements which developed during the colonial era. Neither is the fact that there were linkages between the town and the countryside in itself novel – this too was a common feature of such movements. Nevertheless, it is interesting to trace what is specifically 'Witwatersrand' in the origin of this movement, to consider what it tells us about the consciousness of 'houseboys', and to speculate about what cross-fertilisation of ideas there might have been in its development. At least three noteworthy features seem to emerge.

First, Whitesun, as the leader of the movement stated categorically that he had 'learned his theology at Johannesburg'. If this was so, and there is no reason to doubt it, then if offers us further evidence about the important influence which the Bible had in shaping the consciousness of black men on the Rand during this period. Indeed, what is striking is how this biblical message appealed to Africans across the class spectrum – ranging from independent ministers to 'houseboys' and even through to the leader of a criminal gang like the Ninevites.[162]

Second, Whitesun, like those 'disobedient native servants' at Heidelberg after the war was moved by 'Ethiopian' teaching about 'social equality'. Whereas the rural prophet Degomaile was largely concerned about misfortune in the countryside, like tax and rinderpest, Whitesun was more interested in the towns and keener to ask that 'the white people and black become united and drink from the same vessel, as they had one God'.

Here surely was the imagery and concern of a 'houseboy' rather than that of a herdsman. If this and events at Heidelberg are considered, then it would appear that servile status imposed by race did not settle easily on 'houseboys' and that they registered their ideological objections to it.

The third feature of the Whitesun movement which commands attention is the red cloth badges which he encouraged his followers to wear. It is probably true that the use of this colour drew on some symbolism deeply embedded in the culture of the African resistance. At the trial of the prophets a hostile witness – Chief Molala of the Batlapin – said that: 'He did not know what the badges meant, but they were worn in the early days by the fighting men'. But, whatever the truth of this may have been, Whitesun would have seen the selfsame tokens used in very different surroundings shortly before he left Johannesburg for the countryside. In 1907, red handkerchiefs and neckties – the colours of organised labour – were to be seen everywhere as trade unionists sported their symbols during the mineworkers' strike. If, however, Whitesun had failed to spot the tokens and their significance then he could hardly also have missed the red cloth badges of the 'houseboy' gangs that so frightened the whites of Johannesburg in 1908 – the *Amalaita*. Red might have started and ended as the colour of rebellion for Africans in the countryside but, for any 'houseboy' on the Rand between 1906 and 1908, it would always have new overlays and a special depth of meaning.

The 'black peril'

Between 1890 and 1914 the Witwatersrand – and Johannesburg in particular – were swept by periodic waves of collective sexual hysteria. During these violent storms of social tension, sometimes branded as the 'social curse' but more frequently simply known as the 'black peril', white women, on an unprecedented scale, alleged that they had been sexually molested or assaulted by black men. At the very eye of these storms lay the European household and within it relationships between black and white servants on the one hand, and 'houseboys' and mistresses on the other. Nothing so embittered 'race relations' in urban South Africa before the First World War as these 'black peril' scares, and nothing has been so little studied. To understand and place the 'black peril' in perspective, however, it is first necessary to scrutinise the lull before and between the social storms.

Relationships between 'houseboys' and white female domestic servants on the Witwatersrand were, for reasons that have already been explored above, frequently marked by tension and conflict. While this pattern was, on balance, probably the dominant one, it was far from being exclusive. Employers like Sir Matthew Nathan were cognisant of a second and subordinate pattern of relationships. In a talk to the South

African Colonisation Society in 1910 he noted that: 'If the staff was mixed there was a tendency for the white servants to become too familiar with the family or the native servants', and, he pointedly added, 'of these two the latter was less desirable'.[163]

That this secondary pattern of relationships should develop at all, and that when it did so that it should run along essentially class-determined lines, is hardly surprising. In bourgeois and upper-middle-class homes domestic servants laboured for long hours in splendid isolation. In such homes, servants who were kept socially distant from the employing family and given limited access to outside society were constantly thrown into each others' company. It was perfectly understandable therefore that a degree of 'familiarity' should develop between the sexes and that this should be reinforced by the age and status of most domestic servants who were single and between the ages of 18 and 35. Elsewhere in the city, where there were few African women, the social structure also forced black workers to turn their attention to the only other group of females of their own class that were present in significant numbers – the white domestic servants.

It is difficult to recount cases of such class-bound romances across the colour line partly because these involved behaviour that was by its very nature private, and partly because white society frowned on such relationships. Where, for one reason or another, however, such relationships soured and produced open conflict or where they became too visible in an intolerant society, then they eventually also surfaced in the law courts. It is to these latter cases that we have to turn if we want a glimpse into this aspect of relations between domestic servants.

In 1895, Jim Hloywa courted Jessie McTavish, a 'comely' housemaid in service with a manager of a Johannesburg branch of the Standard Bank, Mr Shotter. Jim pursued an allegedly reluctant Jessie through a series of letters which he confidently signed and which he had delivered to the Shotter household via a fellow servant. When, for reasons that are unclear, he threatened Jessie and the relationship became unmanageable, he wrote her a final letter in which he took his reluctant leave. 'Yes, I better just good-bye', he wrote, 'but I really wanted to be engaged with you.' 'I am a Kaffir', he concluded, 'but my money is as much as of a white man.' 'I winned in the sweep last year £10 000.'[164] Similar correspondence initiated by an African can be traced to one of the city's tearooms where white and black served together as waiter and waitress.[165] Such letters – as Jim Hloywa who received six months' imprisonment and 25 lashes with the 'cat' could testify – produced brutal sentences.

When such letters came from the white servants rather than black men, however, they tended to produce shock or outrage, but seldom court cases or tough sentences. In 1898, one 'Joseph' promptly and permanently brought his trial for 'indecent behaviour' to a close when he

announced to a startled court that he was ready to produce a series of letters from housekeeper Edith Simpson in which she invited him to 'come
round and see her'.[166] Again such correspondence was not unique. In
1913 a master was 'shocked' when he found a letter by a white woman
addressed to 'My Dear Thomas' – his 'houseboy'. Rather innocently the
enclosed note simply enquired of Thomas: 'Can't you come and see me
one day, if you can get off?' To prove the authenticity of the note, the outraged master offered to make the letter available for public inspection.[167]
It is possible that such snippets of correspondence simply reveal the tip
of the proverbial iceberg. What is slightly clearer is that at least some of
these relationships produced a depth of feeling and a sense of commitment that went beyond casual sexual encounters.

In 1904 Marcus Matopa and Caroline Dyer both entered domestic
service in a Johannesburg household. From this there developed a relationship which culminated in the housemaid's pregnancy. The couple
then left service and went to live at the 'houseboy's kraal' at Waterval
North near Pretoria. Here the two remained until they were discovered
by a missionary who obligingly reported their presence to local government officials. The court refused to sentence the couple but 'warned'
them and then ordered Caroline back to service with her former employer in Johannesburg.[168] Once more the story is not without a later parallel.
In 1914, a 'Zulu' and a white 'nursemaid' were found living together in
a room in Doornfontein. The couple informed the magistrate that it was
their wish to leave for Kimberley and get married, but the court separated the couple and placed the woman on probation.[169]

This evidence alone suggests that if the development of intimate sexual
relationships between domestic servants in Rand homes was not a common occurrence, then it was not an entirely novel one either. The strongest
support for this contention comes from the government enquiry that was
set up to investigate the last major 'black peril' scare shortly before the
First World War – the commission appointed to enquire into assaults on
women. The commission which sat in 1913 was of the opinion that 'serious consideration' would have to be given to 'the danger of natives working in close contact with white female servants, especially those that have
been imported from Europe'. In the emasculating manner of the colonist,
the male-dominated commission smugly contented itself with the opinion
that where sexual intercourse had taken place between servants, 'the facts
seem to point to sexual perversion on the part of the female'. Apparently
this 'perversion' was widespread enough, however, for it to recommend
that 'European servants should be taught how to treat the native; they
should not touch or allow themselves to be touched by the latter'.[170]
Clearly, amongst new arrivals in the kitchen, the realities of physical proximity and class affinity pulled the sexes together almost as strongly as

acquired colour prejudice pulled them apart.

Just as servants were drawn together in the homes of the more wealthy, so 'houseboys' and mistresses were pushed into each other's company in lower-middle and working-class homes – and for many of the same reasons. Long hours of more or less collective labour in relative isolation forged bonds of common humanity which the crass racism of a prejudiced society could not always overcome. But, despite this similarity between the two situations, the development of a 'houseboy'/mistress relationship was in the end always more difficult to develop and sustain than its white servant/black servant counterpart. Again the reasons for this were largely class-determined. Whereas relationships between domestic servants were ultimately relationships of *equality* between fellow workers and peers, that between 'houseboy' and mistress remained inherently unequal since it was also – in the final analysis – a relationship between employer and employee. In turn it was precisely because the latter relationships were fundamentally unequal that the initiatives for establishing such liaisons differed. Whereas in the servant/servant relationship either party appeared to have been willing to take the initiative, in the 'houseboy'/mistress relationship the employer seems to have been more willing and able to take the initiative.

There is strongly suggestive evidence of such mistress-initiated relationship even before the South African War.[171] What is clearer from more reliable observers, however, is that after the war such relationships were far more frequent. In 1911 many Witwatersrand whites were shocked when it was suggested publicly that mistresses encouraged black servants to sleep with them. Not so the ministers attached to the South African Mission to the Compounds and the Interior. In an editorial in their magazine, the clergymen said that they knew such allegations 'to be true from instances that have come under [our] own observation from confessions made to us by converts'. The 1913 commission of enquiry also admitted that there were instances to support such an allegation, but that the charge was 'baseless in regard to the majority or even a large number of cases'. But if the commissioners had difficulty in finding cases where 'the native was as Joseph and the white woman as Potiphar's wife', then perhaps it was because they failed to consult the black author and journalist Sol T Plaatje. He 'could fill a book on such first hand information about the vicissitudes of houseboys', but, in his work *The Mote and the Beam*, chose to 'select only one story illustrative of the unenviable lot of this class of worker, especially in Johannesburg'.[172]

But while female initiatives in such relationships appear to have been predominant, they were again certainly not exclusive. Black servants occasionally admitted to the affections that they had developed for their mistresses as well as to the sexual advances that they made to them.

These confessions, made under the gravest of possible circumstances, required exceptional courage which is perhaps why they appear to be relatively infrequent. In 1912, for example, one such case occurred in which a 'houseboy' who 'caught hold' of his mistress by the hand and told her that 'he liked her very much', was sentenced to four months' imprisonment with hard labour and five lashes for 'assault'.[173]

Other black servants, however, were probably consciously or unconsciously inhibited from making direct approaches to their white mistresses by the strength of the class barriers that existed between themselves and their employers. In order to overcome these barriers the domestic servants made indirect attempts to secure the sexual favours of their European mistresses – significantly enough, a procedure that seems to be wholly absent from their interaction with other white servants. Some 'houseboys' turned to shady white or Asian traders for various concoctions or for reputed aphrodisiacs like cantharides, 'Spanish Fly'. Yet others placed their faith in traditional love potions obtained from 'witch doctors' or in acquiring so-called 'Malay Tricks' or charms. A favoured procedure seems to have been to put such potions or *muti* into the mistress's tea – something which perhaps casts light on the great Doornfontein tea-drinking scare of 1898 from another angle. In any event, at least some of these ploys appear to have been successful since the 1913 commission reported that there had been instances involving white women where consent to sexual intercourse had been 'extorted' 'by superstitious dread of pretended occult powers on the part of the offender'.[174]

Looking back at the period between 1890 and 1914 then, at least three general observations can be made about the sexual relationships that developed between white women and the black male domestic servants. First, such relationships seem to have developed most readily along class lines – those between 'houseboys' and white female servants being relatively prominent. Secondly, such relationships could be initiated by either partner where servants were involved, but were more frequently at the instigation of the employer in the case of a mistress/'houseboy' relationship. Thirdly, while such relationships were never openly tolerated or considered to be 'normal', they did nevertheless occur on a substantial scale. Given this, it remains to be considered when these developed clandestine relationships or their latent equivalents broke down on a significant scale, and why they should do so.

The first really noteworthy 'black peril' scare in Johannesburg appears to have occurred during spring of 1893. In early September of that year one of the morning newspapers drew the attention of its readers to a series of attempted rapes by trusted black servants who were considered by whites to be 'almost part of the family'. 'Beware of your "houseboy"', cautioned the editorial, 'for under the innocent front may be lurking and lying latent the passions of the panther, and worse!'[175]

This early squall was followed by four years of relative tranquillity during which there was no marked public outcry about such alleged offences. This calm, however, was in marked contrast to the storm that followed. On 3 July 1897 Mrs Anne Lightfoot was raped and then severely assaulted by her 'kitchen boy', Louis, after a dispute over his wages. This notable attack of sexual brutality was followed by widespread hysteria during which the virtues of public hanging for such offenders were vigorously debated.[176] Once the storm had passed, however, it was followed by a lengthy period of calm which lasted until a few years after the South African War.

In 1904, but more especially from late 1905 onwards, there were familiar social rustlings when sporadic cases of 'black peril' were reported in Johannesburg.[177] These stirrings picked up markedly in volume during 1906, and then finally the winds of panic blew relentlessly throughout 1907 and 1908. The height of public concern during this storm appears to have been reached in mid-1907 when the 'Associated Women's Organisations of the Transvaal' approached the government with a plea that, amongst other moves, social segregation be implemented in an attempt to cope with the curse of the 'black peril'.[178]

This time the storm was followed by a brief period of calm, only to be disturbed by a most unexpected and violent gust during 1911. On 2 February 1911 a 'governess' was out cycling beyond Orange Grove when she was attacked and raped by an unknown assailant who spoke 'kitchen kaffir'. This attack, which became known as the 'Lyndhurst Outrage', was given sensational coverage in the local press and it really unleashed a storm of acute European anxiety. It was followed by a massive police pass-drive against 'houseboys' and a public meeting which, amongst other measures, demanded a mandatory death sentence for attempted rape by black men.[179] This time, however, the city never really settled down and when yet another sensational rape occurred 14 months later, the full impact of gale-force white fury tore through Johannesburg.

At about midnight on 12 April 1912 Mrs W Harrison was attacked and raped by one or more black men while sleeping in her Turffontein home with two small children. This savage attack, in the middle of a solidly working-class district, produced an immediate white male backlash. Within days a series of meetings was held where revolver-brandishing southern suburbs residents organised themselves into vigilante groups. These groups, barely under the control of the local police, swept through the suburban streets at night, checking on passes and assaulting several Africans they happened to come across. On 23 April, 'someone hanged an effigy of a native from the headgear of one of the southern mines'. 'The dummy could be seen for many miles around and was mistaken [by many blacks] for the real genuine article.' In white eyes these acts of aggression were further justified when three days later Mrs Harrison died – from, as it later transpired, an incorrectly self-administered dose of chloride of mercury.[180]

As the embers of racial hatred continued to flicker in late April and early May 1912, so they were fanned into fuller profile by the sensationalist local press. When it soon became clear that the government and others were less than enthusiastic about what they considered to be an undignified and unnecessary over-reaction by Johannesburg citizens, the *Rand Daily Mail* stepped in to force the state's hand. It organised the largest-ever political petition on the Witwatersrand, and on 9 May 1912 handed over 51 925 signatures to parliament in a demand for government action on the 'black peril'. It was largely this pressure that gave rise to the subsequent commission of enquiry.[181]

Since some of these events were expressly designed to ensure continued interest in such offences, the public's temperature did not readily cool. In late June 1912, one 'John Jacobs' appeared in court charged with the rape of the unfortunate Mrs Harrison. After a protracted trial, Jacobs was eventually found not guilty and discharged.[182] Throughout the remainder of the year, however, there were continued reports of 'black peril' cases and it was only early in the following year, 1913, when such offences were eclipsed by more dramatic political events, that anything approaching 'normality' could be detected in public discussions about such events. Even then, however, the storm had not completely blown itself out. There was a brief and less serious resurgence of 'black peril' hysteria in late 1913, which soon gave way to the more demanding fear of impending war.[183] Such statistical foundations as there were to these waves of mass hysteria before the First World War are to be found in Table 2.

Table 2 Sexual assaults in the Transvaal, 1901-12

Year	Rape	Attempted rape	Indecent assault	Total convictions	Number of charges
1901	0	0	3	3	3
1902	0	1	3	4	5
1903	1	1	2	4	4
1904	1	3	7	11	11
1905	1	4	7	12	16
1906	3	6	8	17	21
1907	3	5	11	19	26
1908	4	5	13	22	30
1909	3	5	5	13	25
1910	0	6	18	24	33
1911	3	12	22	37	46
1912	3	10	20	33	51

[Data extracted from *Report of Commission on Assaults on Women 1913*, para 28.]

In re-surveying these periodic 'black peril' scares that occurred between 1890 and 1914 for their underlying causes then, one outstanding feature seems to emerge. It is clear that the majority of such attacks of public hysteria coincided with periods of stress or acute tension within the political economy of the Witwatersrand as a whole. This broadly observable trend, in itself not particularly helpful in enhancing our understanding, comes into sharper focus and assumes a more meaningful dimension when we examine the context of each of these 'black peril' waves more closely.

The least pronounced of these scares was that of 1893. Significantly enough, it came towards the end of a fairly lengthy period of economic uncertainty on the Rand but at a moment during which Johannesburg itself was still within the clutches of a marked recession. Indeed, on the very day that the *Standard and Diggers' News* printed its 'passions of the panther' editorial on 'houseboys', it ran a second leader in which it commented on the bad times and noted how many working men had been forced to send their wives and children away to live at cheaper centres away from the Witwatersrand.[184]

What was perhaps still shadowy in 1893 became clearer during the next scare which was in the aftermath of the Jameson Raid and the recession which that incursion had helped to precipitate. The Lightfoot rape which lay at the centre of the 1897 scare occurred not only in generally unsettled times, but in the immediate wake of manifestly dramatic events. In the six to eight weeks preceding the attack, the Rand had seen a unilateral reduction in the wages of black miners, the formation of a white mineworkers' union and a series of strikes by both European and African mineworkers.

The syndrome of recession-political uncertainty-industrial action was also to be detected in the following 'black peril' scare between 1906 and 1908. Most of this wave of public hysteria was located in the midst of a serious economic depression and at a time when the British reconstruction administration was handing over power to Botha's *Het Volk* government. More specifically still, it is noteworthy how the crest of public concern in May/June 1907 yet again coincided with a time when the white miners were out on strike.

All of these familiar ingredients, although in much less clearly crystallised form, were also to be found in the final outbreak of 'black peril' hysteria before the First World War. In 1911-2, through 1913 and into 1914 the economy gradually wound its way down into the pre-war recession. Again this period, which followed on Union and led up to the outbreak of the First World War was hardly characterised by its political stability – something that was more especially true of the Transvaal. Finally, the tail end of this 'black peril' scare yet again coincided with a period when Witwatersrand miners were out on strike.

This underlying 'black peril' syndrome was most important because of its direct and specific linkages with the household economies of the Witwatersrand. It meant that the major 'black peril' scare occurred at times when the incomes of white middle and working-class families were falling generally. This in turn meant that much of the hysteria was firmly rooted in periods when the wages of domestic servants were falling. But not only were the incomes of employing families generally falling; in the case of many working-class homes incomes actually dried up completely during the strikes of 1897, 1907 and 1913. In consequence, there was an inherently greater risk of the employers defaulting on wage payment due to domestic servants during these periods. In large part then, it is to these underlying structural reasons that we have to turn if we wish to understand many of the so-called 'black peril' cases.

In several cases these economic pressures manifested themselves openly in 'black peril' conflict between mistresses and 'houseboys', and for obvious reasons this was more especially so in working-class homes where these parties most frequently came into direct contact with each other. Although it in itself hardly qualified as a 'scare', it will be remembered that the Lightfoot case of 1897 was triggered off by a dispute about the 'kitchen boy's' wages. In other cases there is also ample evidence to suggest that the actual dismissal, or impending dismissal, of the 'houseboy' was an important contributing factor to the alleged assault. Under such circumstances, it would have been a convenient ploy for a mistress to suggest that she had been sexually assaulted. That white women were consciously capable of resorting to such cynical stratagems was confirmed by the 1913 commission which reported how, in a significant number of cases, 'black peril' charges had and were being trumped up by employers in order to defraud their 'houseboys' of their wages.[185]

But if 'black peril' charges were sometimes consciously manipulated to achieve immediate economic objectives in working-class homes, then it also seems possible that they were more subtly and perhaps even unconsciously used to similar instrumental ends in middle-class homes. It was in these latter situations, where there was a multi-racial staff, that the large majority of sexual offences by 'houseboys' against white female domestic servants allegedly took place.

Given the generally more relaxed and familiar relationships that existed between servants, it is perfectly feasible that black men *did* in fact make more frequent and direct sexual approaches to their fellow female workers. During 'normal' times, when incomes were steady and jobs not at stake, such 'houseboy' advances were no doubt more or less resented and considered to be one of the 'hazards' of the job.[186] In periods of recession, however, the wages of white domestics fell to what they considered to be 'kaffir' levels, thus further reducing the economic distance between

265

groups that were already socially proximate. In addition, such recession-ary periods constantly held out the danger of staff retrenchment, and often it was the white servant that was the first to go. Under these more antagonistic circumstances there were obvious benefits for the white ser-vant if she could succeed in getting the 'houseboy' dismissed first – and a charge of 'black peril' was singularly well suited to this end. The 'houseboy's' dismissal eased pressure on the household's limited avail-able funds for wages and that – together with the gaining of the white family's sympathy through the use of a highly emotive charge – proba-bly secured the European servant her job for some time to come. While it is impossible to prove such a hypothesis conclusively, further weight is lent to it by the fact that 'black peril' charges appear to be totally absent from those households marked by economic stability and security – the homes of the bourgeoisie.[187]

But, although such economic motives can be found to underlie most 'black peril' allegations, they certainly cannot be made to account direct-ly for all such cases. It seems clear that in a significant minority of cases such allegations were used as rationalisations in order to avoid acute personal embarrassment or for other more complex, psychological rea-sons. Again it would appear that the complainants in such cases could have been more or less conscious of their motivations. As we have already noted in passing, there were instances in which white women, for any one of a number of reasons, used 'black peril' allegations as a way of ending relationships with a 'houseboy' that had become unman-ageable.[188] Yet other cases seem to hinge around either the vague or explicitly sensational accusations of adolescent girls within the house-hold – a group that was likely to be particularly sensitive to 'sexual' be-haviour.[189] Many other instances simply derived from women of an extremely nervous disposition who became frightened, or who overre-acted to what would possibly have passed as a minor occurrence in more stable times.[190] But, when all this has been said about a minority of indi-vidual 'black peril' cases, it still remains that these complex human fears and anxieties chose to surface collectively under the very distinctive social and economic conditions outlined above. It was as if at certain times there were witches at loose in suburbia – black witches which a tense and neurotic white society sought to exorcise from its midst.

In part, it was the task of the 1913 commission on assaults to 'smell out' those witches, and this it attempted to do. In the manner of some traditional practitioner it sought to isolate the culprit – in this case the 'houseboy' – and then have him excluded from the community. The 'local segregation of natives in urban areas', the commission concluded in its report, 'is highly desirable'. This powerful proposal was designed to get the 'houseboy' out of the employer's back yard and into a highly regulated system of municipal locations. In addition, the commission also made other suggestions for improved police protection and social control which were designed to cope with the 'problem' of the black male domestic worker.[191]

In the end, however, the 'black peril' commission turned out to be more of an ideological fountain than a political stream capable of cutting new channels of control within urban society. It simply threw up existing ideas into new patterns which interested parties could then point to when seeking justification for behaviour that was ultimately based on economic and political self-interest.[192] The real erosion of the 'houseboy's' position on the Rand came not so much through the commission but through the deeper and more powerful currents of proletarianisation at work in the countryside. Ultimately it was these latter processes which swept new and cheaper labour supplies into the cities and which dislodged the 'houseboy' from back-yard and domestic service sector alike.

For their part, African leaders appear to have been fully aware of the fact that the cry of 'black peril' and the commission which it provoked could be used to achieve and justify more oppressive measures against blacks. Selby Msimang curtly dismissed the white catchword of the day as a 'political term', while Sol Plaatje drew attention to the fact that it was being used in part to provide ideological justification for the Native Land Act. R V Selope Thema and Lerothodi Ntyweyi were equally quick to point out that discussions about the 'black peril' could carry no weight in African circles until such time as they were broadened to include the 'white peril' – the problem of white men seducing black women.[193]

Much of this political infighting passed the 'houseboys' by since they were occupied with more pressing problems. During the worst 'black peril' scares, such as those of 1911-2, many of them stayed indoors for fear of being arrested under the pass laws. The 'houseboys'' most anxious moments of all, however, came after the Harrison rape in Turffontein. Then, in the face of the 'Kaffir Drives' led by the armed white vigilantes, many voted with their feet, fleeing the city for the comparative sanity of the countryside.[194]

But not all of the 'houseboys' were content simply to retreat or defend in the face of white society's various onslaughts. At least some of them must have stayed on to sing an old African work song:

> *Be damn the whites, they call us Jim.*
> *Be damn the whites, they call us Jim.*
> *In spite of the fact that they despise us,*
> * some of their women love us,*
> *In spite of the fact that they despise us,*
> * some of their women love us.*[195]

For many more, however, singing was not enough. At night, and over the weekends they met and organised themselves into armed 'houseboy' gangs. Then, replete with new identities, they poured into the streets of suburbia singing, chanting and openly challenging the society that sought to oppress them. The 'houseboys' were no more. These were the men of the *Amalaita*.

The Amalaita

The origins of organised activity by black domestic servants on the Witwatersrand stretch back directly to the 1890s and indirectly to the very year of Johannesburg's establishment. During the early 1890s, the most important black organisation within the city was a 'secret society' of criminals and robbers known as the *izigebengu* or Ninevites. This 'Zulu'-dominated gang was largely the product of a man who himself had been a 'houseboy' in Jeppe in 1886 and later at Turffontein – Jan Note.[196] While the thrust of later Ninevite activity was clearly of the orthodox criminal variety, it would appear that during the mid-1890s members of the gang were also willing to undertake 'work' in conjunction with, or on behalf of, their 'houseboy' brothers.

In June 1896 a country correspondent of the *Natal Witness* reported certain conversations which he had had with 'natives' who had worked in Johannesburg, 'either at the mines or among resident families'. He reported that the *izigebengu* had been formed by black men to protect their interests 'without recourse to a law court' since the latter procedure could only bring down 'punishment on Kaffirs'. The correspondent then proceeded to recount an example of Ninevite activity with which he had been supplied by his informants:

> When a man has a wrong to redress as, for instance, when his master has 'done him' out of his wages, he makes his grievance known to the *Izigebengu*, some of the members of which are thereupon told off to knock the offending master on the head. These watch their opportunity, and in due course carry out their orders. Reports say that the favourite method is to knock at the door of the former master at night, and if he opens it himself, he is there and then 'settled'. Should someone else open the door, an excuse is made … and another occasion is awaited … '*Ba gwenza*', a man of some standing said, '*ngoba ngu muzi onge na 'mteto*' – They do it because it is a town without law.[197]

Examples of such assaults as well as of burglaries involving 'houseboys' and the *izigebengu* can certainly be found for early Johannesburg.[198] From this it would seem that at least before 1899 the Ninevites performed more of a social banditry function than they have hitherto been given credit for, and that 'Zulu' 'houseboys' figured quite prominently in this movement.

In 1899, however, the outbreak of the South African War forced the *izigebengu* and the 'Zulu' 'houseboys' back to the towns and rural areas of Natal. Many of these men gained employment with the imperial army, but a large number of the younger domestic servants sought work as 'houseboys' in the larger urban centres. By late 1900 these *izigebengu* or *izigelegele* – brigands, as they were sometimes also known – had started to regroup in the suburbs of Durban. In May 1901 the Superintendent of Police, R C Alexander, reported that it was becoming 'a nightly occurrence all over the borough for native lads and young men to parade the streets and roads to the annoyance of everyone', and that they made 'filthy remarks' at passers-by.[199]

These ex-Johannesburg elements soon became a conspicuous part of the Durban scene – a departure which contrasted sharply with the more secretive practices of the older parent gang. The new groups dressed in distinctive wide-bottomed trousers of many colours and paraded through the streets playing music that was 'generally a strange combination of complicated Dutch, English and Native' tunes. The instrument most favoured for this new and vital black music of the cities and the one invariably associated with the gangs, was the mouth-organ. Rival groups from within the city met and regularly challenged each other to organised fights. In addition, many of these gangs went in for organised robbery – usually, but not always, choosing fellow Africans as their victims. As a local newspaper correspondent pointed out, this meant that: 'A white employer might have a kitchen boy or a coachman to work for him during the day while the same individual might prove his assailant, under masque, at night.' It was also thought that it was these exploits which earned the gangs their name – *Olaita*.

The word *olaita*, suggested *Ipepa lo Hlanga* in 1903, presumably came:

> ... from the fact that when they 'hold up' anyone, they ask him to 'light' or '*kanyisa*' – a very familiar term much in use amongst native quack-doctors when asking for '*ugxa*' or retaining fee which is usually paid by the patient before any medical treatment is commenced ... These native desperadoes ... whenever they meet a person, they ask him to 'light' his way by putting his whole purse at their disposal ... If he succeeds in paying up he is said to have 'lighted' his way and is allowed to pass on unmolested.[200]

But while the derivation of the word may be in dispute, it is beyond

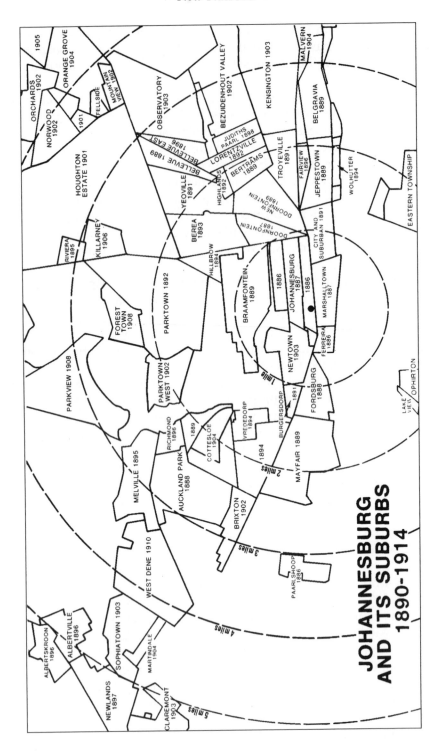

JOHANNESBURG
AND ITS SUBURBS
1890-1914

doubt that the *Amalaita* gangs were already in existence in Durban between 1901 and 1904, and that they presented a challenge to authority – more particularly to the local black police whose endless demands for passes they vigorously resisted.

It comes as rather a surprise therefore to learn that the first *Amalaita* gangs to appear on the Witwatersrand after the South African War were entirely devoid of 'Zulu' members. On second thoughts, however, this is less puzzling than appears at first glance. 'Zulus' returning to Johannesburg in the immediate post-war period appear to have rejoined branches of the older Ninevite organisation rather than incur the displeasure of its well-established leadership by founding new rival gangs.[201] Thus, such elements of *Amalaita* culture as the 'Zulus' did bring to the Rand with them after 1901 were primarily used to re-fertilise the parent gang in its various forms. What other black groups within Johannesburg saw and imitated after the war then, was essentially the old *izigebengu* structure overlaid with the features of the new coastal culture.

One of the first such non-Zulu groups to experiment with *Amalaita* organisation appeared in the eastern suburbs of Johannesburg in 1906. On Sundays, groups of Sotho adolescents, said to be 'church-going boys', staged military-style parades through the streets of part of the city. It was later claimed that these rather spectacular activities soon attracted the attention and additional support of members of other ethnic groups. Unlike the more respectable northerners, however, these later members, including a few 'Zulus', were considered to have been of a 'very low type'.[202]

But no sooner had this ethnically diverse nucleus established itself than it in turn was overrun by a massive new membership. It was these new devotees, the Pedi, and particularly those young men and 'piccanins' that the 1906-8 depression had brought to the cities, that made the Rand *Amalaita* gangs their own. Thus is was at about this time that gang leaders ceased giving commands in English and changed to Sesotho and by 1908 a Johannesburg magistrate was forced to notice that: 'It was a strange thing that almost all the "*Amalaita* boys" came from Pietersburg.'[203] If the *Amalaita* had started as a hybrid outgrowth of Nguni society, then it was subsequently infused with elements of Northern Sotho culture – and Pedi youth culture in particular.[204]

These new gangs drew on earlier and older patterns and then modified or extended them to meet their own requirements. The leader of the *Amalaita* was entitled *Morena* or 'prince', and he was assisted by his captains and sergeants who administered the oath of allegiance to the new recruits – the corporals. The various ranks were signified by means of coloured patches which the *Amalaita* wore on their distinctive 'knickerbocker' trousers. In addition to this, every member wore some or other form of special hat or helmet and a coloured knotted handkerchief around the neck which indicated the particular gang of which he was a member. Finally, each *Amalaita* wore the universal sign of the movement – the red cloth badge. Whistles, mouth-organs, piano accordions, sticks and battle axes forged from modified saddlers' knives rounded off the requirements of a fully equipped *Amalaita* gang which consisted of between 50 and 100 members.[205]

Not all members of the *Amalaita*, however, wore this uniform since there was a further feature to this new youth movement on the Witwatersrand which distinguished it from its coastal predecessor – the fact that it sometimes accommodated both sexes. While it is true that the 1906-8 depression brought the 'piccanins' to town, it was equally noteworthy for the fact that it had pushed the first significant numbers of black women into the Transvaal cities. Many of these young women, aged 15 or more, were drawn to the *Amalaita* and at least some of the gangs – probably composed of age-related sets drawn from Pedi society – readily incorporated them. These women wore their own distinctive matching uniforms made up of a *kop doek* of a colour appropriate to the gang, low-necked blouses, a short 'accordion-pleated' skirt called Scot's *rokkies*, black stockings and high-heeled shoes. Never really equal in number or status to their male counterparts in the movement, the *Amalaita* 'girls' nevertheless formed a significant part of the gangs based in the suburbs or in the more notorious urban locations such as that at the George Goch Mine.[206]

It was also during the depression, and to lesser extent during the next five years, that the *Amalaita* gangs developed particularly rapidly and spread over the larger part of the Witwatersrand. In Johannesburg, the gangs were most strongly in evidence on the eastern and southern fringes of the city – in white working-class suburbs such as Kensington, Bezuidenhout Valley, Ophirton and Turffontein. On the West Rand they were equally conspicuous in the other working-class strongholds of Roodepoort and Krugersdorp.[207] These patterns of distribution and periods of greatest *Amalaita* growth are important because they point to the nature and function of the movement on the Rand.

First, they mean that the *Amalaita* were largely recruited from amongst the most poorly paid 'houseboys', something which, especially between 1906 and 1908, was also a strongly age-related factor. It also means, however, that the ranks of the *Amalaita* were frequently swollen by the many unemployed of the period, and there is certainly evidence to support this.[208] With these features in mind it is easier to understand why it was that the *Amalaita* gangs were so consistently involved in petty crime. It also helps explain why the *Amalaita* were such noted pass forgers, and why in turn there was particularly marked conflict between them and the police.[209] As young men who had lost the battle against poverty in the countryside, the *Amalaita* were always likely to make a more determined stand against the passes and the police which sought to cleanse the cities of the black unemployed.

Second, these patterns mean that *Amalaita* activity was as its height during periods when 'houseboy' wages were falling most rapidly – times that were hardly characterised by good relations between employers and employees. In addition, it is noteworthy how the year of the greatest *Amalaita* activity of all, 1908, came in the wake of one of the more serious 'black peril' crises – that is in a period when black men in general, and 'houseboys' in particular were on the psychological retreat. Given this, the upsurge and form of *Amalaita* activity between September and December of 1908 is less than completely puzzling. In the working-class suburbs of Johannesburg they singled out their immediate employers and perceived oppressors, the white women, jostled them off the side-walks, insulted them, and generally subjected them to a barrage of intimidatory remarks.[210] Similarly, when they came across isolated and unarmed policemen on the beat they surrounded them and sang their war-cry – *Ingoma ya malaita*, 'Song of the *Amalaita*' – or, more pointedly still, *Whole makhoa*, 'Down with the Whites'.[211]

From these activities it seems clearer as to what some of the major functions of the *Amalaita* movement on the Witwatersrand were between 1906 and 1914. In essence it was a movement of young black domestic servants and their unemployed peers born out of hard times in a new and harsh environment. It drew country cousins of both sexes together in unfamiliar urban surroundings by drawing on better-known forms of rural behaviour, and at least one police officer saw in this the original creative function of the *Amalaita*.[212] It was also, however, a movement which sought to give its members who laboured in alienated colonised isolation a sense of purpose and dignity – in short, it transformed 'Saucepan' into a 'Sergeant' in the army of the people. Hardly surprising then that some of the 'worst' *Amalaita* had the best references testifying to the fact that they were 'excellent houseboys'.[213] It was precisely *because* he was such a 'good', 'polite', and servile 'boy' during the day that 'Saucepan' had to become that virile, manly, aggressive 'Sergeant' of the night. It is in this latter light that the *Amalaita* should be seen as the 'houseboys'' liberation army fighting to reassert its decolonised manhood during one of the first major waves of South African proletarianisation. And, as in all struggles involving the deepest of human emotions, the individual battles could be bloody and brutal.

On the night of 12 April 1912 the *Amalaita* 'Chief' of Turffontein, a man named 'Roma' who hailed from the Pietersburg district, rounded up about a dozen male members of his gang and briefed them on their mission. From their meeting place the *Amalaita* proceeded to the back yard of several European households where they called out a further eight female members of the gang – including the 'Chief's' appointed 'Queen', Jokaby. At this point each member of the *Amalaita* had his or her face blackened with soot, and they then marched off under the leadership of Roma to do the night's work.

The gang was brought to a halt outside the Turffontein home of a woman whose husband was away at work on the night shift – Mrs V Harrison. On being asked by one of the female members of the gang why they had been brought there, *Amalaita* lieutenant Marseliba replied:

> We have come to this house on the complaint of a person who complains that he is not being properly treated by the 'missus'.[214]

Then, the women and all but three of the *Amalaita* were posted to act as lookouts. Roma, John and Daniel then forced the bedroom window of the house, entered, and in full view of several members of the gang took turns to hold and rape Mrs Harrison. After equally pointed threats and warnings about the need for secrecy, the platoon of 'houseboys' disbanded.[215]

It was this single act of savagery that did more to unleash the hounds of racial hatred in the suburbs than any other incident before the First World War. It was the Harrison rape that directly gave rise to the white vigilantes and indirectly to the Commission of Enquiry into Assaults on Women in the following year. Yet, for all that, there was not a word about Roma or *Amalaita* gangs when the commission issued its report in 1913. How could there be when the security of the domestic servants' organisation was so stong? It took two full years of police detection including the infiltration of the *Amalaita* and the cynical seduction of some of the female members of Roma's gang before the perpetrators of this crime became known in 1914. In the meantime the white vigilantes of the southern suburbs and the *Amalaita* frequently passed each other by – both parties, in their differing ways, scouring the streets for the witches of suburbia. It was one of South Africa's many tragedies at the time that skin colour in the streets was always easier to recognise than class in the kitchen.

2

AMAWASHA

The Zulu washermen's guild of the Witwatersrand, 1890-1914

Amongst others, there are two aspects to the development of capitalism in southern Africa which immediately capture the interest of the historian who seeks to understand the processes of social and economic transformation that accompany an industrial revolution. The first of these is the very rapidity with which this change was brought about in South Africa. From the time that diamonds were first discovered in the late 1860s up to the First World War – by which time the foundations of a modern capitalist state had been firmly laid – a little more than half a century had elapsed. Compared with the several centuries that it took for a similar transformation to take place in Europe, these five decades constitute a very brief moment – albeit a crucially important one – in our history. The second is how, during this transition to a modern industrial state, most black South Africans were systematically denied access to alternative means of earning an independent livelihood until the point was reached where they had only their labour to sell, and so came to form the largest part of the working class in the new society.

The social historian of the Witwatersrand in general, and of Johannesburg in particular, is constantly reminded of these two themes as he conducts his research, if for no other reason than the fact that the city cannot be artificially divorced from these large-scale processes which helped first to transform the economic system as a whole and then to shape its society. It is not enough, however, to see in the new urban areas the apotheosis of an all-conquering capitalism and to eulogise it accordingly – as do most of the popular historians who see in the story of Johannesburg only the technological triumph of the mining industry or the 'romance' of the Randlords. But nor is it enough for other historians to challenge this vision by presenting a simple picture of 'radical pessimism' which seeks only to highlight the one-way march of Africans or Afrikaners into the working class. The South African transition to capitalism – like that elsewhere – was fraught with contradictions and conflicts and its cities were thus capable of opening as well as closing economic avenues, and there certainly was always more than one route into or out of the working class. Perhaps one of the better illustrations of these complexities is afforded by a study of those black washermen who played a central part in the social and economic life of much of the Witwatersrand between 1890 and 1914 – the *AmaWasha* or Zulu washermen's guild.

For most of the period between 1890 and 1906 the Zulu washermen's guild of the Witwatersrand, not unlike its medieval European equivalents, constituted 'an industrial corporation enjoying the monopoly of practising a particular profession in accordance with regulations sanctioned by public authority.[1] This recognition of the *AmaWasha*, which entailed an exemption from the provisions of the Masters and Servants' Law, served to place this group of self-employed businessmen at the forefront of privileged blacks in an industrialising state which usually sought to confine African economic activity to wage labour in the employ of whites. In addition to being freed from the pass system, members of the guild were also exempted from a local by-law which prevented blacks from carrying weapons, and were further entitled to wear the distinctive turban and uniform of their trade. Finally, in yet another uncharacteristic concession, the authorities allowed the *AmaWasha* to brew as much beer as they required for their own consumption.[2]

The Zulu washermen's guild, again like the earlier European craft guilds, both restricted entry into its ranks and determined the prices charged for its services – powers which gave its members rather distinctive opportunities to accumulate capital. But, despite the fact that many of the guild's members did manage to make considerable cash savings, none of them chose to convert their businesses to employ the mechanised processing techniques of the modern laundryman. Looking back to the countryside from where they had come, rather than ahead to the growing urban areas into which they had temporarily been pushed, the washermen chose to invest their savings in land and cattle rather than in plant and equipment. In a period otherwise characterised by growing African proletarianisation, however, even this form of reinvestment was enough to ensure the washermen a significant measure of economic protection and in parts of rural Natal the *AmaWasha* came to constitute a conspicuously successful stratum in black society. As such, the washermen and their children largely avoided the direct mass march into the working class of the new South Africa which so many of their peers were forced to undertake.

THE RISE OF THE WASHERMEN'S GUILD, 1890-1896

In many societies, but possibly most clearly of all on the Asian subcontinent, there are close links between notions of purity and pollution on the one hand, and that of occupation or profession on the other. Amongst the Hindus of India these perceptions are vividly reflected in the caste structure of society which – amidst countless other examples – ordains a special place for those washermen who undertake to clean the soiled linen of other members of the community.[3] When the first large-scale movement of Indians from the subcontinent to the east coast of southern Africa took place from 1860 onwards, members of that lowly washermen's caste, the *Dhobis*, were amongst the emigrants.

It would appear that *Dhobis* who had emigrated to Natal independently as so-called 'passenger Indians', or who had managed to buy their way out of indentured labour on the sugar plantations, turned to their traditional profession at some stage during the early 1870s. Present-day African informants claim that it was at about this time that Zulu speakers first noticed the turbaned *Dhobis* undertaking the commercial washing of clothes in the Umgeni River. The same informants claim that the Zulus soon noted that there were insufficient *Dhobis* to meet the needs of all the white inhabitants of Durban, and that blacks therefore quickly adopted the turban and entered the business for themselves.[4] What is known with greater certainty, however, is that by 1878 many blacks in

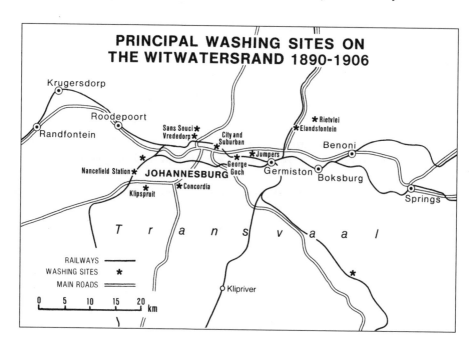

Durban were already undertaking the commercial washing of clothing since the Togt Law of that year sought to peg their earnings at two shillings and sixpence per day.[5] Furthermore, it is clear that from the late 1880s onwards the Durban Corporation regularly issued 'washermen's permits' to blacks.[6] Thus, by the last quarter of the nineteenth century many Africans in Natal and Zululand were already aware of the *Dhobis* and, more importantly, of the income that could be generated through the washing of clothes in the urban areas.

This knowledge of new opportunities to earn cash in the cities came at an important time for Africans since it coincided with a period of accelerated proletarianisation in Zululand and the Natal interior. In many areas, but perhaps more particularly within the triangular region situated between Dundee, Ladysmith and Greytown, the extension of white stock-farming activities, dwindling access to land, a series of cattle diseases and increased taxation combined to force blacks to sell their labour in growing numbers during this period.[7] Up to the mid-1880s, the sluggish growth and modest size of the urban areas that were most accessible to Africans drawn from within the region must have seriously limited the possibilities for would-be washermen. Once gold was discovered in 1886, however, and the rapid and sustained development of the Witwatersrand followed, an exciting new opportunity presented itself to these Africans.

From 1890 onwards Kanyile, Vilakazi, Sithole, Mchunu and Buthelezi clansmen from within this Natal triangle started to peel off the land and to undertake the long march to the Witwatersrand in order to become washermen. Some of these middle-aged tribesmen, who were accompanied by their younger sons, were drawn from the Umsinga district where a system of communal land tenure pertained. Many others however, amongst them the Mchunus and Buthelezis who appear to have dominated the ranks of the *AmaWasha*, came from the families of labour tenants located on white farms in the Weenen district.[8] Once on the Witwatersrand itself, these tribesmen were joined by a smaller number of Hindu *Dhobis* who were also fleeing a political and economic climate that was becoming increasingly hostile to Asians during the early 1890s.

It was not only the demand generated by a mushrooming white population along the line of the Reef, however, that made Johannesburg an obvious target for *Dhobis* and *AmaWasha* alike; there were qualitative as well as quantitative features to the new market which made the town uniquely well suited to the dramatic growth of a washermen's corps.[9] First, as an inland town without the advantage of being sited on a large river, Johannesburg was without any major system of natural drainage which would allow for the ready removal of effluent. For reasons of public health, therefore, the domestic washing of clothing and the tipping of slops into the streets were prohibited early on. Indeed, it was only some 20 years after the town was started in 1906 that the first professionally engineered extensive drainage system came into operation. This in turn meant that for many years the legal washing of clothing was restricted to those streams on the outskirts of the mining town – an inconvenient, tedious and time-consuming practice.[10] Secondly, until some time after the South African War, the bulk of the town's white population was composed of male migrant workers of varying degrees of permanence. These miners, single or separated from their families in Cornwall and elsewhere, were thus without recourse to that female labour which normally undertook the washing and ironing of their clothes.[11]

The economic space created by these distinctly favourable conditions was rapidly filled by the incoming tide of Zulu washermen, and by 1890 there were already a couple of hundred *AmaWasha* at work in the Braamfontein Spruit to the north of the mining camp. By October 1893, when an outbreak of smallpox first occasioned the licensing of the washermen and a slight shifting of their sites, their numbers had risen to over 700. The elapse of two more years saw the growth of the guild outstrip the capacity of the spruit, and by 1898 the *AmaWasha* had extended their operations to four major locations spread around the town. The vast majority of the washermen continued to cluster to the north of the town where the Braamfontein Estate (Sans Souci), Lady Dunbar, Landau and Eastwood sites converged to form what was, in effect, a single Braamfontein-Auckland Park complex. East of the town there was a smaller site at Elandsfontein, while two still smaller sites at Booysens and Concordia served the southern suburbs. In October 1896 an all-time record number of over 1 200 washermen located at eight or more sites paid the shilling licence fee that was necessary to register with the town's health authorities each month.[12]

While the immigrant miners of Johannesburg watched this dramatic increase in the numbers of washermen with a feeling approaching resignation – since there was no real alternative to the service provided by the guild – other Europeans unreservedly welcomed the growth of the new black industry on the Rand. Throughout the 1890s landowners fortunate enough to have streams on their property found that their assets appreciated significantly more rapidly than those of their neighbours. Instead of waiting for the speculative profits that could be realised by the sale of land to the fast-encroaching town, these owners found that they could also look forward to the handsome cash income that could be reaped from rent paid by the washermen during the interim. Louw Geldenhuis, for example, a farm owner and local representative in the *Volksraad* let a small portion of the stream on his property to Lady Drummond Dunbar – the wife of a local health official – at £100 per annum. The formidable

Lady Dunbar, however, recovered more than three times that amount through sub-letting the property to the Zulu washermen. More substantial still was the £350 a year which the Concordia Mining Company obtained from the rental of its property to black washermen during the mid-1890s. Throughout the decade before the South African War, however, it was the coffers of the Braamfontein Estate Company which benefited most from the new industry. By 1895 that Company could afford to pay for the service of a full-time manager as well as for the upkeep of all the plantations on its estate from the £2 400 which it received in rent from the *AmaWasha*.[13] In return for these sizeable sums in rent, the property owners provided the washermen with access to the basic facilities which the *AmaWasha* required to follow their profession. Each washerman paid two shillings and sixpence per week for the right to use the stream, and a further five shillings a week for the privilege of living in a hut on the property.[14] While on the surface of things this monthly rental of approximately 30 shillings from each washerman perhaps did not appear unreasonable, in practice the 'facilities' often turned out to be less than satisfactory.

At each site where laundry was undertaken, the *AmaWasha* cut a series of descending basins or pits along the length of the watercourse and it was in these small dams, in which the dirty discharge of the upper pits served as the 'clean' inflow of the lower, that the actual washing was done. This fundamentally flawed method of site construction ensured that the water used was invariably dirty and discoloured, while a mixture of decomposing soap and mud at the bottom of the pits was said to emit a constant stream of foul-smelling gas bubbles. To make matters worse, the flow of water in certain of the 'streams' was also subject to severe seasonal fluctuations.[15] At Braamfontein-Auckland Park, by far the best developed of the sites, the owners provided eight wood and iron structures to accommodate some of the washermen and a small building in which the laundry could be safely stored overnight. But the small wood and iron huts were often shared by four to six washermen and in 1898 one independent observer described them as 'wretched over-crowded hovels'.[16]

One man's hovel, however, is another man's home and from 1890 onwards a small number of washermen indicated that they considered the sites to be places of semi-permanent residence by constructing their own huts – a practice which also held out the advantage of lower rent. At the Sans Souci site this group of about 80-strong regularly planted crops along the banks of the spruit and also made other efforts to develop gardens.[17] By 1896 this non-migrating core of washermen also held other assets which showed that the Braamfontein site was not being considered simply as a convenient transit camp on a rural-urban-rural journey. In addition to scores of dogs and small numbers of pigs and cattle, the community around Sans Souci also laid claim to 14 horses and four carts. Perhaps even more significantly, the same census showed that besides the 546 Zulu washermen and 14 *Dhobis*, there were also four Indian females and 64 black women resident on the site in 1896.[18] Thus, by the mid-1890s, some of the washing sites were already in the process of transforming themselves into the more familiar type of black 'location' communities to be found elsewhere in and around Johannesburg.

But even this broadening social base could not detract from the fact that in essence these remained *AmaWasha* communities, and this in turn meant that much of the social and economic life on the sites was pulsed and regulated by Nguni custom. What makes the *AmaWasha* of particular interest in this respect, however, is the fascinating manner in which elements of the older Zulu social structure were incorporated into the new urban business community of the washermen's guild. At each site, it was said, an *induna* of 'high rank' and 'comparative wealth' was in firm control of a corps of washermen, and it was he who organised the watch to ensure that the clothes lying around to dry were not stolen from the site. More importantly, it was the *induna* who saw to the 'recruiting of all his own men' and who had the power to fill 'all vacancies'.[19] As the guild grew and the number of places at the most favoured sites declined during the mid-nineties, so the role of *induna* must have assumed increasing importance. Without an *induna* who was willing to act as broker with the site-owner and the municipal authorities, the would-be washerman had little prospect of success. Thus it was after a typical four-month spell of work at the sites in 1895/6 that Geoge Buthelezi, with his *induna*'s prior approval, arranged for his kinsman, Khona Mchunu, to take over from him for a while and 'keep his place warm' until he returned.[20]

Since such alternates or replacements were frequently related, often of a similar age and usually drawn from the same rural areas, it is possible that vestiges of the Zulu regimental system were woven into the fabric of the washermen's guild. An observant journalist noted that when the *indunas* of the various washing sites marched their men into town once a month in order to get their municipal licences renewed, they kept 'perfect time' and proudly sang the songs of their old regiments.[21] It was at these same monthly gatherings on the Market Square that the *AmaWasha* from all the sites around Johannesburg met to discuss their collective business and to pay their respects to the leader of the guild, the formidable Kwaaiman.[22] From 1890 to 1895, Kwaaiman and the senior *indunas* presided over an expanding *AmaWasha* empire which, with the possible exception of the inconvenience caused by the smallpox outbreak in 1893 and the more regular licensing procedure which followed this event, experienced few major upheavals. Much of this changed, however, when the summer rains failed to materialise in 1895 and from then onwards the washermen had growing cause for concern.

While the pits at the crowded washing sites were always somewhat contaminated, their condition became truly disgusting during a drought, and by late October 1895 the local health inspectors had ordered a temporary closure of the main Braamfontein-Auckland Park sites until such time as the pits had been thoroughly cleaned. As drastic was the recommendation that the number of washermen at the Concordia, Booysens and Elandsfontein sites be reduced by half, and that no further licences whatsoever be issued for the two latter sites until the water levels there had improved considerably.[23] This unsatisfactory position, which threatened both the public health and the income of about 150 washermen, persisted throughout the dry summer of 1895. When autumn came, in March 1896, the Johannesburg Sanitary Board saw the need to plan for a longer-term and more radical solution to the problem of the washing sites and duly appointed a sub-committee to examine the question. Once the committee was appointed there was immediate speculation that the washermen would be permanently removed from the town outskirts to a more distant site with a more reliable supply of water.[24] But while such talk might have dampened the spirits of the *AmaWasha* it proved to be much less disconcerting news to at least two other parties – capitalists with an interest in establishing steam laundries and land speculators with an alternative site to offer the Sanitary Board.

In fact, the first steam laundry in Johannesburg appears to have been founded before the drought and washing crisis of 1895/6. In the summer of 1894 one, August Fossati opened a steam laundry on the banks of the Fordsburg Spruit – a venture which operated with seemingly indifferent success for a year or two.[25] It was in late October 1895, however, that an American named William B Hall made the first really serious attempt at running such an industry along modern lines when he floated the Crystal Steam Laundry Company. Hall's scheme, which made provision for the importation of some of the best available plant and equipment from the United States, soon captured the enthusiastic support of several of the town's leading mining and other capitalists. Amongst some of the more prominent shareholders in the 'American Laundry', as it was popularly known, were Otto Beit, Hennan Jennings, Otto Lenz, F O Nelson, G Reunert, E M Sheppard, and G E Webber.[26] Eleven months later – in September 1896 – the Crystal Steam Laundry was in operation next to Lady Dunbar's leasehold property on the Richmond Estate: that is, at the very heart of the territory that had previously been exclusively occupied by the washermen's guild.

But, as the Zulu washermen discovered, bad news seldom travels unaccompanied and no sooner was the idea of the 'American Laundry' mooted than prominent members of the local French and Italian communities proposed the establishment of a rival 'French Laundry'. It is likely that the promoters of this latter scheme drew on the advice of Oreste Nannucci – the managing director of the largest laundry in Cape Town who also had business interests in Johannesburg[27] – as well as that of the less successful August Fossati. Be that as it may, in June 1896 the promoters who had well-developed financial and commercial interests in the young mining town floated the Auckland Park Steam Laundry Company with a registered capital of £12 500. Amongst the more prominent members of this company were Georges Aubert (French Consul in Johannesburg), W E Deplaud, Henri Duval (of the *Banque Francaise de l'Afrique du Sud*), Fernand Pagny, and M A Zoccola (Managing Director of the Grand National Hotel).[28] Yet again this laundry was sited on the Richmond Estate during the latter part of 1896, and this issued the *AmaWasha* with their second direct challenge.

The flurry of financial activity in the mid-1890s, however, was not confined to those associated with the two new steam laundries. Well before it was made officially known that there was to be a search for a single consolidated site for all the washermen some of those in public office, and others with access to privileged information, sought to benefit from the situation. Some time before March 1896 the mining magnate George Goch, assisted by two members of the Sanitary Board – Edward Hancock and H G Filmer – sought to ensure that the washermen's guild would eventually be moved to one of the smaller sites which he owned on the eastern outskirts of the town. Predictably, this manoeuvre soon attracted hostile comment and failed, not least of all because it lacked subtlety. Edward Hancock, besides being the Chairman of the Sanitary Board at the time, was also George Goch's brother-in-law, while the other member – Henry Filmer – was the mine owner's attorney.[29] Likewise, it was also at some stage before the more public discussion of March 1896 that representatives from the Concordia Mining Company sought to persuade certain members of the Sanitary Board that their site was most suited to the needs of the *AmaWasha*. Again, some of Johannesburg's less charitable observers would not have failed to have noticed that Edward Hancock was a leading shareholder in the Concordia Mining Company.[30]

When tenders for the new washing site were eventually submitted to a full meeting of the Sanitary Board in April 1896, however, it was three other proposals that were considered. Of these, only one, Mr Dell's offer of a site to accommodate 1 500 washermen at the farm 'Witbank' on the Klip River, was thought of as a serious proposition; but even then there were serious obstacles to overcome before this proposal could be accepted. Not only was the suggested rental for the new site excessive, but the farm itself was a full two and a half hour rail journey from Johannesburg. This time out of more public-spirited motives, Edward Hancock delayed proceedings, bargained for better terms, and in August 1896 the Sanitary Board eventually approved a modified offer from Dell.[31]

All of these developments – the advent of the steam laundries and the proposed removal of the guild members to Witbank – deeply distressed the *AmaWasha*. On 9 September 1896, while the Dell offer was still awaiting final approval in Pretoria, Kwaaiman took the initiative and informed the Sanitary Board that he and his colleagues strongly objected to any site that was too distant from the town. The Board 'noted' but otherwise ignored this protest, and then proceeded to put great pressure on the Zulu washermen to accept the inevitability of the move to Klip River. Four weeks later the Sanitary Board's health officers refused to issue the washermen with licences that would allow them to operate at the established Johannesburg sites during November. For obvious reasons this action further fuelled *AmaWasha* discontent, and many of the washermen were heard to state openly that they would abandon their profession rather than undertake the move to Witbank.[32]

On 8 November 1896 the members of the guild held a mass meeting on the Market Square and once again instructed Kwaaiman to put their objections to the authorities – this time to A H Smithers, the Sanitary Board's 'Inspector of Natives'. This meeting proved to be no more successful than the earlier one. Smithers curtly informed the leader of the guild that once his members' current licences had expired, all the washermen would wash at the Klip River site or not at all. The news of the ultimatum from the authorities immediately raised a deep and serious division within the ranks of the *AmaWasha*. Within three days of the meeting, however, a small contingent of washermen made the first rail journey to Witbank. The Inspector of Natives, misreading the extent of the rift within the guild, took this as a sign that the majority of the washermen would soon follow and make their way to the Klip River site without further protest.[33]

Between 30 November and 2 December several hundred *AmaWasha* left their old and familiar workplaces, informing the site owners that they no longer wished to be involved in the washing business. Of this large number a few succeeded in obtaining positions as domestic servants, but the vast majority proceeded directly to their homes in the rural areas of Natal.[34] Within 12 hours white Johannesburg lost the services of nearly 40 per cent of the black washermen's corps that usually met its laundry needs. The extent of that loss is reflected in Table 3.[35]

Table 3 Number of washing licenses issued monthly by the Johannesburg Sanitary Board/Town

	1893	1894	1895	1896	1897	1898	1900	1904
January		605			500	521		
February		556			513	388		
March		507			569	458	66	
April		654		845				
May				923		546		
June				939		316		429
July				1 036				
August		683		1 043		233		
September		524					120	220
October	729	591		1 222				
November	635			892		650		
December	556	511	821	498		535		

The swift exodus of such a large part of the washermen's guild soon frustrated many of the town's white residents who now turned to the remaining Zulu laundrymen for help. From 2 December, however, and for a full week thereafter, the overwhelming majority of the remaining *AmaWasha* stayed on at their old central site but went on 'strike' and refused to take in any new work. To make matters worse, the 100-strong contingent of washermen who had moved to the new site at Witbank seized the moment to double the charge for their services. By the end of the week Europeans were either starting to wash their own clothing at home illegally or reluctantly paying the 100 per cent increase to meet the weekly laundry bill.[36]

Then, just when the defiant washermen's action appeared to be seriously inconveniencing the white community, the *AmaWasha*'s resistance started to collapse. From about 8 December 1896 onwards, growing numbers of washermen capitulated and defected to the distant Klip River site.[37] Lack of leadership, the need for cash, the presence of the new steam laundries and 'scabs' at Witbank all combined to undermine the morale of the *AmaWasha*, and by the last week of 1896 most of the washermen's guild was at work in the Klip River.

THE *AMAWASHA* ON THE DEFENSIVE, 1897-1906

There were several obvious reasons behind the *AmaWasha*'s objection to being moved out to Witbank in late 1896, and of these the most fundamental was the desire to maintain cheap and ready access to their customers of long standing. It was this common-sense consideration which lay at the base of the washermen's unsuccessful protest, and in order to more fully appreciate the reasons behind their resistance it is helpful to consider how the move to Klip River threatened their economic well-being.

While still situated on the immediate outskirts of Johannesburg, the Zulu washermen enjoyed a working week with a predictable rhythm to it. The first day of the week was usually devoted to the collection and delivery of bundles of washing. While a half-dozen or so washermen made use of their horses and carts for this purpose, the majority of guild members simply slung the large bundles over their sticks and made the two to five-mile journey into town once or twice on foot. Monday was also usually the day on which the *AmaWasha* collected their fees from their customers. The remainder of the working week – from early Tuesday morning until late Saturday afternoon – was spent on the actual laundering operations; a routine that was only broken by the occasional mid-week special afternoon delivery. Sunday, invariably a day of rest of leisure, rounded off a strenuous week.[38]

Working within this pattern, an average washerman processed three bundles of clothing a day or about 18 bundles per week, and since the charge for a load of washing varied between four and five shillings, this usually generated a weekly income of about £3. This gave each washerman a monthly average income of £12 which, during the prevailing four-monthly spell of migrant labour, yielded a gross income of about £48. Against this, however, the washermen had to offset certain unavoidable costs which, over the same four-month cycle, came to a little more than £7 .[39] Thus, after a typical tour of duty on the Witwatersrand, a returning member of the washermen's guild could look back on a gross profit of about £48. An outline of these transactions is shown in Table 4.

Table 4 Income and expenditure of a Zulu washerman over a four-month period between 1890 and 1896

Income		Expenditure	
60 bundles of washing		Initial Sanitary Board registration fee	1s 6d
per month at 4/-		4 licences at 1/- per month	4s 0d
per bundle for		Hut rental at £1 per month	£4 0s 0d
four months	£48 0s 0d	Site hire at 2/6 per week	£2 0s 0d
		1/3 pass exemption fee at	
		per year	£1 0s 0d
	£48 0s 0d		£7 5s 6d

These gross figures, however, provide no more than a mere outline since they do not take into account some of the other more tangential 'business' transactions which did much to raise the washermen's real income. Throughout the years the *AmaWasha* occupied the 'locations' close to the town sites, they and the women who lived with them derived a considerable income from the illegal sale of beer which they, as members of the guild, were permitted to brew for their own consumption but not to market commercially.[40] An additional source of income, in cash or kind, was the spoil that accrued to less scrupulous washermen who stole or sold their customers' clothing.

From mid-1894 A H Smithers, the Sanitary Board official responsible for the *AmaWasha*, was constantly beset with complaints by Europeans about the loss of their laundry. By late 1895 these complaints reached such a volume – well over 100 a month – that the Inspector of Natives recommended the appointment of a full-time official to deal with all such cases. While many of these losses could be attributed to individual thefts by washermen, there were also occasions when it was clearly undertaken on a more systematic basis – as when, in 1894, Smithers recovered no less than ten 'missing' bundles of clothing during a single surprise inspection at a washing site. Most organised of all, however, was the regular selling of clothing to a gang of 'Peruvians' – Russian or Polish Jews – in 1895. Since the peddling and second-hand clothing trade in the town was firmly in the hands of East European immigrants, these 'Peruvians' would have been well placed to dispose of large quantities of clothing in the retail trade. It was quite conceivable, therefore, that a white miner who had sent his laundry for washing to the guild would end up having to repurchase his own garments from a second-hand clothing dealer in the city centre![41]

While it is difficult to estimate how much additional revenue a washerman could raise through the sale of beer or second-hand clothing, there are clear indications that this involvement in 'informal sector' opportunities was becoming increasingly important prior to the move to Klip River. But here again, this income had to be offset against necessary overhead expenditure – such as the cost of food while at the working sites and, after 1895, the cost of rail transport between Natal and the Transvaal. Even when all these factors are taken into account, however, it would still appear that before 1896 a washerman could reasonably be expected to have a net income of between £40 and £50 after four months' labour on the Witwatersrand. Since most members of the guild undertook two such spells of labour each year, it meant that each washerman could take back cash savings of between £80 and £100 to the rural areas every 12 months. Income of this order placed the AmaWasha in a rather exceptional socio-economic category and not surprisingly their children, when subsequently questioned about their fathers' position in rural society, deemed the washermen to be 'wealthy'.[42]

But much of this changed rapidly once the guild was forced to move to the Klip River site in 1896. The move significantly increased the washermen's overhead costs, seriously disrupted their work rhythm and badly undermined their sources of supplementary income. Above all else, however, it was the Netherlands South African Railway Company, the NZASM, and the cost of transport which threatened to financially cripple the *AmaWasha*. Washermen now had to meet the cost of rail transport for the two and a half hour journey between the Witbank site and their customers, and this necessitated a substantial cash outlay. In addition to this the guild members were, for some months, also obliged to pay a charge for all bundles of laundry exceeding 50 lbs in weight. Undoubtedly it was the direct costs incurred in this manner that did most to keep the *AmaWasha* away from the new site. The Sanitary Board readily acknowledged this problem and consistently put pressure on the railway company to reduce its charges. When the NZASM did eventually agree to reduce its prices there was an immediate, albeit modest increase in the numbers of washermen willing to make use of the Klip River site.[43]

It was not only the direct cost of NZASM transport which adversely affected the fortunes of the washermen's guild, however, it was also the quality and frequency of the service provided by the railway company which did much to undermine the washermen's productivity. For several weeks an indifferent NZASM management was content to allow the *AmaWasha* and their bundles to be carried in empty coal trucks – a somewhat clinical and inappropriate service for those engaged in the laundry industry. More serious still was the manner in which an infrequent rail service disrupted the washermen's work and business rhythm. During the first two months at Witbank there was only a twice-weekly service between the new site and Johannesburg and even when this did improve to a more regular and reliable daily service, in March 1897, it still did not fully meet the guild's needs.[44] The railway company's timetable made it simply impossible for a washerman to make a return journey to the site as well as undertake all his deliveries and collections within the town in a single day. In short, the *AmaWasha* had to spend a great deal more time travelling and less time working, and ultimately this reflected itself in much reduced turnover.

But in addition to the above, there were at least three other formidable disadvantages to be faced by the washermen who made the move to the Klip River site. First, once at Witbank the washermen for a variety of reasons could no longer plant crops or keep the gardens to which they had become accustomed at the old sites and this, coupled with the fact that they now had to make most of their purchases at a local store which could not offer competitive urban prices, meant that they were forced to spend more money on food than had previously been the case.[45] Second, since their 'location' was now well beyond the town and cut off from the normal weekend influx of visitors and customers, beer-selling ceased to be a profitable side-line. Indeed, the appearance of a white-owned canteen at the new washing site meant that the *AmaWasha* were reduced from being small-scale producers of alcohol to simple consumers.[46] Third, the Witbank site was isolated, centralised and under the direct supervision of four black policemen and a much-feared Constable Botha of the ZAR police.[47] This greatly reduced the chance of any sustained involvement in the illegal second-hand clothes trade.

Thus, caught in the economic scissors of increased costs and falling revenue, the members of the guild responded like any orthodox businessmen and increased their prices. From the first week in December 1896 the washermen put up their prices from four shillings to eight shillings for a bundle of washing in an attempt to cope with the new cost structure that had been imposed upon them – a 100 per cent increase. From that point on, the *AmaWasha*'s regular clients found that their laundry needs were being less efficiently dealt with by a smaller number of washermen at prices substantially higher than anything they had been called upon to pay before. This was a situation that was ripe for exploitation by those who possessed the necessary capital to acquire machinery for modern mass-processing techniques. Thus, although the Rand generally was in a state of economic recession after the Jameson Raid, this part of the service sector continued to expand. Whereas there were only two steam laundries in Johannesburg in late 1896, by April 1898 there were at least half a dozen in operation. While the black laundrymen were away, the white capitalists seized the chance to play.

One of the first of the new enterprises, the Melrose Steam Laundry, was opened to the north of the town on the banks of the Jukskei River in April 1897. The promoters of this company realised, as did others at the time, that while capital might be harder to find during a recession, the same was true of labour. They thus set about recruiting workers from amongst those *Dhobis* who were making their way to the Witwatersrand in increasing numbers after 1895.[48] Through offering these east coast Asian immigrants accommodation, rations and a small cash wage, the laundry owners soon acquired a stabilised labour force for their new venture.

While the *Dhobis* at Melrose were undoubtedly poor they were, however, far from being totally demoralised by their vulnerable economic position. Within weeks of the laundry opening the workers came out on an unsuccessful strike against what they considered to be an exploitative piece-work system that had been introduced by the management.[49] After this unsteady start, the laundry continued to make slow but steady progress. By 1899 its workers were sufficiently settled for them to ask the owners to grant them a site on which they could construct a Hindu temple so that their religious needs could be met. This request was granted and the temple-cum-school no doubt further assisted the stabilisation of the work-force.[50] The Melrose Laundry continued to operate right up to the depression in the 1920s while the small corrugated-iron Siva Subramanian Temple still stands today amidst the rather incongruous surroundings of the city's opulent northern suburbs.

But in the Johannesburg of 1897 poverty and bitter distress were not confined to the Asian or African communities – something of which several white charities were only too well aware. The Johannesburg Relief Committee, like most of its Victorian counterparts, however, was reluctant to 'pauperise' the unemployed by simply providing charity to the needy. It therefore cast about for a scheme which would avoid the moral pitfalls associated with 'indiscriminate relief' and at the same time offer help to some of the many destitute Afrikaner families in the western suburbs of Burgersdorp and Vrededorp. Noting the absence of the *AmaWasha* from nearby Braamfontein, the Committee struck upon the idea of establishing a laundry which, while running on a non-profit basis, would offer some employment for urban poor whites.[51]

In mid-1897 the members of the Johannesburg Relief Committee therefore approached the Kruger government for a site on which to locate the laundry which it hoped would employ indigent Afrikaner women. The State President and his colleagues viewed the project with some sympathy, granted the necessary site in Vrededorp and – in September of the same year – set up the *Maatschappy tot nut van het Algemeen* to act as governing body of this charitable institution.[52] The Committee, however, was particularly slow in pushing ahead with the scheme and when the South African War broke out two years later the land granted by the Kruger government had still not been utilised.[53] But despite the failure of the Relief Committee to provide Afrikaner women with more formal employment, many other women – some of them white, many others Coloured and black – took up the hand-washing of clothing as a means of earning a living from 1897 onwards.[54]

As if somehow to add insult to the absent Zulu washermen's economic injury, however, the most important developments of all continued to take place on the Richmond Estate at the very centre of their old Braamfontein-Auckland Park washing site. Here, the rudimentary industrial complex established during the booming business climate of 1895/6 was severely shaken by the 1897 recession but nevertheless survived to make further headway. The Crystal Steam Laundry only remained in business in 1897 through being able to secure an additional loan of £1 500 from the American-linked firm of Chaplin and Manion

Ltd.[55] Thereafter, under the guidance of F O Nelson, the laundry recovered to make steady progress right up to the outbreak of war.

Next door the Crystal Laundry's sister factory, the Auckland Park Steam Laundry, was rather less fortunate. By late 1897 the 'French Company' was in serious trouble with its property being firmly bonded to a Parisian financier.[56] Then, just when all seemed lost, the Company found buyers to take over the venture as a going concern. In January 1898 the Auckland Park Steam Laundry was refloated as the Palace Steam Laundry Limited with a major part of the new company's capital of £8 000 being provided by two local men – A C Reich and Edmund Fordtran. But here too at least some of the new capital appears to have been raised in the United States since the De Boer family of Illinois were reported as holding shares to the value of £1 500 in the new company.[57] Under its new lease of economic life the Palace Steam Laundry made steady progress and functioned until at least 1920.

At about the same time that these developments were taking place at the Richmond Estate, however, the two steam laundries were joined by a third enterprise of a related sort – a soap factory. In February 1897, the Kruger government granted a butcher, H Woolf, and others, a concession to process tallow obtained from Transvaal animals into household and other soap. On the strength of this, Woolf floated the Transvaal Soap Company with a nominal capital of £10 000 but since finance was hard to raise during a recession, the company was restructured in November 1897 in such a way as to allow it to operate with a more modest working capital of £4 000.[58] Unfortunately for Woolf and his partners the rinderpest epidemic in the same year prevented the company from readily obtaining all the tallow it required. Despite this difficult start, the company went into production in 1898 and manufactured increasing quantities of soap during the next ten years. In 1908 the Transvaal Soap Company was again restructured and in 1912 the factory at Richmond was acquired by the international giant, Lever Brothers.[59]

The members of the washermen's guild, viewing these developments from the splendid isolation of Witbank in 1897, had good reason to be distressed. Despite the prevailing uncertain economic conditions the two large steam laundries, three or four other medium-sized enterprises and a small number of hand-washing establishments run by members of the Cantonese community were all making significant inroads into a market that had previously been overwhelmingly dominated by the Zulu washermen.[60] But while developments at the Richmond Estate undoubtedly depressed the *AmaWasha*, it was also true that such hope and optimism as they retained for a return to the town also emanated from the old Braamfontein-Auckland Park complex. For right from the time of the expulsion of the guild from the town a small number of defiant washermen had stayed on at one of the old sites at Richmond. It was this splinter group of the guild, aided and abetted by the site-owners, who fought the Sanitary Board, undermined the viability of the Klip River establishment and who were ultimately responsible for the restoration of much of the old order.

In December 1896, when the vast majority of the *AmaWasha* were making the move to Witbank, Lady Drummond Dunbar persuaded 60 washermen hiring a site from her to remain on the property. While the economic advantage of such a stay obviously appealed to the washermen, they were less confident about the legal consequences which would follow if they should follow their old profession without the necessary Sanitary Board licence. Lady Dunbar, however, promised that she would ensure their legal protection provided that they agreed to take out passes under the law that was generally applicable to Africans. This the washermen agreed to and, abandoning their privileged position as pass-exempt guild members, they duly enrolled as Lady Dunbar's 'servants' and continued to follow their calling.[61]

The Sanitary Board was quick to take up this challenge and immediately prosecuted those washermen operating without the necessary licence. Lady Dunbar and the site-owners, however, struck back by contesting the legal right of the Board to withhold licences and by organising a public petition for the return of the *AmaWasha* and the cheaper laundry service which they provided.[62] Over the next six months a series of intermittent skirmishes between the Sanitary Board and Lady Dunbar took place in the courts. Then, a decisive legal battle was fought when the case of two of Lady Dunbar's 'servants' – Stephanus and Inzonda – was referred to the High Court for a final decision.[63] On 8 July 1897 the High Court ruled in Lady Dunbar's favour and immediately the site-owners put out the word that the *AmaWasha* would be safe and welcome to return to their old places for work. Within four weeks so many of the washermen had left the Klip River site that the store there was forced to close down for want of business. By early September there was not a single washerman left at Witbank.[64]

The Zulu washermen returned to Johannesburg with undisguised pleasure in 1897 and at once reverted to charging their formerly competitive price of three to four shillings per bundle of washing. The majority of the washermen found their way back to their favourite sites at Braamfontein-Auckland Park which were now conveniently – if not hygienically – supplied with warm soapy water discharged from the plants of the Crystal and Palace Steam laundries. Others, including yet more *Dhobis* who had arrived from the east coast, went elsewhere or made their way to new sites that now developed at Langlaagte and near the Jumpers mine.[65]

Yet, for all their delight at being back in their old haunts, the washer-men found that certain important changes had taken place during their absence at Witbank – changes that greatly weakened their economic position. By 1898 the washermen's corps had been reduced to half of its size in 1896, and this – as well as the fact that there were now no less than six laundries in town undertaking the washing and ironing of clothing at four shillings per dozen items – in large part reflected the damage inflict-ed by the move to Klip River.[66] There had also been a series of other developments, however, which in the long run proved to be at least as serious for the washermen. The move to Witbank had split the ranks of the *AmaWasha* and badly undermined the unity of the guild, and it was really only once they had returned to Johannesburg that it became apparent just how much of their former cohesiveness and discipline the washermen had lost. The guild members no longer enjoyed the benefits of having an undisputed leader such as Kwaaiman, with the result that their frequent collective marches into Market Square and the meetings to which they gave rise declined, and this in turn made for a more isolated existence at the various washing locations. This loss of internal control manifested itself in the growing number of reports of theft, gambling, drinking and violence that came from the washing sites between 1897 and the outbreak of war.[67]

The Johannesburg Sanitary Board and its successor in late 1897, the town council, viewed these deteriorating conditions at the old washing sites with some dismay. It was not so much the decay in the social con-ditions within these black communities which disturbed the white authorities, however, as the fact that the washing pits themselves remained as disgusting and unhygienic as ever.[68] But, still smarting from the legal blows inflicted on it by Lady Dunbar's lawyers, the council was powerless to effectively control the sites and it was thus forced into for-mulating a new set of by-laws in September 1897. This set of by-laws extended the council's jurisdiction to cover washing sites 'adjoining' the town as well as those within it – a manoeuvre which would allow the municipality to control independent washermen as well as those employed as 'servants' by site-owners. In addition, the new regulations reinforced an earlier provision which required a washerman to wear a numbered brass badge on his left arm, and increased the cost of a wash-ing licence from one shilling to two shillings and sixpence per month. It was only in late 1898, however, that the Executive Committee of the *Volksraad* got around to approving these draft regulations, and it was only in April 1899 that they were eventually published in the *Government Gazette* and became legally binding.[69] With such belated legal backing, it was hardly surprising that A H Smithers complained bitterly about his inability to control the washermen in the period leading up to the outbreak of the war.[70]

When war was declared in October 1899 the large majority of *AmaWasha* left the sites for their rural homes in Natal and in many cases sought and found work with the invading British forces.[71] A non-migratory core of about 120 washermen, however, stayed on at the washing sites where they were joined by other black men and women stranded by the war. This heterogeneous population which, in addition to the working washermen, now included several professional liquor-sellers and prostitutes, became increasingly difficult to control between 1899 and 1902.[72] Not only were there the by now normal allegations of theft, gambling and immorality, but once the mines reopened with a seriously depleted African mine labour supply, there were also bitter complaints that washing locations adjacent to mines – such as those of George Goch, Jumpers and Concordia – offered a refuge for drunken black miners.[73]

After the British occupation of Johannesburg in May 1900, the incoming administration at once addressed itself to the problem of urban African communities in general, and to the question of the washermen and the washing sites in particular. In this regard, it would appear that the new authorities set themselves the task of achieving three overlapping objectives between 1900 and 1904. First, as a matter of some urgency, they set out to 'clean up' the washing locations by expelling the beer-brewers and liquor-sellers who significantly reduced the productivity of the black labour force on adjacent mines. Second, they sought to establish effective legal control over the washermen themselves, as well as the washing sites. Third, and in the longer term, they desired to enhance control and segregation by attempting to get all urban Africans to live in a single consolidated location.

In October 1900, a proclamation signed by the Military Governor decreed all washing sites to be within municipal jurisdiction and empowered the authorities to remove all persons other than registered washermen from the sites and place them in the location that had been established near Vrededorp during the pre-war years.[74] It seems possible that these powers contributed to the closure of the Jumpers and George Goch washing sites shortly thereafter. What is known with greater certainty is that it only took the municipality and the government a further 12 months to move in and destroy the oldest, and by now most central of all the washing sites in Johannesburg – that at Sans Souci in the Braamfontein-Auckland Park complex.[75]

Towards the end of 1901 the Sans Souci washermen were informed that no further licences would be issued for their site and that they should immediately remove themselves to the old 'Kaffir Location'. This announcement was accompanied by the news that the new British pass law – unlike the old Republican legislation – did not make provision for a pass-exemption for 'those coloured persons earning their living independently of a white master'.[76] These measures threatened to remove some of the remaining independent *AmaWasha* from their competitive central site in the town and arbitrarily reduce them to the menial status of 'servants' in the new economy. In February 1902 *induna* Mahlangu and others – on behalf of the Sans Souci washermen – petitioned the Commissioner of Native Affairs, Sir Godfrey Lagden, for relief from these oppressive measures. The petitioners pointed out to Lagden that they had occupied the site in question since 1890, that many of them had erected houses and lived there permanently, that the cheap service which they provided was favoured by a significant section of the white population, that their crops were still ripening in the ground and that any move would expose them to considerable hardship.[77] The Commissioner of Native Affairs allowed the washermen to reap their crops. In April 1902 the Sans Souci *AmaWasha* moved from their central site – not to the 'Kaffir Location' as Lagden had hoped, but to the notorious washing location at Concordia.[78]

This partially successful act of evasion by the Sans Souci washermen was made possible by certain legal loopholes that continued to exist during the transition from a military to a civil administration in the city. From late 1902 onwards, however, the Milner administration steadily prepared the way for local government authorities to further regulate the activities of any *AmaWasha*. In August 1903 representatives from the government and the Johannesburg and Pretoria town councils held a conference to draft yet another special set of by-laws to deal with, amongst other issues, washermen, locations and steam laundries. Finally, in October 1903, these regulations were approved, and the municipal authorities were fully empowered to deal with the 'problem' of the washermen and their 'private locations'.[79]

Early in 1904, before these regulations could be effectively enforced, Johannesburg was struck by an outbreak of plague and as a precaution against the spread of the disease the Plague Committee ordered that the largest part of the old 'Kaffir Location' be razed to the ground. It was in response to this measure and the immediate problems which it created that the municipality hastily acquired the farm Klipspruit some 13 miles from town.[80] Urban blacks were deeply distressed by these developments and further alarmed by the rumour that the imposition of a strict quarantine would confine them to the Witwatersrand even after they had completed their labour contracts.

This sense of unease, through a combination of chance and design, transformed the usual Sunday afternoon gathering of blacks and others at the Market Square into what the press termed a 'Native Mass Meeting' on 27 March 1904. As a group who had already experienced the effects of one expulsion from the town in 1896, and as small businessmen who stood to lose at least as much as black workers from any new move, the turbaned *AmaWasha* figured prominently at this meeting – leading the crowd in chanting and singing at a venue where they had gathered many times before. After the meeting had been addressed in Zulu by J S Marwick, the crowd, somewhat reassured by the general tenor of his remarks, quietly dispersed.[81] The Assistant Secretary for Native Affairs, however, had been very careful to make no promises in his speech and, in May 1904, all the washermen – together with hundreds of other blacks – were sent to the 'emergency camp' at Klipspruit.[82]

Neither the administrative harassment of the washermen within Johannesburg between 1901 and 1903, nor the evacuation of the remnants of the guild to Klipspruit in 1904 helped to solve one of the city's most basic problems – the continuing need for more satisfactory public laundry facilities. Throughout the period, therefore, there was much criticism of the old washing sites and pressure put on the Council to erect alternate facilities that were cheap, conveniently situated and hygienic.[83] Thus, when the plans for an extensive gravitation sewerage system were formulated in 1902, a scheme for public wash-houses in the working-class suburbs of Burgersdorp and Fordsburg was also mooted.[84] The latter project, however, which in some ways closely resembled the earlier *Maatschappy tot nut van het Algemeen*, never came to fruition.

For their part, capitalists operating within the service sector of the economy viewed these developments between 1901 and 1904 with some enthusiasm since their net effect was to marginally increase the competitiveness of the more centrally situated steam laundries. Not only were their prices becoming more competitive, but the large influx of whites into Johannesburg in the immediate post-war period left the steam laundries with a much expanded market. In several cases this made for business complacency and some of the laundries were accused of developing a 'take it or leave it' attitude towards customers.[85] For most laundry owners, however, this was the most opportune moment to expand their businesses and between 1901 and 1904 the majority of the larger enterprises extended their premises and acquired new plant and equipment.[86] It was also during the same period that a second specialised laundry complex started to develop in the valley to the immediate east of Doornfontein where there was a plentiful supply of water. Here the Lorentzville Steam Laundry and other smaller enterprises established themselves.[87]

But once again, the most significant industrial development of all took place at the old Braamfontein-Auckland Park sites. By the end of the war the Crystal or 'American' Laundry, which had previously operated with an extensive credit system, found itself in severe financial difficulties. The majority of shareholders in the company, however, sensing the improved business climate, were most reluctant to wind up the business and place it under liquidation. Instead, the directors suggested that the company be amalgamated with a smaller laundry owned by F O Nelson and then be refloated as a larger consolidated venture. Since Nelson was already a prominent shareholder in the Crystal Laundry there was no insurmountable obstacle to this strategy and after a shareholders' meeting in July 1902 the new Rand Steam Laundries came into being.[88] As the driving force in the new venture Nelson put the old company's mining connections to good use and systematically secured the mines' boarding-houses and single quarters' laundry contracts for the new venture.[89] Building on this solid foundation of mining-house business the immediate financial future of Rand Steam Laundries was assured and by late 1902 the company employed over 100 white and Malay women workers in the main plant at Richmond.[90]

The Zulu washermen, once more viewing the growing strength of city steam laundries from a position of barren economic isolation – this time the Klipspruit camp in June 1904 – could have found little cause for comfort in these developments. But in the weeks that followed they became more optimistic as hundreds of blacks successfully deserted the camp and re-established themselves in the city. The *AmaWasha*, whose very livelihood depended on a swift return to the urban areas, needed no further prompting and by August 1904 the last of the washermen had left Klipspruit and made the 13-mile journey back to Johannesburg. On this occasion, though, their re-entry was less successful than it had been when they returned from the farm Witbank in 1897 since they were now confronted with more sophisticated barriers of urban segregation legislation which effectively denied them access to the oldest and most central washing sites. Thus, most of the new sites which the 220 licensed washermen came to occupy at Claremont, Craighall and Langlaagte between 1904 and 1905 were further away from their white customers than ever before. Of the older sites only one – that at Concordia – was successfully reoccupied during this period.[91]

But the reoccupation of these more peripheral urban sites by the remaining *AmaWasha* and their families did not perturb the authorities as it might have done, since they knew it to be only a temporary setback in a grander design. At the very moment that urban blacks were deserting the emergency camp and making their way back to Johannesburg, the municipality was laying long-term plans to develop a permanently segregated community at Klipspruit. By June 1904 the Town Engineer had provided the council's Public Health Committee with detailed estimates for the cost of building a complex which would include a 'Native Location', an 'Asiatic Bazaar' and a separate 'location' and laundry for 460 'washboys'.[92] The small-business component provided for in this scheme pleased the council since it meant that not only would the venture be largely self-supporting, but that it actually stood the chance of becoming income-generating.[93] The idea of segregation being paid for by the segregated held enormous appeal for white administrators. By early 1906, an ironing-room, a fenced-in drying site and the first of 100 specially designed concrete wash tubs had been erected at Klipspruit.[94] With blind ruthlessness and staggering cynicism the council prepared to move the washermen for the last time – this time to an uneconomic washing site that shared its setting with the municipal sewerage works.

THE DECLINE OF THE INDEPENDENT ZULU WASHERMEN, 1906-1914

The fragmented clusters of *AmaWasha* that remained in Johannesburg in 1905 appear to have been less than enthusiastic at the prospect of being moved out to the new municipal sewerage farm with its adjoining well-policed laundry complex,[95] and when the town council started to put pressure on the washermen to move to Klipspruit in 1906 many of the more fatalistic amongst them responded as their predecessors had in a somewhat similar situation nearly a decade earlier and simply abandoned their businesses. This time, the departing Zulu washermen also took with them the added burden of anxiety about the Bambatha rebellion that was sweeping through parts of rural Natal.

Others, however, perhaps the surviving members of the old non-migrating core of the guild, chose instead to partly resist the town council's pressure to move to Klipspruit. In late 1906 or early 1907, about 75 washermen under the *induna* Charlie Kanyile made their way to the long-deserted washing site to the east of the city on the farm Elandsfontein. This site, on the property of an impecunious farmer named Deyzel, still fell just outside of Johannesburg's newly extended municipal boundaries. Deyzel, in return for a monthly rental of between £60 and £80, made the washermen welcome on his farm. Kanyile and his cohorts made use of this 'rural' base to tout for business in the city – a practice which the municipal officials were only willing to tolerate while there were insufficient concrete washtubs available at Klipspruit. In time-honoured fashion this group of *AmaWasha* also supplemented their income by selling beer to the inhabitants of the nearby municipal compound at Rosherville.[96]

In general, however, the overall effect of the enforced move to Klipspruit in 1906 was – as in 1896 – to cause a reduction in the numbers of washermen. Sudden moves out of town, for health-cum-segregation reasons, were shattering blows to small black businessmen whose livelihood depended on providing a cheap service to whites in urban areas. Whereas the municipality had issued a monthly average of 262 washing licences in 1905 while the washermen were still occupying sites adjacent to the city, by the following year, when the first moves to Klipspruit had been effected, this figure had dropped to 199. Thereafter, with the exception of 1907, there was a steady annual decline in the average number of licences issued to the Zulu washermen each month. By 1914, a monthly average of only 93 washing licences was being issued to blacks at work in the Klipspruit municipal laundry. These figures are reflected in Table 5.[97]

Table 5 Washing licences granted at Klipspruit municipal laundry, 1906-14

Year	Total issued	Monthly average	Municipal revenue
1905	3 152	262	£778 0s 6d
1906	2 392	199	£598 19s 6d
1907	2 436	203	£609 11s 0d
1908	2 068	172	£517 0s 0d
1909	2 040	170	£510 0s 0d
1910	1 804	150	£451 0s 0d
1911	1 752	146	£438 0s 0d
1912	1 540	128	£385 0s 0d
1913	1 316	109	£329 0s 0d
1914	1 124	93	£281 0s 0d

Several factors contributed to the gradual demise of the washermen's business after 1906. At the time that the municipality enforced the removal of the washermen from their old sites it also took the opportunity to triple the fee charged for the monthly licence from two shillings and sixpence to seven shillings and sixpence – a move designed to help recoup some of the £3 500 spent on the Klipspruit laundry as swiftly as was possible. Initially the town council simply ignored the washermen's complaints about this dramatic increase in price, but once 300 washing bays had been completed in 1907 and it became apparent that the laundry was likely to be permanently saddled with excess capacity, the councillors were forced to rethink the position.[98] After a protacted delay, the council eventually agreed to reduce the fee to five shillings per month as from July 1908 in the belief that this action alone would be sufficient to coax a further 100 washermen out of the rural areas and back into their urban businesses.[99]

The washing licence itself, however, was not the single most important factor in a new cost structure that slowly throttled business at Klipspruit. As had been the case at Witbank ten years earlier, it was the absence of cheap and efficient rail transport that did most to ruin the small businessmen who had been relegated to a segregated site miles out of town. Besides having to meet the cost of a return rail fare to

Johannesburg, the washermen were once again charged for the bundles of clothing they carried – this time at the rate of sixpence per 100 lbs, with an additional sixpence for every further part thereof.[100] The bill for transport alone thus ran at between 10 and 15 shillings per month, and it was hardly surprising therefore that a spokesman for the washermen could complain in 1907 that 'the railway took all their profits'.[101] In addition to this, the washermen were also called upon to pay for the hire of commercial 'trolleys' to help them transport washing within Johannesburg, and to pay for rickshaw pullers to help them move the heaviest bundles from Nancefield Station to the Klipspruit laundry.[102]

But, also as before, there was another and equally unpleasant side to the washermen's economic plight after 1906 – falling revenue. Some of this could be accounted for by the loss of customers which the washermen suffered as a result of providing a less efficient service. During this period the washermen repeatedly passed on customers' complaints to the authorities about 'spoilt work' that arose from the indiscriminate throwing about of completed laundry by railwaymen, or of losses sustained because of the inadequately protected storage space at Braamfontein Station. More important, though, was the reduction in turnover that was occasioned by an inconvenient railway timetable which seriously eroded the washermen's working hours.[103] Perhaps most important of all, however, was the fact that the removal to Klipspruit took place during the worst period of the economic depression that engulfed the Witwatersrand between 1906 and 1908. The marked decline in white working-class incomes during this period ultimately also affected the prices which the Zulu washermen could charge for their services. Thus, whereas three shillings constituted the minimum charge for a bundle of washing in the years before 1905, by 1909 it constituted a maximum, with charges ranging all the way down to one shilling a bundle.[104]

The Johannesburg Town Council – with the single exception of the small reduction in the licence fee noted above – showed little compassion for the remnants of the washermen's guild that it had bundled out into the economic wilderness in 1906. Having invested the ratepayers' money in the Klipspruit laundry, the council proceeded to behave with the single-minded determination that any ghetto landlord would have been proud of. In October 1907 it put pressure on the remaining washermen at Elandsfontein to make the move to Klipspruit by refusing to renew their licences. When this failed to make Charlie Kanyile and his men undertake the move to the municipal laundry the Town Clerk successfully appealed to the Director of the Government Native Labour Bureau to have the defiant washermen removed from Deyzel's farm under the Squatters Law. Even then about 20 of the washermen continued to resist the authorities by moving even further afield to the farm

Rietvlei from where they sought to service the white townships of the East Rand. By December 1907, however, Kanyile and the majority of the group had given up the struggle and reluctantly gone to work at the Klipspruit laundry.[105]

Once the city had been effectively cleared of immediate competition from the *AmaWasha* there were new opportunities for rival small businessmen and larger capitalists to consolidate their hold over the laundry services within Johannesburg. Amongst the first to benefit from the segregation imposed on the Zulu washermen were members of those 'non-white' ethnic groups not expelled from the inner city. The very act of creating the Klipspruit laundry made it economically possible for poorer members of the Chinese and Asian communities to enter and stay in the laundry business – an ironic development which the town council, under pressure from the White League, a racist association of small European traders, could hardly have enjoyed.[106]

Whilst there had been a small Chinese community in Johannesburg since at least the mid-1890s, there was a significant increase in its numbers between 1902 and 1909. Most of the new immigrants were Cantonese speakers who had entered the Transvaal illegally from the Cape and elsewhere in the immediate post-war period.[107] Culturally distinct from their fellow countrymen who laboured underground on the Rand mines during part of the same period, the majority of these 'free' Chinese found their way into the city's retail trade as grocers.[108] A minority, which lacked the necessary capital to enter the retail trade, however, chose instead to establish itself in the more demanding laundry business. Significantly, the greatest opportunity for expansion by this latter set of entrepreneurs came only after the Zulu washermen had been pushed out of the city. Whereas there were only about a dozen Chinese laundries in Johannesburg in 1904, by 1907 there were over 40 and as late as 1914 there were still 46 such establishments in the city.[109]

Most of the Chinese laundries were located in the heart of Johannesburg in the older and less affluent suburbs of Fordsburg and Jeppe. Within these central areas they succeeded in providing a relatively cheap service for white workers since they avoided transport costs by refusing to undertake the collection or delivery of laundry.[110] By the time that the most serious phase of the 1906-8 depression had set in, many of these small hand-laundries had already started to make the transition to more substantial businesses employing up to a dozen or more workers.

At least some of the employees in the Chinese laundries were former members of the Zulu washermen's guild – a development which left white Johannesburg largely unmoved.[111] What did distress some elements of the local middle class, though, was the fact that poor white women in the self-same laundries worked side by side with their Chinese employers and fellow black workers. But if the general social proximity distressed them then what truly horrified them were those cases in which such women workers developed intimate relationships with their employers – hardly the most surprising turn of events given the fact that the local Chinese community was almost exclusively male.[112]

It was therefore partly out of racism and partly out of the desire to dress the open sores of unemployment during an economic depression that the various schemes for public wash-houses were resuscitated in 1907. The establishment of public laundries in Vrededorp/Fordsburg and Jeppe, so it was reasoned, would simultaneously achieve two socially desirable objectives. First, it would place young white girls beyond the reach of the so-called 'Yellow Peril', and second, it would provide badly-needed employment for European women and widows in those suburbs where the greatest concentrations of the urban poor were to be found.[113] Yet again these projects – like those mooted earlier – failed to materialise and the Chinese hand-laundries continued to provide both employment and a service in white working-class areas for several years thereafter.

While the Chinese captured the most central potion of the city's laundry market, however, the more peripheral suburbs fell to the Indian washermen. After the establishment of Klipspruit, *Dhobis* and former steam laundry workers who had managed to accumulate sufficient capital, acquired horses and carts and opened small hand-laundries.[114] Using Newclare in the west and La Rochelle-Rosettenville in the south as bases, these laundrymen successfully toured the outlying white working-class areas in search of business. Between 1906 and 1914 at least 20 and perhaps as many as 50 such small Indian-owned businesses joined in the struggle to win a share of Johannesburg's laundry market.[115]

The serious competition provided by the new Indian and Chinese laundries within the city cut two ways. While it undoubtedly carved out a sizeable portion of the market previously served by the Klipspruit washermen, it also managed to slice off a hefty chunk of the steam laundries' business – and this was particularly noticeable between 1906 and 1908 when the need for cheap services was at a premium. As the economic climate started to improve in 1909, however, so there were ominous signs that the larger and better-capitalised enterprises were set for a further round of expansion which would effectively hold off the challenge from below.[116]

Rand Steam Laundries was yet again in the very forefront of these developments and by 1910 it had 13 branches spread along the Reef, operated a fleet of 33 delivery vans, and employed a work force of 200 white women and 100 black men at its central Auckland Park works.[117] Signs of expansion were also evident at the rival Lorentzville industrial complex where, between 1910 and 1911, first-generation immigrants from Holland, Germany and Scandinavia floated no less than three new companies – the International, Model and New York steam laundries.[118] By 1912 Johannesburg's steam laundries – after a battle dating back all the way to 1897 – were for the first time in full command of the Rand's laundry market and confident enough to embark on the first of many price-fixing exercises.[119]

Out at Klipspruit, all this urban capitalist and small-business expansion left its collective imprint – perhaps most starkly of all in the declining numbers of Zulu washermen noted above. Unfortunately for the washermen it was not only the rival laundries that increasingly attacked their livelihood in the years before the First World War; they were also undermined by socio-economic changes that occurred within the white working-class home itself. As early as 1902-3, for example, advertisements for rotary washing machines had appeared in the local press under the caption 'No More Wash Boys Needed!'[120] More damaging still was the combined impact that servants and housewives had on domestic labour between 1902 and 1914. Important changes in the white family structure during this period, as well as the declining cost of 'houseboy' services, meant that an increasing number of domestic chores – including the washing of clothes – could be cheaply undertaken within the working-class home, thus rendering paid outside assistance unnecessary.[121]

It was thus a group of already besieged washermen who were relegated to the economic wilderness of Klipspruit in 1906. Although nowhere near as powerful as they had been during the heyday of the guild, the remaining *AmaWasha* were acutely aware of the fact that they were slowly and certainly being stalked by economic death and in three successive years – 1906, 1907 and 1908 – they complained bitterly to the Johannesburg Town Council about the disadvantages of the new municipal laundry.[122] Virtually all of their objections were ignored. By early 1909 there was substantial discontent amongst the inhabitants of Klipspruit location and amongst those in the very forefront of the ranks of the frustrated stood the turbaned Zulu washermen.[123]

In early June 1909 the *AmaWasha* and others put pressure on the chairman of the local branch of the Transvaal Native Congress, Kyana, to arrange yet another meeting between the inhabitants of Klipspruit and the authorities. Three weeks later the washermen and other blacks duly met with municipal officials and a senior officer of the Transvaal police. On this occasion, however, the government – concerned about reports emanating from the ghetto – took the precaution of also sending along a representative to the meeting. At this gathering the washermen once more paraded their complaints about rail fares, site charges and the fact that the pervasive smell of sewerage penetrated their laundry and so lost the customers.[124] The government official at the meeting, W Pritchard of the Native Labour Bureau, took careful note of these objections in order to monitor the municipality's response. A deafening silence ensued.

When the council did eventually respond five months later, in November 1909, it did so with a provocative arrogance that was breathtaking. Through the Superintendent of the location, Lloyd, the municipality curtly informed the washermen that it intended to *raise* rather than lower the charges for transport between Klipspruit and Johannesburg. With a degree of patience that Job could only aspire to, the washermen yet again set about petitioning the authorities. This time they pointedly avoided the town council and directed their appeal to the government.[125]

The government officials assigned the task of enquiring into the long-standing grievances reported back in the clearest terms possible. The 'Complaints Officer' attached to the Native Affairs Department in Johannesburg pointed out that the Zulu washermen 'were forced to live in the location' under conditions that were not only unpleasant but positively injurious to their health.[126] The Chief Pass Officer in the city, Edward Wilson, while also concerned about considerations of public health at Klipspruit, was equally anxious to establish the deeper reasons underlying the municipal moves against the *AmaWasha*. Wilson came to the conclusion that the provocative decision to raise rail charges was premeditated, and that the action flowed from a 'white labour policy' which was 'causing the council deliberately to make conditions impossible for the Zulu washermen'.[127]

On the basis of these very critical reports the Secretary for Native Affairs, W Windham, wrote to the Town Clerk on 20 November 1909, pointing out the 'very serious nature' of the black grievances and stating that the government felt 'the urgent necessity for breaking up the location at Klipspruit and accommodating the native residents elsewhere'.[128] While the Council felt unable simply to ignore this advice, it was unwilling to undertake the radical steps proposed by Windham. In order to placate the Secretary for Native Affairs and blur the issues, however, the council arranged instead for the hapless Lloyd to be replaced as the Superintendent of the location and for yet another meeting to be held with the inhabitants of Klipspruit.

This 'absolutely informal meeting' was held in the presence of Windham at the location early in 1910. The washermen and others had yet another opportunity to put their case, while the government officials assured them that – in the future – the council would listen most carefully to their grievances. If the council did listen it certainly did not act, and shortly thereafter the Transvaal government officials concerned were absorbed into the Union's new civil service. The noose of segregation around the black laundrymen's necks was never loosened and the 1910 meeting concluded with the remnants of the Zulu washermen's guild singing their way into economic oblivion to the strains of the national anthem.[129] By 1934 there were a mere 14 Zulu men at work at the municipal washing site, and in 1953 the city council finally closed the Klipspruit laundry, content in the knowledge that the capital cost of the segregated facilities had been more than covered by the rentals paid by the washermen over nearly five decades.[130]

CONCLUSION

There can be little doubt that in the development of a modern industrial state in South African one of the clearest, most vivid and deeply traumatic processes evident is that of the proletarianisation of the African population and the creation of a largely black working class. But while this is understandably seen as one of the dominant themes in the economic development of the subcontinent, it should not leave observers insensitive to important variations on the theme, since both the route into the working class and the pace at which the march was conducted could vary significantly.

Some of these variations arose from contradictions that emerged during the period of early capitalist development on the Witwatersrand. Amongst these was the fact that, during the formative era, the mining industry was largely reliant on 'single' or at least unaccompanied European migrant male workers for the bulk of its skilled and semi-skilled labour requirements. This in turn meant that, in a socio-economic system characterised by rapid growth and enormous scale, capitalism was denied one of its central struts – the nuclear family which reproduces the next generation of workers. One of several important consequences of this situation in which men found themselves without women was that a significant market for domestic services developed on the Rand during the two or more decades between the discovery of gold and the First World War.

The possibilities offered by this relatively lucrative and dramatically expanding market for personal services were swiftly appreciated by those blacks experiencing the ravages of proletarianisation in the South African countryside. Zulu-speaking males in nearby Natal were amongst the first to exploit an economic opportunity which allowed them the chance to earn an income without entering the mining industry as unskilled labourers. Partly modelling themselves on the Hindu *Dhobis* whom they had seen operating on the east coast and partly drawing on elements of their own social structure, these men bound themselves into the Zulu washermen's guild of the Witwatersrand.

This small economic space which appeared in the cracks of a developing capitalist system offered itself only once as a means of escaping the working class – and then only very briefly since the gap closed up almost as rapidly as it had opened. Yet, within a crucial period of 16 years between 1890 and 1906, sufficient Zulu males squeezed through this escape hatch into the world of small-scale business for them and their children to avoid subsequent crushing as workers, and for them to con-stitute a distinctive stratum of the rural society to which they returned. A man like Bhamu Buthelezi, who started life as a labour tenant on a white farm in the Weenen district, subsequently became a washerman on the Rand between 1893 and 1908, accumulated sufficient capital to buy himself land in the Bergville district, and eventually helped to educate his children to the point where they had no need to resort to wage labour in order to earn a living.[131] Bhamu Buthelezi was no exception. On the very farm where he bought land, 'Hambrook', he was joined by at least three other former washermen – a Dhlamini and two Vilakazi brothers – who also managed to acquire property.[132]

Just how different these small black businessmen were from the majority of their fellow countrymen can be illustrated in two ways. First, it can be seen mirrored in the complaint that an *AmaWasha* spokesman made to the authorities during one of the meetings held at Klipspruit during 1909. At a time when most blacks were being swept *off* the land, the washermen were in the distinguished position of being able to object to being 'unable to pay off any debts on their farms or property in Natal'.[133] More striking still perhaps was the very different 'complaint' registered by a white Bergville farmer some years later. In 1918, George Coventry stated in evidence before the Native Lands Committee that:

> 'Hambrook' is 811 acres. 22 heads of families bought it. They are not satisfied with that; they are talking to and encouraging all natives around to rent from them at £2 a hut, advising them to stop working on the farms. The head of that farm, Ephraim, has boy-cotted us for labour. They boycott us unless they get a certain wage. These last two years they had kept labour from going to us. It is registered in the name of a syndicate, but since they have paid for it, it has been subdivided and each one has a certain number of acres, and has a number of rent-paying tenants on his piece. A Kraal which has been with me for nearly 30 years is being continu-ally approached to leave and go there. They admit that we have been just and good to them. One or two use fertilisers and copy us and have improved.

Mr Steward then added:

They all use fertilisers and plant in rows and scarify. 'Hambrook' is about the best piece of native cultivated land I have seen. The natives who want to buy land are those who are going to improve.[134]

Clearly, the brief and restricted business opportunity that opened up on the Rand between 1890 and 1914 was capable of producing at least one minor rural wave that ran counter to the dominant tide of proletarianisation in the countryside.

The Zulu washermen, however, were not alone in possessing an eye for the economic chance on the Witwatersrand. Indeed, the very presence and success of the washermen's guild in Johannesburg during the mid-nineties alerted others with greater financial resources to the economic possibilities of the service sector, and led – from 1896 onwards – to the establishment of a growing number of steam laundries within the town. These capitalist enterprises, situated on the very sites at which the guild was most active, at first found it difficult to compete with the cheaper service provided by the washermen. It was during the course of this struggle, however, that laundry owners discovered that, indirectly, their businesses profited from new state policies which were designed to exercise greater control over urban Africans. Immediately after the British occupation of the Transvaal the Milner administration made strenuous efforts to close down the existing washing sites within the city and to concentrate the activities of the *AmaWasha* into a single segregated site. This series of administrative measures progressively undermined the washermen's business and in 1906 eventually culminated in the expulsion of the remaining members of the guild to Klipspruit.

It was this removal to Klipspruit which, in the end, did much to hasten the demise of the *AmaWasha*. But even here capital, class and colour interacted in a way which makes South Africa characteristically complex since the very act of segregating these small black businessmen created residual economic opportunities for other urban ethnic minorities. Once the *AmaWasha* were tightly bound by the uncompetitive cost structure of a site some 13 miles out of town, their business fell not only to the large steam laundries but to smaller hand-laundries which sprung up in and around the city. Groups of frustrated Europeans watched, with considerable annoyance, as the economic space forcibly vacated by the Zulu washermen was swiftly filled by Chinese and Indian laundrymen.

While aspirant or existing European tradesmen were angered by the arrival of this set of Chinese and Asian competitors, other whites in the middle classes with less at stake were more deeply disturbed by the interracial contact that tended to develop amongst workers of all colours who undertook collective labour in the new establishments. In particu-

lar, many Europeans were shocked by the reports of intimate relationships that sometimes developed between poor white women workers
and Chinese employers in the city's small hand-laundries. Thus, while
the state effectively separated the Zulu washermen from several of their
long-time *Dhobi* colleagues through the creation of Klipspruit in 1906, it
was left to the local women's organisations to attempt to remove white
women from Chinese laundries during the depression and the years
thereafter. To the extent that these efforts enjoyed a measure of success,
Johannesburg's working class became further divided along racial and
sexual lines between 1906 and 1914.

In conclusion then, it may be noted that Zulu speakers were at least as
quick as any other immigrant group on the early Witwatersrand to spot
a new economic opportunity and exploit it. The structure which these
small black businessmen developed during the early period drew on
'Zulu', and to a lesser extent Indian society, and manifested guild-like
characteristics. While the techniques which the *AmaWasha* employed
rendered them increasingly vulnerable to capitalist competition during
the years that followed, the decline of the Zulu washermen's guild was
greatly hastened by the advent of urban segregation. In South Africa
class and colour seldom missed an economic funeral.

3

THE MAIN REEF ROAD INTO THE WORKING CLASS

Proletarianisation, unemployment and class consciousness amongst Johannesburg's Afrikaner poor, 1890-1914

No labour party can be really formidable unless it is based on profound discontent and radical grievances; and the annoyances of the Johannesburg proletariat are, as compared with those of Europe, like crumpled rose-leaves to thorns.
JOHN BUCHAN, 1903

Historians will be amongst the first to acknowledge that much work remains to be done before our understanding of the industrial revolution which transformed southern Africa in the late nineteenth and twentieth centuries is more rounded. While the development of the country's productive resources, the processes of class formation and the rise of class consciousness have been broadly sketched for the region as a whole, there are many areas in our social and labour history which remain unexplored. For those who are interested in the industrial heartland of the regional economic system – the Witwatersrand – the situation is more promising. The dramatic emergence of large-scale primary industry on the Rand, the struggle of unionised white workers and the mobilisation and control of a pool of cheap black labour have all been relatively well documented. But, even here, where the spotlight of scholarly enquiry has done much to illuminate the drama of capitalist development and class conflict, there are parts of the stage that remain in darkness.

Amongst several of the more important actors still stranded in these shadows are the Rand's urban Afrikaners.[1] In the existing literature, the proletarian origins of this group are invariably traced to the changes which capitalism wrought in the Transvaal countryside in the years around the turn of the century. Thereafter we tend to lose sight of these

sons of the soil for a decade or more – until 1907 – when they are por-
trayed as unhesitatingly entering the mining industry as 'scab' labour
during the strike of that year. The implication is thus that most Afrikaners experienced a direct change in status from that of rural *bywoner* to
that of urban worker and that in the intervening period, spent largely
offstage, members of the group became 'dependent upon the usual
means available to such marginalised strata – beggary, whatever doles or
charity were available, and perhaps the occasional odd job'. It is further
suggested by some that such Afrikaners had a strong aversion to manual labour, and by another that they constituted 'an extremely disorganised stratum with little power on their own to enforce even limited economic demands'.[2]

While this view may have something to commend it, it is so schematic that it immediately prompts a number of questions from those who are
in search of more persuasive answers to some of the problems relating to
the issues of proletarianisation, unemployment and class consciousness
during this period. Clearly, there is no group or class that simply waits
patiently in the wings to play its part until such time as it is summoned
on to the stage of economic development by a blast on the trumpet of history. How exactly did Afrikaners manage to survive in the decade or
more of darkness before 1906-8? Did *bywoners* really only manage to
exchange the grinding poverty of the Transvaal countryside for the
debilitation of urban unemployment when they undertook the move to
the Witwatersrand at the turn of the century? Were burghers who had
significant political access to the state from 1881 to 1899, from 1907 to
1910, and to a lesser extent thereafter, truly as disorganised and powerless as we have been led to believe? In Johannesburg – that cauldron of
class conflict where capital and labour were daily pitted against each
other – were the Afrikaners of Burgersdorp, Fordsburg, Newlands and
Vrededorp only capable of manifesting the fickleness of the lumpenproletariat or the opportunism of the nationalists in their struggle?

In this essay an attempt will be made to advance three sets of related
arguments which may go some way towards clarifying our understanding of some of these issues. First, it will be suggested that a significant
number of the former *bywoners* were – by making use of varying combinations of state-aid, craft skill and small capital – capable of establishing
themselves in the local community either as the providers of services or
as petty commodity producers. These largely self-employed Afrikaners
were thus able to avoid the labour market for several years, and it was
only once their enterprises had been eclipsed by larger-scale capitalist
developments that they became proletarianised. In the Transvaal therefore, capital had to conquer many Afrikaners not once, but twice, before
they succumbed to the position of wage labour – first in the countryside

and then in the towns. Secondly, it will be suggested that these unemployed burghers were far from being powerless. Indeed, such was the threat posed by them and other unemployed workers to the developing capitalist system on the Witwatersrand that it called forth a significant response from mine owners and state alike in the form of charity and public relief works. It is thus the Randlords' and their lieutenants' involvement in charitable acts and associations – at least as much as their more formalised policy towards the employment of unskilled white labour – that is in need of analysis when we seek to understand the mining industry's response to the Afrikaner unemployed of the Reef towns. Thirdly, it will be suggested that this Afrikaner corps in the reserve army of labour demonstrated its capacity for organised resistance from an early date, and that in this struggle it manifested an essentially working-class consciousness. Moreover, the nature and extent of this consciousness was at least sufficiently well developed for it to present a local challenge to the dominant ideology of nationalism and that the Afrikaner ruling class was thus forced into an early attempt to co-opt and defuse it.

THE RISE OF AFRIKANER URBAN ENTERPRISE AND SELF-EMPLOYMENT, 1886-1906

The discovery of gold and the emergence of Johannesburg must have presented itself, at least initially, as a new and open-ended economic opportunity to many in the Transvaal towns and countryside during the last quarter of the nineteenth century. Amongst the very first arrivals at the mining camps of the Witwatersrand there were therefore several Afrikaners, and of these a small number soon established themselves as claim holders and successful diggers. These aspirant mine owners, however, were soon confronted with two of the many formidable barriers which the infant industry erected – the need for capital and technical know-how. It was largely because of their inability to cope with these problems that most Afrikaner diggers soon sold their claims to established foreign capitalists who did possess the necessary finance and contacts with which to acquire both mining machinery and expert advice. Thus, although some Afrikaners were able to establish a foothold in the industry which was to dominate Kruger's Republic, and that evidence of that pioneering presence lingered for some years thereafter in the form of the names of some of the mines and companies such as the Meyer & Charlton and the Paarl-Pretoria Syndicate, there were no Afrikaner Randlords at the turn of the century.[3]

In Afrikaner eyes, this absence of representation amongst the new urban bourgeoisie of the Rand was hardly compensated for by the existence of a 'Dutch' strand in the middle class comprised largely of attorneys, teachers, civil servants, legal agents, doctors, notaries, clergymen and traders. The majority of these, however, were well-educated professionals drawn from the older and more developed south, and as such their presence hardly offered testimony of any new-found mobility amongst native-born Transvaalers. As for the traders, their small number pointed to another set of limitations which confronted many Afrikaners – vigorous competition from other immigrant groups with greater commercial experience, the importance of English as the dominant language of economic discourse and, perhaps more familiarly, a lack of capital or compensating credit arrangements with the powerful coastal merchant houses.[4]

With most of these avenues to large and smaller-scale capital accumulation long since closed to them, the majority of the Rand's poor and uneducated Afrikaners were forced to seek a niche for themselves somewhat lower down in the economic structure. In this search they received some assistance from the state in the period prior to the outbreak of the South African War. The Kruger government's insistence that only burgers be eligible for service in the police force meant that by 1899 close on 900 young Afrikaner males had secured positions as Zarps, despite the fact that a fair percentage of them were illiterate. Others managed to find employment at the most elementary level in the civil service, but even here some of the limitations noted above caught up with them. Thus, of the 60 employees in the Johannesburg Post Office in 1897, only 20 were Afrikaners since, or so it was suggested by a section of the local English press, Afrikaners usually lacked the 'technical' knowledge necessary to make a success of such positions.[5]

Beyond the limited protection afforded by the public sector, the employment prospects facing the jobless Afrikaner were even bleaker. The availability of a larger and cheaper pool of black labour, the dominance and ethnic exclusiveness of immigrant English miners who organised themselves into a trade union, and the lack of industrial skills and discipline which confronts any first generation of proletarians all combined to preclude Afrikaners from successfully seeking work in any numbers with the largest employer of labour on the Witwatersrand – the mining industry. Apart from the couple of hundred burghers taken on as an experiment by the Eckstein group during the worst of the depression years in 1897, there was no significant Afrikaner presence in the mine labour force during the pre-war years.

Yet, despite these limited opportunities, each successive year saw hundreds more Afrikaners undertaking the journey to the Witwatersrand, and this influx was particularly marked in the decade or so that elapsed between 1896-7 and 1906-8. This sustained movement to the urban areas hardly constituted the twitchings of so many Transvaal lemmings making their way to almost certain economic death. Nobody – least of all the former *bywoners* – needed to be reminded that their expulsion from the countryside had been caused largely by a plague of locusts, intermittent drought, cattle, diseases, the upheavals occasioned by the war and the extension of capitalist agriculture. But whatever the immediate cause of their plight, the Afrikaner poor knew – as the poor know everywhere – that when virtually all is lost, the chances of survival are always marginally better in the city than in the countryside. In this case, however, economic instinct was supplemented by the knowledge that a number of their kinsmen had already managed to establish a precarious foothold in certain sectors of the rapidly developing urban economy.

For at least some of these Afrikaners the very means by which they abandoned the countryside proved to be their immediate salvation in the cities. Between the late 1880s and the early 1900s, transport riding offered many rural refugees a living. Before the extension of the railway lines from the coast to the Rand in 1892-5, or the more comprehensive coverage of the Transvaal by a system of branch lines by the First World War, the services of transport riders were in constant demand in order to ensure that the vital flow of machinery to the mines and food to its workers remained uninterrupted. Like the workers, however, the mining machinery also had to be 'fed' and thus the transport of coal from the collieries beyond Boksburg and Brakpan opened up a further set of opportunities within this field. Within the towns themselves yet other Afrikaners were employed in the movement of various commodities by ox-wagon while the remainder used the smaller but sturdier 'scotch cart' to ferry stone, cinders and other materials to road works, building sites and brickyards.[6]

In several respects these former *bywoners* were obviously well placed to capture these new business opportunities as they presented themselves. Skills previously acquired with ox and wagon, the limited need for capital and an intimate knowledge of the Transvaal terrain were but some of the factors which allowed for an early Afrikaner dominance of the transport sector. Although it is impossible to be precise about the numbers involved, contemporary sources suggest that in its heyday transport riding afforded 'general' and sometimes even 'lucrative' employment for thousands of impoverished burghers.[7] What is known with greater certainty is that by the early 1890s the sector was sufficiently prosperous for it to attract considerable attention from the Kruger government. In late 1891, the State President persuaded the *Volksraad* of the need to impose a toll of 30 shillings on each wagon carrying loads of up to 6 000 lbs along the Republic's main roads.[8] This contentious measure, which in various forms remained in operation until at least 1895, proved to be a considerable source of revenue to the state. Over a four-month period during 1894, for example, over £9 000 flowed into the state coffers via the tolls.[9] Given this, it is easier to understand why Kruger and some of his closest colleagues were reluctant to abolish the tolls even though such a move would undoubtedly have earned them a measure of political popularity in the countryside.

But the State President's firmness in the case of the transport riders contrasted sharply with his treatment of a second and less prosperous group of Afrikaners engaged in the transport business – the urban cab drivers. In 1889, the *Volksraad* granted A H Nellmapius the exclusive right to operate an animal-powered tramway within Johannesburg. While this concession was obviously meant to provide the rapidly expanding town with a measure of cheap public transport, it also provided Boer agricultural producers with a ready market for draught animals and fodder, and for this reason Kruger consistently opposed later attempts to electrify the system. It was largely as a result of this latter conflict of interests that Johannesburg for many years had to tolerate an underdeveloped public transport system, and it was only in 1906 that the city eventually acquired an electric tramway. In the intervening decade and a half, the urban economy offered a living to those willing to operate horse-drawn cabs in the city.[10]

Former *bywoners* with horses, small 'Cape carts' and the necessary skills were amongst the first to seize the opportunity of becoming owner-drivers of cabs. Poorer kinsmen who could muster the skills but not the other necessary accoutrements of the trade found themselves positions as drivers for the more fortunate. Throughout the 1890s, Johannesburg's cab trade expanded steadily as the city grew and its horse-drawn tramway became increasingly unequal to the task of providing adequate public transport. By the mid-1890s the local authority was issuing over 1 500 licences to cab drivers annually, and of these several hundred were assigned to the Afrikaners of Fordsburg and Vrededorp. The members of the Sanitary Board were aware, however, that this growing dependence on private transport rendered urban commuters vulnerable to the financial demands of the cab trade and this problem reached acute proportions during the depression of 1896-7 when the Board, in an attempt to protect the interests of its constituents, sought to halve the fees which cab drivers were entitled to charge within the city limits. The cabbies responded to this threat with an appeal to the government, where Kruger – ever mindful of *his* political constituency – defended the trade against the proposed action by the Board. It was thus longer-term consequences of the tramway concession that allowed many Afrikaners to find a place of economic refuge in the cab trade before the South African War, and then, to a lesser extent, up to 1906.[11]

In addition to transport riding and cab driving, there was one other field of economic enterprise in which newly urbanised Afrikaners managed to establish themselves with some success after the discovery of gold – that of small-scale brick manufacture. From the late 1880s through to the end of the post-war reconstruction period, many former bywoners found that their knowledge of local clays and brickmaking and drying techniques could be put to profitable use in the rapidly expanding towns of the Witwatersrand. While these opportunities opened up to a greater or lesser extent all along the Reef, they were obviously once again most marked in the city with the largest and most spectacular development of all – Johannesburg.

Twenty-four months after the arrival of the first diggers on the Rand in 1886, Afrikaners were already at work making the bricks which helped to transform the mining camp into a more substantial town. In late 1887, the Republican government purchased a portion of the farm Braamfontein with the intention of using the stream which flowed through the property as a source of drinking-water for the growing number of new arrivals. The south-western bank of the *spruit*, however, also had rich deposits of clay and poor burghers soon approached the state with a request that they be allowed to manufacture bricks on the site. The Kruger government, uncertain as to the permanence of the new gold-fields, agreed to this request with the proviso that each of the applicants pay the state a monthly fee of five shillings for a 'brickmaker's licence' in lieu of rent.[12]

This site, known simply as the Brickfields at first, and then – from 1897 onwards – more formally as Burgersdorp, was soon converted into a hive of Afrikaner industrial activity as the landscape became dotted with hundreds of 'puddle machines', brick moulds, kilns, horses and carts. The poorest of the former *bywoners* usually entered the new industry on the lowest possible rung of the economic ladder – as workers employed by their better-established countrymen, earning between eight and ten shillings per 1 000 bricks manufactured. The more fortunate, with access to a limited amount of capital, usually started out by erecting or purchasing an animal-powered puddle or pug machine – the large wood and metal-encased cylinder in which the clay was mixed prior to being moulded by hand and then baked into bricks. These machines, which were usually attended by two or three black men, were capable of turning out between 2 000 and 3 000 of the superior type of 'stock' bricks per day, or up to 4 000 of the poorer quality known in the trade as 'slops'.

But since brickmaking was essentially a two-phase production process, the producers of raw bricks frequently had to enter into contracts with adjacent kiln owners in order to get their bricks baked and distributed. It would thus appear that it was this latter group – the kiln owners – who constituted a relatively privileged stratum amongst the brickmakers. In addition to operating their own puddle machines, the kiln owners also had adequate numbers of horses and 'scotch carts' which enabled them to distribute the finished product to local building contractors. Yet despite the potentially dominant economic position which the kiln owners commanded within the industry, the Brickfields community does not appear to have been characterised by marked social differentiation amongst Afrikaners. Restricted access to raw materials, keen competition and the cross-cutting ties of kinship no doubt all helped to ensure that there was, as one observer put it, 'no aristocracy' amongst the brickmakers.[13]

As might be expected, however, the overall prosperity of the Brickfields during the 1890s was largely governed by the booms and slumps which the local building industry experienced; something which in turn simply reflected the more fundamental influence which the changing fortunes of the mines exercised over the local economy. The brickmakers thus benefited from the initial flush of development which Johannesburg experienced in the years immediately after 1887, but by 1890 – along with the mining industry – were suffering a recession. When this recession started to lift in late 1891, however, it heralded the advent of a sustained building boom in the city which lasted into the early months of 1896.[14] The price of 'stock' bricks on the local market moved sympathetically and thus rose from £2 15s 0d per 1 000 in 1888 to £3 3s 0d in 1895, and then to an all-time high of £4 10s 0d in early 1896.[15] This peak of prosperity in 1895-6, however, was followed by the post-Jameson Raid depression which ensured that the price of bricks eased considerably between 1897 and the outbreak of the South African War. Some of these economic contours can also be traced in Table 6 which lists the number of new buildings erected each year within the Johannesburg Sanitary Board/Municipal area in the decade between 1894 and 1904.[16]

Table 6 New buildings erected in Johannesburg Sanitary Board/Municipal Area, 1894-1904

Year	Number of new buildings
1894	1 236
1895	2 538
1896	1 491
1897	1 058
1898	444
1899	600*
1900	–
1901	79
1902	1 072
1903	3 000
1904	7 883

*Estimate

By 1892 the Brickfields, originally envisaged simply as a temporary industrial site for impoverished burghers, had acquired a substantial measure of permanence and become the major point of entry into the local economy for the poor, unskilled and unemployed drawn from a wide variety of backgrounds including Europeans, Asians, Chinese, 'Cape Malays' and blacks. Over the next 24 months the area became increasingly congested until it became such a cause for concern to the Sanitary Board's health inspectors that they had to use force to prevent new houses being erected on the marshy ground that was already badly pitted and liberally endowed with pools of stagnant water.[17] Such was the poverty in the countryside and the boom in the city's building industry during the mid-1890s, however, that these efforts proved to be largely in vain. By 1895 not only had the density of population in the Brickfields experienced a further increase, but brickmaking activity had also spread to other sites within greater Johannesburg such as Ophirton, City & Suburban, Booysens and Turffontein.[18] The heart of the industry, though, remained at the original site spread along the Braamfontein spruit, and when the census was conducted in 1896 it revealed that the Brickfields had a population of over 7 000 people of all races and over 1 500 brickmakers who, between them, owned over 1 200 horses and mules and about 450 wagons.[19]

By the mid-1890s the position had thus been reached where brickmaking ranked as the third-largest industry in the Transvaal, being behind only mining and agriculture in terms of the number of people it employed. But despite the industry's remarkable growth and the prosperity of 1895-6 in particular, these small proprietors faced an increasing number of problems as the decade progressed. With the larger independent operators each requiring the services of between 20 and 30 black workers for their businesses, the brickmakers, along with other employers, felt the impact of rising wages as competition for African labour stiffened before 1895.[20] Other difficulties arose from faltering clay deposits and from the substantial losses which were incurred during periods of exceptionally wet weather, such as in the summer of 1893.[21] All of these labour and production problems, however, paled into insignificance when compared with the threat that proved to be one of the most menacing of all which the Afrikaner brickmakers of Braamfontein had to face – insecurity of tenure.

When the Kruger government first granted burghers the right to make bricks along the Braamfontein *spruit* in late 1887, it was the occasion for a minor influx of poor Afrikaners who immediately took the opportunity to erect small cottages on the site. Amongst these and subsequent inhabitants the idea soon took root that their right to squat on the property was secure, provided only that they continued to pay the monthly licence fee to the government. This somewhat comforting train of thought was rudely interrupted in 1889 when local civil servants chose to remind the brickmakers that the land was liable to expropriation without compensation a short notice. The brickmakers, who did not take readily to this idea, appealed to Pretoria with some success. In November 1889 the State President and members of his Executive Committee agreed that a parcel of 200 stands should be surveyed in the Brickfields, and that the poorest burghers should be entitled to the undisturbed occupation of these sites for a period of two years on payment of a monthly licence fee of five shillings.[22]

In June 1892, however, the Executive Committee decided that a portion of the Brickfields should be expropriated and that the land should be put at the disposal of the Netherlands Railway Company for use as a marshalling yard. This move further alarmed the brickmakers who now constituted themselves into the Braamfontein Brickmakers' Association which immediately petitioned the government for the grant of a 99-year lease on the site. Despite this plea the government proceeded with its plans and duly handed over the expropriated land to the railway company in May 1893. This action, however, proved to be most unpopular with the local burghers, and the government soon felt the need to placate some of its more irate constituents. In December 1893 the Executive Committee thus sanctioned the surveying of a further parcel of 160 stands in the Brickfields – sites which were then made available to some of the poorest Afrikaners at a fee of half-a-crown per month.[23]

Having secured this minor concession from the state the brickmakers remained undisturbed at their business for the next 30 months as they took advantage of Johannesburg's mid-nineties' building boom. Then, just as the price of stock bricks reached its peak, the shadow of uncertainty again fell over the Brickfields. In May 1896, it was reported that the Sanitary Board and the Netherlands Railway Company had joined forces in an appeal to the government to put a stop to all brickmaking in Braamfontein – the local authority because it had long complained about overcrowding and its attendant evils in that quarter of the town and the NZASM because of its desire to proceed with its plans for a marshalling yard. This plea apparently elicited a sympathetic hearing in Pretoria since, a few weeks later, the railway company erected a fence across its portion of the expropriated property in the Brickfields – a move which effectively denied the brickmakers access to one of the few remaining local sources of clay.[24]

The brickmakers' response to this development was swift, if not entirely successful. Within hours of the fence being erected they persuaded some of the town's building contractors to finance a trip to Pretoria and within days a delegation was briefed to put their case to the State President. When the burghers met Kruger on 16 June 1896 they impressed upon him the hardship and unemployment that would follow if the site along the Braamfontein spruit were closed down. The State President, however, was reluctant to allow the brickmakers' activities to jeopardise the badly needed expansion of railway facilities in Johannesburg. Kruger therefore informed the burghers that the Brickfields site would soon be closed down, but he also gave them his assurance that his government was aware of its responsibilities and that it would find them an alternative site for their industry.[25]

When this news was formally relayed to a small meeting in the Brickfields a week later, it met with a chilly reception. The brickmakers felt that it would be economically disastrous for them to vacate their central Braamfontein site for a more distant location which would escalate their transport costs and render them less competitive. They were also of the opinion that as burghers their needs should receive priority over those of a 'foreign' company, and that at very least they should be given ample opportunity to wind down their businesses in the Brickfields.[26]

The government took note of this sullen tone, but did not allow it to deflect it from its purpose. The majority of the brickmakers were given until the end of July to vacate the site, and at the end of this period several of the departing Afrikaners established themselves on the residential stands that were made available to poor burghers in the newly proclaimed township of Vrededorp. One small group of brickmakers, however, was allowed to stay on at the Braamfontein *spruit*, and in the end it was only some two years later – in December 1898 – that all such industrial activity in the Brickfields finally ceased.[27]

This did not mean that Kruger had forgotten his pledge to the unhappy brickmakers. Indeed, at the very moment that the burghers were being forced to close down their industry in Braamfontein, the government was busy acquiring an alternative site some way from the city centre for them. The brickmakers, who had previously voiced their disapproval of any attempt to move them to a more distant location, were by now sufficiently desperate to clutch at any opportunity which presented itself. Thus, in order to secure this gain and avoid any charge of ingratitude that might emanate from Pretoria, over 200 burghers signed a petition agreeing to the move to the new site provided that it was speedily expedited. By late 1896 many of the Afrikaner brickmakers were again at work, but this time on the Alberts brothers' farm, 'Waterval', some six miles to the north-west of Johannesburg.[28]

Within a matter of weeks of their occupying the new site the brickmakers had the worst of their original suspicions confirmed – namely, that the relocation at Waterval had badly blunted the competitive edge which they had previously enjoyed at Braamfontein by pushing up transport costs. Never slow to react politically, the burghers saw in this the occasion for yet another appeal to Kruger and his colleagues. This time the brickmakers set out to persuade the government that their economic survival depended on the establishment of a rail link between Waterval and the city centre. After several months of intensive lobbying these agitational efforts eventually bore fruit, and in December 1898 the Executive Committee agreed that tenders be called for the construction of a branch line that would link Waterval to Johannesburg via Fordsburg, the Brickfields and Vrededorp.[29] But, before the scheme could be implemented war broke out and the burghers were thus denied their economic life-line to the city.

After the war the brickmakers quickly regrouped to resume their business. As early as December 1902 it was reported that there were between 30 and 40 'factories' operating in the Waterval area and that the industry employed 500 white men and many more black workers. Predictably enough, the Afrikaners now proceeded to play a far less prominent part in the lobbying activities of the industry and when the Waterfall Brickmakers' Association was formed in the same month, its executive was dominated by English speakers. The new association immediately took up the old issue of railway facilities for the brickmakers, the unfair trade practice which allowed several companies on mining property to continue manufacturing bricks within the inner-city area, and the need for a more stringent pass system to help control the industry's black labour force.[30]

In general, however, the years after the South African War saw a decline in the activities of Johannesburg's independent brickmakers. At Waterval, some of the small producers got a stay of economic execution as the city's suburbs extended northwards in the period before the First World War, thereby reducing transport costs and partly restoring some of the competitive edge which these brickmakers had once enjoyed in the trade. It was also largely as a result of this expansion that a dozen or more Afrikaner brickmakers and their families – amongst them such local notables as the Grundlinghs, the Andersons and the Steenkamps – were able to survive into the twenties, and in a few exceptional cases well beyond that. W H Brummer, the Newlands blacksmith who supplied most of these remaining brickyards with hand-crafted equipment, continued to receive occasional orders for puddle machines right into the 1950s.[31]

CAPITALIST DEVELOPMENT AND THE GENESIS OF AFRIKANER URBAN UNEMPLOYMENT, 1890-1908

The dramatic eruption of capitalist gold mining on the Witwatersrand in the late 1880s immediately confronted the government of the small South African Republic with a new and challenging set of demands. Foremost amongst these was the urgent need to provide the land-locked country with adequate links to the coastal cities if the mines were to be allowed to import the supplies of food, fuel and machinery that were vital to the development of the infant industry. Kruger and his colleagues were not slow to respond to these demands and the decade before the South African War saw a remarkable expansion in railway facilities on and to the goldfields. In March 1890 the so-called 'Rand Tram' which ran from Boksburg along the line of reef was opened and this made for the cheap and efficient distribution of coal supplies to the mining industry. Thirty-six months later, in January 1893, Johannesburg was linked to Cape Town by rail, and within a further 36 months there were also lines extending to Delagoa Bay (January 1895) and Durban (October 1895). Thereafter followed a more sedate period of consolidation and by the outbreak of the First World War the greater part of the Transvaal was serviced by a system of branch lines.

This opening of the economic arteries to the new industrial heartland of southern Africa, however, effectively drained the life blood from long-distance transport riding. Then, as if the advent of the railways were somehow not enough to bear, Kruger's toll system and the natural disaster of rinderpest came to add their distinctive burdens to those in the trade. These blows, delivered as they were by the hand of God and the hand of man, combined to make the years between 1890 and 1896 particularly disastrous ones for the Rand's transport riders. But the transport riders, as befitted brave and God-fearing men, did not take all this

punishment lightly and on occasion they chose to strike back powerfully at the hand of man.

In 1892 it was reported from Vereeniging that large boulders had been
placed across the new railway line from the Cape, and that this was considered to be the work of several angry transport riders who had been
forced to vacate the areas a result of the arrival of the iron horse. It was
the Transvaal tolls, however, that did most to anger burgher agricultural
producers and transport riders, and members of both of these groups
spent a considerable amount of time and effort in avoiding or circum-
venting the toll-houses by taking cross-country routes to their markets.
Where these tactics were not possible, the men sometimes took more
direct action. At Daspoort, near Pretoria, a group of masked Boers seized
the toll-keeper in early April 1894 and, after binding and gagging him,
handcuffed him to a nearby tree before dynamiting the toll-gate. Almost
exactly a year later, the finger of suspicion was again pointed at the
transport drivers when the toll office near the Ferreira Battery on the
Kimberley Road exit from Johannesburg was burnt down under mysterious circumstances.[32]

But in the end, of course, neither the dynamite of Daspoort nor the fire
of Ferreira's could overcome these developments and thousands of
transport riders were forced to seek further refuge in the urban economy.
In Johannesburg, many sought shelter from the icy economic blast by
turning to intra-city transport in the form of 'trolley driving', whilst
some of those who were fully proletarianised got work as drivers on the
horse-drawn tramway.[33] Even in these nooks and crannies, however, they
were soon made to realise that the winds sweeping the country heralded not simply a passing storm of economic competition, but the advent
of a full-scale capitalist winter. The introduction of the traction engine,
the eclipse of the horse-drawn tramway and competition from cheaper
Coloured labour all helped to swamp these struggling survivors and
deposit them in the pools of permanent poverty to be found in
Burgersdorp, Vrededorp and Newlands. Until well into the first decade
of the twentieth century, transport riders continued to form one of the
most conspicuous categories amongst the Witwatersrand's Afrikaner
unemployed.[34]

Those poor burghers who managed to establish themselves in
Johannesburg's cab trade before the South African War fared marginally
better than their transport-riding cousins – largely because, as we have
noted above, the ruling Afrikaner bourgeoisie sought to protect the City
& Suburban Tramway Company as a market for its agricultural producers. But, while this made for a relatively inefficient public transport system, and by so doing gave cab drivers a certain amount of room for economic manoeuvre, it did not indemnify the small-scale operators against

all the vicissitudes of capitalism. Thus in 1896 the tramway company, while riding on the crest of the mid-nineties boom, decided to extend the length of its track by 25 per cent. This development, when coupled with the dramatic surge in the prices of draught animals and fodder which came in the wake of the rinderpest epidemic, made 1896 and 1897 economically shattering years for the cabbies. The number of registered cab drivers in the city fell from 1 200 in 1896 to 700 in 1897 as 500 men were thrown out of work in a period of 12 months. This blow fell particularly heavily upon the poorest section of the Afrikaner community where many of the men had long relied on shift work in the cab trade to provide them with a measure of casual employment. Moreover, it came at a moment when broader capitalist transformation was also sealing off other traditional lines of retreat for the burgher poor – transport riding had already passed its zenith and the Brickfields were in the throes of being closed for the move out of town.[35]

It is true that in the immediate post-war period the cab drivers gained some breathing space as Milner's reconstruction government examined the concession which Kruger and his colleagues had granted to the City & Suburban Company. Poor Afrikaners, however, found it increasingly difficult to maintain their foothold in the trade as they were confronted with the competition provided by an influx of Lithuanian immigrants on the one hand and the spiralling cost of acquiring and servicing cabs on the other. But Afrikaner and immigrant cabbies alike suffered when the reconstruction authorities opened the new electric tramway system in 1906, and then again in 1909, when the City Council first allowed motorised taxis to cruise the streets of Johannesburg. Over this 36-month period a further 600 cab drivers were thrown out of work, and once again the tide of unemployment unceremoniously dumped most of these men in the suburbs of Fordsburg, Vrededorp, and Newlands.[36]

The city's Afrikaner brickmaking community, as we have already seen, was thrust aside to make way for the needs of an expanding economy when, in 1896, the small producers were forced to abandon their Brickfields site in order to accommodate the marshalling yards of the Netherlands Railway Company. Although it was undoubtedly the subsequent move to Waterval that did most of the short-term damage to these Afrikaner businesses, the eclipse of the 'puddle machine' operators was ultimately assured by what was perhaps a more predictable development – the rise of capitalist brickmaking companies making extensive use of Victorian technology.

In April 1890, a mere 24 months after the first burgher brickmakers had established themselves along the banks of the Braamfontein *spruit*, Johannesburg's first modern brickmaking factory went into production. The Braamfontein Brick & Potteries Company, employing two specially recruited artisans from Koblenz in Germany, four local whites and 44 Africans proved to be most successful, and it was soon joined by similar concerns as other capitalists sought to benefit from the rapid expansion of the building industry during the early nineties. By 1893 there were at least three other large companies seeking to supply the mining town's seemingly insatiable appetite for bricks – the Rand Brick & Tile Company, Robert Kuranda's Doornfontein Brick Company and, somewhat further afield, Lewis & Marks's Vereeniging Brick & Tile Company.[37]

The even more spectacular building boom of the mid-nineties saw large amounts of additional capital being invested in the brickmaking industry. Predictably, the ubiquitous Sammy Marks was amongst the first to detect the signs of a heightening demand for bricks and in 1894 the Vereeniging Brick & Tile Company responded to the challenge by importing larger plant and equipment from the English firm that supplied most of southern Africa's needs for brickmaking machinery – Fawcetts of Leeds. Over the following two years in particular, but right up to the outbreak of war, new firms continued to enter the industry; most notably the Patent Artificial Stone Syndicate (1895), the Johannesburg Brick & Potteries Company (1896), the Ophirton Brick & Tile Works Ltd (1897), and the South African Contracting Association (1899).[38]

In the immediate post-war period these earlier companies were joined by a few more entrants to the industry such as the Eclipse Brick Works (1902), the City & Suburban Brick Company (1903), and Donovan's Brick Works at Newlands (1903). This pattern of measured growth was broken, however, when Johannesburg's building industry once again went through an explosive spurt between 1903 and 1905. From an average of ten large concerns supplying the city's need for bricks in 1902-3, the number rose to over 20 during the boom of 1903-5 as several middle-sized producers entered the market, and then slumped back to about ten during the depression of 1906-8. Thereafter, from 1909 to 1914, the figure tended to remain more or less constant as the ten larger firms reasserted their dominance over the local market for bricks.[39]

This stark cataloguing of the rise in the number of brickmaking companies, however, does not in itself reveal the nature and extent of the damage which these new capitalist enterprises inflicted on their smaller Afrikaner competitors. Firms such as the Patent Artificial Stone Syndicate, the Ophirton Brick & Tile Company and others established their works on mining property. This not only provided them with large customers on their doorsteps, it also accorded them all the benefits that came with protected central sites at precisely the moment that the burgher brickmakers were being forced to move out of town. While this legal manoeuvre was undoubtedly within the letter of the law which did not encompass mining property, it certainly infringed the spirit of a municipal regulation which forbade all brickmaking within a three-mile radius of the city centre.[40]

But the real damage derived not so much from the advantage which capitalist firms enjoyed in terms of transport costs as from the competitive edge which mechanised production techniques afforded them. The brickmaking machinery with which Fawcetts supplied their clients was capable of both increasing production and reducing the need for manual labour. The plant installed on the Lewis & Marks property in 1896, for example, had the capacity to produce 20 000 bricks a day 'with the minimum of hand manipulation'. Likewise, when the South African Contracting Association opened its new works for public inspection in 1899, it was noted that the 'manual labour required is reduced to a minimum', and that in terms of 'labour saving appliances' the plant was 'a model of ingenuity'.[41]

The full extent and effectiveness of this capitalist onslaught against the small producers is perhaps best reflected in the changing fortunes of the Johannesburg Brick & Potteries Company. Floated with a capital of over £125 000 in the year that the Afrikaner brickmakers were expelled from the city centre – 1896 – this venture was designed to become the local giant of the brickmaking industry. Amongst many other capitalists, this project attracted the interest of Adolf Epler and Samuel Evans, and in subsequent years both of these mining-house notables served as directors of the company.

Although Johannesburg Brick & Potteries along with other companies struggled financially during the recession years of 1897 and 1898, its highly mechanised plant soon enabled it to produce bricks more cheaply than its rivals – a development which drew accusations of unfair trade practice. Whatever the truth of these allegations, the fact remained that from 1897 onwards the company was able to submit the lowest tenders in town, and by so doing won the lion's share of the larger contracts – including, for example, that to supply the Public Works Department of the *Zuid Afrikaansche Republiek*. Thus at the very moment that Kruger's government was attempting to rescue the burgher brickmakers from economic oblivion by providing them with an alternative site at Waterval, it was also forced to award its business to the Afrikaners' capitalist rivals in the city centre.[42]

Immediately after the war the directors reconstructed the company and the additional capital resources generated by this move were used to acquire new clay deposits at Heronmere as well as modernised plant and equipment. By late 1902 Johannesburg Brick & Potteries had the capacity to produce over 60 000 bricks per day at rates even cheaper than those ruling before the war. Samuel Evans – a full partner in H Ecksten & Co – used this competitive edge as well as his wide range of powerful contacts to help the company win large contracts from, amongst others, the Royal Engineers, the Johannesburg municipality and the Milner government. In 1903 the company made a profit of £6 000. In the following year, however, the post-war housing boom helped the company to an even more spectacular performance as it recorded a profit of over £10 000 and declared a dividend at 25 per cent – and that despite the fact that it had cut the cost of its bricks by half during the preceding 12 months. This relentless expansion made Johannesburg Brick & Potteries the undisputed leader of the local brickmaking industry between 1897 and 1914.[43]

The shadow of this and other capitalist successes fell over areas which, as we have seen, were already struggling in the gathering gloom of unemployment. Most of the small brickmakers who had somehow managed to survive the move from Burgersdorp could not withstand this fierce blast of post-war competition. Some battled on in the economic twilight, hoping that the trams would be allowed to convey bricks when the new public transport system was extended to the north-western suburbs in 1906 – the last echo of Kruger's scheme to provide Waterval with a rail link to Johannesburg.[44] Others sought work in the brickyards of the large companies, only to find that imported machinery destroyed jobs almost as swiftly as the building boom created them.[45] The majority, however, joined the ranks of the workless, and when the full darkness of unemployment eventually settled over Fordsburg, Vrededorp and Newlands in 1906-8, there were brickmakers as well as transport riders, cab drivers and former Republican civil servants in the queues at the soup kitchens.[46]

AFRIKANER CLASS CONSCIOUSNESS AND THE RESPONSES OF MINING CAPITAL AND THE STATE, 1895-1914

Throughout the late 1880s and the early 1890s there was always a measure of white unemployment on the Rand in general and in Johannesburg in particular. As was to be expected in a new town based on a single industry, the large majority of the unemployed were miners who were thrown out of work by the periodic slumps in the mining industry as investor confidence rose and fell spectacularly in the period prior to the relatively sustained development of the deep levels. In 1889, for example, it was reported that white miners were experiencing great difficulty in finding jobs, and in the serious recession of 1892-3, E P Rathbone – hardly an uncritical observer of the working classes – wrote of how: 'It is heart-breaking to see the number of literally half-starved, competent, sober, intelligent miners that we cannot possibly find work for.' Even in 1894, when the economy had once again experienced an upturn, J T Bain of the Witwatersrand Mine Employees' and Mechanics' Union estimated that there were over 2 000 men out of work in Johannesburg alone.[47]

Two related features characterised these early periods of unemployment on the Rand, First, it was noteworthy how, in the years before the Jameson Raid, these immigrant miners had little to turn to by way of large-scale organised assistance or relief. While Rathbone's Rand Labour Bureau which was opened in 1892 undertook to place miners and others in employment in return for five per cent of their first month's wages, such an organisation was – by its very nature – incapable of making serious inroads into what was, after all, a structural problem and not simply a lack of market intelligence on the part of work-seekers. In 1893 J T Bain and his colleagues in the labour movement sought a potentially more radical solution when they unsuccessfully appealed to the Kruger government to give consideration to the possibility of opening state mines in an attempt to cope with the problem of white unemployment.[48]

Given these failures, most of the English miners were forced into seeking more personal solutions to their plight, and for the more fortunate some relief came from casual employment gained as barmen, waiters, billiard makers or bookmakers' assistants in the town. Many of the older and less fortunate, however, were reduced to vagrancy, while some of the younger and more daring turned either to petty crime or highway robbery in order to make a living – the latter group in particular constituting the subject of an exciting chapter in the history of the early Transvaal.[49]

Secondly, it is also noteworthy how relatively few Afrikaners there were amongst the Rand's chronically unemployed in the years before 1895. In part this can be accounted for by pointing to the smaller number of Afrikaners who made their way to the Rand permanently between 1888 and 1894, and the proportionately limited percentage of the overall population of Johannesburg which Afrikaners formed during this period.[50] Probably more important, however, is the fact that these years also coincided with the period during which transport riding, cab driving and brickmaking made their greatest strides within the city. This does not mean that there was an absence of poverty or unemployment within the Afrikaner community – the distress of some of the Brickfields poor on the one hand, and the occasional presence of young highwaymen with names like Van Greuning and De Koker on the other, testify to that – but rather that these sectors of the local economy were capable of absorbing and retaining much of Johannesburg's unskilled Afrikaner labour between 1886 and 1895.[51]

For an extremely complex set of social, political and economic reasons, however, both sets of features noted above rapidly gave way between 1895 and 1897. The development of the deep-level mines, the 'Kaffir Boom' of 1894-5, and the new rail links to the Reef all helped to draw thousands more British and other miners to the Witwatersrand. While some of this new influx of labour was absorbed during the 'Kaffir Boom', much of it simply served to swell the ranks of the reserve army of labour, and more especially so during the recession of 1896-7.[52] During the same period some of the Randlords, operating at first through the Transvaal National Union and later the South African League, sought to extend their programme of agitation against the Kruger state by developing a popular base. As part of this latter campaign to woo the Rand's English workers – a significant number of whom tended to show pro-Kruger sympathies as part of their struggle against capital – these mine owners lent their support to schemes for the more organised relief of the local unemployed. Amongst the more important of these schemes were the Present Help League, established in 1895 with the generous help of Lionel Phillips, and its extension service – the Revd Kelly's Relief Stores – which received substantial support from the same Randlords' overtly political organisation, the Reform Committee. Thus from the mid-nineties onwards the struggle for the support and control of Johannesburg's unemployed was becoming increasingly politicised and the Kruger government showed its prompt appreciation of this fact by temporarily suspending the operation of Kelly's Relief Stores in the days immediately following the Jameson Raid.[53]

At the same time that these intertwining processes were unfolding into their more recognisable forms of organised charity and relief work, an equally complex set of developments was also taking place elsewhere in Johannesburg and in the Witwatersrand's hinterland. The mid-nineties were particularly disastrous years for many Boer agriculturalists and their *bywoners* as locusts, drought and particularly rinderpest dealt them successive blows. This acute rural distress occasioned a new and dramatic increase in the flow of poverty-stricken Afrikaners to the Rand between 1895 and 1897. But, as we have seen elsewhere, this was precisely the period during which the local economy and particularly the sectors we have focused on – transport riding, cab driving and brick-making – was experiencing a recession and thus least capable of absorbing an influx of unskilled labour. Thus these three years saw an unprecedented increase in the number of unemployed Afrikaners in Johannesburg.

By the mid-1890s, therefore, an acute and somewhat contradictory phase had been reached in the development of the city's white unemployment crisis. While such organised charity and relief work as did exist was largely directed towards the 'single', skilled, unemployed

English immigrant miner, the greatest poverty and hardship existed amongst the families of unskilled, unemployed Afrikaner workers. This paradox, or at least the full extent of it, was at first not fully appreciated by either the mine owners or the state although the *Volksraad* did, in May 1897, set up a commission to investigate the need to provide assistance to the burgher poor. This commission made such desultory progress, however, that it was left to a small number of local Afrikaner activists – notably I D de Vries and P C Duvenhage – to grapple with the problem of destitution in the city's western working-class suburbs.

On the morning of 23 July 1897 a group of 25 unemployed Afrikaners from these suburbs decided to draw a leaf from the pages of English working-class struggle when they set out to march to Pretoria in order to lobby their representative in the *Volksraad*, A A Dieperink, about the problems of local unemployment. But Dieperink, who was much put out by the arrival of the marchers in the capital city, persuaded the men to accompany him on a train journey back to Johannesburg where they would discuss the matter. On the same evening, however, the marchers forced the *Volksraad* members to address a meeting of over 1 000 needy burghers held in Vrededorp. At this meeting Dieperink agreed to personally examine the extent of poverty in the suburb during the course of the following morning, and to urge upon the state the need for an immediate public works programme – in particular, a scheme to develop more fully the Main Reef Road.[54]

It was also in the immediate wake of this meeting that the Johannesburg Relief Committee was called into being by De Vries, Duvenhage and about a dozen other Afrikaner notables including, amongst others, the lawyers Barent Malraison, S H van Diggelen and J C Smuts. During the following week the members of this committee debated the virtues of various schemes which could possibly help alleviate burgher unemployment and on 6 August 1897 a deputation of three was sent to Pretoria to seek the State President's support for the proposed steam laundry for white women workers in Vrededorp, and the Main Reef Road works.[55] Kruger gave De Vries and his colleagues a sympathetic hearing, but urged upon the deputation the need to widen its base and increase its authority by co-opting certain local government officials onto the committee. This the members of the committee readily agreed to, and on 9 August they decided to move further in the same direction by inviting all the editors of the Johannesburg newspapers to serve on the committee.[56]

Then, just at the moment that the Relief Committee had carefully completed laying the foundations of its structure, its efforts were struck by an ideological bombshell which came from the most unexpected quarter. On Saturday morning, 14 August 1897, the most radical and sympathetic of the local pro-government newspapers, the *Standard and Diggers' News*, ran an openly hostile and provocative editorial:

> If we were convinced that local destitution was as terrible as some folks would fain make it out to be, we should be the last to seek to belittle it. But as far as we have yet been able to judge, it appears to us that far too much is being made of a few sporadic cases of genuine penury and want. 'The poor ye have always with you.' In every community – and especially in a town with Johannesburg's characteristics – there is always to be found a considerable residuum of poverty-stricken people – those who, through various causes, fall out of the fighting ranks and join the stragglers at the rear.[57]

Getting into its full Victorian stride, the editorial then proceeded to draw the familiar distinction between the 'deserving' and 'undeserving' poor, and to argue that the degree of local unemployment was simply the 'normal' and to be expected in any modernising and mechanising economy.[58] 'It is simply hysterical folly,' the leader writer concluded, 'to declaim under an illusory supposition that abnormal destitution exists.'

These claims incensed De Vries, Duvenhage and some of the other more militant members of the Johannesburg Relief Committee, and within hours of the newspaper appearing on the streets these men had arranged for a meeting of the burgher unemployed in the Market Square. By mid-morning, between 500 and 600 Afrikaners drawn from Burgersdorp, Fordsburg and Vrededorp were in attendance when De Vries and Duvenhage led a relatively orderly procession down Loveday Street towards the city offices of the Relief Committee amidst shouts of 'Berlin! Berlin!' Once the crowd reached this destination it paused and 'demonstrated' outside the offices for several minutes.[59]

From there, however, the men turned towards the Harrison Street works of the *Standard and Diggers' News*, and it was at this stage that the procession was joined by more of the local unemployed, curious bystanders, and by others whom the newspaper later chose to describe as some of the European 'flotsam and jetsam' of the city. By the time the leaders of the procession were met by the acting editor of the newspaper, Joseph van Gelder, the crowd had swollen to between 2 000 and 3 000 people, and its conduct was becoming less orderly. De Vries and Duvenhage then 'invited' the editor to address the marchers on his views about unemployment.[60]

Van Gelder spoke to the crowd and offered to insert the names, addresses and 'handicrafts' of all the unemployed in the columns of his newspaper – not a particularly helpful suggestion to indigent burghers who wanted his editorial support for a state public works programme.

He then proceeded to tell the gathering of more than 2 000 that Mr Blane, a mining engineer, 'was ready to engage ten good men at once at five shillings a day, sleeping accommodation included'. But since the majority of the unemployed were unskilled Afrikaner males with their own homes, it was perhaps understandable that 'the offer met with considerable disfavour'. By this time there were already sporadic shouts of '*maak hom dood*' – 'kill him', and some scuffling within the ranks of an increasingly impatient procession. Hearing this, Van Gelder again addressed himself to De Vries and Duvenhage, who promptly extracted from him the same pledge that they had earlier forced from Dieperink under slightly different circumstances – the promise that he would undertake a personal tour of inspection of the western suburbs in order to assess the nature and extent of Afrikaner poverty. When this 'agreement' was announced to the assembled ranks of the unemployed, however, it did little to appease them. Some members of the procession grabbed Van Gelder and dragged him across the road, and when a fight flared up in a nearby section of the crowd the police swiftly intervened to form a bodyguard for the editor whom they eventually hustled into the safety of the back yard of the Palace Hotel. With the immediate object of their displeasure removed from their focus, the temper of the marchers abated somewhat, but even so it was several hours before the crowd finally dispersed.[61]

Both the composition of this crowd and the militancy of its leadership took the editorial staff of the *Standard and Diggers' News* by complete surprise. 'We had expected the English-speaking variety,' van Gelder admitted in the columns of the following Monday morning's edition. The acting-editor also acknowledged that after his trip to Fordsburg and Vrededorp he was convinced that there were cases of 'real distress', and that a significant part of this could be attributed to the collapse of employment opportunities in the Brickfields. Still smarting from the trouncing which he had experienced at the hands of De Vries and Duvenhage, however, he also went on to note that 'professional agitation will never alleviate suffering' and was further of the opinion that 'nothing of a practical nature was attained' by the 'demonstration'.[62]

Van Gelder was wrong. For several months before this 'demonstration' sensitive observers of the local scene had been noting with increasing concern the rapid growth of white unemployment in the city and the potential which this held for radical action. By the end of the first quarter of 1897, the 'plague of vagrancy' and 'rampant street begging' of late 1896 was giving way to a more aggressive posture on the part of the unemployed. On 2 April 1897, for example, *The Comet* pointed out how the level of local unemployment was becoming dangerously high and that, 'unless remedial steps of some kind are very quickly taken the police will be face to face with an uncommonly nasty problem'. Within two weeks of this observation having been made the point was underscored when a fire broke out in a Market Street shop and a large crowd of whites promptly smashed the windows of an adjacent outfitter and looted the premises. The march of the unemployed to Pretoria and the fracas outside the *Standard and Diggers'* offices in which a pro-Kruger and alleged supporter of the working classes escaped with his life thus contributed to a developing pattern of mass action. As such it left the Transvaal ruling classes with a clear message, and this in turn meant – contrary to Van Gelder's opinion – that a good deal of 'a practical nature was attained' in the wake of the 'demonstration'.[63]

Within four days of the 'demonstration', J P FitzPatrick – acting on behalf of H Eckstein & Co – had agreed to employ 200 unskilled Afrikaners on surface work at the Crown Deep mine. In addition, Eckstein's also approached the Kruger government with the offer to take on a number of younger Afrikaner males between the ages of 16 and 20 in order that they might be given the necessary training which would enable them to cope with underground work. Eckstein & Co were soon joined by the Robinson and Consolidated Gold Fields groups, and by early September 1897 Johan Spaan of the Johannesburg Relief Committee could proudly point to the fact that over 500 unskilled burghers had been found positions on the mines.[64] Although Afrikaners did not look upon this opportunity as providing them with long-term employment – indeed the majority of those engaged on underground work soon left the mines – their militancy had at least forced the Randlords to acknowledge and respond to the claims of this new generation of Transvaal proletarians to employment within the premier industry of the Boer state.

The Kruger government, too, moved 'with commendable promptitude in regard to the question of relief to the indigent' and within days of the 'demonstration' the state gave its approval, in principle, to the proposed steam laundry for workless women in Vrededorp, a scheme for an 'industrial school' which would train some of Johannesburg's Afrikaner youth, and the Main Reef Road project which would provide work for the Rand's unemployed burghers.[65] Of these various schemes, however, it was only really the last one which provided substantial relief to the poor of the city's western suburbs in the period before the war. Between early 1898 and late 1899 the Kruger governmental allocated over £30 000 for the Main Reef Road works and this in turn provided short-term employment for hundreds of Afrikaners.[66]

But if the events leading up to the affray outside the *Standard and Diggers' News* in August 1897 had instantly commanded the attention of Randlords and the Kruger government, then it also managed to concentrate the minds of the local shopkeepers wonderfully. In the wake of the march by the unemployed through the city's streets and past their shops, W Hosken of the Chamber of Commerce, Sam Foote of the Witwatersrand Licensed Victuallers' Association and J W Quinn – the city's foremost baker and a member of the local Sanitary Board – all became closely involved in the activities of yet another newly formed charitable association, the Rand Relief Committee, and supported its efforts in the western suburbs with donations in cash or in kind. It was also these men who persuaded Eckstein & Co, Consolidated Gold Fields, Robinson, A Goerz & Co, Farrar, S Neumann & Co and Lewis & Marks to extend their existing support to the relief programme by making further substantial cash donations to the Rand Relief Committee. Thus, by taking their struggle onto the streets of Johannesburg, the Afrikaner and other unemployed in the town managed to extract significant concessions from the state, the mine owners and the local petty bourgeoisie between 1897 and 1898.[67]

When confidence in the Rand was partially restored during the last quarter of 1898 and the early months of 1899, the local economy revived somewhat and employment prospects for skilled workers in the mining industry brightened considerably. This and the state's continuing public works programme for unskilled burgher labourers did much to help alleviate the crisis of white unemployment and by mid-1898 class tension within the city had eased significantly. The mine owners and shopkeepers, who earlier had willingly shared the burden of providing relief to the Afrikaner and other poor, now made repeated efforts to pass the full responsibility for providing aid to the local indigent to the Kruger government. When these efforts failed, the affairs of the Rand Relief Committee were wound up in September 1898. Thereafter, much of the charity and relief work in the western suburbs fell to the churches and other voluntary associations. By early 1899 the editorial nerve at the *Standard and Diggers' News* had been sufficiently restored for the newspaper to run a cautiously worded leader on another well-worn Victorian theme – the problem of 'Indiscriminate Alms Giving'.[68]

This situation, however, changed again when war was declared in October 1899 as most of the immigrant miners left for the coastal cities and the Afrikaner men left to join their commandos for the coming struggle in the countryside. This exodus significantly altered the class composition of the city, or in the more genteel words of L S Amery, it meant that for the war years 'a large percentage of the normal inhabitants of Johannesburg were either very poor or very rascally'.[69]

Amongst the 'very poor' whom Amery had noted there were many of the wives and children of burghers who were congregated in the

Brickfields, Vrededorp and, to a lesser extent, Fordsburg. It was these families who, in the period immediately prior to the war, had been amongst the principal beneficiaries of the state's Main Reef Road scheme and they were thus amongst the first to suffer when all organised relief operations were suspended. Within a month of the outbreak of hostilities the plight of these families was such that Afrikaner women in the Brickfields were forced into the sporadic looting of unoccupied homes and business premises in the city. In order to contain this assault on private property, the Republican officials who had been left in charge of the city were forced into setting up a new fund for the relief of the local poor. Thus in the months leading up to the British occupation of Johannesburg, the city's remaining merchants and shopkeepers were again called upon to channel donations in cash or in kind down increasingly familiar avenues. This they did – some no doubt simply out of compassion, others out of the desire to help defuse the possibility of further militant independent action by Afrikaner women.[70]

When this source of relief was cut off through the arrival of Lord Roberts and his troops in June 1900 the response of the Afrikaner destitute and the 'rascally' was once again swift and unambiguous. Within days of the city being handed over to the British army, the Imperial troops were called upon to suppress a new – and far more serious – outbreak of looting by 'some of the poor Dutch' and 'the riff-raff of the foreign population' in the western suburbs.[71] After this, there were no further serious wartime incidents of this kind in the city – partly because there was an occupying army to draw on to help protect private property, and partly because the British authorities took urgent and energetic action under the provisions of martial law to rid the town of nearly 2 000 'undesirables' whom it either imprisoned or deported.[72]

These events of 1899-1900, like the earlier ones in 1897, did not escape the notice of Johannesburg's ruling classes who now saw in the imperial intervention the opportunity to engage in a round of radical social engineering which could do much to rid the inner city of its concentration of Afrikaner unemployed and its even more volatile lumpenproletarian element of all colours. As early as February 1902, J W Quinn, a member of Milner's nominated town council and Chairman of its Public Health Committee advocated that the Brickfields, Burgersdorp and a portion of lower Fordsburg be declared an 'Insanitary Area', expropriated, demolished and redeveloped. Quinn was also quick to point out to his fellow councillors that it was particularly opportune to move in this direction while the burghers were still away on commando or else detained in the camps as prisoners of war.[73]

It was not simply the city baker's thoughts that were running in this direction, however. In the boardrooms of the mining companies some of the more influential Randlords were also thinking about the need to plan for the arrival of the army of unemployed which would make its way to Johannesburg when the war ended. 'The argument which I could not press in public but which we use in private and in council,' FitzPatrick confided to his partner Wernher in July 1902, 'is that many thousand men who will be disbanded here within a few weeks and who may be without means of subsistence, must be regarded as an extremely serious possible danger.' 'If they become a starving and disorderly rabble', he warned, 'it will cost us money, exertions, repute and stability ten times what it may cost to tide them through the period until they can be absorbed into the working community.'[74] These strictures echoed loudly in the ears of Milner and his young officials and the reconstruction administration responded swiftly to these suggestions.

In September 1902, a mere six months after Quinn had first publicly announced the possibility of an enquiry into the Brickfields-Burgersdorp-Fordsburg area with a view to eventually expropriating it, the Governor of the Transvaal appointed a commission to examine the problem. The town council's case – in essence also the reconstruction government's case since the former was still a nominated rather than an elected body – was lead by Quinn as Chairman of the Public Health Committee and by Milner's choice as Johannesburg Town Clerk, Lionel Curtis. It was Curtis, however, drawing on his experience at the London Country Council and his knowledge gained as Honorary Secretary to the Mansion House Committee on the Dwellings of the Poor, who really masterminded the authorities' case. Modelling his approach along the lines of the Westminster Housing of the Working Classes Act of 1890, Curtis and his colleagues carefully steered the Johannesburg Insanitary Area Improvement Scheme Commission to the conclusion that – largely on grounds of public health – the buildings under consideration should be demolished. Shortly after the commission reported in 1903, the city's oldest Afrikaner industrial site, already eclipsed by larger capitalist developments and reduced to a residential area for the 'labouring classes and the dangerous classes', was forced to give way to the redeveloped industrial and business sites of Newtown. This, together with the rapid escalation of rents during the post-war housing crisis, did much to push some of Johannesburg's Afrikaner unemployed into the outlying suburbs such as Newlands during the reconstruction era.[75]

But if it was largely Lionel Curtis who responded to Quinn's suggestions in respect of the 'Insanitary Area', then it was Milner himself who paid most attention to FitzPatrick and the other mine owners' warnings about the need to exercise careful control over the unemployed in the immediate post-war period. As Governor of the newest British colony he therefore established the Rand Refugee Department and it was largely this arm of the state, operating with a government grant and mining-house money, together with the older Present Help League which continued to be privately funded, that did most to provide charity, relief and temporary shelter for hundreds of semi-skilled English workers during the earliest months of demobilisation.[76]

By late 1902, however, Milner – already hard-pressed by Whitehall about the cost of the war and reconstruction – was of the opinion that the full burden of meeting these costs could legitimately be passed on to FitzPatrick and his friends. Moreover, he and Lionel Curtis who was even more familiar with the role and function of the Charity Organisation Society in London felt the need to centralise all relief operations on the Rand in order to avoid duplication of effort and to minimise the problem of 'indiscriminate alms giving'.[77] Thus in January 1903 the Refugee Department and the Present Help League were moulded into a single organisation – the Rand Aid Society – with Milner as its patron and R W Schumacher, Carl Hanau and J W Quinn, amongst others, serving on its board of trustees.[78] For at least the next two decades the Rand Aid Association, with the active financial support and guidance of the more far-sighted mine owners, virtually dominated Johannesburg's organised relief programmes.[79]

The reconstruction government and the Randlords thus entered the first months of the post-war period with some equanimity – soothed in the knowledge that the problem of the Afrikaner proletariat in the 'Insanitary Area' on the one hand and the threat posed by the unemployed English miners on the other were both well under control. Indeed, there was at least one of Milner's young officials who was so confident that there was sufficient social grease on the squeakier wheels of Rand capitalism that he could foresee no future for white working-class radicalism. 'No labour party can be really formidable unless it is based on profound discontents and radical grievances,' wrote John Buchan in 1903, 'and the annoyances of the Johannesburg proletariat are, as compared with those of Europe, like crumpled rose-leaves to thorns.' 'There is,' he concluded, 'too strong a force of social persistence in the city to suffer it ever to become the prey of a well-organised gang of revolutionaries.'[80]

If this somewhat hasty judgement served subsequently to embarrass an older and much wiser Buchan in 1907, 1913 and 1922, then there was admittedly little to suggest that he was wide of the mark between 1903 and 1905. As FitzPatrick and his colleagues had hoped, many of the skilled and semi-skilled workers were gradually reabsorbed into the working community during this period, with the Rand Aid Association successfully taking the sting out of much of the class antagonism during the intervening spell of unemployment. The unskilled Afrikaner workers, for their part, used the delay in the introduction of the electric tramway and the post-war building boom to re-establish themselves – albeit on a diminished scale – in their old jobs as cab drivers, brick-makers and casual labourers. The effect of this latter development was to remove temporarily the plight of the urban Afrikaner worker from the view of not only the British administration but also from the former Afrikaner ruling class which at that moment was engaged in the task of politically reconstituting itself. Thus, when Louis Botha addressed the 'Boer Congress' held in Pretoria in May 1904 he was of the opinion that – as far as the Afrikaner poor were concerned – there were only two cat-egories of importance that had to be catered for – the former Republican civil servants in the towns and the ex-*bywoners* in the countryside.[81]

This brief interlude in the struggle came to an end when, from late 1905 onwards, the Rand economy rapidly slid into a full-scale depression. Early in 1906 the electric tram made its first appearance in the streets of Johannesburg and over the next 12 months hundreds of Vrededorp cab drivers as well as scores of others in associated trades such as coach-builders, blacksmiths, farriers and harness-makers were thrown out of work. More serious by far, however, was the dramatic collapse of the building industry as the post-war housing boom came to an end. While this took a predictable toll on hundreds of small brickmakers and their workers in Albertskroon and Newlands, it also rendered thousands of bricklayers, stonemasons, carpenters, electricians, plasterers, painters and handymen in other working-class suburbs unemployed. Redun-dancies on this scale were inevitably reflected in reduced consumer demand and this in turn cost scores of clerks and shop assistants their jobs. Within a matter of months the streets of the city assumed an aspect which had last been seen a decade earlier in 1896.[82]

On this occasion, however, Johannesburg's ruling classes had the ben-efit of an institutionalised monitoring agency which could provide them with an early warning of any unusual build-up in the size of the Rand's reserve army of labour. In March 1906 the Rand Aid Association addressed a letter to Lionel Phillips in which it alerted him to the fact that the new situation would demand resources well in excess of its current government and municipal grants and appealing to him to enlist the sup-port of his company. But even Wernher, Beit & Co's substantial grants – then and later – as well as those of other Randlords were not sufficient to the task of social control during a period of deep depression.[83] The Rand Aid Association thus also urged another of its influential members, the Mayor of Johannesburg and the man immediately responsible for the city's welfare, W K Tucker, to approach the state for further assistance.[84]

In May 1906 Tucker warned Milner's successor in Pretoria, Selborne, that the problem of unemployment in the city was sufficiently serious to merit the urgent attention of the government. The new governor who was at least partly convinced by the Mayor's arguments duly appointed a seven-man commission of enquiry to examine the problems of poverty and unemployment in the colony. When the Transvaal Indigency Commission met for the first time in November 1906, however, it was led by a familiar team of social engineers which revealed that it was Johannesburg rather than the colony as a whole which was of concern to the state. In addition to having J W Quinn as its chairman, the commission was also served by Lionel Curtis, his successor as the city's Town Clerk, Richard Feetham, and yet another of Milner's choices for the task of reconstruction, Phillip Kerr.[85]

This political response to the plea of Johannesburg's ruling classes, however, did little to improve the economic lot of those most immediately affected – the unemployed – who became increasingly anxious as the year drew to a close. Early in December 1906 hundreds of skilled and semi-skilled workers without jobs gathered on the Market Square to discuss their dilemma and at the conclusion of the meeting formed themselves into the 'Unemployed Organisation' under the leadership of Joseph Hale. This body, which was largely composed of the unemployed drawn from the building and allied trades, met at irregular intervals throughout the month in an attempt to solve the problems of its members. The Unemployed Organisation regularly called on the municipality or the government to initiate a public works programme, or in more reactionary vein, appealed to these employers to discharge black workers and take on white men in their place. At a mass meeting held on Boxing Day, for example, it passed a resolution calling on the government 'to remove all coloured men from pumping stations, lamp-cleaning, light porterage and stores tending, and such other work as may fitly be done by white men, and fill the vacancies thus created with Europeans'.[86]

Tucker and his fellow councillors who were closer to these meetings of hundreds of the unemployed in the city centre than the outgoing British administration in Pretoria read these signs with growing concern and in mid-December 1906 the Johannesburg Town Council did indeed take on several hundred unskilled labourers – including a few score Afrikaners – into a local public works programme. In addition to this, the Mayor unsuccessfully approached the Chamber of Mines with a formal request that it consider the possibility of taking on some of the local citizens who were jobless.[87]

Within three weeks of these developments, however, on 4 January 1907, Tucker was again approached by a delegation from the Unemployed Organisation and this time with a far more disturbing request.

Hale and his colleagues now wanted the town council to make available to them a central camp site in order that the members of their organisation might enjoy rent-free accommodation whilst they searched for work. But the Mayor, who was already concerned about the security of the city, refused to entertain a proposition which would – for the foreseeable future – concentrate a large number of the unemployed on a single site. Instead, Tucker put new pressure on the authorities in Pretoria to consider a state public works programme which would draw off some of the unemployed from Johannesburg.[88]

In the weeks that followed, Hale and his colleagues developed a two-pronged strategy to increase their pressure on the ruling classes. On the one hand, they deliberately escalated the demands which they made of the Rand Aid Association in order to embarrass the authorities and hasten the announcement of a state public works programme. On the other, they exploited one of the few major divisions amongst the Randlords by approaching J B Robinson with the request that *he* come to the financial assistance of their members. The latter move reaped an immediate dividend. Robinson – ever anxious to extend his feud with the Chamber of Mines – promptly made £5 000 available to the members of the Unemployed Organisation. As part of their efforts to provide the unemployed with accommodation Hale and his committee used some of this grant to acquire 18 large tents – this despite the fact that they were still without the use of a camp site.[89]

On 14 February 1907 the government finally made its long-awaited announcement about relief works for the Rand's unemployed. This work, which had to be applied for through the offices of the Rand Aid Association, would take the form of road building in the Rustenburg district where the unemployed would also be provided with food and tents. In addition to this, those who enlisted would be paid a small cash wage for their services but, in an attempt to prevent an influx of unemployed from other parts of South Africa, this would be restricted to the sum of two shillings per day.[90]

The prospect of earning two shillings a day on road works at Rustenburg did not elicit much enthusiasm amongst Johannesburg's unemployed. When asked about their opinions, however, the members of the Unemployed Organisation at first simply said that the offer was unsuitable for married men who were unwilling to desert their families during such hard times, while some of the younger men were of the opinion that they would only be in a position to leave the city after they had voted in the election. Hale, disappointed with the government's response, then appealed to Selborne to provide his members with the camp site which the town council had earlier refused them. On 15 February the Governor replied, pointing out that all public property in Johannesburg was under the control of the town council and that in any event all such requests should – in the first instance – be directed through the Rand Aid Association.[91]

By this time the members of the Unemployed Organisation were both tired and angry – tired of making unproductive appeals through official channels and angered by the miserly response of the state to their insistent pleas for help. Despite this, the committee directed one final appeal for a camp site to Selborne. On Friday morning, 16 February, Hale summoned the unemployed to a meeting on the Union Ground and in the address that followed he lost no time at all in making what he considered to be the central points. 'It was a disgrace,' he said, 'that the Government should ask white men to work for less pay than they would offer a Kaffir.' Because of this insulting offer, it was now vital for them to acquire a camp site and 'whether consent came or not they would have the ground, and have it that day'. Hale assured his audience that he already had a site in mind and that it was 'Parktown way'. Amidst growing applause he told the unemployed: 'It might be that it was Sunnyside – the Governor was away and his house was unoccupied.' Finally, Hale warned the 'big people' in the Transvaal that they should not be surprised to see 'before the month was out, such an upheaval in the country as they had never anticipated'. The meeting closed on this militant note with the crowd dispersing to await a reply from Selborne. When no reply had been received by late afternoon the unemployed regrouped and over 700 men and eight families marched into the city centre where they seized and occupied – not the Governor's official residence – but the Braamfontein Show Ground which was under municipal control.[92]

These developments – the formation of the Unemployed Organisation, the soliciting of the J B Robinson gift, the organised attempts to embarrass the Rand Aid Association, the plea for a public works programme and the seizure of the Show Ground were all followed with great interest by the unemployed of Vrededorp. Indeed, several Afrikaners had been party to at least one of these events when, on 14 February, 400 men had simultaneously invaded the offices of the Rand Aid Association to demand food before being persuaded to disperse by their leaders.[93] The seizure of the Show Ground, however, held little appeal for the Afrikaner unemployed – in fact, it left them in somewhat of a quandary since as home-owners in Vrededorp they had no immediate need for shelter, while the creation of an exclusive camp for the workless in effect denied them access the Robinson relief funds.

On the morning following the seizure of the Show Ground, therefore, about 80 of the Afrikaner unemployed under the leadership of a former lieutenant in Kruger's State Artillery, N P Oelofse, met on the Union Ground to discuss their predicament. Oelofse opened the meeting with

more disturbing news for the Vrededorp unemployed. The local committee of *Het Volk* – deeply suspicious that the Rand Aid Association was an
instrument of their political opponents, the Progressives – was of the
opinion that no loyal Afrikaner should accept relief from that agency until
after the election. He thus urged all those present who had previously
received assistance from the Rand Aid Association to return such goods
or food to that body or face the possibility of being disenfranchised when
Het Volk assumed office in a few days' time.[94] The meeting agreed to this
suggestion which left the Afrikaners with no alternative but to extract aid
from the remaining non-Progressive source of relief in the city – the
Robinson fund. Four days later, on 22 February 1907, some of the
Afrikaner unemployed of Vrededorp – drawing on the lessons which
they had learned earlier in the month from the Unemployed Organisation
– invaded the nearby Braamfontein camp where 'they demanded from
the Committee their share of the provisions, and a just share of money out
of Mr J B Robinson's gift'. After a heated argument Hale and his committee agreed to 'register' these men and once the Vrededorpers had been
issued with provisions they 'departed without coming to blows, being
content with a battle of words'. Thereafter, the Unemployed Organisation
continued to provide relief not only to its immediate camp followers composed largely of English artisans but to such 'registered' outsiders who
consisted mainly of unskilled Afrikaner workers.[95]

A week later the Johannesburg Town Council, which had succeeded in
keeping a remarkably low profile throughout these events, met for the
first time to consider the seizure of the Show Ground. Tucker and his colleagues, however, like a reporter from the *Transvaal Leader*, did not fail to
notice that 'there were many ex-soldiers in the camp, well used to discipline'. The Mayor and town councillors therefore settled on the prudent
policy of non-confrontation with the members of the Unemployed
Organisation, and decided instead to redouble their efforts to absorb the
local unemployed into a municipal or state public works programme.
Accordingly, throughout late February, March and April 1907, the council steadily retrenched hundreds of black labourers earning two shillings
a day and systematically replaced them with unemployed whites who
were paid between five and six shillings per day for the same tasks.
Much to Tucker's and the ratepayers' relief, the additional expenditure
incurred through this racist manoeuvre was partly, although not wholly,
subsidised by the new *Het Volk* government. It thus cost hundreds of
blacks their jobs and thousands of pounds in hard cash in an attempt to
reduce the level of white unemployment and its attendant threats in
Johannesburg during the first quarter of 1907.[96]

But if this municipal-state strategy blunted the initiative of the reserve
army of labour as a whole, then it certainly did not succeed in removing

the cutting edge of class consciousness from the Braamfontein camp. Here, skilled workers steeped in a trade union tradition proved more difficult to absorb into the cheap unskilled labour of a public works programme than their unskilled counterparts in Vrededorp, and the numbers in the camp only diminished slowly from 700 in February to 460 in April. It was thus this more concentrated and self-conscious core of the workless that presented itself as a natural constituency for the socialists of the newly formed Independent Labour Party (ILP) to cultivate. From mid-March onwards Joseph Hale, in the face of more radical and persuasive arguments by J T Bain, Archie Crawford and W C Salter, found it difficult to retain control over his increasingly militant followers. On 8 April Hale appeared before the Transvaal Indigency Commission and gave evidence which the majority of his members considered to be insulting or prejudicial to their interests. He and his committee were swiftly deposed from the leadership of the Unemployed Organisation, and replaced by what the camp inhabitants, after the style of the 1906 Russian election, termed the 'New Duma'.[97]

On 1 May 1907 a column of several hundred of the unemployed under the leadership of Archie Crawford marched into Pretoria to seek an audience with the Colonial Secretary, J C Smuts, in the hope that they would be able to persuade the government 'to employ white labour at fair wages', at a place closer to their 'natural field of employment'. But, as I D de Vries and P C Duvenhage had discovered a decade earlier, Smuts was never very enthusiastic about the idea of Johannesburg's unemployed marching into the Transvaal capital. When Crawford and the members of his deputation met the Colonial Secretary a day later they found Smuts as firm as ever. The government was reluctant to pay more than two shillings a day as a basic wage to the unemployed, but it would – if the men were willing to find their own food – consider raising this to three shillings and sixpence. The Colonial Secretary 'was sorry to have to send them as far as the Zoutpansberg district, but it was being done only after the fullest enquiries'. He felt that they should consider this new offer and he concluded the meeting with a warning to the men that they should not become a public 'nuisance' and that if they did there would be 'law for all'.[98] Crawford's deputation then withdrew. At a meeting held on the racecourse later in the afternoon a full gathering of the unemployed unanimously rejected Smuts's latest proposal and then set out on the long march back to the Rand. But by the time they had reached Johannesburg the spotlight of public attention had already swung away from them to focus on a new and more serious manifestation of class conflict.[99]

On the same day that some of Johannesburg's unemployed marched into Pretoria, 1 May 1907, the white miners at Knights Deep on the East Rand went on strike when the management insisted that they undertake the supervision of three rather than two drills during the course of their duties underground. This demand from the mine owners' middlemen held obvious long-term structural consequences for white labour in the industry, and within a little more than a week the strike had spread, with the active encouragement of the Transvaal Miners' Association (TMA), to several of the largest mines on the central Rand. On 22 May, the TMA deemed the strike to be 'general' and it was thus extended to include all those mines along the length of the Witwatersrand that were affiliated to the Chamber of Mines.[100]

These moves by organised labour meant that all mines – with the exception of those controlled by the still recalcitrant J B Robinson – were nominally affected by the strike. Thus, while Robinson donated £2 000 to the strikers' fund for the support of their dependants, many of the mine owners were forced to look around for an alternative supply of white labour which would enable them to defeat their working-class challengers. The Randlords were encouraged in this search by the knowledge that they would not have to look very far. Since at least 1897 the mine owners had been aware of the growing Afrikaner corps within the Rand's reserve army of labour – not least of all because they had periodically been called upon to help defuse its militancy through their involvement in organised charity. Now, with a *Het Volk* government in power, the Randlords sensed the exciting prospect of being able to combine political expediency and economic self-interest by employing Afrikaners as strike-breakers. And when the mine owners sniffed nationalism, their journalistic mouthpiece sneezed patriotism. 'No patriotic South African,' *The Star* announced to its readers on 22 May, 'is likely to complain that the burden of indigency is being shifted from the men of the country to the sojourners from overseas.'[101]

The Chamber of Mines started its campaign to shift the burden of indigency to the 'sojourners from overseas' by recruiting the modest amount of Afrikaner scab labour that was needed during the early days of the strike from areas well beyond the Witwatersrand – in the Pretoria, Potchefstroom and Kimberley districts.[102] This, according to *The Star*, had the virtue – amongst many others – of helping to break down the barriers that existed between 'town and country, race and race'.[103] But as the strike spread and enveloped some of the central Rand mines during mid-May, so the mine owners' agents cast increasingly envious eyes in the direction of the larger and more proximate pools of untapped proletarian labour that lay in the urban areas of Vrededorp and Newlands.

The Transvaal Miners' Association and its closest political ally, the

Independent Labour party (ILP), opposed the introduction of scab labour by the Chamber of Mines with a two-pronged counter-attack. On the one hand, senior officials from these organisations donned their velvet gloves and toured the rural centres explaining the origin of the strike to Afrikaners, appealing to them to support the miners' cause by refusing to accept the job offers that were now being made to them by the Rand capitalists.[104] On the other, rank and file members back on the Witwatersrand used the more familiar iron fist to intimidate and assault those Afrikaners who had been foolish enough to reject advice that had been offered to them in good faith.[105] It was this same combination of tactics which was used with indifferent success throughout the strike that was quickly brought into play when the TMA and ILP first sensed that the Chamber's agents were turning their attention to Johannesburg's western suburbs as a possible alternative source of white labour for the mines.

On 11 May 1907 *De Volkstem* carried, in Dutch, an 'Important Notice to all Afrikaners' on the Rand. This notice, inserted into the newspaper at the request of the TMA, outlined the cause of the current industrial dispute and appealed to all Afrikaners – as 'fellow South Africans' – not to harm the miners' cause. Over the next three or four days the TMA followed up this initiative by holding a series of meetings in the western suburbs of the town. At Vrededorp on 14 May N Mathey and M Trewick of the Miners' Association addressed a well-attended meeting held at the government school. Here, the audience listened attentively to the miners' case but, significantly, the meeting ended without any clear statement of support from the audience. The meeting held at Newlands on the following afternoon, however, was far more satisfactory from the miners' point of view – perhaps not least of all because the TMA had taken the precaution of having the meeting addressed and run by an Afrikaner striker from the Langlaagte Deep mine. Here the audience agreed that no Afrikaners should become 'blacklegs'.[106]

The silence that followed the Mathey-Trewick meeting in Vrededorp, however, was followed by two weeks of intense political ferment within that community. Immediately after the address by the two TMA officials, the Vrededorp Vigilance Association called a meeting of its own under the chairmanship of S A Smit to discuss the issues raised by the strike. This meeting revealed the deeply ambiguous feelings that the oldest urban Afrikaner proletariat in the Transvaal entertained about the new conflict. Many and possibly most of those present felt that the strike afforded them a desperately needed chance to secure employment, but at the same time they feared the strikers' capacity to protect their jobs – the TMA's iron fist. The leader writer at *The Star* probably assessed this strand in the Afrikaners' thinking correctly when he noted that: 'Vrededorp is rather too near the scene of action to proceed without circumspection.'[107] Others at the meeting, however, were of the opinion that as members of the working class they should show solidarity and support the miners in their struggle against the capitalists. Faced with these diverging viewpoints, Smit and his closest advisers drafted a skilful compromise. The members of the Vrededorp Vigilance Association would agree not to act as 'scab' labour provided that the TMA first provided them with an assurance that 'when the strike was over the union would assist Afrikaners to get work on the same terms as British miners, the former agreeing not to work more than two machines or work for a lower rate of wages'.[108] This offer was duly conveyed to the Transvaal Miners' Association shortly after 15 May.

Five days later, when the Vrededorp Vigilance Association had still not received a reply from the TMA, Smit and the unemployed again met to discuss what the correct course of action should be. This time Smit suggested that they should seek the advice of their *Het Volk* Member of the Legislative Assembly, Johannesburg's former principal public prosecutor under the Kruger government, Dr F E T Krause. Krause's response to the predicament of the unemployed came in the form of an open letter addressed to his constituents:

Gentlemen,

It has come to my notice that in consequence of the strike on certain mines certain persons have advised you to support the strikers by not going to look for work on these mines. As I consider it my duty as your representative to inform you what my attitude is under the circumstances, I wish to say that, although I have great sympathy with the strikers, I believe that you will not be justified not to go out and look for work. My earnest advice therefore is, do not allow yourselves to be persuaded, but go and look for work wherever you can get it. Take care, however, that you obtain a guarantee from the employer that you will not be discharged after a short time, and do nothing to lower the amount of wages.

I understand that a resolution to this effect has already been taken. I have the honour to be,

Yours faithfully,
F E T Krause[109]

This letter did much to nudge the hesitant Afrikaners towards accepting positions on the mines as scab labour.

Following the receipt of this letter on 21 May 1907, between 150 and 200 of the Vrededorp unemployed once again assembled under the leadership of S A Smit. This time the Afrikaners formed themselves into a single body of men and marched to the offices of Consolidated Gold Fields in the centre of the city where their delegates attempted to negotiate for employment under conditions similar to those that prevailed before the strike. Before these discussions could be finalised, however, this formidable contingent of Afrikaners was spotted – not by the members of the TMA who were away at picket duty on the mines, but by R L Outhwaite, W Lorimer and J F Back of the Independent Labour Party. These three ILP stalwarts persuaded Smit and his followers not to make any final decision about accepting employment on the mines until such time as they had all had a chance to have a further discussion with Krause. The phalanx of unemployed thereupon withdrew and marched back to Vrededorp for a meeting with Krause accompanied by the three socialist watchdogs.[110]

At their meeting with the *Het Volk* MLA, the ILP contingent attempted to persuade Krause that his advice to his constituents had been primarily motivated by political considerations and that as such it was likely to jeopardise future co-operation between English and Afrikaner workers. Krause responded by saying that he had acted simply to ensure the economic well-being of his constituents, and by pointing out that in any case 'complaints had been made to him by Afrikaners that they had not been able to get work *before* the strike because the British miners objected to their presence on the mines'. In short, the attitudes of the immigrant miners before the strike as well as the TMA's refusal to respond to the proposal put to it by the Vrededorp Vigilance Association during the strike both suggested that the English miner was no particular friend of the Afrikaner unemployed. This information may or may not have come as news to Outhwaite and his colleagues but, in either event, it left them with little effective reply. Making the best of what was rapidly becoming a most unpromising situation, the ILP members again pleaded with the unemployed to 'defer action' – this time so that they could make further representations to the TMA with the request that it 'define' its attitude towards accepting Afrikaners as fellow mineworkers after the strike. Once more the men of Vrededorp agreed to wait.[111]

The following morning the strike was declared to be 'general' and Prime Minister Botha responded by dispatching imperial troops to the Witwatersrand. Over a week later, Johannesburg's Afrikaner unemployed were still awaiting a reply from either the TMA or its ILP intermediaries. The reply never came. On 25 May *De Volkstem* lent its editorial support to the advice which F E T Krause had been offering his constituents. The newspaper – like the *Het Volk* MLA before it – pointed out that it was not only the Randlords but also the muscle of the immigrant miners that had hitherto blocked the Afrikaner's entry into the mining industry:

... up to the present, there has not been the slightest consideration given to the Afrikaner's claim to the better positions on the mines. Most of the companies have given in to the English miners' wish that their countrymen be given exclusive access to such bread-winning opportunities.[112]

De Volkstem was of the opinion that, under the circumstances, the local unemployed owed the Transvaal Miners' Association no favours and that Afrikaners should go out and seek work – making sure that they were not being used only as strike-breakers by demanding a two-year contract from the mining companies.

It was only after this point had been reached that urban Afrikaners in any numbers decided to take up employment in the mining industry. While their country cousins had readily grasped at the job opportunities that had been presented to them from the earliest days of the strike, Johannesburg's Afrikaner unemployed had – through a mixture of fear and class consciousness – hesitated before accepting work as 'scab' labour. From 25 May onwards, however, a growing number of men from Vrededorp took up work at nearby mines such as the Crown Deep and the Crown Reef. The TMA responded by publicly posting the names of 'blacklegs' on the Market Square of adjacent Fordsburg, but when – on 1 June – the all-important SA Engine Drivers' Association also refused to come out in support of the union, the miners lost their battle and the strike gradually disintegrated.[113]

It is estimated that between May and June 1907 some 2 000 to 3 000 Afrikaners gained employment in the Transvaal's premier industry for the first time, and of those a couple of hundred were undoubtedly drawn from Vrededorp and Newlands.[114] As the strike slowly drew to a close, however, scores – if not hundreds – of Afrikaners also *left* the mining industry. Some were cynically dismissed by mine managers once the strike was over while others left of their own accord because of their distaste for the hard, unfamiliar and dangerous work underground. Many others – as has often been suggested – lost their jobs 'because of their inefficiency'.[115] But amongst the many who left there were also several who were forced out by a campaign of organised terror mounted by a group of immigrant miners.

In early June several Afrikaners received anonymous letters typed in red ink which threatened them with dire consequences if they did not immediately relinquish their newly gained posts on the mines. The style, frequency and distribution of these letters left some observers – including one who had been sympathetic to the TMA's struggle – with 'the opinion that there is existing some kind of society whose efforts are directed towards intimidating employees in this nefarious way'.[116] What is significant about those cases that were reported in the press, however, is that virtually all of them relate to those Afrikaners who were permanently resident on the Witwatersrand rather than those who had been recruited in the rural districts during the course of the strike. In large part this can be accounted for by the fact that such Afrikaners tended to live with their families in the suburbs and that because of this they could be more readily isolated and got at than their 'single' country cousins who lived in the massed shelter of the boarding-houses on the mining properties.[117] What it also suggests, however, is that the fully proletarianised urban Afrikaners were more likely to cling to their jobs and that they therefore presented the immigrant miners with a greater challenge than that posed by the less committed newcomers from the countryside. This hypothesis is perhaps further strengthened when we consider how, in the case of the resident Afrikaners, the 'red ink' warnings sometimes evolved beyond mere 'intimidation' into fully-fledged attempts at murder.

At dusk on 12 June a miner named Redlinghuis was cycling towards his home at Klipriversberg in southern Johannesburg when, near Regent's Park, three men armed with revolvers opened fire on him, discharging nine shots. Redlinghuis escaped with a leg wound and minor injuries. Two days later, as the early-morning shift was changing at the Simmer East shaft on the East Rand, a crowd of men wielding revolvers forced miners Oosthuizen and Van der Merwe to jump on their cycles and flee at great pace down a deserted footpath. On rounding a corner, the cyclists 'were brought heavily to ground by coming into contact with a rope which had been placed across the road'. Here again, the men were lucky enough to escape with minor injuries.[118]

Others – although admittedly not Afrikaners – were less fortunate. Twelve hours after the attack on Oosthuizen and Van der Merwe at Boksburg North on 14 June a house occupied by three English miners who refused to support the strike was demolished by a dynamite explosion. Although the owners of the house – a shift boss and his family – were unharmed, one of their lodgers, a miner from the New Comet named Webb Richard, was killed by the blast.[119] It is possible that this attack on the East Rand, where the strike originated and was always most strongly supported, also served as the 'model' for an attempt on the lives of a family of Afrikaner miners in Johannesburg two weeks later.

On 25 June 1907 the Goosen family of the corner Third and Locatie Streets, Vrededorp, received an anonymous typewritten letter containing the familiar 'red ink' threats. Sam Goosen and his two adult sons – all miners – ignored these warnings to give up their newly acquired positions on the nearby Crown Reef. When the father and his two boys woke up to go on shift early on the morning of 2 July, they discovered an unexploded charge of one and a half pounds of gelignite, a faulty detonator and 70 inches of fuse attached to the window sill of their home.[120] In this case, thanks to the defective detonator, the family escaped injury.

All of these incidents, however, were well publicised and it is certain that they, as well as many of those cases that remained unreported, must have left the desired impression on those who had been employed as 'scab' labour during the strike.[121] But, whatever the cause, the fact remains that by the last quarter of the year many, if not most of those urban Afrikaners who had gained employment during the course of the strike, were again jobless. This meant that by late 1907 unemployment and discontent amongst the inhabitants of Vrededorp – and to a lesser extent amongst other groups within the city – had again reached a level that was considered by some to be dangerously high. This time the ruling classes attempted to cope with the rumblings from below with a more broadly based response.

Between August and December of 1907 Vrededorp was invaded by the agents of largely middle-class organisations seeking to cast the women and children of the suburb into a more proletarian mould which, they believed, could open gateways to a new and more industrious life for the poor whites of the city. The South African Women's Federation, for example, besides running a much-appreciated soup kitchen, attempted – with less success – to establish 'cottage industries' in the hope that this would help produce 'a contented and self-supporting population' in Vrededorp.[122] The newly formed Undenominational Benevolent Society, under the patronage of Mrs Louis Botha tried – also unsuccessfully – to build on an idea that had first been put to President Kruger by the members of the Rand Relief Committee a decade earlier: namely, that a public laundry be erected in the suburb which would not only provide work for unemployed Afrikaner women, but also draw off some of those already working, 'with a danger to their morals', in the small hand-laundries of Indian and Chinese employers.[123] The Salvation Army, for its part, concentrated on a 'practical scheme of industrial training' for the older children of Vrededorp, teaching them printing, needle-work, drawing and woodwork.[124]

These schemes, however, produced neither an immediate nor an adequate flow of funds to the starving families of the western working-class suburbs and nobody was more aware of this than the still hard-pressed Mayor of Johannesburg, W K Tucker. It was largely for this reason that Tucker and his fellow councillors agreed to extend the municipal relief works by taking on additional white men to work on the development of the city's water-borne sewerage system. Thus during the closing months of 1907 some 240 whites – including many from Vrededorp –

were engaged as pipe-makers in lower Fordsburg or as trench-diggers in Braamfontein at piece-work rates which averaged out at about five shillings per day.[125]

When this round of temporary and restricted municipal employment came to an end it heralded the advent of a new and even more serious crisis for the Afrikaner unemployed of the city. Early in 1908 the government attempted to partly alleviate the deepening distress in the western suburbs when it appointed R Shanks and S A Smit as Inspectors of White Labour in Johannesburg. Amongst others, it was the duty of these officials to assess the extent of local destitution and, where possible, to place the most needy in government employment. Unfortunately for the two inspectors, however, such opportunities as were offered by the state were both limited and financially unrewarding when compared with the municipal relief schemes – something which in turn reflected the fact that while the government had to cater largely for the landed Afrikaners of *Het Volk*, the Johannesburg municipality had to live with the working classes and the Independent Labour Party. In particular, the offer of work on the construction of the Pietersburg railway line at three shillings and fourpence per day 'plus mealie meal' proved to be most unpopular with the Rand's reserve army of labour. Thus, while the appointment of Smit might have swept one Afrikaner from the more radical ranks of the Vrededorp unemployed into the arms of officialdom, it apparently did very little for the remainder of the unemployed in the suburb.[126]

Throughout the first two months of 1908 the poor of Vrededorp vainly awaited the announcement of some new relief scheme, their awful plight made bearable only by the continued issue of rations by the Rand Aid Association. Then, in mid-February, disaster struck. The Rand Aid Association, which since October 1907 had been operating on an expanded scale with a special grant made to it by Wernher, Beit & Co and the Witwatersrand Native Labour Association, came to the end of these emergency funds. This forced the Association to retract its efforts to within the 'normal' limits set by its more modest municipal and government grants. In the last week of February the Rand Aid Association 'had to strike off the list of recipients the names of the representatives of about one thousand people'. Within days this drastic action reflected itself in the starvation and despair of the Afrikaner unemployed.[127]

On Saturday afternoon, 1 March 1908, the Vrededorp unemployed met under the leadership of three men – Paul Das, Editor of *De Transvaler*, ex-Field Cornet M J Bekker and L Minaar – to discuss the latest crisis confronting their families. At this meeting it was decided that the Colonial Secretary should be petitioned in order to determine what possible assistance the government could offer the Afrikaner poor of the city. Before this could be formally organised, however, Das took it upon himself to visit Smuts and point out to him the gravity of the situation in Johannesburg, and on the following Monday evening the editor of *De Transvaler* reported back on his informal discussions with the Colonial Secretary to a meeting of some 200 of the unemployed.[128]

Das knew that he would be addressing an aggressive white working-class audience and his speech reflected this. He told the meeting that 'General Smuts appeared to have no idea that the distress in Johannesburg was so acute or widespread as it was'. He related how, when the Colonial Secretary attempted to fend off criticisms of neglect by pointing to the Inspectors of White Labour, he countered by telling Smuts that 'Mr Smit was one of those who drove around in cabs and looked down on the Afrikanders working in the streets in the town' – i.e. on those employed as trench-diggers in the municipal sewerage extension scheme. If *Het Volk* could not accommodate their immediate needs, he suggested, then 'the Ministers of the Government should drop £1 000 each from their salaries for the benefit of the poor people'.[129]

Then, getting into his stride, Das extended his speech along popular ILP 'white labour' lines when he pointed out to the meeting that he had asked General Smuts 'whether an Act should not be passed prohibiting the employment of Kaffirs by the Johannesburg Municipality'. When Smuts drew attention to the employment possibilities that existed on the construction site of the Pietersburg railway line, Das responded with a deft nationalist ideological deflection which avoided the more fundamental issues of locality and wage rates. 'Such an offer,' Das told his Vrededorp audience, 'was most insulting to the Afrikander nation. A man who called himself an Afrikander should not go and work for 3s 4d per day and a bag of mealie meal per month. The sting of the whole thing lay in the offer of mealie meal. It was placing them on a level with Kaffirs.' [130]

But the editor of *De Transvaler* had not made his way to Pretoria simply to criticise a *Het Volk* leader; he had also gone to offer some constructive advice. He had put it to Smuts that the government should consider the 'establishment of labour colonies on lines similar to that on which Kakamas Colony' in the Cape was run, but the Colonial Secretary was not particularly enthusiastic about that suggestion because of the government's indifferent success with its own Middelburg scheme. Smuts did, however, agree to think about other ways in which some of the urban Afrikaner unemployed could be placed back on the land. Das rounded off his speech by relating some of the other ideas which he had put to the Colonial Secretary, and the meeting closed with the election of a deputation composed of Messrs Das, Minaar and Bekker who would attempt to meet Smuts formally as soon as was possible.[131]

These new stirrings amongst the unemployed in the western suburbs rang all the old alarm bells for the ruling classes in the town hall. Johannesburg's new Mayor, James Thompson, was as aware as his predecessor that a high level of unemployment and the simultaneous collapse of organised charity in the city constituted a particularly explosive social mixture. Within 48 hours of Das's meeting with the Afrikaner unemployed therefore, Thompson made two moves in an attempt to help defuse the rapidly developing crisis. First, the town council again extended its relief works programme by agreeing to immediately include the Ferreirastown and Marshalltown districts into the municipal sewerage scheme. In three days, between 5 and 7 March 1908, 240 married men earning five shillings a day were taken on as trench-diggers while hundreds of other disappointed applicants had to be turned away. It was noted that, of those employed, 'a very large proportion were Dutch-speaking citizens, and a little enquiry showed that some had come in from as far out as Maraisburg and Sophiatown, though undoubtedly the majority were from Vrededorp'. Second, the Mayor called a meeting of 'representatives of public bodies and benevolent institutions, members of Parliament and prominent citizens' to discuss the crisis.[132]

The swift responses by the editor of *De Transvaler* and the Mayor of Johannesburg to the new situation, however, left at least one set of local leaders somewhat flat-footed and embarrassed – the *Het Volk* MLA for Vrededorp, Dr F E T Krause, and the hapless Inspector of White Labour, S A Smit. Krause, both by training and temperament, found it hard to relate to the majority of his working-class constituents and to empathise with their problems. As a lawyer, he was much more at home in the House of Assembly where, between 1907 and 1908, he and Smuts did much to steer through the Vrededorp Stands Ordinance and its subsequent amendments which enabled his constituents to acquire the freehold rights to their properties from the Johannesburg Town Council.[133] Smit, by contrast, was usually much more closely involved with the local community and had come to earn for himself the unofficial title of 'Mayor of Vrededorp'. His recent elevation to the position of Inspector of White Labour, however, not only placed him on the *Het Volk* payroll but also succeeded in temporarily alienating him from many of his more radical supporters. Both he and Krause therefore felt the need – although for somewhat different reasons – to show that they too were aware of and concerned about the plight of the Afrikaner unemployed. To this end they too called a meeting to discuss the situation.

This meeting, which reflected some of the embryonic class tensions within Vrededorp society as well as the problems which *Het Volk* experienced in dealing with this relatively radical Afrikaner proletarian constituency, took place on the evening of 6 March 1908. Krause, who opened the meeting, made a lengthy appeal to the government to come to the aid of those former Republican civil servants such as the Zarps who were now unemployed by providing them with a pension – an old *Het Volk* plea which possibly contributed, some six months later, to the appointment of the South African Republican Officials' Pensions Commission.[134] As a former principal public prosecutor in Johannesburg, Krause was particularly well known to the one-time members of Kruger's police force, several of whom resided in Vrededorp.

The Inspector of White Labour, however, knew that Vrededorp's most urgent problem centred around the need to find employment for the vast majority of its unskilled workers, rather than the need to secure the longer-term security of a score or more former civil servants. In his address, therefore, Smit made a conscious effort to recover some of the ground which had been lost to Paul Das and his colleagues by advocating more radical solutions along the lines pioneered by the Independent Labour Party. The Inspector of White Labour – possibly in an attempt to distance himself from his new *Het Volk* masters – opened his speech with the populist suggestion that the government ministers accept a reduction in salary in order to benefit the poor. Smit then went on to suggest an improved and expanded public works programme, the need for land settlement schemes to help absorb the urban unemployed, and he closed his address with a plea for state-owned gold mines which would give Afrikaners the more permanent local employment which they had so long hankered after.[135]

But despite this valiant attempt by Smit, both he and Krause knew by the end of the evening that they had failed to seize the initial political moment in the new crisis, and that they had therefore lost the majority of Vrededorp's support to the editor of *De Transvaler*, Minnaar and Bekker. Krause thus closed the meeting with a somewhat sour warning to his constituents about the activities of Das and his colleagues. As a rather bemused observer from the English press noted in his report: 'There appears to be a regrettable difference amongst the poor Dutch of Vrededorp as to the rival claims of two gentlemen who are anxious to be spokesmen.'[136]

The following morning's news did not bring the beleaguered MLA for Vrededorp or the Inspector of White Labour much joy either as they discovered that, hours before they had held their meeting, the Colonial Secretary had formally received their rivals Minaar and Bekker – Das, unfortunately, being unable to attend. Smuts, who remembered all too clearly his previous meeting with a deputation from the Rand's indigent under the leadership of Archie Crawford, had long been worried by the inroads which ILP socialists had been making amongst the urban Afrikaner unemployed and he thus welcomed the two men from Vrededorp 'and urged them not to be led away by interfering agitators, but to look after their interests themselves'. This Minaar and Bekker proceeded to do with some skill, and in a remarkably conciliatory meeting the Colonial Secretary went out of his way to accommodate most of the points they raised – a development which tended to leave Krause even more stranded than before.[137]

The men from Vrededorp raised four major issues in their discussions with Smuts, starting with those closest to home. First, both Minaar and Bekker contended that the appointment of S A Smit as a 'Government Inspector' had been 'unnecessary, and that in any case he was not the most satisfactory man for the post'. The Colonial Secretary agreed to investigate the matter. Second, 'the question of the minimum wage that should be paid for white unskilled labour was then discussed at considerable length'. Here, there appeared to be a difference of opinion amongst the members of the deputation. While Minaar favoured a minimum wage of 15 shillings per day, 'Bekker disassociated himself from his *confrère*'s suggestion, and thought seven shillings and sixpence to ten shillings a day would give satisfaction'. Both of these figures must undoubtedly have come as a shock to Smuts, but he did indicate that the government was rethinking its position on this very important question and that the figure of seven shillings and sixpence was probably a reasonable one. Third, Minaar and Bekker pointed out to their *Het Volk* leader that while the position had improved somewhat since the strike of the previous year, Afrikaners were still not getting their fair share of jobs in the mining industry. The Colonial Secretary said that he would shortly 'visit the Rand and interview the mining people on their behalf'. Fourth, the question of land settlement schemes was discussed and Smuts indicated that while this possibility had been receiving the government's attention for some time, it now intended to implement such plans with all possible haste. 'In conclusion, General Smuts said he was very glad indeed that they had come to him with their grievances. He would always assist impoverished Afrikaners as far as possible, and also the working-class people as a whole.'[138]

Minaar and Bekker left the meeting delighted with the progress they had made with the new friend of the working class and returned to Johannesburg where, at five o'clock on the afternoon of 7 March 1908 on the vacant stands adjoining Bekker's home, the two men related to the assembled unemployed of Vrededorp what had transpired at their meeting with the Colonial Secretary. The Afrikaner unemployed, many of whom in the first instance simply wanted bread, were greatly relieved to hear that Smuts had promised that he 'would certainly look after those who had no food'. They were further cheered by the news of the other schemes that had been discussed with the Colonial Secretary and in general there was a feeling 'that the fog of depression and misery was lifting, and that the people were anticipating work for all those at present idle'.[139]

Smuts, who must have been pleased to hear that reports of his meeting with Minaar and Bekker had done much to 'restore confidence in the Government's promise of assistance' amongst the Afrikaner unemployed, now sought to consolidate *Het Volk's* position by indicating that he would also travel to Johannesburg in order to attend the Mayor's emergency meeting on 9 March. This meeting attracted not only Smuts and H C Hull from the government's front bench, but more than a half-dozen Members of the Legislative Assembly, George Goch, L S Reyersbach and Lionel Phillips for the mining industry, representatives from various charitable organisations, virtually all of the town's ministers of religion, various other prominent citizens and the government's two Inspectors of White Labour. Perhaps the only prominent local person conspicuously absent from this important gathering was the unhappy and politically isolated Member of the Legislative Assembly for Vrededorp – F E T Krause.[140]

The meeting was opened with an address from the Chairman of the Transvaal Indigency Commission, J W Quinn, who dwelt on the familiar distinction between the deserving and undeserving poor and then proposed the appointment of a broadly based committee to deal with the problems of unemployment in Johannesburg. The tone and direction of the debate that followed, however, was set by three speakers affiliated to the Independent Labour Party who pointed out that 'charity was a safety valve for capitalism' and that more radical solutions ought therefore to be sought. Councillor Wilfred Walker, who had been closely involved with the municipality's relief works programme, was of the opinion that most of their difficulties stemmed from the fact that they 'were attempting to build up the country on the foundation of the niggers'. Harry Sampson, MLA, and yet another councillor, J J Ware, took this as their cue to propose an unsuccessful amendment to Quinn's motion which urged the government to open a state mine worked exclusively by white labour and to offer those of the European unemployed who were 'stranded' on the Reef a free rail passage out of the country.[141]

In his reply to these speeches and one in between by Lionel Phillips, the Colonial Secretary sought to steer a course which avoided a head-on collision with the representatives of either capital or labour. Smuts acknowledged that, as far as the economy was concerned, it was possible that 'the foundation might be rotten' – an admission which accommodated the many ILP members present. He continued to warn the advocates of a 'white labour' policy that the government's experiments on the railways had hardly been an unqualified success and that 'it was one thing gradually to introduce a principle the value of which they understood and believed in, and it was quite another to upset the whole economic condition of society'.[142] It was precisely because he did not want to upset the whole economic condition of society that the Colonial Secretary then appealed to the mine owners – not 'in a spirit of criticism, but in a spirit of genuine goodwill and fellow-feeling' – to do their duty and take on more unskilled workers. Then, in a glance over his shoulder at his own and more immediate political constituency, Smuts offered a lengthy outline of *Het Volk*'s plans for a land settlement scheme. The Colonial Secretary rounded off his address by strongly supporting J W Quinn's plea for the appointment of a broadly based committee to tackle the problem of local unemployment.

The Rand Unemployed Investigation Committee (RUIC) which came into being as a result of this meeting temporarily ousted the Rand Aid Association and for the next 18 months – until the economy again improved in mid-1909 – it became the controlling relief agency in Johannesburg. The creation of RUIC marked a shift from a relatively narrowly focused charity drive mounted by the mine owners and the state, to a more broadly based effort by the ruling classes in which they were forced to acknowledge the need to provide both relief *and* jobs for the unskilled whites of the city's western suburbs. While at one level this might simply be interpreted as a pragmatic change from above in the ruling classes' strategy for dealing with the reserve army of labour during a depression, at another – and deeper level – it also demonstrates just how serious and vibrant the challenge from below was during this period of marked class struggle. From being solely the objects of charity under the Rand Aid Association, organised elements of the white working class became partners – albeit very minor partners – in the planning of relief and job-creating possibilities under RUIC. At least some of these realities were reflected in the composition of the new committee which was constituted from: The Mayor of Johannesburg – James Thompson (Chairman), the President of the Chamber of Mines – Lionel Phillips, the Chairman of the Mine Managers' Association, the Mayors of the different municipalities along the Reef, the Chairman of the Indigency Commission, a Government Inspector of White Labour – R Shanks, two delegates from the Rand Aid Association, the Chairman of the Trades and Labour Council, and two representatives of the Unemployed Organisation (by now a full affiliate of the ILP) – Harry Sampson and Wilfred Walker.[143]

Three days after its formation on 11 March 1908, the members of this formidable committee met for the first time in an attempt to ease the problem of unemployment in Johannesburg and some of the smaller Reef towns. As representatives of the potentially largest employers – the mines and the municipality – Lionel Phillips and James Thompson played the dominant roles in the deliberations and the two men soon agreed on the central elements of what was to become RUIC's major plan for job creation. The municipality, which already had some 400 men at work as trench-diggers on its sewerage system would, through the good offices of the Chamber of Mines, offer all of these men who had demonstrated their willingness and capacity to undertake hard manual labour permanent positions as unskilled workers on the mines. This manoeuvre would enable the municipality to take on and test a further 400 unskilled workers who would, in their turn, make their way to the mines where they would eventually be absorbed into the permanent labour force. In addition to this, RUIC would, through the relevant government departments, place smaller numbers of unskilled workers on the Main Reef Road works at Krugersdorp and on railway construction sites in the Transvaal countryside.[144]

In the last week of March 1908 the Johannesburg municipality started to implement the RUIC plan when it paid off all 400 of the men who had hitherto been employed as trench-diggers on the sewerage system. The members of this group, some of whom had been earning the minimum of five shillings a day but many of whom had managed to make between 10 and 15 shillings per day on piece-work, were then offered permanent positions as unskilled workers on those mines that were most accessible from the city's western suburbs.[145] Of these 400 men, 70 were unwilling to work on the mines under any circumstances and thus only 330 indicated their readiness – in principle – to give the offer further consideration. Of these 330 who reported to the mines on the first day. However, a further 198 refused to proceed when it became apparent that the positions they were being offered entailed working underground.[146] This meant that in the end – for one reason or another – only 132 of the original trench-diggers made the transition to the mines. The municipality which in the interim had reopened its books to accommodate 400 new trench-diggers was swamped with applications from over 1 500 unskilled workers – as before, the large majority of these being Afrikaners.[147]

Meanwhile, the 132 erstwhile trench-diggers who had been allocated to hand-drilling operations on the mines at piece-work rates were rapidly becoming disillusioned. Within 48 hours of their new jobs commencing, it became clear to these men that they had been forced to exchange unskilled manual labour in the open air at ten shillings a day, for dangerous semi-skilled work underground at rates which – at best – would allow them to earn two to three shillings a day.[148] This supposedly new deal for the unemployed during the darkest days of the depression aroused intense anger amongst a section of the working class which now believed that it was being cynically used in an experiment by the Chamber of Mines to undercut 'kaffir labour'.[149]

Early on the morning of 3 April, instead of reporting for work, the 132 former trench-diggers – most of whom were from Vrededorp – together with 150 or more of the city's unemployed met on the Market Square to discuss these grievances. At the end of the open-air discussions, a deputation of four under the leadership of G Murray of the Unemployed Organisation was elected to put their views to the Chairman of RUIC. While this four-man delegation set out to interview James Thompson, however, the column of 200-300 unemployed set out on a noisy demonstration of their own through the city centre. Marching and shouting their way through the financial quarter, the former trench-diggers and their followers paused only to vent their spleen at 'the bloodsuckers of Corner House' before turning towards Braamfontein where the municipal works on the sewerage system were still in progress with the aid of a new set of largely Afrikaner workers. Here the demonstrators successfully used a combination of persuasion and intimidation to convince the replacement trench-diggers to down tools 'until the dispute was settled'. The demonstrators then made their way back to the Market Square to await the report of the delegation which they had sent to the Chairman of the Rand Unemployed Investigation Committee.[150]

Murray and his team, in militant mood, met James Thompson and three of his fellow RUIC members – Shanks, Walker and Sutherland – in the library of the municipal offices. Murray pointed out to the Mayor that the 400 former trench-diggers considered that they had been 'deluded out of their sewerage jobs' into a cheap labour experiment by the 'bloodsuckers of Corner House' and his friends in the Chamber of Mines. All the men demanded to be reinstated in their former jobs which, as ratepayers, they in any case considered to be 'their own work'. Furthermore, Murray pointed out, 'certain unemployed who left their trenches to go to the mines had said that if anyone attempted to finish their trenches they still had a pick shank to clear them out of it'.[151]

The Chairman of RUIC and his colleagues were both dismayed and alarmed by these allegations of the fighting talk with which they were accompanied. Wilfred Walker, in particular, was concerned that the ILP would lose its credibility with the unemployed and strongly defended the town council against the charge that it had knowingly sent the former trench-diggers into a Chamber of Mines cheap labour experiment. Thompson assured Murray and his men that RUIC would consider the position as speedily as possible but, he concluded, 'violence was not going to help them, and if there was anything of the sort the responsibility was with them'. The deputation then withdrew.[152]

Back on the Market Square Murray related these proceedings to the

assembled unemployed who, after further discussion, passed two resolutions. The first, of a more general nature, called on the government to
examine 'the ignominious way in which the white workers of
Johannesburg had been treated after they had shown their willingness to
do servile labour'. The second, which more specifically reflected the sentiments of the men drawn from Vrededorp, called on the Prime Minister
and the Colonial Secretary to present themselves in the city 'to meet the
masses in order that they could show cause why land was not opened up
for the purposes of agriculture, and why work should not be immediately supplied to starving white workers'. Then, still angry, the men
abandoned the city centre and made their way to the Braamfontein
trenches to make sure that nobody worked until such time as 'a settlement' was arrived at.[153]

The outline of a settlement was reached within 24 hours. On the afternoon following their demonstration the unemployed were informed by
James Thompson that Shanks, the Inspector of White Labour, had – on
behalf of RUIC – negotiated the basis of a new arrangement with the
mine owners. In terms of the new scheme the former trench-diggers
would no longer be called upon to work underground at rates that competed with black labour, but would instead be allocated to surface jobs
which would enable them to earn between three and five shillings per
day. This suggestion apparently proved acceptable to the unemployed
who, after the proposal had been formally approved by RUIC a few days
later, returned to work.[154]

Over the next 18 months, as the economy gradually improved from April
1908 to October 1909, RUIC retained control over Johannesburg's reserve
army of labour without further major conflict. Besides co-ordinating the
city's relief operations so as to avoid the problem of 'indiscriminate charity', RUIC during the same period succeeded in placing 550 men on government public works, 652 on the municipality's relief works and over
3 000 men in positions as unskilled workers on the mines. The latter exercise, however, no longer held much appeal for the mine owners and
RUIC officially described the results as being 'disappointing' while the
work was seen as simply constituting 'another form of charity'. In addition to this a couple of hundred urban Afrikaners were placed on various land settlements in the Transvaal countryside after the Indigency
Commission had presented its report in July 1908.[155]

All of these jobs, however, as well as the conditions attached to them,
had been won from the ruling classes during the course of the struggle
that had been waged by the unemployed and the workers from late 1906
onwards, and nowhere had that struggle been more intensely fought

than in Vrededorp. Between 1906 and 1908, a substantial part of the Afrikaner proletariat that had been developing in the city's western suburbs since 1896 came – for the first time – to self-consciously view itself as part of the working class. To the distress of certain *Het Volk* notables in general, and the hapless F E T Krause in particular, these ideas continued to flow through a large part of Vrededorp's political channels for some time after the storms of the depression had passed.

Amongst the first to detect this development in the political thought of the Afrikaner workers was the Chairman of the Vrededorp Vigilance Association, S A Smit. From at least the time of the miners' strike Smit had shown considerable interest in the labour movement and when he and Krause had been left politically up-staged by Das and his colleagues in early 1908 this interest increased. Although he never came out openly in support of the Labour Party between 1907 and 1910, Smit consistently encouraged its activities while, at the same time, he sought to avoid a head-on confrontation with Afrikaner nationalists. In July 1908, for example, it was Smit who presided at the meeting when the Labour Party first sought to establish a branch in Vrededorp. On this occasion he 'criticised the attitude of the Nationalist Party towards the working class interests on the Rand'.[156]

It was also during the same year, 1908, that S A Smit was returned as a town councillor for Vrededorp. This election not only reflected the grass-roots support which Smit enjoyed in the constituency, it also succeeded in thrusting him into even more direct contract with the numerous Labour Party activists on the council. From *Het Volk*'s point of view, however, this growing tendency for urban Afrikaners to sympathise with the labour movement was unfortunately not confined to the Rand; it also manifested itself to a considerable degree in the only other sizeable pool of Afrikaner workers in the Transvaal in Pretoria. By mid-1909, when the economy had improved somewhat and the leadership had more time to reflect on such matters, *Het Volk* was giving serious consideration to the problem of Afrikaner working-class consciousness.

Early in October 1909, at the Empire Hall in Pretoria, *Het Volk* launched an 'independent' Dutch Labour Society named *Arbeid Adelt* – 'Labour Ennobles'. In his opening address to a meeting attended by over 300 workers the Chairman, J J Naude, pointed out that the need for 'a Labour Society for Dutch-speaking people had been felt for a long time'. The essential difference between the new organisation 'and the English Labour Party was that in *Arbeid Adelt* most of the members were unskilled'. While the existing labour movement would continue to look after the interests of the skilled workers, such as the English craftsmen, *Arbeid Adelt* would protect most of those who were unskilled or unemployed – the Afrikaners. Naude, a long-time activist amongst the Pretoria unemployed, then went out of his way to deny allegations that the new organisation was simply 'a daughter of *Het Volk*' by saying that *Arbeid Adelt* had 'nothing to do with politics' – a claim that was promptly denied by one of the next speakers, Advocate Gregorowski MLA, who bluntly stated that as far as he could see all those present were 'good members of *Het Volk*'.[157]

Back on the Rand, F E T Krause – and to a lesser extent S A Smit – were quick to spot the possibilities which the new organisation could offer them in Vrededorp. A Dutch labour society under the control of *Het Volk* which could help arrest the drift in sympathy towards the Labour Party held obvious appeal for Krause who was always somewhat at a loss as how to best deal with his volatile working-class constituency. For Smit, on the other hand, an involvement in *Arbeid Adelt* would help to maintain his balance on the tightrope that he had been walking between the labour movement and *Het Volk*. Both men thus readily agreed to support the new organisation when it sought to expand to Johannesburg.

On Saturday night, 16 January 1910, Krause presided over the inaugural meeting of *Arbeid Adelt* held at the government school in Vrededorp. This well-attended gathering followed a familiar pattern. After the chairman had indicated the desire of the new organisation to protect the interests of unskilled and unemployed workers, J J Naude outlined the remaining objectives of the association which already had 700 members – laying particular stress on *Arbeid Adelt*'s efforts to get the children of the poor trade apprenticeships. E Rooth MLA and J Alleman, Government Inspector of White Labour on the Railways, then rounded off the addresses for the evening – the former emphasising that the society was 'a non-political body' and the latter pointing out that the 'heads of the administration' were 'very sympathetic' to the movement and that they could therefore look forward to the co-operation of the government.[158]

Vrededorp gave the promoters of the new labour society an enthusiastic reception. Both as unskilled workers and as members of the unemployed these men knew, from bitter first-hand experience, the strengths and weaknesses of a labour movement that was narrowly constructed around craft unionism. In *Arbeid Adelt* then, these Afrikaners saw the possibility of becoming involved in a wider working-class movement on a sustained basis – an opportunity which had previously always been denied to them as they staggered through one capitalist crisis after another. At the end of the meeting, therefore, they decided to appoint seven members to the local committee of *Arbeid Adelt* and to open an office for the organisation in Tol Street. Within two weeks the Vrededorp branch of *Arbeid Adelt* boasted a membership of 100 while back in Pretoria the promoters spoke enthusiastically about expanding the movement to Boksburg, Germiston and Krugersdorp.[159]

But if in 1910 the Afrikaners of the Rand already knew about the limitations of craft unionism, they were only beginning to experience what the nationalist embrace of a working-class movement entailed. Within days of the opening of the Tol Street office it became clear to the workers, and particularly the unemployed of Vrededorp, that their hopes and ambitions were being channelled down all too familiar government avenues – the Inspector of White Labour, relief works on the railways or the land settlement schemes. The sense of disillusionment which this caused spread rapidly through the community and by mid-March the majority of members of the 'labour society' had come to the conclusion that it was simply a 'propaganda arm' for *Het Volk* and taken the active step of resigning from the organisation. In Vrededorp, *Arbeid Adelt* was all of a six-week wonder.[160]

The collapse of *Arbeid Adelt*, followed shortly thereafter by the absorption of *Het Volk* into the South African Party as the Union came into being, once again left the Afrikaner workers of Vrededorp without any obvious party-political brokers. In a community where poverty and unemployment continued to remain at a high level, however, the need for relief and jobs did not wait on national political developments and nobody appreciated this more than the indefatigable S A Smit. Throughout the period 1908-11, and indeed for some years thereafter, Smit made skilful use of his position on the town council to place many of his poorest constituents on the municipal relief works – trench-digging on the sewerage system by now having become an almost permanent feature of Johannesburg's unskilled labour market for whites.[161]

Whether it was his growing indebtedness to his colleagues on the town council or the space created by the departure of the Transvaal nationalists for the debating chambers of Cape Town – or, more likely, a combination of both – S A Smit during this period came, to an ever-increasing degree, to see his political future as resting with labour. On 1 July 1911, at a large meeting in Vrededorp, 'the only Afrikander who had ever been behind the scenes at Trades Hall', finally took the plunge and publicly joined the Labour Party. Given Smit's considerable personal popularity amongst Afrikaner workers, the Labour Party looked upon this formal act of allegiance by the 'Mayor of Vrededorp' as an event of considerable political importance.[162]

In the rowdy municipal election meetings that followed, however, Smit soon discovered that while most of his supporters had turned left with him, there were still a significant number of stragglers on the right who hankered after nationalism. In an attempt to cope with this problem Smit was forced to call in an old political debt and ask F E T Krause to campaign on his behalf. In an ironic reversal of roles, Vrededorp audiences now heard an unlikely Krause singing the praises of Smit, and in a distinctly lower key, those of the Labour Party. As the political reporter of *The Star* noted with wry amusement: 'Mr S A Smit is performing a gymnastic turn which involves hanging to the Nationalists with his feet and gripping the Labour Party with his hands.'[163]

But the purists of the Labour Party had no taste for such political gymnastics and in May 1912 Smit was forced to resign from the party. This time several of Smit's supporters stayed on and did not immediately follow their spokesman back into the arms of the South African party, and thus right up to the outbreak of the war the Labour Party continued to enjoy a significant following in Vrededorp. Smit in the meantime continued his drift to the right when, in July 1914, he and a number of his supporters abandoned the South African Party in order to establish a new branch of the Nationalist Party.[164]

As always, however, this pronounced fluctuation in Vrededorp's political weather was ultimately determined by the underlying realities of an economic climate which – although to a lesser degree than in 1896-7 or 1906-8 – continued to be dominated by poverty and unemployment. Neither this ongoing political ferment nor its economic causes were lost on Johannesburg's ruling classes who continued to view this volatile white working-class community with a mixture of fear and genuine concern. Thus when the town council was forced, through financial constraints, to curtail its expenditure on the maintenance of this reserve army of labour by 1914 – by abandoning its expensive municipal relief works which had been running continuously since 1906, and by ceasing to contribute to local charitable bodies such as the Rand Aid Association – it was particularly anxious that the state should assume the burden of poor relief.[165]

In its submissions to the Relief and Grants-in-Aid Commission in May 1914, the Johannesburg Town Council contended that the unskilled workers of the western suburbs, 'instead of getting into other spheres of employment became a powerful influence in municipal elections to secure an increase in their wages, the standard of which was now six and sixpence'. More specifically, it was suggested that in Vrededorp:

> ... there was growing up a population poverty stricken, ignorant, and a danger to the community. This population was the bane of all political effort. Every political party truckled to this mass of voters and endeavoured to find employment for them. The mass had overturned every political party, and would overturn any political party which might be in power unless a remedy was provided to remove their appalling poverty and degradation.[166]

More eloquent testimony to the strength and vitality of this section of the Afrikaner working-class struggle could hardly be constructed. If it had been necessary, however, members of Kruger's government, the Milner administration, *Het Volk*, *Arbeid Adelt*, the Labour Party and the South African Party could all have offered additional evidence of Vrededorp's restless search for political shelter. But then perhaps it is inevitable that, under capitalism, the poor and the unemployed should be politically homeless.

CONCLUSION

For some Afrikaners, the discovery of gold on the Witwatersrand during the mid-1880s opened up a limited range of economic opportunities which allowed them to become directly involved in the subsequent development of the mining industry. Of these, several were farmers who used the sale of their land as the economic device with which to secure a share in the new mining ventures. Others, more numerous and with notably less success, attempted to negotiate the more difficult terrain that lay between the status of 'digger' on the one hand, and that of mining company shareholder on the other.

But for the vast majority of Afrikaners – who in the earliest years could become neither mine owners nor unskilled workers in the industry – the discovery of gold brought, at best, rather more indirect opportunities. The growth of the Witwatersrand as a produce market, for example, hastened the arrival of capitalist agriculture in the countryside and while this certainly strengthened the position of many Afrikaner farmers it simultaneously impoverished hundreds of their *bywoner* tenants. Even for the distressed members of this latter category, however, the emergence of the Rand offered some economic consolation during the closing years of the nineteenth century.

In the decade between 1886 and 1896 in particular, and to a lesser extent in the years thereafter until 1906, the growth of Johannesburg allowed thousands of poor *bywoners* to establish a precarious economic presence in the city in the fields of transport riding, cab driving and brickmaking. Despite the vulnerable economic position which they occupied within the local economy, the members of these groups were sufficiently successful in their sale of goods and services for Afrikaner unemployment to remain at a relatively low level throughout the first decade of the city's development. It was only after the transport riders had been defeated by the railways, the cab drivers by the electric tramway, and the small brickmakers by the capitalist companies that chronic and extensive Afrikaner unemployment became a notable feature of the urban areas. The significance of 1896-7 as a date in the history of Afrikaner proletarianisation lies not only in the increased flow of *bywoners* to the towns occasioned by a new series of rural disasters, but in the fact that it also marks the point where these sectors of the urban economy started to collapse in the face of broader capitalist development. On the Witwatersrand there was thus an urban as well as a rural road into the Afrikaner working class and it is therefore insufficient to simply note 'the increasing number of "poor whites" drifting into the towns'[167] or to chart 'rural failures'[168] when attempting to account for its growth.

As might be expected, those Afrikaners who found themselves being pushed down the urban road into the working class vigorously resisted the process of proletarianisation – the transport riders in several instances resorting to sabotage. The cab drivers and the brickmakers instead made use of their political access to the Kruger government in various attempts either to deflect or delay the capitalist onslaught to which they were being subjected. In these efforts they were not always entirely unsuccessful. The cab drivers undoubtedly helped to delay the introduction of the electric tramway system in Johannesburg while the brickmakers obtained both an alternative site for their businesses as well as the promise of a rail connection from the Kruger government. But, in the end, the demands of an expanding capitalist economy assured the economic demise of transport riders, cab drivers and brickmakers alike.

Once they had been forced into the reserve army of labour as unskilled workers, however, these Afrikaners showed – both before and after the South African War – that they had lost little of their capacity to resist. During periods of crisis, such as 1896-7 and 1906-8, angry unemployed Afrikaner workers took to the streets – sometimes with, but usually without the support of their more skilled European counterparts – to bring home the extent of their plight to the ruling classes. It was largely through these militant demonstrations that the poor of Vrededorp extracted concessions in the form of charity, relief works or white labour experiments from the mine owners, the municipality and the state.

Organised charity's origins in Johannesburg lay, in the first instance, in an attempt by a section of the mine owners to exert political influence and control over unemployed English miners via the Present Help League in the period leading up to the South African War. After the war this programme was slightly modified and placed on a more established basis when Milner and the mine owners – drawing on the model of the Charity Organisation Society in London – established the Rand Aid Association to help cushion the blow of unemployment in the years after demobilisation. But, although the Present Help League and the Rand Aid Association had both been created with the 'single' skilled English craftsman in mind, both organisations found that with the passage of time the bulk of their resources had to be devoted to married unskilled Afrikaner workers. After reconstruction and the assumption of power by *Het Volk*, the mine owners and the government – for different reasons – lost some of their enthusiasm for the work of the Rand Aid Association. It was partly as a result of this, and largely because of a new and vigorous thrust by the Afrikaner unemployed, that the Rand Unemployed Investigation Committee came into being in March 1908. The latter organisation, which was constituted from a more broadly based coalition of class interests, reflected a stark political reality – namely, that after 1906 it was the unskilled workers of Vrededorp who did most to determine the nature and pattern of charity in the city. In Johannesburg, as elsewhere, 'charity' was *won* from the ruling classes – it derived from class struggle in the streets rather than from benevolence in the boardroom.

But perhaps even more significant than these gains made in the realms of charity were the achievements of the Afrikaner unemployed in obtaining 'relief work'. In the 28-year period under review here, the state and the Johannesburg municipality were, between them, forced to maintain relief works for at least ten of those years. Large sections of the Main Reef Road (1898-9), most of the trenches for Johannesburg's water-borne sewerage system (1906-14), and portions of the rail network in the Transvaal countryside (1906-14) were all constructed with white labour drawn from Fordsburg, Vrededorp and Newlands. Unemployed Afrikaners, however, did more than merely secure work as unskilled manual labourers: through exercising their political muscle they also did much to determine the wage rates attached to these jobs. This action not only increased wages for such unskilled labour between 1906 and 1914; indirectly it also materially influenced the mining industry's experiments with cheap white labour in 1897 and 1908. The 'failure' of Afrikaners to accept positions as unskilled mineworkers at 'economic rates' during periods of recession can only be understood within the context of their success in achieving alternative employment at higher wages on relief works. It is only by neglecting to examine these important dimensions of the class struggle that one could come to the conclusion that during this period poor whites were 'an extremely disorganised stratum with little power on their own to enforce even limited economic demands'.[169]

It was during the course of this struggle – first while resisting the ravages of proletarianisation, and then while attempting to win employment at a living wage – that urban Afrikaners came to perceive themselves in class terms. Given the pace of capitalist development on the Witwatersrand at the turn of the century, this consciousness did not take long to emerge. In 1893 the Braamfontein brickmakers pointed out in a petition to Kruger that they were 'poor people whose sole income derived from brickmaking', and that if they were not afforded a measure of state protection the entire industry would rapidly fall into the hands of the 'rich speculators'.[170] In 1896 the cab drivers appealed to the State

President and the Members of the Executive Committee as the 'protectors of the working classes'[171] in an attempt to maintain the tariff structure in their trade; while eight months later, in August 1897, the police had to come to the rescue of the editor of the *Standard and Diggers' News* who had incurred the wrath of angry unemployed Afrikaner workers demonstrating in the city centre.

Immediately after the South African War there was further recognition of the threat which Johannesburg's Afrikaner unemployed posed to the ruling classes. Acting in accordance with Milner's political maxim that 'among civilised peoples of more or less equal size that one will be, as it will deserve to be, the strongest, which is most successful in removing the causes of class antagonism in its midst', the incoming British administration embarked on a programme of social engineering to disperse the city's working classes.[172] It was partly as a consequence of this that the racially integrated inner-city ghetto of Burgersdorp gave way to Newtown, and that most of the Afrikaner unemployed found themselves concentrated in Vrededorp.

But, for all this, Vrededorp remained one of the principal sources of class antagonism in Johannesburg and, as half-a-dozen political movements discovered to their cost between 1906 and 1914, one that was notoriously difficult to win and control. In their restless search for political direction the unskilled Afrikaner workers of Vrededorp demonstrated not only an aggressive working-class consciousness, but also a considerable degree of acumen – as when in 1910 it took them six weeks to try on and reject the yoke of a nationalist-dominated labour movement. That in the succeeding decades the same workers should have fallen prey to the nets of a narrow nationalism is one of the many tragedies of South Africa.

4

THE REGIMENT OF THE HILLS
– *UMKOSI WEZINTABA*

The Witwatersrand's lumpenproletarian army, 1890-1920[1]

Since the mid-1960s, and particularly since the publication of Fanon's *Wretched of the Earth*, sociologists and political scientists with an interest in the Third World have been debating the revolutionary potential of those heterogeneous groups that are marginal to society and which are collectively termed the 'lumpenproletariat'.[2] In an adjacent discipline but with a predominantly different geographical focus, scholars like Gareth Stedman Jones, George Rudé and Eric Hobsbawm have skilfully explored aspects of marginality in European history.[3] Despite the fact that several of these scholars share a common intellectual tradition and interest, there has been little cross-fertilisation between these distinct fields of research. This is hardly surprising since Third World social structures and European historical case studies cannot be expected to articulate particularly well. What was required were Third World case studies.[4]

Within the context of this broadly defined problem, the social historian of South Africa seems to have a special responsibility and the opportunity for particularly stimulating research. South Africa was the first country in Africa – and the only one with nineteenth-century roots – to undergo a fully-fledged industrial revolution. Within 75 years of gold being discovered on the Witwatersrand in 1886, capital transformed the face of the subcontinent and generated successive social formations which left an increasingly well-entrenched white ruling class. Those same transforming processes prised black South Africans off their land, separated them from their families, reduced them to the status of workers, and then ruthlessly reallocated them to the towns. There, on the bureaucratic leash of the pass laws, they were soon exposed to two sociologically similar institutions which served the rapidly industrialising economic system partic-

368

ularly well – the prisons and the mine compounds.[5] In a matter of decades, and sometimes perhaps within the space of even a single generation, Africans could successively be pastoralists, peasants, proletarians or prisoners. No blacks could have found this downward socio-economic spiral comfortable, and in those cases where the time-span was telescoped the experience must have been singularly traumatic. If ever there was scope for the study of 'marginality' then surely it is here.

This study, then, will be generally concerned with those marginalised black groups who at the turn of the century made their way to the heart of industrialised South Africa – the Witwatersrand. More specifically, it will focus on an association of men who, at different times between 1890 and 1920, called themselves 'The Regiment of the Hills' (*Umkosi Wezintaba*), 'The Regiment of Gaolbirds' (*Umkosi we Seneneem*), 'The People of the Stone' (*Abas'etsheni*), '*Nongoloza*', or 'Ninevites'. Through this study it is hoped to gain greater insight into the emergence of the black lumpen-proletariat, understand one of its more identifiable formations, access its potentialities and limitations, and to speculate on a form of African resistance hitherto neglected in South African historiography.

'THE REGIMENT OF THE HILLS', 1890-1899

In 1867, a Zulu woman named Nompopo presented her husband with a new son. The boy, one of six children born to the couple, evidently caused something of a stir on his arrival since his parents christened him Mzoozepi – meaning: 'Where did you find him?' Shortly after this event, the father, Numisimani Mathebula, must have considered that his grazing lands in Zululand had become inadequate since he moved his wife and children onto land owned by a Mr Tom Porter, 'near to where the River Tugela takes its course from the Drakensberg'. Numisimani, however, continued to spend most of his time at a kraal near Mzimkulu where he was an *induna* or headman whilst his dispersed family worked on the Porter farm in return for the use of land.

In 1883 the 16-year-old Mzoozepi Mathebula undertook his first six-month spell as a migrant labourer when he entered employment as a 'garden boy' with Mr Tom J of Harrismith. During the following three years he again undertook a spell of labour in Harrismith, this time acquiring new skills as a groom in the employ of a certain 'Mr M'. It was thus in about 1886, when he was 19 years old, that Mzoozepi once more entered service with Mr Tom J as a groom. It was also at this juncture that events occurred which helped to shape the future course of Mzoozepi's life, and the story is best told in his own words:

Before I had finished the first month of this employment one of the horses got lost. On informing my master of this he accused me of being negligent and blamed me for it and told me to go and look for it. I told him that as I was working in the garden on that day he could not hold me responsible for the loss, as all the horses were out grazing alone. He then threatened to place me in gaol if I did not go out and look for the horse that was missing, so I searched but did not find it. He then told me to go back to my kraal and work for Mr Tom P again, and added that Tom Porter would then bring to him the value of the horse that was lost. This amount would represent my wages for about two years ... On return I asked my brother whether it was the law, and whether he thought it fair that I should work and have my wages kept back to pay for the horse which I did not lose. He told me that I must work or they would put me in gaol and added that he did not want to see me there. I told him that I could not work for what I did not lose ...'[6]

Unimpressed with his brother's suggestion and aggrieved by what he felt to be an obvious injustice[7] the young Mathebula decided to escape from his 'employer'. When Tom Porter sent him and another black servant to the new Witwatersrand goldfields later in the same year, he took the opportunity to desert and to give himself a new name – Jan Note.

The transformation of Mzoozepi Mathebula to Jan Note was neither instant nor painless. For 12 months the young man was employed as a 'houseboy' in the Johannesburg suburb of Jeppe, and throughout this period he continued to fulfil his familial obligations by sending cash remittances to his mother via the many migrant friends who were making the journey back to Natal. The problem of Tom J's missing horse, however, pursued him relentlessly and more especially so when his elder brother came to work in the same town in about 1887. In yet another attempt to rid himself of his persecutors, Mzoozepi handed his brother £3 which was to be paid to Tom J in final settlement of the latter's loss. The brother willingly accepted this money, but he also insisted that Mzoozepi accompany him home so that he could be present when the cash was handed over to the white man. This the younger brother refused to do. Increasingly cynical about the European's sense of justice, Mzoozepi decided instead to once more make use of the cover provided by the sprawling mining town and search for new employment in a different suburb.[8]

The independent-minded young Note was, of course, not the only one to perceive Johannesburg as a centre of comparative freedom and opportunity in the late 1880s. Black and white migrants drawn from throughout southern Africa and Europe had come to the Witwatersrand in their thousands in the belief that if they could not make their fortunes then they would at least gain steady employment in the mushrooming town. For many the latter – and more modest – objective was easily achieved. For others, however, the problem was that the early mining economy not only boomed – periodically it slumped. As one of the Johannesburg newspapers editorialised in 1895: 'In South Africa it is invariably a case of feast or famine, of boom or bankruptcy. The happy medium is seldom hit.'[9] The effect of this constant influx of immigrant labour, when compounded by marked economic slumps, was to constantly 'marginalise' the most vulnerable lower echelons of the working class.[10] Yesterday's immigrant and today's worker were tomorrow's unemployed. It was at least partly for these reasons that redundant miners, unemployed clerks, failed businessmen, ex-colonial troopers, and a large number of deserters from the British armed services[11] transformed themselves into pimps, card-sharps, canteen pianists, bottle collectors, billiard markers, fences, skittle-alley attendants, petty thieves, burglars, safe robbers, illicit liquor sellers or highway robbers.[12] When Jan Note moved from Jeppe to Turffontein and 'got a job as a kitchen boy and groom to four single men who were living in a house at the foot of a hill near a small railway station'[13] he unconsciously stumbled across one of the many entrances to the 'white' underworld.[14]

Two of his new employers at Turffontein, Tyson and McDonald, gave the black servant some rather curious instructions and in return offered to remunerate him comparatively generously. He was not to allow any of his black friends near the house, he was to attend to the horses most carefully and just in case the groom failed to understand the message they showed him a revolver and threatened to shoot him should he disobey. Jan Note did not disobey, but he did observe that his new employers kept rather strange hours:

> After breakfast the four men would go out at about 8 or 9 a.m. on their horses and would return at midday for dinner and remain at home until it was dusk. They would then go out again and not return until about midnight. They always seemed to bring back some money with them and I used to see them counting it at night.[15]

It presumably took the young man very little time to realise that he was in fact being employed by a gang of European criminals but, at a wage of £6 per month, he would have been equally quick to appreciate the virtue of silence.[16]

It was probably during 1888, after a few months of 'loyal' service, that Tyson first invited Note on an expedition. In the succeeding months, still cast in the role of black servant, Note joined the gang on several expeditions, serving a criminal apprenticeship by observation. He saw how Tyson and his men held up passenger coaches and robbed white travellers, ambushed the company carts that conveyed the workers' wages to the more isolated gold mines[17] and how the *abathelisi* or 'tax collector' trick could extract small but constant sums of cash from black workers. Here the gang would approach a party of African travellers pretending to be policemen, demand to see a document such as a pass or vaccination certificate, handcuff the victims while 'inspecting' them, and then remove their money before releasing them. In this case the gang simply did what countless official state robbers – border guards, police, customs officials and railway conductors – did to migrants throughout southern Africa.[18]

Whilst learning these basics of the criminal craft Note was presumably willing to tolerate his role as 'servant'. Crime and the colour bar, however, were not readily compatible. Given the size of the gang's takings and his modest wage, as well as his pride and well-developed sense of justice, it did not take Note long to become discontented with his lot as white man's 'boy'. In the belief that there were probably greater earnings to be made if he worked with criminals of his own colour, Note decided to break with Tyson's gang and to seek out the members of the Witwatersrand's black underworld.

Working his way along the particular ethnic cleavages of black society with which he was most familiar, Note soon discovered that most of the Reef's Zulu-speaking petty thieves and minor criminals – the *izigebengu* – did not live within the more densely populated urban areas. Hounded and harassed in the towns by the police and pass laws, most of the *izigebengu* had taken refuge in the nearby Klipriversberg hills immediately to the south of Johannesburg.[19] There, living in the kloofs and caves of a place they called 'Shabalawawa' some 200 men, women and children had placed themselves under the leadership of a man named Nohlopa who hailed from Kwabe in Zululand.[20] At the heart of this loosely knit community, however, there was also a more hardened core of brigands and it did not take long for a man with Note's talent and spirit to bring himself to the notice of these *izigelekeqe*. Within a short period of time Note attained the position of *induna* within the community, acting as Nohlopa's closest adviser and assistant.

It was probably at some time during 1889 that the community at Shabalawawa first started to experience a series of organisational and ideological tremors in their mountain stronghold. First, the inhabitants were startled to learn that their leader, Nohlopa, had been arrested and convicted for breaking into a tailor's shop in Kerk Street, Johannesburg. A second surprise also lay in store for them. While serving his sentence Nohlopa learned to read and write and spent a considerable amount of his time studying the Bible. On his release he returned to the Klipriversberg and, after discussions with Note, announced to the assembled ranks that he no longer wished to be associated with the underworld and that in future he would spend his time preaching to his black brothers on the Rand. This decision left the *izigelekeqe* under the undisputed leadership of Jan Note for the first time.

Shortly after these events the new leader started to do a little reading of his own. Using that same splendidly ambiguous text that had so influenced Nohlopa – the Bible – he derived inspiration which drove him in a radically different direction.[21] It was the Old Testament book of *Naham* which particularly impressed Note and in it he read 'about the great state Nineveh which rebelled against the Lord and I selected that name for my gang as rebels against the Government's law'.[22] To this generalised ideological vision Note added vital paramilitary conceptions, sending the really powerful shock waves through Shabalawawa which transformed it from a loosely organised underworld community into the more tightly knit *Umkosi Wezintaba* – the Regiment of the Hills. As Note himself put it later:

> The system I introduced was as follows: I myself was the *Inkoos Nkulu* or king. Then I had an *Induna Inkulu* styled lord and corresponding to the Governor-General. Then I had another lord who was looked upon as father of us all and styled *Nonsala*. Then I had my government who were known by numbers, number one to four. I also had my fighting general on the model of the Boer *vecht* general. The administration of justice was confided to a judge for serious cases and a landdrost for petty cases. The medical side was entrusted to a chief doctor or *Inyanga*. Further I had colonels, captains, sergeant-majors and sergeants in charge of the rank and file, the *Amasoja* or *Shosi* – soldiers.[23]

'This reorganisation', the 'king' pertinently pointed out, 'took place in the hills of Johannesburg several years before the 1899 war was dreamed of.'

Just how extensive, active or successful Note's reorganised *izigelekeqe* were, however, is extremely difficult to assess. What is generally known is that the decade leading up to the Anglo-Boer War was a particularly successful one for highway robbers in the South African Republic.[24] This is more especially true of the early 1890s, prior to the arrival of the railways on the Witwatersrand, when there were large African labour flows which brigands could capitalise on. In 1890, for example, it was estimated that about 3 000 black workers made their way on foot to the goldfields each month,[25] and in 1892 the mining magnate Hermann Eckstein estimated that there were about 1 000 Africans on the move between

Johannesburg and Kimberley at any one time.[26] Migrant labour on this scale, much of it funnelling through the Klipriversberg, must have made the environs of Shabalawawa a particularly happy hunting ground for highway robbers.[27] It is unlikely that the Regiment of the Hills failed to claim its share of the workers' wages that passed through the country-side.

Within Johannesburg itself there are also some tell-tale signs which point roughly in the direction of Shabalawawa. Early in 1890, for example, the *Standard and Diggers' News* complained about the activities of a well-organised gang of 'Zulu' burglars in the town.[28] Court cases arising from the *abathelisi* trick – especially those involving 'policemen' with their own 'ranks' – are even more suggestive.[29] More concrete still is Jan Note's own testimony that the gang penetrated the prisons of the South African Republic where it gained recruits and taught prisoners – including black miners and 'houseboys' – the organisational structure of *Umkosi Wezintaba*.

Although much of this early activity of the organisation was essentially of an anti-social nature, it was not exclusively so – a fact which testified to Note's influence and the more broadly based notions of justice which concerned the Regiment of the Hills during its formative years. In June 1896, for example, a country correspondent of the *Natal Witness* recounted how certain Zulu speakers who had worked in Johannesburg had reported to him how Africans there had formed themselves into a 'secret society' in order to protect themselves against injustices. His informants told him:

> When a man has a wrong to redress as, for instance, when his master has 'done him' out of his wages, he makes his grievance known to the *Izigebengu*, some of the members of which are thereupon told off to knock the offending master on the head. These watch their opportunity, and in due course carry out their orders. Reports say that the favourite method is to knock at the door of the former master at night, and if he opens it himself, he is there and then 'settled'. Should someone else open the door, an excuse is made ... and another occasion is awaited ... '*Ba gwenza*', a man of some standing said, '*ngoba ngu muzi onge na 'meteto'* – They do it because it is a town without law.[30]

Unfortunately, this illustration which resonates so strongly with the experience of the young Mzoozepi Mathebula, is the only example we have of this aspect of Note's organisation in the period before the South African War.

Much of the evidence relating to this early period, however, is scattered, fragmentary and circumstantial; and on balance it is probably best to see the years 1890-9 as simply constituting a broadly formative period for the Ninevite organisation. Up to the outbreak of the war, the Regiment developed in one of those 'types of human society which lie between the evolutionary phase of tribal and kinship organisation, and modern capitalist and industrial society'[31] and probably consisted largely of migrants and landless labourers.[32] Like the Mafia its origins lay in the countryside[33] and the early community of men, women and children at Shabalawawa operated in a rural milieu on the margins of the Witwatersrand where a state, with as yet limited coercive capacity, could not readily control its members. But under the new leadership of Note, the *Umkosi Wezintaba* had already begun its transformation into an essentially urban and exclusively male organisation based within the prisons and urban areas.[34]

Both the pace and trajectory of that transformation, however, were greatly enhanced by subsequent events and processes and of these three were of particular importance. First, the war itself and the social upheaval which it occasioned left its imprint on the Ninevite membership. Second, the development of the post-war organisation was largely fashioned within the context of an economic system that was industrialising more rapidly than ever before. Third, and most importantly, this accelerated economic development was accompanied – and in part made possible – by a marked increase in the coercive capacity of the state and the mining industry. It was because of this heightened coercive capacity that the Ninevites in the post-war period, to an ever-increasing extent, found themselves thrust into those exclusively male institutions which served the industrialising system to well – the prisons and the mine compounds. The influence of all of these factors could be detected as, after 1902, the Regiment of the Hills gave way to 'The People of the Stone' and '*Nongoloza*'.

'PEOPLE OF THE STONE' AND *NONGOLOZA*, 1902-1906

One of the initial effects of the war of 1899-1902 was to disperse a large part of the labouring population of the Witwatersrand throughout southern Africa. In the earliest months of the conflict thousands of migrant workers poured into the towns seeking travelling passes and some means of organised transport to their rural homes. It seems reasonable to assume, therefore, that the general air of tension and anxiety also permeated into the ranks of the *izigelekeqe* in the Klipriversberg. Most of Note's men led a parasitic existence which relied on the regular robbery of small bands of migrant workers making their way through the countryside. The long-term viability of this mode of operation, however, was threatened by rapid large-scale movements and by a war which would probably terminate the flow of migrant labour altogether. For these and other reasons the inhabitants of Shabalawawa joined the black throng making its way into Johannesburg.

This sudden influx of impoverished black workers, infused with a strand of professional criminals at a time when the resources of the state were even more strained than usual, helped in the proliferation of crime in the town. The Kruger government thus had at least a partial interest in ensuring that most of the 'surplus' black population was evacuated to its rural hinterland as soon as possible. On a single day in October 1899 over 3 000 workers boarded the train for Mozambique whilst hundreds of others walked to the borders of the Republic. The workers from Natal and Zululand, however, found themselves in a slightly different situation, and as one author has noted:

> The office of J S Marwick, the Natal Native Agent in Johannesburg, was surrounded by thousands of African workers, aware that no arrangements had been made for their return home, and anxious lest their earnings be confiscated before they left the Republic.[35]

The predominantly Zulu-speaking crowd that congregated outside Marwick's office constituted the most natural meeting place for Note's troops and it seems that when the Agent got permission to march these migrants to the Transvaal-Natal border several of the *izigelekeqe* inserted themselves in the refugee column. Immediately after the war, the Natal African newspaper, *Ipepa lo Hlanga*, claimed that Marwick's party contained 'many persons of disrepute', including a 'self-organised gang of native desperadoes'.[36] It appears, therefore, that some of the most important of the criminal elements on the Witwatersrand complex were spread to other parts of southern Africa during the early months of the war.[37]

But if the beginning of the war saw the dispersal of Africans, there was ample opportunity for them to regroup as the conflict unfolded. Much of this regrouping was involuntary as the war threw together existing criminal elements and more law-abiding peasants experiencing the trauma of large-scale social upheaval. Several thousand rural people thus found themselves herded into the concentration camps set up by the invading British authorities. Many of those in need of a livelihood, including petty criminals, were employed in a variety of occupations by the British army – significantly, of those who subsequently joined the ranks of the Ninevites many gained their first experiences of both crime and urban conditions while serving with the British troops.[38] Those who found their way to prison stood the risk of being conscripted for service with military units in Natal, while on the Witwatersrand itself the most important meeting place was at the Ferreira Deep Mine compound where the army established a reception centre for 'vagrants' who were compelled to earn the five shillings necessary for a pass by stone-breaking.

By their very nature the concentration camps, prisons and compounds exercised a high degree of control over their black inmates. This was not solely a wartime exigency, for in several important respects these institutions served as models for those labour-repressive instruments that continued to function under the post-war administration. As has been noted in one study of the war and its subsequent effects on blacks:

> The Milner regime extended the pass department, created a system of courts to deal with breaches of masters and servants legislation, introduced a scheme to register the fingerprints of all mining employees to help identify workers who deserted, and established regulations to prohibit mining companies recruiting workers in labour districts. The possibility of African workers exchanging employers to find the most congenial working conditions was therefore considerably reduced.[39]

In 1903 the mining companies contributed to this coercion when they tightened up the functioning of their compounds, and in 1905 the new British administration opened the Cinderella Prison on the East Rand which – amongst other things – supplied local mines with convict labour.[40]

The web of coercive legislation and its supporting institutions of compounds, courts and prisons, besides reducing the mobility of black workers, also had some unintended consequences. Constant infractions of the pass laws in an industrial system with an increased law-enforcement capacity produced a labouring population characterised by its high degree of nominal 'criminal' experience, ensuring that the working class had great familiarity with the two similar institutions of prison and compound. Labourers and lumpenproletarians were forced to rub shoulders to a greater extent than they might otherwise have done. The pass laws and the newly efficient police system drew *all* Africans, law-abiding and law-evading alike, into the Witwatersrand complex and kept them there. It was perhaps predictable, therefore, that when Note's organisation re-emerged after the war it was more urban-based than before and that its natural home would be the prison-compound complex.

It is possible that the post-war Ninevite organisation first re-emerged amongst the 'stone-breakers' at the Ferreira Deep Mine compound. What is known with greater certainty, however, is the fact that the organisation existed in unmistakable form in other prisons immediately after the war. In 1904, J S Marwick – by then Assistant Secretary for Native Affairs in the Transvaal – had noted its presence in the prisons where its members referred to themselves as the 'People of the Stone'.[41] But from at least the same date, and more especially during the depression years of 1906-8, 'loafers', 'vagrants', the unemployed, petty criminals and those without passes also joined the society under yet another name for Jan Note – Nongoloza, the man with the piercing eyes. Whereas the People of the Stone met in prison, it would appear that those who joined *Nongoloza* did so in abandoned prospect holes, disused mine shafts, derelict buildings or old quarries.[42] By 1906 the Ninevite organisation was thus already operating on two fronts – one based inside and the other outside of the Witwatersrand prisons.

Despite the different conditions under which they operated, the People of the Stone and the *Nongoloza* shared important features which betrayed their common origin. Both associations were clearly based on the model devised by Note, and the *Abas' ethsheni* and the members of *Nongoloza* alike pledged their allegiance to him as 'king'. Moreover, both arms of the Ninevite organisation manifested a high incidence of homosexuality, particularly so after the post-war Chinese indentured labourers began to leave the compounds and be replaced in larger numbers by black migrant workers.[43] The mines as well as the prisons successfully excluded women from urban life and by 1906 when, under pressure from the missionaries the Chamber of Mines conducted an enquiry into 'unnatural native vice', it was:

> … common legend throughout the mines that a Shangaan named 'Sokisi' [possibly George Schoko, a noted Ninevite leader] had, while in prison [Cinderella?] practised unnatural vice, and that he had introduced the custom of keeping *izinkotshane* [boy wives] at the Brakpan Mines, from whence it spread until at the present day there is no doubt it is commonly practised throughout all the mines on the Witwatersrand.[44]

But for all the similarities between these two arms of the movement, the Ninevites did not achieve the same degree of organisation, unity and discipline before 1904 as they were to in the succeeding years. While this early stage of relative fluidity in the structure of the organisation can to some extent be explained by the dislocations caused by the war, it can perhaps also be partly accounted for by the absence of the man who the authorities claimed was 'held in superstitious veneration by the rank and file[45] and who was greeted in a hushed voice with the salute usually reserved for Zulu royalty – '*Bayete*'.[46] That 'short thick-set Zulu', about 30 years of age and apparently 'with no appearance to command respect'[47] was, of course, Jan Note.

THE NINEVITES IN THE ASCENDANT, 1906-1912

Regrettably, very little is known with any certainty about Jan Note's movements during the war or in the years immediately thereafter. It is just possible that the leader of the underworld for some time became a member of a gang of bandits – the 'Brigands of De Jager's Drift' – who terrorised a large part of northern Natal with a series of spectacular armed robberies during mid-1903.[48] Certainly the half-dozen bandits included amongst their number one *Nkulu Zulu* who, along with other members of the gang, was sentenced to a long term of imprisonment at Dundee in the same year.[49] If *Nkulu* was Note, however, he must have escaped from his Natal prison shortly thereafter since there is no doubt whatsoever that the chief Ninevite was back on the Witwatersrand 12 months later. In November 1904, a short-term prisoner appearing before the Johannesburg Prison Enquiry Commission gave a vivid account of how Note personally exercised control and discipline over fellow black inmates.[50]

On his release from prison in Johannesburg, Note and eight of his recruits formed a new gang which for several months during 1906 operated with considerable success as store and house-breakers in the Standerton district. But by early 1907 the police were getting sufficiently close to these *izigelekeqe* for the members of the gang to decide to disperse into northern Natal and Zululand. A few months after this Note was arrested and sentenced to another term of imprisonment in the Volksrust prison on the Natal-Transvaal border.

This small prison, however, held few terrors for Nongoloza and in mid-1908 he and two of his fellow inmates – William Masaku and 'Ben Cronje' – broke out of the Volksrust prison and into the local magistrate's court where they stole two revolvers and 75 rounds of ammunition before making their escape from the town. Further north-east, at the village of Wakkerstroom, the three men entered a home and fired at its elderly white occupant who resisted their demands for cash. The noise of the shooting soon attracted the attention of neighbours and when the local police sergeant and a European volunteer attempted to corner and arrest the invaders, the Ninevites again opened fire before staging a successful retreat. From there the three made their way north along the Swaziland border before turning towards the eastern Transvaal mining town of Barberton.

The unheralded arrival of the Ninevites in Barberton coincided with the more boldly proclaimed preparations for a civil reception to be held in a local hotel. At nightfall Note and his two black accomplices let themselves into the hotel dining-room where, after their long journey, they proceeded to make merry on the food and drink set aside for the white dignitaries of the following day. On leaving the premises, however, they were spotted by an African policeman who in a heady moment chose to pursue the Volksrust fugitives – a foolish decision since Nongoloza promptly rewarded him with a bullet through the leg. But, as in Wakkerstroom, the noise of the shooting attracted further attention and this time a slightly inebriated Note and Ben Cronje were captured – William Masaku successfully eluding the police for a further six months. Soon thereafter Note appeared in court charged with escape from lawful custody and several counts of attempted murder, and was sentenced to life imprisonment. From Barberton the authorities transported Note to Pretoria where they not only consciously placed him in the local prison, but also unconsciously dumped him within convenient distance of the very heartland of Ninevite country – the Witwatersrand's urban prison-compound complex.[51]

Within Pretoria Central Prison and more particularly within that section set aside for long-term black offenders – the so-called 'Reserve Camp' – Note at once set about the task of forging for himself a new and highly disciplined Ninevite corps. With the loyal and ruthless support of fellow black notables such as Meshine ('Government'), Jinoyi ('Fighting General'), Charlie ('Doctor') and Jim Dunde ('Judge'), Nongoloza and his followers ensured that the period 1908-10 was one of the most troubled and turbulent in the history of the prison.[52] Once he had reasserted his right to the title of *Nkosi Nkulu* or Great King within the prison, however, Note proceeded to extend his criminal empire to embrace the larger part of the Transvaal – from Pretoria in the north to Klipriver in the south, from Heidelberg in the east to Potchefstroom in the west. This he achieved over the next 48 months by uniting under his leadership various criminal gangs entrenched in regional strongholds and more especially those of the adjacent Witwatersrand.

To the immediate west of Johannesburg, Note succeeded in gaining the allegiance of 'Chief' George Schoko (alias 'Kleintje') and his gang which, centred on the abandoned prospect holes in the vicinity of Canada Junction, specialised in *abathelisi* robberies of workers making their way to and from the West Rand. Not far from this Nongoloza was supported by another important 'Chief' – Sam Nyambezi (alias 'Joseph') who, along with his followers, used the Crown Deep Mine compound as a base from which to raid and plunder the black townships to the southwest of the city. East of Johannesburg Note's most trusted follower was one Jan Mtembu who by 1912 was located at the Premier Mine near Pretoria, while within the Cinderella Prison at Boksburg – a nerve centre for the entire organisation – the Ninevites were under the control of Jim Mandende, a Xhosa who had been personally appointed by the *Nkosi Nkulu* when he had won his spurs back in the days of the South African

Republic. In the far south-east Nongoloza was represented by yet another 'Chief', Jacob Xaba, whose gang inhabited the open countryside between the mine compounds of Brakpan and Nigel and lived by robbery and stock theft. The amazing Note not only succeeded in uniting these five important brigand chiefs under his command, but by 1912 he could also rely on the support of at least ten other 'fighting generals' based in the mine compounds all along the line of reef.[53] At the height of his criminal career Nongoloza could count on the support of between 750 and 1 000 strongly committed Ninevites, the large majority of them being Zulus, but also including amongst their number Shangaans, Basutos, Xhosas and Swazis.[54]

That Note possessed extraordinary charisma seems beyond doubt. But even criminal empires are not built on personality alone and they also have more mundane requirements such as the need for communication. Nongoloza made sure that his wishes reached the Ninevite troops through an elaborate system of signals which could reach most corners of the Witwatersrand and which was ultimately based on the constant ebb and flow of pass offenders. New prison arrivals would pass on information of the organisation's outside activities while discharged prisoners – usually making their way to one of the half-dozen rickshaw yards in Johannesburg – would convey Note's wishes from prison. These 'rickshaw boys', whose occupation ideally suited them to the task, would then pass the messages on to the communications officers of the various gangs. Thus, Nkuku (alias 'Forage'), 'office boy' in the Number Two gang at Randfontein, apparently used to collect messages from the *Nkosi Nkulu* via a certain Mpilempile in a Jeppestown rickshaw yard.[55] Not all messages, however, passed via these intermediaries described by the police as 'recognised agents who disseminate orders and instructions to the members of the gangs outside'.[56] 'Top secret' or 'operations' information occasionally passed directly between gang leaders. Promotions within the organisation, for example, were sometimes discussed in letters between 'generals' from different regions[57] and mere 'office boys' or 'messengers' were not allowed access to such privileged information. Nongoloza's criminal army appears to have made use of a sophisticated two-tier communication system.

But while it was one thing for the *Nkosi Nkulu* and his 'generals' to issue orders, it was quite another to ensure that they were obeyed and the Ninevite army, as much as any other, had need of a disciplinary code to control its tough and sometimes individualistic troops. In this case, as in that of the communications system, it was the ceaseless flow of urban blacks into the prisons that enabled the army of the underworld to function. Although the organisation operated both inside and outside of the prisons, disciplining of the ranks for the most part took place within the confined space of the communal cells that characterised the Transvaal penal system – here there was no place to hide from Ninevite justice. Nongoloza and his officers could rest assured in the knowledge that sooner or later an infringement of the pass laws would inevitably deliver any defiant troops to their prison 'court'.

Lesser offences under the Ninevite disciplinary code centred on matters of status, privilege and prison etiquette. Any member who developed a fully fledged homosexual relationship with an *umfana* (boy), before having officially attained the rank of *ikhela* (Zulu male in traditional society with the chief's permission to marry), for example, stood to be tried before a 'magistrate'.[58] and to be punished by the withdrawal of prison privileges such as tobacco, food or sex. Those with rank who contravened the code stood to be demoted and also to sacrifice certain benefits while in prison.[59] More serious offences were immediately referred to superior courts where there were 'judges', 'prosecutors', 'doctors' and 'jurymen'. Charges brought in these higher courts invariably centred on breaches of Ninevite security, and the sentences were harsh and bloody. Those found guilty of passing on trivial information to the police or prison authorities could consider themselves lucky since they would simply have their front teeth knocked out. But more serious transgressors stood the risk of being stabbed through the shoulder blades with sharpened nails or of being sentenced to the equally unpleasant alternative of 'ballooning'. This consisted of tossing the victim with the aid of a blanket to greater and greater heights and then, at a prearranged signal, removing the blanket and allowing him to plummet to the concrete floor of the cell.[60]

Another form of severe punishment was the dreaded *shaya isigubhu* – the systematic beating of the ribs with clenched fists. 'Tomboek' Umfanawenduku, who was in the Pretoria prison at the time of Nongoloza, offered a first-hand account of this particular Ninevite ritual:

> The penalty inflicted as a rule is anything from three to ten blows. But before this penalty is inflicted they call their Doctor who is also a member of the gang, and he feels our pulse and orders the punishment reduced if he thinks the person is not very strong. He will reduce it from ten to five. I have on two occasions been assaulted in this manner, the first time it was at Pretoria. I had already joined their society when I was ordered to be tried as I was a native constable in the Transvaal Police prior to my arrest. I was taken before the Magistrate, a prisoner named 'Toby', and he punished me for being a native constable and sentenced me to be punished by means of the 'sigubu'. I was to receive twenty blows on each side of the ribs with clenched fists. A Doctor named Charlie, also a hard

labour prisoner, was called to examine and he ordered the punishment reduced to ten blows only. I was then taken into the middle of the room and told to stand straight up with my hands folded, and four members who rank as private soldiers detailed by the Captain. The four soldiers get around you, one at the near and front of you, and the Captain then orders them to attention. They then clench their fists and when he orders 'present arms' they extend their arms in a fighting attitude and continue this until he gives the order of 'sigubu' when each of the soldiers starts punching you from side to side until the Captain gives the order 'halt'. This is a very severe punishment and often when you cough a person brings up blood through the effects …[61]

But even the coughing of blood that came with *shaya isigubhu* was considered insufficient punishment for the worst offenders of all – for them only death was enough.

Unfortunately, we have few cases at present available which show precisely what the exact nature of the 'crimes' were that warranted the death sentence under the Ninevite code. One hapless victim, Matshayli Zungu, a Zulu miner from the Cason compound, had the misfortune to accidentally cross the path of a Boksburg branch of the Ninevites – a particularly tough gang composed of 14 members who included amongst their number several veterans from Pretoria Central and 'Blue Sky Gaol', Cinderella Prison. On being 'invited' to join the gang and choose himself an *inkhehla* Zungu made the fatal mistake of refusing. The 'Government' and the 'General' conferred briefly for a moment and then the 'General', Elijah Mazinyo, pronounced, 'I sentence you to the rope.' Zungu was promptly strangled with a handkerchief[62] after which the gang half-concealed the body in a hole in the wall of a nearby slimes dam. The affair ended with the arrest and execution of the 14 Ninevites.[63]

But the apparently random choice of a victim and the crudeness of the execution mark the Zungu murder as exceptional. More frequently, as one of the Witwatersrand detectives most familiar with the organisation noted, 'The orders for murder are … against natives who have formerly belonged to the gang and afterwards turned police informers.'[64] The police believed that some of these had been killed through having large doses of powdered glass administered to them, a refined procedure when compared with 'the rope',[65] while the same detective described what was perhaps the most cunning Ninevite method of all:

In prison, the death sentence is carried out in the following manner. The prisoner is strangled with a wet towel. The Executioners then chew mealies (maize) and stuff it down his throat. I am told that

383

natives so found have been certified cause of death [*sic*] due to choking whilst eating mealies.[66]

Thus in 1912 Nongoloza controlled an army which knew what his directives were and one which possessed a ruthlessly implemented if not universally understood disciplinary code. Those who are in control of armies, however, have not only to possess power, they also have to be seen to possess and exercise it. How were men who considered themselves to be 'judges', 'generals', 'doctors' and 'captains' to be distinguished from the ordinary mass of prisoners and proletarians herded into the conformity of 'total institutions'? Where did a compound or prison number end and a Ninevite begin?

In several respects this problem must have been as its most acute within the depersonalised culture of the prisons; nevertheless a new immate of the communal cells soon learnt who were the Ninevites and who, for example, the 'Scotlanders' were – a rival gang noted for their rejection of homosexuality.[67] The followers of Nongoloza were distinguished from the latter groups by the sacrifices of food and tobacco which the 'troops' made for their 'officers' and by their show trials and rituals. By 1912, however, an even more visible sign was invariably associated with the leaders of Note's army – the large 'IS' sign on the prison jacket which distinguished those prisoners serving an indeterminate sentence.[68] This insignia of the underworld elicited its own twisted form of respect in a twisted institution.

It was in the comparatively relaxed compounds and their immediate peri-urban surroundings, however, that the Ninevites could most fully and freely develop many of the more obvious features associated with an army. In the sub-culture of *Nongoloza* the 'troops' used their own distinctive slang: a 'bird' was an ignorant person, a 'buck' was a victim, the gang was the 'stone' and a person who 'came with the horses' was not to be trusted since he was either a spy or a policeman.[69] Like many soldiers Note's men had a reputation for their indulgences – in this case drinking the powerful working-class concoction called *ukhali* or smoking *dagga* (marijuana). In this connection it was perhaps also significant that the troopers referred to each other as *mgusas*, the flashily dressed members of a drinking society.[70] Outside of the immediate confines of the compound the soldiers of the underworld invariably carried sticks or coshes and drilled in time to the instructions of an 'officer' who brandished a knife.[71] Up to about 1910 the most distinctive part of the Ninevite uniform was apparently the hat, which was later discarded and by 1912 *mgusas* could most easily be recognised by the way in which they kept their trousers closely pinned to their ankles by the means of bicycle clips or string.[72]

Unlike some of its modern counterparts Jan Note's 'army' was not all dressed up with nowhere to go and very little to do. Its central concern was crime and its members knew exactly how to set about that business. The main thrust of that activity, however, seems to have shifted slightly between 1908 and 1912 as a subtle change in the rank-and-file composition of the Ninevite army took place.

Between 1906 and 1910 – but more especially between 1906 and 1908 during which period much of rural Natal was beset by the Bambatha rebellion and the Rand plagued by a serious economic depression – the police described the majority of Ninevite 'soldiers' or *amakhehla* as being recruited from the 'vagrant class'.[73] Many of these 'vagrants', pushed out of the rural economy and unable to be absorbed into the urban labour force, sought refuge in the more inaccessible *kopjes* of the central Witwatersrand area or even further afield in the eastern or western Transvaal, in mountain caves.[74] Working from these strongholds the Ninevites set to work concentrating on the *abathelisi* trick and various forms of armed robbery. Although the monotony of this pattern was sometimes broken with expeditions of house burglary most of this crime was directed against people – usually fellow Africans. The more urban of these bandits, however, were particularly vulnerable to arrest under the pass laws and as one detective noted:

> These vagrants have often told me that they have no fear of gaol, as it is much better than being outside where they are continually harassed by the police and asked for their passes.[75]

While this was perhaps something of an overstatement it was nevertheless true that this particular rural intake of Nongoloza's army soon learnt the need for a more sophisticated defence against the Transvaal pass system.

By 1910-11 many of these Ninevites had discovered that they could keep the police at bay by taking refuge in those large industrial forts which the state itself had assisted in developing – the mine compounds. Designed to keep people in, the compounds also effectively kept the police out.[76] In 1912 a frustrated Deputy Commissioner of Police noted that the continual police harassment of urban 'vagrants' for passes had 'driven [the Ninevites] into the mine compounds where they enlist as labourers and where they can enjoy all protection that is extended to registered mine boys ....'[77] Within this quasi-prison environment Nongoloza's recruiting officers – the so-called *MaSilvers* who took their name from one of Johannesburg's most notorious pimps of the 1890s, Joseph Silver – had a field day. As the economy improved through 1910-11 they steadily recruited new migrant workers into their 'army' and when the drought of 1912 pushed yet more peasants in the direction of the mines the Ninevites consolidated their new industrial base.

As migrant workers in the compounds rather than 'vagrants' in the surrounding hills started to join Note's organisation in greater numbers, so its criminal focus started to shift. By 1912 much of Nongoloza's army concentrated on store and housebreaking as its principal activity. Partly as a result of the shift in base noted above, the organisation's primary objective had become property rather than people. These Ninevite expeditions to acquire property became highly professional and sophisticated. At Randfontein, no burglary would take place until the 'number two gang', composed of juniors under the supervision of a *landdrost* ('magistrate') and a 'lieutenant', had filed its reconnaissance report. Only then would the older men and the senior officers who constituted 'number one gang' go out, usually to burgle an isolated store or home and invariably carrying with them the tools of their trade – screwdrivers, files, crowbars, jumpers, keys and occasionally guns. Thus tools that were employed underground for the benefit of the mine owners by day became instruments for the use of the worker-criminals by night. In addition such Ninevite squads would seek to avoid recognition and spread their operations by working different 'patches' and by swapping passes with units based in neighbouring territories. Nongoloza's followers in Heidelberg, for example, did much of their best work on 'borrowed' passes in the Boksburg North district.

As a result of these criminal sorties substantial quantities of loot, usually in the form of money or clothing, flowed into the mine compounds. How were these goods distributed? At first sight the fragmentary evidence seems promising for the reader in search of 'social bandits'. It is known that members of Nongoloza's army frequently shared clothing, including stolen property;[78] and also that after one Ninevite gang broke into Schwab's Eating House and Mine Store in 1912, the members returned to the compound and 'all the boys in the room were awakened and asked to have some meat as they had a bag full of it'.[79] However, the sharing of clothing is a common practice amongst the poor and the working classes, and in any case this appears to have been confined to gang members. Moreover, as far as the second report is concerned, meat deteriorates rapidly, and the apparent generosity of the Ninevites might have been born of a calculated need to minimise the risk of betrayal. None of this can therefore simply be construed as evidence of a type of 'Robin Hood' generosity.

It is certainly true that the Ninevite leaders did distribute patronage and occasional gifts to their followers, while the fact that they were called 'chiefs' by some also hints at a traditional redistributive function. However, once again there is no real evidence of any major redistribution of goods and it would appear that the leaders kept back a substantial part of the loot for themselves. Jan Note, in what was undoubtedly an exaggeration, claimed to have accumulated 'bags of money' but the same could hardly be said for most of his followers.[80] Such minor redistribution as did occur within the organisation appears to have been an incidental function of certain social relationships within the structure of the movement.

The lot of the poorest Ninevites of all – the *abafana* or boys – for example, was only marginally improved by their Ninevite membership. These, the hundreds of young lads between the ages of 13 and 16 who entered the Witwatersrand compounds during this period, constituted the poorest-paid workers in the industry and immediately attracted the attention of the *MaSilvers*. As an observer of the compounds noted in 1909:

> When new squads of boys came in the picaninnies are watched with anxious eyes, and proposals are made at the earliest opportunity, and 'matches' are made, and 'trueness' and 'fidelity' are demanded, and failure brings about a disturbance, and likely a row.[81]

These boys became the 'wives' of the *amakhehla* or soldiers in Nongoloza's army and were expected to play a similar role to that of more orthodox Zulu wives. Thus besides being sexual partners, the boys would clean, sew and cook, but no 'wives' would be allowed to participate in the economically more important criminal activities.[82] In return for their domestic services the *abafana* would receive gifts and money from their Ninevite husbands, and would usually be given their *khehla's* portion of the loot for safe-keeping.[83] It was to the limited extent that the poorly paid *abafana* benefited from such gifts that there was a marginal redistribution of goods amongst the Ninevites. But, in general, we can conclude that there is little evidence of a conscious egalitarianism in the Ninevite philosophy and that if anything the criminal spoils were distributed unequally within a hierarchical organisation.

This structured inequality, however, in no way dampened Ninevite enthusiasm for the movement or undermined the members' loyalty to Nongoloza. By mid-1912, when the Ninevite organisation was probably at its most developed, it was said to be gaining 'further adherents daily'.[84] Over two decades, Jan Note and his followers had developed an army with almost 1 000 members, a sophisticated system of communication, rigid discipline, subtle defences and a set of well-defined criminal objectives. From a motley group of peasant marginals who sought refuge from the police in the Klipriversberg had emerged a well-organised lumpen-worker alliance that held criminal control in the very heart of industrialised South Africa. Months before politically conscious blacks met

to form the African National Congress, a black army on the Witwatersrand with branches as far afield as Bloemfontein, Kimberley and
Pietermaritzburg was delivering a serious challenge to a repressive and
privileged white state.

Almost predictably, the severity of that challenge was first felt on the
East Rand where Cinderella Prison, a major stronghold of Nongoloza's
followers, was located. This prison disgorged a steady stream of offenders who had completed medium to long-term sentences – including
many Ninevites – into the surrounding areas. An ironic twist in the operation of the pass law system, however, ensured that many of these men
in Jan Note's 'army' found it difficult to get any distance beyond 'Blue
Sky' on their release, and this in turn meant that the Boksburg and
Benoni districts acted as reluctant hosts to some of the country's most
hardened professional criminals. Furthermore, as we have noted above,
after 1909 many Ninevites made conscious use of the pass laws in order
to gain employment in the nearby mine compounds. As a frustrated
Minister of Native Affairs was forced to note in 1913, 'it will be recognised that our powers are limited by the provision of Section 40 of the
Pass Regulations [which] requires that the released criminal be given the
opportunity of re-engaging himself'.[85] The net result of all of this was
that the East Rand experienced what the local Public Prosecutor termed
'frequent waves of crime' – especially housebreaking, robbery and
assault.[86]

On 20 June 1912 the officer commanding the Benoni police informed
his superior officer that the build-up of Ninevite strength in the district
had reached 'most serious' proportions.[87] Two days later the District
Commandant for the East Rand, Inspector M A Hartigan, brought the
matter to the attention of the Secretary of the Transvaal Police, pointing
out that Nongoloza's army had 'now attained a numerical strength and
organisation sufficient to warrant its receiving prompt and energetic
attention',[88] and from there the matter was referred to both the
Commissioner of Police and the Attorney General. By the end of the year
Nongoloza's army was under ministerial scrutiny and government was
examining 'government'. What had galvanised the state into action was
not simply the mounting Ninevite attack on property, serious as that
was; it was the fear that its law-enforcement capacity in the compounds
and cities was being seriously undermined. It had made the unpleasant
discovery that it could no longer rely on two of its most important sets
of collaborators – the *onongqayi* or black police and the industrial or compound 'police' – in running a labour-repressive economy.

The day-to-day functioning of the Witwatersrand's mining system
was secured by specially selected and uniformed black compound
'policemen'. These management lackeys with state support were respon-

sible for the discipline of the African labour force and for supplying the authorities with a constant stream of politico-economic intelligence.[89] Outside the compound gates the pass laws were enforced by their equally unpleasant fellow collaborators – the *onongqayi*, of whom, in his contemporary account, *Life Amongst the Coloured Miners of Johannesburg*, the black journalist, F Z S Peregrino had this to say:

> For a picture of the average Zulu policeman at Johannesburg I would depict this: A creature, giant-like and large as to proportions, ferocious and forbidding of aspect, most callously brutal of action and irredeemably ignorant.[90]

There was little love lost between these black collaborators and most African miners – and Nongoloza's men singled them out for particular, sometimes unmerciful attention, thereby, albeit in a largely apolitical fashion, helping to paralyse some of the black working class's most immediate oppressors.

The state was both concerned and dismayed by this paralysis. The police were shocked to learn that at the York Mine, Krugersdorp – a West Rand storm centre where, as early as January 1908 a party of 50 armed Ninevites had launched an open attack on three white constables who had attempted to interrupt their manoeuvres – 'everybody in the compound belonged to the society' by 1912, 'including the police boys'.[91] By August 1912 the Deputy Commissioner of Police was seriously considering the possibility of the *onongqayi* being infiltrated or otherwise demoralised by Nongoloza's army; and in January 1913 he informed his superiors in Pretoria that, 'I do not consider that the native police is at present capable of dealing effectively with native criminals.'[92] At the apex of its power the Ninevite challenge to the black collaborating arms of the state achieved, at very least, a stalemate situation. An increasingly powerful South African state had no taste for stalemate situations.

THE DECLINE OF THE NINEVITES, 1912-1920

On 16 December 1910 two prominent Ninevites – 'Chief' George Schoko, alias 'Kleintje', and Jim Ntlokonkulu, known in the underworld as 'The Giant with the Crooked Eyes' – set out for 'work' on the Main Reef Road in time-honoured fashion, assisted by two trusted lieutenants. At about noon they intercepted three black miners making their way to Maraisburg and immediately went into the *abathelisi* routine. Posing as detectives they first asked to see the workers' passes and then demanded their purses. When the workers refused to hand over their money,

Schoko and his men assaulted them with sticks and overpowered them. They then relieved two of the workers of £28 in gold, and administered a thrashing to the third who was unwise enough to be penniless. The Ninevites then returned to their 'fort' in the prospect holes near Canada Junction.

The victims, however, made their way to the Langlaagte Police Station and reported the robbery to Detective Duffey and Constable King – the latter a veteran of the 1908 attack at the York Mine. Duffey and two of the miners set out towards Maraisburg in pursuit of the attackers, whilst King and the third worker searched the Canada Junction area. King had the misfortune to find what he was looking for. No sooner had he ordered the Ninevites out of their hiding place than he was attacked and fatally stabbed in the head. The terrified worker fled back to Langlaagte and reported the constable's murder.[93] After a nightlong search police eventually discovered King's body thrust into an ant-bear hole.

This brutal attack on a white official aroused widespread European indignation. The black journalist who wrote later that: 'Public and police alike felt that Ninevism, that cynical challenge to authority [had to] be wiped out', was probably only slightly overstating the case.[94] Members of the public, the Fire Brigade, Prisons Department officials, the Police Band and over 300 policemen attended King's funeral.[95] Determined to find the killers of the constable, Major Mavrogordato (CID) assigned one of his most able officers, Detective A J Hoffman, to the case on a full-time basis.

Despite thorough and protracted searches of the usual Ninevite haunts south-west of Johannesburg, Hoffman enjoyed little immediate success in his hunt for Schoko and Ntlokonkulu. This was hardly surprising. Both Ninevites, 'feeling the heat' near Johannesburg, had migrated elsewhere in search of 'work', Schoko choosing Kimberley, the only large city outside the Witwatersrand which offered him the type of prison/compound complex with which he was most familiar and Ntlokonkulu opting for the country life, eventually making his way to the far south-east of the Reef where he placed himself under 'Chief' Jacob Xaba.

But almost a month after King's murder, Hoffman's arrest of 'vagrants' and scouring of criminal haunts started to pay off when he received information to the effect that the wanted men were in the vicinity of Vlakfontein. On the night of 18 January 1911 he, Detective Probationer H G Boy, and a team of black assistants tracked a group of suspects towards Hartley's farm. The first thing they found was 'a dying heifer from which the hindquarters had been cut' – a sign of Jacob Xaba's catering arrangements for a bandit get-together.[96] Following the trail they came upon a hut, the Indian inhabitants of which 'were bewailing the loss of their money, poultry and clothes'.[97]

Eventually, at about 2 a.m. they came across Xaba, Ntlokonkulu and the main Ninevite party preparing a sheep for roasting. On the approach of the police the Ninevites fled. Hoffman himself gave chase and, assisted by a *nongqayi* arrested Xaba. Boy tracked the remainder of the fleeing Ninevites and towards daybreak arrested the 'Giant with the Crooked Eyes' – Ntlokonkulu – near a mine pumping station.[98]

The capture of Xaba was an achievement for which both Hoffman and Boy received rewards and commendations. Furthermore, within hours of his arrest 'The Giant with the Crooked Eyes' added to the detectives' success when he told them that Schoko had been involved in a fight in Kimberley, and was lying in hospital there recovering from stab wounds in the stomach.[99] 'Kleintje' was arrested soon afterwards. Within 40 days of the King murder three of the most notable Ninevite leaders had been taken into custody and Nongoloza's army was on the defensive.

In March 1911 Jacob Xaba was sentenced in the Johannesburg Supreme Court to three and a half years' imprisonment with hard labour for stock theft. Shortly afterwards Schoko and Ntlokonkulu were sentenced to death for the murder of Constable King and executed in Pretoria. In August David Ganda and Jim Nomkehla, the most prominent remaining members of Xaba's unit, were arrested and prosecuted for housebreaking, attempted murder and murder in the Heidelberg district. Worse was to follow for Nongoloza's army. In a specific attempt to deal with black professional criminals the government legislated for the above-mentioned 'indeterminate sentence'[100] and when Sam Nyambezi appeared in court in February 1912 on seven counts of robbery and public violence, his case was promptly dealt with in terms of the new provision, whilst 15 members of his gang were sentenced to lengthy periods of imprisonment.

By early 1912 then, the state had already started to make inroads into the Ninevite organisation, and particularly into its leadership. Even so, its success was piecemeal and largely unintentional since the police were as yet unaware of the depth, breadth or extent of the Ninevite army. They were not fully cognisant of the linkages between the gangs controlled by Schoko, Xaba and Nyambezi or of their overriding loyalty to Nongoloza. They were shocked into fuller knowledge by the unsavoury events of May and June 1912.

On the night of 12 May 'Governor' Jim Swazi, 'General' Bill Langalene and 'Colonel' Bill Frisby set out from the Cason Mine compound for a criminal sortie into the Boksburg district. By the end of the evening, for motives that are not clear, this close-knit Benoni-based Ninevite squad had murdered a black policeman named Tsobana using a gun they had acquired from one 'Apricot'.[101] Two evenings later, 'General' Charlie Mxotshwa of the New Kleinfontein compound – who it was said could

call on as many as 100 'soldiers' as far afield as Nigel – marched a squad
of Ninevites into the Brakpan district in search of suitable robbery victims. As they approached the railway station they were asked by a white
miner, Owen Duffy, who was making his way to the single quarters of
the Brakpan mine, to help carry his mattress. The unfortunate Duffy was
clubbed to death, however, and his goods ransacked. The Ninevites
found only a key and a knife.[102]

These two brutal East Rand killings, within days of each other, jolted
the police into action, and it was while enquiring into them that
Detectives W Futter and H G Boy first came to appreciate the magnitude
of Nongoloza's army. The publicity of the subsequent trials produced
further public concern and, by mid-June, the Ninevites were receiving
parliamentary attention.[103] In the wake of these events the state started to
attack the 'army' in earnest. At first the government looked solely to the
police for the destruction of the Ninevites. Some Ninevite notables such
as Xaba, Schoko and Nyambezi had already been accounted for, and the
police consolidated on this start by building up a sophisticated picture of
the organisation and its *modus operandi* by infiltrating informers into the
compounds of several East Rand mines – a precaution that reaped benefits on at least one occasion.[104] But, as senior police officers were quick to
point out, what point was there in rounding up Nongoloza's followers in
the morning when Cinderella Prison disgorged another squad of committed followers, confined by the pass laws to the area, in the afternoon?
What was the purpose of arresting and punishing members of the organisation when it was the very act of imprisonment that brought them into
most immediate and disciplined contact with the leadership of the
movement? Action was required not only on the Witwatersrand alone,
but within the prison system itself.

In September 1912 the Minister of Justice instructed the Director of
Prisons, Roos, to convene a conference of prison superintendents in
Pretoria to formulate recommendations for dealing with the Ninevites in
prison. The resulting resolutions contained a predictable blend of 'stick
and carrot' measures – plenty of stick and very little carrot. Amongst the
reforms suggested was that the 'best classes' of black prisoners be
allowed to associate more freely where exercise yards were available and
'that single cells for separation at nights be provided as far as possible'.
The flow of Ninevite intelligence was to be disrupted by removing well-
known leaders to Robben Island and replacing black warders with
Europeans, while membership of prison gangs was to become a punish-
able 'offence' and Prisons Boards were to be asked 'not to recommend
remission of sentence to known members of these gangs'.[105]

These measures presaged a sharp decline in the strength and discipline of the Ninevite leadership. Nongoloza was naturally concerned

when he found that a growing number of his most able 'generals' were being confined to prison during 1912 and was particularly perturbed by the indeterminate sentence passed on Sam Nyambezi. Jan Note himself was due to appear before the Prisons Board later in the year and stood to forfeit the chance of a remission of sentence if Ninevite activities persisted unabated.[106] Some time after February 1912, therefore, he sent out a message that he 'wanted things kept quiet for a while as he was endeavouring to get his sentence reduced'.[107] Thus Detective Hoffman had only part of the story when he noted in August that: 'Most of the leaders are at present in gaol, and consequently we have a lull in serious crime.'[108]

But the Prisons Board that met on 8 July 1912 decided not to make any recommendation in the case of Jan Note, choosing instead to reconsider the matter in a year's time. This seems to have constituted a serious blow to the hopes and plans of Nongoloza who had by now been in the Pretoria Prison for at least four years. Moreover it laid the basis for the authorities' most powerful attack of all on the organisation: shortly after the Board met, Nongoloza was 'befriended' by his European gaoler, Warder Paskin, through whom the Prisons Department dangled the prospect of future sentence remission if the King of Nineveh would not only renounce the movement but also work for the state. On 27 December 1912, Nongoloza capitulated. In a statement to the Director of Prisons, he explained:

> The new law and the new prison administration have made me change my heart … I am quite prepared to go to Cinderella Prison or any other prison where the Ninevites say they get orders and to tell them that I give no orders even if it costs me my life. I would tell them that I am no longer king and have nothing to do with Nineveh.[109]

In late 1913 the man who could at one stage muster 1 000 lumpenproletarian troops on the Witwatersrand, and who had the unquestioned support of 'generals', 'captains' and 'lieutenants' over hundreds of square miles in South Africa's industrial heartland, became a 'native warder' in the Department of Prisons. The oppressed became oppressor, the gaoled the gaoler. Note served his time until 1917 as warder first at Cinderella and later Durban Point Prison, and later still, in the mid-1920s, was said to be back in Pretoria working as a 'warder' at the Weskoppies Mental Hospital.[110]

Not even Nongoloza's defection nor the other measures taken by the state were sufficient to ensure the total disintegration of the Ninevite army. While the nexus of pass law, compound and prison remained intact at the heart of a repressive political economy, there continued to be a host culture more than capable of sustaining such movements.[111] But the state's various measures did cripple and fragment the Ninevites and by late 1914 the Minister of Justice, N J De Wet, was confident that the authorities held the upper hand.[112]

During the decade that followed on Nongoloza's 'conversion', however, the state was never able to relax its hold. The effect of the First World War on the Ninevite movement has yet to be studied but it is clear that the remnants of the black underworld army continued their own particular struggle in the compounds and prisons while the empire's troops were engaged on other fronts. The Ninevites who murdered Matshayeli Zungu in 1915 for example, were drawn from the compounds of four mines – the Angelo, Comet, Cason and Driefontein. In the immediate wake of the Great War a resurgence of the movement took place for the same reasons that had facilitated its development after the South African War: the value of real wages had dropped markedly and this hardship was felt particularly acutely by the black population; further 'marginalisation' and an increase in crime took place; and the state's apparatus for controlling the pass laws operated more efficiently once the war no longer diverted most of its energy. More Africans became 'criminals' and the prison population expanded proportionately. In 1919 the Ninevites were certainly active both in and outside the Kimberley prisons[113] and were also reported to be present, albeit in embryonic form, at the Noordhoek Prison in the Cape. That they were still capable of making ambitious plans is evident from the report of one Prison Superintendent – the officer in charge of the Durban Point Prison – who reported in 1919:

> At the early part of this year a Ninevite affair was discovered, wherein it was planned to throw the European warders overboard from the ferry boat whilst crossing the bay. This was happily nipped in the bud and the ring-leaders punished with salutary effect.[114]

The succeeding years, however, did see a gradual decline in the more broadly based Ninevite movement. As yet there is no evidence to show that the organisation was present in its original form in the mine compounds after 1919 and it appears to have become increasingly confined to the prisons proper. During the inter-war years its presence continued to attract official notice – at Barberton Prison in 1927 and at Durban Point Prison eight years later in 1935. At some point after the Second World War the prison-bound Ninevites experienced another minor round of reorganisation and almost 100 years after Mzoozepi Mathebula first sought refuge in the hills of the Witwatersrand the remnants of Nongoloza's army continued to function within the South African prisons as the much-feared '28 gang'.[115]

CONCLUSION

In his study of 'social banditry' Eric Hobsbawm has noted that it is:

> ... usually prevalent at two moments of historical evolution: that at which primitive and communally organised society gives way to class-and-state society, and that at which the traditional rural peasant society gives way to the modern economy.[116]

But, he adds: 'the only regions in which it cannot be easily traced are Sub-Saharan Africa and India'. The social historian of South Africa is at once tempted to place the 'Regiment of the Hills' in the context of these observations. There are at least three reasons for this. First, the years between the mid-1880s and 1920 fit Hobsbawm's description rather neatly. The fall of the independent African states, the rise and decline of the black peasantry, imperial intervention and capitalist expansion, the formation of Union and the Natives' Land Act of 1913 are only some of the historical high-water marks which lap against the processes which Hobsbawm has described so vividly.[117]

Second, the Zulu-dominated Ninevites were essentially rural people with ties of kinship and custom – again not unlike the groups which Hobsbawm describes. The presence of a 'chief' at the head of the gang, but more especially of the *ikhehla* point strongly towards Zulu custom and traditional society; the language of the 'urban' Ninevites was strongly flavoured with rural metaphor and they spoke constantly of 'buck', 'birds', 'farms' and 'men who came with horses'; and, to the extent that they did have a programme at all, the leaders were not unconcerned with rural objectives – something that was especially true of periods of exceptional peasant hardship such as 1906-8. Umfanawenduka, a one-time Ninevite, told the police that the leaders of the movement constantly tried to 'entice natives to go away into the hills and live with them' and to 'desert from the work on various mines on the Reef'.[118] Jan Note himself, in his 'confession' to Warder Paskin, spoke warmly of this longing and love for cattle and the countryside, and on his release from duty with the Prisons Department in 1917, the government 'rewarded' him with a small 'farm' in Swaziland.[119] The earliest Ninevites can thus partly be seen as landless labourers seeking to return to a peasant life that was being rapidly destroyed; urban bands with a form of rural consciousness resisting proletarianisation.

Third, the age and social groups recruited into the 'social bandits' and the 'Regiment of the Hills' also bear comparison. In the case of the latter, these similarities are brought into even sharper relief if they are set in the light of Mzoozepi's early experiences, the shattered Zulu military system and the rapid expansion of European commercial agriculture in Natal at the turn of the century. Hobsbawm writes of the social bandits:

> Again, certain age groups – most obviously the young men between puberty and marriage – are both mobile and less shackled by the responsibilities of land, wife and children which make the life of the outlaw almost impossible for adult peasants. It is indeed well established that social bandits are normally young and unmarried. Men marginal to the rural economy, or not yet absorbed or re-absorbed into it, will be drawn into banditry, notably ex-soldiers, who, with herdsmen, form probably its largest single occupational component. So will certain occupations which maintain a man outside the framework of constant social control in the community, or the supervision of the ruling group – e.g. herdsmen and drovers.[120]

Although we do not yet know the detailed socio-economic background of the first Ninevites there is an enticingly familiar ring to these words.

But the similarities promptly end when we consider Hobsbawm's outline of what he considers to be the central characteristics of the groups which he has examined:

> The point about social bandits is that they are peasant outlaws whom the lord and State regard as criminals, but who remain within peasant society, and are considered by their people as heroes, as champions, avengers, fighters for justice, perhaps even leaders of liberation, and in any case as men to be admired, helped and supported.[121]

With the possible exception of a brief period during the early 1890s, the Ninevites were no band of peasant outlaws eliciting the admiration, help or support of their people.

In the industrial revolution that engulfed southern Africa after the discovery of diamonds and gold there was a particularly rapid succession of social formations. In the midst of these traumatic changes there was no time for the landless to linger in the countryside. Those suffering most acutely from the ravages of proletarianisation were swept into the migrant labour system and carried to the cities and compounds. South Africa's 'peasant outlaws' – still carrying some of the conceptual baggage of the countryside – came to town with the rest of their kinsmen. There, living literally and figuratively on the margins of industrial society, they were transformed into essentially urban gangs. No wonder they were difficult to trace in this particular part of sub-Saharan Africa – they were living in the prospect holes, abandoned mine shafts, derelict buildings and caves surrounding the towns – far from their rural homelands.

Hounded and harassed by the pass laws in the centre of the 'white' cities, these lumpenproletarian groups struck at the most vulnerable members of the industrialising system – the black migrant workers making their way home with wages. On the geographical margin of the Witwatersrand they stole and plundered from fellow Africans or terrorised the inhabitants of the urban black 'locations'. As such they were feared, hated and resented by the majority of proletarians or migrant workers. Here there was no room for help, support or admiration. Where the Ninevites did come into close contact with urban institutions they were usually of the most depressing, authoritarian and dehumanising sort – the prisons and the mine compounds. These institutions provided the Ninevites with rich recruiting grounds since in South Africa miserable wages and endless pass law convictions ensured that today's proletarian was tomorrow's prisoner. As exclusively male institutions the prisons and compounds also provided a host culture readily able to sustain organised violence and homosexuality. Perhaps more than anything else it was these institutions that ensured that this part of sub-Saharan Africa produced not social, but profoundly *anti-social* bandits.

But the role of Nongoloza's men should not be minimised simply because they were not 'social bandits' or because most of their activity was directed against fellow Africans. Nor is their part in South African working-class history so unimportant as to warrant only a single cursory line in a standard reference work.[122] Certainly the Ninevite leaders had a low level of political awareness, but they were able to perceive their followers as being in a state of rebellion in an unjust society. To the extent that its activities were directed away from members of the black working class and towards white property, the organisation saw itself as redressing the balance between the exploiters and the exploited, the haves and the have-nots, the powerful and powerless in a markedly inegalitarian and racist society.[123] Under the leadership of one charismatic man and professional criminals, there developed a powerful and sophisticated organisation which welded together lumpenproletarian elements and part of the working class. At the height of its development before the First World War, the Ninevite army – albeit for essentially non-political motives – succeeded in seriously challenging the black collaborating arm of a white-dominated state. For these reasons, if for none other, we should reassess the resistance and revolutionary potential of the lumpenproletariat in South Africa's historical evolution.

NOTES

PART ONE NEW BABYLON

1 THE WORLD THE MINE OWNERS MADE

1   See P Richardson and J J Van-Helten, 'The Gold Mining Industry in the Transvaal, 1886-1899', in P Warwick (ed), *The South African War* (London 1980), pp 18-19.
2   A Pratt, *The Real South Africa* (London 1913), p 166.
3   See R V Kubicek, *Economic Imperialism in Theory and Practice* (Duke University Press, Durham NC 1979), p 24.
4   *Ibid*, p 40.
5   G Blainey, 'Lost causes of the Jameson Raid', *Economic History Review*, 18, 1965, p 353. See also, Richardson and Van-Helten, 'The Gold Mining Industry in the Transvaal, 1886-1899', p 27.
6   Kubicek, *Economic Imperialism in Theory and Practice*, p 43.
7   For an analysis of the repressive functions of the compound system see C van Onselen, *Chibaro* (London 1976), pp 128-86.
8   For some of the difficulties arising from the use of this concept see R Johnson, 'Three Problematics; elements of a theory of working class activities', in J Clarke, C Critcher and R Johnson (eds), *Working Class Culture* (London 1979), pp 201-37.
9   See also, however, G Stedman Jones, 'Class Expression *versus* Social Control? A critique of recent trends in the social history of "Leisure"', *History Workshop*, 4, 1977, pp 163-74.
10 'Eerste Fabrieken', *Standard and Diggers' News*, 14 May 1889.
11 For a fuller discussion of this complex topic see Part Two, Chapter 1, 'The Witches of Suburbia'.
12 For a schematic outline of Nellmapius's career in the Transvaal see H Kaye, *The Tycoon and the President* (Johannesburg 1978).
13 Richardson and Van-Helten, 'The Gold Mining Industry in the Transvaal, 1886-1899', p 28.
14 Kubicek, *Economic Imperialism in Theory and Practice*, pp 43-4.
15 See R Mendelsohn, 'Blainey and the Jameson Raid: The Debate Renewed', *Journal of Southern African Studies*, 6, 2, 1980, p 162. See also Richardson and Van-Helten, 'The Gold Mining Industry in the Transvaal, 1886-1899', p 28.
16 Richardson and Van-Helten, 'The Gold Mining Industry in the Transvaal, 1886-1899', p 20.
17 Blainey, 'Lost causes of the Jameson Raid', p 359.
18 For a brief discussion of the *bewaarplaatsen* problem see Mendelsohn, 'Blainey and the Jameson Raid: The Debate Renewed', pp 161-2.
19 Blainey, 'Lost causes of the Jameson Raid', p 359. See also, however, Mendelsohn, 'Blainey and the Jameson Raid: The Debate Renewed', p. 165.
20 D Bransky, 'The Causes of the Boer War: Towards a Synthesis', unpublished paper delivered to the Workshop on South Africa, Oxford 1974, pp 10-11.
21 See Part One, Chapter 2, 'Randlords and Rotgut'.
22 'To the Relief', *Standard and Diggers' News*, 19 August 1897. See also Part Two Chapter 3, 'The Main Reef Road

into the Working Class'.

23 Richardson and Van-Helten, 'The Gold Mining Industry in the Transvaal, 1886-1899', p 34.

24 For an excellent analysis of the role of gold in the international economy at the turn of the century and some of its implications for the Transvaal see S Marks and S Trapido, 'Lord Milner and the South African State', *History Workshop*, 8, 1979, pp 50-80.

25 Transvaal, *Annual Report of the Chamber of Mines 1895*, p 75.

26 See Part One, Chapter 3, 'Prostitutes and Proletarians'.

27 Much of this episode can be reconstructed from the following items in the *Standard and Diggers' News*: 'We'll Import Abigails', 26 December 1896; 'The Witwatersrand Boarding-House Keepers' Protection Association', 9 January 1897; 'Hotel Employees – Indignation Meeting', 27 February 1897; and Henry Percival to the editor, 25 March 1897.

28 H J and R E Simons, *Class and Colour in South Africa, 1850-1950* (Harmondsworth 1969), p 61.

29 This, and much of the section that follows, is heavily reliant on Peter Richardson's detailed account of the mining industry in the post-war period. See P Richardson, 'Coolies and Randlords: The Structure of Mining Capitalism and Chinese Labour, 1902-1910', p 5. (Unpublished seminar paper, Institute of Commonwealth Studies, University of Oxford, 1979).

30 'Between 1899 and 1910, for example, there was a sharper decrease in the average grade of ore mined on the Witwatersrand than at any other period between 1887 and 1965. The grade of ore sent to the mill declined from a ten-year annual average of 11.748 dwts per ton between 1890 and 1899, to an annual average of 6.572 dwts per ton in 1910.' Richardson, 'Coolies and Randlords', p 1.

31 For some of the reasons behind this see D Denoon, 'The Transvaal Labour Crisis 1901-1906', *Journal of African History*, VII, 1967, pp 481-94.

32 The importance of the output maximisation and cost minimisation programme in the post-war period has been well illustrated in F A Johnstone, *Class, Race and Gold* (London 1976).

33 Richardson, 'Coolies and Randlords', p 2.

34 *Ibid*, p 3.

35 *Ibid*, p. 11.

36 For a thorough appreciation of the complex and sophisticated manner in which the mine owners set about the task of moulding a society that would meet the needs of primary industry during this period see B Bozzoli, *The Political Nature of a Ruling Class: Capital and Ideology in South Africa 1890-1933* (London 1981). See especially Chapters 1 and 2.

37 See D Denoon, *A Grand Illusion* (London 1973).

38 For an account of the wartime plight of the Rand refuges see D Maclaren, 'The Politics of Discontent: The Grievances of the Uitlander Refugees, 1899-1902', *Journal of Southern African Studies*.

39 J Ramsay Macdonald, *What I Saw in South Africa* (London 1902), p 103.

40 For a wider and slightly more systematic discussion of some of the elements of this problem see E P Rathbone, 'The Problem of Home Life in South Africa', *19th Century Review*, August 1906, pp 245-53. For an appreciation of Rathbone's important role as an ideologist for capitalist development on the Witwatersrand during this period see B Bozzoli, *The Political Nature of a Ruling Class*, pp 26-35.

41 Transvaal Colony, *Report of the Commission Appointed to Enquire into and Report on the Johannesburg Insanitary Area Improvement Scheme, 1901-03*. Letter from E M Showers to the Town Clerk, Johannesburg, 12 February 1902, p 10.

42 *Ibid*.

43 Transvaal Colony, *Report of the Johannesburg Housing Commission 1903*, p 1.

44 See Part Two, Chapter 1,'The Witches of Suburbia'.

45 See Part Two, Chapter 2, '*AmaWasha*'.

46 See especially V Markham, *South Africa, Past and Present* (London 1900), pp 375-6.

47 See L Phillips to Lord Selborne (Private), 24 January 1906, in M Fraser and A Jeeves, *All That Glittered* (Cape Town 1977) pp 147-50.

48 *Ibid.*

49 *Report of the Transvaal Leasehold Townships Commission 1912* (U.G. 34-1912). A more detailed study of this neglected subject would also have to take into consideration some of the following evidence: *The Financial Relations Commission (Transvaal), 1906; The Townships Act, 1907; The Townships Amendment Act No 34 of 1908; The Townships Amendment Act No 30 of 1909;* Transvaal Colony, *Mining Regulations Commission 1910,* Vol 1, pp 63-6, 71; and *Report of the Small Holdings Commission (Transvaal)* (U.G. 51-13).

50 See especially, 'Holdings and Homes', *The Star,* 8 November 1912.

51 L Curtis, *With Milner in Africa* (Oxford 1951), p 260.

52 See especially, *Report of the Small Holdings Commission (Transvaal) 1912,* para 16, pp 8-9.

53 *Ibid.* Even this latter figure, however, was considered to be too low for a developing capitalist economy.

54 Transvaal Colony, *Final Report of the Mining Relations Commission* (Pretoria 1910), pp 77-86.

55 P Warwick, 'African Labour during the South African War, 1899-1902', unpublished seminar paper presented at the Institute of Commonwealth Studies, University of London, October 1975.

56 See Part Two, Chapter 1, 'The Witches of Suburbia'.

57 'Problem of Poverty – Inequitable Municipal Doles', *Rand Daily Mail,* 25 May 1914.

58 W C Scully, *The Ridge of the White Waters* (London 1912), pp 207-14.

59 Lionel Phillips to Lord Selborne (Private), 24 January 1906, in M Fraser and A Jeeves (eds), *All That Glittered,* p 148. See also Phillips's suggestion at the time of founding the Johannesburg Art Gallery that fellow capitalists should give generously to the cause in order to help 'counteract those tendencies which provide an exaggerated sense of hatred in the minds of the "have nots" against the "haves"'. *Ibid,* L Phillips to J Wernher, 30 May 1910, pp 224-5.

60 This exercise has been performed in a most skilful and suggestive manner in the English context in G Stedman Jones, 'Working Class Culture and Working Class Politics in London 1870-1900; Notes on the Remaking of a Working Class', *Journal of Social History,* 1974, pp 461-508.

2 RANDLORDS AND ROTGUT, 1886-1903

1 See for example George Rudé, *Paris and London in the 18th Century* (London 1969).

2 Unlike the pavement artist, no researcher is ever in the position where he can honestly say, 'all my own work'. This is especially true of this study, and I am indebted to many people for their help – including the editors of *History Workshop.* I would particularly like to thank Belinda Bozzoli, Martin Legassick, and Stanley Trapido for valuable discussions and also for making research material available to me. I would also like to thank Juan Esteban, Wolf Mersch and Yury Boshyk. Their excellent Portuguese, German and Ukrainian I have distorted to my own ends.

3 D Mitrany, *The Land and the Peasant in Rumania* (Oxford 1930), p 490.

4 P I Lyaschenko, *History of the National Economy of Russia to the 1917 Revolution* (New York 1949), p 411. See also W L Blackwell, *The Beginnings of Russian Industrialization 1800-1860* (Princeton 1968), p 56.

5 *Novi Ukrainski Pisni Pro Hromadsku Spravu, 1764-1880* (Geneva 1881),

pp 111-12; S Podolynsky, *Fabryki i remesla na Ukraine* (Geneva 1881), p 130.

6   See H Bechtel, *Wirtshaftsgeschichte Deutschlands* (Munich 1956), pp 25-6; G Stolper, *The German Economy 1870-1940* (New York 1940), p 37. Also, H Rosenberg, *Probleme der Deutschen Sozialgeschichte* (Frankfurt 1969), p 68; H W Graf Finckenstein, *Die Entwicklung der Landwirtschaft in Preussen und Deutschland* (Würzburg 1960), pp 144-5.

7   *South Africa* (London) 90, 510, 1 October 1898, p 28.

8   By 1899 this dumping of spirits in Africa had reached such proportions, and produced such cut-throat competition, that the major European powers were forced to seek an agreement. *See Correspondence respecting the African Liquor Traffic Convention, signed at Brussels, 8 June 1899* (HMSO, Command 9335, July 1899, Africa No 7).

9   *Standard and Diggers' News (hereafter: S & DN)*, 10 May 1895.

10 See F J Potgieter, 'Die Vestiging van die Blanke in Transvaal 1837-1886', *Archives Year Book for South African History*, 2, 1958, p 94.

11 In part these import duties simply encouraged smuggling – particularly of the cheap Cape Colony brandy known as 'Cape Smoke'. See, for example, the activities of J D Bosman of the Paarl Wine and Brandy Company, as reported in *S & DN*, 24 January 1891. Also, the Goldberg case in *S & DN*, 15 July 1891. See also note 34 below.

12 Editorial, *S & DN*, 29 October 1892.

13 See Miss Annie Russell's account of 'Early Transvaal Towns', republished in *S & D N*, 20 April 1894.

14 *S & DN*, 31 July 1893.

15 C T Gordon, *The Growth of Boer Opposition to Kruger 1890-95* (London 1970), p 36.

16 'Report of Special Liquor Committee' in *Chamber of Mines of the South African Republic Tenth Annual Report for the year ending 31 December 1898*, p 110. (This report runs from pp 108-15, and is hereafter cited as

'*S L C Report 1898*'.)

17 *Report of the Transvaal Concessions Commission*, Part II, Minutes of Evidence, p 71. (HMSO, Command 624 of 1901. Hereafter: *Command 624*.)

18 *Command 624*, p 717. See also *Report of the Transvaal Concessions Commission*, Part I, p 99. (HMSO, Command 623 of 1901. Hereafter: *Command 623*.)

19 *Command 624*, June 1901, p 75. From 1894 to 1898 the glass factory ran at a diminishing loss each year. By 1898 the loss was down to £2 356 for the year, and the directors expressed every hope that it would produce a profit during 1899. See the report on the Hatherley Company in *South Africa*, 42, 544, 27 May 1899, p 482.

20 *S & DN*, 14 May 1899.

21 For detailed descriptions of Hatherley see *S & DN*, 14 December 1899, and 5 May 1890.

22 *Command 624*, June 1901, p 74.

23 *S & DN*, 14 and 24 December 1889; 5 May 1890; 30 May 1891.

24 *Command 623*, June 1901, p 99.

25 See for example J N Bovill, *Natives under the Transvaal Flag* (London 1900), p 47. Also R C F Maugham, *Portuguese East Africa* (London 1906), p 283. Perhaps the most valuable evidence, however, is contained in 'Extracts from the Report of Dr Serrao De Azevedo on the Health Services of the Province of Mozambique', in Transvaal, *Report of the Liquor Commission 1908*, annexure 4, pp 116-17.

26 *Report for the year 1894 on the Trade of the Consular District of Mozambique* (F O Series No 1537) p 4.

27 *Report for the year 1895 on the Trade of the Consular District of Mozambique* (F O Series No 1760) p 4

28 J N Bovill, *Natives under the Transvaal Flag*, p 47.

29 A Davis, *The Native Problem* (London 1903), p 186.

30 W C A Shepherd, 'Recruiting in Portuguese East Africa of Natives for the Mines', *Journal of the African Society*, 33, July 1934, p 254.

31 See *Command 624*, June 1901, p 72.

For issued share capital see
C S Goldmann, *South African Mining
and Finance* (Johannesburg 1895),
Vol 2, p 206; also *S & D N*,
14 November 1892.

32 *South African Who's Who 1909*, pp 107,
147, 139 and 144.

33 Registrar of Companies, Zanza
House, Pretoria, File T669, 'The
Eerste Fabrieken Hatherley Distillery
Ltd, list of shareholders and their
respective holdings as at
31 December 1901'. See also
Command 624, June 1901, p 72. See
also J Ploeger, 'Die Maatskappy
"Eerste Fabrieken in die Zuid
Afrikaansche Republiek"', *Historia*,
Jaargang 2, 1957, 123. (Hereafter: 'Die
Maatskappy'.)

34 *South African Who's Who 1909*, p 144;
Transvaal Leader, 24 August 1899.

35 'Cape Smoke' was so called partly
because rolls of crude tobacco were
actually used in its preparation. See
for example Fisher Vane, *Back to the
Mines* (London 1903), p 169; also note
11 above.

36 *Command 624*, June 1901, p 73. Also,
SLC Report 1898, pp 109-10.

37 *SLC Report 1898*, p 110.

38 *Report for the year 1894 on the Trade of
the Consular District of Mozambique*
(F O Series No 1537) p 15.

39 Companhia do Assucar de
Moçambique, *Relatorios e Contas das
Gerencias de 1895 e 1896*, p 8.

40 *SLC Report 1898*, p 110 and p 115. See
also J Ploeger, 'De Maatskappy',
p 124.

41 Companhia do Assucar de
Moçambique, *Relatorios ... 1895*, p 24.

42 See *S & DN*, 30 August 1894; *SLC
Report 1898*, p 110.

43 Compare the list of distilleries in
*Report for the year 1894 on the Trade of
the Consular District of Mozambique*
(F O Series No 1537) p 36, with that
in *The Delagoa Directory for 1899*
(Lourenço Marques, 1899), p 34.

44 *Report for the year 1895 on the Trade of
the Consular District of Mozambique*
(F O Series No 1760), p 12.

45 *SLC Report 1898*, pp 110-11.

46 For ships and cargoes to Lagos see

T Welsh, 'Contrasts in African
Legislation', *Journal of the African
Society*, 6 January 1903, p 199.

47 *SLC Report 1898*, p 111.

48 Initially, of course, these cheap
imports of potato spirits also hampered local distilleries within
Lourenço Marques. See for example
S & DN, 20 October 1892. For the
consumption of German potato spirits within Mozambique see *Report for
the year 1894 on the Trade of the
Consular District of Mozambique* (F O
Series No 1537), p 36. For the role of
potato spirits on the Witwatersrand
see L S Amery (ed), *The Times History
of the War in South Africa 1899-1900*,
Vol 1, p 121.

49 Welsh, 'Contrasts in African
Legislation', p 199; *Report for the year
1895 on the Trade of the Consular
District of Mozambique* (F O Series
No 1760), p 11.

50 *Transvaal Leader*, 29 May 1899.

51 *Transvaal Leader*, 23 May 1899.

52 Apparently the first prosecution
under the ZAR Trade Marks Act
occurred in 1893 when the local
agents for Spenglers Gin (Rotterdam,
Holland) instituted legal proceedings
against S Feinberg. The findings of
the court in this case are unknown.
See *S & DN*, 16 September 1893;
Transvaal Leader, 23 May 1899.

53 For these recipes see *Transvaal Leader*,
23, 24 and 25 May 1899.

54 *S & DN*, 29 April 1890.

55 Figures from the following sources:
F Jeppe (ed), *Jeppe's Transvaal Almanac
for 1899*, p 46; *S & DN*, 12 October
1892; and *Report of the Chamber of
Mines for 1898*, p 134.

56 *S & DN*, 30 April 1889, 6 March 1890.

57 For examples of these activities see:
S & DN, 19 December 1889; 20 April
1891; 12 October 1892; *Report of the
Chamber of Mines for 1895*, p 76.

58 *S & DN*, 23 July 1889.

59 In the case of Johannesburg see
S & DN, 1892.

60 *S & DN*, 27 June 1894; 9 April 1889.

61 *S & DN*, 26 September and 28
November 1892.

62 For the Transvaal Temperance

Alliance see *S &DN*, 27 July and 26 August 1892.

63 *S & DN*, 11 June and 24 August 1891; 28 November 1892.

64 'It is not, however, contended by the Chamber that there should be total prohibition': *Report of the Chamber of Mines for 1895*, p 77.

65 In this analysis I have drawn on the extensive and detailed interpretation offered by Belinda Bozzoli in her study, 'The Roots of Hegemony; Ideologies, Interests, and the Legitimation of South African Capitalism, 1890-1940', D Phil thesis, University of Sussex, 1975, especially pp 26-84.

66 *S & DN*, 20 April 1891.

67 *S & DN*, 12 September 1889.

68 *Report of the Chamber of Mines for 1895*, p 76. See also *S & DN*, 13 February 1894.

69 Gordon, *The Growth of Boer Opposition*, pp 196, 31. See also J Fisher, *Paul Kruger* (London 1974), p 161.

70 For an example of Kruger's sales to Hatherley see *S & DN*, 30 April 1890; and 'Orange Wine' advert, *S & DN*, 31 May 1894.

71 D E Schutte to the editor, *S & DN*, 11 October 1894. For further background information on the Zarps see *S & DN*, 17 December 1892; 10 February 1894; 14 May 1895.

72 See the report of the Chamber of Mines' deputation to the Minister of Mines on this point, *S & DN*, 5 March 1891.

73 See Montagu White's remarks in *S & DN*, 24 August 1891.

74 *S & DN*, 11 June 1891; L S Amery (ed), *The Times History of the War in South Africa 1899-1900*, Vol 1, p 121. For specific names and cases see, for example, *Transvaal Leader*, I June 1899 and 11 July 1899.

75 E P Rathbone to the editor, *S & DN*, 23 May 1891.

76 For an example of a European death in Pretoria, allegedly caused by the consumption of Hatherley products, see 'R N' to the editor, *S & DN*, 10 November 1891. After noting that a white corpse had been dragged away by the police, 'R N' observed: 'Is it not time this poison was officially recognised in the British Pharmacopoeia? I would suggest first, that the name remain as it is, that the active principal of the drug be known as Nellmapatine, and that the person under its influence be described as being Nellmapnatised'.

77 Fisher Vane, *Back to the Mines*, p 179.

78 Bovill, *Natives under the Transvaal Flag*, pp 36-7.

79 See especially G Blainey, 'Lost causes of the Jameson Raid', *Economic History Review*, 1965, pp 350-66.

80 *Report of the Chamber of Mines for 1895*, p 75.

81 For the official extimates see *Report of the Chamber of Mines for 1896*, p 117, and *Papers relating to Legislation affecting Natives in the Transvaal* (HMSO, Command 904, January 1902), p 26. For unofficial estimates see, for example, *South Africa*, 90, 516, 12 November 1898.

82 J Scoble and H R Abercrombie, *The Rise and Fall of Krugerism* (London 1900), p 95.

83 See *S & DN*, 28 April 1890; 11 June 1891.

84 See *Report of the Chamber of Mines for 1895*, pp 74, 78, and *Report for 1896* pp 136-7.

85 Landdrost van den Berg consistently fought the illicit liquor dealers and for this he earned the support of the mine owners and J C Smuts. See J van der Poel and W K Hancock (eds), *Selections from the Smuts Papers*, Vol 1 (Cambridge 1965), pp 194-5. (Hereafter *Smuts Papers*.) It is interesting to note that van den Berg was the only Republican civil servant to continue in service with the Milner administration after the South African War; see D Denoon, *A Grand Illusion* (London 1973) p 45.

86 See *S & DN*, 3 September 1889; 6 May 1890; 14 July 1891.

87 See Gordon, *The Growth of Boer Opposition*.

88 For the mine owners' case see J P FitzPatrick, *The Transvaal from*

Within (London 1899) p 235.

89 Gordon, *The Growth of Boer Opposition*, p 235.

90 See *S & DN*, 8, 9 and 21 August 1894.

91 See *S & DN*, 11 and 19 September, 4 October 1894.

92 For events surrounding the Trimble and Donovan affair see *S & DN*, 12 and 29 January, 1 February and 8 May 1895.

93 See *S & DN*, 11 and 19 September, 4 October 1894. Also FitzPatrick, *The Transvaal from Within*, p 98.

94 *Report of the Chamber of Mines for 1896*, p 117.

95 W S Cohn to the editor, *S & DN*, 5 May 1899.

96 Ploeger, 'Die Maatskappy', p 125. More generally see *Command 624*, June 1901, p 73.

97 *S & DN*, 21 March 1894.

98 This dominance of a petty-bourgeois organisation by mercantile capital eventually led to substantial conflict and to Heymann's resignation. See *S & DN*, 5, 19 and 22 January, 30 March and 6 April 1895.

99 Ploeger, 'Die Maatskappy', p 124.

100 Ploeger, 'Die Maatskappy', p 125; *Command 624*, June 1901, p 73.

101 Ploeger, 'Die Maatskappy', pp 125-6. See also *S & DN*, 6 November 1894.

102 For the placement of the shares on the Bourse see Ploeger, 'Die Maatskappy', p 126. For the names of those on the Paris and London Committees, see 'Annual Report on Hatherley Distillery' in *South Africa*, 497, 614, 29 September 1900, p 612.

103 Ploeger, 'Die Maatskappy', pp 125-6; *Command 624*, June 1901, p 73.

104 W S Cohn to the editor, *Transvaal Leader*, 5 May 1899; Ploeger, 'Die Maatskappy', p 126.

105 Ploeger, 'Die Maatskappy'; *The Delagoa Directory for 1899* (Lourenço Marques), p 34.

106 Joaquim Mouzinho de Albuquerque, *Moçambique 1896-98* (Lisbon 1899), pp 132-3.

107 Ploeger, 'Die Maatskappy', p 124.

108 Report of J E Evans, British Vice Consul at Johannesburg, as noted in *South Africa*, 40, 518, 26 November 1898, p 434.

109 *S & DN*, 31 July 1893.

110 W F Bailey, 'The Native Problem in South Africa', *National Review*, 28, 1896, p 546.

111 See E B Rose, *The Truth about the Transvaal* (London 1902), p 48; *Transvaal Leader*, 30 June 1899.

112 Rose, *The Truth about the Transvaal*, p 49.

113 Examples from *Transvaal Leader*, 19 June 1899; *South Africa*, 42, 544, 27 May 1899, p 476.

114 *Transvaal Leader*, 19 June 1899.

115 See *Transvaal Leader*, 29 April 1899, and *South Africa*, 37, 478, 17 February 1898, p 350.

116 *Transvaal Leader*, 8 May 1899.

117 *Transvaal Leader*, 30 June 1899.

118 For Pastolsky and 'Schutte' see *Transvaal Leader*, 1 and 2 May 1899.

119 *Transvaal Leader*, 8 June 1899.

120 For snippets of information on Nathanson see *S & DN*, 23 June, 11 and 17 August and 13 October 1894, and 7 May 1895.

121 Reports on the Globus and Shapiro trial are contained in the following editions of the *S & DN*: 16, 17, 23 and 28 October, and 1 and 30 November 1893.

122 *S & DN*, 10 February 1894.

123 *Transvaal Leader*, 8 May 1899. See also the State Attorney's strongly worded letter to the Boksburg Public Prosecutor in van der Poel and Hancock (eds), *Smuts Papers*, Vol 1, p 192.

124 *Smuts Papers*, Vol 1, p 192.

125 *Transvaal Leader*, 5 June 1899.

126 See for example *South Africa*, 40, 522, 27 December 1898, p 624, and 42, 545, 3 June 1899, p 560.

127 For this and other organisational features of the 'compounds' see the following: *Transvaal Leader*, 1 May 1899 and 5 June 1899; *South Africa*, 40, 517, 19 November 1898, p 356, and 42, 546, 10 June 1899, p 629; Rose, *The Truth about the Transvaal*, p 48.

128 See H Fox Bourne, *The Native Labour Question in the Transvaal* (London 1901) pp 29-30.

129 *Report of the Chamber of Mines for*

1898, p 103.

130 *Ibid*, p 102.

131 For a detailed outline of these events and correspondence see *Report of the Chamber of Mines for 1898*, pp 103-7, 124.

132 *SLC Report 1898*, p 112.

133 *Ibid*, pp 109, 112.

134 *Smuts Papers*, Vol 1, p 191.

135 See *Transvaal Leader*, 23 June, 4 and 15 July 1899.

136 W S Cohn to the editor, *Transvaal Leader*, 5 May 1899.

137 *Transvaal Leader*, 1 May 1899.

138 See *Transvaal Leader*, 8 May 1899; Rose, *The Truth about the Transvaal*, pp 49-50. For events at the Jumpers Mine see *Transvaal Leader*, 5 June 1899. And State Attorney Smuts instructed his Boksburg Public Prosecutor: 'If the private detective bureau traps a liquor shop, you must do your utmost to assist it.' See *Smuts Papers*, Vol 1, p 192.

139 See *Transvaal Leader*, 29 April 1899; *South Africa*, 42, 545, 3 June 1899, p 560.

140 *South Africa*, 42, 548, 24 June 1899, p 743.

141 For church support see for example *Transvaal Leader*, 10 May 1899; *South Africa*, 42, 546, 10 June 1899, p 588.

142 *Transvaal Leader*, 17 May 1899.

143 *Transvaal Leader*, 16, 17 May 1899.

144 *Transvaal Leader*, 15 May 1899.

145 *Transvaal Leader*, 22, 24 May 1899.

146 At the premises of Joffe and Abelheim: see *Transvaal Leader*, 18 May 1899. At Friedman, Tiverski, Pastolsky and Katzen's 'Grahamstown Bar', and at the Queen's Hotel: *Transvaal Leader*, 10 June 1899.

147 *South Africa*, 42, 546, 1 June 1899, p 629.

148 See *Transvaal Leader*, 1, 16 May and 8 June 1899.

149 *Transvaal Leader*, 8 May 1899.

150 The above narrative is based on *Transvaal Leader*, 5 and 15 June 1899.

151 For example, Eli Rabinovitz and A Kantor were sentenced to a fine of £100 or eight months' imprisonment with hard labour: *Transvaal Leader*, 29 April 1899.

152 See *Transvaal Leader*, 4 July 1899; *South Africa*, 43, 558, 2 September 1899, p 508.

153 *South Africa*, 42, 556, 19 August 1899, p 396; Rose, *The Truth about the Transvaal*, p 50.

154 Sources for the above four paragraphs: *Transvaal Leader*, 17 and 25 May 1899; *South Africa*, 42, 548, 24 June 1899, p 708.

155 *Transvaal Leader*, 26 August 1899.

156 *South Africa*, 44, 563, 7 October 1899, p 8.

157 *Ibid*.

158 *South Africa*, 50, 647, 18 May 1901, p 391.

159 *South Africa*, 47, 614, 29 September 1900. See also *South Africa*, 50, 647, 18 May 1901, p 390.

160 *South Africa*, 47, 614, 29 September 1900, p 620.

161 *South Africa*, 55, 712, 16 August 1902, p 476.

162 *South Africa*, 46, 591, 21 April 1900, p 125.

163 Amery (ed), *The Times History of the War of South Africa*, Vol 1, p 122.

164 These 'undesirables' disembarked in London where the Metropolitan Police initially refused to allow them entry rights. Thomas Cook and Son were instructed to give them each a one-way ticket to their country of origin, and £1 for food for the journey. Only 50 accepted this offer, and the remaining 100 were ultimately allowed to enter London, *South Africa*, 48, 609, 25 August 1900, p 398.

165 *South Africa*, 47, 614, 29 September 1900, p 627, and 49, 635, 23 February 1901, p 433.

166 This 'achievement', however, was not solely due to the Military Governor. The Governor was, on at least one occasion, pressured on this issue by Alfred Milner. See Bodleian Library, Oxford, Milner Papers, Vol 47, Diary, 11 June 1900, p 40.

167 *South Africa*, 47, 605, 28 July 1900, p 201.

168 J T Darragh, 'The Liquor Problem in the Transvaal', *Contemporary Review*, July 1901, p 126.

169 Darragh, 'The Liquor Problem',
    p 126; *South Africa*, 50, 649, 1 June
    1901, p 457.
170 Darragh, 'The Liquor Problem', p. 125.
171 *Ibid*, p 133. This theme died hard in
    the Transvaal and was resuscitated
    when Chinese labour supplies were
    no longer assured. See Transvaal,
    Report of the Liquor Commission 1908,
    p 103 (particularly the 'reservations'
    of T N de Villiers and G G Munnik).
172 *South Africa*, 52, 667, 5 October 1901.
173 Welsh, 'Contrasts in African
    Legislation', p 199.
174 *Command 904*, January 1902, p 25.
175 *Ibid*, p 26.
176 *South Africa*, 50, 651, 15 June 1901,
    p 583.
177 *Command 623*, June 1901, p 99.
178 *South Africa*, 57, 739, 21 February
    1903, p 610.
179 All quotations from *South Africa*, 59,
    761, 25 July 1903, p 260.
180 Speech read by F Perry to the
    Fortnightly Club, 1 November 1906,
    on 'The Transvaal Labour Problem'.
    (My emphasis.)

3 PROSTITUTES AND PROLETARIANS, 1886-1914

1 R J Evans, 'Prostitution, State and
   Society in Imperial Germany', *Past
   and Present*, 70, February 1976, p 106.
   Nowhere is this argument more-
   clearly stated, however, than in the
   writings of Alexandra Kollontai. See
   especially 'Prostitution and Ways of
   Fighting It', in A Kollontai, *Selected
   Writings* (London 1978), pp 261-75.
2 *Ibid*, pp 114, 128. See also E J Bristow,
   Vice and Vigilance (London 1977),
   pp 154-5.
3 Calculations derived from
   Johannesburg Sanitary Board,
   Johannesburg Census 1896, Part I,
   'Population in Detail'.
4 *Ibid*. See also, however, M S
   Appelgryn, 'Prostitusie in die Zuid
   Afrikaansche Republiek', *Codicillus*,
   13, 1, May 1972, pp 26-9, and L Freed,
   *The Problem of European Prostitution in
   Johannesburg* (Johannesburg 1949),
   pp 6-7.
5 J A Hobson, *The War in South Africa*
   (London 1900), pp 9-10.
6 Editorial, *Standard and Diggers' News*
   (Hereafter: *S & DN*), 15 February
   1897.
7 Para based on: M S Appelgryn,
   'Prostitusie in die Zuid Afrikaansche
   Republiek', p 26; G N van den Berg,
   'Die Polisiediens in die Zuid
   Afrikaansche Republiek',
   Potchefstroomse Universiteit vir
   Christelike Hoër Onderwys
   (PUCHO), D Litt thesis 1972, p 660;
   and Johannesburg Public Library
   (JPL), Johannesburg City Archive
   Collection (JCA), Box 214,
   'Constitution of the Johannesburg
   Sanitary Board', Articles 40 and 56.
8 Kimberley had, of course, experi-
   enced its greatest influx of prostitutes
   in the 1870s. For a fictionalised
   account, see for example J R Couper,
   Mixed Humanity (London, no date).
   See also note 9 below.
9 JPL, JCA, Box 200 A, *Reports and
   Extracts from Reports of Medical
   Practitioners, Kimberley, on the
   Necessity of Proclaiming the Contagious
   Diseases Act, No 39 of 1885, in the
   District of Kimberley, as submitted to the
   Kimberley Borough Council*, (1891),
   pp 1-6. On the functioning of the CD
   Act in the Cape see also for example
   'A Question of Health', *S & DN*,
   9 August 1899.
10 The presence of these Japanese pros-
   titutes was noted in the *S & DN* of
   15 February 1894. It seems possible
   that these Japanese women were
   drawn to South Africa by the diamond boom in Kimberley – see
   K Miyaoka, *Shofu-Kaigai Ryuroki*
   (Tokyo 1968), pp 181-2. (This reference was very kindly made available
   to me by Dr D C S Sissons of the
   Australian National University.)
   There were certainly still Japanese
   prostitutes active in Kimberley in the
   early twentieth century. See 'Japanese
   Interpreter Wanted', *The Star*,
   20 March 1903.
11 For this reason there were frequent
   complaints about prostitutes living
   behind so-called 'coffee shops' and

canteens. Usually, it was the black or Coloured prostitutes who drew white criticism. See, for example, JPL, JCA, Box 209, F van Bardelien to Chairman and Members of the Sanitary Board, 28 September 1893; or the cases of Coloured prostitutes Lizzie Abrahams and Emily Brewis who lived behind the 'Newcastle Bar' as reported in the *S & DN* of 28 December 1894. Perhaps the best description of early bars and bar-maids, however, is to be found in 'Johannesburg by Night', *S & DN*, 24 July 1893.

12 For some of the linkages that devel-oped between pubs and prostitutes in England see for example J J Tobias, *Crime and Industrial Society in the Nineteenth Century* (London 1972). For a list of some of the local bars at which prostitutes were most in evi-dence see the meeting of the Liquor Licensing Board as reported in *S & DN*, 20 March 1895.

13 For an account of the early rise and influence of the WLVA see Part One, Chapter 2, 'Randlords and Rotgut'. For the canteen keepers' view of prostitution see editorials in the *Licensed Victuallers' Gazette* of 17 October 1896 and 20 February 1897. See also, 'An Impudent Petition', *S & DN*, 5 March 1897.

14 See *S & DN*, 14 July 1891, and JCA, Box 216A, Asst Landdrost N van den Berg to Sec and Members of the Sani-tary Board on 6 and 9 September 1893.

15 As one index of Australian immigra-tion see the figures on the increase in the volume of mail between the two countries as reproduced in *S & DN*, 18 May 1895. On Cornish miners and the impact of a declining price of tin, see, for example, *S & DN*, 14 June 1895.

16 For an analysis of the impact of the German East Shipping Line on the Transvaal liquor trade see Part One, Chapter 2, 'Randlords and Rotgut'.

17 See R Evans, 'Prostitution, State and Society in Imperial Germany', pp 106-16.

18 See M Gilbert, 'The Jews of Austria-Hungary, 1867-1914', in his *Jewish History Atlas* (London 1969), p 77; E Bristow, *Vice and Vigilance* (London 1977), pp 177-81; and Irving Howe, *The Immigrant Jews of New York* (London 1976), pp 96-101.

19 See W T Stead's *Satan's Invisible World Displayed – A Study of Greater New York* (London, 1898). This work, in fact, constituted the 1898 edition of Stead's *Review of Reviews Annual*.

20 See Stead, *Satan's Invisible World*, pp 37-42.

21 For the South American connection see Bristow, *Vice and Vigilance* (London 1977), pp 181-6. There were, of course, also a small number of pimps and prostitutes who moved between South America and southern Africa. See for example the case of Robert and Ester Schoub in 'A Gambling Affair', *Johannesburg Times*, 18 August 1896.

22 'A Pimpsverein', *S & DN*, 7 December 1898.

23 JCA, Box 244, 'List of Brothels in Johannesburg, 1895', and related cor-respondence.

24 JCA, Box 244, Bleksley to Docey, undated and related rough returns dated September and October 1896.

25 This para based on the following items drawn from the *S & DN*: Editorial, 3 July 1896; 'The Social Sore', 24 September 1896; 'Trades Carnival', 12 November 1896; and 'The Public Shame', 22 July 1897.

26 This para based on the following items drawn from the *S & DN*: Editorial, 3 July 1896; 'The Social Sore', 24 September 1896; 'Public Indecency', 15 October 1896; and 'Disgusted' to the editor, 11 December 1896. See also 'The Social Evil', 1 October 1898.

27 Para based on: 'A Little Private "Hell"', *S & DN*, 18 August 1896; 'The Social Evil', *The Critic*, 23 October 1896; and 'Notice of Removal' and 'A Relief' in *S & DN* of 21 October 1898. For some continu-ities in this regard see also, L Freed, *The Problem of European Prostitution in Johannesburg*, p 9.

28 See 'Table Public Shame', *S & DN*, 22 July 1897. Also, interview with Mr S R Naidoo at Lenasia on 19 March 1977; and interview with Mr Mchwaneki Sibiya at Eshowe, 27 April 1977. For a similar rickshaw linkage operating in Natal see *South African Native Affairs Commission 1903-5*, Vol 3, para 21, 938, p 292, evidence of C W B Scott.

29 See 'A Reign of Terror' and 'A Pimpsverein' in the *S & DN*, of 13 July 1897 and 7 December 1898. See also the report in the *S & DN* of 2 November 1899. The term 'speculator' for pimps and other criminals appears to originate in New York gangland activity. See Jacob A Riis, *How the Other Half Lives* (New York 1971), p 180. At least some of the Bowery gangsters who came to Johannesburg brought the appellation 'speculator' with them. See, for example, the 'profession' of David Krakower as cited in Transvaal Archives Depot (TAD), Pretoria, ZAR Criminal Cases, ZTPD 3/115, State *vs* Joe Silver, Sam Stein and others.

30 See, amongst other references in the *S & DN*, the following items: 'The Case of Lemaire', 8 October 1897; 'A Gambling Raid', 24 February 1898; 'Guardians of Girls', 6 October 1898; and 'Satan's World', 5 November 1898. Also TAD, Jhb Criminal Landdrost's Papers, Vol 1940, Leon Lemaire to Messrs Schutte, Van den Berg and Dr Krause, 5 October 1899.

31 See for example 'A Gambling Raid', *S & DN*, 24 February 1898. For the origin and use of the name 'Louis' for German pimps see R J Evans, 'The Women's Movement in Germany', D Phil thesis, University of Oxford, 1972, p 41.

32 See for example the case of Johan Janssen as recounted in the *S & DN* of 16 July 1898.

33 For a selection of such cases see the following items drawn from the *S & DN*: 'A Wanton's Bully', 28 September 1896; 'Our Demi-Monde', 7 October 1896; 'A Dusky Don Juan', 21 October 1896; 'A Score

of Them', 17 November 1896; and 'The Nigger as "Macquerot"' (*sic*), 17 November 1896.

34 See for example the relationship between 'Jacob' and Louise Roger, a 47-year-old prostitute from Burgundy as recounted in the following items drawn from the *S & DN*: 'The Purity Crusade', 10 September 1897; 'Under the *Ontucht* Law', 11 September 1897; 'Black and White', 20 October 1897; and 'A Judge's Crusade', 20 October 1897.

35 JPL, JCA, Box 216, Medical Officer of Health, 'Report on Smallpox Inspection', 1 January 1893; and JCA, Box 218, District Surgeon's Report to Chairman and Members of the Sanitary Board, October 1894.

36 In 1895, Dr Liebaert was involved in attempts to legalise prostitution on the Witwatersrand. See, TAD, ZAR, SS Vol 5141 (1895). For his work amongst local prostitutes see for example the account in the *S & DN* of 15 September 1896. For an example of Dr Villettis's work, see the certificate issued to 'Miss Lily' of 'Silvio Villa' in TAD, ZAR, Jhb Landdrost, Vol 1852 (1898), the State *vs* Auguste Roger.

37 See for example JPL, JCA, Box 200A, A H Bleksley, Sanitary Superintendent, to Chairman and Committee, Sanitary Board, 31 January 1895; and JCA, Box 221, Health Inspector's Annual Report for 1895.

38 The Social Sore', *S & DN*, 24 September 1896.

39 In 1897 a three-bedroomed house used as a brothel in central Johannesburg could fetch a rent of up to £40 per calendar month – a sum well in excess of a white miner's wages. See, R Hodges to editor, *S & DN*, 12 May 1897. This process of expulsion appears to have been particularly marked in late 1896. For a selection of complaints see: 'Householder' to editor, *Johannesburg Times*, 10 August 1896; and 'An Englishman' to editor, *S & DN*, 26 September 1896.

40 *The Critic*, 23 October 1896. See also

the comment of the Chief of Police in
S & DN, 1 October 1898.

41 Most of this evidence derives from
Bleksley's censuses of 1895 and 1896
(see notes 23 and 24 above), and then
tracing these addresses through the
property registers in the Rand
Registrar of Townships Office,
Johannesburg. On the *Banque
Française*, however, see also 'Great
Ontucht Plot', *S & DN*, 15 February
1899, and on the Rand Investment Co
see TAD, ZAR, Jhb Landdrost's
Collection, Vol 1940, W A Miller (Sec)
to Public Prosecutor, Johannesburg,
22 March 1899.

42 See 'An Impudent Petition', *S & DN*,
5 March 1897. The *Volksraad* in turn
took great care when it debated this
legislation. See 'The Public Shame',
S & DN, 1 July 1897. The first landlord to be prosecuted, one Charles
Rittmann, appeared in court in early
1899, see 'The Morality Law',
S & DN, 10 January 1899.

43 Para based on: TAD, SS, Vol 5141,
File 3541/95. See also JPL, JCA, Box
244, 'Notes re Regulations on Houses
of Ill-Fame'.

44 This para based on: JPL, JCA, Box
224, 'Notes re Houses of Ill-Fame';
and JPL, JCA, Box 221, Protestant
Ministers' Assoc of Johannesburg to
Members of the Jhb Sanitary
Committee, 18 September 1895. For
some of the background to Josephine
Butler and her thinking see Bristow,
Vice and Vigilance, pp 4-6, 75-93.

45 Para based on: JPL, JCA, Box 222,
Carl von Brandis and others to
Chairman and Members of the Jhb
Sanitary Committee, 8 April 1896;
and TAD, SS, Vol 5141, File 12731/95.
See also, M S Appelgryn, 'Prostitusie
in die Zuid Afrikaansche Republiek',
pp 26-7.

46 Para based on the following items
drawn from the *S & DN*: 'Four Sinful
Sisters', 2 October 1895; 'The Social
Sore', 24 September 1896; and 'The
Social Crusade', 19 November 1896.

47 JPL, JCA, Box 244, Members of the
Deputation to Chairman and
Members of the Jhb Sanitary

Committee, 7 October 1896.

48 *Ibid*. See also 'The Social Sore',
S & DN, 8 October 1896.

49 *Ibid*.

50 Para based on the two following
items which appeared in the *S & DN*,
'The Social Sore', 10 October 1896;
and 'The Social Sore – Regulation
Not Approved', 14 October 1896. It is
significant that on this occasion too it
was not Bleksley – but senior politicians on the Sanitary Board – who
got involved in the redrafting
process. See JPL, JCA, Box 244,
E Hancock and others to Chairman
and Members of the Sanitary
Committee, 14 October 1896.

51 See TAD, SS, Vol 5141 (1895)
P J G Meiring (Chairman) and
N McCulloch (Sec) to His Honour
and the Executive Committee,
24 October 1896. On the origin of the
White Cross League see Bristow, *Vice
and Vigilance*, pp 94-101. It was also
no doubt the old but largely informal
linkages between the White Cross
movement and the YMCA which
partly accounted for McCulloch's
interest, involvement and inspiration.
See Bristow, *Vice and Vigilance*, p 136.

52 The Revd C Spoelstra, *Delicate
Matters – Open Letter addressed to Dr
F V Engelenberg* (Johannesburg,
December 1896).

53 'The Public Morals', *S & DN*,
15 February 1897.

54 This para based on items in *S & DN*,
9 March 1897, *Johannesburg Weekly
Times*, 13 March 1897, and the *Cape
Times*, 19 March 1897. The arrival of
these women in Cape Town – and to
a lesser extent in Durban – naturally
aroused some anxiety in the coastal
cities. See for example 'Migrated
Maidens' or 'In Adderley Street' in
S & DN, 17 and 20 March 1897.

55 Para based on the following items
drawn from the *S & DN*: 'Fun in Fox
Street', 18 August 1896; 'A Reign of
Terror', 13 July 1897; 'Police and
Morals', 21 September 1897; 'The
Social Ulcer', 20 November 1897; 'In
Commissioner Street – Brave Show of
Revolvers', 8 February 1898; and

'Blackguard Syndicates',
30 September 1898.

56 Crime reporters found it noteworthy
that whenever members of the
Morality Squad appeared in court
they invariably entered the box 'in
collarless and generally unkempt
condition suggestive of slovenliness',
Johannesburg Times, 11 June 1898.
Since the majority of these policemen
earned only £14 per month in a notoriously expensive city this condition
was more likely to be a function of
poverty than lack of self-respect. See
especially Landdrost van den Berg's
remarks in 'The Ontucht Plot',
S & DN, 17 February 1899.

57 See, for example, the case of Sarah
Segal in 'A Pimpsverein', in *S & DN*,
7 December 1898.

58 Joseph Silver is the subject of a forthcoming biography which the author
is currently researching. An idea of
the man and some of his
Johannesburg activities, however, can
be gained from some of the following
items drawn from the *S & DN*: 'A
Pimpsverein', 7 December 1898;
'Ontucht Raid', 10 January 1899; 'The
Seamy Side', 11 January 1899; 'The
Great Ontucht Plot', 2 February 1899;
'Ontucht Freemasonry', 9 February
1899; and 'When Police Fall Out',
16 February 1899.

59 See especially in the *S & DN*: 'A
Pimpsverein', 7 December 1898, and
'Ontucht Freemasonry', 7 February
1899.

60 On Salus Budner alias Julius Budner
alias Joe Gold, see, amongst others,
the following items drawn from the
S & DN: 'A Pimpsverein', 7 December 1898; 'Great Ontucht Plot',
7 February 1899; 'Ontucht
Freemasonry', 7 February 1899; and
'The Morality Law', 22 February 1899.

61 *Ibid.*

62 See, in *S & DN*, 'A Pimpsverein',
7 December 1898; and 'Great Ontucht
Plot', 15 February 1899.

63 See for example the editorial in the
S & DN, 15 October 1896: 'It is a
notorious fact that women make the
public parks a hunting ground to

supply houses of ill-fame, and young
girls of tender age are continually
approached by procuresses who hold
out tempting visions of an immoral
life'. See also Part Two, Chapter 1,
'The Witches of Suburbia'.

64 See for example the following items
drawn from the *S & DN*: 'Most Moral
Cape Town', 10 November 1896;
'Rand Women Traps', 12 July 1897;
and 'Saintly Stellenbosch', 18
November 1897.

65 Amongst others, see for example the
following items drawn from the
S & DN: 'An Infamous Traffic',
27 April 1897; 'Rand Women Traps',
12 July 1897; 'A Horrible Trade',
1 October 1897; 'Decoyed to the
Rand', 17 November 1897; and 'The
Police Service', 12 November 1898.

66 The entire Kreslo story was recounted, in some detail, in 'Decoyed into
Sin' in the *S & DN*, 7 June 1899.

67 Some of the relevant information can
be gained from the following entries
which appeared in the 'Police' column of the *London Times*: 8 February
1898, 17 February 1898, 25 February
1898, and 18 March 1898. See also,
however, the entry under the 'Central
Criminal Court', *The Times*, 2 April
1898.

68 For some sources on French pimps in
Johannesburg, see note 30.

69 On Bertha Hermann's role in New
York City see W T Stead, *Satan's
Invisible World Displayed*, pp 126-9. In
Johannesburg see: TAD, ZAR,
Staatsprokureur, Gehieme Minutes,
Vol 193, File 1197/98, Statement by
F E T Krause, 5 November 1898. See
also, in *S & DN*, ' "Satan's World" ',
5 November 1898, and 'The Ontucht
Law', 24 November 1898.

70 On French 'white-slavery' activities
on the Rand see: TAD, ZAR,
Staatsprokureur, Gehieme Minutes,
Vol 193, File 1197/98, Statement by
Detective J J Donovan, 4 November
1898. The clearest and most detailed
example which we have of this type
of French operation, however, comes
from the Cape in 1901. See the
Preliminary Examination of Joseph

Davis (Russian 'Artist') and Marguerite de Thiesse ('modiste'), appearing on a charge of procuring Antoinette and Julienne Jacqmin for immoral purposes. Cape Archives Depot, Attorney General's Papers, Vol 3118, Proceedings of the Supreme Court.

71 Para based on: 'Our Erring Sisters', *S & DN*, 27 September 1895; 'The Public Morals', *S & DN*, 31 January 1898; TAD, Jhb Landdrost, Vol 1939, Det A Burchardt to Chief Detective P de Villiers, 17 August 1899; and TAD, Law Dept, Attorney General File 172/06, Chief Det Inspector T E Mavrogordato to the Commissioner of Police, 12 February 1906.

72 See the statements of Georgette Carpentier, Maria Buffans (signature unclear) and Yvette Vervat in TAD, Jhb Landdrost, Vol 1852, Criminal Cases, State *vs* August(e) Roger, January 1898.

73 *Ibid*. See reports filed by Detectives E H Maher and P J van der Heever over the two-week period.

74 See 'The Morality Law', *S & DN*, 16 July 1898.

75 See, for example, either 'Fordsburg Items' or 'Humbugged by a Harlot' in the *S & DN* of 25 October 1895 or 28 January 1896 respectively. The classic dilemma of the brothel customer in these circumstances, however, is well illustrated in the anonymous letter of 'A G B' to the Head of the Johannesburg Detective Force, 14 June 1896 in TAD, Jhb Landdrost's Papers, Vol 502, Speurpolisie, Inkomende Stukke. See also, 'Rand Morality Law', *S & DN*, 5 August 1898.

76 'Scene at the Station', *S & DN*, 18 April 1898.

77 Krause felt that prostitution was 'a necessary evil which, while it could not be eliminated, could certainly be controlled'. See N van den Berg, 'Die Polisiediens in die Zuid Afrikaansche Republiek', p 661. Drs Coster and van Leeuwens's influence on Krause are clear from TAD, ZAR, State Attorney, Secret Minutes, Vol 193,

File 1197/98. In later years Krause apparently continued to hold strong opinions about prostitution. In 1908, for example, while a Member of Parliament, Krause chose to defend a notorious ex-'American Club' pimp by the name of H Epstein against charges laid under the Morality Act. His successful defence of Epstein drew stinging criticism to Krause's head and it seems unlikely that financial gain would have been his sole motive for accepting this brief. See 'The Pimp H Epstein' in the *South African Pink 'Un*, 27 June 1908; and 'What the Magistrate Said', *Transvaal Critic*, 24 July 1908.

78 See 'The Ontucht Law', *S & DN*, 24 November 1898.

79 In his defence of some of the inhabitants of 'Sylvio Villa' in October 1895 for example, Attorney J J Raaf told the Magistrate that 'these people were a sort of safety valve, especially in a mining community such as Johannesburg', and that if these activities were stopped entirely 'it would open the way to all manner of indecent assaults and bestial crimes'. 'Four Sinful Sisters', *S & DN*, 2 October 1895.

80 This finding naturally produced considerable controversy. See the following central pieces in the *S & DN*: 'Black and White', 20 October 1897; 'A Judge's Crusade', 20 October 1897; and 'The Kafir's Enemies', 21 October 1897.

81 On the operation of the Morality Law during this period see especially 'A Foul Tammany' and 'The Public Service' – editorials in the *S & DN* on 8 October and 12 November 1898 respectively. For an overview of changes in the Morality Squad over this period see 'The Ontucht Law', *S & DN*, 24 November 1898. On Donovan's accusations against Krause (allegations which in part involved Bertha Hermann), see TAD, ZAR, SP, Gehieme Minutes, Vol 193, File 1197/98, statements by Donovan, Krause and others.

82 Some of the more important editori-

als in the *S & DN* during this campaign included: 'A Dead Letter', 29 April 1897; 'The Public Shame', 1 July 1897; 'A Reign of Terror', 13 July 1897; 'Police and Morals', 21 September 1897; 'Blackguard Syndicates', 30 September 1898; and 'The Social Evil', 1 October 1898.

83 'The Morality Law', *S & DN*, 28 September 1898.

84 See 'The Morality Law', *S & DN*, 14 October 1898; and *Der Locale Wetten der Zuid Afrikaansche Republiek* (1899), pp 304-6.

85 See especially 'The Morality Law', *S & DN*, 15 October 1898.

86 Para based on: 'The Public Shame', *S & DN*, 15 October 1898; TAD, ZAR, SP, Gehieme Minutes, Vol 193, File 1197/98; and *A Young South African – A Memoir of Ferrar Reginald Mostyn Cleaver, Advocate and Veldcornet* (Johannesburg 1913), edited by 'His Mother'.

87 *A Young South African*, pp 2-3, 19. For Krause's friendship with Broeksma see also E J Potgieter (ed), *Standard Encyclopaedia of Southern Africa*, Vol 6 (Cape Town 1972), p 457.

88 *A Young South African*, pp 2-3, 19-22. For an example of Skirving's work see 'The Great Ontucht Plot', *S & DN*, 15 February 1899. For Burchardt's contribution see for example the following items in the *S & DN*: 'When Police Fall Out', 16 February 1899, and 'The Ontucht Plot', 17 February 1899.

89 This para based on the following items drawn from the *S & DN*: 'A Pimpsverein', 7 December 1898, and 'The Great Ontucht Plot', 2 February 1899. Note that in these cases Krakower usually appears under the name 'Dave Davis' – his underworld alias.

90 Para based on a study of the following items in the *S & DN*: 'A Pimpsverein', 7 December 1898, and 'The Morality Law', 30 December 1898. Also TAD, ZAR, Jhb Landdrost's Collection, Vol 1827, State *vs* Dave Davis, Henry Rosenchild and Morris Rosenberg.

None of this, of course, escaped Cleaver who noted: 'Here was a pretty mess! Crime rampant, every source of reaching it closed; the very forces of the State assisting it!' *A Young South African*, p 21.

91 *Ibid*. See also 'The Seamy Side – Shuttlecocked' and 'The Seamy Side' in the *S & DN* of 9 and 14 December 1898 respectively.

92 Joseph Silver to the editor, *S & DN*, 10 December 1898.

93 See 'The Morality Law – Charge of Procuration', *S & DN*, 30 December 1898. Cleaver's tactics are perhaps best described by himself: 'To make a long story short, there occurred a split in the ranks of the enemy. Of this I made such use that within a month of the day I started on the job I had packed the Head-centre of the New York pimps in gaol'. *A Young South African*, p 22.

94 This para based on a study of the following items in the *S & DN*: 'The Seamy Side', 14 December 1898; 'Ontucht Raid', 10 January 1899; 'The Seamy Side', 11 January 1899; 'Brewing on Morality Intriguers', 25 January 1899; and 'When Police Fall Out', 16 February 1899. See also *A Young South African*, p 23.

95 'Ontucht Raid – Sensational Arrests', *S & DN*, 10 January 1899, and 'The Seamy Side', 11 January 1899. See also, TAD, ZAR, Criminal Cases, ZTPD 3/115, State *vs* Joe Silver and Sam Stein; and State *vs* Jenny Stein and others.

96 This picture of Cleaver's actions is built up from a series of telegrams sent by the Second Public Prosecutor to J C Smuts and contained in TAD, ZAR, SP, Vol 195, File 244/99, File 251/99, File 307/99 and File 313/99. See also, however, 'The Seamy Side', *S & DN*, 11 January 1899, and *A Young South African*, p 23.

97 See 'The Great Ontucht Plot' and 'The Morality Law' in *S & DN* of 7 and 22 February 1899.

98 *Ibid*. See also *A Young South African*, pp 3-23.

99 For Silver's cleverly devised letter –

which attempted to exploit the differences between Cleaver and Krause, see TAD, ZAR, Jhb Landdrost's Collection, Vol 1720, J Silver and S Stein to The Hon Mr Dietzch. See also the following in the *S & DN*: 'Great Ontucht Plot', 7 February 1899; and 'Great Ontucht Plot', 15 February 1899.

100 See the following items in the *S & DN*: 'Great Ontucht Plot', 15 February 1899; 'When Police Fall Out', 16 February 1899; 'The Ontucht Plot', 17 February 1899; 'The Ontucht Scandal', 18 February 1899; and 'Perjury Epidemic', 23 March 1899. On Silver, Stein and Lizzie Josephs's attitudes see the letter cited in note 99 above, and 'A Dynasty Overthrown', *S & DN*, 6 April 1899.

101 See TAD, ZAR, Criminal Cases, ZTPD, 3/115, State *vs* Joe Silver, Sam Stein and others. See also *A Young South African*, p 23.

102 See TAD, ZAR, Johannesburg Landdrost's Archive, Vol 1824, State *vs* Joe Silver, 13-20 September 1899. See also the small item reported in the *S & DN*, 22 September 1899. The name given in certain black prison gangs to the officer responsible for procuring young African boys for homosexual relationships is 'MaSilver'. See Part Two, Chapter 4, 'The Regiment of the Hills'.

103 *S & DN*, 2 November 1899; and allegations made by the Cape Town Public Prosecutor in 'Morality Law', *The Argus*, 23 September 1904.

104 *A Young South African*, p 3, and 'The Second Raad', *S & DN*, 24 August 1899.

105 *S & DN*, 2 November 1899. See also TAD, Johannesburg Landdrost's Archive, Vol 1940, Leon Lemaire to Messrs Schutte, Van den Berg and Dr Krause, 5 October 1899.

106 For a brief summary see 'A Question of Health', *S & DN*, 9 August 1899.

107 Some of this is reflected in Robin Hallett's 'Policemen, Pimps and Prostitutes – Public Morality and Police Corruption: Cape Town, 1902-1904'. Unpublished paper presented to the History Workshop Conference, University of the Witwatersrand, Johannesburg, 2-7 February 1978.

108 On H J Dempers see 'Social Purity League' and 'The Morality Act' in *The Star*, 18 July and 28 August 1903. Dempers and his partner in law, van Ryneveld, also had certain professional dealings with Joseph Silver in relation to the management of the latter's 'properties'. See Cape Archives Depot, AG 1531/12984, State *vs* Joe Lees alias Joe Silver, 30 August 1904, p 20. On the other events recounted in this paragraph see Hallett, 'Policemen, Pimps and Prostitutes', and Cape Archives Depot, AG Vol 1902, Acting Commissioner of Police, District 3, Annual Report for 1901.

109 Cited in Hallett, 'Policemen, Pimps and Prostitutes', p 4.

110 Hallett, 'Policemen, Pimps and Prostitutes', p 5. For a lengthy and detailed account of the passage of the 'Morality Act', however, see 'Social Reform' and 'Suppression of Vice' in the *Diamond Fields' Advertiser*, 13 and 22 October 1902.

111 Elements of the Silver saga are to be found in the following items reported in the *Bloemfontein Post*: 'The Burglary', 26 November 1902; 'The Morality Muddle', 19 January 1903; 'The Reign of Terror', 19 January 1903; and 'Joe Silver Convicted', 21 January 1903. See also *Laws of the Orange River Colony 1900-1906*, Ordinance 11 of 1903, pp 686-92. For movement to Johannesburg see for example the travels of Max Harris as recounted in Cape Archives Depot, Cape Supreme Court, Criminal Records, September-October 1904, evidence of M Harris, p 28.

112 On the 1897 influx see note 54 above. Alexander's evidence on this matter was given before the *South African Native Affairs Commission, 1903-05*, Vol III, p 647, para 28 285. On Pietermaritzburg see *ibid*, evidence of C W B Scott (solicitor), p 292, para 21 937; and various small items as reported in *Ipepa lo Hlanga*, 24 May

1901.

113 Natal Archives Depot, Pietermaritzburg, Durban Corporation Collection (uncatalogued), Police Report Book No 6. See reports by R C Alexander dated 6 July 1900; 31 July 1900; 4 October 1900; 6 January 1902; 5 January 1903; and 6 April 1903. See also 'The Immorality Act – Prosecution in Durban', *The Star*, 9 October 1903.

114 *South African Native Affairs Communication 1903-05*, Vol III, evidence of J L Hulett (p 164, para 20 174); R C Alexander (p 647, para 28 285), and C W B Scott (p 292, para 21 937). See especially, however, TAD, Colonial Secretary, Vol 139, S O Samuelson, Under-Sec for Native Affairs to Sec for Native Affairs Natal, 13 June 1902.

115 On 'French' prostitutes catering for the troops see TAD, South African Constabulary (SAC), Vol 22, File 8/67, Major T E Mavrogordato to Commissioner of Police, 11 July 1908. Baden-Powell was sufficiently concerned about the men of the SAC's morals that he arranged for the British White Cross Society to forward them a special consignment of reading in the hope that it would help keep them chaste. See Bristow, *Vice and Vigilance*, p 138.

116 On the 'Immorality Trust', see TAD, Law Dept, AG File 172/06, E H Showers, Commissioner of Police, to Sec Law Dept, 2 May 1905; TAD, SAC, Vol 22, File 8/62, Chief Detective Inspector to Commissioner of Police, 6 July 1908; and TAD, Law Dept, AG 172/06, 'Copy of Minute dated 8 May 1906 by Acting Chief Detective Inspector, CID, to Commissioner of Police, Johannesburg'. On others named, see TAD, SAC, Vol 23, File 8/96 (1908), 'CID – List of persons who habitually take houses for brothels'. Compare this 1908 CID list with the original membership of the 'American Club' as reproduced in '*Ontucht* Freemasonry', *S & DN*, 7 February 1899.

117 See G K Turner, 'The Daughters of the Poor', pp 45-61. See also, however, G J Kneeland, *Commercial Prostitution in New York City* (New York 1913), p 80.

118 For the origins of the NY Independent Benevolent Association see G K Turner, 'The Daughters of the Poor', p 48. For the connection of some of its members with the Johannesburg underworld – notably Max and Louis Souvina and P Jacobs – see *New York World*, 22 December 1912. (I am indebted to Ed Bristow for this reference.) On the Souvina brothers' activities in Johannesburg, see TAD, Law Dept, AG File 172/06, Commissioner of Police to Sec, Law Dept, 25 January 1906. There is also an account of the Souvina brothers' prior and subsequent activities in G J Kneeland's *Commercialised Prostitution in New York City*, pp 82-4.

119 For the more general background to Parisian prostitution and sexuality during this period, see T Zeldin, *France, 1848-1945*, Vol I, *Ambition, Love and Politics* (Oxford 1973), especially pp 305-14. On Paris as a 'white-slave' *entrepôt*, see G K Turner, 'The Daughters of the Poor', p 46. On the different nationalities of women 'exported' to South Africa during this period see also A Flexner, *Prostitution in Europe* (New York 1914), p 93. For similar reports at the South African end during this post-war period, see L Freed, *The Problem of European Prostitution in Johannesburg*, p 9.

120 National Archives of the United States of America (NA of USA), Washington, DC, Dept of Commerce and Labour, Bureau of Immigration and Naturalization, File 1-G, 52484, 'Braun European Reports', October 1909. (Once again I am indebted to Ed Bristow for drawing this source to my attention.)

121 On Le Cuirassier in Cape Town, see Cape Archives Depot, Cape Supreme Court, Criminal Records, May-July 1904, Rex *vs* Thor Osberg, evidence of Max Harris, p 16, and Valentine Dufis, pp 23-24. Also Cape Archives

Depot, Cape Supreme Court, Criminal Records, September-October 1904, Rex *vs* Charteris, evidence of Alexander Clark, p 42.

122 In 1908 Le Cuirassier was in Vladivostok. See NA of USA, Dept of Commerce and Labour, File 1-G, 52484, 'Braun European Reports', October 1909. One of Freed's informants on the early history of Johannesburg prostitution claimed that 'Japanese prostitutes were also imported in order to meet the requirements of the Chinese labourers who were employed on the mines'. L Freed, *The Problem of European Prostitution in Johannesburg*, p 9.

123 G K Turner, 'The Daughters of the Poor', p 48. Even before the Russo-Japanese War, however, there were some pimps turning up in local circles who had Chinese experience – notably one 'James Lee', known in the local trade as 'Japanese Hersch'. For the sketch of 'Lee', and an account of an assault on him by Joe Silver, see 'Joe Silver Again', and 'Lee's Story – He comes from Pekin', in *Bloemfontein Post*, 23 January 1903. It seems possible that 'Lee' – like Silver – might have fled Kimberley when the Cape Morality Act came into force in late 1902. If so, there were certainly Japanese prostitutes left behind in Kimberley. See 'Japanese Interpreter Wanted', *The Star*, 20 March 1903.

124 On these earlier groups and the origin of the term *Karayuki-San*, see note 10 above. For the service which these Japanese ladies provided Chinese miners on the Rand, see TAD, Law Dept, AG Vol 367, Enquiries and Inquests 1906-1909, 'Confidential Enquiry into alleged unnatural practices amongst Chinese Coolies', September 1906, evidence of C D Stewart given on 10 September 1906. (I am indebted to Peter Richardson for making this source available to me.)

125 Such as denying vice traffickers orthodox burial rights within the community. On this and other actions taken by Hertz, see unpublished manuscripts by G Saron entitled 'The Communal Scene, Pathology: The White Slave Trade and Liquor Offences', and '"The Morality Question" in South Africa'. These essays, which Mr Saron very kindly made available to me, are incorporated in his history of South African Jewry.

126 TAD, CS, Vol 595, Joseph H Hertz to Private Secretary, Lord Milner, 25 January 1902, with appended petition.

127 TAD, CS, Vol 595, Assistant Private Secretary to J T Lloyd, 28 February 1902.

128 The CID, of course, did not fail to point out this lack of co-operation during the subsequent months. See TAD, Law Dept, AG File 172/06, 'Extract from Annual Report, CID, 1904/05'.

129 Para based on: TAD, CS, Vol 139, Governor (Natal) to Acting Prime Minister (Natal), 24 May 1902; and Under-Secretary for Native Affairs (Natal) to Secretary for Native Affairs, 13 June 1902. Also TAD, CS, Vol 151, Attorney General to Lieutenant Governor, 25 September 1902.

130 TAD, CS, Vol 151, AG, No 12640, Attorney General to His Excellency, The Lieutenant Governor, 25 September 1902.

131 TAD, LTG, Vol 1, File No 2, Lieutenant Governor to His Excellency, The Governor of Natal, 24 October 1902. It is possible, however, that these agitations did produce some minor concessions from Milner and Solomon, since a few weeks later 'barmaids' were banned in Johannesburg. See 'The Banning of the Barmaid', *Diamond Fields' Advertiser*, 10 November 1902 and the small item reported in *The Star*, 15 November 1902.

132 TAD, CS, Vol 595, Onslow to Governor, 7 February 1903.

133 This para based on: TAD, LTG, Vol 1, File No 2, Will Gordon Sprigg

(YMCA), Secretary to the 'Morality Committee', to His Excellency, Hon Sir Arthur Lawley, 16 March 1903, and *ibid*, Will Gordon Sprigg to The Town Clerk, Johannesburg, 26 March 1903. See also 'The Evening Sitting – Immorality Draft Ordinance', *The Star*, 23 June 1903; and *Ordinances of the Transvaal 1903*, pp 315-24.

134 See especially TAD, LTG, Vol 1, File No 2, Will Gordon Sprigg to The Town Clerk, Johannesburg, 26 March 1903.

135 See *South African Native Affairs Commission 1903-05*, Vol IV, Evidence of T E Mavrogordato (CID), p 863, para 44 514; and TAD, SNA, NA 776/06, J S Marwick to Secretary for Native Affairs, 28 February 1906.

136 G J Kneeland, *Commercialised Prostitution in New York City* (New York 1913), p 80.

137 Showers' views are spelt out in some detail in TAD, Law Dept, AG File 172/06, Commissioner of Police to Sec to the Law Dept, 2 May 1905.

138 Para based on: TAD, Law Dept, AG File 172/06, E H Showers to Sec to the Law Dept, 25 January 1906, appended 'Copy of Report from Mr Mavrogordato re Immorality'; L Freed, *The Problem of European Prostitution in Johannesburg* p 10; G K Turner, 'The Daughters of the Poor', p 48; and G J Kneeland, *Commercialised Prostitution in New York City*, pp 80, 83.

139 Para based on the following items drawn from *The Star*: 'Raising the Fallen', 25 July 1904; 'Raising the Fallen', 4 February 1905; 'Our Fallen Sisters', 19 October 1907; 'Immorality at Pretoria', 13 November 1908; 'House of Mercy', 7 April 1909; and 'Social Purity', 24 March 1914. On the background to such 'rescue homes' as they developed in Britain during the Victorian era see Bristow, *Vice and Vigilance*, pp 66-78.

140 This para based on the following letters in TAD, Law Dept, AG File 172/06: H Ternant, Sec to the Law Dept, to Commissioner of Police, 12 January 1906; Commissioner of

Police to Sec to the Law Dept, 25 January 1906; Commissioner of Police to Sir Richard Solomon, 27 January 1906; and Commissioner of Police to Sec to the Law Dept, 12 June 1906.

141 See TAD, Law Dept, AG File 172/06, 'Copy of Minute dated 8 May 1906 addressed by the Acting Chief Detective Inspector, CID, to the Commissioner of Police'. See also TAD, SNA, Vol 63, File NA 776/06, J S Marwick, Native Commissioner, Central Division, to the Secretary for Native Affairs, 28 February 1906.

142 TAD, Law Dept, AG File 172/06, E H Showers to Sec to the Law Dept, 12 June 1906.

143 TAD, SAC, Vol 23, File 8/96, T E Mavrogordato to Commissioner of Police, 21 May 1907.

144 For these returns see TAD, Law Dept, AG File 172/06, Form III – 'Return of Brothels at Johannesburg and Pretoria as at 21 May 1907'. In general, Mavrogordato appears to have minimised police corruption in the post-war period by only allowing senior officers to conduct raids on brothels. See TAD, Law Dept, AG File 172/06, Acting Commissioner of Police to Sec to the Law Dept, 22 May 1907. Mavrogordato, however, was fully aware that a certain amount of bribery persisted, and he also had clear ideas of the tariffs involved. See his evidence to the Select Committee on the Police Bill as reported in 'Detectives Pay', *The Star*, 20 March 1911. The list of these pimps' names is derived from a variety of sources, but particularly from the Transvaal Police 'Special Circular' Series of 'List of Persons deported from the Transvaal under the Immigrants Restriction Act, 1907', copies of which are to be found in TAD, Justice Dept, Vol 34, File 3/228/10, 1900-1910.

145 TAD, SAC, Vol 23, File 8/96, T E Mavrogordato to Sec to the Law Dept, 19 August 1908.

146 For Krause's views on the law and morality at this time see his contribu-

tion to the debate on the Criminal Law Amendment Bill in *Transvaal Legislative Assembly Debates 1908*, col 1423-1425.

147 Para based on TAD, SAC, Vol 22, File 8/62, T E Mavrogordato to The Commissioner of Police, 6 July 1908; TAD, SAC, Vol 23, File 8/96 T E Mavrogordato to Secretary, Transvaal Police, 18 August 1908; 'The Pimp, H Epstein' in *The South African Pink 'Un*, 27 June 1908; and 'What the Magistrate Said' in *The Transvaal Critic*, 24 July 1908.

148 *Ibid.*

149 TAD, SAC, Vol 23, File 8/96, T E Mavrogordato, Deputy Commissioner of Police to Secretary, Transvaal Police, 19 August 1908.

150 TAD, SAC, Vol 23, File 8/96, T E Mavrogordato to Secretary, Transvaal Police, 16 October 1908.

151 On deportations see TAD, Law Dept, AG File 172/06, T E Mavrogordato to The Commissioner of Police, 12 February 1906; *ibid*, T E Mavrogordato to Secretary, Transvaal Police, 16 October 1908; and TAD, Justice Dept, Vol 34, File 3/288/10, 'Special Circular' Series, 'Lists of Persons deported from the Transvaal under the Immigrants' Restriction Act 1907'. See also W C Scully, *The Ridge of the White Waters* (London 1911), p 221. As early as late 1909 some of these deportees from the Transvaal started to reappear in important roles in the vice capitals of Europe. See for example the cases of Max Malitzky and Mrs Margarete Weiss as reported in NA of USA, Washington, DC, Bureau of Immigration and Naturalization, File 1-G, 52484, 'Braun European Reports', October 1909.

152 See TAD, Justice Dept, Vol 34, File 3/288/10, 'Approximate Number of Prostitutes in Johannesburg and along the Reef on 18 July 1910'; and *ibid*, 'List of Reputed Pimps still in Johannesburg', June 1910.

153 On employment possibilities and conditions of service, see the evidence of the following witnesses to the *Transvaal Indigency Commission 1906-1908*: Lieut/Col O'Brien, paras 1497-1502; Sister Evelyn, paras 1743-1757 and paras 1882-1886; Revd A M Kriel, paras 1948-1951; and Dr T B Gilchrist, para 5635. See also, however, the particularly illuminating survey on 'Starvation' as reported in the *Transvaal Leader*, 4 June 1908. On prostitution in Fordsburg and Vrededorp see *Transvaal Indigency Commission 1906-1908*: Lieut-Col O'Brien, paras 1449-1453; Sister Evelyn, para 1708; Dr T B Gilchrist, para 5648 and para 5704. The possibility of sexual advantage being taken of female factory workers was, of course, not a new one. Law No 11 of 1899, the *Ontucht* Law, in Section 9, made provision for the punishment of immoral acts committed 'by managers or overseers in working institutions, work places or factories, with their minor servants or subordinates'. See *Laws of the Transvaal 1901*, p 1060.

154 TAD, Law Dept, AG File 172/06, 'Return of Brothels at Johannesburg and Pretoria, 21 May 1907'; and TAD, SAC, Vol 23, AG Circular Letter No 49 of 1908 – appended updated letter from Inspector W Cartlidge to the Deputy Commissioner of Police.

155 The case of Susan Broderick who was 'sold' to various Afrikaners in Vrededorp before being 'sold' to Ho King is recounted in TAD, Justice Dept, Vol 109, File 3/153/11. See also 'The Yellow Peril', *Transvaal Chronicle*, 13 February 1911.

156 Para based on: TAD, Justice Dept, Vol 34, File 3/288/10, 'Approximate Number of Prostitutes in Johannesburg and along the Reef on 18 July 1910'; 'List of Reputed Pimps still in the Transvaal, 1910'; and 'Summary of Work done under Ord 46 of 1903 and Act 16 of 1908 from 1 July 1909 to 30 June 1910'.

157 UG 51-13, *Report of the Small Holdings Commission (Transvaal) 1913*, p 12.

158 Para based on: TAD, SAC, Vol 23, File 8/96, Commissioner of Police to Secretary, Law Dept, 24 August 1908;

and JPL, 'Minutes of Meetings of the Witwatersrand Church Council, 26 July 1909-2 June 1913'.

4 JOHANNESBURG'S JEHUS, 1890-1914

1   This intention is expressed clearly, and at some length, in 'Memorandum on the Present and Future Boundaries of Johannesburg' in L Curtis, *With Milner in Africa* (Oxford 1951), p 260.

2   See J P McKay, *Tramways and Trolleys* (Princeton 1976), especially pp 5-6, 51-2, 71 and 80. Also S B Warner, *Streetcar Suburbs* (Cambridge, Mass 1962).

3   HMSO, *Report of the Transvaal Concessions Commission*, Part 1 (Command 623 of 1901), para 4. Also, Transvaal Archives Depot (TAD), Gov Vol 463 'Johannesburg City & Suburban Tramway Concession', Statement signed by S Neumann, London, 22 October 1901.

4   TAD, Gov Vol 463, 'Johannesburg City & Suburban Tramway Concession', 22 October 1901.

5   *Ibid.*

6   See also Part One, Chapter 2, 'Randlords and Rotgut'.

7   See TAD, SS Vol 5085 (1895), 'List of Continental Shareholders'; Gov Vol 463, 'Jhb City & Suburban Tramway Concession', 22 October 1901; and J P McKay, *Tramways and Trolleys*, p 145.

8   Paragraph based on the following sources: TAD, SS Vol. 5084 (1985), Directors, Jhb City & Suburban Tramway Co Ltd, to His Honour, The State President and Executive Council, 9 October 1896; 'Tramway Company – General Meeting', *Standard and Diggers' News* (hereafter: S & DN), 26 February 1897; Johannesburg Public Library (JPL), W P Howarth, 'Tramway Systems of Southern Africa; Historic Notes and Extracts' (Mimeo 1971), p 19 (hereafter: 'Tramway Systems of Southern Africa'); and HMSO, *Command 623 of 1901*, para 7.

9   Table constructed from: TAD, SS Vol 5084 (1895), Directors, Jhb City & Suburban Tramway Co Ltd to HH The State President and Executive Council, 9 October 1896, and HMSO, *Command 623 of 1901*, para 7.

10   See J P McKay, *Tramways and Trolleys*, pp 25-6; TAD, SS Vol 5084 (1895), Directors, Jhb City & Suburban Tramway Co Ltd to HH The State President and Executive Council, 9 October 1896; and TAD, Gov Vol 463, 'Jhb City & Suburban Tramway Concession', 22 October 1901.

11   *Ibid.*

12   See J P McKay, *Tramways and Trolleys*, pp 51-83.

13   Howarth, 'Tramway System of Southern Africa', p 19, and TAD, SS Vol 5083, Chairman, Jhb City & Suburban Tramway Co Ltd to State Secretary, 18 July 1896.

14   D M Wilson, *Behind the Scenes in the Transvaal* (London 1901), p 141.

15   *Ibid*, pp 141-2.

16   In this regard it should be noted that while the City & Suburban Co nominally held a right to carry goods on their trams, the Kruger government never allowed it to exercise this right – probably in an attempt to protect Afrikaner transport riders. See TAD, Gov Vol 463, 'Jhb City & Suburban Tramway Concession', 22 October 1901.

17   See Part One, Chapter 2, 'Randlords and Rotgut'.

18   J P McKay, *Tramways and Trolleys*, p 145. The Baron also held a watching brief over the City & Suburban Co through a nominal one-share holding in the horse-drawn tram company – see TAD, SS Vol 5085 (1895), 'List of Continental Shareholders', p 18.

19   D M Wilson, *Behind the Scenes in the Transvaal*, p 42. Wilson incorrectly puts this figure at £500 instead of £5 000.

20   National Archives of the United States of America, Washington, Despatches from United States Consuls in Pretoria 1898-1906, Vol 1; Petition from W Keller and others to C E Macrum, 17 October, 1898.

21 TAD, SS Vol 5083 (1895), J Berlein to State Secretary, 18 July 1896.

22 TAD, SS Vol 5085 (1895), C S Goldmann to Secretary, 12 September 1896.

23 TAD, SS Vol 5084 (1895), C S Goldmann to State Secretary, 23 September 1896.

24 For a selection of such letters see TAD, SS Vols 5083-5085.

25 TAD, SS Vol 5084 (1895), Chairman and Directors, City & Suburban Tramway Co Ltd to HH The State President and Executive Committee, 9 October 1896.

26 For the general background to this see C T Gordon, *The Growth of Boer Opposition to Kruger 1890-5* (London 1970), pp 35-57.

27 See the rather flamboyant account of D M Wilson, *Behind the Scenes in the Transvaal*, pp 142-5.

28 See the following editorials in the *S & DN*: 'Tifts and Trams', 1 July 1897, and 'Those Terrible Trams', 9 July 1897.

29 National Archives of the United States of America, Washington, 'Despatches from United States Consuls in Pretoria, 1898-1906', C E Macrum to State Secretary, 19 October 1898.

30 See 'Tramway Company – General Meeting', *S & DN*, 26 February 1897.

31 'The Tramway Company – The Annual Meeting', *S & DN*, 5 March 1898. See also TAD, Gov 463, 'Jhb City & Suburban Tramway Concession', 22 October 1901.

32 JPL, Johannesburg City Archive (JCA), Box 213, Cab Owners to Chairman and Members of the Sanitary Committee, 10 January 1891.

33 See *Johannesburg Census 1896*, Order VI, p 39. See also 'Johannesburg Jehus', *The Star*, 19 February 1898.

34 *Johannesburg Census 1896*, pp 44-7. For the names and addresses of the majority of businessmen involved see *Longland's Johannesburg and District Directory 1896*, entries on the following pages: 185, 207, 240, 263, 267 and 277.

35 Para based on: TAD, Jhb Landdrost Collection, Spesiale Landdrost Vol 93, Sophia Untembu to Chief Landdrost, 30 May 1891; JPL, JCA, Box 217, S van As to Sanitary Superintendent, 2 October 1894; JPL, JCA Box 218, S van As to Chairman and Members, Central Smallpox Committee, 27 October 1894; and items in *S & DN*, 5 September 1895, and *Johannesburg Times* of 8 and 10 June 1897.

36 'Johannesburg Jehus', *The Star*, 19 February 1898. See also – on the earlier period – W H Somerset Bell, *Bygone Days* (London 1933), p 137.

37 As early as 1890 a battery-powered tram ran at Beaconsfield on the diamond fields, and a full electric tram service was introduced to Kimberley and Cape Town. See Howarth, 'Tramway System of Southern Africa', pp 2, 37 and 47. In Kimberley, however, much of the structural unemployment of Coloured cabbies derived from the closing down of mining companies during the depression. Between 1888 and 1890 the number of cab licences issued in Kimberley fell from 631 to 489. See Cape of Good Hope, *A7-91*, Office of Issuer of Licences, Appendix E, p XI. I am indebted to Rob Turrell for drawing these statistics to my attention.

38 These names are not meant to be fully representative of the 'Malay' community on the Rand. In fact, they simply include the names of the most visible literate cabbies of the 1890s. See for example JPL, JCA Box 213, Petition to Chairman and Members of the Sanitary Board, 10 January 1891; or TAD, SS Vol 4934, Petition to HH The State President and Executive Committee, 8 December 1896.

39 *Ibid*. See also 'Cab Proprietors' in *S & DN*, 27 February 1897; 'Johannesburg Jehus', *The Star*, 19 February 1898; and 'Incompetent Cab Drivers' in *The Sportsman and Dramatic News*, 15 August 1899.

40 There is clear evidence of the increasingly important role of Afrikaners after this date. Note, for example, the

address in Dutch to the meeting of
'Cab Proprietors' in *S & DN*,
27 February 1897, and the fact that a
'Dutch Representative' was included
in the delegation sent to see the State
President. See also 'Johannesburg
Jehus', *The Star*, 19 February 1898.

41 On Jewish involvement in cab driv-
ing see G Simonovitz, 'The
Background to Jewish Immigration to
South Africa and the Development of
the Jewish Community in the South
African Republic between 1890 and
1902', University of the
Witwatersrand, B A Hons disserta-
tion 1960, p 16. (Hereafter:
Simonovitz, 'The Jewish Community
in the South African Republic, 1890-
1902'.) On the liquor trade see Part
One, Chapter 2, 'Randlords and
Rotgut'.

42 Para based on: JPL, JCA Box 213,
Petition to Chairman and Members
of the Sanitary Board, 10 January
1891; 'Meeting of Cab Owners',
S & DN, 7 May 1896; TAD, SS Vol
4934, Petition to HH The State
President and Executive Committee,
8 December 1896; and JPL, JCA Box
232, Petition to Chief Inspector of
Vehicles, 23 February 1899.

43 See items in the *S & DN* of 7 and
8 May 1896; TAD, SS Vol 4934,
Petition to HH The State President
and Executive Committee,
8 December 1896; 'Cab Proprietors'
in *S & DN*, 27 February 1897; and
Johannesburg Times, 4 August 1897.

44 Collectively these areas formed the
western working-class complex of
early Johannesburg. However, some
of these patterns managed to survive
Milner's era of construction. See, for
example, *Longland's Transvaal
Directories of 1903 and 1908*, p 552 and
491 respectively.

45 'Meeting of Cab Owners', *S & DN*,
7 May 1896, and 'Cab Proprietors',
S & DN, 27 February 1897.

46 For the tendency of railways to
expand the need for horse-drawn
cabs see F M L Thompson,
'Nineteenth Century Horse Sense',
Economic History Review, 29, 1, p 65.

I am grateful to Ian Phimister for
drawing this source to my attention.

47 See 'Tramway Company', *S & DN*,
26 February 1897, and 'Johannesburg
Jehus', *The Star*, 19 February 1898.

48 'Tramway Company', *S & DN*,
26 February 1897, and 'Johannesburg
Jehus', *The Star*, 19 February 1898.

49 'Cab Fares', *S & DN*, 2 March 1897.

50 'Meeting of the Cab Owners',
S & DN, 2 May 1896.

51 *S & DN*, 5 September 1896.

52 'The Town is inclined to be very
grateful to the Sanitary Board if the
war it is waging against exorbitant
cab-fares results in the confusion of
the Jehu' – 'The Cab Question',
S & DN, 23 September 1896.

53 See 'Cab Proprietors', *S & DN*,
27 February 1897, and 'Cab Fares',
S & DN, 2 March 1897.

54 For an example of continued complaints see 'How We are Bled',
S & DN, 2 July 1897.

55 As late as August 1897 the cab drivers were still operating the alliance
by circulating a petition against the
introduction of the electric tram in
both the town and the countryside.
See report in the *Johannesburg Times*,
4 August 1897.

56 Para based on: *Longland's
Johannesburg and District Directory
1890*, p 101; JPL, JCA Box 213, Cab
Owners to Chairman and Members,
Sanitary Board, 10 January 1891;
*Longland's Johannesburg and District
Directory 1896*, p 277; 'Cab
Proprietors', *S & DN*, 27 February
1897; 'Johannesburg Jehus', *The Star*,
19 February 1898; and the advert for
'Thornton's Trolley and Cab',
S & DN, 2 December 1898.

57 This para based on: 'Johannesburg
Jehus', *The Star*, 19 February 1898;
'Johannesburg Cabmen', *The Star*,
7 January 1907; and an interview
with Mr Isadore Sagorin at
Turffontein, Johannesburg, on
15 August 1978. (Interview conducted by C van Onselen and Mr S Kahn,
and hereafter referred to as 'Sagorin
Interview'.)

58 As one local journalist put it: 'The

"Cape cart" is dropping into disfavour, and the winter of its existence
is already autumned.' 'Johannesburg
Jehus', *The Star*, 19 February 1898.

59   *Ibid*, and Sagorin Interview,
     15 August 1978.

60   'Johannesburg Jehus', *The Star*,
     19 February 1898.

61   *Ibid*. See also 'Discontented Drivers',
     Transvaal Leader, 14 January 1903;
     E Humphrey to Editor, *Transvaal
     Leader*, 17 April 1902; and Sagorin
     Interview, 15 August 1978.

62   'Our Cabs and "Cabbies"', *S & DN*,
     25 February 1899.

63   'Johannesburg Jehus', *The Star*,
     19 February 1898.

64   J P FitzPatrick to J Wernher, 25 July
     1900, in A H Duminy and W R Guest
     (eds), *FitzPatrick* (Johannesburg
     1976), p 274.

65   *Ibid*.

66   Curtis, *With Milner in South Africa*, p vii.

67   For Curtis's most explicit statement
     about this see *With Milner in South
     Africa*, p 256. For further background
     to the work and context of the
     Octavia Hill schemes see Gareth
     Stedman-Jones, *Outcast London*
     (London 1971), pp 193-6.

68   See the Curtis diary entries for March
     and April in *With Milner in South
     Africa*, pp 203-18. See also Major
     O'Meara's 'Note on Proposed
     Reconstruction, Johannesburg
     Municipality', 15 April 1901, cited in
     Sir John Maud's *City Government*
     (Oxford 1938), p 119.

69   Extract from 'Johannesburg Muni-
     cipality – Memorandum on the
     Present and Future Boundaries of Jo-
     hannesburg'. Reprinted in full in Cur-
     tis, *With Milner in South Africa*, p 260.

70   *Ibid*, pp 257-73.

71   Curtis, *With Milner in South Africa*,
     p 217.

72   See *Command 623 of 1901*, and TAD,
     Gov Vol 463, 'Jhb City & Suburban
     Tramway Concession', 22 October 1901.

73   Curtis, *With Milner in South Africa*,
     pp 258-73.

74   *Ibid*, in C Headlam (ed.) *The Milner
     Papers*, Vol 2 (London 1933), pp 276-7.

75   Johannesburg, *Mayor's Minute 1901-3*,
     p 8.

76   *Ibid*. See also J Maud, *City
     Government*, p 119.

77   For some public responses to these
     delays see the following examples
     drawn from *The Star*: 'Trams at Last',
     21 June 1902; 'The Tramways',
     3 September 1902; and 'An Elector' to
     editor, on 'Electric Tramway Silence',
     7 March 1904.

78   Johannesburg, *Mayor's Minute 1905*,
     p 9. Also J Maud, *City Government*,
     p 119.

79   Para based on: S Court, 'The Progress
     of Johannesburg', *Addresses and
     Papers read at the Joint Meeting of the
     British and South African Associations
     for the Advancement of Science 1905*,
     Vol 4, Appendix 9, p 186;
     Johannesburg, *Mayor's Minute 1913-
     15*, p 93; and J Maud, *City
     Government*, p 120.

80. Para based on: Johannesburg,
     Mayor's Minute 1905, p 8; S Court,
     'The Progress of Johannesburg',
     p 171; J Maud, *City Government*,
     p 120; and 'Notes and Comments',
     The Star, 27 July 1909.

81   Data derived from Johannesburg,
     Mayor's Minute, covering the period
     from 1904 to 1914.

82   Para based on: 'Work for the
     Council', *The Star*, 17 January 1902;
     'Cab Drivers' Union', *Transvaal
     Leader*, 24 April 1902; 'Discontented
     Drivers', *Transvaal Leader*, 14 January
     1903; and Johannesburg, *Minutes of
     the Town Council Meeting*, 28 January
     1903, pp 1276-7.

83   Para based on the following reports
     in *The Star* of 17 January 1902: 'The
     Cab Service', 'Work for the Council',
     and 'Assault on a Cab Driver'. See
     also, however, Johannesburg, *Mayor's
     Minute 1907*, p 99, 'Comparative
     Statement of Convictions against Cab
     Drivers from 1 January 1905 to
     30 June 1907'.

84   Para based on: 'Transvaal Refugee
     Committee – Monthly Report', *The
     Star*, 13 March 1902; Johannesburg,
     *Minute of the Town Council Meetings
     1902*, p 378 and p 951; and
     'Discontented Drivers', *Transvaal*

Leader, 14 January 1903.

85 See: 'The Cab Service', *The Star*, 17 January 1902; 'Cab Drivers' Union', *Transvaal Leader*, 24 April 1902; and Johannesburg, *Minutes of Town Council Meetings*, 28 January 1903, p 1277. By 1905 at least one black cab owner remained in business – one William Beukes. See TAD, SNA Vol 60, NA 3681/05, 'List of Letters of Exemption Granted'.

86 *Ibid.*

87 See, 'Work for the Council', *The Star*, 17 January 1902.

88 Simonovitz, 'The Jewish Community in the South African Republic, 1890-1902', pp 63-6.

89 Afroim Sagorin who arrived in Cape Town in 1902 was one example of such an immigrant. Born at Wilna in 1885, Sagorin was conscripted into the Russian army in the mid-1890s and spent the duration of his military service attending to the horse of a colonel in the Cossack Regiment. At the end of his military service the young Afroim made his way to South Africa where he already had two elder brothers. After trying unsuccessfully to get work as a cab driver in Cape Town, where proficiency in English was a requirement for a licence, Afroim made his way to Johannesburg late in 1902. Here he learnt English, as well as the cab and horse trade, through Jimmy Green who later became a mayor of Johannesburg. Green accompanied the young Lithuanian immigrant on the 'box' of the Victoria and translated the customers' instructions into Yiddish until such time as Sagorin had sufficient mastery of the new language. With the example of an older brother already making a living as a produce merchant, Afroim eventually also accumulated sufficient capital to enter the related business of buying and selling horses. In later years Afroim Sagorin and his sons came to run one of Johannesburg's most successful saddlery and harness businesses. Sagorin Interview, 15 August 1978.

90 Simonovitz, 'The Jewish Community in the South African Republic, 1890-1902', p 15.

91 In addition to the customary objectives of any union, the association sought to 'establish harmony and good fellowship, and to provide legal and monetary assistance to deserving members'. See 'Cab Drivers' Union', *Transvaal Leader*, 24 April 1902.

92 'Cabmen's Grievances', *Rand Daily Mail*, 14 October 1902.

93 Para based on: 'Cabmen's Grievances', *Rand Daily Mail*, 14 October 1902, and TAD, Lt Gov 68/75/82, William Kingsley to the Lieutenant Governor of the Transvaal, 22 November 1904.

94 This para based on: 'Discontented Drivers', *Transvaal Leader*, 14 January 1903, and 'Cabby's Grievances', *Rand Daily Mail*, 16 January 1903.

95 Para based on: Johannesburg: *Minutes of the Town Council Meetings*, 28 Janaury 1903, pp 1276-7, 'The New Cab Tariff', *Transvaal Leader*, 17 April 1903; W N Kingsley to the editor, *The Star*, 20 April 1903; and 'Cab Drivers and their Methods', *The Star*, 27 May 1903.

96 Sagorin Interview, 15 August 1978. Also, interview with Mr Ben Gaddie at Greenside, Johannesburg, on 10 April 1977. From these interviews and other material it is also clear that cab owners frequently set 'traps' for their drivers. See for example 'Cabby and his Fare', *S & DN*, 24 September 1897.

97 Sagorin Interview, 15 August 1978. The cab drivers also had a long history of bribing the police and municipal officials. For a selection of examples see: 'The Cab Question', *S & DN*, 23 September 1896; 'The New Cab Tariff', *Transvaal Leader*, 17 April 1903; 'Cab Drivers and their Methods', *The Star*, 27 May 1903; and 'Bribing an Official', *Transvaal Leader*, 7 December 1905.

98 For this background information see: 'Johannesburg Jehus', *Rand Daily Mail*, 15 July 1905; 'The Cabmen's Strike', *The Star*, 17 July 1905; 'Jehus

on Strike', *Rand Daily Mail*, 17 July 1905; and 'The Owners' Point of View', *Rand Daily Mail*, 20 July 1905.

99 See 'Cabmen on Strike', *Transvaal Leader*, 17 July 1905; 'Jehus on Strike', *Rand Daily Mail*, 17 July 1905; and 'The Cab Strike Ends', *Transvaal Leader*, 18 July 1905.

100 The two preceding paras based on: 'The Cabmen's Strike', *The Star*, 15 July 1905; 'Cabmen on Strike', *Transvaal Leader*, 17 July 1905; 'Jehus on Strike', *Rand Daily Mail*, 17 July 1905; and 'Cab Strike Sequel', *Transvaal Leader*, 18 July 1905.

101 See Leibel Feldman's Yiddish work, *The Jews of Johannesburg* (South African Yiddish Cultural Federation, Johannesburg 1956), pp 137-41. I am most grateful to Mr G Saron for drawing this work to my attention and generously providing me with a translation.

102 Para based on: 'The Cabmen's Strike', *The Star*, 17 July 1905; 'Cabmen on Strike', *Transvaal Leader*, 17 July 1905; and 'Jehus on Strike', *Rand Daily Mail*, 17 July 1905.

103 Para based on: 'Without Prejudice' and 'Jehus on Strike', in *Rand Daily Mail*, 17 July 1905; 'The Cabmen's Strike', *The Star*, 17 July 1905; and 'The Cab Strike Ends', *Transvaal Leader*, 18 July 1905.

104 'The Cabmen's Strike', *The Star*, 17 July 1905. See also, 'The Cab Strike', *Daily Express*, 18 July 1905.

105 *Ibid*. See also W N Kingsley to the editor, *The Star*, 22 July 1905.

106 See 'The Cab Strike', *Daily Express*, 18 July 1905, and 'The Cab Strike', *Rand Daily Mail*, 19 July 1905.

107 'The Cab Strike', *Rand Daily Mail*, 19 July 1905, and 'The Cab Strike', *Transvaal Leader*, 19 July 1905.

108 *Ibid*.

109 See especially 'Owners Support Drivers' in *The Star*, 19 July 1905, and 'Cabmen's Union', *The Star*, 24 July 1905.

110 'The Cabmen's Strike', *Rand Daily Mail*, 19 July 1905.

111 'Cab Strike Ends', *Transvaal Leader*, 20 July 1905.

112 'The Owners' Point of View – An Official Statement', *Rand Daily Mail*, 20 July 1905.

113 'Cabmen's Union', *The Star*, 24 July 1905.

114 See the following items drawn from *The Star*: 'The Electric Trams', 14 February 1906; 'The Trams', 3 April 1907; 'The Tramways', 5 April 1907; and 'Johannesburg Cabmen', 7 January 1907. Statistics derived from Table 4.2.

115 The first attempt at introducing a form of taxi service in Johannesburg dated back to immediately after the war. See 'Prospectus of the Johannesburg Motor Car Company', *The Star*, 19 August 1902.

116 Para based on the following: 'Motor Taxi-Cabs', *The Star*, 17 December 1908; 'The First Taxicab', *The Star*, 5 February 1909; 'Taxi Please!', *Transvaal Leader*, 9 February 1909; 'The Taxi in Johannesburg', *The Star*, 8 April 1909; 'Taxi-Cab Owners', *The Star*, 15 September 1909; and 'How we Travel', *The Star*, 17 August 1909.

117 Para based on: 'Johannesburg Cabmen', *The Star*, 7 January 1907, and 'Cab Sir', *The Star*, 4 January 1913.

118 See *Report of the Transvaal Indigency Commission 1906-1908*, evidence of S J Halford, p 9; Acting Commissioner of Police, paras 1508-13, and Dr T B Gilchrist, paras 5638-9. Given his experiences in charity work in London it is perhaps predictable that Lionel Curtis was a member of this commission. Curtis was thus in the position of introducing the electric tram to the city and then having to investigate at least some of its structural consequences.

119 See the following items in *The Star*: 'Jehus on Strike', 7 October 1908; 'Cabmen's Strike', 8 October 1908; and 'Cabdrivers' Strike', 19 October 1908.

120 See especially: 'Cab Owners and Drivers – Complaint against the Council', *The Star*, 21 December 1911; 'Cab Sir', *The Star*, 4 January 1913, and 'Notes and Comments', *The Star*, 19 February 1914.

PART TWO: NEW NINEVEH

1 THE WITCHES OF SUBURBIA

1   J Cook, *Maids and Madams: A Study in the Politics of Exploitation* (Johannesburg 1890). The two most accessible of the surveys are: E Preston-Whyte, 'Race Attitudes and Behaviour: The Case of Domestic Employment in White South African Homes', *African Studies*, 35, 2, 1976, pp 71-89, and M G Whisson and W Weil, *Domestic Servants* (Johannesburg 1971).

2   D Katzman, *Seven Days a Week* (New York 1978). Amongst other works relating to domestic service in England, the following were found to be useful: J Burnett, *Useful Toil* (London 1974), L Davidoff, *The Best Circles: Society, Etiquette and the Season* (London 1973), P Horn, *The Rise and Fall of the Victorian Domestic Servant* (Dublin 1975) and, of course, F Thompson, *Lark Rise to Candleford* (London 1973).

3   J Jean Hecht, *The Domestic Servant Class in Eighteenth-Century England* (London 1956), p xi.

4   B Doyle, *The Etiquette of Race Relations: A Study in Social Control* (New York 1971).

5   *Johannesburg Census* 1896, Order IV, p 38.

6   *Ibid*. See also *The Star*, 9 January 1897, and *Longland's Johannesburg and District Directory 1899*, pp 262-263.

7   *The Star*, 27 January 1897.

8   For an indication of a base line of wages see 'Hotel Employees' in the *Standard and Diggers' News*, 27 February 1897 (hereafter abbreviated to *S & DN*). More generally, see the excellent article on 'The Cost of Living – The Servant Problem', in *The Star*, 27 January 1899.

9   *Ibid*.

10 *Ibid*.

11 In 1896 there were 553 black women in employment in domestic service in Johannesburg. See J J Fourie, 'Die Koms van die Bantoe na die Rand en hulle posisie aldaar, 1886-1899', MA thesis, Randse Afrikaanse Universiteit, December 1976, p 141. See also, *S & DN*, 27 March 1896. For Coloured women in domestic service see, for example, *S & DN*, 14 September 1898, or *The Star*, 27 January 1899.

12 L Davidoff and R Hawthorn, *A Day in the Life of a Victorian Domestic Servant* (London 1976), p 81.

13 For the origin of registry offices see J Jean Hecht, *The Domestic Servant Class*, p 19. In Johannesburg, see *Census* 1896, Order IV, p 38, and *Longland's Johannesburg and District Directory*, 1899.

14 See *S & DN* of 9 January 1897, 27 February 1897 and 25 March 1897.

15 See for example the letter to the editor of *The Press* (Pretoria) by the labour leader J T Bain, reproduced in *S & DN*, 1 February 1894.

16 *S & DN*, 16 August 1898.

17 *The Star*, 27 January 1899. See also *S & DN*, 28 August 1897.

18 Thus Martharina van Wyk (see 16 above) deserted from service in order to become a waitress in Pretoria. Mrs C M Venn, a 'Rand Pioneer', brought a German maid with her from the coast in the 1880s. 'But "Matilda" was soon spirited away by a barkeeper with the offer of a handsome salary.' 'Lady Pioneers on the Rand', *South African Lady's Pictorial*, 2, 13, September 1911, p 45. For an example of a housemaid-cum-prostitute in Johannesburg, see the case of Mathilde Young in Cape Archives Depot, Attorney General's papers, Vol AG 1026, German Consul General to Attorney General, 31 July 1903. This combination of servant and prostitute was not, of course, confined to mining towns. See also P Horn, *The Victorian Servant*, pp 133-135.

19 *The Star*, 27 January 1899 and Mrs Lionel Phillips, *Some South African Recollections* (London 1899), p 116.

20 'Lady Pioneers on the Rand', *South African Lady's Pictorial*, 2, 20, April 1912, p 18.

21 A R Colquhoun, *Dan to Beersheba*

(London 1908), p 268.

22 This pattern of wage trends has been established from widely scattered fragments of newspaper and other material throughout the period. Some of the more helpful items include: H Lionel Tangye, *In New South Africa* (London 1896), p 88; 'Native Wages Question' in the *Johannesburg Weekly Times*, 26 December 1896; 'Hotel Employees' in *S & DN*, 27 February 1897; 'Houseboys' Wages' in *The Star*, 3 May 1897; and 'Kaffir Domestics' in the *S & DN*, 25 October 1898.

23 *Ibid.*

24 *The Star*, 3 May 1897.

25 See for example *Johannesburg Weekly Times*, 26 December 1896; 'Nil Desperandum' to the editor, *The Star*, 13 July 1898 and 'RED' to the editor, *S & DN*, 27 October 1898.

26 *The Star*, 3 May 1897.

27 *Command 1895, Further Correspondence relating to the Affairs of the Transvaal and Orange River Colonies* (HMSO London 1904), Appendix 1, p 342.

28 Again, this information is culled from a wide variety of sources containing fragments of evidence. Amongst the more helpful were 'At the Street Corner' in *S & DN*, 23 October 1895 and 'Kaffir Domestics' in *S & DN*, 25 October 1898.

29 S Marks, *Reluctant Rebellion* (Oxford 1970), pp 128-130.

30 For employers' complaints about the high turnover of labour see 'Kaffir Domestics' in *S & DN*, 25 October 1898, and several letters addressed to the editor of *The Star*, 6 December 1904.

31 See 'Moneyless Kitchen Boys', *S & DN*, 9 October 1899.

32 See for example *S & DN*, 12 October 1899.

33 See 'Female Emigration' in *The Star*, 30 April 1902. Predictably enough this influx led to a shortage of cheap labour in domestic service in Cape Town in the post-war period. See 'The Servant Problem' in *The Star*, 5 December 1904.

34 *Report of the Small Holdings Commission (Transvaal) 1913* (UG 51-13), p 12. For the expansion in the demand for domestic servants which this engendered in white working-class homes see for example Madelaine Alston, *At Home on the Veld* (London 1906), p 69.

35 For examples, see *The Star* of 15 March 1902, 17 April 1902 and 18 September 1902.

36 See 'Women's Immigration' in *The Star*, 28 April 1902, and 'The Needs of South Africa' in *The Star*, 30 April 1902. See also Transvaal Archives Depot (TAD) Gov, Vol 146, Enclosure No 2 in Transvaal Despatch No 102 of 12 February 1902 and TAD Gov, Vol 150, Acting Sec, Tvl Immigration Office to Private Sec, HE The Governor, 11 May 1904.

37 See 'Women's Affairs' in *The Star*, 18 February 1905. Also, Lady Knightley of Fawsley, 'The Terms and Conditions of Domestic Service in England and South Africa', *Imperial Colonist*, Vol IV, No 48, December 1905, p 139.

38 See for example 'Householders' to editor, *The Star*, 19 July 1902. More importantly, see 'Loafing Kafirs – The House Boy Question' in *The Star*, 16 August 1902.

39 For 'houseboy' wages between 1902 and 1906, see TAD Gov, Vol 150, Acting Sec, Tvl Immigration Office to Private Sec HE The Governor, 11 May 1904, p 2, and *The Star*, 29 November 1904, 1 December 1904, and 21 December 1906. For estimates of the number of 'houseboys' in employment in Johannesburg in 1905-6, see W H Vivian, 'The Cost of Living in Johannesburg', *Imperial Colonist*, IV, 39, March 1905, p 27, and Philip Hammond to editor of *The Star*, 20 December 1906. In a talk on 'Natives as House Servants' in February 1909, A R Hands gave 30 000 as an 'official' estimate – see University of the Witwatersrand Archives, CPSA, AB 767, Diocesan Board of Mission Minutes 1905-21. In an election speech in 1911, the Treasurer of the Union Government

suggested that there were 150 000 'houseboys' employed in Johannesburg and Pretoria. See *The Star*, 18 October 1911. *The Report of the Commission Appointed to Enquire into Assaults on Women in 1913* (UG 34-13), however, estimated that there were about 90 000 domestic servants employed on the Rand (para 42, p 14).

40 TAD, SNA, File NA 1008/02, Major H J A Eyre to all Camp Superintendents, Circular No 46, 30 April 1902.

41 M Streak, *Lord Milner's Immigration Policy for the Transvaal 1897-1905* (Rand Afrikaans University Publication, Series B1, January 1969), pp 44-45. In 1903 it was estimated in an article in the *Quarterley Review* that there were 43 000 more men than women in the Transvaal – see report in *The Star*, 14 August 1903.

42 This paragraph is based on: 'Women's Immigration', *The Star*, 18 April 1902; S. African Emigration, *The Star*, 21 April 1902; 'Women's Immigration – South African Expansion Committee', *The Star*, 28 April 1902; and 'The Needs of South Africa', *The Star*, 30 April 1902. Also, *Transvaal Administration Report for 1905*, Immigration Dept, pp J1-J7.

43 *Ibid*, and Streak, *Milner's Immigration Policy*, p 44-45.

44 *Imperial Colonist*, II, 5 May 1903, p 54. For this Irish preference see also *The Star*, 30 December 1913.

45 Table constructed from the following sources: TAD Gov, Vol 146, 'Extract from Report by the Secretary of the Transvaal Immigration Office', Johannesburg, dated 29 January 1904; TAD Gov, Vol 150, Acting Sec, Tvl Immigration Office to Private Sec, HE The Governor, 11 May 1904, p 1; and *Transvaal Administration Reports 1905*, Immigration Dept, p J4.

46 Evidence of Mrs Marian Logan (SACS) to *Transvaal Indigency Commission 1906-08* (TG 13-1908), para 8571 and 8597, and *Imperial Colonist*, IX, No 114, June 1911. See also 'Imported English Girls' in *The*

Star, 14 January 1910.

47 See P Horn, *The Rise and Fall of the Victorian Domestic Servant*, pp 23-5, or L Davidoff and R Hawthorn, *Victorian Domestic Servant*, p 77. This 'exporting' of domestic servants thus met with English resistance; see Mrs Evelyn Cecil, 'The Needs of South Africa', *The Star*, 30 April 1902. For distaste of domestic service in South Africa amongst white women, see Lady Knightley of Fawsley, 'The Terms of Conditions of Domestic Service in England and South Africa', p 137, or *Transvaal Indigency Commission 1906-08*, para 1743.

48 City of London Polytechnic, Fawcett Library, Mss Vol 41, *South African Colonisation Society Reports 1903*, p 52. See also *Imperial Colonist*, 11, 6 June 1903, p 66.

49 Countess of Selborne, 'Demand for White Nurses in the Transvaal', *Imperial Colonist*, X, 127, July 1912, p 119.

50 TAD Gov, Vol 150, Acting Sec Tvl Immigration Office to Private Sec, HE The Governor, 11 May 1904, p 2, and *Transvaal Indigency Commission 1906-08*, para 1948 and statement by Dr T B Gilchrist, p 240. By WW1 secondary industry was already sufficiently advanced for authorities to despair of successfully 'importing' white female domestics; see *Report of the Commission appointed to Enquire into Assaults on Women 1913* (UG 39-13), para 123.

51 Fawcett Library, Mss Vol 41, *South African Colonisation Society Report 1904*, p 80.

52 See for example 'Notes and Comments' in *The Star*, 14 December 1908 and Miss C Nina Boyle on 'The White Servant Question' to editor, *The Star*, 18 December 1908. It was estimated that within the first five years of the scheme, one in three immigrant domestics got married. See evidence of Mrs Marian Logan (SACS) to *Transvaal Indigency Commission 1906-08*, paras 8576-8577. The problem, of course, pre-dated the SACS. On 27 January 1899, *The Star*

noted of the white female domestic servant: 'If she is at all good looking she had no trouble in getting a husband, and as a rule one who can give her a much more exalted position than she could ever dream of in the Old Country.'

53 *The Star*, 18 October 1911. It was also for this reason that advertisements for white servants in the 'Situations Vacant' column were frequently forced to carry the reassuring phrase 'boy kept' if they wished to attract respondents. See examples in *The Star* of 29 August 1903, 7 December 1903 and 28 January 1904.

54 See 'JD's' letter to 'Lady C', reproduced in the *Imperial Colonist*, II, 6 June 1903, p 69.

55 See H M Downes to editor, *The Star*, 3 December 1904 and two other letters to the editor in *The Star*, 6 December 1904. Clearest of all, however, is M Wilkinson to editor, *The Star*, 8 December 1904.

56 Edgar P Rathbone to editor, *The Star*, 23 November 1904. Also, 'Native Servant Question' by Rathbone in *The Star*, 8 December 1904.

57 Central events in the EDNLA scheme are recorded in the following newspaper accounts: E P Rathbone to editor, *The Star*, 23 November 1904, H M Downes to editor, *The Star*, 3 December 1904, and E P Rathbone to editor, *The Star*, 8 December 1904. See also editorials of *The Star* in the following issues: 5 December 1904, 7 December 1904, 9 December 1904 and 27 December 1904. The full prospectus of the EDNLA was published in *The Star*, 8 December 1904.

58 For the decline of the scheme, see E P Rathbone to editor, in *The Star* of 15 and 27 December 1904. Also, 'Native Domestic Servants' in *The Star*, 24 January 1905.

59 This paragraph is largely based on the following reports in *The Star*: 'White Domestic Servants', 5 March 1907; 'Unemployed Women', 14 March 1907; and 'Women's Problem – The Domestic Servant', 17 October 1907.

60 Nina Boyle, a noted middle-class activist, thus wrote to the editor of *The Star* on 18 December 1908: 'My own scheme, that legislation should be introduced for the compulsory training and employment, as in workhouses at Home, of the children of those who habitually live on charity, seems to me a reasonable and satisfactory one, though neither original nor sensational. It would ensure a supply of white women servants, would spur many chronic idlers to effort, and would lift a large class from degradation into decency.' For an excellent analysis of how these operated in contemporary England, see Gareth Stedman-Jones, *Outcast London* (Oxford 1971).

61 'Notes and Comments', *The Star*, 8 October 1908.

62 See for example *Transvaal Indigency Commission 1906-08*, paras 1761-1768.

63 *The Star*, 10 March 1906. See also 'Transvaaler' to editor, *The Star*, 7 April 1909.

64 For this pattern of reasoning, see the report on a public meeting entitled 'Black Peril' in *The Star*, 2 July 1908. For specific connections with domestic training, see M C Bruce (Sec Native Girls' Industrial School Committee) to editor, *The Star*, 10 December 1908, and later, *Report of the Commission appointed to Enquire into Assaults on Women 1913*, para 138.

65 For information on the Church Industrial Schools, see University of the Witwatersrand Archives, CPSAAB 767, Diocesan Board of Mission Minutes 1905-21, 'Natives as House Servants', talk given by A R Hands at meeting held on 4 February 1909. This is supplemented by information drawn from the following items in *The Star*: M C Bruce to editor, 2 July 1908; 'Kaffir Housemaids', 11 December 1908; 'Native Women – The New Movement', 17 March 1909; 'Native Women', 20 March 1909; and 'The Hull Tax', 18 October 1911.

66 *Ibid*. See also, however, D Gaitskell,

'"Christian Compounds for Girls": Church Hostels for African Women in Johannesburg, 1907-1970', *Journal of Southern African Studies*, 6, 1, 1979, pp 44-49. For a black perspective on the scheme and some of the other reasons that lay behind its failure, see the leading article on 'Domestic Service' in *Ilanga Lase Natal*, 24 November 1911.

67 'Do you think that the majority of young Native females who come to work get ruined by white men? Yes, very nearly all of them; very few escape – not more than ten per cent.' R C Alexander, Superintendent of Police, Durban, in evidence to *South African Native Affairs Commission 1903-05*, 111, para 23 292, p 647. In the Transvaal, see the opinions of William Letseleba (Chairman of Transvaal Native Union) as expressed in his correspondence with the Governor-General and reproduced in *The Star*, 24 October 1911. Most specific of all, however, is S T Plaatje on 'Miscegenation' (*Pretoria News*, 30 January 1911), reprinted in T J Couzens and B Willan (eds), *English in Africa* (Grahamstown), 3, 2, September 1976, p 83. Plaatje's contention that white male employers – and especially those of British descent – seduced black servants while their wives were away from home for various reasons was subsequently confirmed by a later enquiry. See *Report of the Commission appointed to Enquire into Assaults on Women 1913*, para 18.

68 For an account of some of these attitudes and activities, see for example 'Krugersdorp' in *The Star*, 16 November 1908.

69 For the full range of these attitudes, see the following items in *The Star*: M C Bruce to the editor, 10 December 1908; 'Kaffir Housemaids', 11 December 1908; M Wyndham to editor, 18 December 1908; and several letters to the editor, 13 February 1908.

70 See 'The Servant Problem' and 'Kaffir Housemaids' in *The Star* of 23 January 1908 and 11 December 1908.

71 See Carole Cooper, 'Land and Labour in the Transvaal c 1900', MA African Studies, University of London, September 1974, pp 27-34.

72 For general information on these firms, see TAD, SNA, Vol 82, 371/08 and SNA File No 2259/08. Also, *The Star*, 24 November 1908.

73 See 'The Servant Problem', 'Piccanins for Domestic Service' and 'Piccanins – The Government Registry', all in *The Star*, 23 January 1908.

74 See TAD, SNA File 2259/08, H Payne, Inspector Native Affairs Dept, to Director, Govt Native Labour Bureau, 27 August 1908. Also *The Star*, 29 January 1908.

75 'Piccanins', *The Star*, 13 February 1908.

76 See for example 'Piccanin House Boys', in *The Star*, 3 February 1909.

77 This paragraph is based on the following items drawn from *The Star*: 'Native Domestic Labour', 2 November 1907; 'Piccanins', 23 January 1908; Henry Adler to editor, 11 April 1908; 'Piccaninies', 24 November 1908; and the item 'House and Shop Natives' in the weekly 'Commercial Affairs' column of 17 July 1909.

78 Drawn from the following items in *The Star*: H W Hartland on 'The Wages Question' to editor, 31 October 1907, and 'House and Shop Natives', 17 July 1909. See also, TAD, SNA, NA 4199/07, Mrs J L Robinson to Gen Louis Botha, 9 December 1907.

79 Paragraph based on the following items from *The Star*: 'Common Sense' to editor, 6 February 1911; 'Town and Reef', 8 August 1911; 'Disheartened' to editor, 8 May 1912, and 'Black Peril', 30 December 1913. The wage rate is drawn from *Report of the Small Holdings Commission (Transvaal) 1913*.

80 *Ibid*.

81 See 'Labour Problem' and 'The Hull Tax' in *The Star* of 17 and 18 October 1911.

82 'Abolish the Houseboy?', *Rand Daily Mail*, 1 May 1912.

83 In 1911 it was estimated that it would

cost £40 to fully equip a house with electric appliances of a wide range. See 'Household Electricity' and 'Commercial Affairs' in *The Star*, 15 July 1911. The prognosis for the electric cooker can be found in 'Solving the Servant Problem', *The Star*, 18 March 1912. Public consumption of electricity continued to lag, however, and in late 1912 the city council was forced to spend £140 in a campaign to advertise the benefits of domestic electricity, see *The Star*, 8 August 1912. For several decades, however, white South Africans were extremely slow to switch to electric appliances.

84 See Carole Cooper, 'Land and Labour in the Transvaal c 1900', MA thesis, p 27. See also, *Report of the Commission appointed to Enquire into Assaults on Women 1913*, para 105 and paras 131-138.

85 See the following items in *The Star*: 'House and Shop Natives', 17 July 1909; 'Englishwoman' to the editor, 4 February 1911; and 'The Cost of Living', 27 January 1914. See also *Report of the Economic Commission* (UG 12 of 1914), para 24.

86 *Ibid*. In its editorial on 27 January 1914, *The Star* noted: 'Another item that differentiates Rand habits from English is the extent to which natives are employed as servants by the families of artisans ... We are strongly convinced that it is to local production, coupled to some extent with a *change in the habits of the working classes*, that we must look for a real and permanent cheapening in the cost of living.' (Author's emphasis.)

87 Paragraph based on the following items: 'Doings and Darnaway – High Life Below Stairs', *S & DN*, 1 July 1896; 'White Servants' Contracts', *Rand Daily Mail*, 30 January 1903; 'Situation Vacant', *The Star*, 12 August 1903 and 8 March 1904; 'Master and Servant', *The Star*, 2 March 1906; and 'Epstein Divorce' in *The Star*, 21 and 24 August 1906.

88 *Ibid*. See also the following items in *The Star*: 'The Cost of Living',

27 January 1899; 'Immigration of British Women', 5 February 1903; and 'Town and Reef', 8 August 1911. For an example of an employment profile of a Rand housemaid, see Annie Walkman's evidence in the 'Epstein Divorce' in *The Star*, 21 August 1906.

89 Paragraph based on: 'Charge of Assault', *S & DN*, 4 March 1899; 'White Servants' Contracts', *Rand Daily Mail*, 30 January 1903; 'Johannesburg Housekeepers', *The Star*, 20 October 1903; and 'Servants: How to Treat Them', *The Star*, 29 November 1912.

90 These two paras based on: 'Girls on the Rand', *Diamond Fields' Advertiser*, 31 March 1898 and TAD, Gov, Vol 146, 'Extract from Report by the Sec of the Tvl Immigration Office', Johannesburg, 29 January 1904. In the same file see also 'Distress in South Africa', an extract from the *Edinburgh Evening News*, 16 December 1903. See also 'Girls' Friendly Society', *The Star*, 25 November 1905. For background to the Society see Horn, *The Rise and Fall of the Victorian Servant*, pp 106-7.

91 See the letters by 'JHC' and 'JD' reproduced in the *Imperial Colonist*, II, 6, June 1903, pp 68-9. See also 'Housewife' and 'Observant' to editor, *The Star*, 18 October 1907 and 1 July 1910.

92 The problem of 'Jack being as good as his master (of a similar colour)', was an old one in the colonies. See for example the article on 'The Domestic Servant' in *S & DN*, 8 May 1891. For a clear statement of the two possible patterns of relationships, see Sir Matthew Nathan's comments in the *Imperial Colonist*, VIII, 102, June 1910, p 84. Also Mrs Phillip's, 'A Three Months' View of Women's Opportunities and Work in South Africa' in *Imperial Colonist*, IV, 37, January 1905, p 6. For an example of employer resentment of servant transgression of class boundaries, see 'Housewife' to editor, *The Star*, 18 October 1907.

93 See especially the superb letter from

'May Ann' to editor, *The Star*, 21 October 1907. See also 'Disheartened' to editor, *The Star*, 8 May 1912.

94 See for example 'Women's Affairs – Mistresses and Maids', *The Star*, 18 February 1905.

95 For some accounts of accommodation of white female domestics see: 'Housing the Women', *The Star*, 13 March 1902; 'Immigration of British Women', *The Star*, 5 February 1903; 'Abolish the Houseboy?', *Rand Daily Mail*, 1 May 1912; 'Servants: How to Treat Them', *The Star*, 29 November 1912; *Report of the Commission appointed to Enquire into Assaults on Women 1913*, para 98; and 'Did not Know it was a Crime', *Transvaal Leader*, 18 July 1914.

96 On the duties of a cook-general see: 'Women's Immigration 11' and 'Mistress' to editor in *The Star* of 18 April 1902 and 22 October 1907. For an account of some of the problems of laundry work in the Johannesburg household see: 'The Cost of Living', *The Star*, 27 January 1899; 'Johannesburg Housekeepers', *The Star*, 20 October 1903; 'Women's Affairs', *The Star*, 18 February 1905; and 'A Question of Colour' in *Transvaal Leader*, 30 December 1908.

97 Paragraph based on: Lady Knightley of Fawsley, 'The Terms and Conditions of Domestic Service in England and South Africa' in *Imperial Colonist*, IV, 48, December 1905, p 138; 'Housewife' to editor, *The Star*, 18 October 1907; and 'A Mistress' to editor, *The Star*, 22 October 1907.

98 'Servants: How to Treat Them', *The Star*, 29 November 1912. Loneliness was not, of course, simply a product of the South African situation – it was, in part, inherent to the job. See P Horn, *The Rise and Fall of the Victorian Servant*, pp 105-6.

99 See *Transvaal Administration Reports for 1905*, Immigration Dept, Annex 8, p J6. Also, 'JC to Lady C' reproduced in *Imperial Colonist*, II, 6 June 1903, pp 59-60.

100 See for example H Lionel Tangye, *In New South Africa* (London 1896), p 88, or Mr Diamond in *The Sun*, *quoted in S & DN*, 5 December 1896.

101 For white nursemaids and their duties, see the following items drawn from *The Star*: 'The Cost of Living', 27 January 1899; 'Situations Vacant', 12 August 1903 and 28 January 1904. See also *Imperial Colonist*, V, 60, December 1906, p 175, and 'Letter to Lady Knox' in *ibid*, X, 124, April 1912, pp 70-1.

102 *The Star*, 23 January 1908.

103 Latter half of para based on: 'Jan and the Nurse Girl', *The Star*, 13 October 1908; 'Transvaaler' to editor, *The Star*, 7 April 1909; The Countess of Selborne, 'Demand for White Nurses in the Transvaal', *Imperial Colonist*, X, 127, July 1912, pp 118-19. See also the letter from 'A Mother' reproduced in *Ilanga lase Natal*, 3 November 1911.

104 Phillip Hammond to editor, *The Star*, 11 March 1909. For earlier Hammond views on the same subject, see his letter to the editor, *The Star*, 20 December 1906.

105 *Imperial Colonist*, VIII, 102, June 1910, p 84.

106 'Housewife' to editor, *The Star*, 2 November 1907. For further problems associated with the socialisation of children, see Mrs H H Oldroyd on the 'Servant Question' in *The Star*, 1 May 1912, and *Imperial Colonist*, X, 127, July 1912, pp 118-19.

107 See the following: 'Nemesis' to editor, *S & DN*, 23 August 1897; H Lionel Tangye, *In New South Africa* (London 1896), p 88; and Adele le Bourgeois Chapin, *Their Trackless Ways* (London 1931), p 115.

108 Editorial on 'The Kaffir Problem', *S & DN*, 13 October 1897.

109 Para based on: 'Housewife' to editor, *The Star*, 9 February 1911; 'Mr Burton's Statement', *The Star*, 24 April 1912; and *Report of the Commission appointed to Enquire into Assaults on Women 1913*, para 109.

110 For some accounts of the 'houseboy's' duties see, for example, Lady Knightley of Fawsley, 'The Terms and Conditions of Domestic Service in

England and South Africa', p 138 and Philip Hammond to editor, *The Star*, 30 December 1906.

111 This para based on: 'The "Laita" Gangs', *Ipepa lo Hlanga*, 20 November 1903; A Scott to editor, *The Star*, 24 February 1908; 'Tonight's Meeting', *The Star*, 7 February 1911; *Imperial Colonist*, IX, 19, November 1911, p 26; and 'Vrededorp's Views', *Rand Daily Mail*, 1 May 1912.

112 This para based on: 'Assault on a Woman', *The Star*, 22 February 1902; C M Dantu (Sec, Jhb Branch APO) to editor, *Transvaal Leader*, 7 February 1911; Sybil Cormack Smith, 'The Wrong Way to Manage Black Servants', *Imperial Colonist*, IX, 19, November 1911, p 25; *Report of the Commission appointed to Enquire into Assaults on Women 1913*, paras 110 and 111; and S T Plaatje, 'The Mote and the Beam' (1912) in T J Couzens and B Willan (eds), *English in Africa, op cit*, pp 90-1.

113 For further information on these relationships see below, section on 'The Black Peril'.

114 See 'Nemesis' to editor, *S & DN*, 23 August 1897; 'Kaffir Domestics', *S & DN*, 28 October 1898; and 'An Englishwoman' to editor, *The Star*, 5 March 1907.

115 See *S & DN*, 11 September 1895; 'Another Suffering Householder' to editor, *The Star*, 1 December 1904; and 'Fit Via Vi' to editor, *The Star*, 9 May 1912.

116 See 'A Bibulous Burglar', *S & DN*, 26 January 1899; 'Charge against a Native', *The Star*, 9 September 1905; Mrs J Roberts to editor, *The Star*, 1 September 1908; and 'Abolish the Houseboy?', *Rand Daily Mail*, 1 May 1912.

117 See especially the excellent descriptions in 'Loafing Kaffirs – The Houseboy Question' in *The Star*, 16 August 1902. See also *Report on the Commission appointed to Enquire into Assaults on Women 1913*, para 98 and para 152.

118 See 'At the Street Corner', *S & DN*, 23 October 1895; 'Housewife' to edi-

tor, *The Star*, 2 November 1907; TAD, SNA, NA 4199/07 Mrs J L Robinson to General Louis Botha, 9 December 1907; and J J Yates to editor, *The Star*, 4 September 1912.

119 Para based on the following items drawn from *The Star*: Mrs J Roberts to the editor, 1 September 1908; 'Native Women', 20 March 1909; and Bertie C Simes to the editor, 8 May 1912.

120 Para based on: 'Another of the Same', *The Star*, 3 February 1906; J Bold to editor, *The Star*, 6 February 1906; M C Bruce to editor, *The Star*, 10 December 1908; and Ambrose Pratt, *The Real South Africa* (London 1913), pp 8, 17-18 and 53.

121 Fawcett Library, Mss Vol 41, *South African Colonisation Society Reports 1903*, p 25.

122 'Yesterday's Trials', *The Star*, 15 March 1902.

123 'Women's Immigration', *The Star*, 28 April 1902.

124 For the Anna Herrmann case, see: 'Notice', *The Star*, 16 January 1903; 'Master and Servant', *The Star*, 30 January 1903; and 'White Servants' Contracts', *Rand Daily Mail*, 30 January 1903.

125 'Master and Servant', *The Star*, 2 March 1906; and 'Master and Servant', *The Star*, 6 March 1906.

126 'Notes and Comments', *The Star*, 7 March 1906.

127 J Bold to editor, *The Star*, 6 February 1906. For earlier examples of complaints by employers, see 'A Grievance', *S & DN*, 2 October 1896; and 'Sufferer', *S & DN*, 21 January 1897.

128 See especially William Letseleba (Chairman, Tvl Native Union) to Governor General, reprinted in *The Star*, 24 October 1911, and *Report of the Commission appointed to Enquire into Assaults of Women 1913*, para 142.

129 *The Star*, 23 February 1914.

130 For examples see the following items drawn from *The Star*: 'Attempted Murder at Boksburg', 4 April 1902; 'The Pass Law Case', 1 February 1906; and 'Mark it "Good"', 17 January 1913.

131 Para based on, amongst other fragments: 'Native Wages Question', *Johannesburg Weekly Times*, 26 December 1896, and 'XYZ' to editor, *The Star*, 17 November 1908.

132 For black male servants see for example: 'He Helped Himself', *S & DN*, 10 August 1895; 'Attack on Mr Webb', *S & DN*, 16 August 1895; and especially 'Izegebengu', *The Star*, 16 June 1896; and 'Native Violence', *The Star*, 17 June 1896. The comments of the cook-general are taken from 'Women's Affairs – Mistresses and Maids', *The Star*, 18 February 1903.

133 *Report of the Commission appointed to Enquire into Assaults on Women 1913*, para 120.

134 Even before the South African War some employers gave their white female servants revolvers to protect themselves against the 'black peril'; see Mrs Lionel Phillips, *Some South African Recollections* (London 1899), p 50. For other examples see: 'Jan Note's Life and Introduction to Crime' in *SA Department of Justice Annual Report 1912*, pp 238-40; 'Insolent Native', *The Star*, 10 January 1912; and 'Charge against a Native', *The Star*, 14 March 1912.

135 For examples of assaults on domestic servants see: 'The Kafir Problem', *S & DN*, 13 October 1897; also the following items drawn from *The Star*: 'Police Court Cases', 7 February 1902; 'Guilty: Yet Not Guilty', 16 October 1907; 'Lashes Awarded', 13 March 1912; and 'Attacked his Employer', 22 December 1913.

136 Para based on the following items drawn from *The Star*: Mrs J Roberts to the editor, 1 September 1908; 'Employers' Responsibilities', 18 November 1908; and 'Servants: How to Treat Them', 29 November 1912.

137 See for example 'Alleged Theft by a Servant', and 'Connoisseur in Smokes', in *The Star* of 17 August 1902 and 9 November 1911.

138 'Fanakalo' is one of the many great unexplored areas in South African social history. However, for a few observations, see '"Kitchen Kaffir" – The Esperanto of South Africa', by 'Umlungu', in *The Star*, 18 July 1913, and C van Onselen, *Chibaro* (London 1976), p 152.

139 For Victorian naming practices, see P Horn, *The Victorian Servant*, p 113. In *The Star* of 4 July 1912 a journalist gave a short list of some of the African 'names' that appeared on the court roll of the Criminal Sessions and commented: 'The names betray a high range of intellectuality on the part of the white people who christened the boys.'

140 For examples see: 'Kafir Domestics', *S & DN*, 25 October 1898; or 'One of the Suffering Householders' to editor, *The Star*, 8 December 1904. For gifts of clothing to white servants see for example 'Charge against a Lady's Maid', *The Star*, 18 July 1903.

141 This and other points are well made in M G Whisson and W Weil, *Domestic Servants* (Johannesburg 1971), pp 40-3.

142 See for example the great editorial battle between *The Star* and the *Standard and Diggers' News* in *S & DN*, 'The Kafir Problem', 13 October 1897. For other examples of European resentment of blacks' dress see: 'Nil Desperandum' to editor, *The Star*, 13 July 1898; 'Loafing Kafirs', *The Star*, 16 August 1902; TAD, SNA, NA 4199/07; Mrs J L Robinson to Gen Louis Botha, 9 December 1907; or 'As Others See Us' to editor, *The Star*, 30 April 1912.

143 'Chatelaine' to editor, *The Star*, 16 February 1911.

144 This para based on: 'The Kafir Problem', *S & DN*, 13 October 1897; 'The "Black Peril"', *Transvaal Leader*, 22 September 1908; Charles O'Hara to editor, *The Star*, 30 April 1912; and 'A Shop Window Evil', *Rand Daily Mail*, 7 January 1914.

145 Para largely based on: 'The Kafir Problem', *S & DN*, 13 October 1897; 'A Mother' to editor, *The Star*, 1 November 1907; and TAD, SNA, NA 4199/07, Mrs J L Robinson to Gen Louis Botha, 9 December 1907.

146 TAD, SNA, NA 4199/07, Mrs J L Robinson to Gen Louis Botha, 9 December 1907. Remainder of the para based on: 'The Kafir Problem', *S & DN*, 13 October 1897; 'The Native Question', *The Star*, 23 January 1902; and Mrs J Roberts to editor, *The Star*, 1 September 1908.

147 'Women's Affairs – The Domestic Bogey', *The Star*, 17 February 1906. The remainder of the para based on: 'Women's Immigration', *The Star*, 28 April 1902; 'Women's Problem – The Domestic Servant', *The Star*, 17 October 1907; 'Householder' to editor, *The Star*, 24 October 1907; and 'To be Mistress of the House', *The Star*, 21 September 1910.

148 *The Imperial Colonist*, II, 5 May 1903, p 54.

149 See: H Lionel Tangye, *In New South Africa* (London 1896), p 86; 'White Servants' Contracts', *Rand Daily Mail*, 30 January 1903; and 'Women's Affairs', *The Star*, 18 February 1905.

150 Para based on: H F Hunt Phillips to editor, *The Star*, 17 June 1896; 'A Grievance', *S & DN*, 2 October 1896; 'The Pass Law Case', *The Star*, 1 February 1906; Mrs J Roberts to editor, *The Star*, 1 September 1908; and *Report of the Commission of Enquiry appointed to Enquire into Assaults on Women 1913*, para 92. This problem of a suitable 'character' – and its solution – was not restricted to the Transvaal. See P Horn, *The Victorian Servant*, p 45.

151 For examples see: 'The Domestic Servant Question', *S & DN*, 5 December 1896; 'Yesterday's Trials', *The Star*, 17 April 1902; 'Charge against a Lady's Maid', *The Star*, 18 July 1903; and 'Connoisseur in Smokes', *The Star*, 9 November 1911. Again, of course, this practice is not confined to servants in the colonial situation. See P Horn, *The Victorian Servant*, pp 138 and 146.

152 See for example 'He Helped Himself', *S & DN*, 10 August 1895, or 'Attempted Murder and Robbery', *The Star*, 4 April 1902. See also the final section of this essay on the

Amalaita.

153 For complaints about black 'insolence' see: 'Pay the Boys by the Month', *Johannesburg Weekly Times*, 26 December 1896; 'The Kafir Problem', *S & DN*, 13 October 1897; 'Householders' to editor, *The Star*, 19 July 1902; 'Loafing Kafirs', *The Star*, 16 August 1902; and 'A Mother' to editor, *The Star*, 1 November 1907. The evidence in note 156 below also pertains to this problem.

154 'The Revd C A Lane and the Coloured People', *The Star*, 25 October 1904.

155 *Transvaal Leader*, 12 July 1906. On the Zululand disturbances, see S Marks, *Reluctant Rebellion* (Oxford 1970).

156 For examples see the following items drawn from *The Star*: 'Police Court Cases', 7 February 1902; 'Time to Reflect', 25 November 1909; 'Trouble with Houseboy', 3 April 1911; 'Mark it "Good"', 17 January 1913; 'Struck a Woman', 25 August 1913; and 'With a Table Knife', 2 December 1913.

157 'Native Crime', *The Star*, 27 December 1913.

158 For rural cases see for example, 'A Would-be Poisoner', in *The Star* of 22 October 1904 and 9 December 1904. For Witwatersrand cases see the following items in *The Star*: 'Alleged Attempted Murder', 14 August 1903; 'Mistress and Servant', 23 August 1907; 'Guilty: Yet Not Guilty', 16 October 1907; and 'House Boy in Trouble', 26 November 1907.

159 'Kafir Servants and Witch Doctors', *S & DN*, 6 December 1898.

160 For some examples of this drawn from Natal see *South African Native Affairs Commission 1903-5*, III, paras 20 089, 20 174, 23 722, 24 630, 26 783, 29 944 and 31 907.

161 As yet I have been unable to trace the original High Court proceedings of this case. All quotes from the movement here and in subsequent paragraphs are taken from the following reports in *The Star*: 'Native Fanatics', 12 August 1909; 'The Taungs Incident', 13 August 1909; 'Ethiopianism', 14 August 1909, and

'The Bechuana Prophets',
9 November 1909.

162 See Part Two, Chapter 4, 'The
Regiment of the Hill', p 175.

163 *Imperial Colonist*, VIII, No 102, June
1910, p 84.

164 See reports in the *S & DN*, 12 October
1895, and 'Jim loved the White Girl',
14 October 1895.

165 Waiter 'Joe', with the assistance of
friend 'John', wrote as follows to an
unmarried fellow waitress: 'Oh my
dear friend, I am sore for you. I like
your hand so dearly. I love you very
much. I do not know what to do with
you because I love you.' This letter
was worth a fine of £3 or one
month's imprisonment. See 'Native
Insolence', *The Star*, 22 August 1913.
Predictably enough the 'tea-rooms'
had their fair share of 'black peril'
scares. See for example 'Native and
White Girls', *The Star*, 23 August
1911. (See also note 50 above and
text.)

166 'A Peculiar Case', *S & DN*, 19 July
1898.

167 'Colonist' to editor, *The Star*,
8 February 1913.

168 See following items in *The Star*:
'Black and White', 23 August 1904;
'Black and White', 21 September
1904; and 'Under the Morality Law',
27 October 1904. See also reports in
the *Pretoria News* of 24 August and
29 October 1904.

169 'White Woman and Native', *The Star*,
17 July 1914, and 'Did not know it
was a Crime', *Transvaal Leader*,
18 July 1914.

170 *Report of the Commission appointed to
Enquire into Assaults on Women 1913*,
paras 112-13 and 139. (Hereafter,
*Commission on Assaults on Women,
1913*.)

171 See, for example, 'A Shocking
Scandal', in *S & DN* on 22 and 23
June 1898.

172 See *Africa's Golden Harvests*, March
1911, p 8; *Commission on Assaults on
Women 1913*, para 112; and
S T Plaatje, 'The Mote and the Beam',
p 90.

173 'Impudent Native', *The Star*,

27 August 1912. See also 'Woman's
Screams', *The Star*, 2 October 1912.

174 This para based on: 'Selling Love
Philtres', *The Star*, 24 September 1902;
'Pretended Love Medicine', *The Star*,
19 April 1907; *Africa's Golden
Harvests*, April 1907, p 14; 'The Black
Peril', *Transvaal Leader*, 26 May 1908
and 27 May 1908; 'Story of
Witchcraft', *The Star*, 29 May 1908;
'Love Potion Trick', *The Star*,
16 September 1908; 'A "Medicine"
Case', *The Star*, 16 September 1908;
'The Black Peril', *Transvaal Leader*,
22 September 1908; and *Commission
on Assaults on Women 1913*, paras 40
and 198.

175 *S & DN*, 15 September 1983.

176 For the Lightfoot case and some of
the subsequent developments, see
the following items drawn from the
S & DN: 'Hanging too Lenient',
30 July 1897; 'Hanging too Merciful',
30 July 1897; 'Public Hanging',
20 August 1897; and 'Public
Hanging', 23 August 1897.

177 For some examples reported in *The
Star* see 'A Night Intruder', 27 May
1904; 'Charge against a Native',
9 September 1905; or 'Charge against
a Kaffir', 19 September 1905.

178 For an extract of the AWOT petition,
see TAD, SNA, NA 1924/07. For
some of the background to this see
the following items in *The Star*:
'Guild of Loyal Women', 19 April
1907; and 'The Black Peril', 7 June
1907.

179 For these events see, amongst other
items in *The Star*, the following: 'The
Black Peril', 3 February 1911; 'Views
of the Workers', 4 February 1911;
'The Mass Meeting', 7 February 1911;
'Vigilane of the Police', 7 February
1911; and 'The Voice of the Rand',
8 February 1911.

180 For this and other events see: *The
Star*, 13 April 1912; 'Black Peril', *The
Star*, 20 April 1912; 'Black Peril', *Rand
Daily Mail*, 20 April 1912; 'Black
Peril', *The Star*, 23 April 1912; 'The
Turffontein Drive', *Rand Daily Mail*,
24 April 1912; 'Mrs Harrison's
Death', *The Star*, 13 June 1913; and

'Turffontein Outrage', *Transvaal Leader*, 3 May 1914.

181 See, amongst other items, the following drawn from the *Rand Daily Mail*: 'The Public and the "Black Peril"', 26 April 1912; 'Only a Few Days More', 1 May 1912; 'Kaffir Drives', 2 May 1912; and 'The Petition and After', 9 May 1912. See also 'Something Achieved', *The Star*, 10 May 1912. On the role of the press during these crises, see *Commission on Assaults on Women 1913*, para 26.

182 See the following items drawn from *The Star*: 'Black Peril', 2 May 1912; 'Turffontein Outrage', 13 January 1912; and 'Turffontein Case', 23 August 1912.

183 For the late 1913 scare see, amongst others, the following items drawn from *The Star*: 'Father's Fight', 2 December 1913; 'Is "Mushla" Insulting?', 5 December 1913; 'Native at the Door', 22 December 1913; 'Attacked his Employer', 22 December 1913; and 'Native Crime', 27 December 1913.

184 'Hanging too Lenient', *S & DN*, 30 July 1897.

185 *Ibid*. The remainder of this para is based on material drawn from the following items in *The Star*: 'The Black Peril', 24 June 1907; 'The Black Peril', 27 April 1908; 'White Woman Attacked', 29 April 1908; and 'Is "Mushla" Insulting?', 5 December 1913. Also *Commission on Assaults on Women 1913*, para 120. This interpretation, however, has been criticised for being 'functionalist' – see T Keegan, 'Black Peril, Lapsed Whites and Moral Peril: A Study of Ideological Crisis in Early Twentieth Century South Africa', unpublished paper, January 1980. It remains unclear, however, how Keegan's remarks, which are based on a study of rural 'black peril' on Orange Free State farms, help us to understand urban 'black peril' cases in white working-class Witwatersrand homes.

186 Thus white domestics did not always instantly draw the attention of their employers or the police to what they considered to be minor sexual advances. For examples of such approaches and delays in reporting them see: 'The Social Pest', *S & DN*, 27 August 1897; 'The Black Peril', *The Star*, 24 June 1907; 'Kitchen Boy Again', *The Star*, 2 September 1907; and 'Alleged Assaults', *The Star*, 1 October 1907.

187 For examples of 'black peril' cases involving white and black servants, see *ibid*, and 'A Night Intruder', *The Star*, 27 May 1904; 'Charge against a Native', *The Star*, 9 September 1905; 'Black Peril Again', *Rand Daily Mail*, 15 September 1908; 'White Woman's Complaints', *The Star*, 2 November 1908; 'Servant Girl's Complaint', *The Star*, 18 May 1911; and 'Lashes Awarded', *The Star*, 13 March 1912.

188 See notes 164 and 166 above, and 'Assaulting a Lady', *The Star*, 8 May 1912. Also S T Plaatje, 'The Mote and the Beam', p 91.

189 See 'Charge of Assault', *S & DN*, 4 March 1899 and the following items drawn from *The Star*: 'Servant Girl's Complaint', 18 May 1911; 'Lashes for Native', 26 November 1912; 'House Broken Into', 16 October 1913; 'Early Morning Alarm', 13 July 1914; and 'Black Peril', 21 July 1914.

190 A good example of this is to be found in the letter from 'An Unprotected Daughter' to editor, *The Star*, 30 November 1911. The author recounted her morning journey to work: 'I looked at the passing people, white and black, and my eyes caught those of a big black man, who in an instant gave me a wicked laugh, and, drawing his thick black lips into a round, thrust out the tip of his red tongue at me, and passed on!' One does not have to be a psychologist to guess at the sort of fear being expressed here. For a further example, see 'Houseboy Sentenced', *The Star*, 2 December 1913. More generally on this problem, see *Commission on Assaults on Women 1913*, para 26.

191 *Commission on Assaults on Women 1913*, paras 140-161.

192 Such as the Randlords, for example.

R W Schumacher consistently made use of the later 'Black Peril' scares to try to cope with another recession activity – the illicit selling of liquor to African workers. See for example 'The Curse of the Rand', *The Star*, 14 May 1912. Since the Chamber of Mines saw to it that it was well represented on the enquiry into the 'black peril', Schumacher's concern was also driven home in the report. See *Commission on Assaults on Women 1913*, paras 51-9 and 80-5.

193 Para based on: H Selby Msimang to editor, *Evening Chronicle*, 2 October 1913; S T Plaatje, 'The Mote and the Beam', p 92; R V Selope-Thema to editor, *Transvaal Leader*, 12 June 1912; and J J Lerothodi Ntyweyi's correspondence on 'Whites and Blacks', published in *The Star*, 15 September 1911.

194 See for example 'Vigilance of the Police', *The Star*, 7 February 1911, and 'The Turffontein Drive', *Rand Daily Mail*, 24 April 1912.

195 From T Makiwane, 'African Work Songs' in L Hughes (ed), *An African Tragedy* (New York 1974), p 99.

196 See Part Two, Chapter 4, 'The Regiment of the Hills'.

197 'Izegebengu – A Native Secret Society', *The Star*, 16 June 1896.

198 See especially the attack on J N Webb reported in *S & DN*, 16 August 1895, and 'Native Violence', *The Star*, 17 June 1896. For a remarkable court confession by an ex-'houseboy' izigebengu, see 'Attempted Murder and Robbery', *The Star*, 4 April 1902.

199 'Native Labour', *Ipepa lo Hlanga*, 24 May 1901.

200 See 'The Laita Gangs or Native Brigands', *Ipepa lo Hlanga*, 20 November 1903, and 'Native Hooligans at Durban', *The Star*, 26 October 1904. Jeff Guy, however, has drawn my attention to Harriette Colenso's suggestion that the *Amalaitas* might have considered themselves to be 'all-right-ers'. See National Archives, Pietermaritzburg, Colenso Collection, Box 76, Harriette E Collenso to Aunt Eliza (Bunyon),

13 September 1911. This suggestion is made all the more forceful by the fact that Harriette Colenso was basing her observation on her visit to Pretoria.

201 See Part Two, Chapter 4, 'The Regiment of the Hills'.

202 'The Growth of the Amalaita', *Rand Daily Mail*, 11 September 1908.

203 *Ibid*, and 'Passless Natives – A Strange Coincidence', *The Star*, 22 September 1908. See also, however, E Mphahlele, *Down Second Avenue* (London 1959), pp 100-1.

204 Many Amalaita activities such as fighting, music playing, petty thieving and age-solidarity are elements taught and experienced in Pedi initiation schools. In this sense it seems likely that the Amalaita gangs partly performed an important social function for Pedi youngsters who, during the recession, lost access to the traditional initiation schools. See G M Pitje, 'Traditional System of Male Education among Pedi and Cognate Tribes', *African Studies*, 9, 2 and 3, June and September 1950, especially pp 71-2 and 107-9.

205 Para based on: 'The Growth of the Amalaita', *Rand Daily Mail*, 11 September 1908; 'Native Hooligans', *The Star*, 29 September 1908; 'Amalaita at La Rochelle', *The Star*, 23 November 1908; and 'Rand Police Courts', *Rand Daily Mail*, 10 May 1914.

206 For female *Amalaitas* see: 'The Growth of the Amalaita', *Rand Daily Mail*, 11 September 1908; 'Amalaita', *The Star*, 18 November 1908; 'Native Women', *The Star*, 20 March 1909; and 'Magistrate's Cases', *Transvaal Leader*, 6 May 1914. The idea that these were possibly age-related sets comes from comments made by the Revd Porches. See 'Missionary Conference – Amalaita and Native Girls', *The Star*, 5 August 1910.

207 See 'Native Hooligans', *The Star*, 7 September 1908; 'Rand Police Courts', *Rand Daily Mail*, 10 September 1908; 'The Amalaita', *Rand Daily Mail*, 12 September 1908;

'A Native Gathering', *The Star*, 21 September 1908; 'Amalaita Gangs', *The Star*, 4 November 1908 and *The Star*, 16 November 1908.

208 See for example 'Amalaita Again', *The Star*, 15 July 1910.

209 See: 'The Growth of the Amalaita', *Rand Daily Mail*, 11 September 1908; 'Amalaita at La Rochelle', *Rand Daily Mail*, 23 November 1908; and R V Selope Thema to editor, *Transvaal Leader*, 10 October 1913.

210 See especially: 'Native Hooligans', *The Star*, 7 September 1908; 'Native Hooligans', *Transvaal Leader*, 8 September 1908; and 'The Native Trouble', *The Star*, 16 November 1908.

211 'Growth of the Amalaita', *Rand Daily Mail*, 11 September 1908, and 'Amalaita at La Rochelle', *Rand Daily Mail*, 23 November 1908.

212 'Amalaita – Functions of the Society', *The Star*, 18 November 1908.

213 See for example 'The Amalaita', *The Star*, 23 April 1909, and evidence led in the Harrison case, note 215 below.

214 'Rand Police Courts – Amalaita Outrage', *Rand Daily Mail*, 16 May 1914, and 'Magistrate's Cases', *Transvaal Leader*, 10 May 1914.

215 The full story of the Harrison rape case can be pieced together from the following accounts: 'Turffontein Case', *The Star*, 4 May 1914; 'Magistrate's Cases', *Transvaal Leader*, 5 May 1914; 'Turffontein Case', *The Star*, 5 May 1914; 'Magistrate's Cases', *Transvaal Leader*, 6 May 1914; 'Turffontein Outrage: Native Detective's Evidence', *Transvaal Leader*, 8 May 1914; 'Magistrate's Cases', *Transvaal Leader*, 10 May 1914; 'Rand Police Courts – Amalaita Outrage', *Rand Daily Mail* 16 May 1914; and 'Turffontein Case', *Transvaal Leader*, 30 May 1914.

2 AMAWASHA

1 H Pirenne, *The Economy and Society of Medieval Europe* (London 1936), p. 184.

2 For evidence of the washermen's privileged status see: 'The Washboys' Parade', *Standard and Diggers' News* (hereafter *S & DN*), 2 July 1985; 'Wash Boys in Trouble', *S & DN*, 3 August 1895; Johannesburg Public Library (JPL), Johannesburg City Archive (JCA), Box 22, Report of Special Committee chaired by E Hancock to Chairman and Members of the Sanitary Committee, 15 May 1896; and 'Wash Boys' Licences', *S & DN*, 20 June 1896.

3 See for example G S Ghuyre, *Caste and Class in India* (new York 1952), p 8 and p 37; and L Dumont, *Homo Hierarchicus* (London 1970), pp 48-49, p 100 and p 175.

4 Interview with Mr E Kaluse, Johannesburg, 11 February 1977. (Tape deposited in the library of the Oral History Project, African Studies Institute, University of the Witwatersrand, Johannesburg. Hereafter, OHP, ASI, University of Witwatersrand.)

5 *Natal Government Gazette*, 22 July 1878. I am indebted to Prof M Swanson for this and the following reference.

6 See Durban, *Mayor's Minutes* covering the period 1890-1913.

7 S Marks, *Reluctant Rebellion* (Oxford 1970), pp 15-17.

8 Interview with Mr P Gumbi, Johannesburg, 16 April 177; and interviews with Messrs H Buthelezi and N Mchumu, Weenen, 25 April 1977. Tapes deposited OHP, ASL, University of the Witwatersrand. For an indication of the numbers of black males with passes leaving these districts for work in the Transvaal during the mid-1890s see Pietermaritzburg Archives Depot (PAD), Secretary for Native Affairs (SNA), Confidential Papers 1890-1897, File 668/1895.

9 Including the changing white family structure on the Witwatersrand during this period. For a brief discussion of this aspect see Part Two, Chapter 1, 'The witches of suburbia'.

10 For examples see 'Our Washing', *Johannesburg Weekly Times*, 16 January 1897; and JPL, JCA, Box 245,

'Washing Regulations', 1897.

11 See Part II, Chapter 1 above, 'The witches of suburbia' and 'Johannesburg's Wash Tub', *The Star*, 20 April 1898.

12 Figure derived from fragmentary data housed in JPL, JCA, Boxes 220 and 231; and Box 263, Health Officer's Report No 36 for 1895.

13 Para based on: JPL, JCA, Box 217, Manager, Braamfontein Estate Co Ltd to Chairman and Members of the Sanitary Board, 12 November 1894; 'The Wash Boys' Parade', *S & DN*, 2 July 1895; 'Concordia Mining Company', *S & DN*, 23 May 1896; Lady Dunbar to the editor, *The Star*, 31 December 1896; and 'Our Washing', *Johannesburg Weekly Times*, 16 January 1897.

14 See 'The Wash Boys' Parade', *S & DN*, 2 July 1895; and 'Johannesburg's Wash Tub', *The Star*, 20 April 1898.

15 *Ibid*. See also, however: JPL, JCA, Box 263, J Smithers to Chairman, Sanitary Board, 27 October 1894 and Health Department, Report No 36 of 1895; JPL, JCA, Box 221, Health Inspector's Annual Report for 1895; and 'The Washing Sites', *The Star*, 18 November 1898.

16 *Ibid*.

17 Transvaal Archives Depot (TAD), Secretary for Native Affairs (SNA), File 392/02, Mahlangu and other washermen to Sir Godfrey Lagden, 12 February 1902.

18 Johannesburg, *Census 1896*, Part I, Return 2; and Part IX, Returns 1 and 2.

19 See 'The Wash Boys' Parade', *S & DN*, 2 July 1895; and 'Court Cases', *S & DN*, 3 September 1895. See also PAD, SNA, File 1/1/216, Johannesburg Representative's Report for week ended 15 February 1896. I am indebted to Jeff Guy for this reference and others in this series.

20 Interview with Mr R Buthelezi, Mpungu River, Weenen District, 25 April 1977. Tape deposited OHP, ASI, University of the Witwatersrand.

21 'The Wash Boys' Parade', *S &DN*, 2 July 1895. See also various reports on 'Kaffir War Dance' in *S & DN*, 8 December 1898.

22 For reports on Kwaaiman see *S & DN* of 3 August 1895 and 9 July 1896. See also, however, PAD, SNA, File 1/1/216, Johannesburg Representative's Report for week ending 15 February 1896. I am indebted to Jeff Guy for providing me with a copy of this material.

23 JPL, JCA, Box 263, Report No 36, T C Visser to Chairman and Members of the Sanitary Board, 28 October 1895; and Report No 43, A Smithers to Chairman and Members of the Sanitary Board, 28 October 1895. Also, JPL, JCA, Box 221 'A', L H Dunbar to Secretary, Johannesburg Sanitary Board, 6 December 1895.

24 'Health of the Town', *S & DN*, 12 March 1896.

25 JPL, JCA, Box 219, A Fossati to Chairman, Sanitary Board, 25 October 1894; and Box 230, A Fossati to Town Council, 26 April 1898.

26 Registrar of Companies Office (RCO), Pretoria, File on 'Crystal Steam Laundry' (1895); and 'Crystal Steam Laundry', *Johannesburg Weekly Times*, 19 December 1898.

27 See for example the advertisement for Nannucci's business in *S & DN*, 4 March 1896. For a confidential report on Nannucci's suitability for the position of Italian Consul in Cape Town, see Cape Archives Depot (CAD), AG File 965, Commissioner of Police to J B Moffat, Sec to the Law Dept, Cape Town, 30 May 1902.

28 RCO, Pretoria, File T 1313, 'Auckland Park Steam Laundry Co Ltd' (1896). See also G Aubert, *L'Afrique du Sud* (Paris 1897), p 237.

29 See for example L Grahame to the editor, *The Star*, 28 March 1896.

30 'Concordia Mining Company', *S & DN*, 23 May 1896.

31 For the background to the Sanitary Board's acceptance of the Dell offer, see reports of meetings carried in the

following: *S & DN*, 12 March 1896;
The Star, 2 April 1896; *Johannesburg
Times*, 1 August 1896; *The Star*,
12 August 1896; and *S & DN*,
13 August 1896. For details of the
Sanitary Board's accounting regard-
ing the move to the new site see JPL,
JCA, Box 221, 'Comparative
Statement', April 1896.

32 See reports carried in *S & DN*,
9 September 1896 and 24 October
1896.

33 See items reported in *S & DN*,
8 November 1896; *The Star*,
16 November 1896; and *The Critic*,
27 November 1896.

34 See *Transvaal Independent*, 2 December
1896; and *Johannesburg Times*,
10 December 1896 and 15 April 1897.

35 Table constructed from fragmentary
data contained in JPL, JCA, Box 201
and Boxes 220-231; and information
carried in *Johannesburg Times*,
15 April 1897, and *The Star*,
18 November 1898.

36 'Washboys at Witbank', *S & DN*,
2 December 1896. See also reports in
S & DN, 3 December 1896; and *The
Critic*, 4 December 1896.

37 *Johannesburg Times*, 10 December
1896.

38 Perhaps the best account of the washermen's week is to be found in 'The
Washing Site', *The Star*, 18 November
1898.

39 Figures derived from
'Johannesburg's Wash Tub', *The Star*,
20 April 1898, and other scattered
sources.

40 'The Wash Boys' Parade', *S & DN*,
2 July 1895; and TAD, SNA, File
941/02, 'Illicit Liquor Traffic,
Summary of Cases November 1901-
April 20, 1902'.

41 Para based on: JPL, JCA, Box 263,
A H Smithers to Chairman and
Members of the Sanitary Board on
27 June 1894, 18 July 1894, and
1 August 1894. Also items in the
S & DN of 2 July 1895, 25 October
1895, and 12 March 1896; and *The
Star*, 18 November 1898. See also,
'Report of the Superintendent of
Locations', Johannesburg, *Mayor's*

Minute 1905, p 171.

42 Interviews with Messrs H and R
Buthelezi, Weenen, 25 April 1977.
Tapes deposited OHP, ASI,
University of the Witwatersrand.

43 See *Johannesburg Weekly Times*,
26 December 1896; 'The Washing Site
Bogy', *Johannesburg Times*, 15 April
1897; *The Star*, 15 April 1897. When
the Dell proposal was first entertained the suggested rail fare was
three shillings per month. See JPL,
JCA, Box 221, 'Comparative
Statement', April 1896.

44 *Ibid.*

45 JPL, JCA, Box 225, D Margolious to
A H Smithers, 25 August 1897.

46 See for example 'The Washing Site
Bogy', *Johannesburg Times*, 15 April
1897. Contrast this with the former
situation as recounted in 'A Murder
Case', *S & DN*, 7 March 1897.

47 For examples of Zarp Botha's activities see brief reports in the following
editions of the *S & DN*: 25 October
1895, 2 December 1896, 25 February
1897 and 8 April 1897.

48 For the names and origins of some of
these *Dhobis*, who included among
their number Naidoos, Pillays,
Kistens and Chettys, see *British
Parliamentary Papers*, LXVI, *Command
Paper Number 5363 of 1910*, pp 111-112
and 117. Also TAD, Gov Gen, Vol
706, File 15/7, W L Ritch to Under
Sec of State for the Colonies, 7 June
1910, enclosed in Colonial Sec to Gov
General, 18 June 1910; and File
15/47, W L Ritch to Under Sec of
State for the Colonies, 4 August 1910,
enclosed in Colonial Sec to Gov
General, 13 August 1910. I am
indebted to Maureen Tayal for providing me with copies of this material.

49 See advertisement in *S & DN* of
13 April 1897, and 'Doings at
Darnaway', in *S & DN* of 23 April
1897. For further fragments relating
to the Melrose Steam Laundry see
advertisements carried in the *S & DN*
of 4 August 1897 and 26 July 1898.
Also JPL, JCA, Box 231, Secretary,
Melrose Steam Laundry to Secretary,

Johannesburg Sanitary Board, 28 March 1899.

50 Interview with Mr S R Naidoo, Lenasia, Johannesburg, 19 March 1977. Tape deposited with OHP, ASI, University of the Witwatersrand. See also, however, T Naidoo, 'The Temple at Melrose', unpublished typescript, Johannesburg 1978.

51 *S & DN*, 24 August 1897; and *Johannesburg Times*, 24 August 1897.

52 *De Locale Wetten de Zuid Afrikaansche Republiek 1897*, pp 177-179; and 'Johannesburg's Wash Tub', *The Star*, 20 April 1898.

53 'Vrededorp Laundry', *S & DN*, 18 April 1899; and 'Public Wash House Concession', *The Star*, 17 April 1899. See also Part Two, Chapter 3, 'The Main Reef Road into the working class'.

54 Even before the *AmaWasha* had moved out to Witbank there had been a small number of women – often Coloured or European widows – who took in laundry in order to make a living. See for example 'The Wash Boys' Parade', *S & DN*, 2 July 1895. This trend accelerated, however, once the Zulu males went to Klipspruit and the economy slid into the recession of 1897 – see for example *S & DN*, 1 April 1897. More significant still perhaps is the fact that black women started doing laundry at the old sites once the Witbank experiment commenced – see for example Smithers' remarks as reported in *S & DN* of 22 May 1897. After the South African War, and more especially so during the depression of 1906-8, many more European widows took to washing clothes as a means of making a living, sometimes as many as 150 in a single suburb. See for example 'Poor Women', *The Star*, 22 November 1907.

55 'Crystal Steam Laundry', *Johannesburg Weekly Times*, 19 December 1896; and 'Crystal Steam Laundry Limited', *S & DN*, 30 December 1898.

56 'Auckland Park Steam Laundry', *S & DN*, 1 October 1897.

57 RCO, Pretoria, File T 1501, 'Place Steam Laundry Ltd'.

58 RCO, Pretoria, File T 1413, 'Transvaal Soap Company Ltd'.

59 *British Parliamentary Papers*, XXXV, *Command Paper Number 624 of 1901*, evidence of H Woolf, paras 1766-1809. For some of the background to the takeover by Lever Bros see D K Fieldhouse, *Unilever Overseas: The Anatomy of a Multinational, 1895-1965* (London 1878), pp 97-103.

60 For a list of some of these smaller laundries see *Longland's Johannesburg and District Directory 1899*, p 311. That at least some of these laundries dated back to 1897-8 can be deduced from 'Johannesburg's Wash Tub', *The Star*, 20 April 1898. For mention of the Chinese laundries see G Aubert, *L'Afrique du Sud* (Paris 1897), p 237.

61 *Johannesburg Weekly Times*, 16 January 1897.

62 *Johannesburg Weekly Times*, 30 December 1896 and 16 June 1897.

63 For the central events in these proceedings see: *Johannesburg Weekly Times*, 9 January 1897; JPL, JCA, Box 225, Landdrost voor Crimenele Zaken to Sec, Sanitary Board, 13 March 1897; 'Rate-payer' to editor, *Johannesburg Times*, 27 March 1897; *Johannesburg Times*, 15 April 1897; *The Star*, 7 May 1897; *Johannesburg Times*, 19 May 1897; *S & DN*, 22 May 1897; *Johannesburg Times*, 7 June 1897; and *The Star*, 18 November 1898.

64 JPL, JCA, Box 225, D Margolious to Sec, Sanitary Board, 25 August 1897; and *S & DN*, 16 September 1897.

65 Para based on J W Meillon to the editor, *Volkstem*, 23 December 1896; 'Johannesburg's Wash Tub', *The Star*, 20 April 1898; and JPL, JCA, Box 232, Report of Health Officer T C Visser to Mayor and Town Councillors, 13 February 1899.

66 The prices charged by steam laundries appear to have remained more or less constant between 1897 and 1902. Compare G Aubert, *L'Afrique du Sud* (Paris 1897), p 237; and 'A Wash Tub Wanted', *The Star*, 29 July 1902. It was also about this time, i.e. 1897-8,

that black and Malay women (sometimes in small partnerships with members of the *AmaWasha*) first started doing ironing at 7/6d per day plus board. See 'Johannesburg's Wash Tub', *The Star*, 20 April 1898.

67   For some examples see the following selection of items drawn from the *S & DN*: 'Sensation at Sans Souci', 29 January 1899; 'Charge of Murder', 9 June 1898; 'Culture and Kaffirs', 24 June 1898; and 'A Washboy's Woman', 18 November 1898.

68   See *S & DN* of 2 December 1897; and *The Star*, 20 April 1898 and 18 November 1898.

69   On the passage of this legislation see: JPL, JCA, Box 225, H J Filmer to Sec, Sanitary Board, 26 September 1897; JPL, JCA, Box 245, 'Washing Regulations' (1897); and items in *The Star* of 18 November 1898 and *S & DN* of 29 March 1899.

70   See for example JPL, JCA, Box 263, A H Smithers, Fortnightly Report No 30 to Burgomaster, Aldermen and Town Council of Johannesburg, 3 October 1898.

71   Interview with Mr N H Buthelezi, Weenen, 25 April 1977. Tape deposited with OHP, ASI, University of the Witwatersrand.

72   TAD, LAJ, Vol 9, File 574, A H Smithers, Inspector of Natives to Major O'Meara, Acting Burgomaster, Johannesburg, 24 September 1900. I am indebted to Diana MacLaren for drawing this and other reports in this series to my attention. See also, TAD, SNA, File 941/02, 'Illicit Liquor Traffic – Summary of Cases, November 1901-April 20, 1902'.

73   See especially, TAD, SNA, NA 936/02, D R Hunt, Inspector, Native Affairs Dept, to Chief Inspector, 14 April 1902.

74   TAD, LAJ, Vol 9, File 574, Memo by Major O'Meara, 2 October 1900; and enclosed draft proclamation in Smithers's hand.

75   There were at least three good reasons why this particular site was amongst the first targets of the administration. (i) It had long been a notorious centre of beer selling – see note 73 above. (ii) It was ripe for development as a white residential area. Even before the war the Editor of *The Star*, F Dormer, had tried to get the site closed down for this reason. See the note on the Richmond location in *S & DN*, 26 January 1899. (iii) The steam laundry owners would have been less than enthusiastic about this source of cheap competition being so close to them.

76   TAD, SNA, File 392/02, Mahlangu and others to Sir Godfrey Lagden, 12 February 1902.

77   The prospect of a further move by the washermen attracted the attention of yet one more person – Ernest Sheppard, former Field Cornet, Rand Native Labour Association employee and prominent shareholder in the Crystal Steam Laundry. Sheppard unsuccessfully proposed a further Klip River-type settlement for the washermen to the new administration. See TAD, SNA, File 446/02, E Sheppard to Sec for Native Affairs, 22 February 1902.

78   TAD, SNA, NA 2606/02, D R Hunt, Inspector, Native Affairs Dept to Chief Inspector, 14 April 1902.

79   See the following files in TAD, SNA series: NA 2606/02, Memo by Assistant Sec for Native Affairs, J S Marwick, 2 January 1903; NA 1486/03, Town Clerk, Johannesburg, to Sec for Native Affairs, 14 August 1903; NA 1486/03, Draft By-Laws approved by the Public Health Committee; and NA 2606/02, Sec of Native Affairs to Commissioner of Police, 14 October 1903.

80   Johannesburg, *Mayor's Minute 1905*, pp 7 and 9.

81   See 'Native Mass Meeting' and 'Report of the Proceedings' in *The Star*, 28 March 1904.

82   TAD, SNA, NA 1486/03, *Report B of Medical Officer of Health, Washing Sites in Johannesburg*, p 2.

83   See for example 'A Wash Tub Wanted', *The Star*, 29 July 1902.

84   Johannesburg, *Mayor's Minute 1901-1903*, p 33.

85 See 'A Wash Tub Wanted', *The Star*, 29 July 1902; or 'WGP' writing to the editor on 'The Laundry Question' in *The Star*, 13 June 1903.

86 See the following items in *The Star*: 'Laundries', 16 May 1903; 'Palace Steam Laundry', 27 July 1903; and 'Rand Steam Laundries', 26 July 1905.

87 In fact, the seeds of this development were already sown before the war. As early as 1899 the Lorentzville, Bertrams and White Star Laundries were all operating in this part of the town – *see Longland's Johannesburg and District Directory 1899*, p 311. The most significant part of this development, however, took place after the war – see note 86 above.

88 'Crystal Steam Laundry', *The Star*, 22 July 1902. It seems possible that Nelson first acquired a laundry when the original Rand Steam Laundry went into liquidation during the depression of 1897 – see 'Rand Steam Laundry', *S & DN*, 31 July 1897. Nelson's dominant role in the later consolidated venture can be gathered from the company's full name, 'Rand Steam Laundries, F O Nelson & Co'. See 'Laundries', *The Star*, 16 May 1903.

89 When J C Manion visited England later in the same year he left no doubt that the company operated what he called 'a syndicate of mining laundries'. See City of London Polytechnic, Fawcett Library, 'South African Colonisation Collection', Vol 'Early Transvaal Letters', Alicia M Cecil to Miss Russell, 23 October 1902. For the continuing importance of the mines' laundry requirements see for example 'Rand Steam Laundry', *The Star*, 15 October 1910.

90 'A Wash Tub Wanted', *The Star*, 29 July 1902. Judging from the same source it appears that the Palace Steam Laundry employed a complement of about the same size and sexual composition at this time.

91 TAD, SNA, Vol 48, NA 2408/04, *Report of the Public Health Committee on the Location Question 1904*. Report B of Medical Officer of Health, Washing Sites in Johannesburg, pp 1-3.

92 *Ibid*. See also TAD, City of Johannesburg Archive, Vol 402, File 3/60/12/1294, Report of the Town Engineer to the Town Clerk and Location Sub-committee, 20 June 1904.

93 See for example the Superintendent of Locations' remarks in Johannesburg, *Mayor's Minute 1905*, p 171.

94 Johannesburg, *Mayor's Minute 1906*, p IX; and *Mayor's Minute 1907*, pp 25-26.

95 By 1905, the washermen were still 'losing' substantial quantities of laundry at widely dispersed washing sites – see Johannesburg, *Mayor's Minute 1905*, p 171. The original estimates for the costs of the Klipspruit site thus also made provision for an annual bill of £500 for 'police and supervision'. See TAD, SNA, NA 2408/04, *Report of the Town Engineer*, 20 June 1904. Between 1938 and 1953 the remaining 20 or so washermen at Klipspruit continued to be supervised by a municipal policeman, Mr Azariah Gumbi. Interview with Mr P Gumbi, Johannesburg, 16 April 1977. Tape deposited OHP, ASI, University of the Witwatersrand.

96 See various letters in TAD, SNA, NA 3840/07; and 'Faction Fight – Zulu vs Baca', *The Star*, 14 November 1907.

97 Table constructed from data in Johannesburg, *Mayor's Minutes* covering period 1905-17.

98 On the changing cost and capacity of the laundry at Klipspruit see the following: 'The Klip Spruit Farm', *The Star*, 5 November 1907; and the following issues of the Johannesburg *Mayor's Minute, 1906*, p 132; *1907*, pp 25-26; *1908*, p XI; and *1918-19*, p 71.

99 Johannesburg, *Mayor's Minute 1908*, p XI and p 27; and *Minutes of the Town Council 1908*, pp 1, 197 and 1452.

100 On the rising cost of rail transport between Klipspruit and Johannesburg see: Johannesburg,

Mayor's Minute 1906, p 132; 'The Klip
Spruit Farm', *The Star*, 5 November
1907; and TAD, SNA, NA 3820/10,
Complaints Officer, Dept of Native
Affairs to Chief Pass Officer,
10 November 1909.

101 'The Klip Spruit Farm', *The Star*,
5 November 1907. Also, interview
with Mr R Buthelezi, Weenen,
25 April 1977. Tape deposited OHP,
ASI, University of the
Witwatersrand.

102 *Ibid.*

103 'The Klip Spruit Farm', *The Star*,
5 November 1907.

104 TAD, SNA, NA 3820/10, Makaza,
Mkubalo and the other washermen
to the Officer in Charge, Pass Office,
Johannesburg, 7 November 1909.

105 See correspondence in TAD, SNA,
NA 3515/07.

106 Pressure from the White League and
the Fordsburg and Newtown
Vigilance Association was particularly evident at the height of the depression in 1907. Amongst other things,
both of these groups were concerned
that 'the number of laundry licences
issued to Chinese and Coloured persons are on the increase'. See various
documents in TAD, City of
Johannesburg Archive, File A518,
'Asiatic Location'.

107 On the earliest Chinese laundries see
note 60 above. On the issue of illegal
immigrants see for example 'The
Chinese Invasion', *The Star*, 18 June
1903. It is more than likely that several of these Chinese immigrants had
gained experience of the laundry
business prior to their move to the
Transvaal. See for example 'Chinese
in the Cape Colony', *The Star*,
30 April 1906.

108 Perhaps the best description of
Johannesburg's early Chinese community is to be found in Thomas A
See's letter to the editor of *The Star*,
5 January 1904 – 'The Chinaman as
he is – A Compatriot's Defence'. For
a list of Chinese grocers in the city
see for example *United Transvaal
Directory 1911*, pp 1203-1205.

109 TAD, SNA, NA 2408/04, *Report of the*

*Public Health Committee on Location
Question 1904*, Report A of Medical
Officer of Health, p 4; TAD, City of
Johannesburg Archive, File A 518,
'Asiatic Location', 'Report to Public
Health Committee re: Asiatic
Trading', 1907; and *United Transvaal
Directory 1914*, pp 1001-1002.

110 See for example 'Satisfied' to the editor, *The Star*, 17 March 1908.

111 Mr Rwanqana Buthelezi remembers
his father telling him about at least
three such washermen before the
First World War – Petrus Zuma,
Sikhakane Mchunu and Samuel
Dhlamini. Interview with Mr
R Buthelezi, Weenen, 25 April 1977.
Tape deposited OHP, ASI, University
of the Witwatersrand. See also TAD,
GNLB, File 169/647/14/102, Report
No 42 on Washing Site, 25 October
1925.

112 See for example some of the following cases which were reported in *The
Star*: 'Chinese and European', 15 May
1906; 'A Shocking Charge', 9 October
1908; and 'White Girls in the Employ
of Chinamen', 9 February 1910.

113 The moving spirit behind this
scheme was apparently Mrs Pauline
Lotter of the Undenominational
Benevolent Society – see 'Poor
Women', *The Star*, 22 November 1907;
and P Hammond to the editor, *The
Star*, 27 November 1907. By March
1908 the scheme seems to have been
abandoned for want of funds. See the
following items in *The Star*:
'Vrededorp Soup Kitchen', 9 March
1908; 'Another White Woman' to the
editor, 13 March 1908; 'Satisfied' to
the editor, 17 March 1908;
P Hammond to the editor, 20 March
1908; and 'Satisfied' to the editor,
24 March 1908.

114 Such as Mr J R Naidoo, a former
Melrose Steam Laundry employee,
who went into business on his own
at La Rochelle. Interview with his
son, Mr J Naidoo, Johannesburg,
16 November 1976. Tape deposited
with OHP, ASI, University of the
Witwatersrand.

115 See for example the *United Transvaal*

Directory of 1911 and 1914 on pp 1277-1279 and pp 1001-1002 respectively.

116 See especially the item on 'Laundries' in the 'Commercial Notes' of *The Star*, 11 December 1909.

117 'Rand Steam Laundry', *The Star*, 15 October 1910.

118 *United Transvaal Directory 1911*, p 1277. Also interview with Mr P Cohen (ex-Advance Laundries), Johannesburg, 16 November 1976.

119 'Advance in Laundry Rates', *The Star*, 1 June 1912.

120 See items reported in *The Star* of 20 August 1902 or 9 April 1903. See also, however, section on 'Laundry Machinery' in B H Morgan, *Report on the Engineering Trades of South Africa* (London 1902), p 157.

121 These changes, and black servants' resistance to the chore of laundry work are discussed in some detail in Part Two, Chapter 1, 'The Witches of Suburbia'.

122 See for example 'The Klip Spruit Farm', *The Star*, 5 November 1907; and Johannesburg, *Town Council Minutes 1908*, p 1197.

123 TAD, SNA, NA 980/09, unsigned letter to the Protector of Natives, 22 February 1909.

124 TAD, SNA, NA 980/09, Minutes of Meeting held at Klipspruit, Sunday, 20 June 1909.

125 TAD, SNA, NA 3820/10, Makaza, Mkubalo and others to Officer in Charge, Pass Office, Johannesburg, 7 November 1909.

126 TAD, SNA, NA 3820/10, Complaints Officer to Acting Chief Pass Officer, Johannesburg, 10 November 1909.

127 TAD, SNA, NA 3820/10, Chief Pass Officer, Johannesburg, to Director, Government Native Labour Bureau, 11 November 1909. See also, 'Nancefield Location', *Transvaal Leader*, 13 November 1909.

128 TAD, SNA, NA 3820/10, Sec for Native Affairs to Town Clerk, Johannesburg, 20 November 1909.

129 TAD, City of Johannesburg Archive, Vol 24, File A 676, Minutes of an Informal Meeting held at Klipspruit, 17 January 1910. See also TAD,

GNLB, File 59/2238/12/20, Superintendent of Location to Director of Native Labour, 9 December 1919.

130 West Rand Administration Board, NA 5/15, Manager to Medical Officer of Health, Johannesburg, 12 September 1934. Also, interview with Mr P Gumbi, Johannesburg, 16 April 1977. Tape deposited OHP, ASI, University of the Witwatersrand.

131 Bhamu Buthlezi's eldest son – N H Buthelezi – became a member of the South African Police at Weenen, while one of his grandchildren (N H's daughter) went on to study at Atlanta University, Georgia, USA, during the course of 1977. Interview with Mr N H Buthelezi, Weenen, 25 April 1977.

132 *Ibid.*

133 TAD, SNA 980/09, Minutes of a meeting held at Klipspruit on Sunday, 20 June 1909.

134 Union of South Africa, *Minutes of Evidence of the Natal Natives Land Committee 1918* (UG 35-18), p 192. I am indebted to Shula Marks who drew this evidence to my attention.

3 THE MAIN REEF ROAD INTO THE WORKING CLASS

1 The first step to rectify this position was taken by J J Fourie. See his invaluable contribution to E L P Stals (ed), *Afrikaners in die Goudstad*, Deel 1, 1886-1923 (Pretoria 1978).

2 The quotations in this para are taken from a work which specifically seeks to address itself to a historical analysis of 'class formation and class relations' – R H Davies, *Capital, State and White Labour in South Africa, 1900-1960* (Brighton 1979), pp 77 and 101. Davies, however, also subscribes to some – but not all – of the other interpretations offered in this para. See the relevant passages in his work on pp 57, 76, 102-3.

3 This question is explored in greater detail in J J Fourie, *op cit*, pp 19-28.

4 *Ibid*, pp 58-70.

5 This para is reconstructed from fragments collected from several sources. It was noted in the *Standard & Diggers' News* (hereafter, *S & DN*) of 10 February 1894 that: 'The class from which the police is now recruited are the unemployed young Boers to be found in the town and elsewhere ... many can neither read nor write.' See also Commandant D E Schutte to the editor, *S & DN*, 11 October 1894. On Post Office officials, see Transvaal Archives Depot (TAD), Pretoria, SS Vol 5533, R9152/96, 'Opgawe', pp 111-12. Also 'Nationality of Telegraphists', *The Star*, 15 May 1897.

6 For a glimpse into the life of a Transvaal transport rider prior to the advent of the branch-line system, see University of the Witwatersrand, African Studies Institute, Oral History Project, Tape Nos 35 and 36, M S S Ntoane's interview with G K Skhosana at Lydenburg on 7 and 8 September 1979.

7 See for example 'The Problem of the "Arme" Burgher', *The Star*, 30 August 1897, or D Hobart Houghton, 'Economic Development, 1865-1965', in M Wilson and L M Thompson (eds), *The Oxford History of South Africa* (Oxford 1971), Vol 2, p 20.

8 C T Gordon, *The Growth of Boer Opposition to Kruger, 1890-1895* (London 1970), p 30.

9 Gordon is therefore mistaken in his suggestion that the tolls were abandoned in 1892 – C T Gordon, *The Growth of Boer Opposition*, p 30. By way of contrast see for example reports on the tolls in the *S & DN* of 16 June 1894 and 2 May 1895.

10 Para based on Part One, Chapter 4, 'Johannesburg's Jehus, 1890-1914'.

11 *Ibid.*

12 J J Fourie, *op cit*, pp 51-2. Between 1886 and 1891 these sites were rent-free. From the latter date, however, the brickmakers were required to pay two sets of small licence fees. See also J Finch, *To South Africa and Back* (London 1890), p 136.

13 The two preceding paras are based on 'The Brickmaker', *The Star*, 9 September 1896, and an extended interview with W H Brummer in Johannesburg on 31 March 1980. From shortly after the First World War until his retirement in the late 1950s 'Oom Willie' Brummer was the blacksmith in Newlands, Johannesburg, who regularly manufactured 'puddle machines' – the so-called *pokmeule* – and brick moulds for the remaining Afrikaner brickmakers in the city. Of course, even England during the course of the industrial revolution still relied on such 'primitive' machinery. See for example R Samuel's, 'The Workshop of the World', *History Workshop*, 3, 1977, pp 30-1.

14 Some idea of these developments can be obtained from a scrutiny of the following reports in the *S & DN*: 'Building Contractors', 23 May 1892; 'The Building Boom', 18 June 1892'; 'Kuranda & Marais', 27 December 1892; the leading articles of 15 September 1893 and 3 January 1894; and 'Coloured Labour', 30 August 1897. See also, however, the following items in *The Star*: 'The Cry of the Contractors', 20 September 1895; 'The Building Boom', 20 May 1895; and 'The Building Trade', 5 June 1895.

15 These prices for 'stock bricks' were compiled from the following fragments: Johannesburg Public Library (JPL), Johannesburg City Archives (JCA), Box 208, Quotation to build a house supplied by contractors H Smith and D Wood; 'East Rand Notes', *S & DN*, 19 June 1895; 'City & Suburban Notes', *S & DN*, 23 September 1895; 'The Brickmakers', *The Star*, 9 September 1895; 'The Brickmakers', *The Star*, 9 September 1896; and 'Company Meetings', *S & DN*, 29 March 1898.

16 Table compiled from: *Transvaal Leader*, Christmas Number, 1904; and R Krut, '"A Quart into a Pint Pot": The White Working Class and the "Housing Shortage" in Johannesburg, 1896-1906', BA (Hons)

dissertation, University of the Witwatersrand, 1979, p 3.

17 See for example JPL, JCA, Box 218, Health Inspector's Report to the Chairman and Members of the Sanitary Board, 20 November 1894.

18 See especially 'City & Suburban Notes', *S & DN*, 23 September 1895.

19 *Johannesburg Census 1896*, Part XII, 'Occupations', and Part IX, 'Dwellings, Buildings, Live Stock, etc'.

20 For an idea of the size of the African complement at brickyards during the mid-1890s see for example JPL, JCA, Box 263, Folder 113, 'Applications to allow Natives to sleep on premises, 1895'. For the conditions under which such workers lived see for example JPL, JCA, Box 216, Medical Officer of Health, A van Niekerk to Chairman and Members of the Sanitary Board, 24 May 1893; or Report of Inspection carried out at the Brick & Tile Co, 31 May 1893.

21 TAD, SS Vol 4677, Petition by M de Beer and 93 other Brickmakers addressed to His Honour, The State President, and Members of the Executive Committee, 4 April 1893.

22 J J Fourie, *op cit*, p 52.

23 *Ibid* p 53. For additional detail, however, see also TAD, SS Vol 4677, Petition by M de Beer and 93 other Brickmakers addressed to His Honour, The State President, and Members of the Executive Committee, 4 April 1893; and letter to the editor from the Joint Secretaries, The Braamfontein Brickmakers' Association, *S & DN*, 10 February 1894.

24 This para based on: 'Sanitary Board Meeting', *S & DN*, 11 April 1895; *S & DN*, 14 May 1896; 'The Brickfields', *The Star*, 9 June 1896; and 'Poverty Point', *The Star*, 3 September 1896.

25 Para based on: 'The Brickfields', *S & DN*, 15 May 1896; 'The Brickfields Difficulty', *The Star*, 17 June 1896; and 'The Brickmakers', *Johannesburg Times*, 24 June 1896.

26 *Johannesburg Times*, 24 June 1896.

27 See also *The Star* for 11 and 31 July 1896; and *Staatscourant de Zuid Afrikaansche Republiek*, 16 November 1898, p 1609.

28 JPL, JCA, Box 224, V F Schutte (Chairman), M P Koen (Secretary) and other brickmakers to Chairman and Members of the Sanitary Board, 19 August 1896. Also TAD, SS Vol 5735, R12210/96, A J Alberts to Mining Commissioner, 25 August 1896; and L J Alberts to Mining Commissioner, 26 August 1896.

29 TAD, SS Vol 5735, R2553/96, H C Swanepoel and others to Executive Committee, 31 January 1897. See also *ZAR Executive Committee*, Resolution 16, Article 462, April 1898; and Resolution 17, Article 1251, 14 December 1898.

30 'Albertskroon Brickmakers', *The Star*, 8 and 11 December 1902.

31 Interview with W H Brummer, Johannesburg, 31 March 1980.

32 Para based on items reported in the *S & DN* of 24 September 1892, 16 April 1894, and 2 May 1895.

33 Here it is significant to note that while the City & Suburban Tramway Co nominally held the right to convey goods on their trams, the Kruger government never allowed them to exercise this right. This appears to have been one of the few concessions which the Republican government made to the Afrikaner transport riders. See TAD, Gov Vol 463, 'Johannesburg City & Suburban Tramway Concession', 22 October 1901. On Afrikaner employment in related fields see, for example, *Evidence to the Transvaal Indigency Commission 1906-1908* (Pretoria – TG 11, 1908), testimony of Lieut Col O'Brien (Acting Commissioner of Police), para 1445, p 63; and Dr T B Gilchrist, p 24. (Hereafter cited as *Transvaal Indigency Commission 1906-1908*.)

34 See amongst others: 'The Problem of the "Arme" Burgher', *The Star*, 20 August 1897; 'Brick & Potteries Co', *The Star*, 18 March 1902 (introduction of traction engine); *Transvaal Indigency Commission 1906-1908*, evi-

dence of S J Halford, p 9 and
Dr T B Gilchrist, p 240; and *Report of
the Relief and Grants-in-Aid
Commission 1916* (TP No 5 – 1916),
para 35, p 17. (Hereafter, *Relief and
Grants-in-Aid Commission 1916*.)

35 Para based on Part One, Chapter 4,
'Johannesburg's Jehus'.

36 *Ibid*, p 195. More specifically, see
Dr T B Gilchrist's evidence pertaining to Fordsburg in *Transvaal
Indigency Commission 1906-8*, para
5639, p 241. Out of comparative
interest, see also *Report of the
Commission on Pretoria Indigents 1905*,
paras 10 and 12.

37 It would appear that one of the first
and most important of these brick-
works – the Rand Brick & Tile Co –
was started by T M Cullinan who
later developed close connections
with H Eckstein & Co and who
obtained a 'concession' to import
brickmaking machinery from the
Kruger government. See N Helme,
Thomas Major Cullinan (Johannesburg
1974), pp 18-20, and note 42 below.
The remainder of this paragraph is
based on items drawn from the following editions of the *Standard &
Diggers' News*: 9 May 1890, 23 April
1892, 23 May 1892 and 21 September
1892.

38 Para based on the following items
drawn from the *S & DN*: 'Cornelia
Coal Mine', 12 March 1894; 'A Local
Industry', 16 March 1895; 'The Vaal
River Colliery', 13 January 1896;
'Company Meetings – Orphirton
Brick Co', 29 March 1898; 'Company
Meetings – Brick & Potteries Co Ltd,
4 October 1898; and 'A New Brick
Factory' in *The Star*, 3 March 1899.

39 Para based on several fragmentary
sources. A schematic idea of the rise
of the capitalist brickmaking industry
during this period, however, can be
gained from a close examination of
*Longland's Johannesburg & District
Directory*, 1897-9; *Longland's Transvaal
Directory*, 1908-14.

40 See the complaints of the small brickmakers on this score in 'Albertskroon
Brickmakers' in *The Star* of 8 and

11 December 1902.

41 See 'The Vaal River Colliery',
S & DN, 13 January 1896; and 'A
New Brick Factory', *The Star*, 3 March
1899.

42 Two preceding paras based on:
'Company Meetings – Brick &
Potteries Co Ltd', *S & DN*, 4 October
1898; and 'Brick & Potteries
Company', *The Star*, 18 March 1902.
It seems possible that, before the war,
the Brick & Potteries Co operated
with a monopoly right to manufacture machine-made bricks in
Johannesburg. In 1900, Violet
Markham noted: 'The brick and
cement monopolies affect this question [housing] to a large degree.
Machine-made bricks cost no less
than £4 10s 0d per 1 000 or about five
times the cost of bricks in this country.' V R Markham, *South Africa Past
and Present* (London 1900), p 376.
This contention about monopolistic
trade practice was also made in
'Alpha's' letter to the editor, *The Star*,
19 June 1896.

43 See the following important reports
in *The Star*: 'Brick & Potteries
Company', 18 March 1902; 'Company
Meetings – Brick & Potteries Co Ltd',
20 September 1903; 'Brick & Potteries
Co Ltd', 23 September 1905; and
'Brick & Potteries Co – A Successful
Industry', 27 September 1909.

44 'Vrededorp Vigilants', *The Star*,
21 February 1906.

45 See for example the evidence of
Dr T B Gilchrist to the *Transvaal
Indigency Commission 1906-8*, p 240.

46 Unfortunately we do not have a
detailed breakdown of the Afrikaner
unemployed in Johannesburg during
the immediate post-war period.
There is, however, such a breakdown
for Pretoria – an area where capitalist
brickmaking companies also made
noteworthy strides during the post-
war period – and here the evidence
points to a substantial number of former brickmakers amongst the unemployed. See *Report of the Commission
on Pretoria Indigents 1905*, p 3, para
10.

47 Para based on items drawn from the following editions of the *S & DN*: 17 December 1889, 17 July 1893 and 22 January 1894.

48 On these two schemes see items in the *S & DN* of 12 July 1893 and 16 November 1893.

49 For casual employment see, for example, 'Johannesburg by Night' by 'Vagabond' in *S & DN*, 19 January 1895. Many of the Transvaal's highway robbers during the period 1890-3 were unemployed miners waylaying black migrant workers making their way home to the rural areas with their cash wages. See for example the case of J R Lee as reported in the *S & DN* of 18 July 1893. By the mid-1890s this problem was sufficiently serious for the Chamber of Mines to employ its own police force to combat the negative influence which this had on the flow of migrant labour. See Transvaal, *Report of the Chamber of Mines 1895*, pp 69-70; *Report of the Chamber of Mines 1896*, pp 170-1; and D M Wilson, *Behind the Scenes in the Transvaal* (London 1901), pp 196-7.

50 See J J Fourie's useful table, 'Die Trek van die Afrikaner na Johannesburg, 1886-1899 (Mans bo 16 Jaar)', in *Afrikaners in die Goudstad*, p 39.

51 For the van Greuning and De Koker case see *S & DN*, 31 May 1892.

52 The role of cheaper passages from Europe and the rail link to the Transvaal during this period was widely recognised as a contributing factor to the growing number of unemployed on the Rand. See for example *S & DN*, 'Our Unemployed', 7 August 1895; and 'The Distress', 14 August 1897.

53 See *S & DN*, 'Present Help League', 29 November 1895; and 'Kelly's Relief Stores – Still Closed', 27 January 1896.

54 See 'Poverty on the Rand', *Johannesburg Times*, 24 July 1897; and 'Needy Burghers' and 'The Starving Poor' in *The Star*, 24 July 1897. For an excellent account of Dieperink's visit to the western suburbs see, 'Darkest Johannesburg', *Johannesburg Times*, 26 July 1897.

55 The proposed steam laundry eventually gave rise to the establishment of *De Maatschappy tot nut van het Algemeen* and is discussed, in a different context, in Part Two, Chapter 2, '*AmaWasha* – the Zulu washermen's guild of the Witwatersrand'.

56 See, 'Distress in Johannesburg' and 'Rand Relief Committee' in *The Star*, 7 and 10 August 1897. Somewhat misleadingly, this Johannesburg Relief Committee was known locally as the 'Rand Relief Committee', and it should not be confused with a later 'Rand Relief Committee' formed to work primarily in the *uitlander* community in 1898 (see p 130). I am indebted to Diana McClaren for first drawing this important distinction to my attention.

57 'The Distress', *S & DN*, 14 August 1897.

58 For the Victorian basis to these various ideological strands – including that of the residuum – see G Stedman Jones, *Outcast London* (Oxford 1971).

59 'The Indigent', *S & DN*, 16 August 1897. The reference to 'Berlin' in this context is unclear. It is possible, however, that it refers to the demonstration held at the International Congress for Protection of Workers held in Berlin in March 1890 – an event that also coincided with Bismarck's fall from power.

60 See 'The Unemployed', *The Star*, 14 August 1897; and 'The Indigent', *S & DN*, 14 August 1897.

61 *Ibid.*

62 'The Indigent', *S & DN*, 14 August 1897.

63 Para based on: 'Street Begging Rampant', *Johannesburg Weekly Times*, 14 November 1896; 'The Vagrancy Plague', *S & DN*, 20 January 1897; 'The Unemployed', *The Comet*, 3 April 1897; and item in *S & DN* dated 12 April 1897.

64 J J Fourie, *op cit*, pp 82-3.

65 See the following items in the *S & DN*: 'To the Relief', 19 August 1897; and 'Relief for the Poor', 10 September 1897.

66 See J J Fourie, 'Die Geskiedenis van die Afrikaners in Johannesburg, 1886-

67 Para based on 'The Destitution', *S & DN*, 16 July 1898; 'The Destitution', *S & DN*, 20 August 1898; 'The Destitution', *The Star*, 23 August 1898; and 'Rand Relief Fund', *S & DN*, 6 September 1898.

68 *Ibid*. See also 'Indiscriminate Alms Giving', *S & DN*, 27 February 1899. On the alleged 'innate desire' of the Boer population as a whole 'to live on charity' see 'The Boer Population – A Depraved People' *The Star*, 27 January 1899.

69 L S Amery, *The Times History of the War in South Africa 1899-1902* (London 1909), Vol IV, pp 149-50.

70 See, amongst others, the following items drawn from the *S & DN*: 'Wives of Fighting Burghers', 10 November 1899; 'Rand Day by Day', 24 November 1899; and 'Rand Day by Day', 1 December 1899.

71 L S Amery, *Times History of the War*, Vol VI, p 590.

72 *Ibid*, p 594.

73 'Johannesburg Slums', *The Star*, 20 February 1902. See also, however, Quinn's evidence to the *Johannesburg Insanitary Area Improvement Scheme Commission 1902-1903*, para 2839, p 140.

74 A H Duminy and W R Guest (eds), *FitzPatrick* (Johannesburg 1976), FitzPatrick to J Wernher, 5 July 1902, p 333.

75 *Report of Johannesburg Insanitary Area Improvement Scheme Commission 1902-1903*, especially pp 38, 154-5 and 222-3, paras 138-51, 3208-24 and 5220-74 respectively. On the question of inner city rents and the movement of the Afrikaner poor see *Transvaal Indigency Commission 1906-1908*, evidence of Dr T B Gilchrist, p 240 and especially p 242, paras 5666-70; and evidence of Sister Evelyn, p 73, paras 1719-26.

76 See reports on 'The Rand Aid Association' in *The Star* of 9 April 1903 and 5 January 1904.

77 On the role and function of the Charity Organisation Society (COS) in London see G Stedman Jones, *Outcast London*, pp 256-9. That the COS formed the model for the Rand Aid Association seems clear from the editorial on 'The Rand Aid Association' in *The Star*, 9 April 1903. Lionel Curtis was certainly well aware of the role of the COS and the need for such a body on the Rand – see *Transvaal Indigency Commission 1906-8*, p 64, paras 1481-5.

78 'Rand Aid Association – A Year's Work', *The Star*, 29 February 1904.

79 At least one eminent observer was thus off the mark when he suggested that: 'I had that uncomfortable feeling in Johannesburg which one has in so many American cities, that it lacks genuine public spirit. It owes nothing to its millionaires, not even to their charity.' J Ramsay Macdonald, *What I Saw in South Africa* (London 1902), p 102.

80 J Buchan, *The African Colony: Studies in the Reconstruction* (London 1903), p 321.

81 Extract from Louis Botha's speech as reported in *The Star*, 23 May 1904. See also – a few weeks earlier – Sammy Marks's offer to take on the Afrikaner poor as share-croppers on some of his estates; 'Mr S Marks's Offer', *The Star*, 29 March 1904. The reconstruction government, and especially the more conciliatory Selborne, took the point about rural unemployment seriously and attempted to accommodate it. See S Marks and S Trapido, 'Lord Milner and the South African State', *History Workshop*, 8, 1979, p 70.

82 This para is based on several sources, only the principal of which are cited here. On cab drivers, see Part One, Chapter 4, 'Johannesburg's Jehus'. On the building industry and its collapse see: 'How the Poor Live', *Rand Daily Mail*, 29 June 1906; 'Influx of Unemployed', *The Star*, 26 October 1906; statistics as supplied to the *Transvaal Indigency Commission 1906-8* by Joseph Hale (President of the

Unemployed Organisation), p 243; and *ibid*, evidence of W R Boustred (Johannesburg Chamber of Commerce), p 293. On shop assistants, see 'Influx of Unemployed', *The Star*, 26 October 1906; 'The Unemployed', *Transvaal Leader*, 23 February 1907; and 'Poor Whites', *Transvaal Leader*, 27 February 1907.

83 For Rand Aid's approach to Phillips, see M Fraser and A Jeeves (eds), *All That Glittered* (Cape Town 1977), pp 153-5, L Phillips to F Eckstein, 12 March 1906. On subsequent grants from Wernher, Beit & Co and WNLA to the Rand Aid Association see 'Notes and Comments – The Problem of the Desitute' and 'The Present Distress' in *The Star* of 3 and 5 March 1908.

84 'The Unemployed', *Transvaal Leader*, 17 May 1906.

85 The remaining members of the commission were: L S Ferreira, H Crawford, J Reid, J Rissik and F B Smith. See *Transvaal Indigency Commission 1906-8*.

86 'The Unemployed', *Transvaal Leader*, 17 May 1906.

87 Johannesburg, *Minutes of the Public Health Committee*, 19 December 1906, p 140. See also 'With the Workless', *Rand Daily Mail*, 5 February 1907. The Johannesburg Town Council had also apparently taken on a few hundred unskilled workers during the earlier post-war recession of 1903-4 – see J J Fourie, *op cit*, p 77.

88 These proposals – as well as others made later during the depression – included the suggestion that the unemployed be transported to more promising labour markets elsewhere. See especially 'With the Workless', *Rand Daily Mail*, 5 February 1907.

89 Para based on 'Relief Work' and 'The Unemployed', *The Star*, 14 February 1907. This response by Robinson angered many amongst the ruling class, including J W Quinn. See for example Quinn's comments in 'Indigency and Politics', *Transvaal Leader*, 16 March 1907; and his questioning of Joseph Hale in *Transvaal*

Indigency Commission 1906-8, p 243, paras 5709-19.

90 'Relief Work – The Government's Offer', *The Star*, 14 February 1907.

91 Para based on items drawn from the *Rand Daily Mail*, 16 February 1907.

92 Para based on: 'On the Union Ground – A Fiery Speech', *Rand Daily Mail*, 16 February 1907; 'The Unemployed – Seizing the Show Ground', *Transvaal Leader*, 18 February 1907.

93 'The Unemployed', *Transvaal Leader*, 18 February 1907.

94 *Ibid.*

95 'The Unemployed', *Transvaal Leader*, 23 February 1907. See also 'Feeding the Hungry', *Transvaal Leader*, 2 March 1907.

96 See 'Poor Whites' and 'Government Contribution' *in Transvaal Leader*, 27 February 1907; 'Feeding the Hungry', *Transvaal Leader*, 2 March 1907; and 'The Unemployed', *Rand Daily Mail*, 19 March 1907.

97 Para based on: 'The Unemployed', *Rand Daily Mail*, 19 March 1907; 'The Unemployed – ILP Agitators', *Transvaal Leader*, 24 March 1907; 'Unemployed "Stiffs"', *Rand Daily Mail*, 10 April 1907; and 'March on Pretoria', *Rand Daily Mail*, 22 April 1907. For Hale's evidence to the commission see *Transvaal Indigency Commission 1906-8*, p 243.

98 See 'March on Pretoria', *Rand Daily Mail*, 22 April 1907; and 'The Unemployed – The Workless Army', *Rand Daily Mail*, 3 May 1907.

99 See the following items in the *Rand Daily Mail*: 'March on Pretoria', 22 April 1907; 'The Unemployed – The Workless Army', 3 May 1907; and 'Government Offer Rejected', 3 May 1907.

100 E N Katz, *A Trade Union Aristocracy* (Johannesburg 1976), p 131. On the TMA's interpretation of the cause and consequences of the strike see J Mathey's address at 'Another Pretoria Meeting', *The Star*, 17 May 1907.

101 'The "General Strike"', *The Star*, 22 May 1907. As Alan Jeeves has

shown in his '*Het Volk* and the Gold Mines – The Debate on Labour Policy 1905-1910' (Seminar Paper, African Studies Institute, University of the Witwatersrand, June 1980, pp 12 and 18), even before the election, *Het Volk* had approached the Chamber of Mines with a request that it take on Afrikaner miners in the hope that this would help relieve indigency. The Randlords' policy was therefore always likely to meet with the tacit approval of the *Het Volk* Government.

102 For examples of such Afrikaner labour recruited from 'outside districts' during the course of the strike see, amongst others, the following items drawn from *The Star*: 'Dutchmen Repent', 10 May 1907; 'Riot at Langlaagte Deep', 16 May 1907; 'Recruiting at Pretoria', 16 May 1907; 'Wages of Recruits', 17 May 1907; 'Potchefstroom Recruiting', 20 May 1907; and 'Country Recruiting', 24 May 1907.

103 'The "General Strike"', *The Star*, 22 May 1907.

104 See for example 'Feeling at Pretoria – Dutch Labour Available', and 'Another Pretoria Meeting', *The Star*, 17 May 1907.

105 See amongst others the following items culled from *The Star*: 'Dutchmen Repent', 10 May 1907; 'The Miner's Strike – Riotous Proceedings', 16 May 1907; 'Riot at Langlaagte Deep', 16 May 1907; 'Situation Today', 17 May 1907; and 'On the West Rand', 7 June 1907.

106 Para based on: 'Belangryke Kennisgewing aan alle Afrikaners', *De Volkstem*, 11 May 1907; 'A Dutch Meeting', *The Star*, 15 May 1907; and 'Meeting at Newlands', *Rand Daily Mail*, 16 May 1907.

107 'The "General Strike"', *The Star*, 22 May 1907.

108 'The Miners' Strike', *The Star*, 21 May 1907.

109 *Ibid.*

110 *Ibid.*

111 *Ibid.* (My emphasis.)

112 'De Werkstaking', *De Volkstem*, 25 May 1907.

113 Para based on the following items drawn from *The Star*: 'Strike Items', 17 May 1907; 'The "General Strike"', 22 May 1907; 'The Fordsburg District', 28 May 1907; and 'The End of the Strike', 1 June 1907. See also, E N Katz, *A Trade Union Aristocracy*, p 131.

114 Estimate drawn from A Jeeves, '*Het Volk* and the Gold Mines', p 18.

115 E N Katz, *A Trade Union Aristocracy*, p 132.

116 See especially, 'Notes and Comments – Strike Echoes', *The Star*, 13 June 1907.

117 For the accommodation arrangements made for some of these 'single' Afrikaners brought in from the countryside during the strike see for example 'Riot at Langlaagte Deep', *The Star*, 16 May 1907.

118 See the following items drawn from *The Star*: 'Miner Fired At', 13 June 1907; 'Lurking Dangers', 14 June 1907; and 'Further Particulars', 15 June 1907.

119 'Dastardly Outrage', *The Star*, 15 June 1907.

120 'Diabolical Attempt', *The Star*, 3 July 1907.

121 '"Numerous cases of employees receiving intimidating letters are being daily reported"'. 'Notes and Comments – Strike Echoes', *The Star*, 13 June 1907.

122 See 'Charity at Vrededorp – Soup Kitchens and Spinning', *The Star*, 29 August 1907 and 'Work for the Needy – Cottage Industries', *Transvaal Leader*, 16 September 1907.

123 'Helping the Poor', *Transvaal Leader*, 13 November 1907.

124 'Salvation – New Vrededorp Scheme', *Transvaal Leader*, 4 October 1907. This scheme by the Salvation Army was presumably also designed to supplement a drive by employers to give white working-class lads in the city jobs in place of 'Kaffirs'. See for example 'All White – Lads Replacing Kaffirs', *Rand Daily Mail*, 26 August 1907. Of special interest, however, is the experiment which

J W Quinn attempted in his bakery during the depression. See evidence of J W Quinn to *Select Committee on European Employment and Labour Conditions 1913* (Cape Town, SC, No 9 of 1913), pp 457-9, paras 3335-8.

125 'The Unemployed', *Transvaal Leader*, 10 September 1907; 'Work for Whites', *Transvaal Leader*, 12 September 1907; and 'Notes and Comments – The Sewerage Scheme', *The Star*, 30 September 1907. See also the written statement submitted by the Johannesburg municipality to the *Transvaal Indigency Commission 1906-8*, pp 378-9.

126 Para based on: 'We Want Work', *Rand Daily Mail*, 4 March 1908.

127 Para based on: 'Unemployed – Starving and Destitute', *Transvaal Leader*, 2 March 1908 and 'Notes and Comments – The Problem of the Destitute', *The Star*, 3 March 1908.

128 Para based on: 'Unemployed – Starving and Destitute', *Transvaal Leader*, 2 March 1908; and 'We Want Work', *Rand Daily Mail*, 4 March 1908. See also, J J Fourie, *op cit*, p 77.

129 'We Want Work', *Rand Daily Mail*, 4 March 1908.

130 *Ibid*. The irony of this rhetoric lay in the fact that at the very moment that Das was making this speech, some of Vrededorp's Afrikaners were reported as living on 'mealie-pap and water, the mealie meal often begged from Kaffirs'. See 'Unemployed', *Transvaal Leader*, 2 March 1908.

131 'We Want Work', *Rand Daily Mail*, 4 March 1908.

132 Para based on: 'The Starving Poor', *The Star*, 5 March 1908 and 'Problem of the Poor', *Transvaal Leader*, 7 March 1908.

133 Even here, however, Krause found it hard to identify fully with the Vrededorp poor. On being asked whether he considered £15 to be a suitable transfer fee, he replied that he did 'but whether his constituents would be satisfied was for them to decide', *Transvaal Legislative Assembly Debates*, 10 August 1908, cols 1482-3. For a summary of legislation as it

affected Vrededorp between 1893 and 1912 see *Report of the Transvaal Leasehold Township Commission 1912* (UG 34 – 1912), pp 95-7.

134 See *First Report of the South African Republic Officials' Pension Commission*, January 1908, (TG 10 –1909). As has been noted above, the need for pensions was mooted well before the unemployment crisis of 1906-8. Neither Krause nor Smuts, however, would have failed to notice how some of the ex-Republican civil servants such as N P Oelofse and M J Bekker took up prominent roles amongst the more radical unemployed Afrikaners. Thus, both the Vrededorp Stands Ordinance 1906 (as amended 1907 and 1908) and the South African Republic Officials' Pension Commission would have helped to divide this volatile community along class lines during the depression. For Krause's speech see 'The Unemployed Dutch', *The Star*, 7 March 1908.

135 'The Unemployed Dutch', *The Star*, 7 March 1908.

136 *Ibid*.

137 'Problem of the Poor – Government Active', *Transvaal Leader*, 7 March 1908.

138 *Ibid*.

139 *Ibid*.

140 'Indigency Problem', *The Star*, 10 March 1908.

141 *Ibid*.

142 *Ibid*.

143 R H Davies thus gets a good bit more than his dates wrong when he suggests that: 'Indeed, at first (1907-1909) even the co-ordination of "relief work" programmes had been undertaken by a committee of "private" capitalists (the Rand Unemployed Investigation Committee) rather than by a Department of State.' R H Davies, *Capital, State and White Labour*, p 103. For the composition of the Rand Unemployed Investigation Committee see *The Star*, 10 March 1908.

144 Para based on: 'The Unemployed', *The Star*, 12 March 1908; 'The Unemployed', *The Star*, 31 March

1908; 'Unemployed', *Rand Daily Mail*, 1 April 1908; and the evidence of the Secretary to RUIC, H E Sutherland, to the *Select Committee on European Employment and Labour Conditions 1913*, pp 385-9, paras 2721-65.

145 Evidence of H E Sutherland (Sec, RUIC) to *Select Committee on European Employment and Labour Conditions 1913*, pp 388-9, paras 2764-5.

146 Besides their misgivings about an enormous drop in wages which such a move would entail (see below), the fear of contracting miners' phthisis was particularly widespread amongst the Afrikaner poor of Vrededorp at the time. See especially the evidence of R Shanks to the *Select Committee on European Employment and Labour Conditions 1913*, p 393, para 2861. On the numbers involved at the various stages of this operation see 'The Mines and the Unemployed', *The Star*, 7 April 1908.

147 See, 'Unemployed', *Rand Daily Mail*, 1 April 1908; and 'The Unemployed', *The Star*, 3 April 1908.

148 See evidence of H E Sutherland to the *Select Committee on European Employment and Labour Conditions 1913*, p 388, para 2763. See also 'Poor Whites and the Mines', *The Star*, 6 April 1908.

149 'The Unemployed', *The Star*, 3 April 1908. For a selection of Afrikaner responses to this situation, see the extracts reprinted from the 'Dutch Press' in *The Star*, 6 April 1908. Of particular interest is the extract from an editorial in *De Transvaler* in this selection.

150 'The Unemployed – Deputations and Demonstrations', *The Star*, 3 April 1908.

151 *Ibid*. Since it was the braver souls who had made the transition to underground work in the mines, the mayor presumably did not take this threat lightly.

152 *Ibid*.

153 Para based on the following items drawn from *The Star*: 'The Unemployed – A New Scheme', 4 April 1908; 'The Mines and the Unemployed', 7 April 1908; and

'Notes and Comments', 17 April 1908.

154 See the following items drawn from *The Star*: 'The Unemployed – A New Scheme', 4 April 1908; 'The Unemployed', 7 April 1908; and 'Notes and Comments', 17 April 1908. For the first full-length reports on the activities of RUIC, however, see 'The Unemployed', *Transvaal Leader*, 7 August 1908; and 'Rand Unemployed', *The Star*, 16 October 1909.

155 Para based on: 'The Unemployed', *Transvaal Leader*, 7 August 1908; 'The Rand Poor Whites', *Transvaal Leader*, 8 May 1909; 'Rand Unemployed', *The Star*, 16 October 1909; and 'The Dole System', *The Star*, 8 November 1909. See also the evidence of F C Steinmetz (Sec, Rand Aid Association), H E Sutherland (Sec, RUIC) and D P Liebenberg (Inspector of Land Settlements) to the *Select Committee on European Employment and Labour Conditions 1913*.

156 'Labour Propaganda – Missioners in Vrededorp', *The Star*, 1 July 1908.

157 'White Labour – A New Party Formed', *Rand Daily Mail*, 14 October 1909.

158 'White Labourers', *The Star*, 18 January 1910.

159 Para based on the following items drawn from *The Star*: 'White Labourers', 18 January 1910; 'Arbeid Adelt', 1 February 1910; and 'Arbeid Adelt – Constitution and Rules', 31 March 1910.

160 The collapse of the labour society is noted in J J Fourie, *op cit*, p 80.

161 See for example the evidence of H O Buckle, Johannesburg's Resident Magistrate, to the *Select Committee on European Employment and Labour Conditions 1913*, pp 378-9, para 2671.

162 See the quotation from the *Transvaal Leader* of 23 September 1913 and cited in J J Fourie, *op cit*, p 104.

163 'Town and Reef', *The Star*, 27 September 1911.

164 J J Fourie, *op cit*, pp 103-8.

165 See Problem of Poverty – Inequitable Municipal Doles', *Rand Daily Mail*, 25 May 1914.

166 *Ibid*.

167 R H Davies, 'The 1922 Strike on the Rand: White Labour and the Political Economy of South Africa', in P Gutkind, R Cohen and J Copans (eds), *African Labour History* (London 1978), p 83.

168 E Jensen, 'Poor Relief in Johannesburg', *The Journal of the Economic Society of South Africa*, February 1928, 2, 1.

169 Davies, *Capital, State and White Labour in South Africa*, p 101.

170 TAD, SS Vol 4677, M de Beer and 93 others to His Honour The State President and the Executive Committee, 4 April 1893.

171 TAD, SS Vol 4934, Petition to His Honour The State President and the Executive Committee, 8 December 1896.

172 B Semmell, *Imperialism and Social Reform: English Social Imperial Thought 1895-1914* (London 1960), p 181.

4 THE REGIMENT OF THE HILLS -
UMKOSI WEZINTABA

1   World copyright: The Past and Present Society, Corpus Christi College, Oxford, England. An earlier version of this chapter first appeared in *Past and Present: a journal of historical studies*, no 80 (August 1978), pp 91-121. The present essay has been slightly modified so as to incorporate new evidence that has been uncovered in subsequent research. This essay would not have been possible in either form, however, had it not been for the generous assistance of Tim Couzens. I would also like to thank another colleague, Vusi Nkumane, for elaborating on the Zulu terms used in this essay.

2   Amongst others see C Allen, 'Lumpenproletarians and Revolution' in *Political Theory and Ideology in African Society* (Mimeo Edinburgh University 1970), pp 91-115; R Cohen and D Michael's 'The Revolutionary Potential of the African Lumpenproletariat: A Sceptical View', *Bulletin of the Institute of Development Studies* (Sussex), 5, 2-3 October 1973, pp 31-42; and P Worsley, 'Frantz Fanon and the Lumpenproletariat', *Socialist Register 1972* (London 1972), pp 193-230.

3   See G Stedman Jones, *Outcast London* (London 1971); G Rudé, *Paris and London in the 18th Century* (London 1969); and D Hay, P Linebaugh and E P Thompson (eds), *Albion's Fatal Tree* (London 1975). See also the following works by E J. Hobsbawm: *Primitive Rebels* (Manchester 1959), *Bandits* (London 1972), and 'Social Banditry' in H Landsberger (ed), *Rural Protest* (London 1974), pp 142-157.

4   Cohen and Michael are most explicit about this in their essay on 'The Revolutionary Potential of the African Lumpenproletariat', p 41.

5   The sociological parameters of the prison are best discussed in E Goffman, 'On the Characteristics of Total Institutions: The Inmate World', in D R Cressey (ed), *The Prison* (New York 1961), pp 68-106. The sociology and functions of the compound system are fully discussed in C van Onselen, *Chibaro: African Mine Labour in Southern Rhodesia, 1900-1933* (London 1976), pp 128-194.

6   From 'Jan Note's Life and Introduction to Crime', South Africa, *Department of Justice Annual Report 1912* (Pretoria 1913), pp 238-240. (Hereafter, 'Jan Note's Introduction to Crime'.)

7   The origins of Mzoozepi's life of crime thus fit the syndrome as outlined by Hobsbawm in his essay on 'Social Banditry', pp 143-144. Unfortunately we do not know whether peasants viewed Note's life in the same way, but we do know what a noted black journalist – R V Selope Thema – thought about it at a later date. 'Scrutator' [Thema] noted in his column in *Bantu World*, 5 December 1942: 'Jan Note (Mzoozepi) was not an agitator. He was just a human being, driven to desperation by the nature of the pass laws, the dishonesty of a white man, and the unsympathetic attitude of

the police and the magistrates.' See also R V Selope Thema's *The Plight of the Black Man* (Liberty Press, Pretoria n.d.), pp 6-9.

8   'Jan Note's Introduction to Crime', pp 238-9.

9   Editorial, *Standard and Diggers' News*, 31 May 1895. (Hereafter *S & DN*.)

10   See for example the role of this factor in the formation of the white mineworkers' union as reported in the *S & DN*.

11   By its very nature much of this evidence is fragmentary and derives from several sources. A good brief introduction, however, is 'Vagabond's', 'The Streets of Johannesburg by Night', *S & DN*, 19 June 1985. Note too how these groups – especially the soldiers and deserters – conform with those pointed to by Hobsbawn in *Bandits*, pp 33-5.

12   See for example 'Confessions of a Canteen Keeper', *S & DN*, 5 October 1892. For one detailed study of crime, ethnicity and class formation during this period, see Part One, Chapter 2, 'Randlords and Rotgut'.

13   'Jan Note's Introduction to Crime', p 239.

14   See for example *S & DN*, 13 April 1895.

15   'Jan Note's Introduction to Crime', p 239.

16   Jan Note's introduction to crime was thus an almost classic illustration of a process of which the police at the turn of the century were well aware. See for example the evidence of T E Mavrogordato, Acting Head CID, Johannesburg, in *South African Native Affairs Commission, 1903-5*, 5 vols (Pretoria 1906), iv, pp 861-3.

17   These wage robberies and inadequate state protection were the source of constant complaint by the mine owners. See for example Transvaal, *Report of the Chamber of Mines for 1897* (Johannesburg 1898), p 394.

18   Newspapers throughout the 1890s abound with reports of such thefts by state officials. For a selection of examples, see incidents reported in

the following editions of the *S & DN*: 20 March 1891 (ZAR police), 9 August 1894 (NZASM railway officials), and 4 January 1895 (Portuguese border officials). Since such robberies tended to hamper the free flow of labour, the Chamber of Mines complained bitterly about them. See Transvaal, *Report of the Chamber of Mines for 1895*, pp 69-70; and *Report of the Chamber of Mines 1896*, p 170-1.

19   This setting parallels that of many European case studies. See Hobsbawm, 'Social Banditry', p 149.

20   'Statement by Jan Note', in South Africa, *Department of Justice Annual Report 1912* (Pretoria 1913), pp 237-8. (Hereafter, 'Statement by Jan Note'.)

21   This, of course, was the era during which other Africans also started to interpret the Bible in a radical way which frightened the established churches. In particular, it was the decade which saw the emergence of 'Ethiopianism' – black independent churches – and Johannesburg was one such centre. See for example reports in the *S & DN* of 29 May 1895.

22   'Statement by Jan Note', p 238. The book of Nahum is filled with verses which Note perhaps found to be relevant and inspirational. For example, 'Thy people are scattered upon the mountains', *Nahum* iii 18; 'Take ye the spoil of silver, take the spoil of gold', *Nahum* ii 9.

23   'Statement by Jan Note', p 238.

24   So much so that the Chamber of Mines eventually organised its own police force to cope with highway robbers. See D M Wilson, *Behind the Scenes in the Transvaal* (London 1901), pp 196-7. See also note 17 above.

25   See items reported in *S & DN* of 19 February and 28 March 1890.

26   *S & DN*, 2 August 1892.

27   See for example report of a robbery in *S & DN*, 28 June 1895.

28   *S & DN*, 31 January 1890.

29   See especially items reported in *S & DN* of 21 August 1894 and 7 January 1895.

30 'Izigebengu', *The Star*, 16 June 1896.
31 Hobsbawm, *Bandits*, p 18.
32 Classic feeder groups for bandits. See *ibid*, pp 33-5.
33 Hobsbawm, *Primitive Rebels*, p 33.
34 As Hobsbawm has noted of the Mafia: 'Obviously it was a complex movement, including mutually contradictory elements.' *Ibid*, p 41.
35 P Warwick, 'African Labour during the South African War, 1899-1902', post-graduate seminar paper presented at the Institute of Commonwealth Studies, University of London, October 1975.
36 *Ipepa lo Hlanga*, 20 November 1902. My thanks to Peter Warwick who brought this reference to my attention.
37 See P Warwick, 'African Labour during the South African War, 1899-1902'.
38 See especially the evidence of W J Clarke (Chief Inspector, CID, Pietermaritzburg) to *South African Native Affairs Commission, 1903-1905*, 5 vols (Pretoria 1906), iii, paras 27 693-27 696, p 613; and paras 27 801-27 802, p 618. See also, H P Holt, *The Mounted Police of Natal* (London 1913), pp 316-27; my thanks to Jeff Guy who drew this source to my attention. For more detailed case histories, however, see South Africa, *Department of Justice Annual Report 1914* (Pretoria 1915), p 235. Finally, see N Devitt, *Memories of a Magistrate* (London 1934), p 144.
39 P Warwick, 'African Labour during the South African War, 1899-1902'.
40 See J S Marwick's evidence in the case of 'Rex *vs* Mkosi Mkemeseni and 15 Others', p 48, Archbishop Carter's Papers, Archives of the University of the Witwatersrand, Johannesburg. (Hereafter cited as 'Rex *vs* Mkosi Mkemeseni'.)
41 *Ibid*. See also Marwick's observations as reported in 'Jan Note's Reform', *Sunday Times*, 19 September 1915.
42 See Transvaal Archives Depot, Pretoria, Department of Justice, Vol 144, File 1 – No 3/778/12, Statement by 'Forage', 16 June 1912; and

Statements by Detective W W Futter and Detective Probationer H G Boy made on 19 June 1912. (This source hereafter referred to as TAD, File 3/778/12.)
43 According to Jan Note sodomy was already a feature of Ninevite life while the *izigebengu* were still based in the Klipriversberg – see 'Statement by Jan Note', p 238. There is little reason to doubt that homosexuality was also a feature of compound life in the pre-war years. What is also clear, however, is the fact that such relationships became increasingly formal, organised and acceptable in the immediate post-war period. See below.
44 Archives of the Transvaal Chamber of Mines, Johannesburg, 1889-1910, N Series, File N 35, 'Unnatural Native Vice Enquiry, 1907', pp 1-2.
45 TAD, File 3/778/12, M A Hartigan, District Commandant, Boksburg, to Secretary, Transvaal Police, 22 June 1912.
46 *Sunday Times*, 16 June 1912. See also TAD, File 3/778/12, Detective A Hoffman to Deputy Commissioner, CID, Johannesburg, 12 October 1911.
47 *Sunday Times*, 16 June 1912.
48 H P Holt, *The Mounted Police of Natal* (London 1913), pp 316-27.
49 *Ibid*, p 316 and p 327.
50 See evidence of prisoner 'Bc' to Transvaal, *Report of the Commission appointed to Enquire into the Johannesburg Prison 1904-5*, paras 1 268-1 310, pp 61-3.
51 The three preceding paragraphs are based on the following items drawn from *The Star*: 'Native Desperadoes', 7 March 1907; 'Police Exploit', 13 January 1909; and 'Native Criminal Gang', 22 April 1909. See also items relating to the career of Jan Note as reported in the *Sunday Times* of 16 June 1912 and 19 September 1915.
52 See the following items drawn from *The Star*: 'A Gaol Outbreak', 30 April 1908; 'Convicts in Court', 12 May 1908; 'Native Convicts', 14 May 1908; 'Convict Outbreak', 14 January 1910; and 'The Prison Case', 29 January

1910. Also TAD, File 3/778/12.

53 This picture is reconstructed from scattered references in TAF, File 3/778/12.

54 *Ibid.* See especially, however, D M Tomory to the Secretary of Justice, 6 September 1911.

55 TAD, File 3/778/12, Statement by Nkuku, 16 June 1912.

56 *Ibid.* Deputy Commissioner of Police, to Secretary, Transvaal Police, 28 August 1912.

57 TAD, File 3/788/12, Statement by Tomboek Umfanawenduka, 19 June 1912.

58 The status of *ikhehla* and its attendant relationships are best described in *ibid*, statements by 'Office' Josimale (age 13), 17 June 1912; and Tomboek Umfanawenduka, 19 June 1912. Contrast this, however, with the evidence led during the 'Rex *vs* Mkosi Mkemeseni' trial.

59 TAD, File 3/778/12, Statement by Tomboek Umfanawenduka, 19 June 1912.

60 Illustrations of the various forms of punishment employed by the Ninevites can be found in any of the following sources: Transvaal, *Report of the Commission appointed to Enquire into the Johannesburg Prison, 1904-05*, paras 1288-9, p 62; or the following items drawn from *The Star*: '"Convict Chiefs"', 27 January 1908; 'A Brutal Assault', 12 February 1908; and 'Convicts in Court', 12 May 1908. See also, TAD, File 3/778/12, 'Statement as to Position of Native Criminal Gangs in Prison', 1912.

61 TAD, File 3/778/12, Statement by Tomboek Umfanawenduka, 19 June 1912.

62 'Rex *vs* Mkosi Mkemeseni', p 25.

63 See report in the *Cape Times*, 20 August 1915.

64 TAD, File 3/778/12, Detective A J Hoffman to Deputy Commissioner, CID, 12 October 1911.

65 *Ibid*, 'Statement as to Position of Native Criminal Gangs in Prison', 1912.

66 *Ibid*, Detective A J Hoffman to Inspector in Charge, CID, 12 August

1912; and Statement by Tomboek Umfanawenduka, 19 June 1912.

67 For 'Scotlanders' see TAD, File 3/778/12, 'Statement as to Position of Native Criminal Gangs in Prison', 1912; and 'Society in Gaol', *The Star*, 4 August 1914. For an example of conflict between the Scotlanders and the Ninevites, see report in the *Diamond Fields' Advertiser*, 23 May 1919.

68 Much later it was claimed that the state had the Ninevites very much in mind when it first introduced the indeterminate sentence. See leader on 'The Native Criminal', *The Star*, 18 June 1932. For a contemporary description of Cinderella Prison and the 'IS' inmates see for example *Africa's Golden Harvests*, xiv (October 1919), p 131.

69 For a selection of these terms see 'Rex *vs* Mkosi Mkemeseni'.

70 The importance of the word *'mgusa'* was known to at least some detectives – see for example 'Five Natives Charged – Question of Secret Society', *The Star*, 21 August 1913. The importance of drugs within compound culture is discussed in C van Onselen, *Chibaro*, pp 166-74.

71 'Rex *vs* Mkosi Mkemeseni', p 31.

72 TAD, File 3/778/12, Statement by Detective Probationer H G Boy, 19 June 1912.

73 *Ibid*, see especially, Detective A J Hoffman to Inspector in Charge, CID, 12 August 1912; and Statement by Detective W Futter, 19 June 1912.

74 See, amongst other items culled from *The Star*, the following: 'Native Vagrants – A "Herd of Jackals"', 20 August 1908; 'Cave Dwellers', 24 September 1908; 'Cave Dwellers', 20 August 1909; and 'Native Outlaws', 17 November 1909. Perhaps most interesting of all, however, is the 'group of Zulu and other boys who have escaped from the mines' and established themselves in the vicinity of Potchefstroom. See the following items drawn from *The Star*: 'Native Criminals', 9 May 1909; and 'A Mountain Gang', 22 May 1909.

75 TAD, File 3/778/12, Detective

A J Hoffman to Inspector in Charge, CID, 12 August 1912.

76 For precisely this reason 'vagrants' and the unemployed continued to use the compounds as a sort of refuge in the cities. In the case of 'Rex *vs* Mkosi Mkemseni', for example, see the evidence of Matoko Biyela, p 12, and that of Joe Loqoqoza, pp 40-1.

77 TAD, File 3/778/12, Deputy Commissioner to Secretary, Transvaal Police, 28 August 1912.

78 See for example the evidence of Matoko Biyela in 'Rex *vs* Mkosi Mkemeseni', p 15.

79 TAD, File 3/778/12, Statement by 'Office' Josimale, 17 June 1912.

80 'Statement by Jan Note', p 239.

81 *Black and White: The Black Underworld, How it is Created* (Johannesburg 1909), p 1.

82 See evidence led in the case of 'Rex *vs* Mkosi Mkemeseni', p 26.

83 TAD, File 3/778/12, Statement by Tomboek Umfanawenduka, 19 June 1912.

84 *Ibid*, J E Donald, OC Benoni Police, to District Commandant, Boksburg Police, 20 June 1912.

85 *Ibid*, Departmental Memo dated 12 February 1913.

86 *Ibid*, J W Goodman, Public Prosecutor, to Attorney General, 12 June 1912.

87 *Ibid*, J E Donald, OC Benoni Police, to District Commandant, Boksburg Police, 20 June 1912.

88 *Ibid*, District Commandant, Boksburg Police, to Secretary, Transvaal Police, 22 June 1912.

89 For a detailed analysis see C van Onselen, *Chibaro*, pp 128-57.

90 F Z S Peregrino, *Life Among the Native and Coloured Miners in the Transvaal* (Cape Town 1910), p 14; quoted by S T Plaatje in the *Pretoria News*, 11 February 1911. See also Plaatje's attack on Swazi, Zulu and Shangaan police in *Tsala ea Becoana*, 5 November 1910.

91 TAD, File 3/778/12, Statement by Johnson Johannes, 17 June 1912. See also 'Black Hooliganism', *The Star*,

13 January 1908.

92 TAD, File 3/778/12, see Deputy Commissioner to Secretary, Transvaal Police, 28 Jan 1913; and earlier, Deputy Commissioner to Secretary, Transvaal Police, 28 August 1912.

93 See 'Death of Constable King' in *The Star*, 26 April 1911; and a further report in the same newspaper dated 17 December 1912.

94 James Ndlela, 'How the Ninevites were Suppressed', *Umteteli wa Bantu*, 6 January 1934.

95 The King funeral is recalled in *The Star*, 19 December 1912.

96 'How the Ninevites were Suppressed', *Umteteli wa Bantu*, 6 January 1934.

97 *Ibid*.

98 *Ibid*. This account, however, is largely based on TAD, Department of Justice, Vol 117, File 3/780/11, Deputy Commissioner of Police to Secretary, Transvaal Police, 26 January 1911. (Hereafter, TAD, File 3/780/11.)

99 *Ibid*.

100 'The Criminal Native', *The Star*, 10 January 1932.

101 See the following items drawn from *The Star*: 'Mysterious Murder', 13 May 1912; 'Foul Murder', 15 May 1912; and 'Native Policeman's Death', 5 September 1912. See also item reported in the *Transvaal Leader*, 22 June 1912.

102 See the following items in *The Star*: 'Charge of Murder', 11 June 1912; 'Murder of Owen Duffy', 3 September 1912; and 'Murder of Owen Duffy', 4 September 1912. See also items relating to the murder reported in the *Transvaal Leader* of 12 and 19 June 1912.

103 *Sunday Times*, 16 June 1912.

104 TAD, File 3/788/12, Detective A J Hoffman to Inspector in Charge, CID, 12 August 1912. See also 'Rex *vs* Mkosi Mkemeseni'.

105 TAD, File 3/778/12, Secretary for Justice to Chief Commissioner of Police, 3 January 1913.

106 *Ibid*, Secretary for Justice to Director of Prisons, 17 March 1913.

107 *Ibid*, Statement by Nkuku, 16 June 1912.

108 *Ibid*, Detective A J Hoffman to Inspector in Charge, CID, 12 August 1912.

109 'Statement by Jan Note', pp 237-8.

110 This information is drawn from the *Cape Times*, 29 May 1917 and N Devitt, *Memories of a Magistrate* (London 1934), p 144. See also, however, University of the Witwatersrand, African Studies Institute, Oral History Project, interview conducted with the Revd Gideon Sivetye by T J Couzens and A van Gylswyk at Groutville, Natal, on 23 October 1978.

111 Amongst the more important of these were the gang of Pondos and Xhosas set up on the West Rand during the early 1930s under the leadership of 'Chief Hlovu'. See University of the Witwatersrand, Records of the Church of the Province of South Africa, Box 1927, Detective Head Constable H C Boy to the Divisional Criminal Investigation Officer, CID, Witwatersrand Division, 8 January 1930, re 'Secret Society of Pondo Natives known as the Isitshozi Gang'. See also item reported in the *Sunday Times*, 27 October 1935; and B Davidson, *Report on Southern Africa* (London 1952), p 117.

112 TAD, File 3/780/11, Minister of Justice to Justice Ward, 5 August 1914.

113 See various reports in the *Diamond Fields Advertiser* dated: 13 January 1919, 23 May 1919, and 28 May 1919. My thanks to Brian Willan for bringing these items to my attention.

114 South Africa, *Report of the Director of Prisons for 1919* (Pretoria, UG 54-20), p 49.

115 For an insight into modern South African prison gangs – including the descendants of the Ninevites – see the following series of articles in the *Sunday Times Extra* by Brigadier R Keswa: 'King Nongoloza made Women of Men', 26 September 1976; 'The "King" Recruits New Gang – in Jail', 3 October 1976; 'I Saw a Jail Gang Execution', 17 October 1976; 'Secret Salutes Ex-Cons Give a Jail Boss', 24 October 1976; and 'Rival Spoilers were Recruited in Prison', 7 November 1976. See also E R G Keswa's unpublished manuscript, 'Outlawed Communities' (1975).

116 Hobsbawm, 'Social Banditry', p 149.

117 See for example C Bundy, 'The Emergence and Decline of a South African Peasantry', *African Affairs*, lxxi (1972), pp 369-88.

118 TAD, File 3/778/12, Statement by Tomboek Umfanawenduka, 19 June 1912.

119 *Cape Times*, 29 May 1917.

120 Hobsbawm, 'Social Banditry', p 152.

121 Hobsbawm, *Bandits*, p 17.

122 E A Walker, *A History of Southern Africa* (London 1965), p 548.

123 Even black journalists who were usually hostile to the Ninevites recognised this element in Jan Note's career – albeit in a historically inaccurate and somewhat ideological form. 'Scrutator' (R V Selope Thema) thus wrote: 'Although he was helpless and defenceless, he decided to declare "war" against his persecutors. Without arms, he said, he was going to wage a relentless struggle against the white man. He was going to rob him, to break into his stores, burgle his houses and make him uncomfortable in every way possible.' *Bantu World*, 5 December 1942.

SELECT
BIBLIOGRAPHY

MANUSCRIPT SOURCES

Government Archives

Cape Archives Depot, Cape Town
Cape Supreme Court, Criminal Records, September-October 1904, May-July 1904
Natal Archives Depot, Pietermaritzburg
Colenso Collection, Box 76
Durban Corporation Collection (uncatalogued), Police Report Book No 6
Secretary for Native Affairs, Confidential Papers, 1890-1897, File 668/1895
Secretary for Native Affairs, File 1/1/216
National Archives of the United States of America, Washington, DC.
Department of Commerce and Labour, Bureau of Immigration and Naturalization, File 1-G, 52484
Despatches from United States Consuls in Pretoria 1898-1906, Vol I
Registrar of Companies Office, Pretoria
'The Eerste Fabrieken Hatherley Distillery Ltd', File T669
File on 'Crystal Steam Laundry', (1895)
    'Palace Steam Laundry Ltd', File T1501
    'Transvaal Soap Co Ltd', File T1413
Transvaal Archives Depot, Pretoria
    Colonial Secretary: Correspondence, 1901-1911, Vols 1-1028
    Colonial Secretary: Confidential correspondence, Vols 1076-1085
    Colonial Secretary: Confidential correspondence (unregistered), 1901-1907, Vols 1088-1092
    Colonial Secretary: Private Secretary to Colonial Secretary, 1901-1906, Vols 1132-1134
    Government Native Labour Bureau: Uncatalogued Archival Material, 1907-1914
    Secretary of the Governor of the Transvaal: 1901-1910, Vols 1-1371

Johannesburg Housing Commission 1903: Minutes of Evidence, Report, Correspondence, Extracts from the Minutes of the Johannesburg Town Council, Statements

Department of Justice: Miscellaneous Files, 1910-1912

Legal Assistant to the Military Governor 1900-1901: Minute Files L1-L1503

Johannesburg Landdrost: Administrasie, 1886-1900, Portfolios 1-88

Johannesburg Landdrost: Spesiale Landdros, 1886-1900, Portfolios 89-173a

Johannesburg Landdrost: Spesiale Landdros, 1886-1896, Portfolios 604-836

Johannesburg Landdrost: Dranklisensie Kommissie, 1892-1899, Portfolios 248-276

Law Department: Attorney General's Correspondence, 1900-1914, Vols 25-1814

Lieutenant Governor: General Correspondence, 1902-1907, Vols 1-164 and 185-233

Lieutenant Governor: Confidential Correspondence, 1902-1907, Vols 176 and 234

South African Constabulary: 1900-1908, Vols 1-91

Secretary for Native Affairs: Miscellaneous Files

Staatsprokureur: Correspondence, 1886-1900, Vols 1-572

Staatsprokureur: Geheime Minute, 1886-1900, Vols 190-196

Staatsprokureur: Hofpapiere, 1886-1900, Vols 573-753A

Staatsprokureur: Gevangeniswese, 1886-1900, Vols 904-913

Staatsekretaris: Correspondence, 1886-1900, Vols 1148-8796

Other archives

Fawcett Library, City of London
'Early Transvaal Letters', South African Colonisation Society Collection
South African Colonisation Society Reporters, 1903-1904, Mss Vol 41
Johannesburg Public Library
Johannesburg City Archive, Strange Library, Miscellaneous Boxes referring to the period, 1886-1899
University of the Witwatersrand Archives
Archbishop Carter's Papers
Church of the Province of South Africa, Diocesan Board of Mission Minutes 1905-1921, AB 767
Records of the Church of the Province of South Africa, Box 1927

PRINTED SOURCES

Primary sources

Chamber of Mines Reports
  Annual Reports of the Chamber of Mines 1889-1914
Johannesburg Official Publications
  Census 1896
  Mayor's Minutes 1901-1903, 1905-1919
  Minutes of the City Council, 1908-1914
  Minutes of the Public Health Committee, December 1906
  Minutes of the Town Council Meetings, 1902-January 1903
  Report of the Town Engineer 1904
Newspapers
  Standard and Diggers' News, 4 April 1889-31 May 1900
  The Star, January 1902-December 1904
Publications of Her Majesty's Stationery Office, London
  British Parliamentary Papers, Vol LXVI (Command 5363), 1910
  British Parliamentary Papers. Vol XXXV (Command 624), 1901
Correspondence respecting the African Liquor Traffic Convention, signed at
  Brussels, 8 June 1899 (Command 9335), July 1899, Africa No 7
Further Correspondence relating to the Affairs of the Transvaal and Orange
  River Colonies, Appendix 1 (Command 1895), 1904
  Papers relating to Legislation affecting Natives in the Transvaal
  (Command 904), 1902
  Report of the Transvaal Concessions Commission, Part I (Command 623),
  1901
Report of the Transvaal Concessions Commission, Part II, Minutes of
  Evidence (Command 624), 1901
Transvaal Colony Official Publications
  Johannesburg Insanitary Area Improvement Scheme Commission 1902-
  1903
  Laws of the Transvaal 1901
  Ordinances of the Transvaal 1903
  Report of the Commission to enquire into the Johannesburg Prison 1904-5
  Report of the Commission on Pretoria Indigents 1905
  Report of the Public Health Committee on the Location Question 1904
  South African Native Affairs Commission, 1903-1905, 5 Vols, Pretoria
  1906
  Transvaal Administration Reports for 1905
  Vrededorp Stands Ordinance 1906
Transvaal Government (1907-1910) Official Publications
  Evidence to the Transvaal Indigency Commission 1906-1908 (TG 11-08)

Report of the Liquor Commission 1908 (TA 1-1909)
South African Republic Officials' Pension Commission, January 1909 (TG 10-09)
Report of the Transvaal Indigency Commission 1906-1908 (TG 13-08)
Transvaal Legislative Assembly Debates 1907-1910
Union of South Africa Official Publications
Annual Report of the Director of Prisons for 1927 (UG 42-48)
Annual Report of the Director of Prisons for 1935 (UG 28-36)
Department of Justice Annual Report 1912, Pretoria 1913
Department of Justice Annual Report 1914, Pretoria 1915
Minutes of Evidence of the Natal Natives Land Committee 1918 (UG 35-18)
Relief and Grants-in-Aid Commission 1916 (TP 5-16)
Report of the Commission appointed to Enquire into Assaults on Women in 1913 (UG 34-13)
Report of the Director of Prisons for1919 (UG 54-20)
Report of the Economic Commission 1913 (UG 12-14)
Report of the Small Holdings Commission (Transvaal) (UG 51-13)
Report of the Transvaal Leasehold Townships Commission 1912 (UG 34-12)
Select Committee on European Employment and Labour Conditions 1913 (SC 9-13)
Zuid Afrikaansche Republiek Official Publications
De Locale Wetten de Zuid Afrikaansche Republiek 1897
De Locale Wetten de Zuid Afrikaansche Republiek 1899
ZAR Executive Committee, Resolution 16, Article 462, April 1898 and Resolution 17, Article 1251, 14 December 1898

Secondary sources

Directories

Longland's Johannesburg and District Directory 1890
Longland's Johannesburg and District Directory 1896
Longland's Johannesburg and District Directory 1897-1899
Longland's Transvaal Directory, 1903-1908
South African Who's Who 1909
United Transvaal Directory 1908-1914

Select bibliography of secondary sources on the Witwatersrand

Alston, M, *At Home on the Veld,* London 1906
Amery, L S, *The Times History of the War in Southern Africa 1899-1902,* Vols I and IV, London 1909

Anonymous, *Black and White: The Black Underworld, How it is Created*, Johannesburg, 1909

Appelgryn, M S, 'Prostitusie in die Zuid Afrikaansche Republiek', *Codicillus*, XIII, 1, 1972, pp 26-29

Aubert, G, *L'Afrique du Sud*, Paris, 1897

Bailey, W F, 'The Native Problem in South Africa', *National Review*, 28, 1896

Blainey, G, 'Lost causes of the Jameson Raid', *Economic History Review*, 2nd series XVIII, 1965, pp 350-366

Bovill, J N, *Natives under the Transvaal Flag*, London, 1900

Bozzoli, B, *The Political Nature of a Ruling Class: Capital and Ideology in South Africa 1890-1933*, London, 1981

Buchan, J, *The African Colony: Studies in the Reconstruction*, London, 1903

Clearver, Mrs (ed 'His Mother'), *A Young South African – A Memoir of Ferrar Reginald Mostyn Cleaver, Advocate and Veldcornet*, Johannesburg, 1913

Court, S, 'The Progress of Johannesburg', *Addresses and Papers read at the Joint Meeting of the British and South African Association for the Advancement of Science 1905*, IV, Appendix 9

Curtis, L, *With Milner in Africa*, Oxford, 1951

Darragh, J T, 'The Liquor Problem in the Transvaal', *Contemporary Review*, July 1901

Denoon, D J N, 'The Transvaal Labour Crisis 1901-1906', *Journal of African History*, VII, 3, 1967, pp 481-494

Denoon, D, *A Grand Illusion*, London, 1973

Devitt, N, *Memories of a Magistrate*, London, 1934

Duminy, A H and Guest, W R (eds), *FitzPatrick*, London, 1976

Feldman, L (in Yiddish), *The Jews of Johannesburg*, South African Yiddish Cultural Federation, Johannesburg, 1965

Fisher, J, *Paul Kruger*, London, 1974

FitzPatrick, J P, *The Transvaal from Within*, London, 1899

Fourie, J J (ed Stals, ELP), *Afrikaners in die Goudstad*, Deel I, 1886-1924, Pretoria, 1978

Fox Bourne, H, *The Native Labour Question in the Transvaal*, London, 1901

Fraser, M and Jeeves, A (eds), *All That Glittered*, Cape Town, 1977

Freed, L, *The Problem of European Prostitution in Johannesburg*, Johannesburg 1949

Gaitskell, D, '"Christian Compounds for Girls": Church Hostels for African Women in Johannesburg, 1907-1970', *Journal of Southern African Studies*, 6, 1, October 1979, pp 44-69

Goldmann, C S, *South African Mining and Finance*, Johannesburg, 1895

Gordon, C T, *The Growth of Boer Opposition to Kruger 1890-95*, London, 1970

Headlam, C (ed), *The Milner Papers*, Vol II, London, 1933

Hobson, J A, *The War in South Africa*, London, 1900

Jensen, E, 'Poor Relief in Johannesburg', *The Journal of the Economic Society of South Africa*, 2, 1, 1928, pp 26-36

Jeppe, F (ed), *Jeppe's Transvaal Almanac for 1899*

Katz, E N, *A Trade Union Aristocracy*, Johannesburg, 1976

Kaye, H, *The Tycoon and the President*, Johannesburg, 1978

Kubicek, R V, *Economic Imperialism in Theory and Practice: The Case of South African Gold Mining Finance, 1886-1914* (Duke University Press), Durham, NC, 1979

Lady Knightley of Fawsley, 'The Terms and Conditions of Domestic Service in England and South Africa', *Imperial Colonist*, IV, 48, December, 1905

Marais, J S, *The Fall of Kruger's Republic*, Oxford, 1961

Marks, S and Trapido, S, 'Lord Milner and the South African State', *History Workshop*, 8, 1979, pp 50-80

Mendelsohn, R, 'Blainey and the Jameson Raid: The Debate Renewed', *Journal of Southern African Studies*, 6, 2, 1980, pp 157-170

Morgan, B H, *Report on the Engineering Trades of South Africa*, London, 1902

Nimocks, W, *Milner's Young Men: the "Kindergarten" in Edwardian Imperial Affairs* (Duke University Press), Durham, NC, 1968

Peregrino, F Z S, *Life Among the Native and Coloured Miners in the Transvaal*, Cape Town, 1910

Phillips, Mrs L, *Some South African Recollections*, London, 1899

Plaatje, S T, 'The Mote and the Beam' in Couzens, T J and Willan, B (eds), *English in Africa*, 3, 2, 1976, pp 85-92

Ploeger, J, 'Die Maatskappy "Eerste Fabrieken in die Zuid Afrikaansche Republiek"', *Historia*, Jaargang 2, 1957

Potgieter, F J, 'Die vestiging van die Blanke in Transvaal 1837-1886', *Archives Year Book for South African History, 1958*, Vol 2, pp (vii) 1-208

Ramsay Macdonald, J, *What I saw in South Africa*, London, 1902

Rathbone, E P, 'The Problem of Home Life in South Africa, 19th Century Review*, August, 1906, pp 245-253

Richardson, P and Van-Helten, J J, 'The Gold Mining Industry in the Transvaal 1886-99', *in* Warwick, P (ed), *The South African War*, London, 1902

Rose, E B, *The Truth about the Transvaal*, London, 1902

Scoble, J and Abercrombie, H R, *The Rise and Fall of Krugerism*, London, 1900

Spoelstra, Revd C, *Delicate Matters – Open Letter addressed to Dr F V Engelenberg*, Johannesburg, 1896

Streak, M, *Lord Milner's Immigration Policy for the Transvaal 1897-1905*,

Rand Afrikaans University Publication, Series B1, January 1969

Tangye, H L, *In New South Africa*, London, 1896

Thema, R V S, *The Plight of the Black Man*, Pretoria, nd

Trapido, S, 'Landlord and Tenant in a Colonial Economy: the Transvaal 1880-1910', *Journal of Southern African Studies*, October 1978, 5, 1, pp 26-58

Trapido, S, 'Reflections on Land, Office and Wealth in the South African Republic, 1850-1900', in S Marks and A Atmore (eds), *Economy and Society in Pre-industrial South Africa* (London, 1980), pp 350-68

Vane, F, *Back to the Mines*, London, 1903

Van der Poel, J and Hancock, W K (eds), *Selections from the Smuts Papers*, Vol I, Cambridge, 1965

Vivian, W N, 'The Cost of Living in Johannesburg', *Imperial Colonist*, IV, 39, March 1905

Wilson, D M, *Behind the Scenes in the Transvaal*, London, 1901

Select bibliography of other secondary sources

Allen, C, 'Lumpenproletarians and Revolution', in *Political Theory and Ideology in African Society*, Conference Proceedings, Edinburgh University, 1970

Blackwell, W L, *The Beginnings of Russian Industrialisation 1800-1860*, Princeton, 1968

Bristow, E J, *Vice and Vigilance*, London, 1977

Bundy, C, 'The Emergence and Decline of a South African Peasantry', *African Affairs*, 71, 1972, pp 369-388

Burnett, J, *Useful Toil*, London, 1974

Clarke, J, Critcher, C, and Johnson, R, (eds), *Working Class Culture: Studies in History and Theory*, London, 1979

Cock, J, *Maids and Madams: A Study in the Politics of Exploitation*, Johannesburg, 1980

Cohen, R and Michael, D, 'The Revolutionary Potential of the African Lumpenproletariat: A Sceptical View', *Bulletin of the Institute of Development Studies* (Sussex), V, 1973, pp 31-42

Colquhoun, A R, *Dan to Beersheba*, London, 1908

Couper, J R, *Mixed Humanity*, London, n.d.

Cressey, D R (ed), *The Prison: Studies in Institutional Organisation and Change*, New York, 1961

Davidoff, L, *The Best Circles: Society, Etiquette and the Season*, London, 1973

Davidoff, L and Hawthorn, R, *A Day in the Life of a Victorian Domestic Servant*, London, 1976

Davies, R H, *Capital, State and White Labour in South Africa, 1900-1960*, Brighton, 1979

Davis, A, *The Native Problem*, London, 1903

Doyle, B, *The Etiquette of Race Relations: A Study in Social Control*, New York, 1971

Dumont, L, *Homo Hierarchicus*, London, 1970

Evans, R J, 'Prostitution, State and Society in Imperial Germany', *Past and Present*, No 70, 1976, pp 106-129

Fanon, F, *The Wretched of the Earth*, London, 1965

Fieldhouse, D K, *Unilever Overseas: The Anatomy of a Multinational, 1895-1965*, London, 1978

Flexner, A, *Prostitution in Europe*, New York, 1914

Forbes Munro, F, *Africa and the International Economy 1800-1960*, London, 1976

Frankel, S H, *Capital Investment in Africa*, London, 1938

Genovese, E, *In Red and Black: Marxian Explorations in Southern and Afro-American History*, New York, 1968

Ghyre G S, *Caste and Class in India*, New York, 1952

Gilbert, M, 'The Jews and Austria-Hungary, 1867-1914', *Jewish History Atlas*, London, 1969

Goffman, E, 'On the Characteristics of Total Institutions – the Inmate World' *in* Cressey, D R (ed). *The Prison: Studies in Institutional Organisation and Change*, New York, 1961

Gutman, H G, *Work, Culture and Society in Industrialising America*, Oxford, 1977

Hay, D, Linebaugh, P, and Thompson, E P, *Albion's Fatal Tree*, London, 1975

Haupt, G, 'Why the History of the Working Class Movement?', *Review*, II, 1978, pp 5-24

Hecht, J J, *The Domestic Servant Class in Eighteenth-Century England*, London, 1956

Hobsbawm, E, *Primitive Rebels: Studies in Archaic Forms of Social Movement in the 19th and 20th Centuries*, Manchester, 1959

Hobsbawm, E, 'From Social History of Society', *Daedalus*, 100, 1, 1971-1972, pp 20-45

Hobsbawm, E, 'Labour History and Ideology', *Journal of Social History*, 7, 4, 1974, pp 371-381

Hobsbawm, E, 'Social Banditry', *in* Landsberger, H A (ed), *Rural Protest: Peasant Movements and Social Change*, London, 1974

Hobsbawm, E, *Industry and Empire: An Economic History of Britain since 1750*, London, 1980

Horn, P, *The Rise and Fall of the Victorian Domestic Servant*, Dublin, 1975

Hughes, L (ed), *An African Tragedy*, New York, 1974

Katzman, D, *Seven Days a Week*, New York, 1978

Kneeland, G J, *Commercialized Prostitution in New York City*, New York, 1913

Kollontia, A, 'Prostitution and Ways of Fighting It', *in* Kollontai, A, *Selected Writings*, London, 1978

Landsberger, H A (ed), *Rural Protest: Peasant Movements and Social Change*, London, 1974

Le Bourgeois Chapin, A, *Their Trackless Ways*, London, 1931

Lyaschenko, P I, *History of the National Economy of Russia in the 1917 Revolution*, New York, 1949

Marks, S, *Reluctant Rebellion*, Oxford, 1970

Maud, Sir John, *City Government*, Oxford, 1938

Maugham, R C F, *Portuguese East Africa*, London, 1906

Mitrany, D, *The Land and the Peasant in Rumania*, Oxford, 1930

Mouzinho de Albuquerque, J, *Moçambique 1896-98*, Lisbon, 1899

Mphahlele, E, *Down Second Avenue*, London, 1959

McKay, J P, *Tramways and Trolleys*, Princeton, 1976

Pirenne, H, *The Economy and Society of Medieval Europe*, London, 1936

Pitje, G M, 'Traditional Systems of Male Education Among Pedi and Cognate Tribes', *African Studies*, 9, 2, 1950, pp 53-76, and No 3, 1950, pp 150-124

Pratt, A, *The Real South Africa*, London, 1913

Preston-Whyte, E, 'Race Attitudes and Behaviour: The Case of Domestic Employment in White South African Homes', *African Studies*, 35, 2, 1976, pp 71-89

Riis, J A, *How the Other Half Lives*, New York, 1971

Roberts, R, *The Classic Slum*, London, 1971

Rudé, G, *Ideology and Popular Protest*, London, 1980

Rudé, G, *Paris and London in the Eighteenth Century: Studies in Popular Protest*, London, 1969

Samuel, R, 'The Workshop of the World', *History Workshop*, 3, 1977, pp 6-72

Scully, S C, *The Ridge of White Waters*, London, 1911

Semmel, B, *Imperialism and Social Reform: English Social Imperial Thought 1895-1914*, London, 1960

Shepherd, W C A, 'Recruiting in Portuguese East Africa of Natives for the Mines', *Journal of the African Society*, 33, July, 1934

Simons, H J and R E, *Class and Colour in South Africa, 1850-1950*, Harmondsworth, 1969

Somerset Bell, W H, *Bygone Days*, London, 1933

Stedman-Jones, G, *Outcast London: A Study in the Relationship between Classes in Victorian Society*, Oxford, 1971

Stedman-Jones, G, 'Working-Class Culture and Working-Class Politics in London 1870-1900; Notes on the Remarking of a Working Class', *Journal of Social History*, 1974, pp 461-508

Stedman-Jones, G, 'Class expressions *versus* social control? A critique of recent trends in the social history of "Leisure"', *History Workshop*, 4, 1977, pp 163-174

Stolper, G, *The German Economy 1870-1940*, New York, 1940

Thompson, E P, *The Making of the English Working Class*, London, 1963

Thompson, F, *Lark Rise to Candleford*, London, 1973

Thompson, F M L, 'Nineteenth Century Horse Sense', *Economic History Review*, 29, 1

Thompson, L M, and Wilson, M (eds), *The Oxford History of South African*, Vols I and II, Oxford, 1971

Thrupp, S S, 'The Gilds', *The Cambridge Economic History of Europe*, Vol III, Cambridge, 1971

Tobias, J J, *Crime and Industrial Society in the Nineteenth Century*, London, 1972

Turner, G K, 'Daughters of the Poor', *McClures Magazine 1909*, pp 45-61

Van Onselen, C, *Chibaro: African Mine Labour in Southern Rhodesia, 1900-1933*, London, 1976

Walker, E A, *A History of Southern Africa*, London, 1965

Warner, S B, *Streetcar Suburbs*, Cambridge, Mass, 1962

Welsh, T, 'Contrasts in African Leglislation', *Journal of the African Society*, 6, January 1903

Whisson, M G and Weil, W, *Domestic Servants*, Johannesburg, 1971

Worsley, P, 'Frantz Fanon and the Lumpenproletariat', *Socialist Register*, London, 1972

Zeldin, T, *France, 1848-1945, Ambition, Love and Politics*, Vol I, Oxford, 1973

Theses and unpublished papers

Bransky, D, 'The Causes of the Boer War: Towards a Synthesis', Unpublished Paper, Oxford, 1974

Cooper, C, 'Land and Labour in the Transvaal, c 1900', M.A., London, 1974

Evans, R J, 'The Women's Movement in Germany', D.Phil., Oxford, 1972

Fourie, J J, 'Die Koms van die Bantoe na die Rand en hulle posisie aldaar, 1886-1899', M.A., Randse Afrikaanse Universiteit, 1976

Fourie, J J, 'Die Geskiedenis van die Afrikaners in Johannesburg, 1886-1900', D.Phil., Randse Afrikaanse Universiteit, 1976

Hallet, R, 'Policemen, Pimps and Prostitutes – Public Morality and Police Corruption: Cape Town, 1902-1904', Unpublished paper presented to the History Workshop Conference, University of the Witwatersrand, 1978

Howard, W D, 'Tramway Systems of Southern Africa', Mimeo,

Johannesburg Public Library, 1971

Jeeves, A, 'Het Volk and the Gold Mines – The Debate on Labour policy 1905-1910', Seminar Paper, African Studies Institute, University of the Witwatersrand, 1980

Keegan, T, 'Black Peril, Lapsed Whites and Moral Peril: A Study of Ideological Crisis in Early Twentieth Century South Africa', Unpublished paper, January 1980

Krut, R, '"A Quart into a Pint Pot": The White Working Class and the "Housing Shortage" in Johannesburg, 1896-1906', B.A. (Hons.) Dissertation, University of The Witwatersrand, 1979

Naidoo, T, 'The Temple at Melrose', Unpublished paper, Johannesburg, 1978

Perry, F, 'The Transvaal Labour Problem', Speech read to the Fortnightly Club, 1906

Richardson, P, 'Coolies and Randlords: The Structure of Mining Capitalism and Chinese Labour, 1902-1910', Unpublished seminar paper, Institute of Commonwealth Studies, Oxford, 1979

Saron, G, 'The Communal Scene, Pathology: The White Slave Trade and Liquor Offences', Unpublished essay for a study on the history of South African Jewry

Saron, G, '"The Morality Question" in South Africa', Unpublished essay for a study on the history of South Africa Jewry

Simonowitz, G, 'The Background to Jewish Immigration to South Africa and the Development of the Jewish Community in the South African Republic between 1890 and 1902', B.A. (Hons.), University of the Witwatersrand, 1960

Van den Berg, G N, 'Die Polisiediens in die Zuid Afrikaansche Republiek', D.Litt., Potchefstroomse Universiteit vir Christelike Hoër Onderwys, 1972

Warwick, P, 'African Labour during the South African War, 1899-1902', Unpublished seminar paper, Institute of Commonwealth Studies, London, 1975

Interviews

Brummer, W H, Johannesburg, 31 March 1980
Buthelezi, N H, Weenen, 25 April 1977
Buthlezi, R, Mpungu River, Weenen District, 27 April 1977
Cohen, P, Johannesburg, 10 April 1976
Gaddie, B, Johannesburg, 10 April 1977
Gumbi, P, Johannesburg, 16 April 1977
Kaluse, E, Johannesburg, 11 February 1977
Mchunu, N, Weenen, 25 April 1977

Naidoo, J, Johannesburg, 16 November 1976

Sagorin, I, Johannesburg, 15 August 1978 (interview conducted by
S Kahn and C van Onselen)

Sibiya, M, Eshowe, 27 April 1977

Sivetye, G, Groutville, Natal, 23 October 1978 (interview conducted by
T J Couzens and A van Gylswyk)

Skhosana, G K, Lydenburg, 7 and 8 September 1979 (interview
conducted by M S S Ntoane)

INDEX